THE DIARY OF ROBERT WOODFORD,
1637–1641

THE DIARY OF ROBERT WOODFORD, 1637–1641

edited by
JOHN FIELDING

CAMDEN FIFTH SERIES
Volume 42

CAMBRIDGE
UNIVERSITY PRESS

FOR THE ROYAL HISTORICAL SOCIETY
University College London, Gower Street, London WC1 6BT
2012

CAMBRIDGE
UNIVERSITY PRESS

University Printing House, Cambridge CB2 8BS, United Kingdom

Cambridge University Press is part of the University of Cambridge.

It furthers the University's mission by disseminating knowledge in the pursuit of education, learning and research at the highest international levels of excellence.

www.cambridge.org
Information on this title: www.cambridge.org/9781107036383

© Royal Historical Society 2012

First published 2012

A catalogue record for this publication is available from the British Library

ISBN 978-1-107-03638-3 Hardback

SUBSCRIPTIONS. The serial publications of the Royal Historical Society, *Royal Historical Society Transactions* (ISSN 0080-4401) and Camden Fifth Series (ISSN 0960-1163) volumes, may be purchased together on annual subscription. The 2012 subscription price, which includes print and electronic access (but not VAT), is £130 (US $218 in the USA, Canada, and Mexico) and includes Camden Fifth Series, volumes 41 and 42 (published in September and November) and Transactions Sixth Series, volume 22 (published in December). Japanese prices are available from Kinokuniya Company Ltd, P.O. Box 55, Chitose, Tokyo 156, Japan. EU subscribers (outside the UK) who are not registered for VAT should add VAT at their country's rate. VAT registered subscribers should provide their VAT registration number. Prices include delivery by air.

Subscription orders, which must be accompanied by payment, may be sent to a bookseller, subscription agent, or direct to the publisher: Cambridge University Press, The Edinburgh Building, Shaftesbury Road, Cambridge CB2 8RU, UK; or in the USA, Canada, and Mexico: Cambridge University Press, Journals Fulfillment Department, 100 Brook Hill Drive, West Nyack, New York, 10994-2133, USA.

SINGLE VOLUMES AND BACK VOLUMES. A list of Royal Historical Society volumes available from Cambridge University Press may be obtained from the Humanities Marketing Department at the address above.

This volume is dedicated to Raymond and Christine, my parents.

CONTENTS

ABBREVIATIONS

The place of publication is London unless otherwise stated.

Book of Orders	NRO, Records of the Borough of Northampton 3/2, Book of Orders of the Town of Northampton
Bridges, *History of Northamptonshire*	J. Bridges, *The History and Antiquities of Northamptonshire*, ed. P. Whalley (Oxford, 1791)
BRO	Bedfordshire Record Office
CB	Correction Book
Church Survey Book 5	PDR, Survey of the Western Deaneries of the Diocese of Peterborough by Order of Bishop Dee, 1637
CSPD	*Calendar of State Papers Domestic*
Fielding, 'Peterborough'	J. Fielding, 'Conformists, puritans, and the Church courts: the diocese of Peterborough, 1603–1642 (unpublished PhD thesis, University of Birmingham, 1989)
Foster	J. Foster, *Alumni Oxonienses: the members of the University of Oxford 1500–1714* (Oxford, 1891)
Freemen of Northampton	NRO, Records of the Borough of Northampton 6/1, Admissions of Freemen
Gardiner, *History*	S.R. Gardiner, *The History of England, 1603–1642*, 10 vols (1883–1884)
HLRO	House of Lords Record Office
HMC	Historical Manuscripts Commission
Isham, *Diary*	G. Isham (ed.), *The Diary of Thomas Isham of Lamport Kept by Him in Latin from 1671 to 1673 at His Father's Command* (Farnborough, 1971)
Jackson, 'Ship money'	N.J. Jackson, 'The collection of ship money in Northamptonshire, 1635–1640' (unpublished MPhil thesis, University of Birmingham, 1984)
Jones, *Bench*	W.J. Jones, *Politics and the Bench: the judges and the origins of the Civil War* (1971)
Longden, *Clergy*	H.I. Longden, *Northamptonshire and Rutland Clergy, 1500–1900*, 15 vols (Northampton, 1939–1943) and one volume of addenda by G. Anstruther (Northampton, 1952)

Longden MS — NRO, HIL MS 2901.2, H.I. Longden's record of institutions in the diocese of Peterborough, 1542–1823

Longden, *Visitation of Northamptonshire 1681* — H.I. Longden, *The Visitation of the County of Northampton in the Year 1681*, Publications of the Harleian Society LXXXVII (1935)

Markham and Cox, *Northampton* — C.A. Markham and J.C. Cox (eds), *The Records of the Borough of Northampton*, 2 vols (Northampton, 1898)

Metcalfe, *Visitation of Northamptonshire 1618* — W.C. Metcalfe (ed.), *The Visitations of Northamptonshire Made in 1564 and 1618–1619, with Northamptonshire Pedigrees from Various Harleian MSS* (1887)

NCA — Archives of New College, Oxford

NPL — Northampton Public Library, Abington Street, Northampton

NPL MSS — Papers deposited by the NPL at the NRO

NRO — Northamptonshire Record Office

NRS — Northamptonshire Record Society

ODNB — H.C.G. Matthew and Brian Harrison (eds), *The Oxford Dictionary of National Biography*, 60 vols (Oxford, 2004)

PDR — NRO, Peterborough Diocesan Records

Pettit, *Royal Forests* — P.A.J. Pettit, *The Royal Forests of Northamptonshire: a study in their economy 1558–1714*, Publications of the Northamptonshire Record Society XXIII (Gateshead, 1968)

Pevsner, *Northamptonshire* — N. Pevsner, rev. B. Cherry, *The Buildings of England: Northamptonshire* (1981)

Prest, *Barristers* — W.R. Prest, *The Rise of the Barristers: a social history of the English bar 1590–1640* (1986)

PROB 6 — TNA, PCC Administrations

PROB 11 — TNA, PCC Wills

Sheils, *Puritans* — W.J. Sheils, *The Puritans in the Diocese of Peterborough 1558–1610*, Publications of the Northamptonshire Record Society XXX (Northampton, 1979)

Temple of Stowe MSS — Huntington Library, San Marino, CA, Papers of the Temple family of Stowe, letters of Robert Sibthorpe to Sir John Lambe

TNA — The National Archives

Top MS — Bodleian Library, MS Top, Northants, c. 9, manuscript history of Northampton by Henry Lee, town clerk, 1662–1715

VCH — *Victoria County History*

Venn

J. Venn and J.A. Venn, *Alumni cantabrigienses: a biographical list of all known students, graduates and holders of office at the University of Cambridge, from the earliest times to 1751* (Cambridge, 1922–1927), now available at: http://venn.lib.cam.ac.uk/Documents/acad/intro.html

Vestry Minutes

NRO, Vestry Book for the parish of All Saints' Northampton, 1620–1735

Webster, *Godly Clergy*

T. Webster, *Godly Clergy in Early Stuart England: the Caroline puritan movement c. 1620–1643* (Cambridge, 1997)

PREFACE

I would like to thank all those who have contributed to the preparation of this volume. I am grateful to the Warden and Scholars of New College, Oxford, where the diary is held, for permission to publish it, and to their archive staff, Caroline Dalton and Jennifer Thorp, for their great kindness and helpfulness during my work on transcription. It was Richard Cust, the supervisor of my University of Birmingham PhD thesis, who first grasped the significance of the manuscript and then, with characteristic generosity, passed it to me to work on. I owe him a great debt of gratitude for introducing me to historical research in the first place, and for his generous encouragement and intelligent guidance ever since. It is my great good fortune to have also received every kind of kindly support, and mental stimulation, from another eminent historian, Peter Lake, with whom I have discussed the diary at intervals over the last thirty years. These two have been my main sponsors in the quest to publish the document, and have read and commented on my efforts at all stages. I am grateful to several other friends and contemporaries at the University of Birmingham and at the Institute of Historical Research in London, who discussed aspects of the diary with me at various times. Pauline Croft, Andrew Foster, David Hebb, Nigel Jackson, Ian Palfrey, Victor Stater, and Nicholas Tyacke have all expressed interest and encouragement. I am also grateful to John Morrill, who oversaw the publication of my original article in the *Historical Journal*. I would like to thank Ken Fincham, Hester Higton, and Ian Archer for their encouragement and patience in preparing the volume, and Ken for his help with Woodford's Latin. Finally, I want to thank Lilian, without whose love and support in very difficult times none of this would have been possible.

John Fielding
June 2012

INTRODUCTION

The life of Robert Woodford, 1606–1654

A biographical sketch of Robert Woodford is just that. Lacking a powerful patron or connections he was an obscure provincial who left a faint trail in official sources, no private correspondence, and no will. The only significant primary materials from which to construct his life (bar the diary) are the autobiographical essays produced by his son, the religious poet Dr Samuel Woodford FRS (1636–1700).[1] The diarist was born at 11 a.m. on Thursday 3 April 1606 at Old, a village eight miles north of Northampton, and was baptized the following Sunday, the only child of Robert (1562–1636) and Jane Woodford (*fl.* 1583–1641).[2] His father, a modest farmer, had made a socially beneficial marriage to Jane Dexter, the daughter of Thomas Dexter, lord of Knightley's Manor, and his wife Ann (née Kinsman). Robert and Jane had been married at neighbouring Draughton on 2 May 1603.[3] It is tempting to attach religious significance to this decision to marry outside the parish: the rector of Old was the obscure Alexander Ibbs, while the rector of Draughton was Thomas Baxter, a man with contacts in the defunct Kettering *classis* who was presented to the Church courts a year after the wedding accused of refusing to wear the

---

[1] Samuel Woodford left three autobiographical fragments. The first covers the period until 1662 and is printed in L.A. Ferrell, 'An imperfect diary of a life: the 1662 diary of Samuel Woodforde', *Yale University Library Gazette*, 63 (1989), pp. 137–144. Woodford began to write up the remaining two (NCA 9537 and 9494) on 5 September 1678 and they cover the periods until 1690 and 1700. The latter is a copy of the second edition of his *A Paraphrase upon the Psalms of David* (1678). The manuscript autobiographical notes appear in unpaginated sections at the front and the back: F.W. Steer, *The Archives of New College, Oxford: a catalogue compiled by Francis W. Steer* (Oxford, 1974), p. 113.

[2] NCA 9494, section at front; baptismal register for Old. Woodford's grandfather, Edward Woodford (1518–1604), had married Margery Ragdale (d. 1616), and their children included the diarist's father Robert, Henry (1568–1645), who married Joan and had a son William, and Margaret (d. before 1638), whose married name was Wale.

[3] PDR, Archdeaconry of Northampton wills, second series, C168 (will of the diarist's father); *VCH Northamptonshire*, IV (London, 1937), pp. 202–203; D.H. Woodforde (ed.), *Woodforde Papers and Diaries* (London, 1932), loose pedigree at the end; baptismal register for Old (PDR, 246P/1, 6 April 1606); marriage registers for Old and Draughton (PDR, 246P/1, 1603; 107P/1, 2 May 1603); Metcalfe, *Visitation of Northamptonshire 1618*, p. 103.

surplice. However, the evidence for the couple's sacrament-gadding is inconclusive.[4]

Woodford's earliest years were spent at Old, where his playfellow was William Chapman, the son of a local gentleman. Samuel Woodford described his father's education as ordinary. His parents elected to send him to the grammar school at Brixworth, three miles from Old, despite the fact that their village possessed one of its own. Nothing is known about Brixworth school's endowment and little about its pupils. Robert Skinner, a future bishop of Bristol, had attended until about 1605. Woodford mentions only one of his own contemporaries, Robert Yorke, a later attorney. The identity of its staff is similarly obscure. Assuming that Woodford entered at age seven in 1613 and spent several years there, he would have been taught by Mr Elborough, whose identity is uncertain.[5]

When it comes to his level of educational attainment there is more to go on. Woodford developed a facility with the English language; the diary contains several purple passages, usually inspired by Scripture, and the language is at times poetic. He was competent in Latin, using only a small amount of legal Latin but three times quoting passages from classical authors, once from Virgil's *Aeneid* and the same passage twice from Horace's *Epistles*. He was also familiar with Horace's moral odes and even made his own translations.[6] It therefore seems likely that the diarist was the same Robert Woodford who was the friend of Richard Allestree, the almanac publisher based at Derby and Coventry, and who contributed two Latin dedications that were included in the almanacs between 1629 and 1641. Woodford had links with both these towns, and Samuel Woodford stated: 'A Poet I was born, for my father was so before me'. His interest in the ancient world extended to Greece: there is no evidence for his knowledge of the language but he owned a copy of Plutarch's *Parallel Lives* in English.

---

[4] Baxter may not have been a diehard nonconformist and possibly compromised with the ecclesiastical authorities: he certainly continued in post until his death in 1607: Sheils, *Puritans*, p. 54; PDR, CB38, fo. 114r; Longden, *Clergy*.

[5] For Chapman, see Diary, p. 123 and n. 131. The schoolmaster could have been Thomas Elborough (d. 1615) or else John or William. The family were closely connected to the William Greenhills, senior and junior, successive vicars of the parish: D.K. Shearing, 'A study of the educational developments in the Diocese of Peterborough, 1561–1700' (unpublished MPhil thesis, University of Nottingham, 1982), biographical appendix; Longden, *Clergy*; V. Larminie, 'Skinner, Robert (1591–1670)', in *ODNB*; *VCH Northamptonshire*, IV, p. 219.

[6] Alexander Brome included a translation of Horace's moral ode (Book II, number 14), purportedly the work of Samuel Woodford, in his *The Poems of Horace [. . .] Rendred in English Verse by Several Persons* (1666). However, when Samuel reprinted the ode in his own work, *Paraphrase upon the Canticles* (1679), he explained the deception on p. 161, saying that it was the work of his father: H.F. Brooks, 'Contributors to Brome's Horace', *Notes and Queries*, 174 (1938), pp. 200–201. I am grateful to Christina Batey for this reference.

He was well versed in the Bible, and owned a modern devotional aid: the popular catechism written by the famous puritan divine William Ames.[7] He evinced interest in modern European politics, owning histories of France and an unidentified 'imp[er]iall' history (p. 314).[8] He also acquired a popular manual for attorneys written by Sir Edward Coke, and Allestree's almanacs would have been useful in his professional life, but his literary tastes ranged beyond the narrowly vocational. He owned and read books and exchanged them with other literate individuals such as Anthony, an attorney whose surname is not supplied. Given his lack of higher education it is not surprising that he was not up to date with the latest discoveries in cosmology, marvelling to God how 'that glorious lampe of thine the sunne runne dayly about the earth goe forward & turne back againe to light us' (p. 336). However, he was interested in natural phenomena. He did not manifest the Englishman's obsession with everyday weather but recorded what he regarded as unseasonal conditions, meteorite activity, and, on 22 May 1639, an otherwise unrecorded solar eclipse.[9]

Woodford underwent a spiritual conversion in his 'infancy' (p. 396), that is, before the age of seven. The nature of this experience will be discussed below; it is enough to note that he does not attribute it to the influence of any individual. His parents may have been of crucial importance but their opinions do not emerge from the sources. He rarely mentions his father. Robert senior died before the start of the diary, and when Woodford uses the term he is generally referring to his father-in-law. His mother, Jane, on the other hand, was one of the mainstays of his social circle.

To social obscurity we must add professional. As a provincial attorney he was part of the 'lower branch' of the legal profession, where career paths could be vague and informal. Attorneys did not generally undergo the academic education provided by the universities and inns of court, instead relying on vocational training by binding themselves to a senior legal practitioner. Woodford bound himself to John Reading, an Inner Temple barrister with puritan contacts who was to be his only regular patron.[10] Reading lived in the parish

---

[7] I am grateful to Bernard Capp for knowledge of Allestree: B. Capp, 'Allestree, Richard (b. before 1582, d. c.1643)', in *ODNB*; NCA 9494, front section (quotation); Diary, pp. 143, 314.

[8] All page references in the text refer to the diary as reproduced in this volume.

[9] For meteorological observations, see, for example, Diary, pp. 98, 153, 154, 165, 171, 217, 249, 250, 260, 276, 277, 297, 348, 349, 370; for the meteorite, see *ibid.*, p. 351. See also J.F.W. Schröter, *Spezieller Kanon der zentralen Sonnen- und Mondfinsternisse, welche innerhalb des Zeitraums von 600 bis 1800 n. Chr. in Europa sichtbar waren* (Kristiania, 1923).

[10] C.W. Brooks, *Pettyfoggers and Vipers of the Commonwealth: the 'lower branch' of the legal profession in early modern England* (Cambridge, 1986), pp. 152–156; Diary, p. 96, n 2.

of St Peter in the western quarter of the town of Northampton, and possessed another house in the Blackfriars area of London. If Woodford's traineeship was typical, it would have begun around the age of fourteen in 1620 and lasted for six to seven years; he would have lived in his master's houses for its duration. Around 1623 Woodford began to suffer from the financial problems that would dog him for the rest of his life. On 17 October 1638 he noted 'I have bene in this debt & want about 15. yeares' (p. 249). It is likely that the origin of the debt was the fees that he and his parents had paid to Reading. The level of these costs, which has been estimated at between £30 and £80 in 1600, may have risen in the interim.

As Reading's career progressed, so did Woodford's training. Reading held the post of associate clerk of the summer assize on the Midland circuit from 1618 to 1632; he served as undersheriff of the county in 1623, and in 1626 he was called to the bar. He also served as the steward of Northampton, probably from 1632 until 1635.[11] Woodford's time spent with Reading clearly involved an enormous broadening of the horizons of the provincial trainee as he was introduced to the society and culture of other Midland towns and developed his own networks of contacts. In 1637 he encountered Adrian Garner, an apothecary at whose house in Nottingham they had lodged 'in the Circuite' (p. 103). He would also have experienced London itself for the first time as he shuttled back and forth pursuing his master's cases in the royal courts and visiting the Temple; by 1637 he was spending nearly one quarter of his life in the capital.[12] Around 1626 Woodford's period of training with Reading would have been complete but the details of his life before 1635 are few, though he certainly remained in Reading's orbit. Despite disagreements, they remained on good terms, and Woodford continued to rely on Reading (whom he still called master) for employment.

The years 1635 and 1636 were pivotal. On 22 January 1635, at the church of All Hallows, London Wall, he married Hannah Haunch (1617–1699), the daughter of Robert Haunch, weaver and citizen of London, and his wife, Susanna, née Heighes. The minister of the

---

[11] Brooks, *Pettyfoggers and Vipers*, p. 233; J.S. Cockburn, *A History of English Assizes 1558–1714* (Cambridge, 1972), p. 315; TNA, STAC8/139/6; Longden, *Visitation of Northamptonshire 1681*, p. 135; Markham and Cox, *Northampton*, II, p. 570.

[12] For the Readings' house at Blackfriars, see Diary, pp. 131, 175; London was one day's hard ride from Northampton, but Woodford generally made an overnight stop, either at Mr Walker's White Hart at Dunstable (Bedfordshire) or another Mr Walker's Red Lion at St Albans (Hertfordshire). The White Hart dated from at least the sixteenth century: *VCH Bedfordshire*, III (London, 1912), p. 355. Exceptionally, on 19 June 1639, he completed the trip in one day – starting at 5 a.m. and arriving at 8 p.m.

parish was Andrew Janeway.[13] Robert's relationship with Hannah was close, providing mutual support throughout the tergiversations of life and producing fourteen children.[14] The union also brought with it considerable material advantages: Samuel Woodford claimed that 'my Mother brought a considerable Portion to my Father'.[15] It has not been possible to establish the amount of Hannah's dowry but it is clear that Robert Haunch paid it over a long period. He and Woodford normally enjoyed friendly relations. However, during an argument over what Woodford regarded as Haunch's parsimonious accountancy on 18 October 1638, Woodford claimed that there was 'interest due to me from the time that I was married till now for much of the porcon' (p. 250). The Haunches' house, the Two Wrestlers, standing adjacent to Carpenters' Hall, provided Woodford with a base for his frequent stays in the capital, a second home.[16] The Woodfords' first child was born there on 15 April 1636, baptized at the parish church, and named Samuel after his maternal uncle, Samuel Haunch.

On 20 July 1635 Woodford achieved the office of steward of Northampton, which would be the mainstay of his career.[17] Reading admitted neglecting his stewardship owing to the pressure of business: he had in 1635 become the escheator of Northamptonshire and in 1636 chamberlain for the incorporation of the London suburbs.[18] He nominated Woodford as his successor, whereupon the mayor and aldermen elected him by a majority. In his manuscript history of the town, Tobias Coldwell shed more light on the competition for the office: 'A great difference amongst the aldermen about the Steward's place. Mr Pilkington and Mr Woodford, but Mr Woodford

[13]NCA 9494, front section; Guildhall Library, Corporation of London, MS 5083; R. Newcourt, *Repertorium Ecclesiasticum Parochiale Londinense*, 2 vols (1708–1710), I, pp. 256–257.
[14]Only three – Samuel (1636–1700), John (1637–1694), and Susanna (1639–1672) – achieved parenthood and Samuel alone outlived his mother: N.H. Keeble, 'Woodford, Samuel (1636–1700)', in *ODNB*; NCA 9494, 9537.
[15]NCA 9494, front section.
[16]B.W.E. Alford and T.C. Barker, *A History of the Carpenters' Company* (London, 1968), map opposite p. 40; J. Stow, *A Survey of London*, ed. C.L. Kingsford, 2 vols (Oxford, 1908), II, map at back. The Two Wrestlers survived the Great Fire and was let out as tenements by 1678: NCA 9494.
[17]There is a problem over the dating of Woodford's election. The entry made by the town clerk, Tobias Coldwell, in the borough records is dated 20 July 1636 but Thomas Martin's mayoralty (he is described in the entry as mayor) covered the period 29 September 1634 to the same date in 1635. The true date was probably 20 July 1635, to coincide with his term of office: Book of Orders, unpaginated entry at start of volume; Northampton Central Library, 198-10-2797, p. 44.
[18]NRO, D(F) 123; N.G. Brett-James, *The Growth of Stuart London* (1935), pp. 230, 236–237, 284.

carried the place'.[19] Woodford was admitted to the office on condition that he paid William Brooke, the steward before Reading, a pension, though these payments go unrecorded. His defeated rival, Thomas Pilkington, mounted a legal challenge to Woodford's incumbency. Woodford succeeded in seeing this off, and won a much sought-after, and therefore presumably lucrative, office with life tenure. He was now a more established practitioner and took on his own clerk: Hatton Farmer of Towcester served him throughout the period covered by the diary and went on to greater heights than his master, becoming town clerk in 1658 and town attorney by 1660.[20]

In May 1636 Woodford's father died, having already conveyed to his son the house and land he owned at Old, which constituted, in the eyes of Samuel Woodford, 'a meane Fortune if yet of a Fortune it may discerve the name'.[21] The widowed Jane departed to live at nearby Wilby, but Woodford did not settle in the family property, letting it out to tenants instead. In early 1638 Joseph Easton and a Mr Fuller brought New Year's gifts of a brace of capons to their landlord: Easton seems to have paid Woodford £6 10s yearly for his tenancy and to have supplied him with a biannual load of coal. Fuller, whom Woodford describes as an 'ill tennant' (p. 241), is not mentioned again. Woodford's inheritance proved to be the source of great stress as he worried constantly that his creditors would seize it to recover his debts, which by 25 November 1637 ran at a substantial £192. He survived financially only because of a skein of long- and short-term credit, but was frequently behindhand in payments of church dues, tradesmen's bills, and rent.[22] Nevertheless, he was a substantial householder with the rank of gentleman, owing to his office, and possessed high-status objects – a sword, a cane, a watch, a horse.[23] His landholding was enough to qualify him for the shire electorate in 1640, and his assessed share (15s) of the £100 levy ordered by the vestry to pay for a new ring of bells constituted 0.75 per cent of the total. His main creditor was Thomas Watts of Easton Maudit, who held Woodford's fate in his hands. His fear of repossession surfaced when Watts found out about the death of his father, but Watts 'pr[o]mised me not to bringe me in or trouble me for the land' (p. 122). His debts continued at a

[19] Book of Orders, unpaginated entry dated 20 July 1636; Northampton Central Library, 198-10-2797, p. 44 (quotation).

[20] Diary, pp. 97 n. 8, 160, 281, 324.

[21] NCA 9494, front section; in his will, proved by his wife, Jane, Robert senior bequeathed to his son a 'garner' and chest. He described himself as a husbandman: his inventory was valued at £36 12s 6d: PDR, Archdeaconry of Northampton Wills, second series, C168.

[22] Diary, pp. 141, 160, 162, 188, 192, 241, 245, 259, 293, 310.

[23] *Ibid.*, pp. 130, 132, 198, 220, 328.

high level: £214 on 8 December 1638, and £200 by 15 October 1639.
When in May 1639 he was instrumental in conveying one man's land
to another owing to debt, he was thankful 'that I still keepe my fathers
inheritance' because 'if any Creditors should call I should be forced
to doe the like, but Lord helpe me to pay my debts without the sale of
it if it be thy will that the name of my deare father that bred me thus
may not suffer' (p. 303).

By the time of the diary, Woodford had moved from Reading's
home to his own dwelling in the parish of All Saints, the central
and most populous quarter of Northampton. Here he lived in rented
accommodation near the water supply, or Great Conduit, in the
south-east corner of the Market Square.[24] The Woodfords' landlords
were the interconnected Crick and Spicer families, haberdashers and
woollen drapers. The house had originally belonged to George Crick
(d. 1633) but Woodford paid rent to his son, Samuel, and his wife,
Mary, and to William Spicer, who had married George's widow, Ann.[25]
Woodford paid an annual rent of £5, in addition to which he paid
Richard Chapman 18s per annum for stabling.[26] He was vigilant for
opportunities to improve this estate, wanting to move from tenant to
owner-occupier, but was forced by lack of funds to turn down Spicer's
offer in 1637 to sell him the house. On Watts's advice, he considered
selling his patrimony and buying land at Duston near Northampton
which Robert Rich, Earl of Warwick, proposed to sell. He made two
trips to Duston, on 4 December 1637 and 14 March 1638, and even
commenced preliminary negotiations with Warwick's solicitor, but lost
out to another attorney, Francis Cook.[27]

The outbreak of bubonic plague at Northampton in 1638 severely
disrupted family life. The Woodfords opted for flight, a policy made
possible by the presence of Hannah's family in plague-free London.
They instructed their servants, led by Susan ('Sue') Tue, to smuggle the
babies (Samuel and John) out of Northampton in wicker baskets borne
on horseback. Tue set out on 10 April 1638 and the parents followed
on 24 April, leaving their servant Temperance in charge of the house.

[24] *Ibid.*, p. 196; Markham and Cox, *Northampton*, II, pp. 171–172, 196, 252. The Cricks owned
a house, which may have been Woodford's, abutting the Guildhall at the junction of Wood
Hill and Abington Street: Book of Orders, p. 18, and unpaginated entry after p. 611 dated
14 November 1653.
[25] George and Ann had lived adjacent to the Guildhall at the south-east corner of the
square: Book of Orders, p. 18, and unpaginated section at the back, deed of sale dated
14 November 1653; Markham and Cox, *Northampton*, II, p. 172. By marrying a freeman's
widow, Spicer obtained freedom of the borough: Book of Orders, 23 October 1637; TNA,
PROB/11/263.
[26] For rent, see Diary, pp. 141, 162, 165, 245, 267. For stabling, see *ibid.*, p. 171.
[27] *Ibid.*, pp. 139, 186–187; Bridges, *History of Northamptonshire*, II, p. 500.

Hannah remained in London with the children while Robert operated peripatetically, oscillating between the Haunches in London and the house of his friend Thomas Pentlow, at Wilby. Woodford returned to the family home at Northampton alone on 25 October 1638 but the family did not rejoin him there until 15 February 1639. Even then, Samuel remained in London with his grandparents, and the new baby, Sarah, in Edmonton with her nurse. By 1641 both were living with the Haunches: Sarah, who died young, they buried in an aisle of their church. After 1643, Woodford placed Samuel with them for adoption.

Woodford now entered Clement's Inn, the parent institution of which was John Reading's Inner Temple.[28] On 26 November 1638 (following a trial run on 14 June) he decided to rent a chamber at this inn of chancery located near Chancery Lane. Records do not survive but it is clear that Woodford followed the usual practice of leasing jointly with a chamber-fellow, probably Stephen Harvey, a fellow Northamptonshire attorney.[29] Woodford does not seem to have received any formal instruction at the Inn, but certainly benefited from Harvey's knowledge, of whom he wrote that he had been 'a great helpe to me in my affayres' (p. 314). The members were mainly natives of the West Midlands but the East Midlands were well represented: indeed the principal, Godfrey Maydwell, was a native of Northamptonshire.[30] There were plenty of colleagues from Woodford's own area with whom to mix and compare notes: these included Theodore Greene and his junior, Andrew Broughton, who later enjoyed notoriety as the clerk of the High Court of Justice that tried King Charles I. Woodford used his chamber both as an office and as a place to lodge. By 14 February 1639 he had succeeded in obtaining another position, that of almoner for Northamptonshire, again by the good offices of Reading.

From the conclusion of the diary until his death, infuriatingly little emerges from the sources to illuminate Woodford's public life. He does not appear in the records of the Northamptonshire County Committee, but continued as steward.[31] Before 1647 Thomas Pickering, a member of a gentry family from Isham, replaced Hatton

---

[28]Brooks, *Pettyfoggers and Vipers*, pp. 156–157, 164–172.
[29]Diary, p. 294, n. 670.
[30]Maydwell's family came from Geddington. His brother, Lawrence, owned land there and at Cranford, where in 1640 Godfrey presented the minister, John Fosbrooke, to the moiety of St Andrew: J.J. Howard (ed.), *The Visitation of London 1633–1635*, Publications of the Harleian Society XV and XVII, 2 vols (London, 1880, 1883), II, p. 91; Longden MS, 22 May 1640.
[31]Book of Orders, pp. 505, 577, 611; NRO, YZ 5270; Bridges, *History of Northamptonshire*, II, pp. 211–212. One John Woodford was listed as a Northampton Ejector in August 1654, but Woodford's second son was only seventeen years old at that time and apprenticed to his

Farmer as his clerk. The peak of Woodford's career came on 3 December 1653, when Sheriff Peter Tryon appointed him undersheriff of the county. A separate indenture was issued on 11 February 1654, as, over the intervening period, the Cromwellian Protectorate had superseded the Commonwealth.[32]

Details of his private life are similarly scarce. His son Samuel obtained a place at St Paul's school in 1646 through the influence of Susanna Haunch, the boy's grandmother.[33] Samuel went on to Oxford University, supported by a bequest from his grandfather Haunch and an exhibition from the Mercers' Company. Having joined Trinity College in 1653 he soon transferred to Wadham, whose head was a magnet to the Northamptonshire godly. John Wilkins was a preacher praised by his father in 1638, and later a founder member of the Royal Society.[34] The Woodford family continued to benefit from the generosity of its more affluent relations.[35]

Robert Woodford died at Northampton 'of a consumption' on 15 November 1654 and was buried at All Saints' on 17 November, his clerk, Pickering, having died days before. Samuel had become estranged from his father but, after a religious conversion later in life,

grandmother, Susanna Haunch, in London: C.H. Firth and R.S. Rait, *Acts and Ordinances of the Interregnum, 1642–1660*, 3 vols (London 1911), II, p. 973.

[32] *VCH Northamptonshire*, IV, p. 189; TNA, PROB/11/249: Pickering bequeathed 10s each to his master and mistress for mourning rings and 5s each to their children; NRO, Tryon (Bulwick) MSS, T(B) 259/2, 6.

[33] Venn, under Samuel Haunch; NCA 9494, front section; at St Paul's, Samuel was a contemporary of Pepys: M.F.J. McDonnell, *St Paul's School* (London, 1959), pp. 218, 247; C.W. Sutton, 'Cromleholme, Samuel (1618–1672)', rev. C.S. Knighton, in *ODNB*.

[34] NCA 9494, front section; J. Henry, 'Wilkins, John (1614–1672)' in *ODNB*; Keeble, 'Woodford, Samuel'. Woodford's friends Peter Whalley, John Bullivant, and John Parker, the Northampton lawyer, sent their sons Nathaniel (1655), Jeremiah (1656), and Samuel (1656) to Wadham: Isham, *Diary*, p. 200, n. 24, and p. 62, n. 15; Woodforde, *Woodforde Papers*, p. 5; J. Parkin, 'Parker, Samuel (1640–1688)', in *ODNB*.

[35] Woodford was overseer of Haunch's will: he and Hannah were to receive the rents of The Two Wrestlers for the duration of their lives. Robert Haunch (1649), uncle Christopher Haunch (1647), and Susanna (1658), also made bequests to the Woodfords. Susanna bequeathed her apprentice John Woodford's services (he completed his apprenticeship in 1658), and the use of her shop, to her brother, Edmund Heighes, haberdasher. By 1678 John was married with children: he continued to reside in the parish of All Hallows, London Wall. Samuel went on to inherit the estate of his great-uncle Edmund Heighes at Binsted in Hampshire. This side of the family demonstrated their eternal gratitude by their frequent use of the name Heighes. Woodford's daughter Susanna married Daniel Gifford, who, following problems with debts, emigrated to the East Indies, whereupon Samuel Woodford brought his sister to live with him at Binsted, where he claimed she died of grief (and consumption) on 26 September 1672, her son, Samuel, being adopted by her mother and stepfather, Hannah and Robert Guy: TNA, PROB/11/209 (Robert Haunch), PROB/11/253 (Susanna Haunch); PDR, Archdeaconry of Northampton Wills, third series, B, fo. 131 (Christopher Haunch); Keeble, 'Woodford, Samuel'; NCA 9494, front section; NCA 9537, unpaginated, under 23 December 1670.

he set the record straight, acknowledging that he had lost the 'best friend I had in the world', and crediting his father above all with encouraging him in his education. Robert Woodford died landless, as he had feared: Samuel told how his father had bequeathed neither land nor cash, only diaries, 'leaving me & the rest of his children that portion in a Treasury of Holy Prayers & blessings, wch he could never manage to provide for us in Lands & Monys' and 'on wch wee to this day live plentifully'. Samuel confirmed that his father had continued to exercise a godly influence over him, describing how, after his death, he had descended into ungodly company at Oxford.[36] Woodford left no will; in March 1655 Hannah obtained control of the administration of his goods. In 1662 she remarried: Robert Guy, the lord of Holdenby Manor in the village of Isham, was another lawyer but a more successful one, having served as clerk of the peace of Northamptonshire during the Interregnum. She died in early March 1699, outliving Guy and all her children except Samuel, and was buried at Isham. To later generations of Woodfords she was known as 'Mother Guy'.[37]

'To worke out my salvacon wth feare'

Succeeding generations did nothing to counteract the impression of Woodford's historical insignificance: the first of a dynasty of diary-keepers, he seems to have been regarded merely as the precursor of his famous descendant, Parson James Woodforde. Scant interest was shown in the content of his diary, although the Historical Manuscripts

[36] NCA 9494, front section (quotations); NRO, 223P/1, 17 November 1654; Ferrell, 'Imperfect diary', pp. 140–141.

[37] TNA, PROB/6/31, fo. 59. Guy was an assiduous justice of the peace during the Civil War and Interregnum periods, serving on county committees and as clerk of the peace from 1651 until 1660. His first wife had been the daughter of Francis Sawyer of Kettering: their daughter Mary married Nathaniel 'Bunyan' Ponder. Guy's second marriage – to Hannah – took place in London in August 1662 but his main residence was at Isham to the north of Northampton. In 1672, as part of Charles II's Declaration of Indulgence, the house at Isham was licensed as a congregational meeting house. In the same year, the couple adopted Samuel Gifford, Hannah's grandson. Guy's will was prefixed by a godly preamble: TNA, PROB/11/362. He made generous provision for Hannah, for Samuel Gifford, and for Samuel and John Woodford. He made bequests to twenty ministers, or their widows, whose names were to be supplied by Hannah, and enjoined his heir, Francis, to allow his stepmother to live with him until he married: P.R. Brindle, 'Politics and society in Northamptonshire, 1649–1714' (unpublished PhD thesis, University of Leicester, 1983), pp. 134–135; Isham, *Diary*, p. 60, n. 6; G.E. Cokayne and E.A. Fry (eds), *Calendar of Marriage Licences Issued by the Faculty Office 1632–1714*, Index Library 33 (London, 1905), p. 21; B. Lynch, 'Ponder, Nathaniel (1640–1699)', in *ODNB*; NCA 9494, end section; Woodforde, *Woodforde Papers*, index (quotation).

Commission did publish a few entries.[38] The journal dramatically corrects this misapprehension: from the writings of an early modern nobody emerges a compelling study of the puritan psyche and way of life. Woodford's noteworthiness lies in the sheer consistency of his outlook. Every aspect of experience – from thoughts and feelings to the operation of the cosmos – was scrutinized through the same lens of experimental predestinarianism.[39] His Calvinist worldview centred on the belief in an omnipotent and omniscient creator, whose will dictated the history of the universe. Woodford apparently supported the full supralapsarian position on predestination: God had determined mankind's fate before the creation, for purely His own reasons condemning the majority to hell and electing a minority to heaven.[40] Godly professors such as Woodford insisted on the possibility of achieving assurance of their elect status during life. The lives of the elect were known to proceed in a predictable fashion – after an initial awakening or conversion they became increasingly holy over time. Once feeling they were chosen, they persevered in grace and did not fall away. It was the believer's duty to examine his or her own character for the signs of election and to co-operate in the process by inculcating in himself or herself, under God's tutelage, the holy habits of mind and behaviour. This self-analysis was carried out by the conscience (God's 'vicegerent in me' (p. 294)), which possessed the ability to distinguish between the true faith of the elect and the temporary faith achievable by the reprobate.

Woodford had progressed only part of the way on this pilgrimage. He had been converted in childhood by the Holy Spirit, who had made him aware of the sinfulness of his nature and had then proffered the means of salvation, having 'in m[er]cye bestowed the Lord Christ the Cheife of all favors upon me' (p. 161). Using the metaphor of God as bonesetter, he described the rebirth: God had 'made the bones which thou hadst once broken to reioyne againe' (ibid.). God had changed his nature, had broken the old, corrupt, spiritually debilitated man, and from him had fashioned a new, holy being that was no longer inclined to commit the grosser sins. In an alternative description of his conversion derived from the Song of Songs, Woodford referred to himself as the bride and God as the groom who had embraced him and made promises. This refers to the covenant of grace by which

[38] HMC, *Ninth Report* (London, 1883), pp. 493–499.
[39] For experimental predestinarianism and the *ordo salutis* ('way of salvation'), see R.T. Kendall, *Calvin and English Calvinism to 1649* (Oxford, 1979), pp. 51–79; C.L. Cohen, *God's Caress: the psychology of puritan religious experience* (Oxford, 1986), pp. 75–110; P. Lake, 'William Bradshaw, antichrist, and the community of the godly', *Journal of Ecclesiastical History*, 36 (1985), pp. 570–589.
[40] He noted with disapproval that a preacher condemned supralapsarians: Diary, p. 251.

God saved the chosen: it was understood as the action of a testator bequeathing an inheritance to his heirs.[41] According to Woodford's narrative, God had thenceforth accompanied him, sustaining him through his youth, maintaining him 'clenil[y] from many great & scandalous sines which my Corrupt nature would have thrust me into' (p. 396), and delivering him from Satan.[42] He describes a concrete instance of God's deliverance of him from an (unnamed) temptation that had assailed him on 16 October 1634. Three years later he related to a friend 'in private the temptacon which began uppon me this day 3 yeares. oh Lord I blesse thee for thy wonderfull m[er]cye in carryeinge me through it' (p. 125). In assessing his current spiritual state, Woodford allowed himself the necessarily modest judgement that he had indeed grown in grace: he now enjoyed some 'hope of heaven' (p. 338), whereas previously he had enjoyed 'lesse hope of heaven' (p. 161). He referred also to 'heaven & eternall happinesse my everlastinge inheritance' (p. 250). He was not 'voyd of god & grace' (p. 338), and, comparing himself with a prostitute, was 'not as bad as the worst in the world' (p. 186).

He sought to place this quest for good, or war against evil, at the centre of his life: 'one thinge onely is necessary and that we are to seeke the Kingdome of heaven & the right' (p. 268). In a poetic passage he emphasized the urgency of this mission, the necessity not to waste one precious moment of time, and the duty to live in a holy fear of God: 'give me in this my day to worke out my salvacon wth fear [. . .] oh mye god give me to improve every inch of time thou affordest, why should I loose the pr[i]son[er] time that cannot be called back' (p. 336). As a spiritual autobiography, the diary (which was, as we shall see, part of a series) served an important purpose in this project. Woodford recorded his relationship with God, and his struggles both with Satan and with his partly unreconstructed self, which he rebuked: 'I have discoursed wth my soule in the pr[e]sence of god about the folly that its guilty of' (p. 369).[43] Reviewing these experiences enabled him to monitor the progress of his growth in grace and improve his practice of godliness by reference to past successes and failures. To help with this he used two symbols that had been established for centuries. The trefoil (a three-lobed or clover-leaf) symbol served to remind him of his most significant spiritual states, prayers, or formulae; exceptional

[41] *Ibid.*, p. 350; Cohen, *God's Caress*, pp. 47–74.
[42] For Woodford's conversion and spiritual history, see Diary, pp. 161, 165, 258, 396.
[43] For other examples, see *ibid.*, pp. 159, 248, 257, 285.

passages he annotated with two trefoils. The pointing hand symbol drew attention to matters concerning his children.[44]

The elect saint, owing to his or her capacity to live by faith, was joyful: 'a Christian is called to reioycinge, & a good conscience is a continuall feast' (p. 139). At times, when his mind was in this 'holy frame' (p. 338), Woodford detected these characteristics in himself and enjoyed a communion with God. The most powerful instance of this occurred on 17 March 1638, when he experienced 'most great & Ravishinge comforts in secret prayer the Lord even broke in uppon me, he made even his glory to passe before me', affording him a foretaste of heavenly bliss: 'Oh Lord to enioy thy pr[e]sence & to behold thee in thine excellencyes & glory by an eye of fayth is even heaven here uppon the earth'. This spiritual 'high' was so intense that it lasted until the next day. During a dream he experienced a similar level of confidence of salvation: 'I did reioycė in the Lord in spirit with much fayth & dependance on a p[ro]mise as if the Lord was about to p[er]forme it to me' (p. 144).[45] Another aspect of the correct view of the world involved an acknowledgement that one could not earn salvation through one's own virtues, but could only attain it by means of the mercy of an all-powerful God: 'the m[er]cy of the great & gracious god shall shine upon my soule in the face of Jesus Christ to p[ar]don my sinnes' (p. 258). God would alter one's nature: 'The power of the Almighty god through the spirit of the Lord Jesus Christ shall Crucify & kill my strong Corrupcons for his grace is sufficient for me both to forgive & to mortify' (ibid.). On similarly confident occasions, he was moved to tears when optimistic that God had promised to bless him 'though I am nothinge' (p. 181). Again, blessing would come 'not for my merits (which are no better than sinne), but for his m[er]cyes sake' (p. 112). Such intense moments were fleeting: rather more common were brief impressions that his affections had been retuned to holy, as opposed to worldly, frequencies. Then he felt alive and described his affections appropriately as 'quick', 'melting', 'warmed', or 'gracious', and experienced 'eiaculacons in fayth' (p. 221). He experienced the divine presence only intermittently, 'sundry times' (p. 387) over a two-month period in 1641. A budding saint could expect these manifestations to become steadily more frequent and was required to yearn for ever greater grace. Woodford

---

[44] Woodford's pointing hand (W.H. Sherman has named the symbol the manicule) is a basic model with a cuff, and pointing index finger with nail. Both symbols were used by Francis Bacon, Ben Jonson, and, in her journal, by the Northamptonshire gentlewoman Lady Grace Mildmay (d. 1620): W.H. Sherman, *Used Books: marking readers in Renaissance England* (Philadelphia, 2008), pp. 25–52, 169.

[45] For another heavenly vision, this time inducing tears, see Diary, p. 350.

entreated God to appear more frequently and to permit him to 'enioy a holy Comunion with thee, yea a firme Comunion that it may never be broken off any more' (p. 190).[46]

Holy emotions dissipated as Woodford complained to God: 'oh that thou wouldst dwell in the soule of thy servant, why shouldst thou be like a traveller that stayeth but for a night' (p. 271).[47] The fault lay with mankind, who severed the intimacy by sinning. Woodford appealed to God to 'let us not by sinne bereave our selves of thy good p[ro]vidence & blessing' (p. 144).[48] Sin was the prevailing propensity of a corrupt world: Woodford prayed to God that he might 'keep a good conscience voyd of offence both to thee & men' (p. 300). However, residual corruption, and hence the inclination to sin, was present within even the most accomplished saint as his or her inheritance (or 'bias' (p. 324)) from the Fall. Woodford mused on the persistence of briars and thorns, his label for this corruption: 'there is somew[ha]t of the Bryar & thorne in every estate & condicon of this world (brought upon us by o[u]r first defection)' (p. 124). This was the old man, the quality of corruption at perpetual war with holiness within the individual saint. Woodford employs many other names, including the self, the flesh, carnality, the creature, corruption, the world, nature, even death. Internal conflict was a necessary mark of election, proof that carnality did not enjoy uncontested possession of the soul. To make matters worse, Satan exploited this congenital weakness. The believer fought a defensive war engendering a like mentality. Woodford took up various weapons to help him. Faith was a potent defence: he noted that the 'fiery iniections & darts of Satan come thick upon me, the Archer hath shot sure at me wth envenomed arrows, but Ile take the sheild of faith & in the name of god Ile quench & repell them' (p. 271). Faith was also described as a castle, and God as a shield, a refuge, even a rabbit warren.[49]

Woodford sought to demonstrate virtue through the height of his sensitivity to vice: from the list of his sins we can read off the virtues to which he aspired. The regenerate man would be zealous in identifying and extinguishing every last scintilla of impurity in his soul. Woodford was obsessed with his own sinfulness and with maintaining watchfulness to prevent the slightest lapse. Vigilance meant developing a hypersensitivity to the threat of sin so that it might be averted. Having taken receipt of a suit of new clothes, he made a mental note to avoid

---

[46] *Ibid.*, p. 338 (marked with a double trefoil).

[47] He uses the same expression to describe God's concealing Himself from the godly collectively: *ibid.*, p. 289.

[48] For a fuller description of this, see *ibid.*, p. 338.

[49] *Ibid.*, pp. 180, 265. For God as refuge and rabbit warren, see *ibid.*, pp. 184, 399.

pride: 'Lord graunt they may not be a snare to me' (p. 221). While desiring the position of clerk of the peace he wished 'to submit my will to the Lords & not at all to Covet any thinge that is my neighbors' (p. 110). More usually, vigilance took the form of warning himself not to overcharge for his professional services: 'God forbid I should ever put forth my hand to receave the least peny of unlawfull gayne' (p. 388). Sometimes it meant avoiding bad company or various cultural norms in the tavern. On one occasion it meant rejecting a modest business opportunity. The aptly named Mr Pyke had persuaded his wife to make over £1000 to him and called upon Woodford to witness the transaction: he refused 'knowinge that he had wrought her to it by undue meanes' (p. 210). He confessed his actual lapses retrospectively in the diary, although he rarely mentioned the specific commandments breached and sometimes did not put a name to the failing at all.

A key element of the godly outlook was acceptance of an all-encompassing divine providence: the idea that God intervened constantly in the life of the individual and in society generally.[50] All experience was suffused with meaning: even the life of a lowly country attorney was significant. However, it was essential for the incipient saint to exhibit the right interpretation, or sanctified use, of experience or phenomena, to clarify the divine plan as it applied to him or her and to achieve the required dependence on God. Woodford asserted his intention to be dependent: 'I rise & goe & move in the strength of the Lord, or desire to doe so' (p. 280). 'We subsist', he declared to God, 'by thy speciall yea even miraculous p[ro]vidence' (p. 399). The reaction to all events, whether advantageous or disadvantageous, became a litmus test of godliness. The positive side of this was the correct use of mercies or blessings. He acknowledged with thanks every iota of divine providence, from the mundane – obtaining payment from clients – to the intangible – a transitory feeling of happiness or the mental wherewithal to cope with life's difficulties – to the miraculous – protection from looming danger. He recorded praises for his survival after he fell from his horse, for a successful navigation of the forest near Olney in Buckinghamshire, and for his preservation 'goeinge & cominge over Billing Bridge in the great water where I did not well know the way' (p. 171). On the negative side was the correct use of afflictions, which were the saints' universities according to the

[50]Alexandra Walsham has established that providentialist thought was widespread and far from the monopoly of puritans or even Protestants: A. Walsham, *Providence in Early Modern England* (Oxford, 1999). Richard Cust has shown that Charles I himself thought in such terms: R.P. Cust, 'Charles I and providence', in K. Fincham and P. Lake (eds), *Religious Politics in Post-Reformation England: essays in honour of Nicholas Tyacke* (Woodbridge, 2006), pp. 193–208. Woodford mentions the word 108 times.

godly Londoner Nehemiah Wallington.[51] Woodford knew that he was required to regard his problems not as the random and remediless cruelties of fortune but as proof of the didacticism of a loving God striving to effect his spiritual improvement. It was his duty cheerfully to embrace the means of divine chastisement and to search out and correct the sin through which he had offended God and cut the link between them.

Woodford faced serious dangers, disease and war being prominent among them, but by far the most persistent difficulty in his life was his dire indebtedness, the leitmotif of the diary. His reaction to this hardship, profound melancholy, was the wrong response, implying mistrust of God's promises in the covenant to provide for his every spiritual and material need. If contentedness in all conditions was the fruit of faith, then depression, which Woodford referred to as the cares of the world, indicated guilt of the sin of unbelief or rebellion against God. At times he doubted God's probity, expressing 'distrust of the Lord for outward things' (p. 385). His heart was 'ready to be daunted & say it will allwayes be thus I shall never be able to pay but goe backwards rather then forwards, thus infidelity takes hold on me & bringeth worldly sorow whereby I sinne against the bounty & the power of my god' (p. 357). If the godly man kept worries at bay by at all times holding in mind his heavenly inheritance, Woodford allowed his problems to cause him to forget this and to sever the link with God: 'my hart doth not enioy the Lord as form[er]ly, for the thorny cares of the world doe dull my affections often' (p. 132).[52] He was undoubtedly referring to unbelief when he thrice – on 11 and 18 August, and 6 November 1638 – alluded to 'that sinne'.[53] Satan only exacerbated the situation by incessantly reminding him of his predicament and exposing him to temptation: 'these my debts doe stare me in the face, and satan continually iniects them seeing my weaknesse & want of fayth' (p. 267). Occasionally he identified other sins responsible for his debts: pride, profuseness, and idleness in his calling. His fear of ruin could push him to the brink of despair. There was anecdotal evidence that depression could lead to insanity, yet he did not, like Wallington, contemplate suicide.[54] As he approached a crisis he asked rhetorically: 'shall I sink under the burden & suspend my fayth and be discouraged?' (p. 285). He appealed to God: 'wilt thou shew a miracle to the dead' (p. 267).

[51] P.S. Seaver, *Wallington's World: a puritan artisan in seventeenth-century London* (1985), p. 129.
[52] For forgetfulness, see Diary, pp. 182, 250.
[53] *Ibid.*, pp. 227, 230.
[54] *Ibid.*, p. 142. See the cases of Arthur Potter (*ibid.*, p. 265) and the man described by Mr Stancy (*ibid.*, p. 192). See also Seaver, *Wallington's World*, pp. 22, 31, 60.

He drilled himself to accept the correct interpretation of the affliction as God's just and apt punishment of his sins, and was occasionally successful. Debt was a punishment that fitted this crime as it could be equated with sin, a debt owed to God: 'I have not cared for runninge in debt to thee by dayly strivinge against thee, & therefore it is iust with thee I should Runne in debt to men' (p. 142). Debt was the divine correcting rod: 'I kisse the rod & accept the burden' (p. 304).[55] He also used the metaphor of God the alchemist to describe this: 'when thou hast tried us & given us fayth & humilyty bringe us out of the fire as gold' (p. 270).[56] God had imposed hardship in order to teach him the lesson that he should 'live by fayth in regard of outward things, & to be contented in the want of them' (p. 139).

Repentance was the main weapon in the godly's war with sin and the flesh, enabling them to revert to virtue and faith. Woodford repeatedly performed this exercise of self-humiliation, which consisted of various elements neatly summarized in the sermon of a local schoolmaster, Henry Hall: '1 poverty of sp[iri]t & sight of wants 2 sence of them with sorrow & greife 3 hungringe & thirstinge after grace' (p. 146). The godly alone could make constructive use of sin to achieve repentance. In a lesson derived from the minister Andrew Perne, Woodford outlined the way in which contemplation of sin could be used to attain humility, and so turn away from the carnal self back towards a holy disposition: 'we ought to make a good use of sinne to be humbled by it, to goe out of o[u]r selves' (p. 225). He condemned his sins and the worldly nature from which they sprang. The resulting hyperbolic references to his own ungodliness were of course a requirement of the theology. In the most noteworthy of these, he addressed God in a phrase reminiscent of Cromwell's self-appraisal as the 'chief of all sinners': 'I am the vilest & the proudest wretch that ever lived that cannot contentedly submitt unto thee, nay Its a shame that I cannot depend uppon thee after so many p[ro]mises made to me from thy selfe & warnings given to take heed of these cares' (p. 159). Far from growing in grace, it seemed that regression was his lot. After smoking and drinking too much to forget his problems, he lamented: 'I th[r]ive not but am a very starvelinge in grace & godlines & stand as it were at a stay if not goe backward' (p. 324). He compared his own preoccupation with worldly concerns unfavourably with the attitude of the gentiles, although he probably also had in mind the quotation denigrating riches from the pagan Horace.[57] Humiliation climaxed in

---

[55] For another example of the comparison between material and spiritual defects, see Diary, p. 309.

[56] See also Seaver, *Wallington's World*, p. 129.

[57] Diary, pp. 110, 164.

the recognition of his own spiritual impotence and dependence on God's mercy to be saved: 'if I remayne at home restinge uppon myne owne grace or p[er]formances I am utterly lost & damned forever, oh give me a Christ for his sake give me salvation freely' (p. 237).[58] He confessed to God that 'thou mightest glorify thy Justice in my destruccon', and begged that He deal with him 'in m[er]cye' (p. 227). Occasionally, humiliation shaded into surrender: 'Lord I will trust in thee though thou kill me I will lye at thy dore' (p. 136).[59]

In an attempt to induce God to lift his embargo on material wealth, Woodford worked to demonstrate that he had indeed learned his lesson, that God had successfully weaned him from worldly priorities to spiritual. Attempting to express a holy contempt of worldly riches, he wrote 'all earthly things yea the heighth of pompe or heapes of riches & are but dung & drosse in comp[ar]ison of things spirituall' (p. 143). In another passage he screwed up his resolution that 'a Christian in the lowest & worst estate and condition is in farre better case, then a man out of Christ in his greatest wealth and Jollity, and hath more true cause of cheerfullnesse' (p. 139).

In the process of repentance, the concomitant of humility was the disposition described in one of the Beatitudes as hungering and thirsting for grace, praying for God to alter (or heal) one's corrupt (or sick) nature by enduing one with the power to avoid or combat sin, the power of self-abnegation. Woodford asked God to 'increase my fayth empty me of my selfe' (p. 385).[60] He asserted his own spiritual impotence and yearned to access divine grace: 'give me the use of my graces for I am not able to stirre them up my selfe, Lord endue me with strength from on high' (p. 139). The looked-for culmination was God's near perfecting of him in this life – 'oh that I were as holy as an angell of light oh that I could doe thy will in earth as the angells doe it I heaven' (p. 324) – and glorification in the next: 'Lord give us [. . .] weaned affections from the world; Lord give us so to live to thee here that we may after this life be receaved into pa[ra]dise' (p. 124).[61] In a continuation of this metaphor, the solution was to be a weaning from worldly to spiritual affections, from carnal to spiritual breasts.[62] As we shall see, the rule of godly behaviour was moderation,

---

[58] For condemnations of human merit and lauding of divine mercy, see *ibid.*, pp. 112, 216, 227, 388.

[59] For humiliation see *ibid.*, pp. 256, 282; for divine favour being better than life, see *ibid.*, p. 227.

[60] For other examples, see *ibid.*, pp. 236–237, 288.

[61] For living to God forever, see *ibid.*, p. 307. The apocalyptic optimism of 1641 gave rise to a particularly mystical example of this yearning for grace derived from the Old Testament: *ibid.*, p. 388.

[62] *Ibid.*, p. 100.

but immoderation was permitted when yearning for divine love and grace. Woodford prayed: 'make me sick of Love to the Lord Xt' (p. 284). So it was that, alongside his constant prayers for material supply, there were alternative requests for the grace to live by faith in the face of hardship: 'if I can live by fayth in this disadvantage of direfull melancholy surely I should have a most comfortable life if this were removed as one that can dannce in Wooden shoes would surely be more nimble in pumpes' (p. 264).[63] However, the affliction of debt was never removed and led eventually to the repossession of his lands. In the absence of further journals it is impossible to establish whether he reached a spiritual reconciliation with his increasing poverty.

Similarly, Woodford treated the afflictions caused by his family's illnesses as lessons in holiness. The swelling of Hannah's breast following childbirth was said to have resulted from their joint sin of 'deadnes in seeking' the Lord (p. 120), and the children's sicknesses were likewise attributed to parental sin. Woodford emphasized the following passage, referring to one of Samuel's maladies, with the pointing hand symbol: 'thou doest in goodnesse exercise us Lord make us gayners by every passage of thy p[ro]vidence towards us' (p. 333). When they feared that John might lose his sight, Woodford simply asked for pardon of their 'misdoeings' (p. 399). The moral was to love God above all else and to react to divine favour in the correct fashion. Children were seen as blessings, a comfort to their parents. However, the Woodfords' fault lay in their excessive love for their children, which overshadowed their love for God. Human attachments, unlike that between human and God, were to be characterized by moderation. Children were to be loved, but not carnally, for their own sakes, rather as divine gifts, which were to be received with grateful praise, and whose purpose was to stimulate godly action. During one of John's illnesses, Woodford prayed: 'graunt that our harts may sit loose from what ever we possesse, that thou alone mayest dwell in our soules' (p. 103). Referring to the children, he requested God to keep his and Hannah's 'affections from exorbitancy that we may love them in thee & for thee' (p. 104). Their carnal attachment to their children constituted an abuse of divine gifts; he implored God: 'strip us not of the m[er]cyes thou hast bestowed upon us for o[u]r abuse of them' (p. 399). Affliction was designed to correct this wrongdoing. During three bouts of sickness Woodford bargained with God as he did over debt: the three children involved were John, Samuel, and, most poignantly, Thomas, who died aged nine days on 27 August 1640.[64]

---

[63] Further examples of his asking for the faith to bear his predicament: *ibid.*, pp. 142, 228, 264.

[64] *Ibid.*, pp. 103–104 (John), 399 (Samuel), 362–365 (Thomas).

'excercised me wth some affliccon or other & who knowes but this may have a mercy at the end of it' (p. 241).

Woodford bargained with God, sometimes in the form of a conditional covenant of the type he encountered professionally. Both individually and with Hannah, he pledged to regard God's fulfilment of His promise to provide for his material needs as an instance of divine love and to reciprocate with ecstatic praise and a recommitment to divine service. Interestingly, he created physical aides-memoires to remind himself to acknowledge divine beneficence in the event that it materialized. He twice carved his initials into ash trees.[70] More bizarrely, he invented a new genre of religious expression, spiritual toilet graffiti, writing 'CXW. 38. in the house of office for Cares of the world 1638. Resolvinge if the Lord doth helpe me to be put in mind when I shall sometimes come thether to prayse his name' (p. 270). The nature and occasions of such praises beggar the imagination.

Other focuses for meditations that stimulated his faith included the omnipotent divinity and its creation. Addressing God he asked: 'when I looke to thy word, & to the workmanship of thy hands the sunne moone & starres which thou hast made, I will say what ayleth thee oh my soule, [. . .] trust still in god for the Lord Jehovah is the work of ages' (p. 285). Woodford's universe was moral. Even in its ordinary operation it contained homilies for those with eyes to see them: for instance, the diligence of the ant was edifying. Meditation, on the Northampton to Wellingborough road, on the spectacle of hounds chasing a hare, led him to self-condemnation for lack of faith, and reminded him how the sinner was pursued by his own conscience and God's wrath. He also found solace in contemplation of the covenant and sabbath.[71] Perhaps a more surprising heavenly contemplation, given the supposed puritan dislike for any music except psalm-singing, was stimulated by hearing the Daventry wait musicians playing: 'my poore soule in the hearinge of it was lifted up above it to consider of heaven & of that great God who hath put this into the harts of men' (p. 161).

Woodford was keenly aware of his duty to attempt to solve his problems by recourse to normal remedies, not just to God. To combat his depression he tried the spa waters at Wellingborough, which were popular with Charles I, Queen Henrietta Maria, and Cromwell. Woodford partook of the waters on two occasions but to no effect. Next he tested the antimonial cup, a drinking vessel impregnated with the emetic antimony, which was reputed to have properties efficacious against melancholy. On the first occasion it was ineffective, but on the second he noticed a decided improvement. He also took care to

[70] Ibid., pp. 262 (trefoil, a covenant), 234, 237.
[71] Ibid., pp. 167, 256 (trefoil), 397.

obtain treatment for his ill son, John, from a godly apothecary, and Hannah, when afflicted with sore breasts, 'used much meanes but they are ineffectuall' (p. 125), and later consulted Dr Aaron Gourdon about the same malady, who prescribed a purge.[72]

The holy family

Woodford sought to establish religion, rather than traditional dynastic concerns, as the founding principle of his family: 'feare of [God's] name will give beinge and continuacon to a family' (p. 175). He did not regard godly profession as a solitary pilgrimage but as a collective enterprise in which his closest co-religionist and 'yoakfellowe' (p. 278) was the wife provided for him by God through the holy ordinance of matrimony. Hannah, his 'deare & holy wife' (p. 223), possessed a calling equal to his own. Woodford acknowledged this by celebrating his wedding anniversary on 22 January, and in the diary he sometimes emphasized that date (and 3 April, their shared birthday) by conducting a review of their combined spiritual estates. On their fourth anniversary, in 1639, he gave thanks for Hannah and hoped that they might 'live more holily the fifth yeare then before let us & o[u]r family increase dayly in grace' (p. 278). We have already noted the reciprocal comfort that they provided during times of crisis. This suggests a degree of equality in their spiritual status. Woodford was certainly aware of his marital responsibilities, which he heard expounded by the famous Banbury lecturer, William Whateley: husbands 'ought not to be profuse or niggardly or Churlish' (p. 191). Hannah seems to have enjoyed a degree of independence, as when she and the other wives (including the mayoress) went drinking in the town.[73] His absence from Hannah was treated as an affliction from which they might both learn. He prayed God to 'sanctifye the absence of me & my wife from one another to each of us' (p. 215).

The Woodfords, despite their shortage of money, regarded their family not as a burden but as a divine blessing: 'give us such a seed', Woodford asked God, '(when in m[er]cye thou shalt add still to our family) as we may have cause to blesse thee' (p. 148). Indeed,

---

[72] K. Thomas, *Religion and the Decline of Magic* (Harmondsworth, 1973), pp. 113–128; C. Carlton, *Charles I: the personal monarch* (London, 1983), p. 94; J. Morrill, 'Cromwell, Oliver (1599–1658)', in *ODNB*; Diary, pp. 223, 247, 265, 286.

[73] Diary, pp. 302, 339.

God had provided their son Samuel in response to their prayers.[74] However, as divine blessings, the purpose of the children's provision, continuance, or withdrawal, was spiritual, the religious education of the parents. Both needed to prepare spiritually for the birth in order to achieve an appropriately holy frame of mind. Woodford composed dedicated prayers: in Sarah's case while Hannah was in labour. For the mother, birth was a mystical experience: on the brink of Sarah's birth, Woodford asked God to grant Hannah 'strength & patience & a cheerfull spirit & speciall communion wth thee' (p. 403), and himself strove to achieve humility. Susanna's birth evoked an even more intense prayer. It was Woodford's wish that, for Hannah, the birth would be a re-enactment of her own rebirth, her conversion. At the instant of delivery, when the pain (the lot of fallen womanhood) was at its height, Hannah's faith would enable her to apprehend the divine blessing transfiguring grief into joy. He prayed to God: 'let the sence of thy favor come wth the sence of payne, & let thy hand mayd feel her Joy surmount her grief very much let her fayth remayne fixt upon thee immovably' (p. 400). The Woodfords' aspirations for their children were partly spiritual, that they should become saints, but they also expressed more conventional desires for male offspring with 'right shape & forme[,] use of witts' (p. 148), who would be a comfort to their parents. Deformity implied possible divine disfavour, as was confirmed by Woodford's uneasiness over Sarah Crutchley, who was born with extra fingers.[75]

The puritan mother's responsibility extended to suckling her own children, as Woodford acknowledged when he asked for 'the blessinge of the breast as thou hast given us of the womb' (p. 124), but this was not forthcoming. Hannah's breasts were often sore, making feeding impossible. Perhaps aware of godly expectations on the subject, they were reluctant to employ a wet nurse and did so only after taking advice. John was suckled by nurses Woodnot, Heighes, and Emerson. Another local, Goodwife Iblethy, nursed Susanna. With Sarah, the Woodfords used the services of a woman based at Enfield Chase near Edmonton, who was part of a well-established wet-nursing industry on the fringes of the capital.[76]

Pre-eminent among the roles that Woodford envisaged for himself was that of priest within his own family church: 'let my house be a Church & let mount Gerizim be amongst us' (p. 388). The mainstay of his daily routine was a session of prayers, at which the family became

---

[74] *Ibid.*, p. 298.

[75] *Ibid.*, pp. 95, 156, 400–401.

[76] *Ibid.*, pp. 112, 120, 123, 146, 315, 324; L.L. Schücking, *The Puritan Family: a social study from the literary sources* (London, 1969), pp. 67–68.

synonymous with the household. Meetings were attended by Hannah and the infants, Woodford's clerk, Hatton Farmer, and a transient population of household servants, and usually took place either just before or after supper, the former time being preferable '(unlesse some waighty occasion forbid) because freest from drowsiness' (p. 113). He also mentions morning sessions. With Woodford in the chair, the main content of weekday sessions was a reading from Scripture of around one or two chapters. On 12 October 1637 the diary records recommencing the book of Genesis: the goal was a cyclical coverage of the whole Bible. By 15 November the family had reached the twenty-fourth chapter, by 28 November the thirty-third. References to these domestic devotions are infrequent, but by 6 August 1640 the family were starting in tandem the first chapters of both the Old and New Testaments, suggesting that the whole of scripture was covered every two or three years. On Sunday evenings the format was slightly different, consisting of instruction by the head of the family. Woodford, having taken notes at the sermons he attended, would repeat these to the family and then examine them to ensure that they had been paying attention. As he possessed the catechism written by the famous puritan divine William Ames, it is fair to assume that this was used as a teaching aid. Woodford counted his in-laws, Robert, Susanna, and Samuel Haunch, as part of his godly circle, and joined in their family piety when staying with them in London. The Woodfords were also close to Hannah's uncle, Christopher Haunch, who lived near them in the village of Cranford. Woodford had a similarly high regard for his own cousins – Robert Ragdale of Wilby and Gregory Dexter of Old, the radical London printer, colonial governor, and Baptist minister.

Within his miniature godly commonwealth, Woodford also laid claim to the roles of teacher and magistrate. He told God of his intention to prepare his children through religious education for their conversion experience: 'make them instruments of thy glory in their time and enable me to educate them to that end' (p. 124). Exposure to the family devotions would contribute to this, as would personal tuition in the providential mind-set expressed in the diarist's requesting from God the strength to 'singe of thy m[er]cyes & tell them to o[u]r children' (p. 299). This alludes to the practice of teaching not only by formal dogma but also by personal example. Woodford clearly intended to educate his children by reference to divine providences drawn from his own experience and recorded in his diary. Samuel Woodford acknowledged the spiritual value of his father's diaries, admitting that he had been 'piously & Religiously brought up in the knowledge & feare of God' by his parents. If education began at an early age, then so did an authoritarian discipline, provoking one of the servants, Sue Tue, temporarily to walk out in protest at the Woodfords' correction of their eighteen-month-old baby, Sam. As an adult he confirmed the strictness of his upbringing in which his parents 'never let me sin without regret', a seed that was belatedly 'powerfull through the Grace of God to reclayme me'.[77]

The obligation of the godly to form a community and avoid the company of the profane extended to the selection of servants, whose duty was to serve their masters, Woodford asserted to God, 'in thee & for thee' (p. 129). Woodford's choice of clerk, Hatton Farmer, seems to have been successful. He experienced much satisfaction while assessing Hatton's spiritual estate: 'I trust the Lord hath begunne the good worke of grace in his soule' (p. 192). When Hatton lapsed by spending time at an alehouse, Woodford's correction was accompanied by a desire to do him good, mimicking God's chastisement of believers through affliction.[78] This provides an indication of his later treatment of his own children.

The Woodfords' relations with their household staff were considerably less successful, despite their having taken the requisite care to select godly candidates rather than just locals.[79] For example, they employed relations of, or those recommended by, godly friends. Elizabeth ('Besse') Curwyn was the stepdaughter of the Woodfords' godly friend George Curwyn, who, with his wife Elizabeth, later emigrated to Salem, Massachusetts.[80] The six-year-old Besse deserted the Woodfords to return to her mother, and afterwards Woodford noticed that several townspeople were making typically anti-puritan allegations against Hannah. They did 'traduce my wife in layinge the imputacon of haughtinesse of spirit to her charge; and this we suppose to be through the unfaythfullnes of Besse our late servant, & the talkinge of her dame' (p. 123). Woodford's account is further evidence of his kicking against the interpretation of divine affliction required by godly sainthood. Although he accepted that the disobedient servant was an affliction sent to strengthen them, he was reluctant to kiss the rod. He asserted that Besse and others had wronged Hannah, though

---

[77] Diary, p. 152. Quotations are from NCA 9494, front section. Woodford's education of his children had apparently paid dividends. Samuel Woodford's attempts at spiritual autobiography owed much to his father's influence. For instance, two of them (that published in Ferrell, 'Imperfect diary', and NCA 9494) begin with similar appeals for privacy. These two also demonstrate a similar spiritual purpose to his father's volume, namely to provide the autobiographer with assurance and to proselytise his posterity.

[78] Diary, p. 271.

[79] As part of their poor relief provision, the town government attempted to enforce the employment only of Northampton residents as servants: Markham and Cox, *Northampton*, II, pp. 180, 326.

[80] For the Curwyns, see Diary, p. 121, n. 115.

he blunted the accusation by admitting that maligning people was a failing of the town as a whole: 'Lord [. . .] heare our poore prayers in graunting us a sanctified use of this affliccon let us be bettered by it, teach us to goe through good report & evill, & in thy due time Cleare us, & Lord p[ar]don this gen[er]all sinne of us in this towne (traducinge)' (*ibid.*).

Besse Curwyn was quickly replaced by Ann ('Nan') Morris from Towcester, who a week later claimed to be lame and returned home to be replaced by Elizabeth ('Besse') Morris from Kingsthorpe, who lasted only ten days before departing 'in hast' (p. 126). Shortly after, Sue Tue also left in protest at the Woodfords' punishment of Sam. Woodford replaced Besse Morris by sounding out his godly friend William Tompson by letter. Tompson, who lived at Wilby, recommended a girl called Temperance but, despite the promising name, Woodford's problems with servants continued unabated. He employed Richard ('Dick') Odell, the son of a townsman he knew, even though he had been one of Hatton's alehouse companions. Woodford continued to see wayward household servants as divine instruments sent to punish his shortcomings, while insisting on being the offended party.[81] Accepting that the relationship between masters and servants involved reciprocal responsibilities, he was certain that the fault lay on one side only and clearly regarded them as unconverted: 'give them to doe their dutyes to us & we to them take away the rebelliousnes & risinge of spirit that are amongst us, Lord Convert them unto thee make sinne their greatest sorowe that Christ may be their greatest Joy' (p. 339).

Holy duties and ordinances

'Constancy in holy dutyes (p. 146)' or ordinances was a key indicator of growth in grace. When using these catchall terms, Woodford drew a distinction between private and public. The former denoted solitary devotions and the latter collective – family prayers, official church services, even exclusively godly prayer meetings. Private (or secret) prayer stood at the apex of this hierarchy as Woodford implied after attending one sermon, noting that he 'did behold the goeinge of my god in the sanctuary even in this publiq ordinances' (p. 272). The diary captures a life of private prayer and most entries are couched in those terms – extemporary, informal, and shading into spontaneous meditations. His most detailed and lengthy compositions took the

[81] *Ibid.*, p. 309.

form of petitionary prayers in which the believer requested everything from spiritual strength to temporal supply through the intercession of Christ: 'blessed be thy name oh Lord for erectinge this office of peticons that we may in all exigencyes put up our supplications in the name of the Comon savior the Lord xt & receave helpe' (p. 152).[82] Indeed, Christ was the altar upon which the sacrifice of prayers was made. Praise was another mode of prayer he often used, for example when a petition was granted, and by recording such divine answers to prayer he shored up his sense of assurance. Prayer in all its forms was a spiritual activity, but only the worthy could reap its benefits. Rigorous preparation was essential: the mind must be alert, not sleepy, and free from worldly interference as, for instance, when travelling. Attaining efficacious prayers depended on achieving the holy frame of mind in which faith and zeal predominated. Woodford bemoaned his failure to achieve this: 'my prayers have longe wanted that fayth & fervency they have formerly bene offred up with beinge kept downe with the thorny cares of this world, & distraction of businesses' (p. 139). At a godly meeting, the quality of his own contribution was compromised by a similar failure, leading him to condemn himself for dereliction of duty: 'I p[er]formed duty but my hart was very dull & the Lord for my sinnes in too much carking care as I may supose wtheld himselfe much from shininge, Lord accept of my paynfull & straightned prayers' (p. 383).

Public ordinances were nevertheless of crucial importance to his divinity: frequenting sermons was the public practice most associated with puritanism. Woodford's irreducible minimum weekly requirement for sermons did not alter whether he was at home or away. In all circumstances he attended two sermons on Sunday. The only occasion on which he failed to achieve this was 4 March 1638, when the authorities cancelled the afternoon sermon at All Saints' parish. Hannah missed out on one more occasion owing to illness. Furthermore, in Northampton he attended his own parish church and did not usually resort to the trademark godly practice of gadding. The need to do so was obviated by the rich variety of spiritual wares available in his own parish. He gadded only once (9 June 1639), and then in company with the mayor and aldermen, to St Sepulchre's, another town-centre parish, to sample the preaching of a newly appointed incumbent. In contrast with his punctilious Sunday observance, his attendance at the Thursday lecture was infrequent: he records attending on twenty-six occasions. From time to time the opportunity for supplementary sermons arose, but again he regarded attendance at these as optional. He was equally concerned with the *quality* of Northampton sermons, as we shall see.

---

[82] Thomas, *Religion and the Decline of Magic*, pp. 113–128.

Woodford rarely commented on the public prayers provided by these ministers. The occasional exceptions shed light on his expectations of the ministry and on the puritan atmosphere obtaining in his parish. In remarks on two ministers who capitulated to court pressure and went back on godly habits, he expressed a zero tolerance even of occasional conformity with canonical requirements. He voiced his distaste for the Prayer Book service as practised by Charles Newton, whose performance had 'turned somewhat canonicall [he] gave thanks for the S[ain]ts dep[ar]ted' (p. 183). Woodford clearly preferred the extemporary prayers favoured by the puritan ministry. He was willing to forgive Newton an aberration he did not repeat. More serious, however, was the behaviour of William Martin, an apostate who fell from former godliness by practising conformity with canonical ceremonial – 'he bowes at the name of Jesus & stands up at gloria patri' (p. 106) – for which Woodford accused him of backsliding. Clearly such behaviour was abnormal at All Saints'.

In terms of the numbers of sermons attended, Woodford's behaviour during his stays in London was similar to that in Northampton. He always attended two on a Sunday, though he supplemented this with more extras than when at home, and, once only, indulged in five over one week, much less than Wallington's maximum of nineteen.[83] However, the pattern of his sermon-going in the capital was very different from that at home. He almost invariably gadded from his base at the parish of All Hallows, London Wall; and he never mentioned Andrew Janeway, the incumbent there. Woodford attended Sunday sermons in the parish only twice, when he and Haunch had invited Andrew Perne to preach.

His parish of first resort was the godly preaching centre of St Mary's, Aldermanbury, where John Stoughton was the incumbent. Woodford held Stoughton's preaching in the highest regard whether it was his two sermons every Sunday or lectures on Wednesdays and Fridays, and described his sermons as excellent and Stoughton himself as a star. Woodford was equally impressed with his replacement, Edmund Calamy, another nationally famous puritan preacher. Like his predecessor, Calamy invited many other ministers to preach in the parish, such as Simeon Ashe, all of whom received Woodford's praise. Woodford's second choice parish was St Stephen's, Coleman Street, where the future Congregationalist, John Goodwin, was the vicar. Once, Woodford and Haunch travelled outside the city on Sunday to Calibute Downing's living at St John's, Hackney, where Goodwin preached both times. A further two ministers popular with Woodford

[83] P.S. Seaver, *Wallington's World: a puritan artisan in seventeenth-century London* (1985), p. 37.

were Obadiah Sedgwick of St Mildred's, Bread Street, and Joseph Simonds of St Martin's, Ironmonger Lane.

What stands out is the overwhelmingly positive tenor of Woodford's remarks about preachers, whether in London or at home: he was less critical than Samuel Rogers, the professional preacher from Essex.[84] He did not reserve his praise for radical puritans: his taste in preaching seems relatively eclectic. He lauded moderate Calvinists such as Edward Chetwind, Dean of Bristol, and Richard Holdsworth, Master of Emmanuel College, Cambridge. He was impressed with the future Royalist Jeremy Leech, minister of St Mary le Bow, Cheapside, who invited the Northamptonshire minister James Cranford to preach with him. Woodford recorded very few bad sermons in the London parishes. William Martin's replacement at the famous St Antholin's lecture, Budge Row, was described as indifferent. However, the preacher at St Botolph's, Aldgate, who was probably the incumbent, the future zealous Royalist Thomas Swadlin, was such a disappointment that Woodford retreated immediately to Aldermanbury.

Central to Woodford's piety was the ordinance of the Sunday sabbath, which, unlike the saints' days enjoined by the church authorities, was sanctioned by holy writ. His sabbatarianism reflected the divisiveness at the heart of all his divinity, in that only the godly would love the Lord's Day and its activities, while the ungodly mass would despise it. He thanked God 'for thy sabaths which the world loves not' (p. 327). Of course, Woodford engaged in public worship on weekdays, but his sabbath observances were of a higher order in that the entire day was set aside as sacred. He rejoiced that God 'had given us the lib[er]ty of his blessed Sabath, to rest from our labours & to refresh our selves in holy Converse with him in the blessed ordinances' (p. 116). All secular activity was proscribed to allow the ordinances free reign, but mere attendance at, and mechanical utterance of, prayers was inadequate. The effects of these ordinances on the believer were held to be spiritual. In order to participate in 'a holy & a right manner', the individual must be in the correct spiritual state of 'fayth & sincerity of hart' (p. 146, trefoil symbol). To achieve this, preparation was essential. Woodford sometimes prepared (and not only when he proposed to take communion) with a perfunctory prayer on Saturday, occasionally, as most notably on 3 December 1637, followed by a longer version the next morning.

If the optimum state was achieved, then the spiritual benefits of the public ordinances could be dramatic, as Woodford revealed in hoping

[84] T. Webster and K. Shipps (eds), *The Diary of Samuel Rogers, 1634–1638*, Church of England Record Society XI (Woodbridge, 2004), pp. xlii–xlvii.

that the divine 'spirit may come along wth thy word that so every grace may be increased every sinne decayed every affeccon inflamed and rightly placed put wind into my sayles this day' (p. 163). Here is a clear illustration of the idea of the word preached as an edifying boost. Indeed, it functioned actually to dispel evil, as Woodford noted when speaking in praise of the Wellingborough lecture.[85] His most intensely edifying experience resulted from the sermon by Thomas Case on 18 March 1638, concerning the saints' assurance, one of the few performances to approach the potency of secret prayer, although Thomas Ball's efforts on 16 December ran it a close second. A more typical reaction was that he described his mind as being in a holy frame or graciously affected, or with adjectives indicating life, such as 'enlarged' or 'quickened'. Non-holy frames of mind, resulting from faulty preparation, he described with words betokening death, such as 'dull', 'heavy', or even 'dead', and these resulted in self-condemnation for the sin of slackness in duty. In a typical blend of the spiritual and the mundane, he blamed his sleepiness at morning sermon on 'my infirmity of sinnes & want of care to goe to bed early the last night' (p. 181). In its worst form this spiritual dullness could result in Woodford accusing himself of breaching the fourth commandment – he confessed to God his habit of 'prophaninge thy Sabath & ordinances continually' (p. 393). It is an indication of the intensity of the godly reverence for the sabbath that a lack of spiritual rigour was viewed as profanation, and this explains the puritan reaction to the Laudian Book of Sports, which allowed more straightforwardly profane activities.

The sacrament of the Lord's Supper was central to Woodford's piety: he averaged six communions per year (double the canonical requirement) but, given the gaps in the journal, the actual figure was probably higher. He rarely received outside Northampton, the exceptions being once at Wilby and thrice at Aldermanbury, London. The rite's importance to him is demonstrated by his once (on 4 November 1638) choosing to renew his covenant. The significance of this ordinance was more than commemorative: the believer could expect substantial spiritual benefits. He prayed: 'let me this day by fayth eate the flesh & drinke the bloud of the Lord xt' (p. 359), and hoped to be 'alive & quickned & may feele a sensible increase of grace & decay of sinne' (p. 222).[86] Again, only the fit could reap these rewards, and fitness comprised the same repentant qualities that were the goal of all Woodford's piety: he asked God to 'graunt that I may reape benefit by them, give me the fayth spirit & affeccons of a xxian'

[85] Diary, p. 392.
[86] Ibid., pp. 221, 262, 280, 386.

(p. 222). Calamy alluded to these qualities in a sermon expounding Psalm 51: 'The sacrifices of God are a broken spirit: a broken and a contrite heart, O God, thou wilt not despise.'[87]

The rite, though carried out in public, was essentially an internal affair. Woodford carried out the same soul-searching preparation as for the sabbath itself. In the most colourful instances of his preparatory routine, on 2 June and 1 September 1639, he confessed his sins directly to God, instead of via a priest, and strove for a contrite heart.[88] There were also external characteristics to pure communions: the worship should be free of carnality, and the serving minister, who must himself be worthy, might exclude the obviously profane.[89] An unrewarding communion was the result of poor preparation. God withheld himself at the 2 June sacrament owing to Woodford's 'deadnes & coldnesse in dutye' (p. 309), which persisted until Tuesday, when God sent the affliction of disobedient servants to draw attention to the flaw. The concentrated effort involved and the devastating implication of failure is illustrated by a later passage: 'I laboured to have my hart affected but I had little comunion oh my god. oh my god hide not thy face from me' (p. 367).

The godly community

Woodford enjoyed contacts with a variety of godly professors from London and across the Midlands, but his base was the community centred on Northampton, a town notorious for puritanism since the reign of Elizabeth. The network contained some of the leading figures in the lay and clerical elites controlling the town, the most important to mention being Thomas Martin, his wife, Jane, and their eldest son, Samuel. Thomas Martin was the most prominent leader of the godly group in the oligarchy in the first half of the seventeenth century and he was also Woodford's closest friend and ally: indeed, as mayor in 1635 he had driven through Woodford's candidacy for the position of steward in the teeth of considerable opposition from other aldermen. A wealthy woollen draper, Martin had served as mayor in 1616, 1624, and 1634. During his terms of office he had pursued a vigorously godly agenda: in 1624 the corporation had moved unilaterally against

---

[87] *Ibid.*, p. 313 and n. 721.

[88] P. Lake, 'William Bradshaw, antichrist, and the community of the godly', *Journal of Ecclesiastical History*, 36 (1985), pp. 582–585.

[89] Woodford held that ungodly ministers should not be allowed to give communion to the godly (Diary, p. 289), and questioned whether it was contrary to divine law to receive the sacrament in the presence of those who were overtly profane (*ibid.*, pp. 188–189).

alehouses, suppressing many. From 1607 he had also taken the leading role in seeing off repeated challenges from the conformists in the town, led by John Lambe, and in 1628 was reported for holding an illegal conventicle in his house. In 1643 he was elected a justice of the peace for the town and served on county committees.[90] The following year Woodford drew up Martin's will, and was rewarded with a golden ring inscribed 'from a true friend'.[91] Samuel Martin was only slightly less eminent, serving as a churchwarden of the parish in the 1630s, chamberlain of the town in 1638, mayor in 1645 (when Northampton was a Parliamentary garrison), and captain in the militia in 1648.[92]

The Rushworth family was another crucial part of the Woodfords' inner circle. Francis Rushworth and his wife, Joan, were natives of Coventry, and Woodford made social trips with them back to their roots.[93] Francis was an apothecary by trade and part of the next generation of town oligarchs. He served as churchwarden of All Saints' in the decisive years of 1637 and 1638, as mayor in 1643, and was appointed to the county committee.[94] The Sargent family – Roger and his sons, Joseph and William – were equally important. To this vital group we must add the names of Woodford's landlords: Samuel and Mary Crick, and William and Ann Spicer. Crick's father, George, a town bailiff and All Saints' churchwarden, had been accused of illegal conventicling with Thomas Martin. William Spicer was bailiff in 1649: his will was witnessed by the stationer Peter Whalley, another of Woodford's contacts.[95] In 1634 Whalley had been accused by the Privy Council of selling copies of *Histriomastix*, William Prynne's attack on stage plays; he later served as town chamberlain, mayor, and MP for the borough. The Fisher family was also central to the godly scene.

---

[90] Markham and Cox, *Northampton*, II, pp. 115, 304–305, 552. Martin was the nephew of Francis Foster of Whiston, a radical puritan minister deprived for nonconformity in 1605. Martin and the godly had clashed with John Lambe in 1607, and he later led the opposition to Lambe's chancellorship of the diocese, being instrumental in promoting charges against him (with the support of Sir Edward Montagu) to the 1621 parliament, which Lambe survived only by activating his influence at court through the Lord Keeper, John Williams: see Sheils, *Puritans*, p. 81; Longden, *Clergy* (Foster); TNA, STAC8/205/19; Fielding, 'Peterborough', pp. 84–85, 185, 188. Martin was later accused of entertaining the minister John Woods at a conventicle in his house: PDR, CB A2, under dates 29 May 1628, 15 June 1629, and 13 July 1629; NRO, Finch (Hatton) MSS, F(H) 133.
[91] PDR, Archdeaconry of Northampton Wills, third series, A178.
[92] Vestry Minutes, pp. 30–31; Markham and Cox, *Northampton*, II, pp. 441, 552, 568.
[93] Diary, pp. 212–213.
[94] Vestry Minutes, pp. 33–37; Markham and Cox, *Northampton*, II, pp. 17, 441, 552.
[95] Book of Orders, p. 18, also entry dated 23 October 1637; Vestry Minutes, pp. 17, 21, 25, 29, 32, 34, 36, 38; Markham and Cox, *Northampton*, II, pp. 171–172, 441, 552, 561–562; PDR, CB A2, under dates 29 May 1628, 15 June 1629, 13 July 1629; TNA, PROB/11/263; G. Ford, 'Where's Whalley? The search for Sir Samuel uncovers a Whalley–Cartwright alliance in Northamptonshire', *Northamptonshire Past and Present*, 62 (2009), p. 38.

Francis, mayor in 1608 and justice of the peace for the town from 1630 to 1642, supported Woodford in his contest for the stewardship, but his brother John enjoyed a closer relationship with him. A hatter by trade, in 1619 John had been appointed master of the house of correction by the town assembly. In 1635 he had stood accused of preaching to the prisoners in the jail, and he was the only layman noted by Woodford as preaching in the All Saints' pulpit. He was elected mayor in 1640 and served on the county committee. Finally, Woodford numbered his master, John Reading, and his brother Jason among his godly acquaintanceship, though not a third brother, an attorney called Daniel.[96]

One of the defining characteristics of the godly community was its preference for voluntary forms of piety, shading into sociability. The Woodfords, Rushworths, and Martins in particular met constantly at one another's houses, usually over a meal. The purpose of these gatherings was to worship, to demonstrate their distance from the corrupt world, and to achieve collective growth in grace. This is suggested by Woodford's description of a supper conference at his house at which he and Hannah were joined by Francis and Joan Rushworth: 'blessed be the Lord for the priviledges & opportunityes we enioy of meetinge together in peece & Love, oh Lord sanctifye & blesse every meeting of o[u]rs that we may glorify thy name & be instruments of good to one another' (p. 124). At another supper conference at home the Woodfords were in company with the Rushworths and Samuel Martin. Through conference the saints aimed to promote godliness – faith, joy, mutual love, and improvement. Woodford requested God to grant them 'comfort in o[u]r meetinge graunt that we may be cheerfull in the confidence of fayth & direct us to good & wholsome discourse that we may be bettered by it' (p. 166). The result was positive. The outcome was equally upbeat when Woodford attended a supper conference at Samuel Martin's attended by Peter Whalley and their wives.[97] At a dinner conference at the Woodfords' attended by the Rushworths and John Fisher and his wife, the godly schoolmaster Daniel Rogers read a tale from Foxe's *Acts and Monuments*. On a further occasion Woodford joined John Fisher to seek the Lord to address both personal and political problems. Woodford seemed almost to identify this godly network with the visible church: 'Lord [. . .] heare o[u]r poore prayers doe good to thy church blesse us & o[u]r families' (p. 366).

Such examples could be multiplied. Sometimes these consultations assumed a more disciplinary tone: Woodford condemned the

---

[96]Markham and Cox, *Northampton*, II, p. 115; Diary, pp. 95 (and n. 1), 155, 336–337.
[97]Diary, p. 186.

beneficed minister James Lewis for 'his course of company keepinge' (p. 124). This brought about some reformation.[98] Perhaps the clearest example of the spiritual benefits of godly conference is a series of meetings with the Martins. While Hannah was absent during the plague, the Martins and Mary Crick provided food and company, but even more important was spiritual sustenance: during one conference with Samuel Martin, Woodford received valuable counselling about his melancholy; at another they shored up one another's resolve to avoid bad company.[99] The godly also held larger meetings to discuss public affairs, whose subject matter will be discussed later. On occasion, godly conferences could appear to be the urban government at prayer as when Woodford went 'to Joyne in dutye wth gods people' (p. 182). At least ten individuals were present, including the serving mayor, William Collis, his wife and family, the Woodfords, John Fisher, William Turland, and Mrs John Harbert. As with other ordinances, only the spiritually worthy would benefit: Woodford confessed to being 'very dull & unfit' (ibid.), illustrating the spiritual rigour deemed necessary, but the outcome was still positive. Further meetings took place at the houses of Dr James Hart (Lord Edward Montagu's physician), James Fryers, and Thomas Ball, the incumbent of All Saints' parish and leader of the Northampton godly.[100]

The godly network to which Woodford belonged had used its influence in the corporation to appoint Ball, a minister with national clout, who had built up, through the influence of his mentor, Dr John Preston, a network of influential contacts with clergy such as Richard Sibbes, and lay politicians such as Viscount Saye and Sele, the Earl of Warwick, Christopher Sherland, and Sir Gilbert Pickering.[101] Ball then appointed his own subordinates: Charles Newton served as curate from 1632 until 1639, and William Holmes from 1639 until 1645. Daniel Rogers, the son of Daniel, the lecturer of Wethersfield, Essex, served as schoolmaster from 1631 until 1642.[102]

Ball and the corporation had developed the already godly town into an outstanding centre for puritan piety. Woodford's diary is a unique source for the operation of the exceptionally dynamic system of preaching over which Ball presided. He provided two sermons on Sunday – often delivered by him and his curates but frequently by a bewildering array of guests from around the county and country. The

---

[98] Ibid., p. 239.
[99] Ibid., pp. 255, 267–268.
[100] Ibid., pp. 188, 370.
[101] J. Fielding, 'Ball, Thomas (1590–1659)', in ODNB; Markham and Cox, Northampton, II, p. 384.
[102] Diary, p. 107, n. 49.

corporation also required him to maintain a lecturer, but in reality Ball operated the Thursday morning lecture as a combination to which he again invited a host of visitors.[103] His regime also included a communion celebrated on the first Sunday in the month. In total, Woodford heard sermons by thirty-two different ministers, but even this tally is an underestimate. We have already noted the powerful effect on him of a sermon delivered by the visiting divine Thomas Case. Unsurprisingly, Woodford heard Ball more often than any other, and his remarks were invariably complimentary. Andrew Perne was another of his favourite preachers. Perne's efforts were never regarded as anything less than profitable, several times as excellent, and twice earned him the accolade of being a star. Three visiting divines delivered sermons that affected Woodford strongly: an unnamed preacher, William Rathbone, and Henry Hall.[104]

Woodford reserved his criticism for sermons he encountered outside his own parish: for example, in other town-centre parishes, staffed by conformists. When he visited Giles Thorne, Sir John Lambe's client, at St Sepulchre's, his conclusion was negative: 'it appeares by his sermon what he is, Lord weed up the darnell & the Cockle' (p. 310). He also tested the water at St Giles's parish, where George Colson was the curate to Richard Holbrooke, a Church court official. He could only bring himself to stay for part of Colson's Christmas Day sermon because there was 'but litle in it' (p. 154).

The Thursday lecture and Sunday observances allowed Woodford to mix with godly contacts, both lay and clerical, from Northampton's hinterland. After the conclusion of public duties, the congregation dispersed into a number of dinner parties to discuss, among other topics no doubt, the contents of the sermons they had just heard: we have already seen how good sermons stimulated Woodford to take notes for later repetition. After Henry Hall, schoolmaster of Paulerspury, had delivered one of the Sunday sermons, he attended a supper conference held at the Woodfords' with Joan Rushworth. The day after Richard Trueman, the vicar of Dallington and son of the godly saddler, had delivered a Sunday morning sermon at All Saints', Woodford and his mother dined with him on venison pasty at

---

[103] The lecture differed from those held in many market towns in that it was not held on a market day but on Thursday, which had been of civic significance as far back as the Order of 1571. From May 1630 the mayor and aldermen met fortnightly after the lecture to discuss town affairs. The lecture (which dated from 1629 and perhaps even from Jacobean times) occurs in the records in 1654. In 1656 Alderman John Gifford elicited the help of Sir Gilbert Pickering and Cromwell's son-in-law, Lord John Claypole, to support the ministers in the town, and the last reference to it is in March 1658: Markham and Cox, *Northampton*, I, p. 128; II, pp. 49, 400; Fielding, 'Peterborough', p. 159, n. 6; Sheils, *Puritans*, pp. 120–122.

[104] Diary, pp. 146, 276, 365.

the Rushworths' house. The lectures provided similar opportunities for godly social interaction. After five separate lectures delivered by Ball, Woodford attended the following dinners: at his own house attended by Henry Hall and Hatton Farmer's mother; again at home to entertain Daniel Rogers, the Martins, and the Rushworths; at Ball's house; at the house of the churchwarden and baker Peter Farren, who wined and dined the whole town assembly; and at Joseph Bryan's, a Gray's Inn bencher, who had invited Woodford's confidant John Bullivant, rector of Abington, his wife, Mary, and the Rushworths.[105]

The lecture attracted devotees from further afield. The most eminent was Robert Rich, Earl of Warwick, who came to hear Ball, his client and ally, preach. However, the most important incomers from Woodford's point of view were his friends Thomas Pentlow and Andrew Perne of Wilby, and Thomas Watts and Henry Allen of Easton Maudit. Woodford befriended two men called Thomas Pentlow who were related to each other. One was lord of the manor of Wilby and married to Elizabeth Jones of London, where the couple owned a second house in Ironmonger Lane. Woodford took refuge at his house in Wilby for several months in 1638 when the plague was in full spate at Northampton. Another held a manor at Broughton.[106] The two Pentlows seem to have agreed in their religious convictions: Pentlow of Broughton had in 1627 presented Andrew Perne, one of Woodford's favourite ministers, to the other Pentlow's parish of Wilby. Perne, who preached in co-operation with fellow ministers on a Sunday – such as his curate, biographer, and convert, Samuel Ainsworth – headed a godly following (including Pentlow and Woodford's cousins, the Ragdales) which had supported the previous incumbent, the notorious puritan John Everard. During the 1630s they clashed with the Church authorities over their gadding to Leicestershire to hear Thomas Hooker preach, their refusal to report gadders who came to hear Perne, and their ceremonial nonconformity.[107]

[105] *Ibid.*, pp. 109 n. 63, 153, 160, 187, 309, 337.
[106] Pentlow of Wilby (d. 1657) served assiduously on county committees and on the bench during the Civil War and Protectorate periods: his memorial inscription at Wilby proudly stated that, after serving for ten years as a justice of the peace, he had finally been made of the quorum. See P.R. Brindle, 'Politics and society in Northamptonshire, 1649–1714' (unpublished PhD thesis, University of Leicester, 1983), pp. 134–135, 138–139, 143, 144, 150–151; *VCH Northamptonshire*, IV, p. 147; TNA, PROB/11/263; *Historical Gazetteer of London before the Great Fire* (London, 1987), pp. 118–125; Bridges, *History of Northamptonshire*, II, p. 156. For Pentlow of Broughton and Weston Favell, who was married to Isabel (née Eakins), see Venn, under William Pentlow; Metcalfe, *Visitation of Northamptonshire 1618*, p. 178; *VCH Northamptonshire*, IV, p. 109; PDR, Church Survey Book 5, fos 13r, 131; TNA, PROB/11/153.
[107] Longden MS, 17 March 1627; Fielding, 'Ball, Thomas'; J. Fielding, 'Perne, Andrew (c.1595–1654)', in *ODNB*; R. Cust, 'Sherland, Christopher (1594–1632)', in *ODNB*; Longden,

This community tended to take control of the religious rites of passage, such as baptism, by performing them in private at home. For the godly, the role of conversion necessarily reduced the importance of the sacrament: Woodford requested God to convert his (already baptized) children: 'make them thine by adopcon' (p. 124). Before Sarah's baptism, he asked that God 'sanctify my child for the ordinance of baptisme & sanctify the ordinance to the child, & make the Child thine owne by grace' (p. 234). Before John's baptism, his father simply wished that the inward grace might go along with the outward sign. Nevertheless, the ritual was still regarded as important: Woodford ensured that his children were baptized within a week or two of birth and requested the vicar to baptize the six-day-old Thomas at home when it was clear that he would not live long. However, the significance was mainly symbolic, marking the children's entry into the community of the godly, and was an occasion for socializing. The Woodfords chose godparents, according to the stipulations of the Book of Common Prayer, although they referred to them by the more acceptable title of witness. Woodford appointed John Reading and his mother, Jane Woodford, as witnesses at John's baptism. Owing to Woodford's unclear instructions as to the child's name, the witnesses bickered when they were asked to supply the name – Joan favoured Robert but Reading prevailed, providentially according to Woodford, with John. While John's baptism was held on a Sunday in the course of normal observances, Susanna's was performed on a Tuesday. Charles Newton conducted the rite and it was thought necessary to provide a sermon, for which purpose Woodford procured Andrew Perne. Daniel Cawdrey provided the baptismal sermon for John and Martha Gifford's child. Woodford acted as a witness to John Bullivant's child, and attended the domestic baptism of Joseph Sargent's.[108] In line with tradition, there was sometimes a celebratory meal consisting of wine and sugarplums.

Churching was the follow-up rite relating to childbirth and here, again, the godly reduced the ceremony, a reintegration of the new mother into the social life of the parish, to an exclusive occasion performed away from the parish church and its ceremonial requirements. After John's birth, Hannah Woodford was churched at home by an unnamed cleric in the presence of the landlords

---

Clergy; PDR, CB 61, under 11 July 1630; PDR, CB A63, fos 192, 408, 417, 425; TNA, SP16/308/52; E. Allen, 'Everard, John (1584?–1640/41)', in *ODNB*; TNA, STAC8/35/3; TNA, SP16/251/25. Robert Ragdale had been excommunicated in 1626 for insulting the local conformist minister: PDR, CB 58, unfoliated, 28 July 1626; PDR, Miscellaneous Book 5b, fo. 2r.

[108] *Diary*, pp. 95–96, 150, 186–187, 323, 370.

(Mary Crick and William and Ann Spicer), John Loe (the godly ironmonger), and his wife, Ann. Charles Newton churched Hannah at home after Susanna's birth in the presence of Mary Crick and the Rushworths; after Thomas's birth, William Holmes performed the ceremony, after which he attended a dinner at the Woodfords' attended by Crick, Christopher Iblethy (the husband of the Woodfords' wet nurse), John Friend the sexton, and Messrs Fery and Johnson, who both acted as parish clerks at various times and may therefore have had an official role in the proceedings.[109]

Godly example

For puritans, the character and experience of individual saints was at least as important as abstract doctrine.[110] When James Lewis preached at the funeral of John Rolles, Woodford noted 'Lord thou art pleased to preach to us by thy word & by example, oh teach to profit' (p. 384). The godly were expected to increase collectively in grace by a process of trading experiences of divine providence in their lives. The most striking example is Andrew Perne's relation of his conversion experience to Woodford. He claimed to have been converted at St Catharine's College, Cambridge, where he had held a fellowship during the mastership of Richard Sibbes.[111] Woodford derived a similar amount of edification from the contemporary example of Thomas Warren of Old, 'on whom I trust the Lord hath shewed much m[er]cy & converted him a sinner from his evill way Hosanna in the highest' (p. 394).

Woodford's co-religionists confided to him instances of the providential intervention of the Holy Spirit in their lives. John Fisher, the evangelist of the jail, related his delivery from the violence of prisoners who had locked him in the dungeon during a jailbreak. Thomas Watts attempted to comfort Woodford about his level of debt using the example of his own deliverance.[112] Woodford reciprocated with edifying tales of his own, sometimes perhaps derived from that list of providences, his diary. The warning at the beginning of the volume shows that the contents were not meant for all eyes. Only fellow professors could be trusted to peruse it: he 'shewed my book

[109] *Ibid.*, pp. 197, 326, 369.
[110] P. Collinson, '"A magazine of religious patterns": an Erasmian topic transposed in English Protestantism', in *Godly People: essays on English Protestantism and puritanism* (London, 1983), pp. 499–526.
[111] Diary, pp. 99–100.
[112] *Ibid.*, pp. 170, 259.

to some Lord deliver me from danger & blesse & prosper thy people'
(p. 362). The godly's daily task of working out their salvation was lent
a historical perspective by reading Scripture or the *Acts and Monuments*,
which permitted the godly to identify themselves as part of a timeless
struggle, as the heirs of past saints, a 'saving remnant' in a corrupt
world and unreformed church.

The pilgrimage that started with conversion ended with death. As
with so many aspects of godly life, the secret was in the preparation.
Woodford strove to be prepared for death, but left no will.[113] Godly
dying, like godly living, was not a private but rather a social, even
theatrical, affair.[114] The death of 'that holy man' (p. 97), Thomas
Freeman of Cranford, was a textbook case: the epitome of a godly
death. The collective nature of godly religion is again reflected in
Woodford's narrative of the deathbed drama. He attended Freeman's
bedside with his mother and Hatton Farmer. In this final act, the
dying professor and the assembled godly conclave provided mutual
encouragement and corroboration of their callings. By this late stage
the spiritual man was expected to have all but banished the carnal.
The signs of election included a love for the godly and a cheerful
enthusiasm for death deriving from assurance. Freeman's will had
already stated his full assurance of salvation and the godly witnesses
now informed Woodford of Freeman's joyfulness: he 'complained that
his body was become a very unfit organ for his soule to worke in he
reioyced much to see us; and seemed no whit afrayd of death but
desired to be dissolved and to be with the Lord xt' (*ibid.*). This was a
staple godly formula. Woodford's group returned the next day to find
Freeman weaker but on the brink of a holy death. Shortly afterwards,
he 'sweetly slept in the Lord' (p. 98). The godly spectators had provided
spiritual comfort and had, by prayer, helped to send him joyfully on
his way, corroborating the dying saint's status as a potent holy man.
Freeman had chosen his parish priest, Robert Lambe, to deliver the
funeral oration. Lambe was the client of Bishop John Williams of

---

[113]However, he did draft that of his friend Thomas Martin, and perhaps had a hand in
its composition. Martin asserted man's impotence ('he cannot p[ro]mise life to himselfe for
one minute'), and his gratitude to God for all worldly and spiritual blessings. He stated
his assurance of elect status (Christ had 'layd up a crowne of immortality for me') and his
expectation of physical resurrection, of being 'cloathed with my Skinne, & with these eyes of
my body shall see my Redeemer': PDR, Archdeaconry of Northampton Wills, third series,
A178.

[114]R. Houlbrooke, 'The puritan death-bed, c. 1560–1640', in C. Durston and J. Eales (eds),
The Culture of English Puritanism, 1560–1700 (1996), pp. 122–144.

Lincoln, and his reputation was mixed. However, those attending the ceremony were unequivocally godly.[115]

The example provided by Woodford's friend Joan Rushworth was less straightforwardly positive. When her final illness took hold, Joan was 'troubled in Conscience' (p. 390) and as Woodford's family was about to begin its Sunday evening sermon repetition the crisis erupted and Samuel Martin arrived to bring Woodford to her bedside. Joan, harbouring doubts about her election, 'was in mighty horror roringe sometimes most hideously & cryeinge out she was damn'd she was damn'd, she should be in hell to all eternity, & that she had neglected so great salvacon' (p. 391). Woodford and Martin played the roles of spiritual physicians. Their joint counsel at the height of the crisis elicited from her a response that demonstrated the required marks of election – love of God and the godly, and the recognition that she had offended God by sin: 'the Lord stayed her in some measure in the midst of her horrors she acknowledged she loved god & his children, & that she had iniured god but he had done her no iniury at all' (*ibid.*). Woodford prayed for her and inscribed the prayer in his diary. He was in no doubt about the significance of this affliction: in wrath God had withdrawn Himself from Joan to teach her humility and encourage her to renewed repentance. Yet Woodford also derived from the incident lessons for himself and the other onlookers, namely to increase vigilance against sin, which had caused God to obscure himself from Joan, and to re-engage with godly values – the necessary mixture of dread and love of the divinity, of confidence and doubt. Woodford does not tell us anything further about Joan's illness but the conclusion appears to have been satisfactory. She died over a week later and Woodford noted that Daniel Rogers preached excellently at her funeral.

If Woodford derived spiritual encouragement from the reality of his fellow professors' lives, then he did equally from the sermons preached after their deaths. Rogers was said to have preached excellently again at the funeral of John Ball, an Oxford scholar whose father, Lawrence, was elected mayor in 1641. Woodford's friend John Bullivant preached at the funeral of a Mrs Wilson. More revealingly, Charles Newton preached at the burial of Goodman Atkins, which suggests that it was not only the wealthy who received such tributes. This also illustrates the process of continuous peer review and assessment by which godly lives progressed. Woodford treated the sermon critically, comparing it with his own knowledge of the subject's life. Newton, said Woodford, had 'spoke very well of who I think deserved no lesse' (p. 188).

[115] Thomas Freeman's will stated that he was 'in hope and full assurance' of resurrection. He also bequeathed money to both ministers of Cranford, Robert Lambe and John Fosbrooke: NRO, Archdeaconry of Northampton Wills, second series, G211; TNA, SP16/266/54.

Godly unity?

Woodford regarded angry divisions in society as sinful manifestations of still carnal natures. When witnessing an argument between non-godly participants, he mused 'while they wrangled, what Jarringe & Contradiccon sinne hath brought into this world Oh Lord let thy gospel be so powerfull upon us that the Lyon may become a Lamb' (p. 127). He condemned himself for anger, having exploded against the ungodly Daniel Reading, expressed 'too much foolish choler' (p. 272) in response to a dinner invitation from the corporation, and, after a drinking session, broken out in 'Corrupt passion' (p. 324) against Edward Chadwick, a professional rival. He was equally furious with servants whom he had instructed to catch his horse.[116] Squabbling among the saints was more serious still, as the godly community was partly defined by its unity. However, to characterize the relationships between the Northampton godly simply as a matter of amicable collaboration is to tell only half of the story. Woodford reveals the group to have been riven by disputes. There were naturally tensions within his own family, whether it was his mother and wife bickering over sugarplums, marital strife, the Woodfords' clashing with Hannah's Uncle Christopher, or Woodford falling out with his father-in-law over money. The godly ideal of moderation in behaviour involved a restraint of humankind's natural passions. After Jane and Hannah's spat, Woodford wrote that God had given his family 'speciall love one to another so I humbly pray thee give us discretion, & power over every passion, that no jarre may at any time come at all to interrupt that true affection betweene us' (p. 96). Inter-godly tensions at work are covered in a later section.

At times the failings of the godly threatened to become public, with the danger of discrediting their profession, especially during the sensitive decade of the 1630s. These underlying tensions came to light when Woodford and Robert Haunch quarrelled with John Reading over the fee that they jointly owed him for obtaining the county almonership for Woodford. Woodford claimed that Reading had demanded £100 at first but had then allowed Woodford to beat him down to £50. He was thrown into a panic by Reading's threat to make the matter public by pursuing the debt in the Court of Requests, and hoped to settle the matter without recourse to the law. One of the justifications for this was that publicity would bring godly profession into disrepute. He was not prepared to accept all the responsibility for this, and apportioned the guilt for the affliction between himself and Reading. He asked God: 'Are we not both thine, pr[e]serve thy gospel

---

[116]Diary, p. 110.

from imputacon, we are both of us vessels wherein there is no pleasure & thou mayest Justly breake us one against another, but oh let us live in thy sight, & let thy m[er]cye pr[e]vent o[u]r ruine' (p. 283). The dispute was successfully concluded by reference to two saintly umpires. Woodford had made use of this form of mediation previously, when he and Hannah had fallen out with her uncle, Christopher Haunch. On this occasion the godly minister William Spencer of Scaldwell fulfilled the role, by whose physicianship the injury to the godly community was 'somewhat cured' (p. 98). That the Woodford *vs.* Reading dispute had come to a head in London perhaps explains the choice of two London clergy – John Stoughton and William Gouge – as referees. Stoughton was doubtless Woodford's selection, while Gouge, prolific writer and minister of St Ann's, Blackfriars, where Reading's London home was situated, was his. The divines suggested a compromise figure of £60, which Woodford paid.[117]

Equally disturbing for Woodford was his falling out with his cousin Robert Ragdale and other Wilby residents engaged in a dispute over leases with Thomas Pentlow, the lord of the manor. Woodford's position was ambiguous since it was his friend Pentlow who employed him to operate the court. He helped the tenants to draw up their statement of grievances, but was distressed to learn that 'my cousin had much abused me & s[ai]d [...] that hell swarmed with Lawyers' (p. 383). Woodford was particularly upset by the fact that fellow godly professors ('those that are good' (p. 378)) were charging him with provoking them to promote a lawsuit against Pentlow, then taking Pentlow's side in the ensuing dispute. Woodford struggled fiercely to accept the right interpretation of the affliction. He strove for the necessary qualities of humility and submission to the divine will, which required him to love his accusers as the instruments of divine castigation of his sin: 'Lord pardon my faylings in any kind, & doe thou blesse those that speake ill of me & doe them good & make me a gayner by it [...] remove pride & pr[e]iudice let us be base & low in o[u]r owne eyes' (p. 379). However, he simultaneously harboured rebellious objections to his opponents' views, whose blameworthiness he contrasted with his own righteousness: 'bringe forth my righteousnes & uprightness her[e]in as the Light' (*ibid.*). From Woodford's viewpoint he was also an offended party, which necessitated a posture of culpability towards God but righteousness towards man. Addressing God he admitted: 'I have deserved ten thousand times more from thee (though not from them)' (p. 383). Claiming to have worked impartially to negotiate an informal compromise, he prayed for his own eventual submission to the scourge.

[117] *Ibid.*, pp. 283, 302, 304, 308.

His opponents, he stated to God, 'are but the instruments thou usest to doe me good by, helpe me to love them' (*ibid.*). The dispute was apparently resolved by agreement rather than litigation, but the ill-feeling between Woodford and the Wilby residents persisted. He hoped for reconciliation, but the axiomatic unity of the godly was not restored.[118]

The godly's relationship with the ungodly

Woodford subscribed to a highly polarized and exclusive view of Christian society, whose members he categorized as either godly or ungodly. As Peter Lake has shown, this was a viewpoint with potentially radical ramifications in which ordinary members of the national Church and society were excluded from the Christian community.[119] Woodford described the godly in orthodox terms and their excluded opponents as being at the opposite pole spiritually – as the reverse of righteous, strict, godly, holy, good, honest, religious, Christian, profitable, converted. The acme of godly behaviour was a mixture of preciseness and prudence, to walk 'holily & precisely & circumspectly' (p. 364). The godly possessed the ability to recognize these qualities in others.[120] However, the diary's descriptions of Woodford's encounters with strangers show that snap decisions were rare. On the road he met 'one Mr Taylor of Birmingham a godly man & his freind, I rec[eive]d much good & comfort in discourse & conference with Mr Taylor' (p. 342). Similarly, he travelled with a Mr Richards, a carrier from Loughborough, 'an honest religious man I hope' (p. 278). A third instance involved a journey with 'an honest man of Titchmarsh one heyes' (p. 170). In all these cases, Woodford felt confident after only a few hours in judging them godly.

His experiences at Clement's Inn show how godly groups could coalesce. Woodford and his godly chamber-fellow, Stephen Harvey, had no sooner installed themselves than they sought out other likeminded men. Harvey, said the diarist, 'hath found out a society of honest younge men in o[u]r house blessed be god for it, Lord increase thy graces in us all' (p. 332). The group, described severally as their honest or Christian society or company, induced a Mr Ratcliff to join them. One night they disputed 'which way we should goe as most

[118] *Ibid.*, p. 392.

[119] P. Lake, '"A charitable Christian hatred": the godly and their enemies in the 1630s', in C. Durston and J. Eales (eds), *The Culture of English Puritanism, 1560–1700* (1996), pp. 145–183.

[120] C.L. Cohen, *God's Caress: the psychology of puritan religious experience* (Oxford, 1986), pp. 148–149.

p[ro]fitable in o[u]r meetings' (*ibid.*); another time the professed aim was to 'seeke the Lord' (p. 333).

Godly taxonomy was not entirely a matter of black and white: there was room for grey. One could never be absolutely certain about a person's status, not even one's own. Woodford requested a meeting with Stephen Chapman, a minister who originated in his home parish of Old but who held a living in Devon, 'whom I did desire to sift because I had heard well of but not from p[er]fect intelligence but his hast[e] beinge much I am not yet satisfyed but I hope very well' (p. 102). In this picture of the judicious Woodford assessing the evidence of godliness presented to him by a member of the clerical elite and finding it wanting there is further evidence that peer assessment was at least as important for the godly calling as individual introspection. There was ample scope for differences of opinion over godliness, and Woodford's verdicts on individuals have the power to surprise. While regarding the moderate puritans Robert Bolton and Joseph Bentham as godly, he perfunctorily dismissed their friend and collaborator, the barrister Edward Bagshaw, as 'a rude man' (p. 191), despite his fierce reputation for opposing Laudianism.

Puritan disapproval of various aspects of contemporary culture is well documented. In a society where drinking and smoking were normal, the godly ideal was not complete abstinence but moderation in carnal pleasures. On one occasion Woodford confessed to God an overindulgence in alcohol: 'let me find cherefullnes in attendinge uppon thee wthout such squeezinge the Creature for that which it cannot yeild wthout thee' (p. 247). His love of tobacco he acknowledged by asking God to 'take off the necessity from my body & the affection from my mind of usinge Tobacco' (p. 236). Wicked alcoholic immoderation might lead to drunkenness, a sin dire in itself but also a catalyst leading to greater wickedness. When Woodford learned that a man had committed adultery he concluded that 'this is a fruit of his drunkennesse' and requested God to 'fence my heart for ever ag[ains]t such abominacons' (p. 257). However, his behaviour does not seem to have differed hugely from the prevailing norm. He noted his frequent shortcomings retrospectively in the journal. Such lapses occurred even when in the company of professors: at Francis Rushworth's house, 'instead of comfortinge my selfe with gods creatures I through want of moderacon was sick' (p. 288). After a meeting at Samuel Martin's, Woodford complained of their collective failings: 'let not our metings be an occasion of excesse, but make us moderate' (p. 298). He later noted the failings of both himself and Simon Moore, the minister: 'I drunke too much wyne wth him for it made me a litle ill afterward' (p. 328).

From time to time Woodford was obliged to interact with unprofitable company, a malign influence over the godly. Such contacts were permissible only if one had a calling. Yet he was sometimes prepared to tolerate this necessary evil, as, when eager to obtain royal patronage, he socialized with two royal servants – Henry Middleton, a sergeant-at-arms, and Mr Winstanley, keeper of the royal apartments at Whitehall. He lamented his failings, of committing sins in bad company, in writing: 'Lord what doe I doe in such Company [. . .] Let not the cares of the world & melancholy cause me to put forth my hand unto evill' (p. 247). He had already described these men as unconverted: at Wilby one Sunday they 'did not like the length of the sermons, Lord convert them unto thee' (p. 242).

Woodford details various characteristics of the ungodly, among which profanity and opposition to godly piety are prominent. Middleton and Winstanley embodied both attributes. However, the stark dichotomy between the godly and the ungodly existed mainly in Woodford's mind: his action was usually limited to recording his regrets. He again internalized his rejection of sinners and their sins after a session at the Swan Inn in Kettering with bad company, consisting mainly of conformist ministers: 'let me never goe into such Company againe unlesse I have a calling' (p. 236). While noting the malign influence of sinful company into which he had fallen at Grafton Regis – conformist ministers and other 'lea[r]n[e]d drunkards' (p. 343) – he drew a nice distinction between their excess and his own slightly better behaviour, which was neither drunkenness nor moderation but still sinful: 'the Lord kept me that I ranne not to the same excesse, [. . .] yet I had cause to be humbled for want of that moderacon that should have been in m[e]' (ibid.).

Woodford found support for his determination to avoid bad company from his friend Samuel Martin after they had both lapsed – in Woodford's case with the town chamberlain, Edward Burgins, whom Martin nevertheless included among his friends. Woodford lamented 'Lord give me I pray thee wholly to forsake & reiect such company', and conferred with Martin, who 'blames himselfe for keepinge company sometime wth those that feare not god in drinkinge wine & takinge tobacco wth them now and then' (p. 255). Both men resolved 'in gods feare & wth his helpe to reforme in that p[ar]ticuler' (ibid.). This resolution seems to have worked in the short term: three days later, Woodford rejected an invitation to socialize with James Lewis at the Swan Inn at Kettering where he had previously fallen into bad company. Yet this was the exception, and he continued to achieve only limited success in avoiding 'occasions of evill' (p. 257).

That negative examples from life could be as potent as positive ones is demonstrated by the story of William Perkins, a former soldier and keeper of the Swan Inn at Northampton. An ungodly death to set against the godly ones, Perkins expired, rumour had it, 'havinge caught a surfeyt wth drinkinge' (p. 302). Woodford attended his funeral for its didactic benefit and does not mention the content of the funeral sermon preached by Charles Newton, but concludes 'make him an example to me & all other that heare of it that we may learne moderacon in the use of thy m[er]cyes' (p. 303).

The telling of jokes and funny stories was another custom to be treated with circumspection. Woodford could appreciate their attraction but was suitably pious about the danger of sin, unlike Daniel Reading and others that had 'a great facultye in merry tales & Jests which I dare not allow my selfe in or least apply or give my mind unto, although they take much with the hearers' (p. 198). He apparently abstained, but his only condemnation was internal. He compared Reading's unprofitable company with the profitable company of his barrister friend Henry Goodere: 'give me more to avoyd the socyety that is not p[ro]fitable as Mr Readinge, Lord blesse & doe good to Mr Goodere whom thou hast endued with the grace of thy sp[iri]t' (p. 336). The attitude towards inherently sinful activities was clearer cut: when two squires, John Syers and Robert Mulshoe, 'played longe here at night' (p. 198) – presumably at cards or dice – Woodford simply refrained and concluded 'Lord convert them' (*ibid.*).

More offensive yet were those aspects of conventional culture that involved misuse of the divine name – swearing and the drinking of healths – as they entailed a direct breach of the third commandment. Woodford restricted his response to opting out of the offensive behaviour. A Mr Meridale invited him into company at an inn and, Woodford conceded, 'showed me much love'; but when the company's behaviour deteriorated he stood aloof: 'they were loose & swearinge, & dranke a health or two which I would not pledge in the Ceremony oh Lord establish me that I never decline thy truth' (p. 130). He thought this sin serious enough to activate his duty of reproof, although he exercised this mainly when away from home among strangers, when the consequences for his own reputation were fewer. He met a 'very wild gent' (p. 315) on the road from London to St Albans, where they lodged together. The next day Woodford took on the role of evangelist, issuing an admonition, and praying for the conversion of the unnamed gentleman. Woodford 'often intreated him to leave his swearinge, Lord convert him' (*ibid.*). Similarly, in company with William Beeley, archdeacon of Carmarthen, he 'opposed a health which he began: blessed be god' (p. 185). At the Swan in Kettering, Woodford acted in concert with Francis Rushworth, who was rather more outspoken than he. The diarist was 'troubled to be in such Company' with the innkeeper, John Baxter, and others, and noted that 'we reproved Baxter the host for his swearinge Lord bestowe grace upon him' (p. 243). This no doubt constituted the shining conversation he promised God. In general, however, the course of normal social interaction was not greatly disturbed.

In his journal Woodford condemned activities that were anathema to the godly – bear-baiting, maypole-dancing, and stage plays.[121] He denounced the University of Oxford during a visit as a sink of iniquity: it was 'p[ro]digiously p[ro]fane I p[er]ceave for drunkennesse swearinge & other debauched Courses, stage playes & Lord reforme these seminaryes' (p. 316). Yet in the 1650s he sent his son Samuel to this 'seminary', which had, in the meantime, been reformed by Parliamentary visitors. In reality, Woodford was willing to apply a degree of latitude when participation in various pastimes was part of the expected round of socializing. Despite his contempt for stage plays he witnessed an interlude called *The New Hunt* during a social visit to Sir Christopher Hatton at his palatial Elizabethan pile, Kirby Hall: 'we saw litle of it cominge late' (p. 238). However, returning to Kirby the next day he was in the audience to witness another interlude, *Masculine Humours*, by the rabidly anti-puritan poet and cleric Peter Hausted. Neither of these works has been traced.

Woodford positively enjoyed several traditional pursuits: like Cromwell and Colonel John Hutchinson he liked music, which he found to be a transcendental experience, and was happy to go bell-ringing at Wilby with Thomas Pentlow and Samuel Ainsworth.[122] He may even have attended the Easter horse race at Northampton Heath on 29 March 1638 with Pentlow and Watts. Clearly a far from dour puritan, he did not find pleasure only in prayer meetings. He relaxed by strolling with his family in Moorfields, London's first civic park, by playing bowls at Wellingborough, and by fishing with Thomas Bacon, squire of Burton Latimer, at his watermill.[123]

Godly attorney

Woodford regarded his profession as a divinely ordained calling. The bedrock of his career was the stewardship of Northampton, to which the corporation had appointed him for life after he had taken the steward's oath. John Reading would have passed on to him a written guide to his duties – the now lost 'Steward's Book of

---

[121] Diary, pp. 118, 179, 316.
[122] J. Morrill, 'Cromwell, Oliver (1599–1658)', in *ODNB*; P.R. Seddon, 'Hutchinson, John (bap. 1615, d. 1664) in *ODNB*; Diary, p. 243.
[123] Diary, pp. 214, 218 and n. 456, 231, 232.

Annual Memoranda of Court Proceedings'. Woodford's court work revolved around the weekly meeting of the Court of Record, at which he served as deputy clerk to the town clerk, Tobias Coldwell, and as clerk to the bailiffs.[124] The mayor presided over the court, which met every Monday except for a vacation in August. Woodford served as a witness to the enrolment in the borough records of important contracts. His income derived from fees: a day's takings ranged from 16s to an exceptional £3. The steward was also clerk of the bailiffs' court, which was the equivalent of the sheriff's court in the rest of the county. Woodford does not make separate mention of the meeting of this court, which probably also assembled on Monday, when several functions converged. The third of his court duties involved keeping the court leet dealing with manorial business and petty crime on behalf of the mayor.

The steward worked closely with the mayor and recorder to organize the administration of urban justice at Northampton's quarter sessions, at which the recorder presided. Woodford co-operated with Mayor William Collis to prepare the business of the sessions, and on 9 December 1637 with the bailiffs to invite to dinner the recorder, Richard Lane, a Middle Temple bencher with court connections, and the county justice of the peace, Dr Samuel Clarke, who was responsible for the Hundred of Spelhoe, in which Northampton lay.[125] The mayor initiated charges against individuals while the steward drew up the necessary paperwork. For example, Woodford's friend Mayor John Gifford required him to draw up such charges against Richard Mottershed for misbehaviour in the Monday court and against Humphrey Ramsden for night walking, drunkenness, and causing an affray: these charges had political ramifications and will be discussed below. Meanwhile Woodford was winning the trust of Lane, as he records presiding over the quarter sessions himself as Lane's deputy.[126]

Performing as the representative of the corporation, Woodford negotiated with individuals and other bodies, most often over charitable bequests to the town. When the legacy bequeathed by Sir Ralph Freeman, mayor of London, to his home town of Northampton was not forthcoming from his son-in-law, Sir George Sondes, Woodford liaised between Mayor Collis and Sondes's cashier. Alderman Thomas Wheatley of Coventry had left an annual amount to be lent to Northampton tradesmen, naming the aldermen of

---

[124] Markham and Cox, *Northampton*, II, pp. 3, 116–117, 533. Woodford had been appointed by the upper chamber of the assembly, the mayor and aldermen (previous mayors).

[125] *Ibid.*, pp. 103–106, 115–116, 130–132, 533.

[126] Diary, pp. 108–109, 163, 310.

Coventry as the trustees of his charity; Woodford was part of a delegation of Northampton aldermen despatched to Coventry to negotiate with the mayor and corporation for payment. Mayor Fowler and the corporation charged Woodford with the task of collecting tax arrears due to the town from the Soke of Peterborough. Having successfully negotiated with the recorder and justices there, he was delighted by the praise that he received from his own aldermen on his return. Similarly, in the plague year of 1638, Woodford represented the town's interests to the justices meeting at the county quarter sessions at Kettering by passing on the corporation's desire to hold the next county sessions at Wellingborough rather than Northampton itself because of the disease.[127]

A variety of miscellaneous duties devolved upon the steward. Together with the recorder he was instrumental in installing the new mayor at Michaelmas. Recorder Lane would read a charge to the new incumbent, after which Woodford tendered the oath of office to him. The steward also made payments on behalf of the corporation – to the minister for his maintenance, to the town wait players, and to messengers delivering royal proclamations from London, although Woodford disputed this last responsibility with the sergeants. The steward acted as clerk to the coroners, who were responsible for investigating sudden deaths, and was expected to attend various civic functions.[128] By virtue of his office, he also exercised the quasi-judicial function of arbitrating disputes. Woodford and Bailiff Benoni Coldwell successfully effected a compromise between Messrs Peach and Hart. Less successful was the attempt of Woodford and Thomas Martin to mediate in a dispute between John Bernard and Alexander Eakins over the keeping of greyhounds. This clearly demonstrates that Woodford's office allowed him to box well above his weight socially, as both were members of the gentry. He and his fellow referees, Thomas Martin and Thomas Morgan, met at the Swan Inn to provide arbitration but failed to prevent the escalation of the dispute, which continued with a scuffle.[129]

The success of Woodford's stewardship hinged on his maintaining a good working relationship with his employers in the upper echelons of the corporation. With this end in mind, he sent a gift of mutton to the town's attorney, Daniel Reading, and dined with him and with Mayor William Collis. He sent a six-gallon 'roundlet of claret' (p. 328) to Mayor-Elect John Danby and a turkey to Recorder Lane.

---

[127] *Ibid.*, pp. 173–174, 239, 253, 276, 319.

[128] Markham and Cox, *Northampton*, II, pp. 112–114, 130–132; Diary, pp. 119, 126, 160, 162, 290, 328, 371, 380.

[129] Diary, pp. 127, 323.

Indeed, Woodford was cultivating Lane and his wife, Margaret, as prospective patrons: he persuaded Lane to appoint him his deputy to keep the court for the Hundred of Hamfordshoe with the hope that, thenceforth, 'this small wheele' would 'turne about a greater' (p. 173), but Spencer Compton, the Earl of Northampton and Lane's patron as lord of the hundred, overruled Lane by appointing his own candidate, John Eakins.[130]

Woodford's relationships with a number of other members of the corporation were, however, problematic. The steward argued constantly with various town officers, many of whom were godly, in disputes that were caused by personal dislike, or social or professional rivalry. He squabbled with Bailiff Benoni Coldwell, a member of his godly network. Though accusing himself of 'rash anger & violent passion' (p. 181), he pleaded in mitigation that he had been provoked. Edward Burgins was another bugbear. A barber by trade, Burgins served as chamberlain of the town, but Woodford regarded him as bad company. However, Burgins's will, which included a godly preamble, shows that he enjoyed godly friendships with Samuel Martin and Joseph Sargent. Woodford's most persistent enemy was the mayor, William Collis, who attended a godly meeting with him and who was regarded as a nonconformist by Sir John Lambe's informer. Woodford and Thomas Martin quarrelled with Collis and the sergeants (Thomas Crutchley, James Fryers, and John Hall, also members of the godly community) over who should pay messengers delivering royal proclamations to the corporation. A greater row erupted over Woodford's objection to the level of Monday court fees authorized by Collis and paid to him by the sergeants. Collis blew hot and cold, and Woodford lamented that he would never win the man's favour: 'I can have small hope of it if I looke unto the disposicon of the man' (p. 150). As a result, Woodford was obliged to appeal to his allies, John Gifford, Alderman Roger Sargent, and Chamberlains Thomas Judkins and Joseph Sargent, but the conclusion of the dispute goes unrecorded.[131]

Woodford's absence from the town during the plague of 1638 strained the relationship with his employers, who remained at their posts.[132] He obtained from Mayor-Elect Richard Fowler a leave of absence from the latter's installation at Michaelmas, but later Woodford feared that Fowler would dismiss him for his absenteeism.

[130] *Ibid.*, pp. 148, 155, 157, 172, 180, 182.
[131] TNA, PROB/11/195; TNA, SP16/474/80; Diary, pp. 126, 127, 129, 150–152.
[132] The corporation stayed put (Diary, p. 206), as did Thomas Ball (Fielding, 'Ball, Thomas'). Francis Rushworth took a shop under the Swan Inn, Kettering (Diary, p. 243), while several of Woodford's neighbours sheltered at Wellingborough (*ibid.*, p. 213).

The corporation may have been placated by Woodford's charitable fundraising efforts on behalf of the stricken town: he supported the relief efforts undertaken, after the appeal of Mayor William Collis for aid, mainly by Recorder Lane, the town attorney, Richard Rainsford, and county justices Drs Samuel Clarke and Robert Sibthorpe. Woodford acknowledged the non-partisan nature of these charitable schemes (these men, we shall discover, occupied the opposite pole from him in politics and religion) while noting the reluctance of the godly justice, Sir Rowland St John, to lend his support. Lane's appeal to the Privy Council had met with a swift response: the county justices of the peace were to raise a weekly contribution of £100 on top of the £48 per week already ordered by Clarke and Lane from the towns within five miles of Northampton.[133] Woodford enhanced this official effort with deeds of his own. He wrote to Mayor Collis giving him permission to contribute the court fees due to him to the relief of the poor and the sick. Enlisting the help of his father-in-law, Robert Haunch, he twice (in June and July 1638) set about raising contributions from Northamptonshire expatriates living in the capital and from Haunch's London friends. He amassed around £70 and £11 respectively. Sir Paul Pindar, a merchant prince and diplomat originating in Northamptonshire, outshone the other donors with a contribution of £50. When transporting the first of these sums into the country by carrier proved prohibitively expensive, Woodford concealed the gold coins in his boots and assumed the responsibility himself. He undertook further money-raising schemes with the help of another Northamptonshire native, the London alderman William Abell, who suggested first a petition to the Court of Aldermen (which foundered on a technicality, despite the support of the mayor, Sir Richard Fenn), and then one to Archbishop Laud (the fate of this latter idea is not recorded). Woodford's fears of dismissal proved groundless and he was welcomed back and allowed to resume his duties.[134]

The tireless search for patronage shows that Woodford aspired to the career progression of a successful attorney. Haunch was a potential source. With his backing and that of Worsley, a friend who was clerk of the Tallow Chandlers' Company, Woodford began manoeuvres to obtain the clerkship of Weavers' Hall, of which Haunch was the upper bailiff in 1636 and 1637. The attempt was abortive but Woodford was equally active back in Northamptonshire, where (though conscience-stricken) he coveted the position of clerk of the peace for the county, which was filled by Francis Gray of Wellingborough. The achievement of such a post usually depended on the gentry's patronage, so when

[133] *Ibid.*, pp. 203–204, 241, 249.
[134] *Ibid.*, pp. 202, 210, 218–220, 230, 252.

the rumour of Gray's illness reached him, he headed immediately to Wellingborough with Pentlow of Wilby, but the severity of the illness must have been exaggerated and Gray survived for years.[135] Sheriff Peter Tryon was responsible for Woodford's belated attainment of the county undershrievalty in 1653, at the end of his career and his life. This apparently new influence in his life may simply have been the posthumous exertion of the influence of his old master, John Reading, who had served as undersheriff in 1623 under Tryon's father, Moses.[136]

In late 1638 Woodford launched a search for employment in the national sphere. After an apparently chance meeting at Wilby with Henry Middleton, a royal sergeant-at-arms, and his companion Winstanley, the keeper of the royal apartments and galleries at Whitehall Palace, Woodford jumped at the possibility of royal patronage. He arranged to rendezvous with Winstanley during his next visit to London and, after enjoying a guided tour of the royal apartments, elicited from Winstanley a promise to obtain for him a position in the king's gift. After prolonged socializing with Winstanley and Middleton in London, Woodford gained an interview with John Benbow, clerk of the patents. At Benbow's house in Green's Lane, Westminster, Woodford rifled through his book and established that reversions had been granted on only three of the seven auditorships of the exchequer. Woodford urged Winstanley to procure one of the reversions for him but, despite further costly oiling of the wheels, Winstanley prevaricated, and the subject disappears from the diary.[137]

There was one occasion on which the search for central patronage was successful: Woodford's purchase of the county almonership from Reading. The episode speaks volumes about seventeenth-century business ethics. Woodford successfully covered it up, but he clearly felt qualms of conscience and prayed to keep his conscience 'ungashd' (p. 283). Above all, he feared being caught. If the matter became public: 'that will discover to the world that I give money for the place & then another may step in & get it from me' (p. 279). Such transactions were regarded as acceptable so long as they were kept secret. On 14 February 1639 Woodford attended the lord high almoner to Charles I, Bishop Walter Curll, at Winchester House, to be confirmed in office. Woodford entered into a bond of £200 with Curll to collect the various forfeitures due to the crown and to submit them to Curll in

[135] *Ibid.*, pp. 97, 131, 219, 221, 229. Haunch had been elected to the livery in 1616 and was chosen as upper bailiff in 1636 and 1637: A. Plummer, *The London Weavers' Company 1600–1970* (London, 1972), p. 451.
[136] Bridges, *History of Northamptonshire*, II, pp. 289, 318; NRO, Tryon (Bulwick) MSS, T(B) 248, 259/6; TNA, STAC8/139/6.
[137] Diary, pp. 242, 246–248, 251.

the Easter and Michaelmas terms. This was no doubt the reason for Curll's meeting with Woodford at Northampton the following Easter, though the diarist gives no details of monies received and makes no further mention of the post. Nor did he express any disquiet at working alongside a bishop who enthusiastically supported Laudian religious reforms.[138] In the end, despite Woodford's receptiveness to the idea of court patronage, his career was not crowned with great success and he remained a provincial attorney.

The perquisites of the stewardship of Northampton were never adequate to Woodford's needs. In consequence, he was constantly engaged in a search for private clients to bring in more funds. There were two categories of work involved in his private practice: court and non-court. He served as the steward for private landlords, which involved keeping their manorial courts (baron and leet), acting as justice jointly with the landlord who appointed him.[139] These courts were at the centre of parish society, and Woodford mixed regularly with landowners and clergymen. Other court work included representing clients at the town's and county's quarter sessions, or before boards of enquiry into damages following natural calamities. His records of the storms raging in Northamptonshire and London in January 1639 and the flooding that hit Northamptonshire in April 1640 also provide interesting data for the study of climate history.[140] The high point of his court work consisted of conducting suits before the central courts based at Westminster Hall and the biannual county assizes. Woodford rarely conducted a case from beginning to end: often he was involved only with the procedural paperwork. His non-court work required him to draw up a variety of legal instruments, concerned mainly with the disposal of property and provision of credit. Other property transactions included arranging the bride's jointure during marriage negotiations and establishing charitable trusts. Still other documents concluded local disputes without recourse to law. Woodford also compiled wills and, when required, witnessed them or supervised their execution.

Kinship and godly networks provided much of this practice. He kept the manorial court at Broughton for Thomas Pentlow and that of Pentlow's namesake at Wilby, and represented the latter in a quarrel with Recorder Lane. He also operated the manorial court for his

---

[138] *Ibid.*, pp. 283–284, 303; M. Dorman, 'Curll, Walter (1575–1647)', in *ODNB*.

[139] C.W. Brooks, *Pettyfoggers and Vipers of the Commonwealth: the 'lower branch' of the legal profession in early modern England* (Cambridge, 1986), pp. 197–202.

[140] Diary, p. 276 (stormy weather); Woodford mentions the flooding of the River Nene at Northampton and of the River Tove at Towcester, and flooding on land owned by Robert Pearson, perhaps at Walgrave, seven miles north of Northampton: *ibid.*, pp. 349, 351.

cousin Gregory Dexter at Old and for Thomas Bacon at Burton Latimer. He represented Peter Whalley in a dispute and conducted court business for William Warren of Old.[141] Woodford owed his employment in three court cases to his godly connections. Thomas Watts employed him in a Chancery suit over property in which the plaintiff was the godly John Temple of Frankton in Warwickshire. Woodford was integral to the organization of Watts's case: he prepared his answer to Temple's initial bill of complaint, scheduled meetings of local commissions at Lutterworth and Banbury to gather evidence, and accompanied Watts to London to a preliminary hearing before Sir Charles Caesar, master of the rolls. He attended the final trial at Warwick assize, at which the verdict went against Watts. Woodford gained further employment by means of Watts's influence with Sir Christopher Yelverton, who stood accused by the dean and chapter of Christ Church, Oxford, of ruining the rectory of Easton Maudit, which Yelverton leased from them. Woodford made a trip to Oxford to dispute with Christ Church's barristers, but does not seem to have been involved in the resulting Chancery suit.[142] Pentlow of Broughton engaged Woodford to act for him in a case in the Court of Wards against his landlady, Philippa Sill. Again, Woodford was prominent in steering Pentlow's case, although he also obtained the counsel of the barrister Robert Tanfield of Loddington. Woodford co-ordinated the meeting of a local commission at Towcester, acted as clerk of the proceedings, and carried the completed records to London. He compiled the briefs used to instruct counsel, and liaised with the barrister, Thomas Kittermaster. Finally, Woodford accompanied Pentlow to Westminster to retain three advocates qualified to act for them in the court: the outcome was successful.[143]

The same process of godly recommendation operated to provide Woodford with court work of a political nature and with non-court practice. Reading was instrumental in Woodford's employment as part of the legal team representing the county gentry against royal revitalization of the forest law. Later, Thomas Bacon retained Woodford to represent him in an acerbic dispute with a conformist faction in his parish. Woodford supervised moneylending transactions for his cousins, the Warren and Ragdale families of Old. He handled other non-contentious work for them, representing them in local administrative matters: he liaised between his cousin Gregory Dexter and the Commission for Charitable Uses, and approached Justice

---

[141] *Ibid.*, pp. 129, 198–199, 243, 299, 319–320, 323.
[142] *Ibid.*, pp. 310–312, 322–323, 325, 334, 339–341, 395, 397–398.
[143] *Ibid.*, pp. 233–237, 249, 277–279.

Francis Downes on behalf of his aunt to request her exemption from the obligation of training an apprentice. For Pentlow of Wilby he provided guidance and paperwork relating to his purchase of property and organized leases for him both as lessor and as lessee. He executed similar lease work for George Coles (to Thomas Ball) and for John James of Olney, Buckinghamshire. He restricted his will-compiling service to godly confidants, owing presumably to the intensely personal nature of the credos contained in such documents. Those which he composed for his father and Thomas Martin are extant: those for Pentlow of Wilby, John Fisher, William Tompson, and George Basse, the latter two also of Wilby, are not. He agreed to act as supervisor of the wills of Thomas Watts and John Loe the ironmonger.[144]

Woodford pursued long- and short-term strategies designed to broaden his client base in what was a keenly competitive market. The names of his rival attorneys – John Eakins, John Danby, Richard Rainsford, Edward Chamberlain, Francis Cook, and Henry Fleming – occur periodically in the diary. During his six-day working week he followed the market days in an area describing a triangle to the north of Northampton. Monday was court day in Northampton; Wednesday was Wellingborough market day; Friday was Kettering market day; Saturday was one of the market days back in Northampton. From August 1640 he added the Tuesday market at Towcester, to the south of Northampton, to his routine. To supplement this weekly schedule he attended the various annual fairs at Northampton, Wellingborough, and Kettering, and the courts: the county sessions at Northampton (or Kettering or Wellingborough), Northampton borough's own sessions, and the biannual assizes. His aim was to follow up on the gentry and aristocratic contacts that he had made to build up a clientele of wealthy patrons. Sir Christopher Hatton entertained him at Kirby Hall, as well as at his hunting lodge in Moulton Park; Sir John Isham offered hospitality at Lamport; John Bernard at Abington. Sir Christopher Yelverton invited him to Easton Maudit; Francis Nicolls entertained him at Faxton. He even enjoyed a friendly conversation with Sir Thomas Cave of Stanford, the patron of Archbishop Laud. In a similar vein, while in London he dined with the merchant, customs farmer, and Laudian church restorer, Sir John Wolstenholme.[145]

[144] *Ibid.*, pp. 105, 152–153, 156, 170, 179, 194–196, 242–243, 259, 274, 285–286, 302–303; TNA, PROB/11/235 (Watts), PROB/11/189 (Loe).

[145] Diary, pp. 155–156, 181, 238 (Hatton); 125–126, 327, 335 (Isham); 125, 161 (Bernard); 108, 158, 229 (Yelverton); 125, 203 (Nicolls); 244 (Cave); 132, 274 (Wolstenholme).

Touting for business paid dividends, and Woodford must have established a reasonably good reputation in the locality. When in Northampton, the royal sergeant-at-arms, John Powell, engaged him to draw up a writ, but most employment came from the local gentry. John Bernard selected him as one of the referees to mediate his dispute with Alexander Eakins, squire of Weston Favell, over keeping greyhounds, but Woodford was unable to translate this initial involvement into court work. After the arbitration broke up in violence, Bernard retained a rival, Francis Cook, to act for him in the resulting lawsuit. Richard Denton employed Woodford to represent him in a dispute in the Court of King's Bench against the quarrelsome Eakins over rights of common. Woodford obtained a prohibition to stay proceedings in a junior court, initiated the case in King's Bench before Lord Chief Justice Sir John Bramston, and had Eakins jailed. When the case came to trial at Northampton assizes, Woodford consulted Recorder Lane, who with Denton found fault with Woodford's handling of the case, but Woodford was vindicated when the jury found for Denton in this case and in a counter-suit launched by Eakins. Sir John Isham, whose wife, Judith, was regarded as godly, though he was not, not only employed Woodford to compile documents for him but also invited him to be steward of his manorial court.[146]

Woodford's private stewarding work was concentrated in two clusters of manors. As we have seen, the first lay within the Northampton–Kettering–Wellingborough triangle and developed mainly from family and godly influence. The second focus was the manor of Grafton Regis to the south of Northampton, near the border with Buckinghamshire. Indeed, Grafton was his most important work of this kind: he kept the courts baron and leet there for the duration of the diary. Grafton's courts were prominent as they lay at the centre of the honour of Grafton, a cluster of manors designated by Henry VIII to support his mansion there. Woodford had obtained the post by the patronage of the owner, Sir Francis Crane (d. 1636), or his French widow, Lady Marie. In March 1640 Woodford enjoyed a sudden increase in stewardship practice from the surrounding manors. Only that of Potterspury did he obtain not through the favour of the patron but by purchase.[147]

The level of Woodford's work fluctuated. Summer was normally a dead time: there was a long gap between legal terms and this was exacerbated by the steward's vacation in August. Added to this was an extra ebb and flow caused by the impact of public crises. The outbreak

[146] *Ibid.*, pp. 127, 133–134, 137, 149, 158, 175, 195, 287, 326–327, 329, 331, 402.
[147] *Ibid.*, pp. 109–110, 136, 148, 170, 210, 260, 293, 343, 347–348, 371–373.

of plague at Northampton in 1638 and the drastic effect of the Bishops' Wars disrupted the markets, fairs, and courts that were the lifeblood of his profession, and caused potential clients to lose confidence: 'people want moneys & those that have it are loath to p[ar]t wth it' (p. 291). There followed a corresponding increase in optimism and business after the elections to the Short Parliament in March 1640 seemed to presage better times ahead. This proved to be the case, as the advent of the Long Parliament brought Woodford a great deal of business.

Religion and current affairs

Woodford was avidly interested in news, an enthusiasm that was greatly assisted by his profession's peripatetic lifestyle. His weekly circuit allowed him access to a wealth of gossip and news from across Northamptonshire and the East Midlands, while the area's position near a key north–south artery relatively near to London, and his own connections with the capital, meant that national, and even international, news was abundant. His London links included letters from Hannah, the Haunches, and others. His contacts included John Dillingham, a Northamptonshire tailor who had moved to the Whitefriars area as a professional newsletter writer, and Woodford's cousin Gregory Dexter junior, a connection with the London press.[148] Most news came, in the diarist's idiom, down from London rather than up from the North Country; however, at John Reading's house Woodford heard of the mistreatment of the godly hero Henry Burton at Lancaster Castle. The outbreak of the Bishops' Wars only increased this traffic. News from York included details of the refusal of Lords Saye and Sele and Brooke to fight the Scots; Henry Sprig's sons, returning from the north to Banbury, showed Woodford the proceedings of the Glasgow Assembly.[149] The availability to Woodford of the Haunches' London house allowed him to witness events of national significance such as Judge Sir Richard Hutton's summing up in Hampden's Case or the triumphant return from jail of Burton, Bastwick, and Prynne, and to meet other figures of national stature, such as the authors of the Covenant, Alexander Henderson and Lord Archibald Johnston of Wariston, whom he encountered at Dillingham's. He experienced the disturbances centring on Archbishop Laud's palace at Lambeth. As he flitted between London and the headquarters of the central courts at

---

[148] *Ibid.*, pp. 103, 141 (and n. 190 on Dillingham), 254, 288, 291, 368.
[149] *Ibid.*, pp. 99, 299, 301, 325.

Westminster Hall, he participated in a vibrant news market, including news of who was preaching at court, developments in Hampden's or Chambers' Case over ship money, the doings of the archbishop or royal family, and proceedings in Parliament.[150]

Woodford analysed the body politic using the various polarities which he applied to society generally: God versus Satan; the converted versus the unconverted. Although he did not use the terms court and country, he clearly envisaged such an opposition but with the terms being understood as ideological poles not geographical locations. He envisaged public affairs as a global, immemorial battle between the religious and ideological poles of Christ and Antichrist, true religion and popery, the essence of all evil.[151] He interpreted the politics of the 1630s as a popish conspiracy to subvert the Church and state: it is not known when he arrived at this interpretation but it certainly predated the diary. In this he shared the viewpoint of the parliamentary opposition leaders of the 1620s.

For Woodford, the key threat was religious, and the most iniquitous government policies were the intensely ceremonialized public ordinances enjoined by the Laudians centring on newly created holy altars. As we have seen, for the godly, pure ordinances involved an exclusive, spiritual worship, and provided a crucial means of maintaining their callings. Laudian worship, in contrast, was seen to be compromised by inclusiveness and to consist of bodily postures invented by corrupt humanity. The honour accorded the altar was regarded as idolatrous and superstitious, misdirecting reverence towards a thing of human invention. Woodford prayed that God would 'extirpate all pop[er]y Idolatry sup[er]stition & p[ro]phanenesse and come forth oh Lord amongst thine adversaryes who doe plott against thee & seeke to defile thine ordinances with base humane inventions' (p. 216). He contrasted the godly's pure spiritual sacrifices with the impurity of Laudian efforts: 'why should we cut off a dogs neck before thee & offer thee swines blood instead of the sacrifice wthout blemish, why should carnall ordinances & an earthly sanctuary still remayne & the worship in spirit & in truth be yet refused' (p. 289). To Woodford, of course, the true altar was Christ himself. Laudian ceremonies were moreover regarded as 'innovations' (p. 182), implying that the Church had been basically sound before their introduction and the godly capable of enjoying pure ordinances within it. He also condemned

---

[150] *Ibid.*, pp. 130–131, 175–176, 200, 274, 281, 377–378.
[151] P. Lake, 'William Bradshaw, antichrist, and the community of the godly', *Journal of Ecclesiastical History*, 36 (1985), pp. 570–589; idem, 'Constitutional consensus and puritan opposition in the 1620s: Thomas Scott and the Spanish Match', *Historical Journal*, 25 (1982), pp. 805–825.

Laudian insistence on full canonical and Prayer Book ceremony, which, at All Saints' Northampton at least, was also innovatory.[152]

Consequently, Woodford gave his wholehearted support to the efforts of the parish and corporation to prevent the creation of an altar at All Saints'. The diocesan bishop, Francis Dee of Peterborough, had been uniquely early in enjoining the construction of railed, east end, altars from 1634. The response of All Saints' had been robust, railing in the communion table but refusing to transform it into an altar, instead placing it tablewise in the chancel, surrounded by the lavishly refurbished seats of the civic oligarchy.[153] Woodford never mentioned this rail, which he found inoffensive as it did not enclose an altar. The authorities had attempted to change this arrangement: in January 1637 Dee's deputy, Dr Samuel Clarke, had tried to force the removal of the table to the eastern end of the chancel, but Dee had been obliged to move it himself into the altarwise position for his visitation in July when he had inveighed against puritans and, with Clarke, had bowed towards the altar.[154] The offence for Woodford lay in the table's altarwise position. He recorded with praise that, on 3 September, the churchwardens, Rushworth and Farren, turned the table east to west at the communion.

As part of the visitation, Dee had commissioned a survey of parish churches from Clarke and Dr Robert Sibthorpe. Both men were part of a firmly entrenched clique of avant-garde conformists, led by Sibthorpe's brother-in-law, Sir John Lambe, which had been active since the late sixteenth century, clashing repeatedly with the godly town.[155] Woodford described this intervention 'by some of the worser sorte of divines & by [ap]p[ar]iters & to observe the standinge of the tables whether altarwise or not & to set them so; oh Lord looke uppon us in m[er]cy it is an evill time' (p. 104). They ordered the churchwardens of All Saints' to demolish the existing rail and the seats in the chancel, and to place the communion table altarwise along the eastern wall and enclose it with a returning rail with kneeling bench attached, at which all parishioners were to receive the Eucharist. On 12 November 1637 Woodford confirmed that the

---

[152] Diary, pp. 106, 183, 270.
[153] K. Fincham, 'The restoration of altars in the 1630s', *Historical Journal*, 44 (2001), pp. 930–931; Fielding, 'Peterborough', pp. 95–118; TNA, SP16/474/80; TNA, SP16/370/51.
[154] PDR, CB A63, fos 430r–432v; TNA, SP16/474/80.
[155] Sheils, *Puritans*, pp. 6–7, 75–76, 87, 126–127; idem, 'Some problems of government in a new diocese: the bishop and the puritans in the Diocese of Peterborough 1560–1630', in R. O'Day and F. Heal (eds), *Continuity and Change: personnel and adminstration of the Church in England, 1500–1642* (Leicester, 1976), pp. 167–187; idem, 'Religion in provincial towns: innovation and tradition', in F. Heal and R. O'Day (eds), *Church and Society in England: Henry VIII to James I* (London, 1977), pp. 156–176; Fielding, 'Peterborough', pp. 57–91.

communion table had been moved to the east end '& there is an iniuncon it seemes to come up to it but Lord establish us in thy truth & for Xt his sake root out all sup[er]stition & Idolatry'. He deemed the proposed second rail offensive as it was to enclose an altar. In contrast, he praised the churchwardens' refusal to rail the table where it stood at the east end when so ordered by Clarke on 16 and 18 December, and repeated this praise on 31 December after they had returned the table to its position 'long wise in the body of the Channcell' (p. 157). As a result, Clarke excommunicated them. The churchwardens appealed to the Court of Arches, but the dean, Sir John Lambe, refused to absolve them, whereupon they petitioned Archbishop Laud, claiming to have completed the work and asking him to direct Lambe to grant them absolution. However, the churchwardens had lied, and Lambe suspended the case. The wardens next appealed to the Court of Delegates, where, remarkably, they obtained an inhibition from the dean, Sir Henry Marten, overturning Clarke's original sentence. Lambe responded with a suit in the Court of High Commission, forcing the wardens to rail the table as originally instructed.[156] Woodford noted on 16 March that 'The Com[munio]n Table is raylinge in to the top of the Chancell & the seates there pulled downe. O Lord destroy sup[er]st[iti]on' (p. 188). This second rail was completed shortly after 17 March, and Woodford now raised the matter to a higher level: 'The rayle in the Chancell is now s[ai]d almost up and its confidently reported that the sicknes is in the Towne' (p. 189).

The godly interpretation of divine affliction applied equally to the world of public affairs, where God intervened to highlight public vices: Woodford interpreted high corn prices, the Northampton floods, a solar eclipse, and meteorite activity in this fashion.[157] Far more serious was the Northampton plague of 1638. He regarded this as punishment for the creation of the altar, and responded in the same way as he did to personal affliction, requesting God to remove the affliction or else to preserve the godly so that they might learn from the episode. Only its destruction would propitiate the divinity. He asked God to 'command thy destroyinge Angell to cease for the Lords sake oh pull downe the abhominacons that are amongst us' (p. 197). Whether consciously or not, Woodford was locating the conflict in historical context: previous outbreaks of plague in Northampton

---

[156]TNA, SP16/381/88; TNA, SP16/370/57; TNA, SP16/378/74; TNA, SP16/474/80; HLRO, main papers, petition of Farren and Rushworth, 6 February 1641; J.S. Hart, *Justice upon Petition: the House of Lords and the reformation of justice 1621–1675* (London, 1991), p. 72.

[157]Diary, pp. 111, 307, 349, 351.

had similarly signalled divine displeasure with public policy.[158] The godly used their informal structures to work through the problem of the plague. Woodford debated the issue with Thomas Martin and Matthew Watts and, during a dangerous visit to the town, with an anonymous woman 'that had lived well who complayned for want of a peck of corne; I went into the towne & wept uppon it & confessed that sinne was the cause of our mourning' (p. 205). The godly were unified in their estimation of the cause of the outbreak. Thomas Ball set out the problem by preaching sermons on Jonah 3, in which the people of Nineveh avoided divine wrath by repenting and fasting.[159] The parish's repentance was noted by Clarke in a letter to Lambe of 17 June 1638, in which he tried to persuade him to inform Laud that 'they now doe what they list in the church service at All Saints in Northampto. Some very lately cut the Rayle or Cancel that was about the Lord's Board in Pieces, and brought downe the Lord's Table into the middle of the Chancel'.[160]

The Laudian altar had lasted less than three months. On 14 April 1639 Woodford noted that the table was 'still' down, and there is no evidence that the altar was ever renewed. The second of Ball's remedial measures, a public fast conducted by himself and Newton, took place on lecture day, 21 June 1638, as Sibthorpe complained to Lambe. The crisis revealed differences among the godly over their response to affliction. Woodford and Francis Rushworth fled Northampton, but those with higher callings – like Ball and the corporation – remained at their posts. For Woodford this realism was clearly a legitimate response, but on a rare visit to the plague-ridden town he chided himself for a lack of faith in divine providence. After fulfilling Ball's criteria, the town still had to wait until February 1639 for the pestilence finally to subside. Then Ball ceased to preach political sermons, perhaps for the first time since 1634, and returned to 'his former manner to set forth a body of religion' (p. 286).[161]

Woodford found confirmation of his interpretation of events in the providential deaths of those who ignored divine chastisement by embracing Laudianism. When George Colson, the curate of St Giles's

---

[158]The 1578 incidence had coincided with the suppression of puritan activity at All Saints' and with unpopular foreign policy: marriage negotiations with the papist duc d'Anjou. In 1606, the issue had been local policy: Mayor (and physician) George Coldwell's suppression of alehouses had brought the plague's ravages to an end. See Sheils, *Puritans*, pp. 123–124; A. Walsham, *Providence in Early Modern England* (Oxford, 1999), p. 140; J.H. Raach, *A Directory of English Country Physicians, 1603–1643* (London, 1962), p. 111.

[159]Diary, p. 253.

[160]The rail was demolished between 9 April and 16 June but probably nearer to the latter date: *ibid.*, p. 197; TNA, SP16/393/15.

[161]TNA, SP16/393/75; Diary, pp. 205–206; PDR, CB A57, unpaginated, dated 11 February 1634; PDR, CB 67, unpaginated, 3 August 1637.

in the eastern part of the town, died suddenly, Woodford remarked that he had refused 'to give the sacram[en]t to those that refused to come up to the rayles' (p. 183). More dramatic yet was the death of Richard Powell, one of the vicars of Pattishall. As an ally of Lambe, Powell headed a Laudian faction in the parish, which clashed constantly with a godly one led by the other vicar, Miles Burkit, over the altar policy, among other things. To Woodford, Powell was 'a p[er]secutinge preist' who had died suddenly 'in the house of office' (p. 270) en route to the Church court, where he had intended to report his parishioners, after first approaching three times an east end communion table. The lesson for Woodford was clear: 'Thus doth the Lord glorifye himselfe in the destruccon of his obstinate enemyes' (ibid.). If the saints were living sermons, then the ungodly were perishing ones and equally likely to convert sinners. He wished that God's 'adversaryes would lay this to hart that they might convert & turne unto thee that thou mightest heale them' (ibid.).

Woodford's opposition to ceremonial was not a case of ecclesiological nimbyism. Popish pollution of ordinances he regarded as a national problem requiring a national solution: his estimation of the threat did not decrease after the demolition of the altar. Indeed, in reality the vast majority of parishes in the town and diocese did possess railed Laudian altars by this time.[162] He declared that 'the whole Kingdome is in a forlorne condicon gods ordinances in many places mixed wth base ceremony & sup[er]stition' (p. 215). God was still punishing other areas, which had not repented like godly Northampton: 'thy Judgments' he told God 'are much abroad the pestilence rageth in the Countrye the small pox in the Citty of London' (ibid.). Woodford concurred with the verdict of John Baynard, who preached at Wilby on 'the causes of the pestilence that now rageth in many places vizt Idolatry Corrupcon of gods worship oppression & oh Lord remove both the Cause & the stroke' (p. 230).

The second aspect of popish antichristian plotting against true religion involved an assault on doctrine and the practical divinity associated with it. Woodford petitioned God for the only solution, a national godly reformation. In this analogy he portrayed God as a thresher, praying Him to 'purge thy floore blowe away the chaffe that is amongst o[u]r doctrine & in o[u]r discipline let pop[er]y

---

[162]Woodford tended to identify his own parish with the town as a whole. Whereas All Saints' had repented, the three adjacent urban parishes had not and were still occupied by Laudians – two of them the appointees of Sir John Lambe – and possessed railed altars. Nevertheless, the pestilence had ceased in all four: PDR, Church Survey Book 5, fos 69, 78v, 80v, 83. The living of St Peter's was held by Dr Samuel Clarke, St Sepulchre's by Richard Crompton, and St Giles's by Richard Holbrooke. The latter two were clients of Lambe: Diary, p. 154, n. 237.

& Arminianisme hide them selfe' (p. 313). Arminianism threatened the predestinarian theology underpinning godly profession. He again conveys the impression that this was an error that had infiltrated the national Church as a whole, and his examples come from varying locations, both high and low. He argued heatedly with Arminians such as William Bernard, a member of the Northamptonshire gentry, and, in St Dunstan's churchyard, London, with an attorney whose Christian name was Anthony. During a business trip to Coventry he dined in the town hall and described how James Naylor 'an arminian & I had much dispute about pr[e]destinacon' (p. 254). Naylor was not alone: Woodford defended God's 'truth but I found few there that favoured it' (*ibid.*). Anti-Calvinism reached to the very apex of the nation. Woodford was a member of the congregation assembled in the presence of the king at the Chapel Royal, Whitehall Palace, to hear a sermon by the royal chaplain, William Beale, a protégé of Laud. For Woodford, Beale embodied the link between the attacks on doctrine and worship. Beale, whose house at Cottingham possessed a 'shamefull Crucifix' (p. 238), preached 'ag[ains]t supr[a]lapsarians & p[ro] Confession to, & absolucon by the Church' (p. 251).[163] Such divinity, with its intense sacerdotalism, threatened Woodford's direct link with God.

Woodford's core piety was everywhere beset by the popish adversary. He encountered ministers who had been silenced by the authorities and noted that Dr Clarke had threatened Richard Trueman, minister of Dallington, with death for daring to speak out against ceremonialism. Andrew Perne's afternoon sermons came under scrutiny from the Church court official, Dr William Roane ('that sup[er]stitious doctor'), who arrived to 'heare & (I doubt) to entrap Mr Pearne' (p. 222). John Stoughton came under far more sustained pressure from Laud, Lambe, and William Juxon, Bishop of London: Woodford referred to Stoughton's harassment by the 'malice of Satan & his instruments' (p. 174). Following his attendance at Stoughton's sermon on the anniversary of the Gunpowder Plot in 1637, Woodford placed the current antichristian threat to Stoughton as simply the latest in a historical series including the Spanish Armada of 1588. He expressed gratitude to God for 'defendinge thy holy gospel & the professors of it especially for kepinge us from the cruelty of [15]88 & this hellish powder plot graunt that thy gospel may still runne & be glorified pr[e]vent & break in peeces all plots & machinacons that are against it' (p. 133).

Woodford singled out Clarke as a key adversary, equating him with Haman, the biblical enemy of the Jews. In 1638 the surrogate

[163]Woodford had lodged at Beale's house on 10 September 1638.

exploited the outbreak of plague as a convenient pretext to reduce the frequency of sermons: as Clarke wrote to Lambe, 'I long since advised the mayor and some of his discreet Brethrē that the Thursday lecture, and sermons on Sundayes in the afternoone, should be forborne in theys Infectious & dangerous tymes'.[164] The diary entry for Sunday 4 March 1638 details Clarke's banning of the afternoon sermon on that day, and explains this as stemming from an infernal conspiracy to undermine true gospel religion, describing a Manichaean conflict in which the adversaries are dominant and the godly a victimized minority. Laudian attacks were again portrayed as novel deviations from previous orthodoxy. However, this impression of Laudianism triumphant was quickly dispelled. Five days later it appeared that Clarke was 'appeased & that things here shall be much as they have bene' (p. 185). Such proved to be the case. The next Sunday, the practice of two sermons was resumed and not interrupted again for the duration of the diary.

Indeed, alongside fear of the popish threat in Woodford's mind ran an estimation of the English Church as essentially sound and capable of providing pure ordinances. He hoped that 'this Kingdome may be still the place of [God's] delight, & that thine ordinances may still flourish' (p. 100). Again, he informed the Lord 'we yet enioy thine ordinances Lord continue them to us & o[u]r posterity forever' (p. 120) and wished that 'thy gospel may still runne & be glorified' (p. 133). His estimation of the intensity of the popish threat was not lessened by Northampton's extraordinary capacity to see off the threat of Laudianism. That this fear persisted in his mind beyond these victories reinforces the view that he regarded popery as a national and no mere local phenomenon. In any case, the Laudians were still in office.

Popish inundation also threatened to overwhelm the sabbath, a matter of divine law specified in the fourth commandment. Woodford regarded government policy as doubly sinful, attempting to sanctify the plethora of saints' days dating from before the Reformation while profaning the genuinely holy sabbath. He never explicitly mentions the Book of Sports (the clergy at All Saints' apparently never read it), but the Book's sanctioning of various recreations was in his mind when he complained of the explosion of profanity: 'why should p[ro]phanenesse be established or countenanced by a law' (p. 289).

---

[164]TNA, SP16/393/15. Bishop Matthew Wren of Norwich had persuaded Bishop William Juxon of London to use the tactic of suspension owing to plague against the Dedham lecturer, John Rogers, in 1636. Juxon failed to reinstate Rogers when the disease subsided: T. Webster and K. Shipps (eds), *The Diary of Samuel Rogers, 1634–1638*, Church of England Record Society XI (Woodbridge, 2004), pp. lxxii–lxxiii.

On the other hand, observing saints' days deprived God of his due. On St Matthew's Day, Woodford expressed the wish that 'we might once leave this dedication of dayes to Saints & dedicate all o[u]r dayes to thee o[u]r god' (p. 327), and on another occasion criticized Charles Newton for praying for dead saints. Woodford experienced direct pressure only in 1639 in Bishop Juxon's London.[165] He related how on 23 May (Ascension Day) his stationer refused to sell him parchment for fear of questioning by the authorities, claiming that the Church was prohibiting secular work on saints' days but not on Sundays. This deprived the subject of his liberty to work for six days a week: such opinions were of course the source of the idea of the protestant work ethic. On St Peter's Day (29 June), Woodford condemned the law as sinful, wishing that 'it may be lawfull by man's law also to worke uppon the Six dayes & not to p[ro]phane the Seaventh' (p. 315). He omitted mentioning any anti-sabbatarianism in Northampton but noted that on 28 October 1639 (Simon and Jude's Day) the Monday court did not take place.

A final defining characteristic of the adversary's divinity was their marginalization of godly profession as radical sectarianism. Laudians described as such any who objected to their version of ceremonialized public worship, so when James Forsyth, minister of Old, 'spake ag[ains]t puritans' Woodford responded with a prayer for the 'rootinge out all Idolatry sup[er]stition & will worship & the restauracon & establishm[en]t of that which is in spirit & in truth' (p. 226). He and the godly regarded themselves not only as orthodox members of the Church of England but as the best part of it, and he reacted sharply against Laudian attempts to 'stayne' them 'with opprob[r]y[um] callinge them puritans, sectaryes' (p. 289).

Woodford envisaged an ideal godly commonwealth, in which national laws corresponded with divine.[166] He stated to God that 'the feare of thy name will give beinge and continuacon to a family & nothinge else can establish a house or a nacon' (p. 175). England was portrayed as having been previously sound. Many of her laws were indeed godly; he prayed God: 'Let thy lawe & o[u]r good lawes fflourish' (p. 314). Woodford subscribed to a clear definition of a godly judge who ruled 'for the fatherlesse & the widow & the oppressed' (p. 288). Set against this notion of good governance was the destabilizing factor of popery, which was equated with oppression. God's church '& our Comon wealth' were in the opposite of a 'right

[165] Webster, *Godly Clergy*, pp. 206–207.

[166] P. Lake, 'Constitutional consensus and puritan opposition in the 1620s: Thomas Scott and the Spanish Match', *Historical Journal*, 25 (1982), p. 808.

and blessed frame' (p. 99) because the same popish adversaries had subverted the country's laws.

As with religious affairs, Woodford perceived matters in black-and-white terms, polarities corresponding to Christ and Antichrist, and worked to fit current events into these categories. His primary secular concern was with the prerogative tax of ship money. At no stage did he express himself in terms of anxiety over relative levels of assessment for the levy. His concern was for the national test case of its legality, that of John Hampden. He followed each stage of the dispute, dividing the judges between the supporters of oppression and popish error (the majority supporters of the royal position) and the minority supporting justice and righteousness. His 'friend' (p. 286), Sir Richard Hutton, was one of only two judges to find against the king, citing the illegality of the tax. Woodford greeted Hutton's verdict with euphoria: 'Justice hutton delivered his opinion freely and playnely against the businesse shewinge it to be contrary to the lawes of the Realme' (p. 200). He compared this with the dithering error of Judge Jones, who 'fluttred in his argum[en]t, meteorlike hunge betweene heaven & earth & yet in the end concluded ag[ains]t Mr hampden' (*ibid.*). He wrote that Oliver St John's defence of Hampden was 'much applauded & hummed' (p. 133) by those present, which much displeased Judge Sir John Finch, a supporter of the tax. Woodford witnessed the deliberations of Justices Sir Robert Berkeley and Sir George Vernon in the Exchequer Chamber. Recording their verdicts in the king's favour, he offered up a prayer that 'Justice & righteousnes may flow downe like a streame in this Kingdome' (p. 176). While in London in June 1639 he also followed the later stages of another high-profile ship money dispute, that of the London merchant Richard Chambers, who, in 1636, had launched a suit in the Court of King's Bench against Sir Edward Bromfield, the Mayor of London who had jailed him for non-payment of the levy. Woodford condemned the tax while asserting the basic rectitude of English laws: 'Lord turne the streame of things for the Lord's sake, oh Let thy lawe & o[u]r good lawes fflourish' (p. 314).

Woodford expressed the same sentiments while observing the impact of the ship money tax on his friends. When William Tompson of Wilby obstructed the official trying to distrain his goods for non-payment of the levy, Woodford prayed to God requesting that the 'great & heavy taxe' be withdrawn, and that the kingdom might live 'in thy feare seekinge the p[ro]motion of thy glorious gospell' (p. 167). At Wilby he witnessed the uproar caused by residents of the village assembling to threaten bailiffs sent by the sheriff to distrain the goods of defaulters: 'the women assembled & some men and affright them, there was much running wth forkes & Cowlestaves & Ah Lord reforme whats amisse both in the church & Comon weale' (p. 240). The protesters included his friend Constable Francis Freeman, who was sent for shortly afterwards by the Privy Council, and Thomas Pentlow later became involved in the dispute. Woodford was also on hand in Wilby when Henry Middleton, the royal sergeant-at-arms, arrived to arrest Francis Sawyer of Kettering, a member of the godly gentry, and William Walker, Chief Constable of Wymersley Hundred, for their vehement opposition to the tax.[167] Woodford believed the arrests to be wrongful. As Middleton departed for London with his prisoners, Woodford repeated his plea tò God to 'show m[er]cye to this Kingdome, amend and reforme what ever is amisse' (p. 243), but his account was rather defensive owing to his decision to associate with Middleton for career reasons. This sensitivity illustrates the general unpopularity of the tax: 'Mr Midle[ton] told me he came to appr[e]hend Mr ffr[ancis] Sawyer (of which I knew nothinge before)' (p. 242). Woodford condemned another form of misgovernment associated with popish oppression: Sir Robert Banastre's harsh treatment of a debtor, whom Banastre told he would treat like a dog, caused the man to commit suicide. Banastre had connections with the court, was the county's most assiduous ship money sheriff, and beautified Passenham church along Laudian lines. Given Woodford's own financial predicament, it is not surprising that he abhorred the sins of usury and extortion, for which he censured Sir Henry Robinson and Thomas Pilkington's widow, Ann.[168]

Woodford included the revival of forest law within his definition of popish oppression, regarding it as an overbearing misuse of the royal prerogative, exemplified by the behaviour of Judge Sir John Finch. As we shall see, Woodford played his part in resisting the forest law. He complained that Finch had prejudged the issue without listening to the objections of the county gentry: he had 'much anticipated us in o[u]r evidence by declaringe what hath bene allreadye adiudged in this Iter in other places which he hath warned the Councell to take notice of' (p. 117). Finch was here referring to previous proceedings in Essex at which the forest policy had been set out. This involved increasing the area of land subject to forest law to medieval levels and then imposing composition fines on landowners for the illegal liberation of land from the operation of that law, a transparent expedient to raise revenue.[169] Woodford confirmed his appraisal of Finch in 1640 when the latter was appointed Lord Keeper. He asked God to 'put *good* men into places' (p. 397, my emphasis). Like the more moderate puritan, Lord

---

[167] Diary, pp. 242 (and n. 528 on Sawyer and n. 529 on Walker), 240 (and n. 524 on Freeman).
[168] *Ibid.*, pp. 164, 272–273, 381.
[169] Pettit, *Royal Forests*, pp. 83–95.

Edward Montagu, Woodford deplored the impact of the second part
of the policy – the revitalization of the forest courts – on the lower
classes of society.'⁷⁰ He saw this as both unjust and ungodly because
the courts 'set very great fines uppon small offences in the forests'
(p. 117). When people 'were fined for cutting downe maypoles in the
forests, it was told them by one on the Kings p[ar]t that they were not
fined for havinge maypoles but for cuttinge them downe in the forest'
(p. 118). At court sessions Woodford asked God to bring 'good out of
evill' (p. 241) and pleaded 'that Justice & right may pr[e]vayle & that
all oppression may cease' (p. 326).

For Woodford the popish plot had been a revolution from the top
down led by the archbishop, the bishops *en bloc*, and the Laudian
clergy. He unequivocally implicated William Laud in the pollution of
ordinances, noting that he 'hath renounced the havinge a hand in
bringing men up to the rayles to receave the sacrament oh Lord thou
art able to bringe shame & confusion of face upon all fauvo[u]r[er]s
& p[ro]moters of sup[er]stitión & Idolatry' (p. 306). Referring back to
the 1630s from the perspective of 1641, he recalled that 'the cursed
B[isho]ps & their Clergy' had been 'as the head' and were now 'as
the tayle' (p. 392). Unlike the Essex minister Samuel Rogers, whose
criticisms of bishops were aimed at errant individuals, Woodford's diary entries of the 1630s constitute a condemnation of episcopacy itself,
about which he never made a positive statement. The bench of bishops
was so riddled with popery that the very institution was discredited.
This left no room for an ideal of a good bishop.'⁷¹ The only person to
merit a favourable remark was Bishop John Williams of Lincoln, an
opponent of the regime but hardly a godly prelate. He prayed on 24
October 1637 'ag[ains]t wicked B[isho]ps, & their hierarchy I prayed
for the establishm[en]t of the gospel here' (p. 220) and later 'ag[ains]t
that hierarchy of B[isho]ps ag[ains]t sup[er]stition' (p. 129).

He took a similarly monolithic view of convocation, noting in late
1637, when a rumour was current that Charles I was about to call
Parliament, that 'there is speech of a convocation of B[isho]pps at
London about the church Cerem[onies] & discipline Lord worke for
the best for thy people' (p. 120). The bishops had used their influence to
build up among the clergy a faction of likeminded adversaries of God.
Addressing God, Woodford described how bishops had 'set up those
whom thy soule hateth' (p. 358). He mentioned only one archdeacon,
whom he said misused God's name in drinking healths. Woodford
singled out various individuals among the episcopate as especially

'⁷⁰E.S. Cope, *The Life of a Public Man: Edward, first Baron Montagu of Boughton, 1562–1644*
(Philadelphia, 1981), p. 148.
'⁷¹Webster and Shipps, *Diary of Samuel Rogers*, p. lxxiii.

infamous, including the Archbishop himself, Bishop Matthew Wren of Norwich, Dee's regime at Peterborough, his successor, John Towers, who issued 'base articles' (p. 318) ahead of his primary visitation in 1639, and Juxon's administration in London. To this list we can add secular 'evil counsellors'. Sir John Finch was unpopular with Woodford for his role in ship money and the forest law, as were the majority of judges giving the verdict against Hampden; Strafford he mentioned only during the Long Parliament.

Woodford held an elevated opinion of the true minister, who was characterized as a watchman or watchdog, tirelessly alert for sin in society, and voluble in its condemnation. Laudian clergy he categorized as counterfeits: ineffective preachers, hostile to the godly instead of to sin, enjoying wealthy livings in idleness, they were unfit to deliver the sacrament to God's people. Why, he asked, 'should dumb dogs that cannot barke remayne snarlinge at thy faythfull servants, why should Idle drones eat the fat & drinke the sweete & serve thy people' (p. 289). Clergy of this stamp were to be found both high and low in the nation. Thomas Turner, Laud's chaplain, preached at St Paul's in support of altars and bowing. William Beale, another archiepiscopal chaplain, preached error in the Chapel Royal. To these we can add local Laudian clergy such as Giles Thorne, Sir John Lambe's client as vicar of St Sepulchre's in Northampton, who in Woodford's estimation 'appears by his sermon what he is, Lord weed up the darnell & the Cockle that the wheate may grow' (p. 310). Woodford dismissed a sermon delivered by George Colson, the curate of St Giles's, Northampton, and noted the presence of a 'sup[er]stitious altar' (p. 154) in the church. The only solution to this problem, he stated on 9 July 1638, was a national reformation of the clergy. He called on God to eject popish adversaries and send 'forth into all the corners of the land and establish in all congregacons able ministers of the gospell that may build up thy church and put all iniquity to silence' (p. 216).

Woodford also reviled Laudian church court informers such as Henry Folwell, who instigated a 'devillish plot ag[ains]t a p[ro]fessor one Mrs Clarke' at the quarter sessions by procuring his servant 'to say he saw another in the act of incontinencye wth her': the servant 'afterward confessed the truth & cleered her innocencye' (p. 204–205). Thomas Pidgeon is an instance of Woodford's elision of the profane, the godly's traditional parish enemies, with the religiously deviant. Pidgeon, a Church court apparitor as well as a carpenter by trade, had been Dr Clarke's ally in creating an east end railed altar at his chapel of Upton, in the teeth of opposition from the churchwardens. After socializing with Pidgeon, Woodford commented that he 'was almost drunke Lord convert that p[er]secuter to thee'.[172]

He held out only a faint hope of conversion for those he saw as enemies of God. When the court official Dr William Roane scrutinized one of Andrew Perne's sermons, Woodford hoped that the gospel would work 'uppon that sup[er]stitious doctor, I besought the Lord for his convercon' (p. 222). When referring to idolaters in general, he was prepared to go a stage further. If they could not be converted he prayed that God damn them: 'come forth oh Lord amongst thine adversaryes who doe plott against thee & seeke to defile thine ordinances with base humane inventions, if they belong unto thee bringe them in, if not confound them oh Lord confound & curse them and all their machinacons' (p. 216).

Popish rot reached to the apex of the English Church and state, the head of both of which was an unrepentant sinner. Woodford prayed for 'the Kings Ma[jes]tye for his Convercon, to inlighten his eyes to stirre him up to drive away the wicked from the throne, & to make choice of such as will be faythfull' (p. 112).[173] The Essex minister Samuel Rogers shared this opinion of Charles I.[174] This was to go much further than to claim that the king had been misled by 'evil counsellors'. The throne was indeed beset by the wicked, but their influence was merely a symptom of the crucial dysfunction, Charles's defective nature. Woodford regarded Charles as ignorant of true religion, as unable to distinguish right from wrong, and as guilty of consistently sponsoring popish error. After a sermon by William Beale, the royal chaplain, Woodford prayed for the establishment of 'true doctrine & a pure worship' and called on God to change the King's nature: 'give him to discerne betweene things that differ' (p. 251). Recording that Bishop Wren had preached at court, he complained: 'bringe those that are faythfull to preach before his Ma[jes]tye with effect & remove the wicked from his throne that it may be established & continue' (p. 175). He focussed on Charles's appointment of court preachers, but the monarch's wider religious and secular patronage was, of course, considerable. The court itself was not regarded as inherently evil: it had been made so by Charles's wrong decisions, which betrayed no fear of God and thus jeopardized his throne, nation, and dynasty ('house' (ibid.)). This final danger was further exacerbated by the poisonous influence of Charles's Catholic wife, Henrietta Maria, for

---

[172] Diary, p. 264 (and n. 587 on Pidgeon).
[173] For other examples see ibid., pp. 173, 297.
[174] Webster and Shipps, Diary of Samuel Rogers, p. lxxv.

whose conversion he prayed, and of her mother, Marie de Medici, whose pending visit to London he anticipated with abhorrence.[175]

In his vision of a godly commonwealth, Woodford envisaged a crucial role for the monarch, ruling like a David or Solomon. In 1638 he recorded the anniversary of Charles I's accession: 'oh Lord graunt him longe to raigne for thee & the good of thy Church & people' (p. 193). The king was a patriarch with a sacred responsibility for the kingdoms and churches committed to his care by God. On his tour of the privy apartments in Whitehall Palace, Woodford saw 'the 4 gospells the acts of the apostles & the Apocalipse in books all sett forth wth pictures' and prayed for Charles 'make him a nursinge father to the Kingdomes committed to him' (p. 246). Contrast this respect for the institutions of monarchy and judiciary with his contempt for that of episcopacy. The key criterion of a rightful king and dynasty was adherence to divine law. A true king feared God, promoted true religion and justice, and warded off popish error and tyranny. He prayed to God: 'let holy doctrine & pure worship be set up, & let Justice flow downe like a streame, that the throne may be established' (p. 358).

Woodford's respect for monarchy led him to extend much more charitable goodwill towards Charles than towards other sinners: he failed to mention the sumptuous railed altar in the chapel royal at Whitehall, for instance.[176] He strained to see the good in the king: 'make him a blessed instrument of thy glory in these churches let his eyes scatter all Idolatry pop[er]y sup[er]stition & p[ro]phanenesse let the good be accepted of him' (p. 298). However, conversion seemed an unlikely prospect: the nation needed ministers who would preach before him 'with effect' (p. 175), but Charles appointed only the enemies of God. It might be necessary for God to intervene directly through affliction. On 29 November 1637 it was rumoured that the king was sick. Woodford fantasized about a newly converted king, who would do away with popish superstition. A defining characteristic of a godly king was his inclination to rule in partnership with Parliament, and Woodford yearned for Charles to summon one.[177] His estimation of this institution was lofty. Court and country might be riddled with popery but Parliament was not: he associated it with the positive ideological pole of a godly commonwealth, and had supreme confidence in its ability to correct the wrongdoings of the Personal Rule.

[175] Diary, pp. 246, 358.

[176] K. Fincham and N. Tyacke, *Altars Restored: the changing face of English religious worship, 1547–c.1700* (Oxford, 2007), pp. 177, 227–228.

[177] Diary, pp. 144–145.

Woodford's attitude towards the war with Scotland developed over several months. His first mention of the crisis, on 27 April 1638, was vague. For personal reasons he feared the outbreak of hostilities, which might cause his creditors to call in their debts while simultaneously undermining his ability to repay them by devaluing his property.[178] Around 2 January 1639 his opinion crystallized, after John Dillingham showed him the proceedings of the Glasgow Assembly, which had responded to Charles I's attempted imposition of a new Prayer Book with godly revolution, abolishing episcopacy and establishing a Presbyterian discipline. The diarist never mentioned this origin of the uprising. To Woodford the cause of the conflict was the popish corruption of the English government. He wished for peace certainly, but more importantly for an English reformation to eject popery, on 22 January petitioning God to 'pr[e]vent the warre wth Scotland I pray if thou seest good however let thy truth & gospell be established in power & purity amongst us'. Remarkably, various examples of pro-government propaganda – particularly the royal proclamation of 27 February asserting that the Scots 'strike at the Roote of monarchicall governm[en]t' (p. 288) – convinced him that the English regime was the aggressor, the Covenanters his godly fellow sufferers under oppression. Official condemnation of the Scots as traitors intensified in Woodford's mind the pre-existing notion of a popish conspiracy, proving to him by 6 March that popish control of state policy had become near total. He complained that 'The opposers of god & true religion have said we will devoure at once; they are in our hands, now shall we pr[e]vayle' (p. 289). He therefore prayed for the destruction of Babylon, the popish Antichrist. Of course Woodford had already made up his mind on the subject of episcopacy, owing to what he saw as its complicity in the popish plot, and he undoubtedly regarded the conflicts as the Bishops' Wars, although he never used the phrase. He also identified secular oppression in the regime's conduct of the war, applauding the opposition expressed by the 'godly & gracious' Lords Saye and Sele and Brooke (p. 301), who refused to fight for the king or to swear an oath of loyalty that lacked parliamentary authority.

Events were judged to have come to such a pass that God had hidden His face from a sinful nation. He now intervened directly. This Woodford discussed with John Bullivant: 'how iustly the Lord may bring uppon us the Judgem[en]t of the sword' (p. 295). He and his godly London friends were persuaded that God would lift the affliction once the Church had repented: 'the Lord will surely looke uppon his poore church in the end, when his church is fit for deliverance & when ungodly men have filled up the measure of their sinnes' (p. 307).

---

[178] *Ibid.*, p. 271.

Woodford's state of mind combined a desire for holy patience with a militant faith in final victory. Though the prospects seemed grim, he informed God that 'thou hast given us thy word to be neare unto us even in o[u]r mouthes, & we have the mind of Xt. Oh give us fayth to make all o[u]r owne' (p. 289). He considered fleeing from this affliction as he had from the plague, but was delighted at the Truce of Berwick, which concluded the first war. The anticipated reconciliation gave some optimism of a royal volte-face resulting in the redress of the grievances of the Personal Rule. Woodford fervently hoped that it demonstrated 'much Love from the Kinge to' the Covenanters and that henceforth God's 'church & people' would gain 'dayly more & more grace in the eyes of his Ma[jes]ty', while he would now 'frowne uppon the wicked and such as have evill will at Sion' (p. 312). There was some hope that the Antichrist had suffered a setback: 'Lord confirme & sanctifye this peace unto us let it be of moment, a meanes to advance thy gospell & to disappoynt Antixt & his cursed adherents' (p. 314). The resumption of godly reformation by the reconvened Glasgow Assembly no doubt confirmed this.[179]

Running parallel with Woodford's idea of an activist piety was an activist citizenship embodying the duty of Christians to promote virtue and reprove sin. He expressed admiration for individuals and groups who voiced opposition to government policies. Nationally, he applauded the high-profile stand taken by Hampden, Lords Saye and Sele and Brooke, the City of London, and the trio of 'holy livinge Martirs', Burton, Bastwick, and Prynne (p. 377). This extended to his cousin Gregory Dexter, a London printer who, Woodford asserted to God, had 'adventur[ed] himselfe much in thy cause' (p. 384) by printing Prynne's *Instructions to Church Wardens*, for which Dexter suffered in the Court of High Commission.[180] Such high expectations informed Woodford's criticism of the magistracy (Mayor William Collis and the assembly) for capitulating to Dr Clarke even to the extent of allowing the banning of a single Sunday afternoon sermon. His expectations of the ministry were particularly high. As the best solvent of evil was preaching the gospel, Woodford reserved his praise for those ministers who persisted, despite pressure from the authorities, in preaching frequently, expounding Calvinist themes, and denouncing popish error. He applauded sermons condemning superstition delivered by Richard Trueman, Thomas Ball, and Benjamin Tompkins at Northampton, and two unnamed ministers at Aldermanbury in London.[181] He singled out for particular acclaim

[179] *Ibid.*, p. 325.
[180] For Dexter, see *ibid.*, p. 367, n. 867.
[181] *Ibid.*, pp. 100, 154, 182, 219.

John Stoughton and Andrew Perne. He commended the latter to God as one of the 'Champions for thee, even great Apolloes' (p. 100). Discussing the potency of Perne's performances he hoped the 'gospell might breake forth that the bright shininge of it might enlighten all the world, that Pop[er]y like dagon may fall before it' (p. 228). Others were acclaimed for their analysis of the times as ones of imminent persecution by the enemies of true religion, in which it was necessary to organize against oppression. Woodford expressed emphatic approval for sermons by Saye and Sele's suspended chaplain, John Mayo, in one of which, according to a hostile observer, he preached on the text 'Grow in Grace was very vehement in his use of reprehension saying these ar[e] decaying tymes wherein many did oppose those who grow in grace but they must have fellowship one with another and fortifie themselves against evill tymes'.[182] John Wilkins advocated 'pr[e]paracon for p[er]secucon' (p. 165); and James Cranford encouraged his audience to 'stand for the truth in times of greatest darknesse & danger' (p. 292). Woodford applauded his courage: 'this was a word in season Lord uphold him & stand by him in his troubles & dangers' (ibid.).

Woodford's own response to the Personal Rule involved a resolution to remain in England and within the existing Church structure. He rejected for now the drastic reactions embraced by more radical godly groups, such as those who thought separation was essential to achieve pure ordinances. His views were influenced by his position at the centre of a long-established puritan community: he encountered outright separatism only in London, where he discussed the current state of religion with Nicholas Tew and others, 'all unlesse one of them sep[ar]atists or greatly inclininge' (p. 313). Woodford's conviction of the deep penetration of popery, and his dislike of the popish residue in the half-reformed English Church, had substantially convinced him of the case for separation but he was not yet prepared to take the final step: 'my hart doth much hate or distrust the antichristian power that is amongst us and vayne ceremonyes & some weake rudim[en]ts yet why I should sep[ar]ate because of some imp[er]feccons I am not yet wholly convinced oh Lord enlighten me' (ibid.).

He felt the same misgivings over emigration. He discussed the issue with Henry Hall, schoolmaster of Paulerspury, and a Mr Shepherd. Woodford, unlike the Essex minister Samuel Rogers, was not enthusiastic about New England, apparently sharing the opinion of Rogers's half-brother, Daniel Rogers, the schoolmaster of Northampton, that departure was unnecessary.[183] He mentions

---

[182]TNA, SP16/474/80.
[183]Webster and Shipps, *Diary of Samuel Rogers*, pp. xx, 97, 99.

without judgement two families emigrating to Massachusetts: George and Elizabeth Curwyn headed for Salem; William Sargent later served as lay minister at Barnstaple.[184] These views were perhaps explained by his essential optimism about Parliament's willingness to remove the deficiencies in Church and state. It remains to be seen what actions, other than wishing for the summoning of a parliament, were open to provincial individuals opposed to government policy.

Woodford's contest with popish influence began with prayer, which, at times, he used as a weapon, praying *against* the episcopal bench without hoping for its conversion. He also participated in the collective response of the Northampton godly, which fell back, as instructed by some preachers, on its voluntary structures, which were now put to work on public issues. Such meetings provided mutual support in times of danger and aimed to co-ordinate individual responses into a unified effort. During the town's struggle to avoid the altar policy, Woodford attended a meeting at which Mayor William Collis and his wife were present: 'I am now to goe Joyne in dutye wth gods people to beseech the Lord for helpe in this evill & troublous time [...] Lord heare our poore prayers for thy poore church & for our selves' (p. 182). In another example of collective petitionary prayer, he and Hannah joined a group of 'gods people' at Ball's house who were 'seekinge the Lord in the behalfe of his church & o[u]r selves' (p. 370).

Government religious policy was a lively topic of conversation in the county. There was much debate among the godly over the seriousness of the threat of popery and the right response to make to it. Woodford debated ceremonies with Daniel Rogers, with godly groups in Northampton and London, and even with godly strangers on the road. In Northampton he attended two conferences on the subject on the same day. The first took place at James Fryers's house, where, accompanied by Thomas Martin and Martin Tompkins, Woodford interviewed Thomas Case, a Norfolk minister under suspension for nonconformity. The second occurred at the house of the physician Dr James Hart, and was attended by Thomas and Matthew Watts. The conference at Hart's further exposed the pressure brought to bear on godly unity by the policies of the 1630s: 'we had argument about kneelinge at the sacrament, & whether it is lawfull to communicate wth knowne p[ro]phane p[er]sons & about bowinge' (p. 188).

Woodford and friends lent their support to the principled stand against the altar policy made by the churchwardens, Rushworth

---

[184]Diary, pp. 121 (and n. 115 on Curwyns), 176, 194; R.L. Greaves, 'Lothropp, John (bap. 1584, d. 1653)', in *ODNB*; G.A. Moriarty, 'Genealogical research in England: Gifford: Sargent', *New England Historical and Genealogical Register*, 74 (1920, 1921), pp. 231–237, 267–283.

and Farren: indeed, the parish paid their expenses in the case.[185] Woodford praised their repeated turning of the communion table into a non-altarwise orientation within the first rail, and their rejection of Clarke's instruction to create a railed altar at the east. The churchwardens 'answered him boldly' (p. 151), giving their reasons in 1641: the authorities had no 'Authority so to doe either from Rubrick or Cannons'.[186] On the day of Rushworth's excommunication for refusal to create a railed altar, he and his wife, Joan, attended a supper conference at the Woodfords' with Samuel Martin (during Rushworth's absence in London on account of the dispute, the Woodfords had taken care of Joan). Yet the yearned-for unanimity was not achieved. Even in Northampton the issue of conformity could divide godly opinion. After a supper conference at the Woodfords' attended by the Rushworths, Samuel Martin, and his wife, Woodford chastised Joan Rushworth in the diary for her unhappiness over her husband's stand against Dr Clarke. Joan, he wrote, was 'to blame in beinge heavy & sad to see her husband goe on wth such resolucon in the busines against dr Clarke. Lord strengthen his hands that he may not be discouraged' (p. 183).

What of the Christian's duty to reprove sin? Lacking the protection of a powerful patron, Woodford was acutely aware that the expression of his political views, some of which were actionable, was fraught with danger, and therefore inscribed a plea for privacy at the start of the diary, which he showed to the godly alone. He did not apply to himself the same high standard that he used for national politicians or those with higher callings. As with social manners so with politics, the obligation to speak out was activated only infrequently: conduct was to be dictated by moderation and prudence. When the commissioners arrived at Northampton to order the creation of an altar, he noted, quoting a favourite godly passage from Isaiah 59:15, that 'it is an evill time & the prudent hold their peace, who so dep[ar]ts from evill maketh himselfe a prey' (p. 104).

This caution was only overridden when challenged directly on a matter in which divine law was at stake: on two occasions Woodford found himself in potentially very dangerous circumstances and responded with a degree of courage. The first was when socializing at Sir Christopher Hatton's, a courtier and patron of Laudian ministers. After dinner he fell into conversation with Hatton's conformist chaplain, James Longman. The topic turned to religion 'the times & altars & bowinge to them he favors & maynteynes those innovations' (p. 181); as it happened, this was the time when the construction of

---

[185] Vestry Minutes, pp. 36–37.
[186] HLRO, main papers, petition of Farren and Rushworth, 6 February 1641.

the altar was under way at All Saints'. At first Woodford resolved to be circumspect 'so to carry my self that he might not p[er]ceave my opinion' (p. 182). Finally goaded beyond endurance, he expressed opposition on the basis of religious conviction – idolatry was an abominable sin: 'the fire brake out, & I spoke in the behalfe of gods true & sp[irit]uall worship, though with as much discrecon as I could & thought fitt' (*ibid.*). He had still not given full vent to his feelings. He wished to avoid danger, but prepared himself to be persecuted, as instructed by the preachers, by asking God to cultivate in him the necessary capabilities to make his opposition effective: 'if in thy p[ro]vidence thou hast ordeyned that I shall be called forth to witnesse to thy truth, I beseech thee give me knowledge & wisdome & fayth & courage & resolucon & patience' (*ibid.*).

On the second occasion, Woodford found himself outnumbered by Arminians attacking predestination at the council house in Coventry, but this time chastised himself for imprudent zeal: 'the Lord much moved my hart to defend his truth but I found few there that favoured it, I was too earnest & hasty in my argum[en]t' (p. 254). Fortunately for Woodford, his mettle was never put to the test. In contrast, his condemnation of actual Roman Catholicism seems to have been carried out in an atmosphere bordering on conviviality. Encountering Lord Brudenell's Catholic kinsman, Woodford 'used what arguments I could to convince him of his error & prayd unto the Lord in his behalfe' (p. 201) and lodged with him. During a visit to Thomas Bacon's Catholic relation, George Poulton, squire of Desborough, Woodford recorded supping 'wth a demure priest which was there as I was informed, we had much discourse of gen[er]all papists in divinity' (p. 298).

Woodford's actions are often a matter of speculation. In view of his written intolerance of occasional conformity among the clergy and the prevailing mood of anti-Laudian nonconformity obtaining at All Saints', where Ball fended off attacks on his preaching and led determined opposition to ceremonial, it is likely that Woodford seldom, if ever, practised ceremonial conformity. He took a similarly hard line on lay conformity, describing the Laudian Humphrey Ramsden as a 'sup[er]stitious wretch' (p. 101). We can state with a degree of confidence that he was never required to receive communion at the rails of an east end railed altar. During the period of the first rail, the churchwardens repeatedly brought down the communion table and set it pointing east to west. The fully Laudian second rail and altar lasted only three months, during which time Woodford received communion once. He alternated between two seats, one of which was situated in an 'Alley' (p. 197) in the nave, where he sat with the town sergeants by virtue of his office. During the plague he chose to sit with

Hannah in their own seat, which, if it was one of the tall, formerly collegiate pews, may have made concealment of their postures easier. We cannot pronounce definitively on Woodford's practice: puritans were infamous for mental equivocation, and there were ways to evade the spirit of Laudianism.[187]

A similar problem is encountered when trying to assess his response to secular policies such as ship money. Northamptonshire was one of the most recalcitrant counties, while Northampton itself paid virtually nothing, even towards the writ of 1637. Woodford may in addition have been able to exploit his constant absences to evade payment, but unsurprisingly he furnishes no details. There exists a single recorded instance of his secular resistance: he defaulted over payment of coat and conduct money. Lord Lieutenant John Mordaunt, Earl of Peterborough, sent a warrant for his arrest to Wilby on 29 July 1640. The constable of Wilby, William Lord, returned the warrant saying that Woodford could not be found, and the diary is silent on his whereabouts.[188]

Woodford expressed his ideological opposition to government policy through the pursuit of his calling, in which he sought to counteract oppression. He played a part in the county's opposition to the revival of forest law, liaising between senior counsel – John Whitwick, Edward Bagshaw, and Geoffrey Palmer – and the county gentry, who seem to have been united in their resistance. His landlord, Samuel Crick, provided their accommodation in Northampton.[189] In Woodford's view, the county objected to the defence presented by Whitwick, their chief advocate, finding it too submissive, the consensus being that counsel should protest. Whitwick's submission, he complained, 'was not well liked on the counetryes p[ar]te, it was done so lengthy who would have had a submiss[ion] wth p[ro]testacon' (p. 118).

When he agreed to act for his godly friend Thomas Bacon, squire of Burton Latimer, Woodford was drawn into a truly bitter clash.[190] Bacon's pre-eminence had long been challenged by a group led by the rector, Dr Robert Sibthorpe, whose viewpoint encompassed personal

---

[187]After a conference with Daniel Rogers at Ball's house, Woodford noted with approval that the schoolmaster 'seemes to loath vayne Ceremonies' (p. 164). Ramsden confirmed Rogers's nonconformity, accusing him of administering the communion without a surplice to sitters and himself receiving the sacrament 'wth thone hand on his heade, & kneeling on thone knee': TNA, SP16/474/80.

[188]Jackson, 'Ship money', pp. 134–135, 195–196; TNA, SP16/461/53.

[189]Diary, p. 118.

[190]I rely heavily on V.L. Stater, 'The lord lieutenancy on the eve of the Civil Wars: the impressment of George Plowright', *Historical Journal*, 2 (1986), pp. 279–296; and Jackson, 'Ship money', pp. 32–45.

identification with the king and Laud, conformist divinity, ardent anti-puritanism, and an infamous dedication to royal absolutism. The conflict had ranged over various issues including rights of common, pew allocation, and altar creation, but now centred on ship money.[191] In 1638 Bacon retained Woodford to act for him in a Star Chamber case in which he was the defendant and Sibthorpe's ally, George Plowright, the promoter. Faced with Plowright's commitment to collecting the tax, Bacon and others had in 1635 employed delaying tactics, before, with the support of Sheriff Sir John Dryden, referring the matter to the Privy Council. Sibthorpe had activated his influence at court through Sir John Lambe, and Bacon had stood accused of leading a seditious, puritan, conspiracy – counselled by Dryden, Richard Knightley, and Edward Bagshaw – to sabotage the tax.

Woodford acted for Bacon in two commissions for the interrogation of witnesses, one held at Kettering, the other at Daventry. He liaised with Bacon, his brother John, also included in the suit, and Bacon's chosen commissioners, examined witnesses, and completed the paperwork. He produced legal briefs for Bacon's court appearance in conjunction with senior counsel, Geoffrey Palmer, and Bacon even requested him to appear in person in the Star Chamber on 10 May. The attorney's reluctance was due to fear of his opponent: 'I am apt to thinke that dr Sibthorpe will therefore set himselfe against me & ruine me' (p. 305). He tried to persuade himself, with what result is unclear, of his duty to appear, appealing to God: 'I am in my callinge thou canst deliver me from the mouth of the Lyon & from the fingers of the wicked & the violen[t] man' (ibid.).

To Woodford this was much more than an administrative dispute: he was battling evil through the legitimate channel of his calling. Bacon, he said, was 'much oppressed by the malice & violence of wicked men that p[er]secute him Lord I pray thee sanctifye it unto him, & breake this snare' (ibid.). However, at this point Sibthorpe received a check. Lambe abandoned the suit, which had been overtaken by Plowright's impressment as a soldier by the deputy lieutenants, among them Sir Rowland St John, after Plowright, as Constable of Burton, had failed to press his quota of soldiers for the Bishops' Wars.[192] Sibthorpe eschewed traditional methods of dispute resolution, referring the matter to his court contacts and instigating a second Star Chamber case through Plowright against Bacon. Sibthorpe reiterated the theme of a puritan conspiracy led by Bacon, the lieutenants, puritan justices,

---

[191] NRO, 55P/57, pp. 63–71, entry under date 19 July 1633; TNA, SP16/261/fos 85v, 91v, 101v, 109v, 117v, 125v, 174v, 214v, 230; NRO, 55P/68, under year 1637.

[192] Temple of Stowe MSS, STT 1885, 16 May 1639; Diary, pp. 193, 195–198, 206, 230–232, 294.

and even the moderate Lord Montagu, to undermine the king's cause, the collection of ship money.[193] He organized Plowright's case while Woodford organized Bacon's. The latter provided briefs for the Star Chamber hearing on 17 May, at which 'Plowright the p[er]secuter' (p. 306) was found to be at fault and imprisoned.

By virtue of his stewardship of Northampton, Woodford was part of an influential group in the town's government, and here also he was able to combat evil through the pursuit of his calling. When Humphrey Ramsden, a Laudian layman, settled in the town, the godly community co-operated to eject him, with the steward playing his own part.[194] According to Ramsden's account, he had spent the latter half of 1637 in the town, but his enthusiastic ceremonialism had caused the godly of All Saints' parish, a 'nest of Puritans', to revile him as a papist. He had responded by compiling a detailed written account of the parish's nonconformity, but when this was discovered the puritans had mounted a concerted campaign against him and expelled him from the town. A year later, in March 1639, safe in a conformist enclave, he forwarded his denunciation to that 'orthodoxall gent' Sir John Lambe, hoping that he would reduce to conformity the 'malignant refractory spirits who disturb the peace' of the church.[195] Woodford confirmed that the godly regarded Ramsden's ritualism – he bowed when entering and leaving church, as was encouraged by the visitation articles of Bishop Dee – as a popish threat. On Ramsden's arrival in the town, Woodford hoped that the 'sup[er]stitious wretch lately come hether may not doe hurt' (p. 101). The main threat posed by Ramsden was that he might report the nonconformity of the parish, but he might also inflict religious damage by offending godly parishioners with his gestures. Ramsden put the following criticism into the mouth of Charles Newton: 'you offend weak Christians not only those but alsoe did trouble the consciences of strong ones'. The townsmen, led by Newton, Rushworth, and Fery, launched a verbal and violently physical challenge to his practices.[196] He claimed that his hosts in Northampton had reacted with more moderation: John

[193]Temple of Stowe MSS, STT 1890, 3 June 1639.

[194]Diary, p. 101 and n. 22.

[195]TNA, SP16/414/163.

[196]TNA, SP16/474/80. Ramsden said that Charles Newton had criticized him for bowing at the name of Jesus, for standing up at the *gloria patri* and gospel, and for bowing when entering and leaving church. He had further condemned as idolatry Ramsden's worshipping the altar 'before anything'. Francis Rushworth, the churchwarden, said that if he had offended Ramsden 'he served mee right for that I bring new customes into their ch[urch] wch he neither found in the Canons rubricke nor was enjoyned by act of parliament'. Another group of townsmen had sent him the message (via the parish clerk, Fery) that 'there is noe more holinesse in it [the church] than in his owne house'.

Maunsell, Prynne's former chamber-fellow at Lincoln's Inn, and his wife, Susan, tacitly disapproved of his actions, as indeed did Woodford. The diarist even lent him his copy of William Ames's catechism on 26 November 1637. This moderation changed, claimed Ramsden, when Susan Maunsell discovered his written denunciation of the parish's nonconformity.

The mayor, Woodford's friend John Gifford, ordered him to prepare charges against Ramsden, which he was forced to answer before the Laudian justice, Dr Clarke, at the quarter sessions: 'Ramsden the sup[er]stitious fellow was indicted for night walkinge & p[rese]nted for an affray, & beinge 2ce [twice] drunke, oh Lord convert him if it be thy will or remove him from this towne' (p. 108). Again Woodford associated alehouse ungodliness with religious error. Ramsden's account of these events was rather different. Following Susan Maunsell's discovery of his written denunciation, the Maunsells had encouraged their servants to provoke him.[197] When he had struck one of them, Maunsell had thrown him out onto the street. He also countered the charge of inebriation, claiming not to have entered a tavern for months: 'neither ever would if I had lived in Northton xx yeares because I would not give theym the least advantage sith they were so fully bent against for he did drink ergo he is drunk hath beene an argument stronge enough to condemne mee in Northton'.[198] Ramsden was not entirely without friends in the town. Henry Neale of St Giles's parish represented him, and much of his information came from Christopher Young, Dr Clarke's curate at St Peter's parish, and James Forsyth, rector of Old. However these men were not influential enough to protect him and he left shortly afterwards.

The puritan clique encountered more opposition with political overtones. Mayor John Gifford brought charges against Richard Mottershed of Kingsthorpe for miscarriage in his court; Woodford again drew up the paperwork at the town's quarter sessions. In response, Mottershed threatened them both 'to have Mr Gifford & me in the Starr=chamber & to unsteward me' (p. 163). Mottershed was from a recusant family connected to the Church courts, Sir John Lambe, Bishop Robert Skinner of Bristol, the Earl of Northampton, and Archbishop Richard Neile himself.[199] However, there is no evidence that he carried out his threat.

---

[197] Ramsden gave the following summary of the parish's attitude towards him: 'I am smiled at by the ministers & better sort and laught out of the ch[urch] by the vulgar the men are a little more sparinge herein then heretofore but women and boyes were never so forward [...] I am counted a papist they say throughout the towne there cannot be a more scornfull parishe.& censorious people in England': TNA, SP16/474/80.

[198] TNA, SP16/414/163.

[199] Diary, p. 163 (n. 269 on Mottershed).

Woodford was equally committed to combatting the godly's opponents in the town oligarchy. The godly faction in the senior body of the corporation was challenged by one led by John Danby and William Knight. That this opposition was long-standing and partly based on differences of ideas is suggested by the controversy that had arisen in 1627 over the collection of the forced loan. The mayor, William Knight, had appealed to the Privy Council emphasizing his zeal to collect the levy, with repeated claims to be the only commissioner to make the least effort.[200] In contrast, resistance had been rife in the town and county: in Northampton itself the opposition had included clergy such as Thomas Ball and Benjamin Tompkins, the recorder, Christopher Sherland, his deputy, Richard Lane, and Sir Edmund Hampden. The assembly had split along similar lines over Woodford's election as steward in 1635. Woodford's backers were led by Mayor Thomas Martin, and included the aldermen John Gifford, Francis Fisher, Roger Sargent, John Bott, and John Harbert.[201] This left Aldermen Danby, Knight, and Matthew Sillesby in the camp of his rival, Thomas Pilkington, and indeed all three were beneficiaries of Pilkington's will.[202] The identities of other supporters of Pilkington are a matter of speculation: Henry Chadwick and Richard Fowler are likely candidates. The divergence over ideas emerged again in reaction to the policies of the Personal Rule. It was during Danby's mayoralty that the Monday court was suspended on St Simon's and St Jude's day. Mayor Gifford was censured by the Privy Council for his obstructionism over the collection of ship money, while the majority of the assembly blocked the attempt by Mayor Danby, Alderman Knight, and Mayor Fowler to collect coat and conduct money to support the anti-Scottish war effort.[203] Fowler was probably also stopped by the assembly from paying his respects to the general of the English army, the Earl of Arundel, when he passed through the town, until coerced into doing so by a warrant.[204]

During the elections of 1640 the conflict between these town factions, which mirrored similar divisions in the county as a whole, burst into the open. Two weeks before the shire election for the Short Parliament, Woodford was not a floating voter. He prayed God to take the national election process in hand and deflect the adversaries who

[200]TNA, SP16/75/27, 271. I thank Richard Cust for these references; see also R.P. Cust, *The Forced Loan and English Politics, 1626–1628* (Oxford, 1987), pp. 233, 297–298, 301, 309.
[201]Martin was active in securing Woodford's appointment. Woodford reimbursed him for his expenses in travelling to London about the dispute with Pilkington: Diary, p. 160.
[202]PDR, Archdeaconry of Northampton Wills, second series, L120.
[203]Diary, pp. 324, 330; Jackson, 'Ship money', pp. 134–135; Markham and Cox, *Northampton*, II, pp. 436–437.
[204]Diary, p. 293.

were hostile to Parliament: 'give grace & wisdome to the Country & Corporacons to make choyce of gracious & able men & thou blesse the worke in their hands pr[e]vent the plots of thine adversaryes' (p. 336). He rejected the overtures of one potential court candidate, Sir Christopher Hatton, despite having previously received hospitality from him. When the godly candidate, Sir Gilbert Pickering, rode from Wellingborough to Northampton, Woodford joined his entourage: 'I was much affected to see him & prayed in my hart for him & came along wth him' (p. 344). The election was fought on issues of principle. John Crewe won the senior seat without polling, owing to his resistance to ship money, leaving Pickering to contest the junior seat with the court candidate, Deputy Lieutenant Thomas Elmes, Hatton having pulled out. After voting for Pickering, Woodford celebrated his victory, which was 'to the Joy of the harts of gods people' (p. 346). His friends – Pentlow, Ball, Gifford, Martin, and Whalley – actively campaigned for Pickering, who had been the pupil of Ball and Preston. During a later enquiry into the conduct of the election, these men were accused of slighting Elmes's supporters as seditious papists and claiming that Elmes was ineligible to stand because, as a deputy lieutenant, he was questionable in Parliament for his part in pressing troops for the Bishops' Wars. On the other side of the divide were ranged Dr Samuel Clarke, Mayor John Danby, and local magnates with court connections, including the new Lord Lieutenant (the Earl of Peterborough), the Earl of Northampton (and his agent, Richard Mottershed), and the Earl of Westmorland.[205] Woodford hinted at the souring of social relationships brought about by the political tensions revealed at the election. Before the contest he had feared that his revealing his allegiance to Pickering might bring him into jeopardy and prayed 'direct me & defend me from evill that may come uppon me for doeinge that wch is right' (p. 342). Afterwards he noticed that his working relationship with Sir John Isham, which had been amicable despite political differences, had cooled: 'I p[er]ceave his carriage was altered towards me in respect that I was for Sr Guilb[er]t Pickering at the eleccon' (p. 352).

Similar divisions were apparent in the Northampton mayoral elections of 6 August 1640, which Woodford describes in religious terms. His friend John Fisher was elected mayor, with the equally godly Henry Sprig and Martin Tompkins as his bailiffs: 'in despite of all adverse power, to the ioy of thy people & the vexacon of the enimyes of religion & strictnes Lord be with thy servants' (p. 359). Woodford celebrated Fisher's victory 'notwithstanding all the opposicon of

---

[205] *Ibid.*, pp. 342, 344–346, and notes.

Mr danby now Maior Mr Knight & al' (p. 360). There was also considerable opposition to the godly among the freemen.[206]

As the Short Parliament began, Woodford restated his support for the Scots, the solidarity of international Protestantism faced with the ubiquitous threat of popery, and his identification with Parliament as an institution. He claimed a supranational fast had been held in England, Scotland, and Germany, with the purpose of promoting the success of the parliament, and he prayed for 'my deare bretheren abroad in the world' (p. 350). Enormous expectations of Parliament were coupled with continuing fear that the adversary would sabotage the session. He placed the responsibility for Parliament's sudden dissolution, and the reaction to it of London's lower orders, squarely on the shoulders of this adversary. Staying at the Haunches, he experienced in person some of the unrest. Lambeth Palace was attacked, forcing Laud to flee in disguise over the Thames, the White Lion prison was occupied, and those arrested for the attack on Lambeth were sprung from jail.[207] Woodford regarded these instances of mob violence – by the so-called London 'Apprentices' – as unalloyed 'troubles' and 'evills' (pp. 354–355), despite his loathing of the archbishop. While approving of the anti-popery of the rank-and-file soldiery marching north via Northampton, he failed to endorse their undisciplined ferocity. The men were 'vehemently bent ag[ains]t papists & will scarce be ruled by their captaynes. Oh Lord looke uppon us in this nacon reforme what is amisse send forth thy light & thy truth, scatter Idolatry sup[er]stition & p[ro]phanesse for the Lords sake' (p. 357). Woodford the lawyer preferred the parliamentary way of addressing grievances over popular violence.

The episode of the Short Parliament substantiated his theory of a popish conspiracy and confirmed his estimation of the role of the Scots in thwarting it. He explained the role of the invading army as a *deus ex machina*. Its task of purging and purifying the nation was equated with that of the messenger of the Lord described in Malachi 3:1–3. Through this army, he asserted to God, 'thou canst to the shame of thine enimyes bringe destruccon uppon them whence they did least expect it' (p. 361). Many of his godly friends shared this reading. Scottish propaganda was circulating in the area and a clerical conference at Kettering on 25 August, attended by Ball, Perne, and many others,

---

[206] *Ibid.*, p. 373, and n. 887.
[207] *Ibid.*, pp. 349, 352–355, and notes.

lent it their enthusiastic support.[208] A thorough reformation of Church and commonwealth was the only solution to the problem of popery: a return to the status quo was insufficient. Woodford begged God to 'bowe the heavens & come downe & dwell amongst us, & make us a Kingdome of preists a holy nation oh let holy doctrine & pure worship be set up, & let Justice flow downe like a streame' (p. 358).

The process needed to begin with the evil institution of episcopacy, and around 2 August 1640 he called for its destruction by lightning bolt.[209] On the other hand, he still held out a faint hope that the Stuart dynasty might be purified rather than purged. He continued to wish for the conversion of the king, and beseeched God to 'convert his queene unto thee' (ibid.), thus ensuring the orthodoxy of the king's 'royall posterity that they may be famous in Jacob & doe worthily in this our Ephratah' (ibid.). Woodford became more politicized, mobilizing in support of the aims of national oppositionist politicians. At Wellingborough market on 9 September 1640, he obtained a copy of the Twelve Peers' Petition, composed by Pym and St John and signed by Saye and Sele and Brooke, calling for the summoning of Parliament to address grievances both religious and secular. The next day he circulated the document in Northampton. He attended a meeting of knights and gentry in the town at which a similar local petition to the king was drawn up. Woodford signed the document, which was conveyed to Charles at York by Sir Gilbert Pickering, the shire MP, and Richard Knightley, MP for the borough of Northampton.[210]

Woodford's attitude to the Long Parliament was informed neither by localist concerns nor by issues arising for the first time from the Bishops' Wars, but by already well-rehearsed religious and ideological questions originating in his experiences of the 1630s. He continued to push for godly reformation and reiterated his personal identification with Parliament. The godly conference was now allied to explicitly political objectives. On the first day of the session, Woodford and three former town bailiffs, Francis Rushworth, Peter Whalley, and George Goodman, met 'to read pray & conferre, which meetinge we purpose to be constant in if god p[er]mitt, we rem.[embered] the church of god & the p[ar]liam[en]t begininge this day' (p. 373). On the public level, a royal proclamation stipulated a day of fasting – to

---

[208] The meeting was held at the Swan Inn, whose host, John Baxter, Woodford had upbraided for swearing on 29 September 1638, and who now provided much of the information used by Lambe in his prosecution of the clergy meeting at Kettering in the Court of Arches: Fielding, 'Peterborough', pp. 18, 161 n. 24, 220, 226 n. 24, 248–249; Webster, *Godly Clergy*, pp. 231–232.

[209] Diary, p. 358.

[210] *Ibid.*, pp. 368–369.

be observed on 17 November in London and 8 December throughout the kingdom – to remove plague, war, and other divine judgements. Woodford observed both.[211] In London he spent fourteen hours at Aldermanbury listening to Calamy and two visitors preach. Someone reported to him the first fast sermons delivered before the House of Commons at St Margaret's in Westminster by Cornelius Burges and Stephen Marshall. Both thundered against idolatry, profanation of the sabbath, and repression of preaching, and called for the godly to band together in a covenant. Woodford described their efforts as delivering 'glorious things with extraordinary zeale & fervor, this hath bene a heavenly day Lord heare the prayers of thy people worke a holy reformacon' (p. 375), and claimed Parliament was of one opinion. He also observed the fast at Northampton, hearing the curate, William Holmes, preach in the morning and Ball for four and a half hours in the afternoon. In conclusion, Woodford prayed 'Lord remove B[isho]ps & Idolatry & sup[er]stition & pesteringe Ceremonyes & thy plagues out of the Land, & send forth thy light & thy truth' (p. 380).

He was delighted by Parliament's initial burst of legislative activity aimed at liberating the victims of the Personal Rule (in which process he was eager to play an active role) and punishing the perpetrators of its misdeeds. The release of Burton, Bastwick, and Prynne he welcomed as 'the returne of the Captivity from Babilon' (p. 377), and indeed he met both Prynne and Burton at Calamy's church on 29 November. He acted professionally for some of the local victims of the regime, prosecuting the suit of the churchwardens, Rushworth and Farren, at the Grand Committee on Religion, against Clarke and Sibthorpe, and that of Thomas Bacon at the Committee on Ship Money. He also gave assistance to John James in his case against Lambe, Chancellor Thomas Heath, and Dr William Roane for persecution for ceremonial nonconformity.[212] As for the godly's 'Cursed & malicious adversaryes', Woodford consigned them to 'fall before them even as haman before Mordecai' (*ibid.*). He had previously denounced Clarke as Haman, and the bishop's surrogate experienced as sudden a reversal. Lambe, Clarke, and Sibthorpe were summoned before Parliament and punished in the first weeks of its sitting. Woodford celebrated the downfall of many of the highest profile 'evil counsellors' of the Personal Rule: 'the Lord hath done great things allready the Lieu-tenant of Ireland is in the Tower the Archb[isho]p Cant[erbury] under the black rod, the Lord Keeper rune away b[isho]p Wren bound to appeare & 6. Judges' (p. 382).

---

[211] *Ibid.*, pp. 375, 380.
[212] *Ibid.*, pp. 378–379, 382, 387.

However, godly reformation was still jeopardized by the papist party. Woodford reported rumours that the adversary was trying to bribe Charles to dissolve Parliament. The adversary might deceive the Scottish army into withdrawal by falsely promising redress of grievances, and then prevail on the king to dissolve Parliament. The Scots were regarded as guarantors of reform, as underwriters of the Parliament's existence: he feared that 'the mouthes of the Scots will be stopped by granntinge all things & the feare is the p[ar]liam[en]t will not last after their returne' (p. 378). Woodford's sense of utter dependence on the Scots and distrust of royal government is expressed in his approval of the terms of the Treaty of Ripon concluding the Second Bishops' War: 'much good newes from the p[ar]liam[en]t this week I blesse god about 300000li given to their br[ethere]n the Scots that there shall be no pub.[lic] goeinge [?after] &. Lord goe on to build thy temple [amo]ng us' (p. 386). He cemented this bond by meeting in person, at Dillingham's house, Alexander Henderson and Lord Archibald Johnston, two of·the radical leaders of the Covenanters. Shortly afterwards, the Triennial Act received royal assent, causing rejoicing with bonfires in the City of London.[213]

The London Root and Branch petition of 11 December 1640 blamed the oppression of the Personal Rule on episcopacy. Woodford himself composed, between 12 and 31 January 1641, a similar Northamptonshire document, which has not been found. On 26 April 1641 he welcomed with optimism the 'dore of hope that the Lord hath opened for his poore Church in generall & my selfe in particular' (p. 388), and, referring to the bishops, called on God to 'cutt them off roote & branch in one day forever extirpate their hei[r]archy' (p. 389). In mystical Old Testament language, he outlined an apocalyptic vision of a global revolution led by the godly to convert the vast ranks of the non-believers, a missionary crusade climaxing in the defeat of the Antichrist. He was naturally delighted at the apparent victory of the godly over the discomfited Laudian bishops and clergy, but noted that final victory – abolition of episcopacy and outlawry of Laudian worship – had not yet been achieved.

The shelving of the abolition question and the outbreak of the Irish rebellion would have brought about an abrupt reversal of Woodford's expectations and reactivated his fear of antichristian popery. His interpretation of events would have chimed with the thesis of the Grand Remonstrance, causing him to call for Parliament to assume ever greater powers to confront the Antichrist in Ireland or to purge the English nation. We can easily envisage him developing into a committed Parliamentarian, like his friends, as the town quickly

[213] *Ibid.*, pp. 378, 387.

became a garrison.[214] Woodford was clearly at this stage leaning towards Presbyterianism, and when in London he favoured the preaching of Calamy and his following. Most of the ministers with whom Woodford was associated followed this trajectory, as did his father-in-law, Robert Haunch.[215] Meanwhile, in Northampton, the political temperature was rising: on 25 July 1641 the crisis induced Ball to abandon once more his pastoral style of preaching, and to revert to political forms of address: he 'spake as desirous of a reconciliacon of the differences that are now in the towne, Lord reconcile them' (p. 391). The dominant godly faction became ever more militant, on 3 August appointing of itself a public fast 'though not commannded publiquely' (p. 393), at which Ball exercised with John Baynard and William Rathbone. In January 1642 the assembly strengthened the town watch, and in April introduced new by-laws, attempting to restore discipline to its increasingly raucous and disorderly sessions.[216]

The diary

The manuscript diary of Robert Woodford is held by New College, Oxford (NCA 9502). It measures 14.2 by 10.5 by 3 cm. It is bound in limp vellum, which has been re-sewn and reattached, and has a wraparound flap to protect the fore edge, secured with a leather tie. Faint lettering at the base of the flap reads 'III'. On the back cover, and upside-down in relation to the contents of the diary, is the inscription 'Liber Quartus [per] Annos' followed by unclear figures. The edges of the text block are sprinkled with red: the lower edge is inscribed 'Lib IV' and the upper edge with 'AD L[iber] 5 1637. 8.9.40.1'. The diary, then, is the sole survivor of a series, but these markings make it unclear whether it is volume three, four, or five, and whether the series continued further. It is possible to speculate that, if each diary covered four years, Woodford would have begun keeping journals in 1622, 1626, or 1630. The earliest of these coincides roughly with the start of his debt problems, the second with the completion of his apprenticeship, but no final decision is possible.

---

[214]Markham and Cox, *Northampton*, II, pp. 438–442; NRO, Finch (Hatton) MSS, F(H) 133; P.R. Brindle, 'Politics and society in Northamptonshire, 1649–1714' (unpublished PhD thesis, University of Leicester, 1983), pp. 134–135, 143, 144.

[215]See *The Testimony of our reverend Brethren Ministers of the Province of London to the Truth of Jesus Christ And Our Solemn League and Covenant etc. Attested by Other Ministers of Christ in the County of Northampton* (London, 1648); Tai Liu, *Puritan London: a study of religion and society in the City parishes* (London, 1986), pp. 134, 226.

[216]Markham and Cox, *Northampton*, II, p. 454; Book of Orders, p. 69.

The diary contains 588 pages and is approximately 89,000 words long. The first six pages are blank; the seventh contains the following memoranda, separate from the diary itself:

> deb Vrs Johem Clynte de Wychingford in Com Worcester clrs[217] & Lettice ux p deb sup Lease arrer 12 yeares 40s p ann p tythes in Crannesley Leas dat 25° Novbr 21° Jac Cov p soluc reddits so R haunch & Mr h p equal porcon John Clynts alias Clynt Vrs Owen Brabrooke[218] father de Thorpe Malsor in Com Northton husband Johem Atkins de Ketteringe Lynnen dr & Matth Wiseman de Irthlingborow in Com N y V oct ren

The diary begins on the next page. The journal is written in Woodford's own neat hand and covers the period 20 August 1637 to 16 August 1641, suggesting the deliberate organization of four-year diaries.

Woodford did not paginate the book, and made use of four main symbols. The trefoil (either single or double) highlighted spiritually significant passages, while the pointing hand emphasized matters concerning his children. He used a symbol similar to the commercial '@' but with the tail running clockwise to mean 'accusator' (plaintiff), and one similar to the modern ampersand meaning either 'and' or 'etc'. He usually ruled across the page after each entry. There are a small number of annotations by later generations of the family: these stand out clearly from the text and have been ignored.

Woodford admitted that there was sometimes a delay before he wrote up his diary, resulting in faulty recall. He would leave blank ruled spaces for later completion, sometimes (as on 16 January 1637/38) inscribing an aide-memoire in the space. This methodology resulted in occasional minor chronological inaccuracies. Coverage is very full until 29 December 1639 but, thereafter, lengthy omissions are common – the main reason given being weight of professional business but also, occasionally, lethargy owing to depression. On these occasions, either no entries were logged or a single composite one summarized events occurring during the interim. Lacking space in the diary, Woodford inscribed longer, more discursive notes beginning fifteen pages before the end of the volume (the remaining fourteen pages are blank) and working backwards through the diary (but forwards chronologically) until they collide with the diary itself. They are dated and cross-referenced to their main diary entries and cover the period 29 August 1638 to 25 February 1640.

---

[217] John Clynte of Wichenford, clergyman, was disputing the rights to the tithes of Cransley with Francis Downes of Pytchley: Diary, p. 236.
[218] Churchwarden of Thorpe Malsor in 1637: PDR, Church Survey Book 5, fo. 130r.

The diary descended through the line of Woodford's eldest son, Samuel, until, in 1970, Oliver Heighes Woodforde donated it to New College. In the meantime, the other volumes had been lost. Dorothy Heighes Woodforde stated that there had been three occasions when significant quantities of manuscripts disappeared: during the Great Fire of London in 1666, a century later, and in 1909. The last of these can be immediately discounted: when the HMC compiled its report in 1883 the diary was described as the last remnant of, and the last volume in, a series of three.[219] The first occasion can perhaps also be rejected. In 1678 Samuel Woodford celebrated his father's literary legacy and would surely have mentioned the loss of the vast majority of it. The remaining volumes were probably destroyed around 1766, when many family papers were deliberately burned during the custodianship of Samuel Woodforde (1695–1771), the rector of Ansford in Somerset and Parson Woodforde's father: the survival of one volume seems to have been accidental.

[219] F.W. Steer, *The Archives of New College, Oxford: a catalogue compiled by Francis W. Steer* (Oxford, 1974), pp. 112–113; D.H. Woodforde (ed.), *Woodforde Papers and Diaries* (London, 1932), p. xii; HMC, *Ninth Report* (London, 1883), pp. 493–499.

EDITORIAL NOTE

The spelling, punctuation, and capitalization of Woodford's diary have been left unchanged as the sense is generally clear. Wellingborough he spells as variations on 'Wellingborow'; Towcester as 'Toucester'. Christ (either standing alone or as part of Antichrist) is shortened to 'Xt', except in such words as Christian and christened or when forming part of the name Christopher; these he spells as follows: 'xxian', 'xxned', 'xxofer'. The only letter that I have altered is his 'j', which I have changed to 'i' where necessary. In the introduction, Woodford's surname is spelled without a final 'e' because this is the way that he spells the word throughout the diary; the only exception to this applies to later generations of the family. Where editorial additions and explanations have been made they appear either in square brackets or in a note. Some of Woodford's abbreviations and contractions have been expanded in this way: Northampton, which he writes 'Northton', has been rendered 'North[amp]ton'.

Confusingly, Woodford refers to his father-in-law and mother-in-law, Robert and Susanna Haunch, as father and mother, and to his brother-in-law, Samuel Haunch, as brother. However, the identities of individuals can usually be worked out from the context. His father, Robert, died before Woodford started the diary, while his mother, Jane, lived at Wilby, Northamptonshire. The Haunches, on the other hand, were Londoners, living in the parish of All Hallows', London Wall.

The rulings that appear across the page after many entries have been omitted. Of the four symbols that Woodford uses (see the introduction, pp. 12–13, 90), three are described in words in square brackets; the fourth – the symbol like an ampersand – is represented by the ampersand. All places mentioned are in Northamptonshire unless otherwise stated. Woodford did not paginate the diary. Since most of the volume is chronological no pagination has been added; the beginning of a new diary page is announced by a single line space (indicated by an asterisk where it occurs at the bottom of a printed page). The additional entries at the end of the document are dated and cross-referenced to the main diary. References to the diary are given by page number. Woodford used the old style or Julian calendar and started the new year on Lady Day (25 March), so for the period 1 January to 24 March the year has been altered to show the two different styles, as in '24° Martii 1637/38' (the solidus and the date following it having been added).

ROBERT WOODFORD'S DIARY, 1637–1641

who ever finds this booke (if lost) I pray be sparinge in looking into it, & send it to Robte Woodford at [*crossed out:* Northton] Northampton.

20° Augusti. 1637 Sab.[bath]
I prayed alone and I and my deare wife prayed in private this morninge to beseech the Lord for his blessinge uppon the sacrament of Baptisme to our poore child this day that the inward grace might goe a longe with the outward signe &, and that the Lord would make it an Instrument of some service to him in his Church in time to come and a Comfort to us the parents and surely the Lord hath heard us in m[er]cye we prayed not to be hindred in our sanctificacon of his Sabath this day & to order Conveniences &. Mr ffisher¹ preached in the morninge, but my hart somewhat heavy Lord p[ar]don my dulnes.
Mr Ball preached in the afternoone, & had sweet p[ro]fitable doctrine about the p[ro]vidence of God, & I was much affected I blesse the Lord; I was a little troubled when I went to church about the name

---

¹Woodford's friend, Alderman John Fisher, or his son Samuel, a clergyman. Fisher had been a central figure in the Northampton godly scene since at least 1604, when, as churchwarden of All Saints' parish, he had been presented to the Church court accused of omitting to report the corporation's godly incumbent, Robert Catelin, for preaching that 'all that use the signe of the crosse in baptisme ar antechristians and that all that doe kneele at the sacramt of the supper doe comitt idolatrie' (PDR, CB37, fo. 163r). He next appears as master of the house of correction, which had been founded in 1615 as a work creation scheme to relieve the poor, who ground malt. It had been initially situated underneath the Conduit Hall, but by the 1630s had been relocated near to the Bell Inn in Bridge Street. Before Archbishop Laud's visitation of 1635, Sir John Lambe had received a Church court denunciation of Fisher, who had by that time apparently expanded his sphere of competence to include the jail. Deponents accused Fisher of selecting certain prisoners and townspeople in 1634 to congregate in a side chamber, where he 'expounded Scripture or preached unto them' and then prayed for the king, and for the queen 'that god would bring her out of her false Heresie and Confound all Dumbe Dogges wch led her to Antixt' (TNA, SP16/308/52). It is therefore likely that the layman Fisher is preaching here (with dubious legality), and again on 27 September 1640 while mayor. The *ODNB* details two sons called Samuel whose Oxford educations are suspiciously identical and may have been confused. One was chaplain to Sir Arthur Haselrig and a later Quaker writer, the other a godly minister in 1640s Shropshire: S. Villani, 'Fisher, Samuel (bap. 1604, d. 1665)' in *ODNB*; S. Wright, 'Fisher, Samuel (1605/6–1681)' in *ODNB*; Markham and Cox, *Northampton*, II, pp. 108, 115, 177–178; *VCH Northamptonshire*, III (London, 1930), p. 35.

of the Child havinge forgotten to leave word that the name should be
John, but I desired to wayt

wayt on god in that so my mother being one of the witnesses said Rob
but Mr Readinge² named it John; the name by which I and my wife
used to call it before it was borne.

21° Aug. 1637

here was some difference betweene my mother wife and I about
sendinge some sugar plums to Old. But Lord I pray thee make us very
Carefull & wise for time to come as thou hast in m[er]cye given us
speciall love one to another so I humbly pray thee give us discretion,
& power over every passion, that no jarre may at any time come at all
to interrupt that true affection betweene us and Lord I pray thee give
my deare wife harty affection to my poore mother, & wisdome in her
Cariage & expressions not at all

all to [crossed out: doubt of] give her occasion to doubt of it.
Mr ffletcher³ & his wife lay in the towne tonight at the Swan.⁴

---

²John Reading, Woodford's master and patron, was an Inner Temple barrister. He
had married Dorothy Morgan, the daughter of Francis Morgan of Kingsthorpe near
Northampton, in 1616. Morgan was a judge in the sheriff's court of London and the patron
of the conformist cleric Dr Samuel Clarke at St Peter's, Northampton. The Readings'
children included Nathaniel and John, both of whom were Inner Temple barristers:
Longden, *Visitation of Northamptonshire 1681*, pp. 135–136; Longden MS, 2 November 1608; F.A.
Inderwick and R.A. Roberts (eds), *A Calendar of the Inner Temple Records* (London, 1896–1936),
pp. 291–292, 327, 331. Reading enjoyed contacts with the puritan colonists of Massachusetts.
In late 1630, John Winthrop had entrusted to him the legal preparations necessary to settle
his estate before emigration. Reading wrote the following year to Governor Winthrop
concerning the will of another emigrant, Isaac Johnson; the will included Winthrop,
Reading, and John Hampden as executors. In 1631, acting as executor, Reading had
presented Edward Reynolds, a moderate Laudian with godly connections, to the living
of Braunston. The same year he received a legacy from Christopher Sherland, Recorder
of Northampton: W.C. Ford et al. (eds), *The Winthrop Papers*, 6 vols (Boston, 1929–1992), II,
pp. 49–56, 318–319, and III, pp. 36–37; R. Thompson, 'Johnson, Isaac (bap. 1601, d. 1630)',
in *ODNB*; F.J. Bremer, 'Winthrop, John (1588–1649)', in *ODNB*; Longden MS, 11 August
1631; TNA, PROB/11/10.

³William Fletcher of Old, perhaps a solicitor (Diary, p. 235): PDR, CBA63, fo. 306.

⁴The Swan Inn in the Drapery had been listed since at least 1585 and much public
business was transacted there. The county gentry met there on 14 September 1637 to co-
ordinate their response to the crown's forest policy and John Bernard met Woodford there on
business on 20 October 1637. It was used as a base by Sir Gilbert Pickering during his election
campaign for the Short Parliament in March 1640, and by the petitioners supporting the
Grand Remonstrance on 21 January 1642. After 1672 it was used as a Presbyterian meeting
house before being destroyed in the Great Fire of 1675: Markham and Cox, *Northampton*,
II, pp. 306–307; BRO, St John (Bletso) MSS, DDJ 1369; TNA, SP16/489/15; Isham, *Diary*,
p. 318.

22° Aug.
a meetinge to day in the towne about offices Mr Moulshoes[5] I thinke
& Mr Kirkhams[6] our Journey to Mr ffreemans[7] to day hindred by
Mr ffletchers beinge in towne. This eveninge came to towne an
acquaintance of mine Mr Worsley a young man Clerke to Chandlers
company in London & doth much incourage me to seeke the
Reversion of the Clerkship of Weavers hall, whereof my father is
now Master so I have written, Lord direct & order every thinge for
the best for the Lords sake I desire to wayt uppon thee,

23° Aug.1637
we prayed & my mother & I and hatton[8] went towards Cranford
in the morninge hopinge to returne that night when we had seene
good Mr freeman there; but we dyned at Mr Pearnes at Wilby as we
went blessed be thy name oh Lord for the Comforts of him & other
Christians and we came to Cranford about 2 a clock where we found
that holy man Mr ffreeman weake in his bed, & heard how fruitfull &
Cheerfull he had beene all his sicknesse, & then had much precious
& comfortable discourse but complained that his body was become a
very unfit organ for his soule to worke in he reioyced much to see us;
and seemed no whit afrayd of death but desired to be dissolved and
to be with the Lord xt. I went to my Unckles[9] at night to Lodge there
& Mr Spencer[10] came up to me there. I trust the strangeness
******

[5] Robert Mulshoe, lord of the manor of Finedon, was the son-in-law of the godly lawyer
Robert Tanfield, who bequeathed him law books in his will. His son and heir was Tanfield
Mulshoe. With John Syers of Loddington, who also married a Tanfield daughter, he was the
overseer of the will of Joseph Hill, rector of Loddington and a Church court official. It is not
known what office is here being referred to: Isham, *Diary*, p. 150, n. 14; TNA, PROB/11/55;
Diary, p. 196, n. 372; Longden, *Clergy*.
[6] Possibly Robert Kirkham of Fineshade Abbey; the office has not been identified: Pettit,
Royal Forests, p. 90; TNA, SP16/261/117.
[7] Thomas Freeman of Cranford.
[8] Woodford's assistant, Hatton Farmer of Towcester, went on to become Northampton
town clerk (1658) and town attorney (1660). He witnessed the will of John Loe in 1641 and
was a beneficiary of the will of Woodford's lawyer friend, Henry Goodere. Hatton's mother
was Woodford's sometime creditor: Markham and Cox, *Northampton*, II, pp. 70–71; TNA,
PROB/11/189.
[9] Hannah's uncle, Christopher Haunch, lived in the parish of Cranford St Andrew, where
in 1637 he witnessed the will of Thomas Freeman. In 1647, he made charitable donations
to the poor not only of Cranford but of a group of parishes centred on Wellingborough –
Irchester, Wollaston, and Doddington. His will was witnessed by Woodford's clerk, Thomas
Pickering: TNA, PROB/11/109; PDR, Archdeaconry of Northampton Wills, second series,
G211; third series, B131.
[10] William Spencer was a member of Lord Edward Montagu's moderate puritan circle.
Montagu presented him to the rectory of Scaldwell in 1617 and in 1630 William Piers, Bishop
of Peterborough, licensed him to read the Kettering lecture, but it is clear that the Book

betweene my Uncle and us is somewhat cured. Lord increase Christian amity more & more for the Lords sake. Amen.

24° Aug. 1637 [St] Barthol.[omew's] day.

after I had prayed in private for myselfe & mine & and for poore Mr ffreeman I went [*crossed out:* dow] downe to see him, he was Cheerfull and said now he praysed god he had got on the yoake of Christ and that now [*crossed out:* there were] he had but a step to heaven and desired us to helpe lift him up by our prayers, & a little before he dyed, he prayed god be with us all, and prayed when we could not well understand his words, and about 10 of the clock in the morninge he sweetly slept in the Lord without makinge any noyse onely ceased to breath; but, about an houre before he dyed I tooke leave of him, thinking to have gone along presently & he thanked me & desired to be remembered to my wife and prayed the Lord to blesse us, oh Lord in m[er]cye make good this blessinge & prayer of

of thy servant uppon me and mine for the Lords sake Amen.

my mother Closed his eyes at his dep[ar]ture I came away with hatton after dinner, & came home very safe (though wett) I blesse the Lord. Much unseasonable rayne & wet Lord looke uppon us in m[er]cye. I found my wife & children well at home I blesse the Lord, & Johns mouth somewhat amended. The sicknes very hot at Ringstead" still Lord send them helpe & Cure for the Lords sake. Mr Chadwick¹² marryed to day.

25 Aug. 1637

I went to James ffryers¹³ to eate some best beefe in the morninge beinge invited, but I liked not beinge in the company & stayed not longe & went downe to my Masters where they invited me to dinner & I dyned

of Sports (1633) was the last straw for this moderate divine and he abandoned the earlier compromise. In 1634 he was prosecuted in the Court of High Commission for ceremonial nonconformity and for not only refusing to read the Book but for preaching against it: Fielding, 'Peterborough', pp. 124, 130; TNA, SP16/266/54.

"Woodford means the plague, which also doubled the normal death rate at adjacent Higham Ferrers for the years 1637 and 1638. The disease did not spread to Northampton town until 4 March 1637/38 (according to Dr Clarke) or 17 March 1637/38 (according to Woodford): Diary, p. 189; A.N. Groome, 'Higham Ferrers elections in 1640: a Midlands market town on the eve of civil war', *Northamptonshire Past and Present*, 2:5 (1958), pp. 243–251.

¹²Possibly Edward Chadwick, who occurs in the parish accounts from 1628 and served as sidesman in 1635 and bailiff of the town in 1651: Vestry Minutes, p. 21; Markham and Cox, *Northampton*, II, p. 562.

¹³James Fryers was the son of Thomas Fryers, mayor in 1590. He was an active member of the vestry at All Saints' parish 1623–1628, acting as an assessor for various parish rates. He was also one of the town's sergeants: Sheils, *Puritans*, p. 141; Vestry Minutes, pp. 16–21.

there with Mr Johnson[14] &. There is great pr[e]paracons making for the Justice seate, oh Lord set the kingdome in a

a right and blessed frame, that it may goe well with thy Church & our Comon wealth even for the Lords sake Amen. I heare Mr Burton[15] is cruelly used by his Jaylor, Lord relieve & looke uppon them in m[er]cye for the Lords sake Amen. Mr ffreemans man came for the things the wine gowne &.[16] I was graciously affected in publiq & private prayer (I blesse the Lord) this night for my deare wife 2 children & the afflicted church.

26° Aug. 1637
I prayed and went towards Cranford to the burial of good Mr ffreeman; and in the way I put up many prayers for increasinge grace in me & my deare wife, I prayed for my sweete Children; for releife to the poore prisoners for we heare report how hardly Mr Burton is handled at Lancaster & the Lord vouchsafed to heare

heare my poore peticons; when I came to Cranford I there found Mr Pearne & diverse others Christians, Mr Lamb[17] the minister of the p[ar]ish preached at the fun[er]all out of the p[ro]phet.
afterward my mother & I came home and were here in due time & safe blessed be god Mr Pearne came alonge with us about 4 mile of the way & ffr[ancis] ffreeman;[18] & Mr Pearne related to us his opposicon of goodnesse before the Lord pleased to worke, & how the

[14] Possibly the Johnston who seems to have been acting as parish clerk on 24 March 1639.

[15] Henry Burton, who, along with William Prynne and John Bastwick, had been condemned by the Court of Star Chamber for criticizing the religious policies of the Laudian regime: Gardiner, *History*, VIII, pp. 226–234.

[16] Woodford purchased these items in Northampton: Diary, p. 109.

[17] Robert Lambe had been appointed to the rectory of Cranford St John by the patron, Bishop John Williams of Lincoln: Longden MS, 7 February 1629.

[18] Francis Freeman was a leading member of the active godly grouping at Wilby, and related to Thomas Freeman, whose will he witnessed. As patron of Wilby (with Benjamin Cave and John Lord), he had presented Francis Austin as rector in 1609 but he supported the new vicar, Dr John 'Ever-Out' Everard, in a Star Chamber case in 1623 when Austin challenged Everard's possession of the living. Everard was an unusually outspoken godly critic of the Spanish Match. Freeman (with Woodford's cousin Robert Ragdale and John Hackney) was presented in 1630 to the Church courts, accused of gadding to hear the famous puritan minister Thomas Hooker preach at Great Bowden in Leicestershire: PDR, Archdeaconry of Northampton wills, second series, G211; Longden MS, 27 July 1609; E. Allen, 'Everard, John (1584?–1640/41)', in *ODNB*; R.M. Smuts, 'Rich, Henry, first earl of Holland (bap. 1590, d. 1649)', in *ODNB*; PDR, CB61, unpaginated (1630); Webster, *Godly Clergy*, p. 155 and note.

Lord wrought uppon him, & how god wrought in Katherin hall[19] & which did much affect me I blesse the Lord, oh Lord how mighty is thy doctrine accompanied wth thy sp[iri]t and what wonders doth it worke, such changes were never made by philosophy or humane [comman]damments Thy spirit alone can convince the world of sinne of righteousness & Judgem[en]t oh Lord I blesse thee for that mans conversion whom thou hast wonderfully quallifyed & made an Instrument of so much good, Lord blesse his ministery still keepe open his mouth notwithstandinge all the power of the adversary hold him as a starre in thy hand, and blesse him

him to my family still as thou hast done, & Rayse up more Champions for thee, even great Apolloes that may be mighty in the scriptures, and shew thy selfe wonderfull in workinge, that this Kingdome may be still the place of thy delight, & that thine ordinances may still flourish amongst us, that we may suck & be satisfied with the breasts of Consolation; for the Lords sake

my mother and I invited to Mr John Readings to dinner.

27° Aug. 1637 Sab.[bath]

I prayed and went to church, where Mr Trueman[20] preached this morninge, who dealt faythfully and boldly (out of [*crossed out:* 1] 6 deut[erónomy] 4 heare oh Israel &) against Idolatry & sup[er]stition blessed be thy name oh Lord, I beseech thee defend him, and incourage him in thy way against all opposition. Mr Ball had p[ro]fitable doctrine about gods p[ro]vidence in the afternoone; my wife is ill in her breast & otherwise, oh Lord I desire to wayt uppon thee I beseech thee heale her, & graunt she may bringe up the poore infant with

with comfort, & graunt that it may thrive & p[ro]sper; I beseech thee shew me thy glory, & be good to me & mine every way especially

---

[19] Perne's conversion occurred during his fellowship of St Catharine's College, Cambridge (1622–1627), when the prominent godly divine Richard Sibbes was the master: J. Fielding, 'Perne, Andrew (c.1595–1654)', in *ODNB*.

[20] Richard Trueman was the son of the godly Northampton saddler of the same name. He had been the vicar of Dallington near Northampton since his appointment by the Hampshire justice of the peace Sir Henry Wallop in 1625. He had not previously been in trouble with the courts and had dedicated a published sermon to his patrons, Lord Robert (now deceased) and his son, Lord William Spencer. The former, at least, had a reputation as a patron of godly ministers. The sermon stated that these were the biblical last times, in which ordinary men must not be afraid to criticize those in power as John the Baptist had criticized King Herod: Fielding, 'Peterborough', pp. 23–24; Richard Truman, *A Christian Memorandum wherein is Handled the Christian Doctrine of Reproof* (London, 1629), p. 85.

spiritually for the Lords sake the breife for Cranford & Nassington Churches[21] read this afternoone.

Oh Lord I pray thee pr[e]vent that the sup[er]stitious wretch[22] lately come hether may not doe hurt for the Lords sake.

I praid after in private and did beseech the Lord for my poore wife who was very ill wth her breasts & an ague and did intreate that the Lord would please to recover my poore wife, and that it might be a testimony of his m[er]cy to me for time to come, and I did pray that the Lord would please to inable me for reciting the Record tomorrow for scandalous words vile & filthy which I know I was utterly unable for [*crossed out: illegible letter*] about Brigs his wife of Kingsthorpe; and I had gracious answer from the Lord in prayer blessed be thy name oh Lord.

28° Aug. 1637

I prayd & went to the Court after 8 a clock and I found the answere of my poore prayers for my wife was much better I blesse the Lord, & very cheerfull; and when I was about to read the Record I found my selfe very unable for it, but I remembred that I was called to it & I trusted the Lord would helpe me so the Lord in m[er]cy did uphold my hart that I went on with it without any trouble, blessed be thy name oh Lord, it is not in vayne to depend uppon thee, thou art my

---

[21] A brief was a royal mandate recommending contribution towards a charitable appeal. The aim of the appeals in the parishes mentioned, Cranford St John and the exempt prebendal jurisdiction of Nassington, was the repair of their steeples: W.E. Tate, *The Parish Chest: a study of the records of parochial administration in England* (Cambridge, 1974), pp. 120–125; PDR, Church Survey Book 5, fo. 144v; Pevsner, *Northamptonshire*, p. 310; K. Thomas, *Religion and the Decline of Magic* (Harmondsworth, 1973), p. 19.

[22] This refers to Humphrey Ramsden, a Laudian layman who wrote to Sir John Lambe on 20 March 1639 (TNA, SP16/414/163) from Dr William Isaacson's house at Woodford, Essex. Isaacson's father, Henry, was a conformist connected with Wren and Andrewes (P.E. McCullough, 'Isaacson, Henry (bap. 1581, d. 1654)', in *ODNB*). William was the rector of Woodford from 1619 and of St Andrew's by the Wardrobe, London, from 1629, where Lambe himself was buried in 1646 (J. Fielding, 'Lambe, Sir John (c.1566–1646)', in *ODNB*). In his letter, Ramsden referred back to his time of residence in Northampton in 1637–1638. A second document listed in the *CSPD* (TNA, SP16/474/80, wrongly dated 1640) is the 'story herein enclosed' mentioned in the letter: that is, Ramsden's information on the activities of Northampton puritans between 18 May 1637 and New Year's Day 1638, which should correctly be shown as an enclosure to it. The information came from personal experience as well as from local conformist contacts (Woodford has Ramsden arriving on 27 August 1637 and last refers to him on 26 November). Ramsden had heard that Lambe loved the 'ancient ceremonies' used in the primitive Church and now practised by the leaders of the English Church, to which he had been himself converted at St John's College, Cambridge. Ramsden had attended the college (as Lambe had before him) between 1629 and 1637 (see Venn), during the conformist masterships of Owen Gwynn and William Beale.

god in thee will I trust forever and ever our Court was not ended till almost 8 a clock at night.

Mr Attourney our Recorder[23] dr Clerke & were there in the morninge. I dyned with my mother at Mr Rushworths[24] & with Mr Trueman, at venison pasty I blesse the Lord.

29° Aug. 1637

I prayed and went to speake with Mr dan readinge[25] about direccon for a s[ub]p[o]ena ad testificand[um] in the Sess[ions] p[ro] hensman, 6° September next & with Mr danby.[26] I spoke after with Mr Stephen Chapman the minister[27] who sent for me to the hynd[28] whom I did desire to sift because I had heard well of but not from p[e]rfect intelligence but his hast[e] beinge much I am not yet satisfyed but I hope very well oh Lord blesse him & increase grace in his soule for time to come for the Lords sake Amen.

[23]Richard Lane was a Middle Temple bencher with court connections. He had been elected Recorder of Northampton in 1632, having served as deputy to the previous incumbents, Sir Henry Yelverton and Christopher Sherland. However, unlike his predecessors he was not one of the godly. He was appointed attorney general to the Prince of Wales in 1635, defended the Earl of Strafford in 1641 and the twelve imprisoned Laudian bishops in 1642, and the latter year deserted his post as recorder and joined the king at Oxford. The king appointed him Lord Keeper in 1646, but he died in exile in Jersey: D.A. Orr, 'Lane, Sir Richard (bap. 1584, d. 1650)', in ODNB; Prest, Barristers, pp. 230–232, 240–252, 276–277, 374–375.

[24]Francis Rushworth, apothecary, was granted his freedom of the borough in 1631, when he was described as hailing from Coventry. He and his wife, Joan, were central figures among the Northampton godly: Book of Orders, p. 17.

[25]Daniel, John Reading's ungodly brother: Diary, p. 336. Daniel was also a lawyer. He was accused by the corporation of illegal malting in 1641 and in 1642 appointed the (to Woodford) religiously imperfect James Lewis to the living of Duston. In 1648 he represented the corporation and by 1650 had been appointed town attorney. He was married to Mary Harvey, and at his death in 1659 was very wealthy: Book of Orders, pp. 13, 67, 87, 100, 108; Foster; Metcalfe, Visitation of Northampton 1618, pp. 98–99; Markham and Cox, Northampton, II, p. 345; TNA, SP23/108, p. 113; TNA, PROB/11/294.

[26]John Danby, attorney, had served as Bailiff of Northampton in 1605, chamberlain in 1615, churchwarden of All Saints' in 1623, and Mayor of Northampton in 1629 (and would do so again in 1639), had had a seat assigned to him in 1634–1635 when the chancel was rebuilt, and had witnessed Thomas Pilkington's will in 1637. His daughter married John Bullivant, vicar of Abington. His will of 1651 (proved 1654) was witnessed by Woodford's clerk, Thomas Pickering, and instructed that he be buried in the chancel at All Saints' as close as possible to his first wife, Sarah: Markham and Cox, Northampton, II, pp. 552, 561, 567; TNA, PROB/11/232.

[27]Chapman (b. 1591) was the son of Thomas Chapman of Old. A graduate of Christ's College, Cambridge, Stephen had been the vicar of East Budleigh, Devon, since 1631; he was ejected during the Civil War: Venn.

[28]Abraham Ventris's inn, the Hind (or Hart) in the Market Square, had been listed since at least 1585 and was often used for official business such as meetings of the Church courts: Markham and Cox, Northampton, II, pp, 306–307.

I went after & payd Mr Perkins[29] for the wine at the Baptizinge & for Mr ffreemans fun[er]all, when I came home I find my deare Child John very ill & in my apprehens[ion] not like to Live, but Lord I know thy m[er]cye & thy power, I pray thee delight to shew m[er]cye unto me, & if it be thy will continue him unto us so that he may

hereafter bringe glory unto thy name & comfort to us the parents, & graunt that we may walke worthy such a m[er]cy for the Lords sake Amen. Oh Lord I pray thee graunt that our harts may sit loose from what ever we possesse, that thou alone mayest dwell in our soules, & that we may uppon all occasions be willinge to forgoe, & leave the comfort of the creature & labour to find more in thee the Creator for the Lords sake Amen. I received a letter from Mr Greg[30] for money Lord enable me to pay my debts for the Lords sake Amen. I was at the George[31] with Adrian Garner[32] an apothecary in Nottingham, where we use to Lye in the Circuite, and I am glad to understand by him that Mr Coles [sic][33] is still at Nottingham, & hath the liberty of his ministry

30° Aug. 1637
my child still as it was, asleepe, & I heare whisp[er]inge as if it was not like to live

but I have besought the Lord in whose hand alone is our breath, still to continue him to us if it be his will, and make it a comfort to us & an Instrument of his glory in time to come, and I have p[ro]missed that by the Lords helpe it shall be a further ingagement to me to walke with the Lord; I shall receave him againe as given a new. oh Lord I desire to submit to thy good p[ro]vidence in all thy wayes. Lord heare & helpe for the Lords sake Amen. I pray diverse times for my poore child.

---

[29] William Perkins, a former soldier who was the host of the Swan Inn in Northampton: Diary, pp. 141, 219.

[30] One of Woodford's creditors, a Londoner: ibid., pp. 302, 303.

[31] The George Inn had been listed since at least 1585 and was situated on George's Row on the south side of All Saints' churchyard: Markham and Cox, Northampton, II, pp. 306–307.

[32] Garner rose from being a member of the Common Council of Nottingham to be town chamberlain in 1643 and sheriff of the borough by 1646: Records of the Borough of Nottingham, 9 vols (Nottingham, 1882–1956), V (ed. W.T. Baker, 1900), pp. 215, 220, 280, 430.

[33] George Coates was rector of St Peter's, Nottingham from 1617 to 1640; a godly minister, he resisted the erection of a Laudian rail around his communion table in 1636: R.A. Marchant, The Puritans and the Church Courts in the Diocese of York, 1560–1642, (1960), pp. 186, 193–199, 299.

31° Augusti. 1637
My poore child asleep I thinke till this morninge (some few small
wakeninge intervalls excepted) but now it is awaked & hath sucked
Mrs Rushworth this morninge blessed be god. Oh Lord how great is
thy strength & power thou art god alone & there is none beside thee
Blessed be thy name

for the manifestacon of thy strength & Love unto us in this thinge, oh
Lord I pray thee still in m[er]cy Continue unto us o[u]r Children, and
make them blessed Comforts unto us & instruments of thy glory in
due time, & keepe our affections from exorbitancy that we may love
them in thee & for thee, for the Lords sake Amen.
There is a gen[er]all visitacon of Churches in this diocesse[34] by some
of the worser sorte of divines & by [ap]p[ar]iters & to observe the
standinge of the tables whether altarwise or not & to set them so; oh
Lord looke uppon us in m[er]cy it is an evill time & the prudent hold
their peace, who so dep[ar]ts from evill maketh himselfe a prey,[35] oh
Lord send helpe from heaven for the Lords sake The house for the
Justice seate here goes up apace[36] the time appoynted is 18° Sept next
oh Lord order all things for the best for the Lords sake Amen.
1° 7br. 1637
Litle John sucks well blessed be the Lord, and is

is mendinge thanks be to god. my wife troubled with sore & tender
breasts. Oh Lord I beseech thee heale them and make her a Joyfull
mother, and graunt that both of us in the sense of thy m[er]cyes may
have our harts lifted up to thee in prayses for the Lords sake Amen.

---

[34] As part of Bishop Francis Dee's first triennial visitation (July 1637) he commissioned
from Drs Samuel Clarke and Robert Sibthorpe a survey of the churches in the western half
of his diocese. These deputies insisted on railed east end altars, in line with Dee's expressed
requirements from 1634 onwards, and, indeed, the survey revealed that most parishes had
by now complied. The commissioners also ordered the reception of communion there,
kneeling, by minister and congregation. In addition, they drastically reorganized church
interiors to accommodate the novel, altar-focused, worship and insisted on other practices
such as the minister's reading of the second or communion service at the altar and the
reception of communion by newly married couples: Fielding, 'Peterborough', pp. 81–82,
109–118; J. Fielding, 'Dee, Francis (d. 1638)', in *ODNB*; PDR, Church Survey Book 5.
[35] Isaiah 59:15.
[36] The Justice Seat, or principal forest court, was held in Northampton's Market Square.
In his history of the town, Henry Lee said that the court was set up on Bakers' Hill (or
Corn Hill) to the north of the Market Square: *VCH Northamptonshire*, III, p. 25; Markham
and Cox, *Northampton*, II, pp. 570–571; Top MS, p. 104.

My cousin dexter[37] was here & tells me that Mr dr Clarke[38] desires to speak with me to morowe about their busines of the Charitab[le] Uses.

2° 7br. 1637

poore Mr Newton[39] was taken by a pursu[i]vant out of the high Commission, & made to pay about 40s presently, & is to appeare the next tearme, oh Lord looke downe from heaven & see the violence & the wrong that is offered to thine, & rescue them out of the paw of the Lyon for the Lords sake Amen when I went to dr Clarke there I found poore Mr Trueman with him & Mr Burcot[40] his sonne

sonne in law, like a lamb betweene 2 wolves, so since I understand by him that they threaten him that he is like to loose his life for the sermon the good & p[ro]fitable sermon which he preached here against Idolatry the last Sabbath day. Oh Lord defend him & susteyne him for the Lords sake I heare from London to day that the bishop of Lincolne[41] is like to loose his head the next tearme, & its said Mr

[37]Gregory Dexter (*fl.* 1581–1657), lord of Knightley's manor in the parish of Old, was the son of Stephen Dexter (d. 1632) and his wife, Ann (née Turland). Stephen was the brother of Woodford's mother, Jane. Gregory married Isabel (1587–1667) and his heir was Gregory junior, the New England resident. Gregory senior is last mentioned in the will of Dr John Twickten, rector of Corby, a Church court official, 1622–1635. In 1657 Twickten made a bequest to him and to his grandson, Stephen, who had been born in Massachusetts, but not to the Baptist minister, Stephen's father, Gregory junior: PDR, Archdeaconry of Northampton Wills, second series, H, fo. 33; *VCH Northamptonshire*, IV (London, 1937), pp. 202–203; Longden, *Clergy*; NRO, Old parish registers.

[38]Dr Samuel Clarke had been recruited to the Church courts in 1615 by Chancellor John Lambe and had established himself as an adherent of Lambe's brand of avant-garde conformist churchmanship. He had also been promoted by Bishops Richard Neile and John Overall and by Laud himself, who placed him in charge of the diocese in 1634 during a vacancy, and appointed him a commissary for his metropolitical visitation in 1635. He had been chaplain to Prince Charles and King James and had been supported by the Countess of Denbigh, the Duke of Buckingham's sister. He was a friend of Richard Steward, Clerk of the Closet to Charles I: J. Fielding, 'Clarke, Samuel (1582–1641)', in *ODNB*; PDR, CBA63, fo. 333; K. Fincham and N. Tyacke, *Altars Restored: the changing face of English religious worship, 1547–c. 1700* (Oxford, 2007), pp. 186–187.

[39]Charles Newton was curate of All Saints', 1632–1639, and jail preacher from 1635, in which year he was reported to be prepared to lose his place rather than read the Book of Sports. He appeared before the Court of High Commission on 8 October 1637 (Diary, p. 122), but the content of the charges is unknown; Ramsden accused him of administering to sitters, not bowing at Jesus' name, and editing the Prayer Book: TNA, SP16/308/52; TNA, SP16/474/80.

[40]William Burkit was Clarke's son-in-law and an official in the Peterborough Church courts; in contrast, his brother Miles was one of the most recalcitrant resisters of Laudian policy in the county: Longden, *Clergy*; Fielding, 'Peterborough', pp. 105–107.

[41]Bishop John Williams of Lincoln had been suspended from his office in July 1637 after having been 'framed' on trumped-up charges relating to his time as Lord Keeper, partly because he opposed the altar policy: A. Foster, *The Church of England 1570–1640* (London,

Prinne is or shall be sent for to the next tearme to dye Oh Lord worke wonderfully for thy people for the Lords sake Amen.
I pray to be pr[e]pared for the sacrament.
3 ° Sept. 1637 Sab.[bath] sacr.[ament]⁴²
Mr Ball preached very p[ro]fitably this morninge blessed be the Lord; good affections I blesse the Lord especially at the sacram[en]t; Mr ffarren⁴³ & Mr Rushworth had turned the Table East & west blessed be thy name oh

oh Lord for their Courage. Mr Wm Martin preached in the afternoone nothinge so p[ro]fitably oh Lord keepe him from backslidinge, Amen. he bowes at the name of Jesus & stands up at gloria patri⁴⁴ heu quantum mutatus ab illo.⁴⁵

1994), p. 70. Laud and Lambe played the key roles in his downfall; however, Williams is an unlikely hero for the godly: see Fincham and Tyacke, *Altars Restored, passim*; M.D. Slatter, 'A biographical study of Sir John Lambe *c.* 1566–1646' (unpublished BLitt thesis, University of Oxford, 1952), p. 62.

⁴²Humphrey Ramsden stated that Ball administered to at least four unknown sitters, but his view of the magistrates was blocked; Rogers administered to four sitters, and his usher, William Swale, although only a bachelor of arts, administered, without surplice, to four. Newton likewise administered to Nathaniel Benbow (haberdasher), William Bott (linen draper), and Thomas Pendleton (shoemaker). All were members of the Northampton godly but only Benbow had form with the Church courts. He resided in Clarke's parish of St Peter, where Christopher Young was curate, and had served as town bailiff. As early as 1618 Sibthorpe had ordered him to receive communion kneeling. As churchwarden in 1635, he had joined in a presentment of several men accused of ringing the bells at the burial of a notorious drunkard. The following year, in defending himself against a charge of refusing to receive communion, he reportedly claimed that 'he did refuse to receive the Communion for that the minister did require him to come and receive the same at the rayles of the altar' and protested that 'hee is willing to receive the same soe that the Co[mmun]ion table be brought downe into the body of the Chauncell as he conceaveth is required by the auncient order of this Church': PDR, CBA63, fo. 333r–v; PDR, CB48, fo. 69r–v; PDR, CBA63, fo. 266r; TNA, SP16/474/80; TNA, PROB/11/185.

⁴³Peter Farren, baker and member of the Northampton godly, and Francis Rushworth were the churchwardens for All Saints' parish. At Dee's visitation in July the communion table had stood altarwise with its short ends pointing north–south. By turning it east–west the wardens were ensuring that it was an altar no longer: TNA, SP16/474/80.

⁴⁴The passage beginning 'Glory be to the Father' in the Prayer Book service.

⁴⁵'[Heu] quantum mutatus ab illo Hectore qui redit exuvias indutus Achilli' '[Alas], how greatly changed from that Hector who came back arrayed in the armour of Achilles!': Virgil, *Aeneid*, II, lines 274–275. William Martin was an unbeneficed minister; by 1641 he was preacher at Horton: Anon., *A Certificate from Northamptonshire. Touching pluralities. Defect of maintenance. Of not preaching. Of poor ministers* (London, 1641), p. 5.

ROBERT WOODFORD'S DIARY, 1637–1641

My wife Churched this morninge here at home, Mrs Crick[46] William
Spicer & ux[47] Goodman Loe[48] & ux dined with us to day.
Mr Truemans suspencon published in our church to day.
4° Sept. 1637
Court to day & we had here at dinner Mr Rushworth & ux Mr ffisher
of the Gaole & ux, Mr Rogers,[49] I was much affected with the story
of Crow[50] (that so carefully kept his new testam[en]t in his p[er]ills) in
the booke of Acts & mon.[uments] related by Mr Rogers, blessed be
thy name oh Lord for the comfort of good freinds thou art please to
afford us. My M[aste]r went this day towards London.

I was spoken to by my M[aste]r on Satterday last to solicite the busines
of the fforest[51] for the gentry of the Country.

[46]Mary, the wife of Samuel Crick, Woodford's landlord. They owned a haberdasher's
shop.

[47]Ann ('Nan') Spicer was the widow of George Crick.

[48]John Loe (d. 1642) was an ironmonger, and (with his wife, Ann) part of the godly scene in
Northampton. Woodford and Daniel Reading acted as overseers of Loe's will, while William
Spicer, Thomas Crutchley, and Hatton Farmer, served as witnesses. Loe was a freeman of
the borough by 1640: TNA, PROB/11/189; NRO, Finch (Hatton) MSS, F(H) 3501.

[49]Daniel Rogers was the godly master of the free school. He had gained an MA from
Sidney Sussex College, Cambridge, in 1631, and was the grandson of the godly Essex
minister Richard, and half-brother of the diarist Samuel. He was associated with the
Knightleys of Preston Capes (Thomas Dugard met him there in 1633) and a key member of
the Northampton godly (he witnessed Thomas Martin's will in 1644). In 1641 he subscribed
to William Castle's missionary effort to convert native Americans and in 1642 preached the
Wellingborough lecture. By 1646 he was minister at Wootton and by 1658 of Stoke Bruerne.
He married first Dorothy, daughter of Lawrence Ball, and, second, Martha, the daughter
of John Reading: Webster, *Godly Clergy*, pp. 55–56, 233; T. Webster and K. Shipps (eds),
The Diary of Samuel Rogers, 1634–1638, Church of England Record Society XI (Woodbridge,
2004), p. xiii; D.K. Shearing, 'A study of the educational developments in the Diocese
of Peterborough, 1561–1700' (unpublished MPhil thesis, University of Nottingham, 1982),
p. 350; Fielding, 'Peterborough', pp. 166 n. 24, 186–188, 255, 226 n. 9; PDR, Archdeaconry
of Northampton Wills, third series, A178, and fourth series, Book 10, p. 110; British Library,
Add. MS 23,146, fo. 21r; Longden, *Clergy*.

[50]Thomas Morse had reported that in 1555 Gregory Crow had been shipwrecked on a
voyage to Kent and had been forced to jettison all his goods but retained his New Testament.
Having found his money among the wreckage he threw it away, stating 'If the Lord will
save our lives, he will provide us a living'. Rescued by Morse, a merchant operating out of
Antwerp, he related his story to the townsmen there, who duly donated money and clothes
to him: J. Foxe, *Actes and Monuments of These Latter and Perillous Dayes Touching Matters of the
Church*, ed. S. R. Cattley, 8 vols (London, 1841), VIII, pp. 148–149.

[51]Charles I revived the medieval forest laws (which had fallen into desuetude) as an
expedient to raise revenue without recourse to Parliament. Henry Rich, Earl of Holland,
was made chief justice of the forests and placed in charge of the process in the areas
where it was enforced – Essex, the forest of Dean, and the three Northamptonshire forests
of Rockingham, Whittlebury, and Salcey. This took two forms: first, from 1635 the forest
courts were revived to prosecute trespasses against the forest – the Swanimote for lesser

I make doubt what to doe oh Lord direct & order every thinge for the best for the Lords sake Amen.

5° Sept. 1637

I prayed and went [*crossed out:* this morninge] to Sr xxofer Yelvertons,[52] they had almost dyned when I came, but I had very lovinge intertaynement from my Lady Mrs Allen Mr Watts[53] & Blessed be thy name oh Lord for all thy m[er]cys Sr xxofer was from home with whom I went to speake about the forest busines, but I met there with Mr Egleston[54] & Mr Pentlow.[55]

Mr Maior[56] Mrs Maioresse & my M[ist]r[es]s supped here to night wth the Cost they sent I pray to be enabled for the Sessions & Gaole d[e]l[iv]ery to morowe.

6° Sept. 1637

I prayed in private & with my family & went to the Sessions,[57] where ffill[58] was convicted of Baretry[59] & subornacon to periury & where many other foule offences were punished Blessed be thy name oh Lord for good & wholsome Lawes, Lord establish & increase them for the Lords sake. The Lord graciously enabled me this day, Ramsden the sup[er]stitious fellow was indicted for night walkinge & p[rese]nted

offences, the Justice Seat for greater. More controversially, from 1637 the boundaries of the royal forests were arbitrarily extended to their medieval limits, one observer stating, with minimal exaggeration, that the bounds of Rockingham forest were extended from six miles to sixty. It is clear that the scheme was primarily intended to be a windfall tax on the rich or, as Pettit described it, 'quasi-legal extortion': *Royal Forests*, pp. 83–88, 93 (quotation).

[52]That is, Sir Christopher Yelverton. Yelverton's father, Sir Henry, was a Jacobean attorney general, and Sir Christopher had in 1636 entertained Charles I at his Easton Maudit estate. Sir Christopher's will contained an unusually lengthy godly preamble and he and his wife, Ann (the daughter of Sir William Twisden of Kent), supported godly ministers such as Edmund Calamy and the Calvinist bishop Thomas Morton. He was obliged to pay £200 to purchase a pardon for disafforestation, and was later a very obstructive ship money sheriff: Fielding, 'Peterborough', pp. 22–23; TNA, PROB/11/217; Pettit, *Royal Forests*, p. 90; G. Isham, *Easton Maudit and the Parish Church of Saints Peter and Paul* (London, 1962), *passim*.

[53]Henry Allen (and his wife, Helen) and Thomas Watts were friends of Woodford's living at Easton Maudit: Book of Orders, p. 46.

[54]The unidentified Mr Eccleston: see Diary, pp. 170, 229.

[55]Woodford's friend Thomas Pentlow of Wilby, who should not be confused with his kinsman and namesake, who lived at Broughton: see Introduction, p. 37.

[56]Woodford's friend Mayor John Gifford.

[57]This is the town's not the county's quarter sessions, and was conducted by the recorder, Richard Lane.

[58]William Filkins had in 1614 refused to receive communion, claiming that he had not prepared for it: PDR, CB44, fo. 42.

[59]Vexatiously commencing lawsuits, which was the professional offence of attorneys: C.W. Brooks, *Pettyfoggers and Vipers of the Commonwealth: the 'lower branch' of the legal profession in early modern England* (Cambridge, 1986), p. 137.

for an affray, & beinge 2ce[60] drunke, oh Lord convert him if it be thy will or remove him from this towne for the Lords sake Amen.
7° Sept.
I prayed & went to keepe Grafton [Regis] Court, & there I found Mr Bagshaw[61] with whom I had some discourse about

about the fforest busines; I went after Court to my Lady Cranes[62] to remember Mr Bryan[63] & Mrs Bryan to her where I met wth Mr

[60]Twice.

[61]Edward Bagshaw of Moreton Pinckney was a Middle Temple barrister with wide-ranging godly connections stretching back to the puritan divine Robert Bolton and including Francis Nicolls of Faxton, John Sawyer of Kettering, Francis Downes of Pytchley, Sir John Pickering of Titchmarsh, Sir John Dryden of Canons Ashby (uncle of the Restoration poet), and Sir Thomas Crewe of Steane. During the 1630s he was prominent in protecting those godly harassed by the Church courts. For his godly zeal (according to Sibthorpe) John Crewe appointed him Recorder of Banbury. Bagshaw's Lenten reading at the Middle Temple in 1639 criticizing Laudian bishops was terminated by Archbishop Laud himself but earned him great popularity at his inn and political recognition in the form of the Parliamentary seat of Southwark in the Short Parliament. However, by 1641 he had moved towards the king and was thenceforth a Royalist: Fielding, 'Peterborough', pp. 26, 209, 239–240; P.R.N. Carter, 'Bagshaw, Edward (1589/90–1662)', in *ODNB*; M.F. Keeler, *The Long Parliament* (Philadelphia, 1954), p. 94; TNA, SP16/447/33; Temple of Stowe MSS, STT 1880, 28 April 1639.

[62]Lady Marie Crane (d. 1642) was the French widow of Sir Francis Crane (d. 1636), who had been a courtier and head of the Mortlake Tapestry Works. In 1629 he had lent the crown money on the security of ten Northamptonshire manors, including Grafton Regis wherein lay Grafton House in which he came to reside. He had commissioned his other mansion of Stoke Park (which was located in the parish of Stoke Bruerne) from Inigo Jones, and Crane had entertained the king there in 1635. On his death he had bequeathed £500 to Archbishop Laud's restoration of St Paul's Cathedral and allowed his widow, Lady Marie, to live on at Stoke Park, but required her to leave Grafton, which was to be leased out. Clearly, she had not yet done so. After her death the Crane properties passed to Sir Francis's brother, Sir Richard (d. 1645); and in 1643 Grafton was the scene of a famous Civil War siege. The Grafton manorial court was held in the King's Arms, which was owned by Crane's enemy at court, Sir Miles Fleetwood: TNA, PROB/11/105; W. Hefford, 'Crane, Sir Francis (c.1579–1636)', in *ODNB*; Pevsner, *Northamptonshire*, pp. 415–416; Fielding, 'Peterborough', p. 143, n. 48; *VCH Northamptonshire*, V (Woodbridge, 2002), pp. 142–176.

[63]Joseph Bryan (1590–1639) was a Gray's Inn bencher. His father, John, had been a godly Elizabethan mayor of Northampton, who had petitioned Secretary Robert Cecil to protect the corporation's godly minister, Robert Catelin, from deprivation in 1605, and had been involved in a Star Chamber case in 1607 against John Lambe as one of the godly accused of circulating scurrilous poems parodying the Church court's officials. Joseph was closely connected to the godly lawyers Christopher Sherland and Robert Tanfield, and chose Zouch Tate as one of the overseers of his will, which was witnessed by Francis Rushworth, the godly Northampton apothecary, John Bullivant, the godly minister of Abington, and John Speed (d. 1640), the heir of the famous cartographer and himself the first anatomy lecturer at Oxford: TNA, PROB/11/10, 55; Sheils, *Puritans*, pp. 83, 117, 122–123; Markham and Cox, *Northampton*, II, p. 52; TNA, STAC8/205/19; TNA, PROB/11/179; S. Bendall, 'Speed, John (1551/2–1629)', in *ODNB*; Prest, *Barristers*, pp. 346–347.

Bunian[64] as I walked in the hall there I thought uppon Sr ffrancis Crane that was gone who had heaped up treasures, that could not keepe him from death Non domus & fundus non aeris acervus &[65] oh Lord graunt me thy favor which is better then life, outward things cannot secure from the evils of this life & much lesse helpe after death. I am often thinkinge if the Lord would so bringe it about to bestowe uppon me the Clerkship of the peace, what a great temp[or]all m[er]cye it would be to me & how convenient for me, but I desire to submit my will to the Lords & not at all to Covet any thinge that is my neighbors, oh Lord I beseech thee add unto my outward estate if it be thy will as thou hast in wonderfull m[er]cye added to my family & sanctify every m[er]cye to me thy poore servant for the Lords sake Amen. I was angry at the men in the morninge that could not catch my horse Lord p[ar]don it &

adhuc[66] 7° Sept. 1637
heale this corrupcon in me for the Lords sake. This day at Grafton [Regis] I made an assumpsit[67] betweene Mr Butler & Buncher[68] who have referred their Controversy to Sr Miles ffletwode[69] & Mr Bagshawe, & have respectively d[e]l[ive]r[e]d each to other 6d & in conse[centi] inde[70] have p[ro]missed to pay 100li if either of them fayle to p[er]forme their award on this p[oin]te, so as the award be made & published in writinge before All hallow day next.

---

[64] Thomas Bunning was curate of Grafton and Lady Crane's chaplain. He was present at Parliament's storming of Grafton House in 1643, having already been sequestered: A.G. Matthews (ed.), *Walker Revised* (Oxford, 1948), p. 277; *VCH Northamptonshire*, V, p. 76.
[65] Horace, *Epistles*, Book 1, epistle II, lines 47–49; the full quotation reads, 'Non domus et fundus, non aeris acervus et auri, aegroto domini deduxit corpore febris, non animo curas' ('Neither house nor farm, nor store of brass and gold, can banish fever from the ailing body or care from the mind'). It may have been a popular maxim: Burton quoted it in his *Anatomy of Melancholy*, and so did the Shropshire antiquary, Richard Gough: R. Gough, *The History of Myddle*, ed. D. Hey (London, 1988), p. 158.
[66] Still.
[67] Allowing the plaintiff to obtain damages from the defendant when the defendant had caused the plaintiff loss by a failure to fulfil a promise: Brooks, *Pettyfoggers*, pp. 67, 88–89.
[68] Butler resided at Alderton. One Thomas Buncher of nearby Paulerspury had explained his absence from church in 1625 by claiming to be excommunicate: PDR, CB64, fo. 537r–v; Diary, p. 348.
[69] Sir Miles Fleetwood of Aldwincle, a senior official in the Court of Wards, supported the Duke of Buckingham in the parliaments of the 1620s but spoke out against Laudian ceremonies in the Short Parliament of 1640: C.S.R. Russell, *Parliaments and English Politics, 1621–1629* (Oxford, 1979), pp. 16, 129, 168, 173, 199–200, 220, 246, 248; J.D. Maltby (ed.), *The Short Parliament (1640): diary of Sir Thomas Aston*, Camden fourth series XXXV (London, 1988), pp. 16, 20, 35, 73, 134–135, 165; S.M. Jack, 'Fleetwood, Sir Miles (d. 1641)', in *ODNB*.
[70] 'In consequence of which'.

Ramsden was here with Mr Neale[71] to know the p[rese]ntm[en]ts.
8° Sept. a lady day[72] fare here to day
we receaved a letter that my father will be here to morrow, whereof
we are very glad;
I pray dayly for my deare wife & sweete Children, & family Lord
blesse us one unto another for the Lords sake Amen.
I have sent to my mother to come over to morrow

9° Sept. 1637
my father came hether to day safe blessed be god Mr Welsh came
along with him.
oh Lord graunt me much Comfort in my father & mothers & they in
me for the Lords sake Amen. I sold some maslin[73] to day that came
from Old Corne is very deare, Lord p[ar]don o[u]r sinnes & worke a
gen[er]all refermacon that thy m[er]cyes may flow downe in greater
abundance. Poore Nel is in great distresse in travell I prayed for her,
my wife greatly troubled to heare of her misery & danger.
10° Sept. Sab.[bath]
Mr Newton preached in the morninge & Mr Wm Martin in the
afternoone, Lord give me to p[ro]ffit by thine ordinances for the
Lords sake Mr Rushtons[74] 2d sonne henry xh[riste]ned to day

11° Sept. 1637
I rose early this morninge & prayed and had a short grudginge of
direfull melancholly oh Lord heale me of it I pray thee, & worke my
hart to true thankfullnes for the great ease thou hast given me already
for the Lords sake.
My wives breasts are not well & the Child is hardly brought to suck
good Lord I pray thee give us the blessinge of the breast as thou hast
given us of the womb for the Lords sake Amen.

---

[71]Henry Neale (d. 1641), Sibthorpe's former father-in-law, and the member of a
Northampton gentry family with its own chapel in All Saints' church: Metcalfe, *Visitation of
Northamptonshire 1618*, pp. 117–118; TNA, PROB/11/186.
[72]The feast of the Nativity of the Virgin Mary.
[73]Mixed grains – usually rye and wheat.
[74]William Rushton, attorney, succeeded Woodford as Steward of Northampton on the
latter's death in 1654. Rushton's son Henry similarly succeeded his father on *his* death in
1665 and served until 1683. Ramsden claimed that Thomas Pendleton omitted to perform
hat honour (the custom of removing one's hat in church) at this service: Longden, *Visitation
of Northamptonshire 1681*, pp. 181–182; Markham and Cox, *Northampton*, II, p. 570; TNA,
SP16/474/80.

o[u]r 6 bells are gone to Leic[ester] to be new cast[75]
Nurse Woodnot went away.
12° Sept
We prayed & my father & mother tooke Leave to goe to London so I
went with them 2 or 3 miles, & when I came back p[rese]ntly after we
were much affrighted for in dressinge of the Child John found a deepe
hole in the throate of it, which came we supposed by the carelessness
of the Nurse

Nurse, my wife was much troubled & the thinge did much affect me
but we desired both to quiet o[u]rselves in the Lord, for the Lord
his p[ro]vidence is over all, & it is his m[er]cy it was now espied
hopinge that it is not yet mortall. after Mr Spicer[76] had bene here &
the throat was dressed he tooke the breast p[rese]ntly though before
he had bene very averse to it, blessed be thy name oh Lord for all thy
goodness.
graciously affected in prayer with my wife but especially in private
alone, where the Lord did graciously answere me in my poore requests,
and the Lord will surely blesse me, not for my merits (which are no
better then sinne), but for his m[er]cyes sake I prayed for increase of
grace in me & my deare wife, for my poore mother, for the sweete
children the Lord hath given me for gods gracious p[ro]vidence
towards me to add to my outward estate & I was much affected
in prayer for the Kings Ma[jes]tye for his Convercon, to inlighten his
eyes

to stirre him up to drive away the wicked from the throne, & to make
choice of such as will be faythfull. Oh Lord worke mightily for the
Lords sake.

---

[75] In August 1637 a meeting of the vestry ordered the raising of £50 to recast the church
bells: the renewed bells rang again on 13 December 1637. The Leicester bell founder was
Hugh Watts, who was to recast the tenor bell at the parish of Old in 1639: Vestry Minutes,
p. 33; L.M. Middleton, 'Watts, Hugh (1582/3–1643)', rev. A. McConnell, in *ODNB*; Bridges,
History of Northamptonshire, II, p. 203.

[76] John Spicer (apothecary) was the son of Christopher Spicer of Cogenhoe and his wife,
Rachel, the daughter of the puritan radical Percival Wiburn. The elder Spicer had been the
titular rector of Fawsley appointed by Sir Richard Knightley to provide cover for the *de facto*
pastor, the ejected minister John Dod. John Spicer, whose friends included Peter Whalley
and Curate William Holmes, was married to Frances Cartwright. He was elected town
bailiff in 1637: Longden, *Clergy*, Spicer; TNA, SP16/308/52; G. Ford, 'Where's Whalley?
The search for Sir Samuel uncovers a Whalley–Cartwright alliance in Northamptonshire',
Northamptonshire Past and Present, 62 (2009), p. 34; Book of Orders, p. 32.

we began to night to pray our eveninge prayer in the family before supper, wch I find to be best (unlesse some waighty occasion forbid) because freest from drowsiness &

13° Sept. 1637
I am goeinge out this morninge to consult with Captayne Bernard[77] about the forest business oh Lord direct us in it let every thinge be done for the best, give me grace & favor in the eyes of the gentry of the Country & blesse me in my undertakinge for the Lords sake Amen.

I was afterwards with him from whom I find respect & incouragem[en]t to goe on I blesse the Lord.

I was after with Mr Bullivant[78] & Mrs Bullivant who lyes in.

14° Sept. 1637
I prayd, & went after to some gentlemen of the Country at the Swan who met there about the busines in hand, where Mr Cooke[79] received about 20li more, so he hath p[ro]mised to deliver the Records.

---

[77] Woodford always refers to John Bernard (Barnard) (1604–1665), lord of the manor of Abington, as captain. Bernard was the son of Baldwin Bernard and the stepson of Sir Edmund Hampden, one of the leaders of opposition to the forced loan of 1627. John married first Elizabeth (d. 1642), the daughter of Sir Clement Edmondes of Preston Deanery, Secretary of State, and secondly, in 1649, William Shakespeare's granddaughter, Elizabeth Hall: Isham, *Diary*, p. 230, n. 3.

[78] John Bullivant was the rector of Abington, 1628–1651, to which he was appointed by Eleanor Hampden, widow of Sir Edmund Hampden. He was a member of the Northampton godly and was married to Mary Danby: Fielding, 'Peterborough', p. 22; Isham, *Diary*, p. 62, n. 15.

[79] Francis Cook (d. 1638) was an attorney from Kingsthorpe and repeatedly undersheriff of the county, 1628–1638. His wife was the daughter of the wealthy townsman George Coles: *VCH Northamptonshire*, IV, pp. 80–82; Diary, p. 147, n. 208; J.H. Burgess, 'The social structure of Bedfordshire and Northamptonshire 1524–1764' (unpublished DPhil thesis, University of York, 1978), p. 186.

there were Sr xxofer[80] Yelverton, Sr Richard Samwell[81] Mr Craven[82] Mr Nicolls[83] Captain Bernard & Mr Welch & his wife were in the towne & here tonight in the eveninge.

15° Sept.

Mr Tanfeild[84] came to towne to day, & Mr Palmer[85] & Mr Bagshaw were here before who are of Counsell for the

[80] Christopher.

[81] Sir Richard Samwell of Upton was a patron of godly ministers opposing court policies of the 1620s and 1630s (such as Benjamin Tompkins and George Preston) and played a leading part in resisting the forced loan of 1627 and (with Miles Burkit, vicar of Pattishall) the ecclesiastical policies of the 1630s: Diary, pp. 136 n. 180, 210 n. 430; R.P. Cust, *The Forced Loan and English Politics, 1626–1628* (Oxford, 1987), p. 301; Fielding, 'Peterborough', pp. 22, 105–107.

[82] John Craven (1610–1648) had attended the Middle Temple with Bulstrode Whitelocke before marrying Elizabeth, the daughter of Lord William and Lady Penelope Spencer. He had forged close links with his in-laws and had returned to live with them at Althorp in 1637 following a quarrel with Lord Maynard. A Royalist, he was created Baron Craven of Ryton (Shropshire) in 1643. On his death in 1648 he made a bequest to the Arminian Sir Richard Spencer: I.W. Archer, 'Craven, Sir William (c.1545–1618)', in *ODNB*.

[83] Francis Nicolls of Hardwick (with his uncle Sir Augustine of Faxton, d. 1616) was the patron of the moderate Northamptonshire godly divine Robert Bolton, and the overseer of his will, together with other godly friends such as his brother-in-law Edward Bagshaw, John Sawyer, and Francis Downes. Bagshaw dedicated his life of Bolton to Francis Nicolls, who took a leading role in opposing the forced loan and was rewarded with a Northamptonshire seat in the parliament of 1628. During the 1630s Nicolls was associated with divines who spoke out against ecclesiastical policy such as his chaplain, William Clarke, John Baynard, and John Baseley, and was himself pursued by the Church courts for puritan practices. He counted John Reading among his godly friends and had been appointed by Sir John Pickering as the guardian of his son Gilbert, whom he supported in the knight of the shire contest for the Short Parliament: Fielding, 'Peterborough', pp. 26, 129–130; PDR, Archdeaconry of Northampton Wills, third series, A198 (Nicolls); TNA, PROB/11/19 (John Pickering).

[84] Robert Tanfield of Loddington (1584–1639) was a Middle Temple barrister and the son and nephew of lawyers. He acted as counsel to Lord Montagu of Boughton. His godly uncles, Sir William and Francis Tate, had lived at Delapré Abbey just outside Northampton. He was a graduate of that godly seminary Emmanuel College, Cambridge, a godly associate of Sir Simonds D'Ewes, and spoke in his will of his assurance of being one of the elect: TNA, PROB/11/124 (Sir William Tate), PROB/11/46 (Francis Tate), and PROB/11/55 (Tanfield); Prest, *Barristers*, p. 394.

[85] Geoffrey Palmer was lord of the manor of East Carlton, and was himself forced to pay a fine for the disafforestation of his estates. He was a high-flying lawyer, who had been called to the bar in 1623. Although a member of the Long Parliament and a manager of the Earl of Strafford's impeachment, he changed his political allegiance during the debates on the Grand Remonstrance in 1641 (after John Hampden moved to print the document) and became a staunch Royalist. At the Restoration he was knighted and appointed Charles II's attorney general: Isham, *Diary*, p. 15; Pettit, *Royal Forests*, p. 90; L.A. Knafla, 'Palmer, Sir Geoffrey, first baronet (1598–1670)', in *ODNB*.

Country in the great business about the new bounds[86] of the forest.

Mr Chamberlayne[87] here who it seemes is solicitor for Mr Knightley[88] & some other gentlemen.

16° Sept

our Counsell all beinge 6 vizt Mr Tanfeild Mr Bryan Mr Bagshaw Mr Whitwick[89] Mr

Geoffry Palmer & Mr Adams,[90] who are of Counsell for the Country have met together to Consult about the busines I rec[eive]d 5li from Sr

---

[86] This was phase two of the revival of forest law, the extension of the forest boundaries to their medieval limits. In theory, it brought enormous swathes of land and scores more villages within the competence of forest law. From the first, however, the real intention was to raise a lump sum from wealthy landowners. Since the Middle Ages the crown had alienated large areas of forest to private individuals, often withdrawing the land from the restrictions of forest law, and it was for this disafforestation (which Charles I declared illegal) that those individuals were now to compound. The enormous fines imposed on leading noblemen such as the Earls of Westmorland and Salisbury were massively reduced: Pettit, *Royal Forests*, pp. 88–92.

[87] Edward Chamberlayne of Warwickshire, who also held lands in Northamptonshire. He is probably the same who occurs as the Undersheriff of Northamptonshire to Sir John Dryden in 1635 and who was a feodary (a local official of the Court of Wards) who was particularly zealous for the collection of ship money in Leicestershire. In his will he bequeathed law books to his heir and mentioned a son called Knightley Chamberlayne: Jackson, 'Ship money', p. 25; T. Cogswell, *Home Divisions: aristocracy, the state and provincial conflict* (Manchester, 1998), p. 233; TNA, PROB/11/264.

[88] Richard Knightley came from a puritan dynasty based at Fawsley which had sheltered the notorious Martin Marprelate press. With their friends, the Drydens of Canons Ashby, they had consistently supported godly ministers through the tergiversations of the seventeenth century. Knightley protected the eminent John Preston and, through him, was connected to a nationwide godly network led by Viscount Saye and Sele and others including Lord Brooke, John Hampden, John Pym, Sir Arthur Haselrig, Christopher Sherland, Sir Thomas Crewe, John Crewe, Edward Bagshaw, and ministers such as John Dod and Daniel Featley. This network protected godly ministers and organized parliamentary and non-parliamentary resistance to court policy from the 1620s onwards. Knightley had himself led opposition to the forced loan in 1627: Fielding, 'Peterborough', pp. 13–19, 218–219.

[89] John Whitwick (1581–1645) was an Inner Temple barrister and Steward of Coventry. He was a Royalist in the Civil War: Prest, *Barristers*, p. 403.

[90] William Adams of Hardingstone was a bencher of the Middle Temple. Before 1631 he married either Dorothy or Ann, the nieces of Judge Sir Francis Harvey of Hardingstone, and remained close to his wife's family. He was buried in the chancel of the Temple church in 1659: H.A.C. Sturgess (ed.), *Register of Admissions to the Honourable Society of the Middle Temple from the Fifteenth Century to the Year 1944*, 3 vols (London, 1949), I, p. 106; F.A. Inderwick and R.A. Roberts (eds), *A Calendar of the Inner Temple Records*, 5 vols (London, 1896–1936), II, p. 367; TNA, PROB/11/165, PROB/11/171.

John hanbury[91] & 50li from Sr Anthony haslewood,[92] & 3li I rec[eive]d
before from Mr Bernard
I gave 2 peeces to night to Mr Palm[er]
My Lord of Holland who is Lord Cheife Justice in Eyre, & my
Lord ffinch Chief justice of the Comon pleas Judge Jones Baron
Trevor Justice Crawley & Judge Bridgman cheife Justice of the County
Palatine of Chester are all come to towne, & with them of Counsell
for the Kinge Sargeant Whitfeild & the Kings solicitor Litleton[93]
I was a little troubled to see how much Mr Chamberlayne tooke uppon
him in the busines & seemed to slight me much if not exclude me, but
I desired to looke onely to the Lord; And I reioyced much

much and praysed the Lord with much sensiblenes & affection that
he had given us the lib[er]ty of his blessed Sabath, to rest from our
labours & to refresh our selves in holy Converse with him in the blessed
ordinances; & I prayd to be pr[e]pared for it & for them he should
send to speake unto us in his name,
I went with Mr Maior[94] & to attend the Lord of Holland & who Lyes
at the Lady harvyes,[95]

[91] Sir John Hanbury of Kelmarsh was unusually non-partisan in his clerical patronage,
which included the moderate godly ministers Thomas Alford (his chaplain) and Archibald
Symmer, but also Thomas Turner, Archbishop Laud's chaplain. His friendships were just as
wide-ranging. In his will he bequeathed inscribed rings to a large number of people ranging
from the godly Richard Knightley, John Reading, and Edward Bagshaw through moderates
such as Lord Edward Montagu and the Earl of Manchester to the arch-Laudians Sir John
Lambe and Turner: Fielding, 'Peterborough', p. 45; TNA, PROB/11/97.

[92] Sir Anthony Haslewood was squire of Maidwell: Isham, *Diary*, p. 27.

[93] The Justice Seat, the principal forest law court and the only one able to impose fines,
proceeded with almost regal pomp. It had been resurrected in 1635 but had been repeatedly
adjourned until this time, when fines were first imposed. The listed judges and lawyers
were Sir John Finch, William Jones, Sir Thomas Trevor, Sir Francis Crawley, Sir Oliver
Bridgman, Ralph Whitfield (serjeant-at-law), and Sir Edward Littleton (Solicitor General),
who prosecuted John Hampden on the crown's behalf. In addition, fifteen members of the
county gentry formed a grand jury: Pettit, *Royal Forests*, p. 86; J.S. Cockburn, *A History of
English Assizes 1558–1714* (Cambridge, 1972), p. 293; Jones, *Bench*, pp. 19, 20–21, 37, 41–42,
139.

[94] John Gifford.

[95] Either Christian, the widow of Judge Sir Francis Harvey of Cotton End (Justice of
Common Pleas), or Mary, the widow of Sir Francis's son, Sir Stephen, who predeceased
his father. Sir Francis had enjoyed wide-ranging contacts among the godly (John Sawyer,
Francis Nicolls, John Freeman) and non-godly gentry (Sir Anthony Mildmay, Sir Arthur
Throckmorton, Robert Breton, and John Wake): TNA, PROB/11/88; NRO, Finch (Hatton)
MSS, F(H) 4678; TNA, PROB/11/100, PROB/11/106, PROB/11/18; Metcalfe, *Visitation of
Northamptonshire 1618*, pp. 98–99.

17° Sept Sab.[bath] 1637 Sab.[bath][96]
I praied to be pr[e]pared for gods ordinances this day
One Mr hodges[97] preached in the morninge before my Lord of Holland
& the Judges. very well, & my hart was affected I blesse the Lord
Mr hill worthy Mr hill[98] preached in the afternoone Lord make thy
word effectuall uppon us all

graciously enlarged in family dutyes I blesse the Lord.
18° Sept. 1637
no Court to day by reason of the Justice seate.
I pray to be enabled for what is required of me in attendinge the
Justice seate for the Country about the bounds of the forests.
I stayed at Mr Cricks all the morninge about sortinge the Records but
I heare that Justice ffinch[99] in his charge hath much anticipated us in
o[u]r evidence, by declaringe what hath bene allreadye adiudged in
this Iter[100] in other places which he hath warned the Councell to take
notice of:
I went thither in the afternoone, where they set very great fines uppon
small offences in the forests.[101] the time for the bounds is appointed on
Wednesday morninge.

[96] Ramsden claimed Thomas Pendleton again failed to perform hat honour during another
baptism on this day: TNA, SP16/474/80.

[97] Moses Hodges was as yet unbeneficed but was presented to the rectory of Upper Isham
on 2 November 1637 and again in 1653 by Lord Protector Cromwell: Longden MS, 2
November 1637, 1653.

[98] Thomas Hill (with Thomas Ball) had been one of John Preston's inner circle at
Emmanuel College, Cambridge. He obtained his benefice of Titchmarsh on 11 July 1633,
when the godly patron, Sir John Pickering, granted the right to present to his godly
friends Viscount Saye and Sele, Sir Erasmus Dryden, and Robert Horsman: Fielding,
'Peterborough', pp. 18, 31.

[99] Sir John Finch was zealous in enforcing the forest laws, and indeed was an aggressive
exponent of royal authority: A. Hughes, *The Causes of the English Civil War* (London, 1991),
pp. 24, 156; Jones, *Bench*, pp. 139–141; Pettit, *Royal Forests*, p. 86; L.A. Knafla, 'Finch, John,
Baron Finch of Fordwich (1584–1660)', in *ODNB*.

[100] A judge's circuit. This refers to proceedings in the other forest county of Essex, where
the crown had stated that the alienation of forest land had been illegal and had imposed
large composition fines on offenders: Pettit, *Royal Forests*, p. 84.

[101] The fines were mainly for trespasses against Rockingham forest. There were relatively
light fines for trivial thefts of wood (usually for maypoles, as here) or deer; larger ones
for the more serious offences of felling large numbers of trees (Sir Giles Mompesson) or
keeping cattle in the forest (Sir John Wake), through to the high penalties imposed on
the grantees of forest land. William Cecil, second Earl of Salisbury, as the heir of Robert,
the first Earl, was fined £20,000, and the Earl of Westmorland £19,000 for numerous
offences. Other magnates to incur enormous fines included Sir Christopher Hatton, Lord
Thomas Brudenell, the Earl of Peterborough, and Lord Edward Montagu: Pettit, *Royal
Forests*, pp. 86–88.

when men were fined for cuttinge downe maypoles in the forests,[102] it
was told them by [*crossed out:* some] one on the Kings p[ar]t that they
were not fined for havinge maypoles but for cuttinge them downe in

the forest.
19° Sept. 1637
many great fines imposed againe to day. [*crossed out:* I received from Sr
John hanbury & Sr Anthon[y] haslewood 10li to lay out in the busines]
I gave Mr Palmer 2li for a fee. Mr Tanfeild would not take any thinge.
20. Sept
I feed Mr Bagshawe Mr Adams Mr Whitwick Mr Bryan 2li a peece.
It was desired by o[u]r councell to have time till the afternoone & then
till next morninge diverse gents were with the counsell at night, & Sr
xxofer[103] Yelverton gave me 20s for my paynes.
21° Sept
our counsell went on a while, but p[rese]ntly Mr Whitwick made a
submission in the behalfe of the country, which was not well liked on
the counetryes p[ar]te, it was done so lengthy who would have had a
submiss[ion] wth p[ro]testacon.[104]
I gave Mr Chamberlaines man 12s p[ro] br[ev]iat[e]s & 2li 8s to Mr
Crick for the councells dyet &
22° Sept.
The Justice seate continues still but not in such vigor now the bounds
are gayned.[105]

*****

---

[102] This was a common offence, so much so that in 1637 stocks were erected at Wakefield
Walk in the forest of Whittlewood, south of Northampton, for the punishment of wood
stealers: Pettit, *Royal Forests*, pp. 86, 152.

[103] Christopher.

[104] Woodford's account receives corroboration from a surprising source, the private papers
of Thomas, Lord Brudenell of Deene, a Catholic recusant magnate and friend of the king.
Attempting to persuade Charles to abandon the policy, he concurred in Woodford's opinion
of Whitwick's performance, referring to a submission made at the Justice Seat by 'one that
had neither interest in the country nor understood the subjects' rights': NRO, Brudenell, E,
XXIII, 21, Brudenell's draft memorandum dated 1637 and entitled 'Reasons to induce his
Majesty not to enlarge his forest of Rockingham' (quoted in Pettit, *Royal Forests*, pp. 92–93).

[105] That is, now that the royal forests had been extended to their medieval size. In November
1637 commissioners were appointed to compound with forest offenders and in April 1638
landowners were ordered to appear before the commissioners at London House, while
Holland ordered the Surveyor General, Sir Charles Harbord of Potterspury, to confirm the
extent of the new bounds. Only a small percentage of the fines was collected: Pettit, *Royal
Forests*, pp. 88–90.

23° Sept. 1637
The Lord of holland & the Judges are gone out of towne Its s[ai]d the Lord of holland is gone into the forest to surveigh & plot out a R[e]d deere p[ar]ke to morow.
24° Sept. Sab.[bath]
Mr Newton & Mr Ball did both very p[ro]fitably to day blessed be god.
somewh[a]t enlarged in duty this day I prayse the Lord
25° Sept.
Court adiourned to day till Thursday.
26. Sept.
I would give some present to new Mr Maior[106] but want money. Lord I pray thee increase my estate in thy due time for the Lords sake Amen.
27° Sept.
great pr[e]paracon at Mr Maiors for the feast[107]
28° Sept.
Court here to day I got some money I prayse the Lord.
29° Sept.
I pray to be inabled to give the oath[108] & Mr Ball

preached in the morninge before the oath then Mr Recorder[109] gave the new maior a charge and the Lord enabled me to doe my p[ar]te I blesse his name great feasting at the Maiors to day, Mr Collis Maior Mr B[enoni] Coldw[e]ll & John Spicer Bayleifs.[110]

---

[106]William Collis, mercer, had served as a bailiff in 1628, churchwarden in 1636, and chamberlain, 1631–1636. According to Woodford, he died on 18 May 1639. The son of Ursula (the sister of John Crick), he was an integral part of Woodford's godly society, as were his wife and daughter Sarah: Freemen of Northampton, unpaginated, under Collis (dated 1635); Vestry Minutes, pp. 21, 32; Markham and Cox, *Northampton*, II, pp. 552, 562, 567–568; PDR, Archdeaconry of Northampton Wills, second series, Book AE, p. 86.

[107]Mayoral elections took place on the first Thursday in August but the new incumbent did not take up his duties until Michaelmas (29 September): Markham and Cox, *Northampton*, II, pp. 32–34.

[108]On the day of the mayor's proclamation in office, the town assembly was to appear wearing its best clothes to accompany the mayor to All Saints' church, where the bell was tolled thrice. Then proceedings adjourned to the guildhall, where the steward tendered the mayor his oath of office. Finally, the party repaired to the mayor's for the feast: *ibid.*, pp. 30–33.

[109]Richard Lane.

[110]The Coldwells enjoyed a long godly pedigree: Benoni was the brother of Tobias, who was town clerk between 1618 and 1654, and the writer of a manuscript history of the town. Their father, George, had been mayor in 1606 and town clerk from 1592 to 1618, during which time he had been presented before the Church court for sending his son to the free school while the master, Simon Wastell, was excommunicated for nonconformity. Among the godly friends mentioned in his will of 1612, in which he expressed confidence of his election, were Wastell, Robert Catelin (the divine), Dr John Cotta (the physician), and

30 Sept. 1637 there is speech of a convocation of B[isho]pps at London about the church Cerem[onies] & discipline Lord worke for the best for thy people for the Lords sake.

1° Oct. Sab.[bath] Sacram[en]t."'

Mr Porter"² preached in the morninge very p[ro]fitably & Mr Newton in the afternoone, blessed be thy name oh Lord that we yet enioy thine ordinances Lord continue them to us & o[u]r posterity forever for the Lords sake Amen.

2° Octob. 1637

I prayed (though dully) & went to the Court to the New Maior Mr Collis & Bennoni Coldwell & John Spicer Bayleifes.

At my Comminge home I find my wife very ill with her right breast, which (they say) is like to breake my hart is very sad for my deare wife, but what can I doe? oh Lord I desire to make knowne my sorrow to thee my god I beseech thee helpe us I beleive oh Lord that thou art able to pr[e]vent the breakinge of it, Lord pr[e]vent it if it be thy gracious will, sanctifye the feare of it to us p[ar]don our deadnes

deadnes in seeking to thee oh Lord direct [*crossed out:* so] to some meanes which thou wilt blesse if it be thy will and by thy helpe wee thy poore servants will prayse thee for this great m[er]cye, and labor to walke more carefully before thee oh Lord heare & helpe graciously for the Lords sake Amen. I am now goeinge to dinner to Mr Maiors,"³ oh Lord give me comforts & Cheerfullnes & moderacon & favor in their eyes for the Lords sake Amen.

Francis Harvey (the lawyer). In 1608 Coldwell and his sons had been involved in a Star Chamber case against John Lambe, who accused the Northampton godly of circulating scurrilous verses deriding the personnel of the Church courts. A third son, George, was a Northamptonshire clergyman supported by the Tate family of Delapré Abbey. Benoni served as a sidesman in 1633, 1635, and 1641, and (as here) as a bailiff of the town in 1637. John Spicer was the apothecary who had treated Woodford's son John: TNA, STAC8/205/19 and STAC8/205/20; PDR, CB37, fo. 193r; PDR, Archdeaconry of Northampton wills, first series, Book Z, p. 194; Vestry Minutes, pp. 21–36; Sheils, *Puritans*, p.26; Markham and Cox, *Northampton*, II, pp. 562, 570; Longden MS, 12 July 1610 and 16 December 1616.

"'Ramsden claimed that Ball administered the communion to six unknown female sitters, and Newton to a further six including John Smart, hosier, and Samuel Martin: TNA, SP16/474/80.

"²Probably Thomas Porter, who had married Mary Collis, the sister of William, Mayor of Northampton, 1637–1638. He is probably the same as the Flintshire minister mentioned by Calamy. Born in Northamptonshire, he was a Cambridge MA and later a Presbyterian, ordained at Peterborough in 1623: PDR, Archdeaconry of Northampton Wills, second series, Book AE, p. 86.

"³William Collis.

Besse[114] went away to day to dwell with her dame Curwyn[115] and one Nan Morris came to us from Towcester.

3° Octobr. 1637
The quarter Sessions here this day for the Country. I was downe at the Castle[116] Mr Attourney Lane gave the Chardge.
Mr dalbyes business heard in the eveninge.

4° Octob.
Mr Wallop[117] gave me 3s 4d. I moved towards night about Mr Charlets business
I was with Sr Thomas Brooke[118] for the money he owes me but cannot get it, Lord helpe me

to it in thy due time thou seest my necessity & want Lord supplye me graciously for the Lords sake Amen.

5° Oct. 1637
I prayed & p[ro]vided to goe to grafton [Regis] Court. I sent hatton to Sr Thomas Brooke who saith he hath left or will leave order with Mr Collis where he lyes to pay me.
My M[aste]r goes towards London to day & the Ch[ildre]n there to remayne, Lord be with them pr[e]serve them doe them good, & give me favor in their eyes still if it be thy will.

---

[114]Elizabeth ('Besse') Curwyn: see next note.

[115]Elizabeth Curwyn (1611–1668) was the daughter of Alderman John Harbert, the former mayor. She had married a freeman called John White, who had died in 1633, leaving her with two children – Woodford's maid Elizabeth or Besse (1631–1688) and Mary (1632–1675). It was a peculiarity of Northampton's constitution that marriage to the widow of a freeman conferred freedom of the borough. This George Curwyn (Curwin, Corwin) (1610–1685) obtained in 1634 by marrying Widow White, and thereby gained two stepdaughters. George was clearly a tradesman and is seen extending credit to Woodford. The whole family emigrated after 2 April 1638 to Salem, Massachusetts, where Captain Curwyn became a rich merchant. His second wife was Governor Winslow's daughter. See Book of Orders, p. 35; C. Partridge, 'Elizabeth Herbert wife of 1) John White 2) George Corwin', *New England Historical and Genealogical Register*, 150 (April 1996), pp. 190–193; 'Pedigree of Curwen', *ibid.*, 10 (1856), p. 304; Diary, pp. 141, 171, 176, 194; Markham and Cox, *Northampton*, II, p. 311; C.W. Upham, *Salem Witchcraft with an Account of Salem Village*, 2 vols (New York, 1978), I, p. 98; J. Savage, *A Genealogical Dictionary of the First Settlers of New England*, 4 vols (Boston, 1860–62), I.

[116]Northampton's Norman castle, where Thomas Becket had clashed with King Henry II.

[117]Obadiah Wallop was probably related to Richard of Bugbrook, a relation of the Wallops of Farley Wallop, Hampshire, and Wappenham, Northamptonshire, who was under attack from George Jay, the conformist incumbent, for paying salaries to the previous three incumbents, while living in the parsonage and retaining the income, £300 per annum: TNA, SP16/372/110; Metcalfe, *Visitation of Northamptonshire 1618*, p. 48.

[118]Sir Thomas Brooke of Great Oakley was closely allied with the moderate puritan magnate Edward, Lord Montagu of Boughton, and was the patron of the godly minister Archibald Symmer: TNA, PROB/11/99; Fielding, 'Peterborough', pp. 26, 77–79.

I overtooke the Coach when it was a little past Cotton end & rode
before to keepe grafton [Regis] Court intendinge to goe with my
M[aste]r that days Journey, but it seemes they turned Newport[119] way;
Mr Wit[120] was at grafton [Regis], & as we came home he informed me
that he knew of the death of my father & but hath pr[o]mised me not
to bringe me in or trouble me for the land
it hath pleased the Lord in m[er]cy to cure my wives breast without
breaking blessed be thy name oh Lord.
6° Octob.
I prayed and went up to Sr xxofer hatton[121] to dinner where I had good
respect I blesse the Lord, oh Lord I

blesse thee for the favor thou givest me in the eyes of men. Thy
p[ro]vidence doth all things.
Sr John hanbury is made high Sheriffe of the County
7° Octobr. 1637
My want of money still is much and yet the Lord is pleased still to
supply me.
I was in some distresse to day for money to buy p[ro]vision in the
market but god had p[ro]vided that there was left in hattons hand
10s for [crossed out: ffiff] ffill[122] which he refused to receave so it was to
remayne with me, Blessed be thy name oh Lord for this p[ro]vidence.
A clyent one Somes[123] came to me to [crossed out: f] pr[e]pare an office,
I pray to be enabled to that & the p[ro]hibicons for Mr Barnards[124]
[crossed out: Clyents] tennants.
8° Octob. Sab.[bath]
Mr Ball preached morninge & eveninge very p[ro]fitably I blesse the
Lord. Mr Newton beinge gone to appeare at the high Commiss[ion]
I was graciously affected and enlarged in duty
******

[119] Newport Pagnell, Buckinghamshire.
[120] Perhaps Thomas Watts.
[121] Sir Christopher Hatton was a cousin of the Elizabethan Lord Chancellor of the same
name, and a patron of aggressively conformist clergymen. His main residence was Kirby
Hall, a prominent Elizabethan mansion which he was improving over the period 1638 to
1640 with the aid of Nicholas Stone and, possibly, Inigo Jones: Pevsner, Northamptonshire.
Hatton had sat as an MP for Peterborough in the parliaments of 1624 and 1625. He was the
Steward of Higham Ferrers (part of the queen's jointure) from 1636, a fervent Royalist in the
Civil War, and spent many years in foreign exile before the Restoration: V. Stater, 'Hatton,
Christopher, first Baron Hatton (bap. 1605, d. 1670)', in ODNB; Fielding, 'Peterborough',
p. 46; M.F. Keeler, The Long Parliament (Philadelphia, 1954), p. 208.
[122] William Filkins.
[123] Presumably Nathaniel Some.
[124] Probably John's brother, William: S.E.N. Higgins, The Bernards of Abington and Nether
Winchendon, 4 vols (London, 1903), I, pp. 55, 59.

duty this day I blesse the lord.

9° Octob. 1637

a good Court to day I blesse the Lord, where the Lord hath graciously supplied my necessityes. my wife & I often troubled to thinke that diverse in the towne doe traduce my wife in layinge the imputacon of haughtinesse of spirit to her charge; and this we suppose to be through the unfaythfullnes of Besse[125] our late servant, & the talkinge of her dame, however Lord I pray thee heare our poore prayers in graunting us a sanctified use of this affliccon let us be bettered by it, teach us to goe through good report & evill,[126] & in thy due time Cleare us, & Lord p[ar]don this gen[er]all sinne of us in this towne (traducinge) oh Lord teach us to walke worthy the gospel for the Lords sake Amen. our mayd Nan[127] is lame as she saith.

10° Octobr. 1637

my wives breasts sore still wth choppinge[128] [crossed out: illegible word] I pray unto the Lord for cure in his due time my Clyent Some came to me with this P[ro]vidence

11° Octob. 1637

I prayed and went to Wellingborowe, I was wth my mother as I went along and at Wellingborow & wth Mr Pearne as Mr danby & I came back. I and my wife are invited to Mr danbyes to dinner to morow. Johns tongue was cut beinge tongue tyed by Mrs davison.[129] Mr Beeton[130] (they say) is excommunicate, oh Lord helpe thy poore church for the Lords sake Amen. I met with Wm Chapman of Old[131] at Wellingborow & his sonne Wm my playfellowe. Our mayd Nan went away to day, & one Besse Morris from Kingsthorpe came to us,

[125] Elizabeth ('Besse') Curwyn.
[126] 2 Corinthians 6:8.
[127] Ann Morris.
[128] Chapping: cracks in the skin.
[129] Possibly related to Valentine Davison of Butchers' Row, Market Square: PDR, Archdeaconry of Northampton Wills, third series, A 236 (will of William Spencer, 1646).
[130] Robert Beeton was the high constable of Hamfordshoe Hundred. In April 1636 Sibthorpe had accused Thomas Bacon, lord of the manor of Burton Latimer, of combining with 'puritan high constables', including Beeton, to prevent the collection of the ship money tax in Burton. Beeton was also singled out by Sheriff Charles Cokayne as obstructive to the tax and sent for by the Council. This latter dispute, whose conclusion is unknown, was refereed by Sir John Isham and Sir Lewis Watson: Jackson, 'Ship money', pp. 42, 48–49.
[131] William Chapman, senior, attended musters 1605–1619, while one of the same name (either senior or junior) was supported by the priest at Old, James Forsyth, in claiming exemption from the burdens of knighthood in 1631, and occurred as churchwarden in 1634 and 1637: J. Wake (ed.), The Montagu Musters Book 1602–1623, Publications of the Northamptonshire Record Society VII (Northampton, 1935), pp. 7, 205; HMC, Report on the Manuscripts of the Duke of Buccleuch and Queensberry, III (London, 1926), p. 361; PDR, CBA63, fo. 194r–v; PDR, Church Survey Book 5, fo. 135r–v.

Lord make her a good ss[erv]ant to us, & make her thine for the Lords sake.

12° Oct.

we found the office to day at the hind for Nathaniel Some, & the Lord graciously directed me in it, & hath given me some more light into business of that nature.

we began Genesis againe to day. Lord helpe us to p[ro]fit by readinge the scripture for the Lords sake.

13° Oct.

graciously affected in readinge the 3d chapter of Genesis & in prayer; oh Lord there is somew[ha]t of the Bryar & thorne in every estate & condicon in this world (brought uppon us by o[u]r first defection) Lord give us patience & weaned affections from the

the world; Lord give us so to live to thee here that we may after this life be receaved into pa[ra]dise, where never came the accursed thistle or prickinge bramble, and Lord blesse my sweete children thou hast given me make them thine by adopcon give them the use of witts limbes & p[ar]ts & make them instruments of thy glory in their time and enable me to educate them to that end give me necessary supply of outward things for the Lords sake Amen.

I made a bond to day from Tho. Chiles of Ravensden in Com[itatu] Bedf[ord] to Mr ffisher p[ro] 10li payable 14° Apr. next.

Mr Rushworth & Mrs Rushworth supped here to night blessed be the Lord for the priviledges & opportunityes we enioy of meetinge together in peece & Love, oh Lord sanctifye & blesse every meetinge of o[u]rs that we may glorify thy name & be instruments of good to one another for the Lords sake Amen.

I had some discourse with James Lewes[132] about his course of company keepinge Lord sanctifye my poore desires & expressions to him for the Lords sake Amen.

14° Oct.1637

my wives breasts are very sore, oh Lord I pray thee heale them, and give us the blessings of the breasts as

as thou hast in m[er]cye given us the blessings of the womb. Oh Lord thou art able to send health and Cure thou hast heard o[u]r prayers

---

[132] Possibly the minister appointed by Daniel Reading to the living of Duston in 1642, the son of Jeremiah Lewis, godly incumbent of Northampton All Saints', 1616–1628. James was possibly living unbeneficed in St Giles's parish, where in 1632 a parishioner bequeathed him money to preach his funeral sermon. One of that name served in the Church courts in 1634, which would not have improved Woodford's view of him: Longden MS, 8 November 1642; Longden, *Clergy*; PDR, Miscellaneous Book Va, fo. 16r.

form[er]ly, heare them now who art a god that heareth prayers, she hath used much meanes but they are ineffectuall oh Lord say but the word & they shall be cured & make her a ioyfull mother & let us still have occasion to prayse thee even for this m[er]cye too if it be thy will for the Lords sake Amen.

Mr Nicolls sent me 20s this day for my paynes about the forest busines, Lord be blessed for these seasonal supplyes.

15° Octob. 1637 Sab.[bath]

Mr Perkins of Naseby[133] preached here morning & eveninge very p[ro]fitably blessed be god.

16. octob.

I prayed and went to dinner at Captaine Bernards where I found much Love I blesse the Lord.

I came alonge with Mr Bullivant to North[amp]ton, and I declared to him in private the temptacon which began uppon me this day 3 yeares.

oh Lord I blesse thee for thy wonderfull m[er]cye in carryeinge me through it I beseech thee that I may never forget thy goodnesse to me in this but that I may labor to be truly thankfull & to expresse thankfullnes by more fruitfull walking for the Lords sake Amen.

I was wth Mr Bullivant at the George & dranke some wormewood beare, & wth Mr Rushworth I was very ill after I had supped oh Lord p[ar]don my fayling & make me very watchfull for the Lords sake Amen.

17° Oct.1637

I prayed and went to dinner to ffaxton[134] where I found very lovinge intertaynement I blesse the Lord, I went after to Sr John Ishams[135]

---

[133]Thomas Perkins, a Cambridge BA and client of Edward Shuckburgh of Naseby, had resisted Laudian policy by refusing (initially at least) to relinquish his afternoon sermon in favour of a catechism class and by refusing to administer the communion at the altar rails. Instead, he removed the communion table from the rails to the body of the chancel at communion time: Fielding, 'Peterborough', pp. 144 n. 52, 205; PDR, CBA63, fos 320, 381; A.G. Matthews (ed.), *Calamy Revised* (Oxford, 1934), p. 387.

[134]Francis Nicolls's manor.

[135]Sir John Isham of Lamport had amassed a fortune in the 1620s, mainly by moneylending. He was a patron of conformist clergy and numbered Lord Keeper John Williams and Sir John Lambe among his allies. However, he had married the godly Judith Lewin and allowed the famous divine John Dod access to his family for the purposes of preaching and spiritual counsel. During the Civil War he attempted to remain neutral, unlike his more openly Royalist progeny, Justinian and Elizabeth: M.E. Finch, *The Wealth of Five Northamptonshire Families 1540–1640*, Publications of the Northamptonshire Record Society XIX (Oxford, 1966), pp. 33–34; Fielding, 'Peterborough', pp. 57 n. 81, 79; I. Stephens, '"My cheefest work": the making of the spiritual autobiography of Elizabeth Isham', *Midland History*, 34 (2009), pp. 183, 189–191. I thank Isaac Stephens for this reference.

who stayed me with him 2 or 3 houres & expressed very much love to me, oh Lord thine owne good p[ro]vidence hath brought this about give me ever to wayt & depend uppon thee for the Lords sake Amen.

I came home p[ar]te of the way with John Cole[136] who is troubled about the world, but we laboured

laboured to incourage one another in the Lord & found much comfort blessed be thy name oh Lord.

18° Octobr. 1637 St Luke

I prayed and went this day to Wellingborow fare havinge but one 12d with me & leavinge but one 2d with my wife, but the Lord in m[er]cye sent me 8s from Raph Blower & 11s from Guilb[er]t Tebot[137] who overtooke me accidentally uppon the way cominge home; Blessed be thy name oh Lord. So I this day made even with Raph Blower for all things & rec[eive]d of Guilb[er]t Tebot this 11s in p[ar]t paym[en]t.

19° Oct.

Mr Ball preached at the lecture to day very p[ro]fitably blessed be god.

20° Octob. 1637

I prayed and went to the Court, & I moved Mr Maior[138] about an order for the Sargeants payinge for declaracons,[139] but I found not that successe I expected, and Mr Maior seemed to desert me much & the Sargeants Clamord, so that I was much troubled, and when I came home I found o[u]r mayd Besse[140] resolved to be gone in hast[e] & my wife was troubled at it, so in the trouble & fluctuations of my sp[iri]t I desired to make knowne my afflicons to the Lord who enabled me in some measure to looke over them.

---

[136]John Cole was active in the vestry 1628–1633, and had served as a sidesman. The Church court had arraigned him and his wife in 1629 for attending conventicles organized by Jeremiah Warner at the houses of Thomas Martin and George Crick. He served as chief sergeant of the town from 1652 until 1657: Vestry Minutes, pp. 21–30; Markham and Cox, *Northampton*, II, p. 78, 571; PDR, CBA2, unfoliated, dated 15 June 1629.

[137]A freeman of Northampton since 1631, and a beneficiary of the will of Everard Tebbot of Old, possibly his brother: Book of Orders, p. 15; TNA, PROB/11/193.

[138]William Collis.

[139]The corporation paid royal messengers who brought writs and proclamations down from London: Markham and Cox, *Northampton*, II, p. 33.

[140]Elizabeth ('Besse') Morris.

I went after dinner to old Mr Martin[141] to give him thankes for speaking in my behalfe at the Court.

I went after to Cap[tain] Bernard who had appointed to come to speake with me as uppon this day.

so at the swan I met first with Mr Al[exander] Eakins[142] who desired me to speak to C[aptain] Barnard that he might keepe a Couple of Greyhounds under him, so I p[er]ceaved he Jiered, & told him it may be he thought that he might keepe greyhounds as well as the Capt[ain] & then

desired afterward that I would speak to him that he might keep them under his Lady.

but when I met with C.[aptain] Barnard in a Chamber there with Mr Martin Mr Morgan[143] & the Captaynes man word was brought that Mr Eakins desired to speake with him so when Mr Martin was gone he sent him word he might come up if he pleased so he came & carried him selfe very uncomonly, & [crossed out: when] set his arme under his side, & when the Captayn after long patience told him he spoke simply, Mr Eakins replyed he did not say that he spoke sillily whereuppon the Captaine struck him about 3 or 4 blowes with his litle Cane, I was thinkinge while they wrangled, what Jarringe & Contradiccon sinne hath brought into this world

Oh Lord let thy gospel be so powerfull uppon us that the Lyon may become a Lamb for the Lords sake Amen.

*****

---

[141] Woodford's close friend Thomas Martin, the father of Samuel, for both of whom see Introduction, p. 32.

[142] Alexander Eakins of Weston Favell, whose servants were accused of brawling in the belfry of St Peter's church in Northampton in 1634. One Alexander (perhaps the same) died in 1666 at Ringstead (where the family also owned property), leaving money to a kinsman, Henry Raymond, a puritan divine who read a lecture at Ringstead sponsored by patrons from London in which he condemned the Laudian Book of Sports: Metcalfe, *Visitation of Northamptonshire 1618*, p. 178; PDR, CBA63, fo. 150r–v; PDR, Archdeaconry of Northampton Wills, fourth series, X84; Fielding, 'Peterborough', pp. 130, 156, 161 n. 24.

[143] Thomas Morgan (1609–1665), the son of Francis, a barrister whose friends included Edward Bagshaw and whose sister married John Reading. Some of his servants had reportedly refused catechism at the hands of Dr Clarke in 1628. Thomas's grandfather was another Francis, a judge who had been Dr Clarke's patron: Longden, *Visitation of Northamptonshire 1681*, pp. 135–136; TNA, PROB/11/130, PROB/11/133; PDR CB A2, unfoliated, under 23 July 1628; R.M. Serjeantson, *A History of the Church of St Peter, Northampton* (Northampton, 1904), pp. 107, 206.

adhuc[144] 20° Oct. 1637
I wrote to Goodman Tompson[145] about the mayd servant that was
offerd on Wednesday last & I prayed for a good servant.
Mr Rushworth & his wife & Mrs Newton here with some oysters &
blessed be thy name oh Lord.
21° 8br.
I have prayed for the manifestacon of gods good p[ro]vidence towards
us in a servant.
Besse[146] went away to day.
Mr Somes brought me 6li which I have receaved of him to carry to
London.
John not well.
22° Oct. Sab.[bath]
Mr Ball preached in the morninge & Mr Atterbury[147] in the afternoone.
John very ill, but I pray unto the Lord for him, who is infinitely
gracious.

23° Oct.1637
I was downe at my M[aste]rs house in the old study, and thought
uppon the affliccons & thoughtfullnes I had there, & praysed the Lord
who had delivered me. Court to day, and I prayed in a sp[irit]uall
manner before I went to be freed from [crossed out: full-width line] rash
anger & such occasion of trouble as I had the last court so the Lord
graciously heard me blessed be thy name oh Lord.
Mr Maior[148] payd me 3li of the money due to me from Sr Tho[mas]
Brook blessed be thy name oh Lord for it: newes brought us the mayd
will come. I pray to heaven her a blessing.

[144]Still.
[145]William Tompson of Wilby (chapman) was clearly regarded as godly by Woodford.
The overseer of his will (dated 1649) was the radical godly leader Robert Welford of Earl's
Barton, who in 1592 had been accused of supporting the Brownist William Hackett, and
who had been presented for gadding as late as 1634: E.A. Irons, 'A calendar of a court book',
Northamptonshire Notes and Queries, new series, III (1911), p. 239; Sheils, Puritans, pp. 16, 22, 111n,
128–129, 141; PDR, CB64, fo. 44r–v; PDR, Church Survey Book 5, fo. 134r–v. The maid
in question was Temperance (surname unknown) from (possibly) Charwelton (see Diary,
p. 129).
[146]Elizabeth Morris.
[147]Francis Atterbury had been the godly incumbent of the living of Milton Malsor since
1627 and enjoyed the patronage of the lord of the manor there, Stephen Harvey, son of
Sir Francis Harvey: Webster, Godly Clergy, p. 233n; Longden MS, 16 April 1627; TNA,
PROB/11/88.
[148]William Collis.

24° Oct.

I prayed and went to keepe Court at Broughton for Mr Pentlowe[149] hatton went for the mayd to Carleton[150] Mr Bentham[151] was at the Court, I have

adiourned them over to 21° Novembr as I came home I was exceedinglye graciously affected in prayer the Lord pleased to breake in uppon me in a gracious measure I prayed ag[ains]t wicked B[isho]ps, & their hierarchy I prayed for the establishm[en]t of the gospel here, for the increase of gods graces in my selfe & family, & for o[u]r p[ro]sp[eri]ty if the Lord saw fit, & for my sick child of whose health & life I had much feare but I desired to wayt uppon the Lord, so I found some comforts at my coming home I blesse the Lord.

25° Oct. 1637

I stayed at home to day. I went in the afternoone with Mr Ball to Mr Maior nere the Northgate was not very well when I came home. here supped with us Mr Rushworth & ux Mrs

Reading Mrs Newton &.

litle John not well, nor my wife, & so we are advised to have one to suckle the child, so after much debate we are resolved on it, & the Lord in his p[ro]vidence hath sent us one goodwife Emerson that pleaseth us very well & the child hath sucked dayntily blessed be thy name oh Lord, oh Lord I pray thee heale my deare wife & the child & still give us occasion to prayse thee for thy goodnesse.

Temp[er]ance o[u]r mayd came to day, oh Lord make her thy servant & graunt that she may be faythfull to us, & may serve us in thee & for thee. I bought the table of fees of old Mr Sarg[e]nt[152] for 12d, wch tab[le] I suppose to be false in p[ar]t.

26° 8br. 1637

I prayed and came forward for London kept court at grafton [Regis], & by gods m[er]cye

*****

[149] Woodford's friend Thomas Pentlow of Broughton, who should not be confused with his kinsman and namesake, who lived at Wilby: see Introduction, p. 37.

[150] Possibly Charwelton.

[151] The godly minister Joseph Bentham had been appointed to the benefice of Broughton on 24 December 1631 by Edward, Lord Montagu of Boughton, on the advice of the godly ministers Robert Bolton and Nicholas Estwick, although he had been part of his patron's godly coterie since 1617. Bentham was far from enthusiastic about Laudian policies but, like his patron, his response to them was more moderate than that of many of his godly colleagues: J. Fielding, 'Bentham, Joseph (1593/4–1671)', in *ODNB*.

[152] Roger Sargent, mayor of the town in 1625: Cox and Markham, *Northampton*, II, pp. 551–552; Book of Orders, unfoliated, under the year 1636.

am come safe to Brickhill[153] to the red Lyon where one Mr Meridale stayed for me & showed me much love, but they were loose & swearinge, & dranke a health or two which I would not pledge in the Ceremony oh Lord establish me that I never decline thy truth for the Lords sake.

Oh Lord I pray thee blesse my family at home give them health of body & mind inable me to pray for them & they for me, keep us from all terrors & evils restore us together againe with much comfort to the glory of thy name for the Lords sake.

I am now in the greene Chamber at the Lyon, Lord give me quiet rest this night & let thy p[ro]tection & blessing be ever over & with me for the Lords sake Amen.

Mr Lockye is here.

27° 8br. 1637
The Lord hath graciously refreshed me with sleepe this night, blessed be thy name oh Lord; And now oh most gracious father I pray thee goe along with me still in my Journey keepe me from evill blesse my family at home give us againe a Comfortable meeting to the glory of thy name for the Lords sake.

I came alonge from Brickhill with a Lancashire man one Mr Snape, to Islington, where he stayed to Lodge and I came alone to London beinge afraid it beinge darke & the way dangerous but the Lord brought me safe to London blesse the Lord, where I find my father & mother very well I blesse the Lord.

28° Octob.
I prayed and went abroad & have sent away my horse by harry Bodington.

I went after to Guildhall to see the Lord Maior[154] sworne which was done with great solemnity. The Comon Cryer who is also mace-bearer first made 3 proclamacons, with, All manner of

p[er]sons here present keepe silence.
Then the towne clerke or his deputy made 3 times obeisance to the Lord Maior & kneeled downe at the North end of the table, then the mace-bearer makinge like obeisance kneeled downe at the other end, & set his Mace uppon one end, & layd the booke uppon the top of it, then the new Lord stood up & put his hand on the booke & the towne Clerke gave him the oath of supremacy the oath of Allegiance & the oath of Maioralty, then the [crossed out: Chamberlayne

---

[153]Near Bedford.
[154]That is, Sir Richard Fenn, who was in the process of succeeding Sir Edward Bromfield: A.B. Beaven, The Aldermen of the City of London, 2 vols (London, 1908–1913), I, pp. 201, 219.

of the Cittye made 3ce[155] obeysance] old Lord Maior rose & delivered the place to the new, after that the Cittye Chamberlayne made 3ce obeisance & kneeled and delivered a very rich Scepter to the old Maior who kissed it & delivered it to the new, who tooke it & kissed it & layd it downe uppon the velvet Cushion, then the Chamberlayne makinge 3ce obeisance in goeinge backe, brought in the same manner a purse & then a seale; after that the swordbearer makeinge obeisance as before delivered up his sword in the same manner to the old Mayor & he to the new, & the new to the swordbearer againe, And then the Cryer makinge 3ce proclamacon was againe bid to say by the Towne Clerke All manner of p[er]sons here p[rese]nte may now dep[ar]te & give yor attendance againe uppon a new summons.
I dined at my Mistresses in black ffryers

29° Octob. 1637 Sab.[bath]
I prayed and went to heare dr Stoughton[156] morninge and eveninge, who deales honestly & faithfully & boldly.
30° Octob.
I prayed and went to Mr Pentlowe we came after to dyne with my father at weavers hall who is Master of his Company this yeare.
I was to see the Lord Mayor goe in p[ro]cession in [St] Paules.
31° Octob.
I prayed and went to Westm[inster] hall there is much speech of the Morocco embassador[157] who hath brought a p[re]sent to his Ma[jes]ty.

---

[155]Thrice.
[156]Dr John Stoughton was the perpetual curate and lecturer at St Mary Aldermanbury. Rejecting pleas from John Winthrop to accompany him to Massachusetts, Stoughton had staved off attacks from Bishops Laud and Juxon during the 1630s with the help of godly patrons such as Sir Robert Harley. He was a key godly figure on the steering committee for John Dury's ecumenical project and took part (with Thomas Ball) in the compilation of the 'Body of Divinity'. He died in 1639 while preparing sermons for publication dedicated to Henry Rich, Earl of Holland, and to Sir Gilbert Harrison: P.S. Seaver, 'Stoughton, John (bap. 1593, d. 1639)', in *ODNB*.
[157]The Moroccan ambassador, Alcayde Taudar Ben Abdala. The King of Morocco, who was involved in a local conflict, purchased the neutrality of the English fleet by surrendering the European captives of the Barbary pirates: *CSPD*, 1637–1638, p. 476; Gardiner, *History*, VIII, p. 70.

1° Novembr[158]
No hall day to day. I heard dr Stoughton in the afternoone, but stood somewhat farre off I prayd this morninge & went to speake with Mr Robins[159] & when I found him out Mr Weltden by gods p[ro]vidence

came to us, to speake with him, & desired me to goe & dyne with Sr John Wolstenholme,[160] where I had very great & kinde entertaynement, oh Lord I prayse thee for thy good p[ro]vidence towards me continually.
much debate & some difference betweene my father & I concerning Mr Readings money, Lord I pray thee be gracious to us for the Lords sake Amen.

2° Nov. 1637
No hall day. I prayed and went about my occacons, I have bought a sword of John Weston.
[crossed out: I was wth my master who stands]
3° Nov.
I prayed and went to Westm[inster] hall; and moved about my occacons this day with successe I blesse the Lord but my hart doth not enioy the Lord as form[er]ly, for the thorny cares of the world[161] doe dull my affections often, oh Lord looke from heaven uppon me give me to endure this crosse with much fayth & patience yea cheerfullnes, & in thy good time pay my debts for me & blesse me in outward things if thou seest good for the Lords sake Amen.

---

[158] All Saints' Day. Ramsden claimed that Newton had by now returned from the Court of High Commission, that at afternoon prayers he read from Philippians 3 but failed to bow when Jesus' name occurred, and that he persisted in editing the Prayer Book by omitting the Lord's Prayer at morning prayer, and at churching and marriage services: TNA, SP16/474/80.
[159] Richard Robins of Long Buckby, who was associated with Thomas Watts of Long Buckby and Easton Maudit, Woodford's friend and creditor. He was involved (with Watts) in obstructing the work of Sir Robert Banastre, the assiduous ship money sheriff, at Buckby in January 1638. His son, Obedience Robins, was an apothecary who emigrated to Virginia: Jackson, 'Ship money', p. 157, n. 88; M.C. Wilheit, 'Obedience Robins of Long Buckby: a 17th century Virginian', *Northamptonshire Past and Present*, 53 (2000), pp. 7–18.
[160] Henry Weltden was the son of William Weltden of Thornby (d. 1631), who had been a barrister and auditor of the Duchy of Lancaster. Sir John Wolstenholme (1562–1639) was a wealthy merchant and customs farmer; a keen Laudian, he rebuilt Stanmore church in Middlesex: Longden, *Visitation of Northamptonshire 1681*, pp. 236–237; J.K. Laughton, 'Wolstenholme, Sir John (1562–1639)', rev. H.V. Bowen, in *ODNB*; K. Fincham and N. Tyacke, *Altars Restored: the changing face of English religious worship, 1547–c. 1700* (Oxford, 2007), pp. 167–168.
[161] Mark 4:19.

4° Nov.
This morninge Mr St John[162] argued in the behalfe of Mr

Mr hampden about the ship-money, he was much applauded &
hummed[163] by the by-standers, though my Lord ffinch signified his
displeasure for it.
I was not present.
5° Nov. 1637. powder treason day. Sab.[bath]
I prayed and went to dr Stoughtons Church morning & eveninge a
stranger preached in the morninge very honestly & dr Stoughton him
selfe in the afternoone very boldly & worthily, blessed be thy name oh
Lord for such lights Lord continue them & sett up more & greater for
the glory of thy name & exaltacon of thy gospel, in despite of all thy
foes for the Lords sake Amen.
And blessed be thy name oh Lord for p[ro]tectinge & defendinge thy
holy gospel & the professors of it especially for kepinge us from the
cruelty of [15]88 & this hellish powder plot graunt that thy gospel
may still runne & be glorified, pr[e]vent & break in peeces all plots &
machinacons that are against it for the Lords sake Amen.
6° Nov.
I prayed and went to Westm[inster], & gott into the [Ex]Cheq[uer]
chamber (though with some danger in the crowd

Crowd) to heare the rest of Mr St Johns Argum[en]t, who spake
very fully & boldly & gave great satisfaccon to the by standers who
adventured to hum him againe, oh Lord incline the harts of the Judges
to give a right sentence for the Lords sake amen.
One of the Kings counsel is to answere him on Satterday.
after that 2 others are severally to argue for Mr hampden & to be
answered by 2 of the Kings counsell.
7° Novemb.1637
I prayed and went about my occ[asi]ons, we busied about the
suggestions for denton,[164] in the p[ro]hibicon.

---

[162] Oliver St John (1598–1673), Hampden's famous advocate: William Palmer, 'St John, Oliver (c.1598–1673)', in *ODNB*.

[163] Hum: to make a low inarticulate vocal sound as a sign of approbation.

[164] Suggestions were informations recommending a prohibition: that is, the order of a superior court forbidding the proceedings of an inferior in a case falling outside its cognisance. The case referred to is *Richard Denton vs. Alexander Eakins* over rights of common: Markham and Cox, *Northampton*, II, p. 458.

8° Nov.
I prayed and went to Westm.[inster] Richard denton is come to the towne to make oath of servinge the rule on Eakins I drew up an affidavit & he tooke his oath before Justice Croke.[165]

9° Nov.1637
I prayed and went to Westm[inster], and as I came home I met wth Mr Pentlowe of Broughton, who hath bene much affrighted & takinge phisick, for on tuesday he was wth a kinsman who dyed suddenly & the Chirurgeon they sent for s[ai]d it was the sicknesse,[166] I laboured to take the p[rese]nte opportunity & to show him the necessity of p[rese]nte labouringe for grace, Lord blesse that example & my poore words to him for the Lords sake Amen. I was sent for to my Lord cheife Justice[167] about Eakins in the Gaole.
10° Nov.
I prayed and toke horse, but callinge Mr Travell[168] at his lodginge in the well yard nere St Bartholomews I was forced to stay for him so I went to his horse at the flour de luce in ffetterlane[169] & stayd about an houre & came away without him, but baytinge[170] at St Albans he overtooke me so we met with another traveller and came safe though late to the white harte in Dunstable.
I ride uppon a horse of John Cox which came up with Mr Boughton;[171] I prayse god for his good p[ro]vidence towards me in it, & for hearing my prayer.

11° Nov. 1637
we had more company & came safe to North[amp]ton I blesse the Lord, but my horse was much tyred & threw me downe twice but I had no hurt I blesse the Lord.

---

[165]That is, Denton swore by affidavit to present to Eakins the court's order. Sir George Croke was judge of the Court of King's Bench: Jones, *Bench*, p. 125; C.W. Brooks, 'Croke, Sir George (c.1560–1642)', in *ODNB*.
[166]The plague.
[167]The chief justice of the Court of King's Bench was Sir John Bramston: Jones, *Bench*, pp. 125–127.
[168]Possibly Robert Travell, rector of Weston Favell, who was deprived for nonconformity by Bishop Thomas Dove in 1605 and immediately reinstated by his patron (and father-in-law), Richard Leverich; or else Travell's son, Immanuel: Longden, *Clergy*.
[169]The Fleur de Lis, Fetter Lane.
[170]Giving food and water to horses during a journey.
[171]Andrew Broughton of Seaton in Rutland worked for the Northamptonshire attorney Theodore Greene of Marston Trussell and Clement's Inn. In later life, Broughton served as clerk of the High Court of Justice that tried Charles I, whose death sentence Broughton read out. He died in exile in Vevey, Switzerland: S. Kelsey, 'Broughton, Andrew (1602/3–1687)', in *ODNB*.

And the Lord gave me comforts comminge home findinge my family in health & Joyfull at my arrival, blessed be thy name oh Lord for all thy goodnes.

Longstrap[172] a dangerous theife got out[173] of the Towne gaole[174] to night. John is growne much I blesse the Lord.

12° Nov. Sab.[bath]

Mr Newton preached both times very well I blesse the Lord.

but I find the Com[mu]n;[ion] table removed to the very top & there is an iniuncon it seemes to come up to it[175] but Lord establish us in thy truth & for Xt his sake root out all sup[er]stition & Idolatry.

I wanted some money to pay the poore Lord supply me.

13° Nov.

I prayed and went to the Court where I had some supply (I blesse the Lord) about 16s whereof I payd my

my mother about 9s my wife had borrowed 8s 6d of her, & shee 18d of my wife, so she hath 2s more towards 20s arrere of the 40 p[ai]d to besse Rise[176] my mother went to Old to day.

---

[172]Matthew Longstrap was later executed for burglary: Diary, p. 151.

[173]Jailbreaks were a recurring problem in early seventeenth-century Northampton, necessitating expenditure in 1613, 1619, and 1653 to improve security: Markham and Cox, *Northampton*, II, pp. 175–176.

[174]Northampton had three jails and it is often difficult to know which one is being referred to. Here, the town's own jail is clearly intended. It was situated underneath the Conduit Hall, a second town hall built in 1460 which derived its name from its position over the water supply, the Great Conduit. There were, in addition, two jails controlled by the county's justices of the peace: the castle itself and the house of correction. The latter had been instituted in 1615 as a work creation scheme for the relief of the poor, and had also initially been situated under the Conduit Hall. By the 1630s it had been moved to a location at or near the Bell Inn on Bridge Street. The separatist Robert Browne died in one of the three in 1633. The godly repeatedly attempted to make religious provision for the prisoners: Thomas Bradshaw, curate of All Saints', had in 1616 admitted burying executed criminals; John Fisher was reported for preaching to a selected audience of prisoners and townsfolk at (probably) the castle in 1635, and the courts were informed that the curate Charles Newton was soon to take over this jail evangelism; finally, in 1641, Francis Nicolls made provision in his will for monthly sermons at the county jail (at the castle): Markham and Cox, *Northampton*, II, pp. 175–178; *VCH Northamptonshire*, III (London, 1930), pp. 35–36; M.E. Moody, 'Browne, Robert (1550?–1633)', in *ODNB*; PDR, CB41, fo. 24r–v; TNA, SP16/308/52; PDR, Archdeaconry of Northampton Wills, third series, A198.

[175]As part of the church survey of 26 and 27 October, Ball had been ordered to administer the communion only from within the rails to those who came up, and not to leave the rails to administer to any 'factious or disobedient person' (TNA, SP16/370/57), and to provide sufficient communions for the entire parish to receive kneeling at the rails by Candlemas (2 February 1638): *ibid.*

[176]The Rise family of Northampton, Woodford's creditors, were descended from the Richard Rise who occurred at musters in 1591. Elizabeth was perhaps the mother of the brothers – Richard, Harry, and Edward – who ran foul of the law in 1638: J. Wake (ed.),

I rec[eive]d of Grey 6s p[ro] allocac[ion] 3 sup[ersedea]s[e]s[177] p[ro]
Mr Cooke goodman Iblethy[178] desired money of me.
14° Nov. 1637
I went to day to Sr Richard Samwells beinge Com[missione]r wth
him to take a fine of Job Walker et al. & had 3s for my paynes I blesse
the Lord.
Longstrap is againe taken.
Mr Maior[179] sent for me to night, about preparing the Sess[ions]
p[ro]cess.
I [crossed out: have] find it a worke to steere up against my wants but
Lord I will trust in thee though thou kill me I will lye at thy dore for
thou art the most bountifull houskeep, in thy good time pay my debts
& helpe me for the Lords sake Amen. John Loe came wth a bill for
money but I could not pay him. Oh Lord shew me thy arme for I
desire to stay my selfe uppon thy p[ro]vidence.
15° Nov.
greatly affected this morninge in readinge in the family 24 Gen.[esis]
to behold gods gracious p[ro]vidence to

to Abraham & his godly servant & to Isaac &. Oh Lord thou art still
the same, surely I will stay my selfe uppon thee, & wth thy helpe I will
cheerfully wayt for thee.
somewhat subiect to melancholy & the thorny cares of the world
oh Lord [crossed out: send] give me a greater measure of fayth &
cheerfullnes for the Lords sake.
16 Nov. 1637
I prayed and went to grafton [Regis] Court, havinge but 9d not
knowinge whether I should get any thinge or not, but the Lord in
m[er]cye p[ro]vided there for me about 5s or more. Mr Nicolls was
there & Mr Butler absent.
Mr Tompkins[180] it seemes preached here at the Lecture to day.

*A Copy of Papers Relating to Musters, Beacons, and Subsidies etc in the County of Northampton AD
1586–1623*, Publications of the Northamptonshire Record Society III (Kettering, 1926),
p. 36.
[177] A stay of legal proceedings.
[178] Christopher Iblehigh (who was formerly apprenticed to Isaac Greenough, tailor) occurs
as a sidesman of the parish in 1643. His wife occurs in the diary as a wet nurse: Freemen
of Northampton, unpaginated, under Greenough (dated 1623) and Iblehigh (dated 1632);
Vestry Minutes, p. 38.
[179] William Collis.
[180] Benjamin Tompkins (rector of Harpole, 1628–1670) had many godly connections,
including Sir Edmund Hampden and Sir Richard Samwell. In 1627 he had publicly
denounced the prerogative tax known as the forced loan: Longden, *Clergy*; TNA,
PROB/11/53 and PROB/11/23; Fielding, 'Peterborough', pp. 218, 261 n. 9.

I overtooke Goodman denton coming from London with the
p[ro]hibicon.
17° Nov. St hughs fare to day
somewhat subiect to melancholly & cares Lord helpe me; Mr Watts
here to day to whom I am indebted 120li besides the 25li & 19li & the
money which my father himselfe hath rec[eive]d of Mr Robins about
10li which 3 last sumes my father owes him.

Mr Watts tells me my white horse is dead. Lord enable me to beare
every losse & affliccon and to make a sanctified use of all & to pay my
debts for me for the Lords sake amen.
we were at Mr Rushworths to night.
Lord helpe me against my melancholy for the Lords sake
[*left margin: symbol of a hand with finger pointing at this line*] the Candle fell
uppon Sams face nere his eye, Lord be blessed that it burnt not his
eye.
a cutpurse taken to day.
18° Nov. 1637
I prayed though dully.
in great want of money to day.
Mrs Rushworth sent for 20s my wife borowed of her in my
absence and henry Goodere[181] came to whom I am indebted 20s
more
Su[182] went and got 20s of goodwife Iblethy oh Lord looke uppon my
Lowe estate for the Lords sake Amen.

19° Nov. 1637 Sab[bath]
I prayed and went to church and there the Churchwardens demanded
money of me for the poore forenoone & afternoone but I had not
[*crossed out: a farthinge*] any unlesse 2 farthings.

---

[181] Henry ('Harry') Goodere (d. 1660), Woodford's godly friend, was a Gray's Inn barrister
married to Elizabeth Wright of Brixworth but with Northampton friends including Hatton
Farmer and the Bott family. Perhaps originally from Baginton, Warwickshire, he settled at
Cransley, and served conscientiously as a justice of the peace from 1653: *VCH Warwickshire*,
VI (n.p., 1951), p. 23; TNA, PROB/11/301.
[182] Susan ('Sue') Tue was the Woodfords' servant and creditor.

one Mr Mayhoe[183] preached morninge & eveninge very well &
faythfully I blesse the Lord & I had some gracious comforts in hearinge
gods word great conflicts in my hart dayly about depending on god
for my outward condicon, Lord helpe me & susteyne & supply me for
the Lords sake.
Mr Ball is at Sinpston[184] wth his new wife.
goodman Emerson supped here.
20. Nov.
Court to day some supply I blesse the Lord yet ffr & L[185] have not payd
me h[enry] Goodere dyned with me here to day.
my wife & I supped at Mr Rushworths.
21° Nov.
I prayed and went along to Broughton to take the verdict of the jury,
h[enry] Goodere went alonge with me. It rayned almost all the way.
Mr Pentlowe gave me but 10s. Oh Lord I

thanke thee for any supply thou art pleased to afford me.
22° Nov. 1637
I lay somewhat too longe this morninge. I am much troubled with the
thorny cares of this world Lord helpe me from heaven Let me [have]
the comfort in thee a thousand fold which I want in the Creature for
the Lords sake Amen. my horse lookes very poore as if like to dye,
my wife & I much troubled in the thoughts of it & some Jarringe &
rash speeches betweene us, Lord p[ar]don [*crossed out:* & heale] our
sinnes & heale o[u]r natures, & give us faith to wayte uppon thee in
all estates for the Lords sake Amen.

[183] Mayo (Mayhoe, Maiho) was, according to Ramsden (whose information came from
Dr Clarke's curate, Christopher Young), Lord Saye and Sele's chaplain and a minister
whom the authorities had banned from public preaching. John Mayo (1598–1676) was a
Northamptonshire man who had matriculated from Magdalen Hall, Oxford, in 1615, but
had left without taking a degree. Ramsden claimed that on this occasion he preached at
Ball's invitation (who invited him back on 28 December) 'that it is utterly unlawfull to make
or have the picture of Christ his arguments I do not remember the scripture alledged but
mistaken though we have known Christ after the flesh yet henceforth know we him so
no more [2 Corinthians 5:16]' (TNA, SP16/474/80). Woodford heard him preach again in
London on 30 December 1638, after which he emigrated to New England and was ordained
a minister at Barnstaple, Massachusetts, in 1640, where he served as the assistant of John
Lothropp: S.H. Moore, *Pilgrims: New World settlers and the call of home* (London, 2007), p. 197;
R.L. Greaves, 'Lothropp, John (bap. 1584, d. 1653)', in *ODNB*.
[184] Ball's third marriage was to Jane Hatch, the widow of John Hatch (d. 1635), gentleman,
of Simpson, Buckinghamshire: J. Fielding, 'Ball, Thomas (1590–1659)', in *ODNB*; TNA,
PROB/11/169.
[185] 'ffr' is probably James Fryers; 'L' might be John Loe or Thomas Lamport.

Lord continue the beast still to be serviceable to me if it be thy will, & keepe me from such a losse I humbly pray thee.

23° Nov. 1637
up to day presently after 4 a clock [above: trefoil symbol], & subiect I am to melancholy & the thorny cares of the world [margin: trefoil symbol], but I remember a Christian is called to reioycinge, & a good conscience is a continuall feast, and a Christian in the lowest & worst estate and condition is in farre better case, then a man out of Christ in his greatest wealth and Jollity, and hath more true cause of cheerfullnesse. I have prayed unto the Lord to helpe me against my infidelity and melancholly, to give me the use of my graces for I am not able to stirre them up my selfe, Lord endue me with strength from on high, what a wretch am I to be so long in learninge this lesson to live by fayth in regard of outward things, & to be contented in the want of them truly Lord I have a proud & carnall hart Lord pardon & heale inable me to dep[ar]t from every sinne & exorbitancye to denye my selfe, to walke cheerfully & wisely to live by fayth and trust perfectly in thee, and in thy due time I beseech thee supply me payinge my debts for me & p[ro]vidinge for me & mine if it be thy will according to thy p[ro]misses wherein I have desired to trust let all be in m[er]cye for the Lords sake.

Mr Ball preached at the lecture.
Wilby men are still in the spirituall Court[186] & here to day, Lord resine them if it be thy will.
William Spicer came to me at night to offer me his house to buy if I please, but I well knew my disability & therefore did uppon the matter put him off. Oh Lord I pray thee in thy due time provide a house for me thou hast all in thy hand & thou art exceeding gracious & mercifull In thee will I trust p[ar]don my infidelity & want of dependance uppon thee my god for the Lords sake.
24° Nov. 1637
some comforts in gods ordinances this morning I blesse the Lord, yet my prayers have longe wanted that fayth & fervency they have formerly bene offred up with beinge kept downe with the thorny cares of this world, & distraction of businesses
*****

---

[186]This was follow-up action by Bishop Dee's commissioners in the wake of the church survey. At Wilby, the responsible churchwarden was Robert Ragdale, and defects included a failure to rail the communion table, curate Ainsworth's preaching unlicensed, and individuals (including Perne and Pentlow) with seats that were too high: PDR, Church Survey Book 5, fo. 134.

[*margin, next to first word: trefoil symbol*] But Lord p[ar]don all my sinnes & faylings give me fayth & Cherefullnes, & give me favor in the eyes of Mr Watts & my other Creditors, & in thy due time pay my debts for me, and if thou helpe me out of my lowe estate, oh Let me walke humbly before thee make me very thankfull, & helpefull to those in the like want; oh Lord my god though I see no meanes of helpe, yet I will beleive & trust in thy gracious p[ro]vidence, & in thy sure p[ro]misses, thou hast said verily I shall be fed, hast p[ro]missed never to fayle me nor forsake me; Thou hast bene my god hitherto & hast raysed me from the dunghill, I will surely trust in thee for time to come, Lord graunt that I may follow my callinge with diligence & conscience, & may goe away & be no more sad seeminge I have prayed unto thee, and Lord blesse me & my whole family in soule body name basket & store[187] & to thy glory & our owne eternall comfort for the Lords sake
my wife somewhat ill to night I prayed for her

I went downe to Mr Balls in the eveninge and as I was goeinge I prayed for grace & wisdome in his eyes.
25° Nov. [*trefoil symbol*]
Oh my god stretch the wings of thy sure p[ro]teccon over me and my family this day give us this day our dayly bread & forgive us our trespasses that are past & lead us not into temptacon for time to come, oh Lord I pray thee carry me through the occasions of this day in such a manner that I may be freed from distractinge thoughts at night, and let me behold thy good p[ro]vidence this day towards me & mine for the Lords sake Amen.
I have but 2 groats left, Lord supply me I pray thee for the Lords sake. 7 a clock in the morning some sweete comfort in private prayer this morning I blesse the Lord, & some confidence the Lord will p[ro]vide for me, & he brought it into my hart

in prayer that as he had given me a mouth to eat so he had given me a mouth to pray, oh Lord thou art a god that hearest prayers, it is not in vayne to seeke thee, graunt that I may patiently repose my selfe uppon thee for the Lords sake Amen.

[187]Deuteronomy 28:5.

A note of the debts I now owe

To Mr Watts uppon my bond_____		100li
To him for 20li I receaved of Mr Robins_____	X	20li
To William Turland[188] _____	X	20li
to goodwife Chapman of Old[189] _____	X	10li
to Mr Gregg_____	X	5li
to Mr dillingham[190] about_____		4li
to old Mr Martin_____	X	5
to my mother Woodford about _____	X	6li
to Su Tue_____	X	5li
to reckon to Mr Some for_____	X	6li

besides some debts here in the towne about 3li to goodman Iblethy about 30s to Mr heyes[191] about 40s to Mr Curwyn about 3li 10 or more to Mr Crick for rent & all about 10s to goodman Lamporte[192] to

---

[188]A townsman and clearly regarded by Woodford as godly, Turland was perhaps related to Thomas Turland, a Northampton joiner employed in repairing the church in 1634, who witnessed the will of Woodford's friend Richard Trueman, and who occurred in town politics in 1640: Diary, p. 227; Vestry Minutes, p. 31; NRO Finch (Hatton) MSS, F(H)3501.

[189]Frances Chapman (d. 1650) was the widow of Thomas Chapman of Old, who witnessed the will of Woodford's father in 1636, and was the trustee (with Woodford senior) appointed in 1620 by Woodford's kinsman John Ragdale to support his children. Frances was lending money to Woodford at a rate of interest of 8 per cent: PDR, Archdeaconry of Northampton Wills, second series, P104, C168; *ibid.*, third series, A71; J. Wake (ed.), *The Montagu Musters Book 1602–1623*, Publications of the Northamptonshire Record Society VII (Northampton, 1935), p. 7; Diary, pp. 256–257.

[190]John Dillingham was a Northamptonshire tailor related to William Dillingham, rector of Cranford St John (d. 1621), and Thomas Dillingham, rector of All Saints', Barnwell, 1618–1640, and St Andrew's, Barnwell, 1639–1647. Both were connected to the circle of moderate godly clergymen centred on Edward, Lord Montagu of Boughton, and occasionally served in the Church courts. John moved to London, from where he wrote newsletters to Montagu about foreign (and probably also Scottish) affairs. Dillingham was forced to flee to Paris after Archbishop Laud received information that he was sheltering a Scottish knight (possibly Johnston of Wariston: Diary, p. 378) as part of a puritan conspiracy of Scottish and English malcontents to force the calling of Parliament. By 30 November 1640 he was back in London, and by 1643 edited the *Parliament Scout* newspaper, wherein he allied himself with the Parliamentary 'middle group' organized by Montagu's nephew Edward Montagu, second Earl of Manchester, Oliver St John, and others: J. Raymond, 'Dillingham, John (*fl.* 1639–1649)', in *ODNB*; A.N.B. Cotton, 'John Dillingham: journalist of the "middle group"', *English Historical Review*, 369 (1978), pp. 817–834; E.S. Cope, *The Life of a Public Man: Edward, first Baron Montagu of Boughton, 1562–1644* (Philadelphia, 1981), pp. 157–158, 168–169, 184–185, 197; Longden, *Clergy*; Longden MS, 11 June 1617, 24 February 1618, and 16 January 1639.

[191]Robert Heyes (Hayes, Heighes), shoemaker, occurs in the parish records in 1628 and 1632 and went on to serve as bailiff of the town in 1634. Woodford refers to him as cousin, so he must have been one of Hannah Woodford's Heighes relations: Vestry Minutes, pp. 21, 29; Markham and Cox, *Northampton*, II, p. 562; TNA, PROB/11/209 and PROB/11/274.

[192]Thomas Lamport, haberdasher, wrote his will in 1649. He was doubtless related to Richard Lamport, who died in 1654 at the reputed age of 129 years: PDR, Archdeaconry of Northampton Wills, third series, B243; Top MS, p. 107.

h[enry] Goodere 20s. [*last 2 lines and this line bracketed, with the comment:* p[ai]d]
Oh my god Looke uppon me in m[er]cye, I confesse indeed I have not cared for runninge in debt to thee by

[*left margin: trefoil symbol*] by dayly strivinge against thee, & therefore it is iust with thee I should Runne in debt to men, I confesse I have bene proud & profuse & therefore this burden is iustly uppon me, I confesse I have not bene diligent in my callinge, and therefore I am iustly poore, I confesse I doe not beleive and therefore it may be iust with god that I should not be established. But Lord looke uppon me in m[er]cye p[ar]don all my sinnes & faylings, & yet send me helpe if it be thy will relieve me I beseech thee, Lord thou hast all in thy hand and thou art my father, and I am in want I know thou hast a thousand wayes in thy blessed p[ro]vidence to bringe succor to me by surety my eyes shall be towards thee & turned away from the Creature, oh Lord graunt that my debts may waste away this ensueing yeare, & graunt us more plenty I humbly pray thee if thou seest good for the Lords sake Amen. very bare of money to day yet the Lord in m[er]cye supplyed, for as I rem.[ember] once to day not had never a pennye, & then before the pudd

puddings came from Mrs Harvey,[193] I receaved a litle money & was able to give 6d to the messenger, & had a litle to buy mutton, & purposed to be without beefe in the house if no other remedy, yet before night the lord in m[er]cye sent me some more money to buy beefe too, but then I was brought lowe againe, & I know not how to pay the poore to morow then in the eveninge the Lord in m[er]cye sent me more so that I had about 3s or more; Lord be blessed for all thy goodnesse, It is inough that thou feedest me from hand to mouth, even me and mine could I live the life of fayth (which I beseech thee graunt) I might find more comfort in this condicon, haveinge more exp[er]ience of thy m[er]cye dayly then if I had great abundance in my owne keepinge; the Lord will be gracious to me in my debts, Lord deale with me as thou pleasest I am thine, give me fayth contentation & cheerfullnes for the Lords sake

I sent a scroll of my debts to Mr Watts to him to day & showed in it which were my debts & which were my fathers.
Ramsden came to speak with me.

---

[193] Possibly Mary Harvey, the widow of William Harvey of Weston Favell, and the mother of Francis Harvey the barrister: TNA, PROB/11/165.

26. Nov. 1637 Sab.[bath]

Mr hall[194] of Paulerspury preached in the morning & Mr Ball in the afternoone

some comforts in holy dutyes I blesse the Lord; Mr hall & Mr Shepheard were here, & we had much discourse of new England.

Mrs Rushworth supped here with us.

Ramsden the sup[er]stitious fellow came to me to borrow dr Ames his catechisem,[195] oh Lord sanctify it unto him.

27° Nov. Court to day.

I got but litle there; Mr Maior[196] seemes not much to favor me in my fees, oh Lord give me favor before him if it be thy will, & teach me to carry my selfe

selfe in every respect as it becometh a xxian for the Lords sake.

I was at goodman Gibsons[197] after dinner and at Mr ffishers who gave me his will to alter.

Mr Crick sent to borrow 10s of me but I feared I had not enough did not lend it.

28° Nov. 1637

I have prayed in secret with some fayth & hope this morninge I blesse the Lord now Lord blesse & direct me this whole day for the Lords sake Amen.

some gracious affecons in private prayer with my wife and after very much affected in readinge the 32 and 33 chapters of Genesis in the family, to behold gods wonderfull m[er]cye to Jacob: & Jacobs fayth & prayer & & greatly affected in publiq prayer in the family. Ah Lord how sweete thou art thy pr[e]sence is glorious & exceedingly delightfull, all earthly things yea the heighth of pompe or heapes of riches & are but dung & drosse in comp[ar]ison of things spirituall. Lord give me fayth in thee for the Lords sake.

*****

---

[194] Henry Hall was the schoolmaster of Paulerspury: D.K. Shearing, 'A study of the educational developments in the Diocese of Peterborough, 1561–1700' (unpublished MPhil thesis, University of Nottingham, 1982), p. 339.

[195] Woodford was clearly sceptical that Ramsden would derive any benefit from reading the catechism written by the godly divine William Ames, which was dedicated to the sons of Lady Vere and was entitled *Chief heads of divinitie [. . .] in forme of catechising* (Dordrecht, 1612): K.L. Sprunger, 'Ames, William (1576–1633)', in *ODNB*; I. Green, *The Christian's ABC: catechisms and catechizing in England c. 1530–1740*, (Oxford, 1996), p. 219.

[196] William Collis.

[197] Thomas Gibson (fl. 1624–1640): Vestry Minutes, p. 35.

Tho. Lamport came to me for the hire of his horse to London & Charleton,[198] so I payd him 10s blessed be thy name oh Lord for the paym[en]te of that debt; oh Lord still p[ro]vide for me I pray thee till thou supply me againe,

another prisoner came into the Gaole to day one holman[199] a Caurrier for pickinge ones pocket, oh Lord give him repentance & sorrow of hart & fayth to turne unto thee for the Lords sake.

some comforts in prayer at night & in duty I blesse the Lord.

29° Novemb. 1637

[crossed out: oh Lord I pray] a very comfortable Dreame to night wherein I did reioyce in the Lord in spirit with much fayth & dependance on a p[ro]mise as if the Lord was about to p[er]forme it to me.

Oh Lord I pray thee blesse me this day & keep [margin: trefoil symbol] me goe with me to Wellingborow & returne againe with me never fayle me or forsake

me, shew me thy gracious p[ro]vidence this day if it be thy will, & blesse my deare wife my sweete Children & whole family keep us in thy feare under thy p[ro]tection, let us not by sinne bereave our selves of thy good p[ro]vidence & blessing and Lord I pray thee in thy due time pay my debts for me I hinge uppon thee for I have no other helpe in all the world, (thou art better then all the helpes in the world blessed be thy name) and Lord make me diligent in my callinge give me more practise & more abilityes for it, & money to follow it if it be thy will for the Lords sake Amen.

I went towards Wellingborow about 11 a clock and came safe thether I blesse the Lord; I sent 12d in beefe to my Aunt Joane, I met there with my mother & Aunt Mr Pentlow Mr Marriot[200] &

I heare at Wellingborow that his Ma[jes]ty hath bene sick, & hath resolved uppon a Parliam[en]t; oh Lord pr[e]serve him in life & keep him from all conspiracyes & seeinge he is a kinge of so many prayers from his godly subiects, frame his hart for thee, that he may spread thy gospel & estab

*****

---

[198]This refers to his servant, Hatton's, trip to Charwelton on 24 October 1637 and the outward leg of Woodford's trip to London on 26 October, since on 10 November 1637 he states that he was returning on John Cox's horse.

[199]John Holman: Diary, p. 150.

[200]Possibly Nicholas Marriot, who was a member of the grand jury in 1630: Pettit, *Royal Forests*, p. 76; J. Wake, *Quarter Sessions Records of the County of Northampton [. . .] 1630, 1657–1658*, Publications of the Northamptonshire Record Society I (Hereford, 1924), p. 87.

establish it amongst us that he may take away the high places even all Idolatry & sup[er]stition out of the land, and move his hart to call a p[ar]liam[en]t, which (beinge directed by thee) may conclude uppon wholesome lawes for the Kingdome, & may redresse exorbitancyes Lord heare & helpe for the Lord xt his sake

yester [*crossed out:* day] night men were mett cominge from Leicester & one of them Robbed & almost slayne and to night I heare another was met by Robbers & escaped from them hardly but I came home safe I blesse the Lord some comforts with my wife in private prayer & by my selfe in secret.

30° Nov. 1637
Oh Lord keep & blesse me & mine for the Lords sake Amen.
I am troubled about 20s owinge to Goodman Iblethy which Su borrowed, Lord p[ro]vide it for me & graunt

graunt they may not send till we have it I have had great experience of thy m[er]cye in my lowe estate blessed be thy name.
Mr Ball preached to day a preparatory sermon to the doctrine of Justificacon by fayth which he meanes to handle next.
Nan Spicer swooned to night, & my wife called so hastily that I feared she was much affright & was ill afterwards.

1 decembr. 1637
some comforts in private & wth my wife & family.
I was in the afternoone with Mr Rushworth & at the Church.

2° decembr.
some comforts in duty to day I blesse the Lord, and the Lord hath wonderfully supplyed

supplyed me this day, so that I have p[ai]d goodwife Emerson 6s p[ro] John & 6d besides & p[ai]d the 20s to goodwife Iblethy, & bought some meate for to morow, blessed be thy name oh Lord, oh how gracious is the Lord.
But now we have not one penny left in the house of money to spend or lay out (except onely the 11s²⁰¹ which we are to keepe & a few single pence I think). But Lord the exp[er]ience of this day is so fresh that it doth encourage us to trust in thee; Lord helpe us.
Mr Watts advises me to sell at Old & buy at duston Lord direct me for the best for the Lords sake Lord be blessed for the Love & favor of Mr Watts to me.
Lord pr[e]pare us for a blessed Sabbath to morow.

²⁰¹ Undoubtedly the eleven-shilling 'Edward peece' that Woodford was forced to spend on 23 December 1637.

Nurse hes[202] here to night John beinge not very well we feare, Lord keepe him in health for the Lords sake Amen.

[*left margin: trefoil symbol*] 3° dec. 1637. Sab.[bath]
Oh Lord enable me & my house to sanctifye this thy Sabath, not speakinge our owne words thinkinge o[u]r owne thoughts or findinge o[u]r owne pleasure on this thy day; Lord keep out of our harts all thorny and worldly cares; all contrivances for worldly things. Let thy spirit descend into o[u]r soules thy word enlighten us thy love inflame us thy promises stay us and comfort us; helpe us to p[ar]take of every ordinance of the day in a holy & a right manner with fayth & sincerity of hart for the Lords sake.

Mr Bullivant preached in the morninge very p[ro]fitably blessed be the Lord out of 37 ps[alm] 5 commit thy way unto the Lord trust also in him & he will bringe it to passe [*left margin: trefoil symbol*] oh Lord why should I doubt thou art to a christian what he beleives thee to be, oh Lord I beleive helpe my unbeleife surely thou will p[ar]don my sinne and sanctifye my nature more & more, surely thou wilt feed me and cloath me & supply me and my family, I remember thy m[er]cye and blessed p[ro]vidence to Abraham Isaac and Jacob to david to Joseph to Nehemiah to Mordecai hester to thy people in Egipt to poore Ruth &. Oh Lord thou wilt feed

feed me with food convenient for me blessed be thy name; Lord give me more fayth more humility a larger hart to doe good, give me contentacon & the feare of thy name forever
Mr hall preached p[ro]fitably in p[os]t merid[iem] 2 pet[er] ult[imo] [capitulo] & ult[imo] [verso][203] grow in grace & the signes of grace begun 1 poverty of sp[iri]t & sight of wants 2 sence of them with sorrow & greife 3 hungringe & thirstinge after grace[204] 4 constancy in holy dutyes 5 a combat betweene the flesh & the spirit.
In the time of morninge sermon one Mr fflexney[205] a prisoner at Mr Ben[oni] Coldwells for debt got away.
I wanted money for the poore when Mr ffarren the churchwarden demanded it, Mr Ball is at Sinpston.[206]

[202]Perhaps Heyes (Heighes).
[203]2 Peter 3:18.
[204]Matthew 5:6.
[205]William Flaxney occurs in the records in 1656: Markham and Cox, *Northampton*, II, p. 457.
[206]Simpson, Buckinghamshire.

4° dec. 1637
Court to day a very small one Lord supply me for the Lords sake
amen.
I am now goeinge to duston to inquire if my Lord of Warrick[207] sells
there, intendinge if I can meet wth a purchase to advantage my selfe
to sell at Old and buy there; oh Lord thou seest & knowest all things
knowest what will be best, I humbly cast my burden & busines

busines uppon thee, oh my god order every thinge for the best I humbly
pray thee & blesse me in whatever I undertake, I humbly commit my
way unto thee, & desire to trust in thee therefore I beseech thee bring
it to passe if thou seest good ps[alm] 37.5 even for the Lords sake in
whose name & worthinesse I begg every m[er]cye fit for me.
Mr Coles[208] to whom I went was not as home but I met with him
afterward here in the towne, but can understand litle from him but
that diverse are earnest to buy, oh Lord I desire to looke alone to thy
p[ro]vidence.
5° dec. 1637
some comforts in dutye I blesse the Lord & some Contentacon.
I [crossed out: went] was afterward with Mr Judkin[209] Mr Martin Mr
Joseph Sargent & Mr Humphrey, we stayed at wheelowes[210] his at Road

[207] Robert Rich, second Earl of Warwick, was one of the leaders of moderate opposition to
the crown from the 1620s until the Civil War: B. Coward, *The Stuart Age: England 1603-1714*
(London, 2003), pp. 164, 177, 181, 190; S. Kelsey, 'Rich, Robert, second earl of Warwick
(1587-1658)', *ODNB*.
[208] George Coles was a wealthy member of the urban gentry, with lands in Huntingdonshire
and Lincolnshire as well as Northamptonshire. His brother Roger and his wife, Susan, had
in 1636 resisted taking communion kneeling at the altar rails at Samuel Clarke's parish of St
Peter. Coles was connected to several Northampton lawyers: his daughter married Francis
Cook, an attorney from Kingsthorpe; Richard Lane, the recorder, was called upon to
oversee his will, which was witnessed by William Rushton, the future steward, and Matthew
Sillesby, the godly scrivener. Coles's lasting legacy is detailed in a table of benefactions dated
1719, in which it is stated that he had conveyed lands to trustees for charitable uses for
the benefit of the poor. Alms were to be distributed (and a sermon preached) on the first
Thursday after the Purification of the Virgin Mary (2 February): NPL MSS, 420; Markham
and Cox, *Northampton*, II, pp. 363-364; TNA, PROB/11/185.
[209] Thomas Judkin, tanner, was chamberlain of the town from 1635 until 1637 and Joseph
Sargent in 1637. Judkin and his father of the same name were active godly townsmen with
many contacts: Freemen of Northampton, unpaginated, dated 1625; Markham and Cox,
Northampton, II, pp. 551-552, 567-568; Vestry Minutes, pp. 21-34; PDR, Archdeaconry of
Northampton Wills, second series, O34; Sheils, *Puritans*, p. 83.
[210] In 1612, William Wheelowes of Hardingstone had accused (in the Court of Star
Chamber) Edward Mercer, Mayor of Northampton and farmer of the rectory of
Hardingstone, and George and Tobias Coldwell of conspiring to accuse him of the rape of
Margaret Evans: TNA, STAC8/305/9, 10; PDR, CBA20, fo. 207v.

Lane end[211] to meete Mr Ball & his wife but we came away & they overtooke us at Wootton houses; they tooke it kindly; Lord give me favor in

in their eyes if it be thy will.
I spent the 6d that I had in stayinge for them & Mr Rushworth did accidentally lend me halfe a crowne at night, oh Lord I blesse thee for thy p[ro]vidence, goodwife Emerson had 6d of it to night for washinge.
6° dec. 1637
I went not to Wellingboro to day, but in the afternoone I went to see Mrs Lane[212] at Kingesthorpe, where I had kind entertaynemt Lord I pray thee give us favor in their eyes, and bringe about somethinge in thy good p[ro]vidence for the payinge my debts and supplyeinge my necessityes for the Lords sake.
I got nothinge this day but the Lord in m[er]cye lengthens out the oyle & the meale which will through gods m[er]cye extend to another supply; I have now 3d & my wife about 12d Sam not very well Lord heale him for the Lords sake I prayed for him as I went to Kingsthorpe.

7° dec. 1637
I prayed. and am now goeinge to keepe Grafton [Regis] Court 3 weekes Court Lord I pray thee goe with me & p[re]serve me & shew me thy p[ro]vidence for the Lord Xt his sake Amen. I carried but one 3d with me yet the Lord so supplyed me that though I laid out uppon my selfe & horse about 2s, yet I brought along with me about 3s more blessed be thy name oh Lord.
I came alonge with a young man of Leic[ester] from Grafton [Regis].
8° dec. Lady day[213] ffare to day
[six lines crossed out, illegible except first one: somew[ha]t heavy for my wife & I are troubled] for

for time to come, and give us such a seed ((when in m[er]cye thou shalt add still to our family) as we may have cause to blesse thee: for even wth right shape & forme use of witts & & by thy helpe oh Lord we will [two lines crossed out, illegible] for the Lords sake here us thy poore servants Amen.

---

[211]The end of the lane leading from the village of Roade to that of Hardingstone, just south of Northampton.
[212]Margaret Lane (aunt to the poet Thomas Randolph) was married to Richard Lane, Recorder of Northampton and attorney to the Prince of Wales. Randolph dedicated a work to Richard Lane in 1632: D.A. Orr, 'Lane, Sir Richard (bap. 1584, d. 1650)', in *ODNB*; Prest, *Barristers*, pp. 374–375.
[213]The feast of the Conception of the Virgin Mary.

I rec[eive]d of Mr Eakins²¹⁴ to day to Mr Marriots use 4li 14s in full
of the execucon of 5li. I heare that Cap[tain] Bernard hath imployed
Mr Cook in the busines betweene him & Mr Alex Eakins oh Lord I
desire to wayt uppon thy good p[ro]vidence in all my wayes doe me
good for the Lords sake.
I sent Mr Wyne 50s of Mr Marriots money p[ai]d Mr Marriot the rest
& he p[ai]d me for my paynes so we are even.
9° dec.
henry Parnell hath made even with me for the writt I have sent for for
him & ffery:²¹⁵ so we are now even.

Mr Bayleifes & I were this morninge at Mr Attorneyes²¹⁶ & dr Clarkes
to invite them to the Sess[ions] dinner on Wednesday next.
10° dec 1637 Sab.[bath]
Mr Newton preached in the morninge & Mr Ball in the after noone,
very soundly & p[ro]fitably blessed be the Lord.

---

²¹⁴John Eakins, an attorney living at Isham, had been prosecuted in the Court of High
Commission in 1634 (his co-defendant being the lord of the manor, John Pickering, the
father of Woodford's clerk, Thomas) by Robert Weldon, the conformist minister of Stoney
Stanton near Leicester. Weldon had accused him of the puritan practice of refusing hat
honour during the church service, profaning the communion table, and insulting the clergy.
Eakins had been found guilty by the court and fined, but the verdict was later overturned by
the Long Parliament, which stated that the commission had had no competence to try the
case. Eakins had also served as high constable for the Hundred of Higham Ferrers (in which
hundred lay his other estate, at Ringstead), thereby provoking the condemnation of Robert
Sibthorpe in 1636 during the Bacon ship money case. Sibthorpe derided him as one of
Sheriff Sir John Dryden's 'puritan high constables' (TNA, SP16/318/6) bent on sabotaging
the tax, and he was duly arrested by the Privy Council in 1637. The same year he was
named (with Thomas Pentlow) as the overseer of the will of the godly Thomas Freeman
of Cranford. In 1640 he was accused of canvassing for Sir Gilbert Pickering, the godly
candidate for knight of the shire in the Short Parliament. His will (dated 1652) was witnessed
by Robert Guy: *VCH Northamptonshire*, IV (London, 1937), p. 189; TNA, SP16/26, fos 15v,
23v, 39v, 86v, 90r–v, 93v–94v, 121r–v, 127v, 154r–v, 163v, 182v, 192r–v; Longden, *Clergy*; J.S.
Hart, *Justice upon Petition: the House of Lords and the reformation of justice 1621–1675* (London, 1991),
pp. 79–80, 101n; TNA, PROB/11/235; PDR, Archdeaconry of Northampton Wills, second
series, G211; Bodleian Library, Oxford, Bankes MSS, R6.64.18/5 A; TNA, PC 2/47/241;
TNA, PROB/11/355; Longden, *Clergy*.

²¹⁵(William?) Fery served as parish clerk in September 1640, although one Mr Johnston
is seen performing the function in the Diary on 24 March 1638/39. He was possibly the
same Farie of Gold Street who challenged Humphrey Ramsden for bowing on entering
church and who occurs (as Ffayery) in the Diary on 13 September 1640. His wife, Sarah,
died in 1638: J. Wake (ed.), *A Copy of Papers Relating to Musters, Beacons, and Subsidies etc in the
County of Northampton AD 1586–1623*, Publications of the Northamptonshire Record Society
III (Kettering, 1926), p. 155; TNA, SP16/468/76; TNA, SP16/474/80; NRO, 223P/1, All
Saints' burial register, April 1638.

²¹⁶That is, Richard Lane, attorney to Charles, Prince of Wales, and Recorder of
Northampton.

my wife was very ill this morninge, was not at Church in the morninge, I prayed unto the Lord in the behalfe of my deare wife; my wife was very ill at Mr Sargents at the baptizinge,[217] but now somewhat better blessed be the Lord I had some comfort at night in instructinge & examininge my family I blesse the Lord.

11° dec.

I prayed and went to the Court, where Mr Maior[218] continued his unkindnesse to me not stayinge till I had received my money of the Sargents at which

which I was much troubled, but Lord looke uppon me in m[er]cye give me yet grace & favor in his eyes if it be thy will, I can have small hope of it if I looke unto the disposicon of the man, but Lord I know & read but lately how thou didst turne the hart of Laban & Esau to Jacob, I know thy strength & thy m[er]cye is infinite, poore Will Botts[219] cause went ill to day contrary to the opinion of the Court; Lord I pray thee give all thy servants a sanctifyed use of all their troubles for the Lords sake.

my poore child John is very ill with a cold but I pray unto the lord in his behalfe, who is a god that heareth prayers.

12° dec. 1637

I prayed and went about the businesses of the Gaole d[e]l[ive]ry to morow & Sess.[ions]

I pray to be fitted for the inployment to morow the bells here are almost ready to ringe againe.

13° dec. 1637

I prayed and went to the Sessions,[220] where the Lord graciously enabled me.

the proffet of the Sess[ions] very small to day.

Mathew Longstrap for Burglary, & Thomas Nicollson for purse cuttinge were Condemned to day & one John holman burnt in the hand.

I prayed for the poore creatures to be cutt off by the hand of the lawe.

The bells first rang to day since they were new hanged.

---

[217] The baptism of Martha, daughter of Joseph Sargent, Chamberlain of Northampton: NRO, 223P/1, All Saints' baptismal register, 10 December 1637.

[218] William Collis.

[219] William Bott, a creditor whom Woodford regarded as godly, appears as a sidesman from 1641 until 1642. He and Henry ('Harry') Bott were related to Alderman John Bott, who had been mayor of the town in 1630. Ramsden reported William for receiving communion sitting. The case referred to must be Bott's suit against Clayton: Diary, p. 209; Markham and Cox, *Northampton*, II, p. 552; Vestry Minutes, pp. 36–38; TNA, SP16/468/76 and SP16/474/80.

[220] The sessions were for the town not the county.

14° dec.
I complayned to Mr Gifford to day of Mr Maiors[221] usage of me, who dislikes many of his carriages so he will speake to him uppon occasion. Oh Lord be blessed for that mans Love who is my very constant friend. Mr Pearne Mr Pentlow Mr Watts & ux & & diverse freinds here who were at the lecture to day.

15 dec. 1637
The Commission for Charitab[le] Uses to day at the Towne hall. The poore prisoners Longstrap & Nicollson executed to day at Wall back.[222] I rec[eive]d l[ette]rs from London wherein my father much complaynes for want of money, oh Lord supply us both of thine owne fullnes for the Lords sake.
16° dec.
I prayed and went to goodman harrison[223] & into the hog market to have bought a hog, but could not there meete with any so I came back & bought one of Mr Bradford[224] for 35s. Oh Lord be blessed for supplyinge us so graciously.
we killed the hog to night.
The Lord sent me some moneys to supply my necessityes blessed be thy name oh Lord.
The Churchwardens this day sent for before [crossed out: Mr] dr Clarke & & there inioyned to rayle in & fix the table at the East end of the Channcell; but they both refused and answered him boldly, blessed be the Lord oh Lord give them courage & the confidence of fayth & wisdome for the Lords sake.

[221]William Collis.
[222]Henry Lee confirms that an area known as 'Wall Bank' was used for hangings when noting the execution of Leonard Bland in 1651. This probably refers to a stream called the Wallbeck (or Walbeck) which runs through Kingsthorpe Hollow to the north of Northampton on the border of the town lands and Kingsthorpe parish, and which had been the site of a short-lived medieval leper hospital: Top MS, p. 107; Bridges, *History of Northamptonshire*, I, p. 413; *VCH Northamptonshire*, II (London, 1906), p. 162; *ibid.*, IV, p. 82; R.M. Serjeantson, 'The leper hospitals of Northampton', *Natural History Society and Field Club*, XVIII, no. 141 (1915); 'Archaeological sites and churches in Northampton', in Royal Commission of Historical Monuments of England, *An Inventory of the Historical Monuments in the County of Northampton* (London, 1985), V, p. 55.
[223]Robert Harrison, a freeman by 1640: NRO, Finch (Hatton) MSS, F(H) 3501.
[224]Bradford occurs in the vestry minutes in 1628 and is possibly the Thomas Bradford who was harried in the Church courts in 1615 by Robert Sibthorpe for a puritan attitude to the baptismal service. See also the town election for the Long Parliament: Vestry Minutes, p. 21; Fielding, 'Peterborough', p. 73; NRO, Finch (Hatton) MSS, F(H) 3501.

Mr ffarren & Mr Rushworth Churchwardens.[225]

17° dec. 1637 Sab.[bath]
Mr Newton preached in the morninge & Mr Ball at night.
litle John is very ill with a Cold in his lungs & head, but I and my deare
wife have besought the Lord for him with earnestnes & an answere of
peace blessed be thy name oh Lord for erectinge this office of peticons
that we may in all exigencyes put up our supplications in the name of
the Comon savior the Lord xt & receave helpe.
18° dec
I prayed both in pub[lic] private & secret & went to the Court, &
prayed to be d[e]l[ive]red from rash anger, so Mr Maior[226] did oppose
& but the Lord gave me some gracious moderation of spirit blessed
be thy name oh Lord.
The Churchwardens againe with dr Clarke & to day where they were
Taunted & but Lord encourage them.
Mr ffisher sealed and published his will to day in the p[rese]nce of
Mr Sam. Martin Nath. Sharpe & I[227] we supped at Mr Rushworths &
went downe afterward to Mr Balls.

19° dec. 1637
Mr Judkin & Mr Joseph Sargent[228] had of me this day the table of fees
which I suppose to be false in diverse places.
At the night my wife & I were much afflicted at Sues[229] sudden goeinge
away at our correctinge of Sam so I prayed in the distresse that the
Lord would order it for the best.
Oh Lord give us wisdome in o[u]r correction of o[u]r children &
in o[u]r carriage towards them & o[u]r servants for the Lords sake
Amen.
I was at Captayne Barnards to day but he was not at home.

[225] According to the Church court records, Rushworth and Farren appeared before Clarke
on 17 (not 16) December at the Hind Inn. The wardens having failed to comply with their
previous admonition made at the time of the church survey in October, Clarke ordered them
to rail the communion table where it now stood at the east end of the chancel and to call up
the communicants to receive kneeling there: they were given until the first court day after
Christmas to comply. In their petition of 1641 the churchwardens claimed (as Woodford
records here) to have defied Clarke boldly, stating that his demands were contrary to the
requirements of the Book of Common Prayer and the Canons of 1604: TNA, SP16/378/74
and SP16/474/80; HLRO, main papers, petition dated 6 February 1641.
[226] William Collis.
[227] Samuel Martin was the son of Woodford's close friend Thomas Martin: see Introduction,
p. 32. Nathaniel Sharpe was active in the vestry from 1624 until 1633: Vestry Minutes, pp. 15-
36; Markham and Cox, Northampton, II, pp. 52, 562, 568.
[228] The town's chamberlains (accountants): Markham and Cox, Northampton, II, p. 568.
[229] Susan Tue.

Mrs ffarmer hath wrote to intreat me to stay for the 10li for 6 moneths which I cannot doe,

20° dec.

I prayed and went to Cap[tain] Bernards & from there to Wellingborowe and returned safe I blesse the Lord, I came home p[ar]te of the way with Mr Cooke & his two sonnes.[230]

My litle sonne John is very well recovered blessed be thy name oh Lord for hearinge o[u]r poore prayers, oh Lord graunt that we may not sett our affections too much uppon him or any worldly thinge

thinge but graunt that we may Love the Creatures in thee & for thee, I met good Mr Pearne & my cousin cominge from North[amp]ton.

I have sent this day to Mrs ffarmer so shee hath wrote me word she will p[ro]vide it.

21° dec 1637

I prayed and went to church where I heard Mr Ball who preached p[ro]fitably blessed be thy name oh Lord.

I went after to dinner at Mr ffarrens where dyned Mr Maior the Bayleifes[231] & 48[232] or a great p[ar]te of them to eat the brace of does that came from the Lord of holland.

Mr Blomeley came over about the assurances from him to Mrs Pryor[233] we advised with Mr Bryan about them.

a great snow is fallen.

one Medbury a miller is lately found dead at his mill havinge slipped into the water there;

22° dec.

I prayed and rose early to dispatch the ffeoffm[en]t[234] for Mrs Pryor so in the afternoone I went downe

to the house in the South quarter with it where it was sealled and delivered.

---

[230] Cook's son was also called Francis. He married the daughter of Richard Lane. His other son may have been the attorney Tempest Cook: *VCH Northamptonshire*, IV, pp. 80–82.

[231] William Collis, Benoni Coldwell, and John Spicer.

[232] That is, the forty-eight burgesses who formed part of the ruling town assembly: Markham and Cox, *Northampton*, II, pp. 18–20.

[233] A John Blomeley was a beneficiary of the will of Sir Christopher Yelverton in 1654; another possibility is one of the brothers Thomas and Brian Blomeley of Easton Maudit, who were mentioned in a 1660 table of Northampton benefactions as donors to the poor. Mrs Pryor of Hardingstone might be related to John Pryor of All Saints' parish, who last occurs in the records in 1628: Diary, p. 216; TNA, PROB/11/217; Markham and Cox, *Northampton*, II, p. 361; Vestry Minutes, p. 21.

[234] A deed conveying property.

23° dec. 1637
I rose betimes & prayed in private & with my deare wife & then with
my family with some fayth & warmed affeccons (I blesse the Lord)
especially in prayinge & readinge with my family. This day in some
distresse for money, for none came from Captayne Bernard according
to his p[ro]misse; nor from Mrs ffarmer
so in the end I have chang'd the 11s Edward peece²³⁵ but Lord enable
me to redeeme it againe if it be thy will: old Mr Martin is troubled
that I bringe not the 5li for his chardges & Lord enable me to pay him
for the Lords sake if it be thy will, & p[ro]vide for me this vacaccon
time for the Lords sake, & for the tearme too I humbly pray & make
me very thankfull for ev[e]ry m[er]cye for the Lords sake.

24° dec.1637 Sab.[bath]
Mr Newton preached in the morninge & Mr Ball in the afternoone
p[ro]fitably.
a great snow & very sharpe weather.
25° dec. xxmas day.
Mr Ball preached very soundly in the morninge, shewinge that religion
onely to be true which had god for the author actor end & Rule, against
will worship sup[er]stition &.²³⁶
here dyned with me goodman Emerson & ux & his mother goodman
Smith & ux Ned Oakley & ux goodwife Nicolls & her daughter, who
were much refreshed by it, oh Lord I pray thee enable me still that I
may be able to give somethinge to those that are in want for the Lords
sake Amen.
somewhat distracted whether I should goe to Baggington to morow
with Mr Rushworth & Wm Bot, I desired the Lord to direct me.
in the afternoone I heard p[ar]te of a sermon from Mr Colson²³⁷ at
St Gyles, but litle in it there I saw a sup[er]stitious altar, Lord looke
uppon us in m[er]cye I borrowed 32s of Mr Sam. Martin.
*****

---

²³⁵The Woodfords had hoped to save this for a rainy day: Diary, p. 145. It was probably
an angel, a gold coin issued during the reign of Edward VI and by Woodford's time worth
eleven shillings.

²³⁶Ramsden's account of Ball's sermon was rather different: 'Mr Ball often uses very
homely comparisons on Xtmas day s[ai]d many did serve the King for their owne ends that
they may domineer in the countrey but gods children &.': TNA, SP16/474/80.

²³⁷Colson had, since at least 1637, been curate to Richard Holbrooke, the vicar of St
Giles's parish and a Church court official appointed to his living by Sir John Lambe. He
had probably been curate of St Sepulchre's under Richard Crompton, vicar from 1624 until
1639, another Lambe appointee and Church court operative: NRO 233P/107, unfoliated,
under the year 1637; Longden MS, 21 January 1624 and 7 June 1628; NRO 241P/42,
unfoliated, under the year 1634.

26° dec. 1637
I went not along with Mr Rushworth & Mr Bott I bought me [*crossed out:* s] a knife a box &. Lord make me exceedinge thrifty I humbly pray thee
my wife & I sent a breast of Mutton & dyned at Mr dan Readings.
I sent for my mother to day to wilby by Ned Oakley who is come safe I blesse the Lord.
27° dec.
I prayed in secret, & in private with my wife & in publiq & then we went to Mr Maiors[238] to dinner havinge prayed the Lord to direct everythinge in his p[ro]vidence & to give us confidence how to carry ourselves, so we had kind entertaynement to see to, & Love from Mr Ball & who were there. I was with Mr Sam. Martin at night, who was not very well.
28° dec.
Mr Ball preached here at the Lecture & Mr Maiho a very faythfull preacher in the afternoone[239] at

at night we had Jason Readinge an honest man to supper, my Masters brother, we were invited to night to Sr xxofer hattons to dinner to morow Oh Lord I blesse thee for the favor I find from that man & other freinds thou in thy mercifull p[ro]vidence hast raysed up for me give me still grace & favor in their eyes so farre as thou seest good for me for the Lords sake.
[*crossed out:* I pray]
29° dece 1637
I prayed in the morninge in secret, in private with my wife & with my family, and for direction & gods good p[ro]vidence for the day & and afterward I and my wife rode to the parke[240] to Sr xxofer hattons with Mr ffisher & his wife where we dyned with Mr Martin; Mr Cawdrey[241]

---

[238] William Collis.

[239] Ramsden gives this account of Mayo's attendance at Northampton on Holy Innocents' Day (28 December): 'he came agayne [he had preached at All Saints' on 19 November] in the forenoone did stand with his hat on all sermon tyme wt a light browne coat on scarcely like a clergie man and in thafter-noone preached on these words Grow in Grace was very vehement in his use of reprehension saying these ar [. . .] decaying tymes wherein many did oppose those who grow in grace but they must have fellowship one with another and fortifie theymselves against evill tymes': TNA, SP16/474/80.

[240] Hatton lived at Kirby Hall in the parish of Gretton, but this may refer to Moulton Park just north of Northampton. He had obtained a royal grant of this extra-parochial area, which contained two lodges, in 1634: *VCH Northamptonshire*, IV, p. 218.

[241] Daniel Cawdrey was the son of Robert Cawdrey, the author of the first English dictionary, and was a central figure in the Northampton godly community. Appointed rector of Little Billing in 1625, he delivered Sir Edmund Hampden's funeral oration in 1627. In the 1630s he publicly preached in criticism of Archbishop Laud at Kettering and evaded the altar

Mr Ball & ux, & had kind enterteynemt & came home safe I blesse
the Lord.

my wife went after to Goodwife Crutch[ley] who had sent for her to her
labor, & hath a girle which hath 2 litle ioynts or fingers extraordinary
comminge

comminge out of her litle fingers, which is some trouble to us & others
Oh Lord I prayse thee from the very botome of my hart that thou
hast bene so gracious as to bestowe right shape & forme uppon the
Children thou hast given to me, Lord continue thy m[er]cye still in
that kind to us we are not able to make one Joynt or one hayre thou
alone doest all, oh I beseech thee p[ar]don all o[u]r sinnes & faylings
& give us still matter of prayses to thee for thy goodnese for the Lords
sake Amen.

Mr Waters²⁴² hath left with me to [crossed out: day] night 4 Indent[ures]
& a booke to be shewed to the Comm[issione]rs for charit[able] uses.
My wife gave goodwife Crutch[ley] xiid.

30° dec. 1637

I prayed & went about my occasions though not with that dilligence
required.

Mr houghton²⁴³ & divers have bene with me to day but I can receave
no money.

I was compelled to borow 18s more of Mr Sam. Martin; & am
somewhat melancholly but Lord I will trust in thee forever I beseech
thee make good thy sure word to thy servant doe not fayle me

policy by removing the communion table from the rails during the eucharist. In July 1637 he
buoyed up the godly minister John Barker of Pytchley at his execution. Cawdrey also penned
condemnations of the Book of Sports and the altar policy, apologias for which were written
in the 1630s by John Pocklington, but Cawdrey claimed that he was unable to publish his
rebuttals until the 1640s: J. Fielding, 'Cawdrey, Daniel (1587/8–1664)', in *ODNB*.

²⁴² The brothers William and Thomas Waters, of Eastcote in the parish of Pattishall, were
godly attorneys. They had been summoned before the Privy Council in 1632 (William as
Constable of Towcester) at the behest of Lord Lieutenant William Cecil, Earl of Exeter, for
encouraging eight inhabitants of Towcester (including the mayor) to default over payment
of the muster rates and for disrupting the service by delaying payment to the deputy
lieutenants of the money they had received. In October 1636 William admitted pulling
down the churchyard cross at his parish of Pattishall, and both sided with the godly Miles
Burkit in his conflict with his fellow vicar, Richard Powell, a conformist. Both brothers
petitioned the Long Parliament on 21 January 1641 against the Privy Council's verdict in
favour of Powell: TNA, SP16/211/85; PDR, CBA63, fos 404r–v, 427r–v; J.S. Hart, *Justice
upon Petition: the House of Lords and the reformation of justice 1621–1675* (London, 1991), pp. 87–89;
Longden, *Visitation of Northamptonshire 1681*, p. 177.

²⁴³ Thomas Houghton served as an assessor for a church rate in All Saints' parish in 1627,
and by 1656 was serving as a night watchman: Vestry Minutes, pp. 19, 21; Markham and
Cox, *Northampton*, II, pp. 457–458.

nor forsake me for the Lords sake, but feed & cloath me & my
family &

& in thy due time pay my debts for me; hatton came from toucester
to day, & tells me his mother will send me money shortly. I have
sent a warrant by Kening to arrest vernam of Ashby at ffrancis
Perins[244] suite, we bought two couple of Turkyes, great cocks & a
hen [illegible word] all cost about 17s 6d or 18s, & sent the Cocks
to Mr Attourneyes & Sr xxofers[245] by Ned Oakley we have now no
money left in the house but 5d & I am somewhat troubled, but Lord
looke uppon us in m[er]cye & helpe us we desire to trust in thee,
pr[e]pare us for the Sabath & sacrament to morow for the Lords sake
Amen.
31° dec.1637 Sab.[bath] sacr.[ament][246]
somew[ha]t straightened of time this morninge lyeinge too long
somewhat dull in dutyes of the day Lord p[ar]don my deadnes for
the Lords sake.
The Churchwardens have brought downe the Com[mu]n;[ion]
Table to day from the Top & set it long wise in the body of
the Channcell,[247] blessed be thy name oh Lord for incourageinge
of them beare them out in it for the Lords sake if it be thy
will.
I was fayne to desire Mr ffarren to lay downe 9d for
******

[244]The messenger might be Nicholas Kenning of Kisslingbury; the Vernams are John and
Robert of Cold Ashby. Francis Perrin has not been identified, but there were members of
families bearing that name at the neighbouring parishes of Guilsborough, West Haddon,
and Cottesbrooke: PDR, Archdeaconry of Northampton Wills, second series, G217; HLRO,
main papers, 1641; J. Wake (ed.), *A Copy of Papers Relating to Musters, Beacons, and Subsidies etc in
the County of Northampton AD 1586–1623*, Publications of the Northamptonshire Record Society
III (Kettering, 1926), pp. 149–151; PDR, Visitation Book 8, unfoliated, under Cold Ashby.
[245]That is, Richard Lane and Sir Christopher Yelverton.
[246]Ramsden claimed that, at this communion, Ball administered to ten sitters, including
Joseph Sargent (draper), George Goodman, John Friend junior (barber, son of the sexton
of the same name, who had been accused during the 1637 survey of insulting Dr Clarke's
curate, Christopher Young), and John Hall (a sergeant). Newton reportedly administered to
another ten, including Thomas Pendleton and William Bott: TNA, SP16/474/80.
[247]On 16 December, the commissioners had ordered them to confirm their railing of the
table at the east end. Ramsden confirmed that it was the usual practice at All Saints', once
Clarke and Sibthorpe had created an altar there, to bring the table down from the east end
and set it tablewise (short ends pointing east to west) during the communion: *ibid*.

for me at the sacram[en]t; havinge but about 2d about me,

1° Januar 1637/38

I prayed & went to heare Mr Ball preach before I went I made a
Replevin[248] at the instance of John Powell[249] to the Constab[le] & of
Little Billing to replevin certayne Apparell & out of the hands of
Thomas Cowp[er][250] & had for that & the bond to the Sher.[iff][251] 2s
blessed be thy name oh Lord for the seasonable supply.

This day we heare young Mrs Morgan[252] is brought to bed of a sonne,
oh Lord I prayse thee for it that thou givest her comforts after so much
sorow wth so bad a husband Lord sanctify this m[er]cye to them all
for the Lords sake Amen.

to day here dyned with us 4 of my M[aste]rs Children Mr dan.
R.[eading] ch[ildre]n & ffr[ancis] Rushworth & Mrs Crick & Wm his
wife beinge sick.[253]

2° Jan 1637/38

I prayed and went to Sr xxofer[254] yelvertons alone & came thether
before dinner, where was great variety of dayntyes & much good
company Mr Cawdrey, Mr Cranford[255] &

---

[248] A person's recovery of goods wrongfully distrained from him.

[249] Later in the year the Privy Council, incensed at the poor progress of Sheriff Sir John
Hanbury's efforts to collect ship money, censured him and committed him to the custody
of Powell, royal sergeant-at-arms, who then escorted him about his official business until 10
September, when an appeal to the Earl of Manchester, Lord Privy Seal, set in train events
leading to his release: Jackson, 'Ship money', pp. 115, 147.

[250] There was a Thomas Cowper living in Northampton itself. His father had written to
Robert Cecil in 1605 to protect Robert Catelin, the godly minister of All Saints', from
deprivation for nonconformity. Cowper junior had been mayor in 1621 and, with Woodford
and Lawrence Ball, acted as overseer of the will of his fellow godly ironmonger, John Loe, in
1641: Sheils, *Puritans*, p. 83; Markham and Cox, *Northampton*, II, p. 552; TNA, PROB/11/189;
PDR, Archdeaconry of Northampton Wills, third series, B243; Vestry Minutes, p. 21.

[251] The reluctant ship money sheriff, Sir John Hanbury.

[252] Deborah Morgan née Gregory (d. 1681) was married to Thomas Morgan of
Kingsthorpe. Their son was Francis Morgan (1638–1705), who grew up to be a bencher of
the Middle Temple: Longden, *Visitation of Northamptonshire 1681*, pp. 135–136; Isham, *Diary*,
p. 140n.

[253] William Spicer, whose wife, Ann, had swooned on 30 November.

[254] Christopher.

[255] James Cranford had been presented to the living of Brockhall in 1627 by John Thornton
(who, like his neighbours the Knightleys and Drydens, supported the puritan divine John
Dod). Cranford was also connected to the Yelvertons: in 1641 he was to dedicate a sermon
to Sir Christopher's wife, Ann (née Twisden). According to Humphrey Ramsden, Cranford
had preached at the lecture on Ascension Day (14 May) 1637 to a gate of 800 as confidently
as if he had been in New England. Ramsden's most likely source of information (he did
not yet reside in the town) was Christopher Young, Dr Clarke's curate at St Peter's parish.
Ramsden claimed (all quotations are from TNA, SP16/474/80) that Cranford preached
against Laudian fasting ('The kingdom of heaven stands not in meate & drink but in

It was late ere I came out & I was very fearefull as I came home but I prayed & when I was come past litle Billinge & it began to be darke that I doubted of finding the way then I overtooke two on horseback cominge to North[amp]ton & came with them very safe I blesse the Lord but I was much p[er]plext with the Cares of the world as I came here supped with us George Allome & Nell.

daniel Simons[256] marryed to day.

3° Jan

This morninge I am much afflicted with the cares of the world considering my great debts & my small ones, havinge now but 2. twopences in the house & about to goe to Mr Rushworths where I shall meet with Mr ffarren whom I desired to lay downe 9d for me on the Sab.[bath] day.

& seeinge my great store of stuff for my horse & fuell much impayred to wonderment, my base hart

[left margin: trefoil symbol] hart is almost overcome with mellancholly & the cares of the world, oh Lord what shall I say I am the vilest & the proudest wretch that ever lived that cannot contentedly submitt unto thee, nay Its a shame that I cannot depend uppon thee after so many p[ro]mises made to me from thy selfe & warnings given to take heed of these cares, & exp[er]iences of many seasonable supplyes & of the strength of thy mighty arme I beseech thee oh I beseech thee Looke uppon me in m[er]cye, if it be thy gracious will helpe me to pay my debts, if not I pray thee give me Contentacon in this my condicon Lord I wayte uppon thee heare me for the Lords sake Amen.

righteousnes where speaking his pleasure concerning fasting, this comforts, saith he, those who are so much for Ceremonyes', who forced these rites on 'godly ministers for wch they are content to loose their liveings & libertyes'); altars ('Theres now such cringing before the altar as though they had god pent up in a narrow roome whom heaven and earth be not able to containe'); the use of candles ('as though he wanted light who gives light to the sun, moone and starrs'); bowing at the mention of Jesus; the use of singing and organs ('such pr[o]phaning and singing in the church & that organs ar but as childrens calls'); holy churches ('Some attribut too much holynesse to the church but know that a prayer in thy closet thy chamber doore being shut is as acceptable to god as in a church. God is not tyed to places: there is noe holynesse there but in the tyme of p[er]forming holy dutyes no more than there is in consecrated bread that remains after communion'); and bodily worship of god ('God regards not bodily worship sith he is a spirit we must worship him in spirit. The very heathens could say deus est animus. To ye king indeed we may doe reverence because he is visible, but to do so to god invisible hath a show of Idolatrie'): Longden MS, 25 October 1627; TNA, PROB/11/147; Fielding, 'Peterborough', pp. 17–18, 23; Longden, Clergy.

[256]Simons had obtained his freedom of the borough in 1635, after apprenticeship to William Collis, mercer; he served as a sidesman in 1639, and a watchman in 1656: Freemen of Northampton, under 1635; Vestry Minutes, p. 34; Markham and Cox, Northampton, II, pp. 456–459.

I have sent up & downe & am got no money & Mr Watts[257] hath bene
with me for 20li for Mr Balls quarteridge & I have it not; oh Lord give
me fayth & contentacon whatever thou witholdest for the Lords sake
Amen.

4° Jan 1637/38
I prayed and went to church to heare Mr Ball at the lecture.
after sermon Mrs ffarmers 10li came so shee & I are now even, blessed
be god for this supply.

[crossed out: we] I and my wife went afterwards to Mr Bryans to dinner
where dyned with us Mr Bullivant & ux Mr Rushworth & ux Mr
Tempest Cooke[258] & & had kind enterteynement; I went afterward &
payd Mr Martin the 5li he looked for, for his expences in his Journey
to London & in the busines betweene me & Mr Pilk[ington][259] so he
& I are even blessed be god, Lord helpe me still in m[er]cye for the
Lords sake Amen.
we were invited to have bene at Captain Barnards to day at dinner.
ffuller[260] brought his couple of Capons to day.
Mr Pendleton the Shoemaker[261] his sonne dyed this eveninge.

---

[257]At a meeting of the town assembly in 1629 during the mayoralty of Woodford's friend
John Gifford, it had been decided to provide St Thomas's house as a rent-free dwelling
for Thomas Ball, together with an annual salary of £80 (for the maintenance of him and
a curate), and £20 for reading a lecture. This was to be paid quarterly at the time of the
meeting of the town assembly. Lawrence Watts seems to have received this quarterage for
Ball, judging from the entry for 6 January 1637/38 (Epiphany), when Woodford paid Ball
via Watts on behalf of the corporation: Book of Orders, pp. 3, 9.

[258]The attorney Tempest Cook (possibly the son of the attorney Francis Cook of
Kingsthorpe) had obtained the freedom of the borough in 1631 and later witnessed the
will of Sir William Willmer of Sywell, a Royalist, in 1646. He served as town clerk, 1654–
1657: Freemen of Northampton, unpaginated, dated 1631; TNA, PROB/11/198; Markham
and Cox, Northampton, II, p. 570.

[259]Thomas Pilkington, London merchant and former Undersheriff of Northamptonshire,
was Woodford's defeated rival for the post of steward. He had died in 1637 but Woodford and
Martin were still clearly involved in concluding Pilkington's legal challenge to Woodford's
position. Pilkington's brother William was the vicar of Dodford, where he quarrelled with
his conformist patron, Sir Arthur Throckmorton. The beneficiaries of Thomas Pilkington's
will included Matthew Sillesby and Peter Farren: Markham and Cox, Northampton, II, p. 117;
Longden MS, 13 May 1625; A.L. Rowse, Raleigh and the Throckmortons (London, 1962), pp. 280,
289; NPL MSS, 420, 1581; PDR, Archdeaconry of Northampton Wills, second series, L120;
PDR, CBA55, fo. 195; Metcalfe, Visitation of Northamptonshire 1618, p. 129.

[260]Woodford's tenant, mentioned below on 20 September 1638.

[261]Thomas Pendleton served as bailiff of the town in 1628, chamberlain from 1642 until
1644, and mayor in 1648. He served as a churchwarden from 1634 until 1635, when he
reported the parish's failure to carry out Bishop Dee's altar policy. Ramsden mentions him
as a nonconformist who received communion sitting from Newton and failed to do hat
honour during the sacrament of baptism on 3, 10, and 17 September 1637. He was the
leader of Northampton's embryonic shoe industry, which was to receive its initial stimulus

5° Jan 1637/38
I prayed and went to the vestry, where there was grannted another
assessment of 100li to the Churchwardens.[262] Lord enable me to pay
my p[ar]te I was very much afflicted to day with worldly [*left margin:
trefoil symbol*] cares but did strive [*crossed out:* ag] and pray & labor to
beleive against them, I doe much blame my selfe & am greived that I
should be such a wretch as not to depend uppon god with cheerfullnes
for p[ro]vision of those outward things I have remembred how easye
it is for the Lord to

to p[ro]vide for me, oh Lord the time was when I had lesse hope of
heaven, then of those things yet thou hast in m[er]cye bestowed the
Lord Christ the Cheife of all favors uppon me & hast made the bones
which thou hadst once broken to reioyne againe,[263] and I am sure thou
takest notice of my estate & condicon of debt & wants, Lord helpe me
(if it be thy will) for thou art all-sufficient & what ever thou bestowest
graunt that it may be in m[er]cye in answere to my poore prayers
& in p[er]formance of thy gracious p[ro]mises & graunt that I may
behold thy arme & p[ro]vidence in it that so my hart may be filled
with thy prayses all the day longe & my tongue may delight to talke of
thy wonders but however blessed father I beseech thee sanctifye unto
me this my necessitous condicon & put out of my soule these thornye
Cares for the Lords sake.
after I had dyned here I went over to Captayne Barnards, where they
were at

at dinner when I came & had the musiqh of daventry,[264] my poore soule
in the hearinge of it was lifted up above it to consider of heaven & of
that great God who hath put this into the harts of men. Mr Bullivant
was here & one Mr dyer &.

in 1642, when Parliament placed an order worth £1,000 for boots and shoes to equip its
army to suppress the Irish rebellion. By 1648 Parliament had authorized the sale of the lands
of the catholic recusant and delinquent William Baude of Walgrave to pay the bill, but in
1651 Pendleton and others told a committee that £208 was outstanding: Vestry Minutes,
pp. 21–34; Markham and Cox, *Northampton*, II, pp. 551–552; TNA, SP16/474/80; TNA,
SP23/108, p. 113.
    [262]This sum was additional to the £50 assigned in August 1637 towards recasting and
hanging the bells of All Saints': Vestry Minutes, pp. 33–34.
    [263]Based on Psalm 51:8.
    [264]As a corporation Daventry employed waits – professional musicians – to play on official
occasions, but the local gentry also paid them to play privately, as John Bernard did here
(and as Sir Justinian Isham did in 1671). The Brackley waits became embroiled in a dispute
between Sibthorpe and his puritan neighbours in 1639. For the Northampton waits (who
had previously been employed by the Spencers of Althorp), see Diary, p. 380; Isham, *Diary*,
p. 72, n. 25; Temple of Stowe MSS, STT 1880, 28 April 1639.

The Lord brought me safe home though it was somew[ha]t darke I blesse the Lord.

p[rese]ntly after Wm Spicer come to me with his bill of 5li so I p[ai]d him 3li of it & p[rese]ntly after that Mr Sam. Martin sent to me for the 50s I owe him but I could spare but 20s at which I was somew[ha]t troubled, Lord help me in thy due time for the Lords sake Amen. I went & spoke with Mr Martin who is willinge to stay for all his money till next weeke, oh Lord enable me to pay it then for the Lords sake Amen.

6° Januar 1637/38 Twelfth day.

I prayed, & went after to Mr Whalleys,[265] & had some cheerfullnes (I blesse the Lord) to goe about my businesse; I was afterwards with Mr Rushworth Mr Sam. Martin & one Mr Phips &.

Joseph Easton[266] sent his couple of Capons to day

day. I p[ai]d Mr L[awrence] Watts 20li to day for Mr Balls quarteridge at Rob Sillesbyes shop.

Oh Lord I beseech thee helpe me & my father who are both of us in great distresse by reason of debt, for the Lords sake susteyne & comfort us, & ease us in thy due time o god who art exceedinge mercifull & all-sufficient.

Oh Lord pr[e]pare me for thy Sab[bath] for the Lords sake Amen.

7° Januar 1637/38 Sab.[bath]

Oh Lord I pray thee pr[e]pare me for thy blessed ordinances this day graunt that thy spirit may come along wth thy word that so every grace may be increased every sinne decayed every affeccon inflamed and

---

[265]Peter Whalley (1605-1656), a stationer trading in Northampton and Coventry, had been identified by the Privy Council in March 1634 as having sold copies of *Histriomastix* (1632), Prynne's attack on stage plays. Whalley married Hannah Cartwright (1605-1675) and counted John Spicer and the curate William Holmes among his intimates. He served as chamberlain of the town from 1640 until 1643, mayor twice, and MP for the borough in the first Protectorate Parliament. His funeral sermon was preached by the moderate Laudian Edward Reynolds, who dedicated its later publication to John Crewe. Referring back to the 1630s, Reynolds wrote of him: 'he was as is said of Mnason Acts 21: 16 an old disciple a Professor of Religion in the worst times when piety was nicknamed preciseness and he that departed from evil made himself a prey Isaiah 59:15': *Deaths Advantage Preached Last Summer (1656) at Northampton at the Funeral of Peter Whalley the Mayor* (London, 1657), p. 26. Whalley was the progenitor of a dynasty of clergymen and of a historian of the county: R.B. McKerrow (ed.), *A Dictionary of Printers and Booksellers in England and Ireland and of Foreign Printers of English Books 1557-1640* (London, 1910), p. 287; S.R. Gardiner (ed.), *Documents Relating to the Proceedings against William Prynne in 1634 and 1637*, Camden Society, new series, 18 (London, 1877), pp. 58-60; Vestry Minutes, pp. 19-35, 36, 38; Markham and Cox, *Northampton*, II, pp. 441, 551-552, 561-562, 568; Isham, *Diary*, p. 200, n. 24; G. Ford, 'Where's Whalley? The search for Sir Samuel uncovers a Whalley-Cartwright alliance in Northamptonshire', *Northamptonshire Past and Present*, 62 (2009), pp. 31-44.

[266]Easton was Woodford's tenant at Old: Diary, pp. 192, 259.

rightly placed put wind into my sayles this day for the Lords sake and
I beseech thee for his sake also rebuke the melancholly & alienacon of
mind caused in me through distractinge newes & other troubles and
helpe me against unbeleife for the Lords sake.

A stranger one Mr Percivall[267] preached both times very honestly &
p[ro]fitably blessed be the Lord, and I was graciously affected in
dutye I prayse the Lord, greatly enlarged in publiq prayer in the
family & in private, & had power over my worldly Cares I blesse the
Lord.

8° Januar. 1637/38
I prayed and went to the Court which afforded me some supply I
prayse the Lord.
after dinner I p[ai]d Mr hayes 4s p[ro] 2 payre of shoes for my mother
& my wife, beside whats due to him uppon the bill.
my wife & I went to Kingsthorpe to Mrs Morgans wth Mrs dan
Readinge[268] as I went I overtooke Mr Mottershedd[269] who threatens
to have Mr Gifford & me in the Starr=chamber & to [crossed out: un]
unsteward me because Mr Gifford committed him for miscarriage
in the Court when he was Maior & me for drawinge an Inditement
against him about it at the Last Sessions, oh Lord I beseech thee
deliver me from the malice of this man for the Lords sake.
My mother went home to day to Wilby, with Ned Oakley
*****

---

[267]John Percival occurs as the curate of Abthorpe from 1630, when he was presented to
the Church court for stating that the parson, Hugh Alloway, had preached on Christmas
Day 'and spoke of a greyhound of Edward Parsons eating pie meat' (PDR, CB1, fo. 310r).
At the 1637 visitation it was reported that Percival was not a graduate: PDR, X639–642/8,
unfoliated, under Abthorpe; PDR, Church Survey Book 5, fo. 37v.

[268]Mary, the sister of Francis Harvey of Weston Favell (1611–1703), a Middle Temple
barrister and MP for Northampton from 1656 to 1660: Foster; Metcalfe, *Visitation of
Northampton 1618*, pp. 98–99.

[269]Richard Mottershed, attorney, was from a recusant family living at Kingsthorpe and
descended from John Mottershed, the Elizabethan diocesan registrar. Several Mottersheds
served as notaries public in the Church courts, and later members of the dynasty included
Thomas, registrar of the Court of High Commission, and his son Edward, another civil
lawyer and key follower of Richard Neile, Archbishop of York. Thomas was one of
Sibthorpe's allies who signed the certificate of good character for Plowright during the
Burton Latimer ship money dispute. In partnership with Sir John Lambe's factotum in the
courts, Richard Stockwell, Richard Mottershed had in 1628 presented the conformist royal
chaplain Robert Skinner to the living of Pitsford, which he had relinquished only in 1636
when promoted to the bishopric of Bristol: PDR, Instance Book 14, *passim*; PDR, CB40,
fo. 46r; PDR, CB56A, fo. 334; PDR, CB55, fo. 83; *VCH Northamptonshire*, IV, pp. 82–83; B.
Levack, *The Civil Lawyers of England* (Oxford, 1973), p. 257; Sheils, *Puritans*, p. 6; Longden
MS, 22 May 1628; Longden, *Clergy*; Fielding, 'Peterborough', p. 38; TNA, SP16/409/2i.

9° Januar 1637/38
I prayed in private & in the family & went to Oagles[270] house to reckon with Crutchley[271] where was Mr Coldwell Mr Pendleton &. The Sessions are this day at Ketteringe.[272] I was at Mr Balls to night, but he was forth at Oxford, I had good discourse with Mr Rogers who seemes to loath vayne Ceremonies.

10. Jan 1637/38
I prayed & went to Wellingborowe where I spent 1s but got nothinge. Oh Lord I pray thee increase my practise & graunt me abilityes for it. I p[ai]d Nurse 7s this morninge for 6 weeks past. This day I heare that Sr henry Robinson is dead who was a great rich man & a usurer; Non domus & fundus non aeris &[273]
I [crossed out: ha] was incouraginge my selfe in goeinge a longe to wayte uppon god still by fayth & to labor to keepe close unto him, & I remembred what god said to david when he had sinned god sent [crossed out: Ill] the p[ro]phet to him to enumerate

[left margin: trefoil symbol] the m[er]cyes god had bestowed on him, & withall that if they had not bene inough he would have done thus &

---

[270]John Oagles and his son Thomas occur in the records from 1636 until the 1640s: Book of Orders, p. 75; Freemen of Northampton, under Thomas Oagles (dated 1636).
[271]Thomas Crutchley, who, with his wife, Elizabeth was part of Woodford's godly circle, was one of the town's sergeants. He proved the will of the godly saddler Richard Trueman: TNA, SP16/468/76; Cox and Markham, Northampton, II, p. 49; PDR, Archdeaconry of Northampton Wills, second series, G100.
[272]Traditionally, all quarter sessions meetings had been held in Northampton, in the west of the county, until, in 1624, the custos rotulorum, Sir Francis Fane (later Earl of Westmorland), had summoned them to Kettering, nearer to his dwelling in the east. The eastern gentry, led by Lord Montagu, agreed with this removal but resented the actions of Fane, who was regarded as a parvenu. The Privy Council's compromise was that Kettering would thenceforth be host only to one of the meetings, Northampton to the other three. Fane duly held the sessions at Kettering in January 1626 and in 1629 built a new sessions house at his own expense; his son Mildmay Fane continued the policy when he succeeded as custos. Clearly this compromise was operating in the 1630s, with the January meeting still being the one held at Kettering (see also Diary, p. 275): E.S. Cope, The Life of a Public Man: Edward, first Baron Montagu of Boughton, 1562–1644 (Philadelphia, 1981), pp. 104, 109–111, 135, 171; F.W.M. Bull, A Sketch of the History of the Town of Kettering Together with Some Account of its Worthies (Kettering, 1891), p. 16.
[273]This dismissal of Robinson is puzzling, as he seems to have enjoyed a godly pedigree: connected by friendship or kinship to the godly Downes and Tanfield families (as well as to Sir Robert Rich), he supported his local minister, Leonard Pattinson, formerly a leader of the Elizabethan classis at Kettering. During his shrievalty in 1629 Robert Bolton preached the assize sermon, which was later published by Edward Bagshaw. In his will, Robinson expressed no doubts that Christ's merits alone had assured him of the salvation prepared for 'the elect Saints and servants of God': TNA, PROB/11/176; Sheils, Puritans, pp. 41, 54, 97; Bridges, History of Northamptonshire, p.164; Bolton, Two Sermons Preached at Northampton at Two Severall Assizes There (London, 1635), title page.

thus for him,[274] & I receaved much comfort and thought how the Lord had alreadye bestowed many m[er]cyes uppon me, and surely now he sees me in want againe, he hath a thus & thus for me in his due time to supply me. Oh Lord I beleive helpe my unbeleife, & grant that from the pinchinge wants of outward things which I feele I may consider my spirituall wants & weaknesses & be more humbled for them for the Lords sake Amen. I was wth Mr Eakins & Mr Prat[275] at Wellingborow I came home in due time & safe I blesse the Lord notwithstandinge the frostines & slipperynesse of the way.

I was at old Mr Martins at night wth Mr Rushworth & Mr Sam. Martin

11° Jan. 1637/38

Mr Wilkins[276] preached at the lecture to day very p[ro]fitably (I blesse the Lord) uppon pr[e]paracon for p[er]secucon.

I heard afterward Mr S. Martin had bene here & we feared it was for the 50s wch I

I owe him, but I went to him & find him willinge to spare me it a while longer blessed be the Lord; so we had good discourse at his house & he came afterward home with me.

[left margin: symbol of a hand with finger pointing at this line] 12° Jan 1637/38 poore Sam. hath bene very ill this morning with vomitinge &.

so I prayed unto the Lord that gave me him at the first & the Lord hath in m[er]cye given me him againe for he is suddenly recovered blessed be thy name oh Lord.

more occasions of trouble in regard of the things of this life; for Mrs Crick hath bene with me for 34s I owe her, & goodman Lowe hath sent his bill for about 7s which I owe him & I have it not, & my father hath wrote me a very pittifull letter of the straights which he is in in

---

[274]2 Samuel 12:8.

[275]This is possibly Thomas Pratt (junior) of Mears Ashby who served as a sidesman for his parish in 1637 and whose wife, Isabel, had been accused in 1634 of gadding to Wilby, where Andrew Perne was the incumbent: PDR, Church Survey Book 5, fo. 135r–v; PDR, CBA63, fo. 192r–v. Woodford clearly regarded the Mrs Pratt he mentions on 20 and 21 February 1637/38 as godly.

[276]John Wilkins was born in the house of his maternal grandfather, the godly divine John Dod, and, like his grandfather, was a protégé of the Knightley family (on 2 June 1637 Richard Knightley had presented him to his vicarage at Fawsley). Wilkins was also chaplain to their friend Viscount Saye and Sele. Saye and Knightley were among the parliamentary visitors who installed Wilkins as Warden of Wadham College, Oxford. He went on to marry Oliver Cromwell's sister Robina in 1656, and became both President of the Royal Society and a bishop after the Restoration: J. Henry, 'Wilkins, John (1614–1672)', in *ODNB*; Fielding, 'Peterborough', p. 17.

regard of debts, oh Lord I beseech thee looke uppon us in m[er]cye thou art able to ease us in thy due time doe it for the Lords sake &

& [*left margin: trefoil symbol*] in the meane while deliver us from our feares, from arrests & & give us to live by fayth & to goe with cheerfullnes & dilligence about our callings.

we are to have our lovinge freinds Mr Sam Martin & Mr Rushworth & their wives to supper with us to night, oh Lord give us comfort in o[u]r meetinge graunt that we may be cheerfull in the confidence of fayth & direct us to good & wholsome discourse that we may be bettered by it for the Lords sake Amen. Mr Parker[277] was here with me to day.

The Churchwardens are to appeare at the sp[iritual] Court to day.

The Churchwardens decreed to be excommunicate[278] to day for bringinge downe the Comm[uni]on table, to day.

we had comforts in o[u]r freinds at supper to night blessed be the Lord.

13° Jan 1637/38

somewhat distracted with worldly cares to day yet the Lord hath in great m[er]cye releived me

& sent me some supply I blesse thy name oh Lord for this m[er]cye. Mr ffisher & goodman Odell[279] chosen arbitrat[ors] to day betweene Perin & the Vernams have by their award put an end to all controversy betweene them to this time, Vernam hath p[ai]d him 36s in full of all debts & chardges & I have d[e]l[ive]r[e]d to goodman Odell both Peryns bonds by direction to be cancelled

I have p[ai]d goodman Loe his bill of 7s 6d[280]

I prayd in the morninge wth my wife amongst other things about the Churchwardens I heare this afternoone they are delivered & have liberty to bringe downe the table at the administracon,[281] blessed be thy name oh Lord.

---

[277] John Parker of Northampton was called to the bar between 1639 and 1642 as a member of Gray's Inn. A Parliamentarian and active justice of the peace during the 1640s, he was a serjeant-at-law at his death in 1668: P.R. Brindle, 'Politics and society in Northamptonshire, 1649–1714' (unpublished PhD thesis, University of Leicester, 1983), p. 135; Prest, *Barristers*, p. 275, n. 98; TNA, PROB/11/326.

[278] Farren and Rushworth again appeared before Clarke on this day at the Hind. Since they had failed to rail in the table altarwise at the east end (and had in fact brought the table down into the chancel and placed it tablewise during the communion), they were excommunicated: TNA, SP16/378/74.

[279] Probably the father of Woodford's servant, Richard.

[280] For the fire iron (see later in the same entry), as John Loe was an ironmonger.

[281] There is no mention of this victory in the Church court records and, indeed, by 28 January the wardens' excommunication had been published.

goodman Clarke brought us the Iron to hang before the fire,
I have written this day to Mr Watts Thomas Warren[282] my brother Mr
Weston & my father, oh Lord pr[e]pare me [crossed out: f] & my family
for thy Sabath approachinge for the Lords sake Amen

14° Jan. 1637/38 Sab.[bath]
worldly cares were ready to possesse my soule in the morninge so
soone as I awaked but I brought the word of the Lord against them
& they did not much pr[e]vayle I blesse the Lord, I banished them by
remembring the Sabath.
some blessed assistance in the dutyes of the day especially [crossed out:
espec] in publiq at night I prayse the Lord. Mr Newton preached in
the morninge, Mr Ball in the afternoone.
15° Januar.
greatly afflicted this morninge with thorny cares [left margin: trefoil
symbol] they seized uppon me very much, with much melancholly
& sweatinge, but out of the depths I have called unto the Lord the
deliverer who hath oft delivered and yet I trust will deliver oh Lord
helpe my unbeleife for the Lords sake truly Lord I can see no helpe
from an arme of flesh but it seemes to me that I am this last yeare
runne 50 or 60li in debt more then I was before & what Lord shall I
then doe oh how weighty is this affliccon, Lord I desire to

to submit unto it I beseech thee that I may doe it with Cherefullnes, I
desire to cast this burden uppon thee Lord susteyne me, & stay up the
hart of me and my deare wife & fit us for our callings for the Lords
sake. I prayse the Lord I had some enlargement in dutye with my
deare wife, & in secret by my selfe, oh Lord helpe as thou hast done
for the Lords sake.
16 Jan 1637/38 [raised script: Mach[in] Cousin heyes]
I observe gods good p[ro]vidence to me this day in bringing Mr
Machin[283] to me [crossed out: this day] who brought me a busines wherby
I gayned 3s 4d and in enablinge to pay Mr heyes this day.

17° Januar 1637/38
I prayed and went to Wellingborowe where goodman Tompson
resisted the man that would have distreyned him for the shipmoney
oh Lord ease us of this great & heavy taxe if it be thy will and graunt
that the whole kingdome may live in p[er]fect peace & unity in thy
feare seekinge the p[ro]motion of thy glorious gospell and graunt us

---

[282] For the Warrens of Old, see Diary, p. 226, n. 482.
[283] Possibly Edward Machen, a Middle Temple barrister: Prest, Barristers, p. 336.

yet to see p[ar]liaments that may conclude on those things that may be for the glory of thy name & the happinesse of the Kingdome for the Lords sake.

18° Januar 1637/38

I prayed in my family and went with Mr Sam. Martin henry Allen & Mr Rushworth to Coventry and the Lord pr[e]served us graciously in the Journey kept us safe notwithstandinge the dangerous Joye Lane beyond Wi[lle]n[h]all which we went through when it was somewhat darke, & in other places. when we came to Coventry we durst scarce inquire of Mr Ball[284] least we should heare he was dead, but we found him at farre more ease then form[er]ly & we had all much comfort

oh Lord goe on still with the Cure to a p[er]fect recovery if it be thy will to the glory of thy great name & the comfort of those that doe depend uppon him.

Mr Martin & I lodged together, he prayed at night very graciously.

19° Januar 1637/38

I prayed in the morninge with warmed affeccons & much fayth I blesse the Lord.

we were after at Mr Sheriffe Snells[285] but I saw no Relig[ion] there we came after to trinity Church where we heard a sermon the man bowed at the name of Jesus. Mr Martin & h[enry] Allen went for North[amp]ton about 3 a clock in post merid[iem], but I went alonge wth henry Goodere to Baggington to his father in lawes Mr Wales where I found kind enterteynement

20° Januar 1637/38

harry Goodere & I came out in the morninge about 5 a clock, he came alonge with me to Killesby[286] & then turned back, after I was p[ar]ted from him I had very gracious comforts, & did much accuse my selfe in the pr[e]sence of god for my infidelitye & did beseech earnestly of the Lord an increase of fayth & other graces, oh Lord heare me for the Lords sake

p[rese]ntly after I met wth a young man comminge to North[amp]ton who surely is gracious, so we spoke about Communion tables & bowinge &.

---

[284] Brian Ball made his will in January 1638. An apothecary, he chose Samuel Snell to act as a trustee: Lichfield Record Office, D/C/11.

[285] Samuel Snell was added to Coventry's council in 1644 and replaced a Royalist alderman in 1651: Coventry City Record Office, A 14 (a, b), Council Minute Books 1557–1696, A14 (b), fo. 99v. I am grateful to Richard Cust and Ann Hughes for this reference.

[286] Kilsby.

The Lord brought me home safe betweene 11 & 12 a clock, blessed be thy name oh Lord.

21° Januar 1637/38 Sab[bath]

Mr Clarke of ffaxton[287] preached here morninge & eveninge very p[ro]fitably & boldly I blesse the Lord. Lord strengthen him still to stand for thee & for thy truth for the Lords sake Amen.

dr Clarke hath sent forth a sentence of excommunicacon ag[ains]t the Churchwardens here, which is not yet published

22° Januar. 1637/38

Court to day where I found Mr Maior[288] more favourable to me to day then I expected. Oh Lord continue it & increase it still if it be thy mercifull will for the Lords sake Amen. This day I have bene married 3 yeares, blessed be thy name oh Lord for the m[er]cy thou hast shewed me since, Lord blesse me & my whole famyly & Continue our lives still if it be thy will to thy glory & our comfort for the Lords sake goodman Iblethy & ux supped [*crossed out:* at Abington] here to night

23 I prayed and went to Abington to Capt Bernard where I dyned, I had much dispute with Mr W[illia]m Barnard[289] about Arminianisme, oh Lord setle him in thy truth.

Capt Barnard p[ai]d me the Bill of the last tearme for the p[ro]hibicon. I came home from Mr Bullivants with Mr ffarren & the ffarryer.

24° Januar.

I prayed and went to Wellingborowe where I met with some practise I blesse the Lord, from Rob. Worlidge.[290] And Mr Cox of [Mears] Ashby[291] hath incouraged me to get the Court Baron for hamforde

*****

[287] Faxton chapel was attached to the rectory of Lamport, where Sir John Isham's protégé, the Church court official William Noke, was the incumbent. The anonymous *A Certificate from Northamptonshire. Touching pluralities. Defect of maintenance. Of not preaching. Of poor ministers* (London, 1641) claimed (p. 7) that Isham impoverished the living by retaining the tithes, resulting in incumbents who were of a poor standard and did not preach. Francis Nicolls of Hardwick owned the manor of Faxton and maintained William Clarke there, a godly minister who doubled as his household chaplain: Fielding, 'Peterborough', p. 26; *VCH Northamptonshire*, IV, p. 199; Longden MS, 22 November 1636; PDR, Archdeaconry of Northampton Wills, third series, A198.

[288] William Collis.

[289] William Bernard, John's brother, lived at Ecton: Diary, p. 122.

[290] Worlidge was a tenant of Thomas Bacon, squire of Burton Latimer: NRO, 55P/57, p. 69.

[291] Thomas Cox was a landowner from Mears Ashby and a reputed gadder to other parishes according to a presentment of 1633: J. Wake (ed.), *The Montagu Musters Book 1602–1623*, Publications of the Northamptonshire Record Society VII (Northampton, 1935), pp. 73, 146; PDR, Church Survey Book 5, fo. 135r–v; PDR, CBA63, fo. 19r–v.

shoe hundred, I pray unto the Lord about it I came home with an
honest man of Titchmarsh one heyes & we had much private discourse
with much affection I blesse the Lord. [*crossed out:* I & my wife should
have bene at Mr Benoni Coldwells at dinner had we bene at home]
25° Jan 1637/38
I prayed and went this morninge to keepe Grafton [Regis] Court,
where the Lord graciously supplyed me with above 5s cleer gayne
there, blessed be thy name oh Lord.
I came home with a servant of the Lady Cranes [*crossed out:* I dyned
with] we should have dyned at Bayleife Coldwells to day had I bene
at home.
26. Jan
I prayed and went to Olney, lost my way in the forest neare olney but
came hether safe I blesse the Lord, where I receaved of John James[292]
9s in p[ar]te of paym[en]t p[ro] writts & a Lease makinge, he owes
me still of the old reckoninge 6s 8d, & imployed me further I blesse
the Lord, and I had much p[ro]fitable

p[ro]fitable meditacon in my Journey as I went along I prayse the
Lord.
I came afterward to Easton [Maudit] where I found kind
enterteynement from Mr Allen & Mr Watts, and Mr Watts hath given
me much encouragem[en]t, to wayt uppon god, by Informinge me
how he was indebted when he first marryed in 200li & yet god inabled
him to pay it in a matter of 2 yeares oh Lord make me able to beare
this burden & ease me of it in thy due time for the Lords sake Amen.
Mr Eccleston gave me 11s for writinge out the bounds of the fforest
for him the Lord be praysed.

---

[292]John James of Earl's Barton had been prosecuted by Drs Heath, Clarke, and Roane,
and by Henry Alleyn (a conformist ally of Sir John Lambe) for nonconformity to Laudian
ceremonial since 1632, and Woodford was clearly representing him. In 1641 James claimed
that Clarke had previously excommunicated him, despite his having compounded with
the court, and had thereafter, in 1634, promoted a suit against him in the Court of High
Commission. The case was referred to Lambe, who only released James when he had paid
£10 towards the repair of St Paul's and the fees of the Northampton court. Subsequently he
moved to Olney, Buckinghamshire, where Lambe again proceeded against him for gadding
to sermons and entered a caveat preventing him from appealing to the Courts of Arches and
Audience: this was perhaps the result of Laud's rumoured blocking of the appeals procedure
for cases originating in Northamptonshire, Buckinghamshire, and Bedfordshire (see Diary,
p. 382, n. 913). He was thus forced to conform to Laudian ceremonial, especially standing
at the *gloria patri*. He was later excommunicated for holding a conventicle in his house:
Fielding, 'Peterborough', p. 102; HLRO, main papers, James's petition, 9 February 1641;
J.S. Hart, *Justice upon Petition: the House of Lords and the reformation of justice 1621–1675* (London,
1991), pp. 77–78.

The Lord graciously pr[e]served me this day goeinge & cominge over Billing Bridge in the great water where I did not well know the way. [*illegible scribble*]

Mr Watts gave me 6li more for my fathers use which makes 60li to my father besides the 20li I have had over & above the 100li I owe him.

blessed be thy name oh Lord for this mans favor thou hast raysed him up to be an

Instrument of comfort & helpe to me blessed be thy name oh Lord.

27° Januar. 1637/38

I have p[ai]d Mr Chapman[293] 9s for the halfe yeares rent of the stable, & have bought wheate & beefe to day blessed be thy name oh Lord.

blessed comforts often times in dutyes I prayse the Lord with much dependance uppon god in my extremityes & exigents.

I had gracious enlargem[en]t in readinge & prayer this morninge I prayse the Lord.

28° Januar. Sab.[bath]

Mr Newton preached in the morninge & Mr Ball in the afternoone, the excomunicacon was published in thafternoone against Mr ffarren & Mr Rushworth the Churchwardens, Lord looke uppon the times & amend them for the Lords sake.

29° Januar 1637/38

Court to day where the Lord is still pleased to supply me graciously. this afternoone h[enry] Goodere came to towne & he & Mr Rushworth supped with me. I p[ai]d 3s 4d to Mr harberts[294] man for a payre of shoes formerly so he & I are even blessed be the Lord.

I have paid Mr Curwyn 2s res[i]d[ue] of the old reckoninge so he & I are even praysed be thy name oh Lord.

I was at Mr Mayors[295] to night who shewed himselfe very kind to me blessed be thy name oh Lord for hearinge my prayer in any measure.

---

[293] Richard Chapman was active in the vestry from 1622 until 1628: Vestry Minutes, pp. 15–25.

[294] John Harbert was active in the vestry from 1626 and in the corporation – he was mayor in 1629 when he presented Thomas Ball to All Saints': Vestry Minutes, pp. 18–25; Markham and Cox, *Northampton*, II, pp. 551–552.

[295] William Collis.

30 Januar.

I prayed and came forward [*crossed out:* to] towards London this morninge about 9 or 10 a clock with Mr Sea Mr Lambe[296] & h[enry] Goodere & came safe to Dunstable blessed be thy name oh Lord. before I came I payd Nurse all owthinge[297]

due to her [*crossed out:* till, from] to this time.

I left 12d wth my wife to pay Ned Oakley & money to buy hops & for the brewinge & about 5 or 6s to keep house with besides an arrer due from ffryers Lord supply my family graciously for the Lords sake Amen. I prayed at night with Mr Goodere.

31° Januar. 1637/38

Mr Goodere prayed wth me this morninge. we came safe to London I blesse the Lord about 3 a clock in thafternoone where I find my freinds well I prayse the Lord & met here with my uncle heyes & Mr Pyke[298] I pray for favor in their eyes if the Lord see fitt.

I heare that on Satteday last 2 of the Judges vizt Crawley & Weston[299] gave their opinions for the Kinge about the ship money.

1° ffebr.

I prayed and went to Westm[inster] hall where I met wth Sr xxofer[300] yelverton who showed

showed me much favor I prayse the Lord. In the afternoone I went to Mr Attourney[301] who hath p[ro]mised me a deputacon to keep the 3 weeks Court at hamfordshoe when he comes into the Country. blessed be thy name oh Lord & now Lord I beseech thee inable me for it every way and graunt that I may ayme at thy glory in all my accons graunt that I may never trouble my conscience by takinge any fee

---

[296]There are three candidates for the Mr Sea mentioned here: Francis Say of Great Doddington (who married Alexander Eakins's daughter Elizabeth), their son, Alexander (b. 1614), or Francis's brother Thomas, rector of Whiston. Lambe is probably Robert, rector of Cranford St John from 1629 until 1640: Metcalfe, *Visitation of Northamptonshire 1618*, pp. 134, 178; Longden, *Visitation of Northamptonshire 1681*, p. 43; Longden MS, 7 February 1629; PDR, Church Survey Book 5, fo. 130r–v.

[297]That which is owed.

[298]That is, Edmund Heighes of London, haberdasher, Hannah Woodford's uncle. Pyke has not been identified.

[299]Sir Francis Crawley and Sir Richard Weston. The other judges to declare for the king were Berkeley, Vernon, Trevor, Jones, and Finch. Croke, Hutton, Denham, Bramston, and Davenport declared for Hampden: C.S.R. Russell, 'The ship money judgements of Bramston and Davenport', *English Historical Review*, 77 (1962), pp. 312–318: Jones, *Bench*, pp. 139, 143.

[300]Christopher.

[301]Richard Lane, attorney general to Prince Charles: D.A. Orr, 'Lane, Sir Richard (bap. 1584, d. 1650)', in *ODNB*.

there or otherwhere that I shall doubt of, and blesse this small thing
unto me in thy p[ro]vidence I know if thou pleasest thou canst cause
[*left margin: trefoil symbol*] this small wheele to turne about a greater;
doe me good for the Lords sake Amen.
I read till about 12 at night in private and prayed against the inundacon
of pop[er]y & for the Convercon of his Ma[jes]ty Lord heare me for
xt his sake.

2° ffebr. 1637/38. Candlemas day
I dyned with h[enry] Goodere to day at my Cousin Ragdales in
Stayning lane;[302] we went afterward to sermon at dr Stoughtons &
heard him who spake boldly in the name of the Lord & gave comforts
ag[ains]t times of sufferinge. Oh Lord still strengthen his hands &
uphold him & suffer not his malicious enemyes to pr[e]vayle for the
Lords sake Amen.
we went after & heard a sermon in Pauls preached by one dr Turner,[303]
who preached for bowinge at the name of Jesus & towards the altar
oh Lord looke from heaven in m[er]cye to thy poore church behold
& visit this vine for the Lords sake Amen.
h[enry] Goodere supped here & is to lye wth me to night.
3° ffeb.
h[enry] & I prayed & I went to Westm[inster] wth Mr daniel Readinge
&.
I have bene this day encountred againe (as I am dayly) by the cares of
the world, but in the name of the Lord shall I destroy them for surely

surely thou wilt feed & Cloath me, its not in vayne to trust in thee
& wayte uppon thee give me comfort in thee in the worst condicon
whatsoever for the Lords sake & pr[e]pare me for thy Sab.[bath]
approaching I rec[eive]d l[ette]rs to day from Mr Mayor & to Sr
George Sands[304] Lord give me successe for the Lords sake.
gracious Comforts & fayth in private prayer at night I blesse the Lord.

---

[302]Woodford was related to the Ragdale family of Old through his grandmother Mary
Ragdale, who had married Edward Woodford, his grandfather, in 1560. Edward Ragdale,
Woodford's cousin, lived in the parish of St Mary, Staining Lane, of which by 1638 he was a
prominent resident; T.C. Dale (ed.), *The Inhabitants of London in 1638* (London, 1931), p. 120;
D.H. Woodforde (ed.), *Woodforde Papers and Diaries* (London, 1932), genealogical table at the
end.
[303]Thomas Turner was Laud's chaplain: N. Tyacke, *Anti-Calvinists: the rise of English
Arminianism c. 1590–1640* (Oxford, 1987), p. 240.
[304]This letter from William Collis to Sir George Sondes probably concerns the charitable
bequest made by Sir Ralph Freeman to his native town of Northampton. Sondes, who had
married Freeman's daughter and heiress, Jane, was the executor of his father-in-law's will.
Freeman, a wealthy clothworker and merchant, had died in 1634 as Mayor of London, and
had bequeathed £1,000 to be used by local tradesmen and clothiers to provide work for

4° ffebr. 1637/38 Sab.[bath]
I prayed and went to Aldermanbury church where I heard a stranger
preach very faythfully & boldly blessed be thy name oh Lord.
dr Stoughton preached in the afternoone with like faythfullnes &
bouldnes. oh Lord stay them up still & suffer not the malice of Satan
& his instruments to pr[e]vayle against them for the Lords sake.
graciously inlarged in the family in prayer to night I blesse the Lord.

5° ffebr. 1637/38
I prayed & went in the morninge somewhat early to find Mr Simpson[305]
house who is Cashier to Sr George Sands to intreat his helpe about my
letter & so he informed me that Sr George was in Towne & followed
me thether & delivered the letter & hath promised that an answere of
it shall be pr[e]pared by 3 a clock to be sent to Mr wilcox of horton.[306]
I went not to Westm[inster] this morninge stayinge about this busines.
I went at night & have receaved the Answere blessed be thy name
oh Lord so I have inclosed it & written to Mr Maior.[307] Lord give me
grace & favor in their eyes if thou see good for the Lords sake Amen.
6° ffeb Shrove tuesday.

the poor and to augment the stipend of the master of the grammar school. Sondes was the
nephew of Lord Montagu and had been educated by Dr John Preston at Emmanuel College,
Cambridge. Freeman had also enjoyed friendly dealings with Montagu, but had been a
supporter of the Duke of Buckingham, and had bequeathed £1,000 towards Archbishop
Laud's renovation of St Paul's Cathedral. Sondes had already failed to administer Freeman's
legacy properly. In August 1636 the Privy Council summoned him to London following their
receipt of a petition from the Mayor of Northampton, William Knight, complaining that
Sondes was withholding the money. Collis's letter was probably a further reminder. A
later meeting of the town assembly (in March 1638) complained that only £500 had been
received; on 31 October 1640 the assembly despatched Thomas Martin to petition the Long
Parliament for redress, and in March 1641 the assembly resolved to prosecute Sondes for
the balance. His refusal to pay came back to haunt him. In 1655 his home county of Kent
was scandalized by his son's, Freeman Sondes's, execution for the murder of his brother,
George. Local godly clergy blamed the fratricide on the sins of the father, prominent among
which was his misadministration of Freeman's charity: T. Seccombe, 'Sondes, George, first
earl of Feversham (1599–1677)', rev. S. Kelsey, in *ODNB*; W.K. Jordan, *The Charities of London
1480–1660: the aspirations and the achievements of the urban society* (London, 1960), pp. 124, 179, 305,
345 n. 145; Markham and Cox, *Northampton*, II, pp. 350–351; HMC, *Report on the Manuscripts
of the Duke of Buccleuch and Queensberry*, III (London, 1926), p. 362; TNA, PC2/46/337 and
PC2/46/368; TNA, PROB/11/99; Book of Orders, pp. 59–62; TNA, PROB/11/165.

[305]Possibly the John Sampson mentioned as a trusted servant in Sir Ralph Freeman's will:
TNA, PROB/11/165.

[306]Leonard Wilcox of Horton had been Freeman's steward of that manor since at least
1625 and performed the function for the next owner, Henry Montagu, Earl of Manchester.
He may also have been the same attorney who, in 1633, had been the source of anti-papist
rumours concerning Lady Digby: TNA, PROB/11/223; PDR, Church Survey Book 5, fo.
90r-v; *VCH Northamptonshire*, IV, p. 261.

[307]William Collis.

I was graciously affected in private duty this morninge I blesse the
Lord wth much fayth. I went alonge with my M[aster] to blackfryers
to dinner oh Lord I blesse thee for the favor I find in their eyes it is
from thee alone.

Coles & Soudly of derington[308] came to towne to night to prove the
Suggestions.[309]

Mr Mayor came to London to day & met with my letter by the way.

7° ffeb. 1637/38

Bishop Wren[310] preached at the Court to day. Oh Lord bringe those
that are faythfull to preach before his Ma[jes]tye with effect & remove
the wicked from his throne that it may be established & continue as
the dayes of heaven for the feare of thy name will give beinge and
continuacon to a family & nothinge else can establish a house or a
nacon. by gods good p[ro]vidence we have found out an error in
o[u]r Suggestions in due time which came through the want of right
informacon by denton.

Ned Oakley [*crossed out:* went]

8° ffeb. 1637/38

I had a Recovery at Barre[311] to day for one Pettiver[312] a clyent of mine.

9° ffebr

I prayed and went to the hall & have compounded at the alienac[on]
office for the fine to the Kinge uppon the writt of Entry p[ro] pettiver
p[ro] xs

10° ffebr.

I prayed & went to the hall where Judge Bartlet & Vernon[313] went on
wth the argument in the Checquer Chamber about the Ship-money
& have given their opinions as the other two did. oh Lord graunt

---

[308] Derrington near Stafford.

[309] Legal information not given on oath.

[310] Matthew Wren, as Bishop of Norwich, was the most vigorous exponent of Laudian
policies: N.W.S. Cranfield, 'Wren, Matthew (1585–1667)', in *ODNB*.

[311] Gaining possession of some property or right by the verdict of a court.

[312] Woodford's client may be the same Pettiver with whom he later stayed at Kettering
and whom he considered ungodly. This individual may be the John Pettiver (mercer) whose
will was witnessed by Thomas Harris, rector of Kettering, in 1640. It is debatable whether
this is the John Pettiver prosecuted by William Spencer, rector of Scaldwell, around 1629
as 'a Common drunkard and altogether unfit for the company of God's people', who had
reputedly 'come into the Church amongst them that receaved the sacrament and went
out irreverently' and who by April 1630 was reported for standing excommunicate: Diary,
p. 243; PDR, CB61, unfoliated, under 9 July 1629 and 23 April 1630; Longden, *Clergy*.

[313] That is, judges Sir Robert Berkeley and Sir George Vernon: S. Doyle, 'Berkeley, Sir
Robert (1584–1656)', in *ODNB*; D.X. Powell, 'Vernon, Sir George (c.1578–1639)', in *ODNB*;
Jones, *Bench*, pp. 139–143.

that Justice & righteousnes may flow downe like a streame in this Kingdome for the Lords sake.

11° ffebr. Sab.[bath]

dr Stoughton preached eveninge & morninge at his owne Church.

The Churchwardens of o[u]r parish at North[amp]ton came to the towne to day & sent for me at night, the occas[ion] of their cominge to day was necessary as they supposed.

12° ffebr.

I prayed and went to the hall; beinge the last day of the tearme, I am much straighted for moneyes but my desire was to wayte uppon the Lord.

Through gods m[er]cye I brought my businesse to some good head & fit to be left with others.

13° ffeb.

I prayed and came out of towne about 9 a clock & met wth one John Taylor of Warr

Warrington in Com[itatu] Lanc[aster] & one Mr Kinston Taylor & I had much discourse about Mr Burton[314] we came safe & early to dunstable to day blessed be god.

I prayed wth Taylor to night who seemed to be affected with it, Lord worke good in his soule for the Lords sake Amen.

I met about highgate with Mr Wm Sargent[315] George Curwyn & who intend New England Lord blesse them for the Lords sake Amen.

14° ffeb. 1637/38

we came out about 6 a clock I left them at Stony stratford & came safe home blessed be god where I found all my family well I prayse the Lord.

I went to old Mr Martins at night & to Mr Maiors[316] & find much favor I prayse the Lord.

---

[314]Following his condemnation by the Court of Star Chamber, the godly Henry Burton had been imprisoned at Lancaster Castle until November 1637, when he had been moved to Guernsey: K. Gibson, 'Burton, Henry (bap. 1578, d. 1647/8)', in ODNB.

[315]William Sargent, who was active in the vestry from 1628 until 1630, was a haberdasher who, in later life, served as lay minister at the settlement of Barnstaple, Massachusetts: Vestry Minutes, pp. 21–26; R.L. Greaves, 'Lothropp, John (bap. 1584, d. 1653)', in ODNB; G.A. Moriarty, 'Genealogical research in England: Gifford: Sargent', New England Historical and Genealogical Register, 74 (1920, 1921), pp. 231–237, 267–283.

[316]William Collis.

15° ffebr.

Mrs Crick sent this morninge for some money I owe her but I could not pay her; Lord looke uppon me in my lowe estate if it be thy will for the Lords sake.

I went to Grafton [Regis] to day to keepe Court

& receaved some supply I prayse the Lord. I came home with one Owen a minister who hath a vicaradge lately bestowed on him by my Lord Spencer.[317]

my horse is amisse & very poore so that I much feare I shall loose him, it would be a great affliccon to me Lord I humbly submit but pr[e]vent it if it be thy mercifull will.

my wife & I with our pullet went & supped wth Mrs Rushworth who is sad by her husbands absence Lord give them successe in what they are about for the Lords sake.

16° ffeb. 1637/38

Mr hicklinge sent for me to day to the George to borowe 2s 6d of me fearinge his money would not hold out so he had it of me which shall goe towards what I owe him more.

[*left margin: trefoil symbol*] Oh Lord I am in want & know not what to doe for the morowe but I desire to trust in thee Lord releive me in thy due time teach me to live uppon thee with comfort by fayth for the Lords sake Amen.

17° ffeb. 1637/38

I prayed and went in the morninge to Mr Maior[318] to intreat his direccon to ffr[yers] to pay me for some entryes concerning the towne which ffr[yers] denyed, & god gave me favor in his eyes accordinge as I prayed, poore goodwife Cooke was wth me twise for the 5s her sonne hath sent her by me but I had it not, Lord enable me to pay her on munday

---

[317]Lord Henry Spencer of Althorp, the future Earl of Sunderland, was still a minor and under the wardship of his mother, Lady Penelope (née Wriothesley). One John Owen had been curate at the Spencers' home parish of Great Brington since 1634 under her husband, William, the second Baron. Possibly Spencer was now promoting Owen to the rectory of Brington: M.E. Finch, *The Wealth of Five Northamptonshire Families 1540–1640*, Publications of the Northamptonshire Record Society XIX (Oxford, 1966), pp. 55–56, 60, 62n, 65; PDR, CB64, fo. 133r; PDR, X639–642/8, unfoliated, under Brington.

[318]William Collis.

Its told me this day that my Lord of North[amp]ton[319] hath sealled a deputacon to some one to keepe the Court for hamfordshoe which Mr Attourney so lately p[ro]mised me oh Lord I desire to wayte uppon thee every thinge through thy m[er]cye & good p[ro]vidence shall fall out for the best for me Lord bestowe it uppon me if thou seest good for the Lords sake Amen.

one Warren of harleston wanteth a bond that hath bene formerly in the Court here but neither I nor Crutchley can find it Lord I pray thee deliver me from this feare if it be thy will for the Lords sake

Ah Lord how many exigents & affliccons I meet wthall in the world but make me to

to triumph in thee at all times & a gayner by every condicon, & pr[e]pare me for the Sabath for the Lords sake Amen.

my father hath now had 71li of Mr Watts & I [have had] 22li besides my former hundred so Mr Watts is to give us 7 more & it makes it 100.

18° ffeb 1637/38 Sab.[bath]

Mr Newton preached in the morninge & the minister of Grantham[320] a stranger in the afternoone very p[ro]fitably & well blessed be god oh Lord graunt that we may more p[ro]fit under thy glorious gospell which yet by thy m[er]cye we doe enioy then ever we have done formerly for the Lords sake Amen.

19° ffeb.

Court to day where I had some supply of my wants blessed be god.

Mr Mayor[321] deserted me againe to day in a

a businesse I moved in about entryes in towne businesses.

[*crossed out:* 19] 20° ffeb.1637/38

[319]Spencer Compton, second Earl of Northampton, had seats at Castle Ashby, Northamptonshire, and Compton Wynyates, Warwickshire, and was related to the Mordaunts, earls of Peterborough. He was Lord Lieutenant of Warwickshire but was relatively inactive in the local politics of either county – he was above all a courtier on close personal terms with Charles I. The Comptons had a history of supporting conformist ministers, notably Bishop John Towers, Peter Hausted, and Isaac Casaubon: J. Fielding, 'Towers, John (d. 1649)', in *ODNB*; M. Bennett, 'Compton, Spencer, second earl of Northampton (1601–1643)', in *ODNB*; V. Stater, 'Mordaunt, Henry, second earl of Peterborough (bap. 1623, d. 1697)', in *ODNB*; Fielding, 'Peterborough', pp. 40–41.

[320]The minister of Grantham North from 1608 until 1647 was Thomas Dilworth, with Edward Harrys ministering in Grantham South from 1634 until 1638: J.E. Swaby, *Lincolnshire Parish Clergy in the Seventeenth Century* (1883) (typescript held at the Lincolnshire Record Office).

[321]William Collis.

I prayed and went alonge wth Mr Pentlowe to Rugby where good Mr Nalton[322] is preacher there was in the towne a bearebaytinge, which I was greived at & the more because I feared it was done in opposicon to the good man.

our Journey was about Mills wch Mr Pentlow was to buy of one Mr Pratt.[323]

Mr Pentlowe prayed at night.

21° ffebr.

Mr Pentlowe prayed againe this morninge while after we went to breakefast to Mrs Childs house, where I had much comfort in discourse wth her & Mrs Prat two good women. about 11 a clock we came away & rode hard & I got hether in due time before the Judges came in

in (blessed be god for his good p[ro]vidence towards me in it) for so I escaped Mr Maiors anger.

I went after with Mr Maior & the Aldermen to the Judges lodginge, where old Justice hutton[324] shooke me kindly by the hand & is very lovinge to me allwayes blessed be thy name oh Lord for his favor towards me. I am very short of money, & Mrs Crick sends but I cannot help.

Mr ffarren & Mr Rushworth came home to day & have p[ro]cured an Inhibicon out of the delegates though wth much difficulty

22° ffebr. 1637/38

one Mr Alford the high sheriffe Sr John hanburyes Chaplayne[325] preached before the Judges to day very honestly. The Assizes began this morninge the Lord in m[er]cye sent me 3s 4d from the inhabitants

---

[322] James Nalton was the puritan minister at Rugby: J. Eales, *Puritans and Roundheads: the Harleys of Brampton Bryan and the outbreak of the English Civil War* (Cambridge, 1990), p. 157; A. Hughes, *Politics, Society, and Civil War: Warwickshire, 1620–1660* (Cambridge, 1987), p. 81.

[323] This seems to be the same Mr Pratt mentioned on 10 January 1637/38, who has been tentatively identified as Thomas Pratt of Mears Ashby.

[324] Sir Richard Hutton was famous for his protestant piety and popular for his resistance to prerogative taxation. He had led the judges' opposition to the forced loan in 1626 and had refused (even after a personal confrontation with the king) to sanction the Star Chamber prosecution of the imprisoned MPs following the stormy parliamentary debates of 1628 and 1629. In 1635 he had refused to join the other eleven common law judges in endorsing the extension of the levying of ship money to the whole kingdom. While eventually signing under pressure the unanimous judicial opinion of 1637 in favour of ship money, he dismissed the crown's case when Hampden came to trial in 1637 – such a levy might not be made by the monarch without parliamentary consent unless in time of war. This verdict, issued on 28 April 1638 according to Woodford, was widely circulated and greatly applauded: Jones, *Bench*, pp. 125–127; W. Prest, 'Hutton, Sir Richard (bap. 1561, d. 1639)', in *ODNB*.

[325] Thomas Alford was domestic chaplain to Sheriff Sir John Hanbury of Kelmarsh and vicar of Daventry from 1635. Hanbury's will of 1639 stipulated that his loving friend preach the funeral oration: TNA, PROB/11/97.

of Benifeild for takinge off [*crossed out:* a fine] p[rese]ntm[en]t which the Clerke of Assize[326] & Rob[er]te Worlidge p[ai]d me 8s p[ro] the writt & warrant v[e]rs[us] hensman.

Mr Watts lodged [altered from: lodgeth] here [*crossed out:* to] last night, I pray thee oh Lord continue his favor to me still for the Lords sake.

The Inhibicon out of the delegates was published by Mr Newton to day before the Judges,[327] wch made the adversaryes [*blank*]

23° ffebr.

I inquire still about the Stewardship of hamfordeshoe & I heare its gone to John Eakins I pray &

& desire to wayte uppon the Lord. I have no tryalls at all this Assizes, but I desire to cast my care uppon the Lord & to wayte for his good p[ro]vidence oh Lord thou alone art holy & wise & gracious, teach me to trust p[er]fectly in thee for the Lords sake

The cares of the world doe strike soe at the Castle of my fayth, & are ready even to batter it, Lord Uphold me for I desire to trust in thee.

24° ffeb. <u>1637/38</u>

I prayed and went to the Castle where I spoke to Mr Attourney who p[ro]mised to sealle me a deputacon to day, though he heard of John Eakins which he did accordingly, Lord direct every thinge for the best.

Mr Tourney[328] calls uppon me for money excedings and I have it not, Lord helpe me, so he hath given me time till the tearme; Lord furnish me with it then for the Lords sake.

The Judges are gone to day to Warrick[329]

one prison[er] onely condemned & he for a Burglary at Grendon, he livinge at Easton Maudit.

*****

[326] Francis Williamson was the clerk of assize for the Midland circuit from 1633 until 1642, his deputy being John Tourney: J.S. Cockburn, *A History of English Assizes 1558–1714* (Cambridge, 1972), p. 315.

[327] The churchwardens later claimed that Clarke had berated them at the Northampton court because of their appeal to the Court of Delegates (and Newton, the curate, for publishing, as described here, the inhibition issued by that court): 'called yor peticoners Coxcombes dishonest churchwardens and giddy headed fellowes. And that they went to London and told Lyes and offered a false oath' (HLRO, main papers, petition 1641). Sir John Lambe, they said, then reinforced Clarke's effort by initiating a suit against them in the Court of High Commission (which was still current on 6 February 1641), forcing them finally to create the railed, east end altar: Diary, pp. 188–189.

[328] John Tourney was the associate clerk of assize on the Midland circuit from 1633 until 1656: Cockburn, *History of English Assizes*, p. 315.

[329] Cockburn states (*ibid.*, p. 31) that the Midland assize circuit was fixed during the early seventeenth century – commencing at Warwick and concluding at Northampton. However, on this and two further occasions in the Diary (pp. 288, 341), the judges are described moving from Northampton to Warwick.

25° ffeb. 1637/38 Sab.[bath]

somewt sleepy at morninge sermon through my infirmity of sinnes & want of care to goe to bed early the last night oh Lord graunt that I may amend that faylinge

graciously affected in hearinge Mr Ball in the afternoone who preached faythfully against Idolatry & p[er]secuters of xxians I was greatly affected in secret prayer this eveninge I blesse the Lord to teares wth much fayth and the Lord hath p[ro]mised to blesse me though I am nothinge the Lord will freely be gracious to me & will establish me in soule & family will pay my debts I trust in due time & will p[ro]vide outward necessaries for me oh Lord teach me to live by fayth for the Lords sake I prayed for the distressed church of god Lord heare me

26 ffeb.

I prayed and went to Court, where we had very much wrangling one with another especially Mr Bayleife Coldwell & I about the busines of fflexney, oh Lord p[ar]don our rashnes & Cure this

corrupcon of rash anger & violent passion in me for the Lords sake and graunt that I may never break out againe though much provoked. I went to Captayne Bernards in the afternoone but found him not within,

I prayed unto the Lord as I came alonge uppon the way.

poore John Sillesby is in prison, & his goods seised by 2 or 3 fieri fac[ias][330]

The sp[irit]uall Court breathe out Chr[istians]

27° ffebruary 1637/38

I prayed and went afterwards to Sr xxofer hattons to the parke where I had kind entertaynemt from Sr xxofer; oh Lord I blesse thy name for that mans favor to me It was thine owne worke to move his hart towards me at the first & now to continue his favor to me Mr Cawdrey dyned there too.

Mr Longman[331] Sr xxofers Chapleyne & I had much discourse after dinner about the times & altars & bowinge to them he favors &

---

[330] A writ of fieri facias authorized the sheriff to distrain a defendant's goods to the value of money owed. John Sillesby was the son of Matthew Sillesby, a scrivener who had been mayor of the town in 1631, and who had been a leading participant in the godly obstruction of the conformist policies of John Lambe over the period 1614 to 1624. According to Woodford, Matthew died on 28 March 1639. John had been an active parish officer from 1628 until 1635: Fielding, 'Peterborough', pp. 71–72; Vestry Minutes, pp. 21–31.

[331] James Longman was chaplain to Sir Christopher Hatton of Kirby. It was later alleged that he illegally obtained the living of Aynho in 1644 by imprisoning and torturing the Parliamentarian widow of the lord of the manor, Richard Cartwright, at Banbury Castle with the connivance of its governor, Sir William Compton, until she signed away her rights and those of the heir, John. Longman was ejected from the living by Parliament around

maynteynes those innovations, I resolved so to carry my self that he might not p[er]ceave my opinion, but the fire brake out, & I spoke in the behalfe of gods true & sp[irit]uall worship, though with as much discrecon as

as I could & thought fitt; oh Lord keepe me from danger & questioninge if it be thy will, but if in thy p[ro]vidence thou hast ordeyned that I shall be called forth to witnesse to thy truth, I beseech thee give me knowledge & wisdome & fayth & courage & resolucon & patience, let me not feare the face of mortall man for the Lords sake John Eakins began the 3 weeks Court of hamforde shoe here to day.

28 ffebr. 1637/38
I prayed and went to Wellingborowe to day, & met wth many good freinds, my mother tells me shee heares I intend to sell the land at Old oh Lord direct every thinge for the best for the Lords sake Amen.
I went to Mr Pearnes as I came home & from Wilby Mr danby & I came home together safe I blesse the Lord;

1° Martii
Mr Tompkins of harpoll preached at the lecture to day. Oh Lord pr[e]vent the inundacon of pop[er]y & sup[er]stition for the Lords sake Amen.
Old Mr Martin much afflicted wth his eye still.
harry Rise is come to towne & is apprehended uppon the like suspicon of felony for the goods sold here by his brother I rec[eive]d a letter which I suppose is counterfeyt from Richard

2° die Martii 1637/38
somewhat troubled with my old disease of forgetfullnes Lord ease me & helpe me for the Lords sake Amen. I am now to goe Joyne in dutye wth gods people to beseech the Lord for helpe in this evill & troublous time, & I am very dull & unfit Lord put thy spirit into my hart & words into my mouth & graunt that we may cry mightily unto thee so as thou mayest heare us, for the Lords sake.
The Lord was pleased graciously to enlarge me in dutye, & to affect my hart & gave me fayth to beleive in some measure I blesse the Lord. Oh Lord heare our poore prayers for thy poore church & for our selves for the Lords sake Amen.

1646, by which time he had fled to the Royalist headquarters at Oxford, where he became chaplain to New College. He was replaced at Aynho by John Cartwright's candidate, Robert Wild: Longden, *Clergy*; A.G. Matthews (ed.), *Walker Revised* (Oxford, 1948), p. 282; S. Ransom, 'Squire Cartwright and Parson Drope', *Cake and Cock Horse*, IV, no. 5 (1969), pp. 67-73; R.L. Greaves, 'Wild, Robert (1615/16-1679)', in *ODNB*.

There was Mr ffisher William Turland & I, Mrs Maioresse Mr Collis
Mrs harbert my wife goodwife Gibson Sar[ah] Collis Beck Bushell
&.[332]

3° Martii 1637/38
I was in great distresse for money but the Lord in m[er]cye sent me
in the morninge about such time as the m[ar]ket was for butter &
eggs 18d from John Clendon of Wellingborow, & other moneyes for
some declaracons & when goodwife pin came to me for 12d from her
husband I gave her all I had wch was 6d and told her I would come
or send a while after and reckon with her husband; so about

the time of m[ar]ket openinge for Corne the Lord sent me 25s from
Turland of harrington p[ro] resid[ue] recovery so I had to buy a strike
of wheate wch cost me 7s 4d; & to send pin, so I have paid him 5s &
there is 25 behind. Thus the Lord hath graciously carryed me through
this day blessed be thy name oh Lord.
I p[ai]d for milk 22d to Ned Oakleys wife 1s.
Mr Sam. Martin came home to day having bene at London so we
had him & ux & Mr Rushworth & ux to supper.
Mrs Rushworth is to blame in beinge heavy & sad to see her husband
goe on wth such resolucon in the busines against dr Clarke. Lord
strengthen his hands that he may not be discouraged for the Lords
sake.
4° Martii 1637/38 Sab.[bath]
I prayed & went to church where Mr Newton preached honestly &
well, though his prayer is turned somewhat canonicall & gave thanks
for the S[ain]ts dep[ar]ted[333] &.
Mrs Rushworth sent for this morninge to Coventry her father beinge
extreame ill it seemes.
Mr Colson the Curate of St Giles dyed this morning who had so late
before refused to give the sacram[en]t to those that refused to come
up to the rayles. we

*****

---

[332] William Collis, his wife, and possibly his daughter, Sarah, were clearly regarded as godly
despite Woodford's constant bickering with the mayor over official business. Mrs Harbert
was the wife of John Harbert, mayor in 1629; Mrs Gibson, the wife of Thomas Gibson,
who was active in the vestry from 1624 until 1640. Rebecca Bushell was the niece of John
Bushell (d. 1630), cutler and London citizen: Cox and Markham, *Northampton*, II, p. 252;
Vestry Minutes, pp. 15–35; TNA, PROB/11/157.
[333] Newton was under the censure of the Church court: Diary, p. 105, and n. 39. The
Prayer Book prayer for which Woodford is expressing his disapproval is probably that for
'the whole state of Christ's Church militant here in earth', part of the second (communion)
service, which blesses God's 'holy Name for all thy servants departed this life in thy faith
and fear [. . .]'.

we had here no sermon in the afternoone, which thinge hath not bene knowne here in [*crossed out:* many] very many yeares before, it seemes dr Clarke hath forbidden it & its too much obeyed, oh Lord though the adversary this wicked haman[334] & those of the Confederacye seeke to extinguish the light of thy glorious gospell & hate it as the theife hates the dawninge of the day, yet let thy light & thy truth breake forth let the sunne still arise & disp[er]se the foggs that come from the bottomlesse pitt, and make thine enimyes to be ashamed & to lick the dust oh Lord o[u]r eyes are towards thee keep & defend thy poore church & feed it with pure doctrine, oh Lord o[u]r enemyes are many & very mighty & we are weake & few, but though the coneyes be a weake & despicable & feeble folk 30.p[ro]v.[erbs]26. yet they make their houses in the rocks & who can unburrow them, Lord we take sanctuary in thee our god, & if we speake of strength thou art stronge, oh Lord make the adversaryes to know they are but men for the Lords sake I am much afflicted with the cares of the world, oh Lord p[ar]don & remove them for the Lords sake. much afflicted wth thorny cares in publiq prayer at night. Oh Lord give us to Live by fayth for the Lords sake Amen.

I gave harry Rise 6d in the gaole, & 10d to the poore

5° Martii 1637/38
I prayed wth my wife & with my family & in secret wth some comfort & enlargem[en]t I blesse the Lord, & I prayed against rash anger & for gods good p[ro]vidence uppon the day which I have found I prayse the Lord for we had an Indifferent quiet Court, & gaynfull to me I prayse god, & afterwards Guilb[er]t Tebot p[ai]d me the 12s 6d he ought me & Cr[utchley] p[ai]d me the reckonings of the day.
in the afternoone we went to the fun[er]all sermon at St Gyles Mr Ball preached very p[ro]fitably I prayse god. I went downe at night to Mr Balls. I p[ai]d goodman Iblethy 30s in p[ar]te of his bills & 22d p[ro] payre stock[ings] p[ro] ux.
6° Martii
I was up somew[ha]t early to day and have prayed unto the Lord with much fayth though the Lord doth exercise me with great afflicons yet surely the Lord will not forgett to be gracious & will surely blesse me & mine, we are much afflicted in regard my wife knowes not yet whether she be with child so she hath many feares I have prayed unto the Lord to shew m[er]cye unto us & to pr[e]vent & take away our trouble

*****

[334] Haman was the enemy of the Jewish hero Mordecai. He was defeated and executed on the gallows intended for Mordecai.

trouble about it, Oh Lord I acknowledge for o[u]r sinnes & faylings thou might iustly punish us but for the Lords sake p[ar]don them & shew m[er]cy to thy servants even in the things wch we are troubled about for the Lords sake Amen.

Richard Rise came [*crossed out: word starting with* f] to the towne here to day about his kinsman that is now in prison here my wife and I walked to Abington in the afternoone for her healthes sake. Mr & Mrs Bulliv[an]t not at home I was at Captayne Bernards. I supt at old Mr Martins to night.

7° Martii 1637/38
my wife finds some alteracon this morninge & I feare least she went too violently yesterday wch if she be with child may cause her to miscarry & I am somewhat melancholly but I have besought the Lord, to be gracious oh Lord blesse me in my Journey to Wellingborow to day & give me comforts when I returne here for the Lords sake Amen.

I went to Wellingborowe where I met wth Richard Rise who came alonge with me home & supped here I found my wife somewhat better I prayse the

the Lord, who is a god that heareth my poore prayers

8° Martii I prayed & went to Grafton [Regis] Court, & returned safe home I blesse the Lord, one Mr Beely of Stokegolding[335] dyned with us an archdeacon I opposed a health which he began: blessed be god

9° Martii 1637/38
I prayed and went alonge wth Richard Rise to Mr Maiors where met us Mr Bayleife,[336] so they are contented that harry Rise who is in prison shall be released and that the Recognisance[337] for Edward shall not be returned &.

he & harry broke their fast here, Mr Coldwell hath p[ai]d me 5s towards the writts v[e]rs[us] fflcxney.

I heare that dr Clarke is appeased & that things here shall be much as they have bene, oh Lord roote out the sup[er]stition we have already receaved & keepe out the Rest for the Lords sake.[338]

William Bot is very sick.

10° Martii
Mr Watts was here to day, Lord give me still favor in his eyes for the Lords sake.

---

[335] William Beeley (here described as living at Stoke Goldington, Buckinghamshire) was the Archdeacon of Carmarthen, which was under the See of St David's.

[336] William Collis and Benoni Coldwell.

[337] An obligation to perform an act or observe a condition; alternatively, the money pledged as surety for such performance.

[338] Clarke had banned the afternoon sermon on 4 March, but the practice resumed on 11 March.

I have receaved litle money this day, oh Lord susteyne me in my outward estate for the Lords sake.

Mr Ball of Coventry dyed it seemes to day, Lord stay the harts of his freinds uppon thee for the Lords sake

11° Martii 1637/38 Sab.[bath]

Mr Ball preached here in the morninge & Mr Newton in the afternoone.

gracious Comforts in dutye this eveninge I blesse the Lord.

in the time of morninge pub[lic] excercise there was one house[339] taken wth a woman at Blunts he sent to the stocks[340] & she to the Gaole under the Conduicte, and in the time of the eveninge excercise one Wright was taken wth Nel Glover a naughty woman he put in the Gaole & she sent to the house of Correccon,[341] oh Lord p[ar]don their sinnes & give them amendment for the Lords sake. The fruits of sinne are shame, oh what vile creatures we are by nature; blessed be thy name oh Lord that I am not as bad as the worst in the world. my wife & John somewhat ill to day.

12° Martii Court to day. where Mr Maior[342] & I had some difference againe, Oh Lord pr[e]vent it for time to come & give me grace & favor in his eyes if it be thy will, however I beseech thee give me to be as patient as thou requirest I should be for the Lords sake for divisions are a signe that we are still carnall. Lord make us more spirituall.

I and my wife supped at younge Mr Martins where we had gracious comforts in good Conference with them & Mr Whalley et ux.

13° Martii 1637/38

my wife very ill to day & so is litle John, I have besought the Lord for them & for my family. I pray that the Lord would please to direct me to a good pennieworth for some land at duston if he see fit for the Lord of Warrick is about to sell there. Mr Cawdrey preached here this

---

[339]Mr House or Howes has not been definitely identified, although there were brothers of that name (John, Thomas, and Robert) living at Wootton in 1631: PDR, CB1, fo. 410.

[340]Portable stocks had been used since 1634, when soldiers, incensed at the condemnation of one of their number to punishment at the fixed stocks in Market Square, had burned them down: Markham and Cox, *Northampton*, II, p. 196.

[341]For the town jail (under the Conduit Hall) and the house of correction, see Diary, p. 135, n. 174.

[342]William Collis.

afternoone at the baptizinge of a Child of Mr Giffords[343] but I was wth Mr Pulley[344] my Lord of Warricks solicitor Mr Wilso[n][345] Mr Coles &. My Lord of Warrick came late to the towne at night. Nurse Emerson who suckled John hath an ague so we are compelled to weane him, oh Lord pr[e]serve him & blesse him & my whole family for the Lords sake

14° Martii
I prayed and went downe to see my Lord of Warrick first in duston River but as I went I heard my Master was come to his owne house so I went downe to him, & the Lord hath given me grace in his eyes blessed be thy name oh Lord.
I met wth Mr Ball at the River & Mr Newton wth whom I had much discourse about the state of things there. I found my wife indifferent well at my returne I blesse the Lord & John is somewhat better of his cold I prayse the Lord. goodman Atkins[346] dyed this eveninge.

15° Martii 1637/38
Mr Ball preached very well at the Lecture to day blessed be god. my Lord of Warrick was there. Mr hall Mrs ffarmer dyned here to day.
my wife & I are much troubled about her Condicon least there should be in her a false conception, because of that & but we have earnestly besought the Lord oh Lord heare us for the Lords sake.
John is very ill oh Lord recover him for the Lords sake Amen.
I am told to day that Mr Challis would give no answere to John James when he demaunded my money of him that is due about 2li 16s oh Lord I pray thee supply me.

16° Martii
I have earnestly besought the Lord in the behalfe of my deare wife & my poore child John who is very ill & froward, & I have commended my outward Condicon (which is somewhat desperate in regard of my many debts & much charge) to the m[er]cy & good p[ro]vidence of the Lord, who hath surely heard my prayers & will work for the best.

---

[343] The records of All Saints' show Jane Gifford's baptism on the previous day, 12 March 1638: NRO, 223P/1.
[344] Possibly Richard Pulley (d. 1649) of Ingatestone, Essex: TNA, PROB/11/207.
[345] This might be the William Wilson who – along with Daniel Reading and Thomas Adkins – was found guilty by the town assembly in 1641 of various infringements of Northampton's liberties, including illegal malting. He was listed as a servant in the will of the Northampton barrister Joseph Bryan. The two Mrs Wilsons whose deaths the diary records (pp. 274, 384) were presumably related to him: Book of Orders, pp. 13, 67; TNA, PROB/11/179.
[346] There were six Adkins brothers descended from an aldermanic grandfather, Thomas Adkins. These are possible candidates for identification as Woodford's godly townsman. Perhaps the most likely were Thomas, Edward, or their cousin, John; a Peter Adkins also occurs: Metcalfe, *Visitation of Northamptonshire 1618*, p. 60; PDR, Archdeaconry of Northampton Wills, second series, L108.

Oh Lord stay my heart uppon thee give me to wayt for thee in thy
m[er]cyes for the Lords sake.
I have prayed for strength against sinne, for practise for gods good
blessinge & goodman

goodman Atkins was buryed this afternoone & Mr Newton preached
at his fun[er]all, & spoke very well of who I think deserved no lesse.
Mr Rushworth spoke to me for the 15s for the Assessm[en]t[347] but I
had it not Lord furnish me with it & for other necessar[ies]
litle John is very ill and vomits up all he receaves so that we are much
troubled but I have sought the Lord who I trust will heare & helpe,
and Lord we desire onely to depend uppon thee & to submit unto
thee we pray thee doe us good & helpe & recover the poore infant
if it be thy will for the Lords sake Amen. The Com[munio]n Table
is raylinge in to the top of the Chancell[348] & the seates there pulled
downe. O Lord destroy sup[er]stit[i]on.
17° Martii 1637/38
I have prayed this morninge & then I went to meet a [*crossed out:*
suspended] minister a good man Mr Case[349] at James ffryers his house
wth Mr Martin Mr Tomkins[350] Mat[thew] Watts & T[homas] at dr
harts,[351] where we had argument about kneelinge at the sacrament,

[347]Towards the extra £100 voted on 5 January 1637/38 (and due on 10 March) for recasting
and hanging the church bells: Vestry Minutes, p. 34.
[348]Work on creating a railed, east end communion table had now resumed (and was
nearing completion on the next day, 17 March) following Sir John Lambe's and Dr
Clarke's overthrowing, in the Court of High Commission, of the churchwardens' hard-
won inhibition out of the Court of Delegates mentioned in the entry for 21 February:
Fielding, 'Peterborough', p. 97.
[349]Thomas Case of Norwich diocese was a vocal opponent of the Laudian policy of Bishop
Matthew Wren and a future member of the Westminster Assembly. During this period
he had taken refuge in Manchester, where he was evangelizing the surrounding area at
the request of the godly divine Richard Heyrick: R.C. Richardson, *Puritanism in North-west
England: a regional study of the Diocese of Chester to 1642* (Manchester, 1972), pp. 31, 35, 54–55,
150–151; M. Mullett, 'Case, Thomas (bap. 1598, d. 1682)', in *ODNB*.
[350]Martin Tompkins was regarded as godly by Woodford and served as bailiff from 1640
until 1641: Diary, p. 360.
[351]James Hart was an Edinburgh-born physician and client of Edward, Lord Montagu. In
1625 he had dedicated *Klinik or the Diet of the Diseased* to his patron, which Hart had intended
as a companion volume to Robert Bolton's *Some Generall Directions for a Comfortable Walking
with God*, which was dedicated to Montagu in the same year. A member of the Northampton
godly since around 1612, in his writings Hart accepted the description of himself as a puritan.
In 1614 he was presented to the Church courts for neglecting to receive Easter communion
at All Saints' at a time when Dr John Lambe and the conformists had expelled Robert
Catelin, the corporation's minister, and replaced him with the vehemently anti-puritan Dr
David Owen. He was a leading member of that community, in 1631 overseeing the will of
Simon Wastell, the retired headmaster of the free school and leader of godly resistance to
Lambe: Fielding, 'Peterborough', p. 51, n. 32; E.S. Cope, *The Life of a Public Man: Edward,*

& whether it is lawfull to communicate wth knowne p[ro]phane p[er]sons & about bowinge &. Oh Lord I pray thee establish us in thy truth & before thou bringe us to suffer satisfye us thoroughly that we may beare the Crosse with more Comfort; my Child John is still much amisse & doth hardly reteyne any thinge in his stomake & is greivously infested with a cold both in his head & lungs oh Lord I pray thee heale & Cure him if it be thy will & reserve him as an instrument of thy glory in aftertimes &

& give us to make a sanctifyed use of so great a m[er]cye, Oh Lord we receaved him first from thee by prayer & thou hast restored him to us from former illnesses when we have prayed unto thee, Lord heare our poore prayers againe if it be thy will for the Lords sake Amen.

The rayle in the Chancell is now s[ai]d almost up and its confidently reported that the sicknes is in the Towne,³⁵² Oh Lord pr[e]vent it or heale it if it be thy will, if not I pray thee give us to see the rod & him that smiteth with it that we may be bettered by the affliction, and secure I beseech thee (if it be thy will) the house & family of me thy poore servant & the rest of thy servants here from that thine arrowe for thy p[ro]vidence guideth all things, and dispose of us so as we may have food & rayment & necessary sustentacon for the Lords sake Amen.

first Baron Montagu of Boughton, 1562–1644 (Philadelphia, 1981), p. 147; J. Symons, 'Hart, James (d. 1639)', in *ODNB*; PDR, CB44, fo. 63r–v; Longden, *Clergy*.

³⁵²This outbreak of plague hit Northampton and villages to the north of it such as Ringstead (where it may have started: Diary, p. 98), Denford, Holcot, and Old. By Woodford's estimation it lasted for nearly a year. Dr Samuel Clarke gave an earlier date than Woodford (*ibid.*, p. 98, n. 11) for its commencement at Northampton. The death rate (as recorded by Clarke) ran at twenty-six, sixteen (these figures were confirmed by Woodford on 5 June), and twenty-nine per week during the period 27 May to 17 June, peaking around 24 July at forty-two (as recorded in the diary). Woodford did not announce the all clear until 16 February 1638/39, although by 17 November 1638 he recorded that the situation had improved sufficiently for St Hugh's fair to be held, and that only three had died in the previous week. The parish register in the parish of St Sepulchre tells a similar story, giving the dates 29 March 1638 for the commencement and 1 January 1639 for the conclusion. The overall Northampton death toll of 565 means that the outbreak was second in severity in the seventeenth century only to that of 1605 (when the total was 625), since the town escaped the Great Plague of 1665. All Saints' parish, the most populous, naturally bore the brunt of the attack, with 247 fatalities (compared with 411 in 1605). The Privy Council rapidly showed concern, on 10 April writing to the mayor (William Collis) instructing him to prevent the spread of the disease and offering practical advice: Jackson, 'Ship money', pp. 118–121; Markham and Cox, *Northampton*, II, pp. 237–239; TNA, SP16/393/15.

Oh Lord send me money to buy corne for bread this day in due time
if it be thy will for the Lords sake. my wife & Su[353] made up money
inough afterward for the Corne I blesse the Lord.

At night I had most great & Ravishinge comforts in secret prayer
the Lord even broke in uppon me, he made even his glory to passe
before me & p[ro]claymed the Lord the Lord gracious & Oh Lord
to

to enioy thy pr[e]sence & to behold thee in thine excellencyes & glory
by an eye of fayth is even heaven here uppon the earth, I have put upp
many peticons this night unto the Lord in an acceptab.[le] time, The
Lord will surely blesse me & mine. Sam. Collins dyed at night; Mr
Bayleife Coldwells Child borne this last night dyed in the morninge
Lord give us all a sanctifyed use of this thy hand of mortality now
uppon us in the towne for the Lords sake.

18° Martii 1637/38 Sab.[bath]

Mr Ball preached in the morninge, but my hart was very heavy & my
head sleepy Lord p[ar]don my sinne & weaknesse,

Mr Case preached in the afternoone most excellently out of the
6. Heb.[rews] 17. 18. & raysed this poynt That god is abundantly
willinge that the heires of p[ro]mise should have strong Consolation;
which poynt he made good by demonstracons & reasons & applyed it
admirably blessed be thy name oh Lord. Lord enable me to repeate
it p[ro]fitably to my selfe &

& family for the Lords sake.

I was greatly affected in hearinge him, even filled with fayth & Comfort
abundantly like to the Comfort in secret prayer the Last night I blesse
the Lord. Oh how sweet the lord is! Oh come oft & see how gracious
the Lord is, Oh Lord I beseech thee keep my mind in frame let me
ever enioy a holy Comunion with thee, yea a firme Comunion that it
may never be broken off any more for the Lords sake.

O Lord heale my poore Child that is sick if it be thy will, I humbly
sue unto thee as the Centurion & health & sicknes are thy servants say
but to this goe & it goeth to that Come & it cometh, say but the word
& my child shall be healed, & if thou bestowe this m[er]cye I beseech
thee sanctifye it for the Lords sake Amen

19° Martii 1637/38

I prayed and amongst other things to be delivered from passion & and
went to the Court where we had not much wranglinge.

---

[353] Susan Tue.

I went afterwards along wth my Master Mr Reading to Banbury,
we came late thether to the Red Lyon we went after to Nath[aniel]
Readinge at Mrs Wares where

where we found him in his ague fit, I was not very well after supper
with some qualmes for a while but the Lord graciously recovered me.
My M[aste]r told me of one Mr Edward Bagshawe a rude man (whom
I knew well) how he was lately stayed suddenly with a fall from his
horse, Oh Lord graunt me ever thy blessed p[ro]tection.

20° Martii 1637/38
I prayed in the morninge & went afterwards to Mr Sprig,[354] and after
that to the Lecture where Mr Wheatly[355] that good man preached
very p[ro]fitably (amongst other things) shewinge what is required of
husbands to their wives, that they ought not to be profuse or niggardly
or Churlish lord sanctifye it to me for the Lords sake, I went afterwards
along with Mr Bagshawe to his house at Morton Pinckeny, we dyned
first at Mr harfords the schole masters; my M[aste]r stayed at Banbury
this night

21° Martii
I prayed and came early from Mr Bagshawes & safe home I blesse the
Lord where I found my wife indifferent well & my litle John somewhat
better then he was I blesse the Lord, I went after to Wellingborowe,
and found that my mother had bene very ill of an ague but is recovered
blessed be thy name oh

oh Lord, oh my god sanctifye it unto her & all thy m[er]cyes for the
good of her soule for the Lords sake I rec[eive]d 8s more of George
hopkins[356] & 8d of Rob Worlidge in full of all & 2s 6d of George Curtis
in p[ar]te of what he owes me.

22° Martii 1637/38
I prayed and went to holcot to hopkins, & so to Ketteringe fayre where
I could not meet with any imployment, & I had much conflict with
the thorny cares of the world & thoughts of my debts & of the many
payments I have this Lady Day but I prayed unto the Lord often in
the way goeinge & cominge & found much refreshinge comfort in the

---

[354] Henry Sprig was active in the vestry of All Saints' from 1628 until 1638, and was
regarded by Woodford as godly. He was elected bailiff in 1640: Vestry Minutes, pp. 21–34;
Diary, p. 360.

[355] William Whately, the 'roaring boy of Banbury', was lecturer there and also operated a
godly seminary: Webster, *Godly Clergy*, pp. 20, 27–28, 54, 159 (quotation), 160.

[356] George Hopkins of Holcot was probably the son of Thomas Hopkins, the brother-in-law
of the godly alderman John Bryan, both of whom had been prosecuted in Star Chamber
in 1607 by John Lambe for circulating satirical verses about the Church courts: TNA,
STAC8/205/19.

sweet p[ro]mises & m[er]cye of the Lord, The Lord will surely doe
me good Blessed be thy name oh Lord,
I heare that Mr Arthur Potter[357] an old melancholly man is growne
mad, oh Lord pr[e]serve me thy servant ever in my right mind give
me ever the use & exercise of my witts & limbs & sences if it be thy
will for the Lords sake.

23. Martii
Its certaynely reported that the sicknes is in the Towne

I have besought the Lord to prevent the spreadinge of it if it be his
will, or els in his m[er]cye to dispose of me & my family to a hidinge
place & to sanctifye the stroke unto us.

24° Martii 1637/38
we were greatly in extremity for want of money this day & my
wife was compelled to borow what she wanted of Temp[er]ance,
Lord supply our necessitous Condicon for the Lords sake
Amen.
Mr Watts our Lovinge freind gave us this day a strike of wheat & a
dousin of Pudgeons oh Lord I prayse thee for that mans favor it is
from thee I pray thee continue it unto us for the glory of thy blessed
name for the Lords sake.
I had much Comfort & satisfaccon in speakinge with hatton to night
I trust the Lord hath begunne the good worke of grace in his soule oh
Lord goe on with it for the Lords sake.

25° Martii Easter day & Lad[y] Day 1638
Mr Ball preached in the morninge, my wife & I went both to the
sacram[en]t, havinge prayed oft unto the Lord before for a blessinge
uppon his ordinances: & desired to bringe all o[u]r burdens before
him.
Mr Newton preached in the afternoone.

26° Martii 1638
The ffare here to day.[358] one is dead to night one Bryan & its thought
she dyed of the sicknes, & 4 have dyed out of dannts house. Lord
Looke uppon us in m[er]cye for the Lords sake.
I receaved from goodman Tompson to day 5li to be p[ai]d at
London, Easton payd me 6li 10s rent to day: & I have p[ai]d Mr
Sam Martin 28s I ought him & 4d that thother 22s wanted, so

---

[357] Potter had been town bailiff as early as 1605 and served as churchwarden of St Peter's parish in 1635: Markham and Cox, *Northampton*, II, p. 561; PDR, X639–642/8.
[358] The annual fair had been due on 25 March (Lady Day) but had been postponed because this fell on a Sunday.

he & I are even. I p[ai]d to Mr Rushworth 15s for the levy to the bells.

27° Martii
This day Kinge Charles hath raigned 13 yeares Compleate oh Lord graunt him longe to raigne for thee & the good of thy Church & people. I have p[ai]d George Curwyn all blessed be god

28° Martii
I prayed and went to Wellingboro fare where I met wth diverse freinds. my mother hath beene ill of an ague but is now recovered blessed be thy name oh Lord I met there with my uncle hanch.[359]

29° Martii 1638
I was very busy in the morninge & could not intend to goe to the sermon,
Mr Bacon[360] afterwards intreated me to be Clarke to a Commission for him at Ketteringe on wednesday next, I doe see & admire gods gracious p[ro]vidence towards me in supplyinge me & sendinge me

---

[359]Christopher Haunch.
[360]This is the ship money phase of the factional rivalry at Burton Latimer between the squire, Thomas Bacon (1601–1642), and the rector, Dr Robert Sibthorpe. Bacon is here being prosecuted in the Star Chamber at the instance of Sibthorpe's ally, George Plowright, as a result of a rating dispute over the ship money writ of 1635: see Introduction, pp. 79–81. Bacon's father, Edward (1547–1627), had moved from Hessett, Suffolk, and had married the daughter of George Poulton, the Catholic recusant squire of Desborough, and his wife, Elizabeth Isham, the aunt of Sir John Isham of Lamport. Thomas was the eldest of three sons, the others being John – with whom Woodford prayed – and Edmund. Their sister, Ann, had married the conformist clergyman William Noke. Thomas had married Margaret Franklin (d. 1627), the daughter of George Franklin of Bolnhurst, Bedfordshire. After Margaret's death he married one Elizabeth (d. 1648). The family remained close to its Isham kinsmen, Sir John and his son Justinian. Sir John presented Noke to his rectory of Lamport in 1636, while Bacon made Noke a pluralist in 1640 by presenting him to that of Great Addington. During the Civil War he was ejected from both. Bacon also possessed an estate at Long Buckby. According to his monument, after a life involving various hardships ('varias aerumnas'), he died quietly. He was succeeded by his son Edmund: memorial inscriptions in Burton parish church; Isham, Diary, p. 66, n. 45; Metcalfe, Visitation of Northamptonshire 1618, pp. 66, 191; Longden, Clergy, under Noke; Longden MS, under 22 November 1636 and 23 September 1640; TNA, PROB 11/207/162 (will of Elizabeth Bacon); Fielding, 'Peterborough', p. 55, n. 81.

practise I was at the heath[361] in the afternoone with Mr Pentlowe where I met my true freind Mr Watts (Lord continue him so) & divers others.

30° Martii

I was walkinge forth this day wth Mr Martin & Mat[thew] Watts towards Kingsthorpe & we discourst of the present Calamityes & the Case of this towne now in regard of the sicknes feared. Oh Lord provide for us in m[er]cye.

I am in hand with a Lease betweene Mr Coles & Mr Ball blessed be thy name oh Lord

31° Martii

The Lord in m[er]cye hath sent me more imployment to day, Blessed be thy name oh Lord for thy good hand towards me; we have invited the good people that are goeinge for

for new England, Mr Sargent Mr Curwyn & their wives for munday night.

1° Apr. 1638 Sab.[bath]

Mr Ball preached in the morninge & Mr Newton in the afternoone some comforts in duty I blesse the Lord.

2° Apr.

Court to day wch was worth neare 50s to me I blesse the Lord, the Lord hath dealt bountifully wth me I prayse his name. we had much wranglinge to day, I have a base passionate spirit Lord subdue my passion for the Lords sake make me as a weaned child.

o[u]r good freinds goeinge for new England supped with us & Mr Martin & ux & Mrs Rushworth.

3° Apr.

The Sessions here to day but were adiourned after their first goeinge downe to

*****

---

[361] This refers to a horse race. Lord William Spencer and other gentry had in 1632 supplied the set-up costs, and Northampton corporation had purchased the silver cup, which was to be ridden for annually on the Thursday in Easter week. Spencer had encountered opposition from Sir Richard Samwell, who had claimed that the activity offended God, who usually inflicted supernatural punishment on those who bred match horses. Such meetings, Samwell had claimed, bred disorder, which contravened the Book of Sports, and he had refused to contribute. He had received short shrift from his patron, who had stated that Sir Anthony Mildmay and Thomas Elmes kept such horses and prospered, while the king himself enjoyed the sport. Northampton Heath was situated to the north-east of the town, adjacent to the Kettering Road. Later sources in the 1670s mention a race on the same day at Harlestone Heath (or Firs) on land owned by Spencer near Althorp: *VCH Northamptonshire*, II (London, 1906), p. 382; Isham, *Diary*, pp. 99, 100 n. 10, 103; Markham and Cox, *Northampton*, II, p. 539; British Library, Add. MSS 25,079, fo. 101; NRO, Spencer (Althorp) MSS, S(A), A3/3.

to the Castle[362] by reason of the sicknesse here I finished the Lease betweene Mr Coles & Mr Ball & it was sealled at Mr Coles his house. I was a witnesse in the busines betweene Mr Eakins & Captayne Bernard, and spoke as imp[ar]tially as I could in the p[rese]nce of the Lord yet Mr Reading condemned me of mincinge[363] & I went afterward with Mr John Bacon[364] & Mr dousinge[365] to Burton Latimer.
4° Apr. 1638
we went in the morninge to Ketteringe, where the Commissioners met vizt dr Pocklington[366] Mr downes[367] Mr Sawyer[368] & Mr Say[369] the first

[362]The sessions reconvened at Wellingborough on 22 May.

[363]Mincing his words, speaking euphemistically.

[364]The brother of Thomas and Edmund Bacon.

[365]Thomas Dowsing was the vicar of Long Buckby: Longden MS, 13 May 1629.

[366]John Pocklington was a prebendary of Peterborough and a royal chaplain. He was a close friend of Bishop Dee and a dedicated advocate of Laudian policies, his written apologias for which were burned by the public hangman on the orders of the Long Parliament: V. Larminie, 'Pocklington, John (d. 1642)', in *ODNB*; Fielding, 'Peterborough', p. 253; Longden, *Clergy*.

[367]Francis Downes (d. 1640), the owner of the manor of Pytchley, was a younger son of a Lancashire gentry family whose seat was at Wardley Hall, Worsley, and had represented the town of Wigan in the parliaments of 1624 and 1625. Downes and his brother Roger (d. 1638), the squire of Wardley, were members of Gray's Inn. Francis was a justice of the peace and possessed a puritan pedigree: in 1631 he had witnessed the will of the godly divine Robert Bolton, and he had himself acted as a patron to the godly ministers John Baseley and John Baynard (the client of Francis Nicolls). Downes had previously clashed with Pocklington in 1634 over a similar commission, albeit an ecclesiastical one. He and Edward Bagshaw had been deputed by the Court of High Commission to take evidence in the case of the justices of the peace John Sawyer of Kettering (his fellow commissioner here) and Francis Nicolls (both also connected to Bolton), who had been charged with holding puritan conventicles with Nicolls's chaplain, William Clarke; but Pocklington's complaint that Downes had protected the defendants resulted in charges being preferred against Downes. In 1635 Sir John Lambe uncovered evidence that Downes had protected John Fisher's conventicle in Northampton from the attentions of Sibthorpe, and that the godly incumbent at Pytchley, John Barker, had held conventicles with Downes at the manor house, as also at the houses of Goodwife Burley, the wife of Downes's coachman and gardener, and of Henry Wyne, another of Downes's servants. The sympathetic account of Barker's execution for murder at Northampton in 1637, which was found at Pytchley later in the century, had belonged to Downes: Fielding, 'Peterborough', pp. 26, 129–130; Temple of Stowe MSS, STT 1880; *Notes and Queries*, CLXIX (1935), pp. 64–65, 301–302; Lancashire Record Office, WCW 1638 (will of Roger Downes); TNA, PROB/11/183 and PROB/11/241 (wills of Francis and Alice Downes); TNA, SP16/308/52; Prest, *Barristers*, p. 357; NRO Isham (Lamport) MSS, I(L) 2570.

[368]John Sawyer was a godly justice of the peace based at Kettering, a patron of Robert Bolton, and, with his brother Francis and the friends detailed in the previous note, a leader of opposition to crown policy in the 1630s. In 1639, at the height of the First Bishops' War, Sibthorpe complained of Sawyer setting a watch for papists in the town of Kettering and subsequently arguing with Sibthorpe about it at the meetings of the justices of the peace: Fielding, 'Peterborough', pp. 26, 129–130; Temple of Stowe MSS, STT 1880.

[369]This might be Francis Say, squire of Great Doddington. His sister Susan had married the conformist vicar of the parish, Anthony Waters. Alternatively, it could be their brother

& last were for the Kinge & thother two p[ro] Mr Bacon one George
Plowright is the relator, Mr John Bacon & I lay at one Pettivers house
at Ketteringe.

5° Apr.

I wrote to and receaved a letter from my wife to day & I heare that
the sicknesse is at a

a house neare unto mine one dishleyes[370] by the great Conduit, but I
beseech the Lord to spare me & my family if it be his will.

I might not be with the Commission[er]s when they examine on the
Kings p[ar]te

I prayd wth Mr John Bacon at Burton [Latimer] at night.

6° Apr. 1638.

my aunt Woodford[371] was here to day at Ketteringe to intreat me to
speake that they may not have an apprentice so I have spoke to Mr
downes.

we cannot make an end & so have adiourned the Commission till
Wednesday next. Mr Sires[372] & Mr Moulshoe were here to night.

I prayd againe wth Mr John Bacon at Mr Pettivers oh Lord worke
grace in his hart for the Lords sake.

7° Apr.

I rose prettye early & came to holcot to goodman hopkins, & so home
in good time I blesse the Lord.

where I heare two have dyed out of dishleyes house another sick in
one Washingto[n's] house[373] in the drap[er]y Lord helpe us heale us
sanctify thy stroke unto us for the Lords sake.

8° Apr 1638. Sab.[bath]

Mr Newton preached in the morninge and Mr Ball in the afternoone,
I sate in the seate with my wife to day because loath to sit in the

Thomas, the conformist rector of Whiston: Metcalfe, *Visitation of Northamptonshire 1618*, p. 13;
Longden, *Visitation of Northamptonshire 1681*, p. 43; TNA, SP16/375/82; Longden, *Clergy*.

[370]Thomas Dishley had attained the freedom of the borough in 1630: Freemen of
Northampton.

[371]Joan, the wife of the diarist's uncle, Henry Woodford of Old.

[372]John Syers, lord of the manor of Loddington, was the son of the catholic recusant
Robert Syers, and the son-in-law of the godly lawyer Robert Tanfield of Loddington, who
bequeathed law books to him in his will of 1639. With Robert Mulshoe he was the close
friend of the rector, Joseph Hill, a Church court official. Syers was a Civil War Royalist, and
in 1671 bequeathed his own library to Sir Justinian Isham of Lamport: Isham, *Diary*, p. 64,
n. 30; Longden, *Clergy*.

[373]Eleanor, the daughter of Daniel Washington, a tailor who had achieved the freedom of
the borough in 1623, died soon afterwards. Thomas Dishley's son and daughter were buried
on 3 and 6 April: Freemen of Northampton, unpaginated, dated 1623; NRO, 223P/1, All
Saints' burial register, April 1638.

Alley wth the Sergeants [*crossed out:* another] one dead in Washingtons house to day oh Lord command thy destroyinge Angell to cease for the Lords sake oh pull downe the abhominacons that are amongst us that so thou mayest delight to show m[er]cy unto us for the Lords sake.

I have bene very dull & sleepy this day Lord p[ar]don it to me for the Lords sake Amen.

9° Apr. Co[u]rt to day

I prayed against rash anger, & the Lord heard me in a gracious manner blessed be thy name oh Lord.

I have sent Mr Pentlowe the Bill in Chancery ingrossed; I have p[ai]d Mr Trueman all. my mother is come to us to day by gods p[ro]vidence to keep my wife company in my absence.

[*left margin: symbol of a hand with finger pointing at this line*] my sweete Children are to goe towards London to

to morow uppon [*above text: symbol of a hand with finger pointing at the next word*] goodman Lamports horse in wicker baskets wth Su[374] & goodman wright oh Lord blesse them & keepe them defend from danger by thy mighty p[ro]vidence carry them thether as uppon Eagles wings keepe them in health there watch over us all in m[er]cy & bringe us agayne in safty with peace & comfort to this place for the Lords sake.

10° April. 1638.

I prayed and my wife & I went alonge with our Children about as farre as Sinpton Windmill[375] I humbly cast & committed them to the p[ro]vidence of the Lord who I know was able onely to keepe them from dangers.

I went afterwards to holcot to Mr Pearson[376] & William Chapman to take the answere of old hopkins to Lovells[377] Bill.

11° April 1638

I prayed and went early to Ketteringe to meete Mr Bacon & the Commission[er]s uppon the same businesse we sate the last weeke, and at the Red lyon we spent the first day.

12° April

we examined diverse witnesses this day ex p[ar]te def[endan]t. Mr Pentlowe was here.

---

[374] Susan Tue.

[375] Simpson, Buckinghamshire.

[376] Robert Pearson of Walgrave. Robert Wyne, who also held land at Burton Latimer, was one of his tenants: NRO, Isham (Lamport) MSS, IL 1714, 1715.

[377] William Lovell of Burton Latimer. Hopkins may be Thomas, the son of George Hopkins of Holcot, and was probably Lovell's tenant: PDR, Church Survey Book 5, fos 138r, 140r–v.

13° April we examined more witnesses to day ex p[ar]te def[endan]t.
Mr daniel Readinge dyned here he & diverse others have a great
facultye in merry tales & Jests, which I dare not allow my selfe in or
at least apply or give my mind unto, although they take much wth
the hearers, but Lord Ile trust in thee alone for favor & imployment
from men & for abilityes to p[er]forme what I undertake Mr Sires &
Mr Moulshoe played longe here at night Lord convert them & make
them instrum[en]ts of thy glory.

14° April 1638
we examined some few short witnesses (I think) and afterward made
up the Commission; I had prayed before that the Lord would move
Mr Bacon to consider well for my paynes & Losses; so he gave me 5li
I blesse the Lord and then I came to North[amp]ton where I found
that more had dyed of the disease since Munday.
15° April Sab.[bath]
Mr Newton preached in the morninge & Mr Ball in the afternoone.
16. 17. 18. 19. 20. 21. 22. all these omitted by beinge too longe ere I
recorded what had passed.
[*crossed out:* 16 Apr.] 23 Apr.
St Georges fare held here[378] to day though nothinge great by reason
of the sicknesse.[379]
24° Apr.
I prayed & went to the Court & afterward my

my wife and I & [*crossed out:* my] Wm Warren[380] of Old came out for
London, & by gods m[er]cye came well to dunstable to Mr Walkers.
Mr Smith[381] paid me 3li to day for my watch.
Mr Ireland[382] Mr Chamberlaine & Mr Cooke overtook us on the way

[378]The fair was held on Northampton Heath, to the north-east of the town on the Kettering
Road, owing to the plague: TNA, SP16/393/15.
[379]On 1 May 1638 Mayor Collis wrote to Recorder Lane complaining that this decay in
trade had been occasioned by an exaggeration of the severity of the plague. Northampton
traders had been prevented from conducting business in the surrounding countryside:
for example, Sir Hatton Fermor, a justice of the peace, had forbidden any Northampton
men from attending the May Day fair at Towcester. As a result, many Northampton
inhabitants had fled the town, rendering multitudes of labourers unemployed. Alderman
Gifford disagreed with Collis's view that the level of plague had been over estimated: Jackson,
'Ship money', pp. 118–119; TNA, SP16/389/7, 8.
[380]For the Warrens of Old, see Diary, p. 226, n. 482.
[381]Possibly Francis Smith, saddler: TNA, SP16/468/76; NRO, Finch (Hatton) MSS, F(H)
3501.
[382]William Ireland of Sutton Bassett on the Leicestershire border, attorney, was undersheriff
of the county in 1618, 1622, 1632, and 1638: J.H. Burgess, 'The social structure of Bedfordshire
and Northamptonshire 1524–1764' (unpublished DPhil thesis, University of York, 1978),

Richard Tresham[383] went along with us.

25° [crossed out: illegible letter] April. St Markes day.

we prayed & went out somewhat early & layed at Barnet where I met with one Pritchet a North[amp]ton man,[384] & wth Wm. Miller Mr ffosbrooke[385] & we came afterwards to London in due time where we found o[u]r parents Children & freinds very well I blesse the Lord.

26° [crossed out: illegible letter] Apr. 1638.

I slept somewhat ill to night, I prayed & went to Westm[inster] hall & about my occasions

Lord wthout thee I cannot p[ro]sp[e]r therefore I pray thee blesse me make thy face shine uppon me & mine let o[u]r soules thrive & p[ro]sp[er] thou the worke of o[u]r hands for the Lords sake Amen.

[24–29 April crossed out vertically – italicized] *24° April 1638 I prayed and went about my occasions and* [crossed out: *sometimes I meet wth troubles & stormes*] *I kept the Court in the morninge, & afterward my wife & I & Wm Warren came along towards London, we tooke o[u]r Leave of the towne & o[u]r house & commended them & o[u]r selves to gods good blessing & p[ro]vidence & came to dunstable that night to Mr Walkers at the white hart. Lord be praysed for pr[e]servinge us givinge of us health & comfort.*

we left onely Temp[er]ance at o[u]r house.

25. Apr.

we came safe to London where we found o[u]r children well blessed be the Lord.

******

p. 186; Jackson, 'Ship money', pp. 115, 147; M.E. Finch, *The Wealth of Five Northamptonshire Families 1540–1640*, Publications of the Northamptonshire Record Society XIX (Oxford, 1966), p. 33.

[383]Tresham (1611–1683) was the son of William Tresham of Old and Elizabeth (née Isham). William was a member of a cadet branch of the Catholic Tresham family of Rushton: his sister Eliza married the godly Northampton barrister Joseph Bryan. In 1648 Richard witnessed the will of Frances Chapman of Old, presumably some relation of his son-in-law John Chapman, who was later to be Sir Justinian Isham's bailiff: PDR, Archdeaconry of Northampton Wills, third series, A71; Isham, *Diary*, pp. 21–22; TNA, PROB/11/179; Prest, *Barristers*, pp. 346–347.

[384]William Prichard, a freeman of the town in 1640: NRO, Finch (Hatton) MSS, F(H) 3501.

[385]John Fosbrooke, the rector of Cranford St Andrew, a client of Bishop John Williams of Lincoln. Fosbrooke had been a regular preacher at the (now abolished) Kettering lecture; in 1633 he had dedicated a collection of published sermons to his patron, who, he claimed, had attended many of them. His family owned the manor, and he was also connected to the moderate godly in the area: Margaret Tomlin, widow of James Tomlin, a clerical appointee of the Montagu family, named him an executor of her will and made him responsible for the godly education of her children, and Woodford's friend Thomas Freeman made him a bequest in 1637. Fosbrooke was chosen by Bishop Dee to preach at his primary visitation in 1634, in what was an attempt to win over the moderate godly to Laudian policies: Fielding, 'Peterborough', p. 26; Sheils, *Puritans*, pp. 40, 99, 105, 114–115; PDR Archdeaconry of Northampton Wills, second series, M201 and G211.

26° Apr. 1638.
I prayed and went to Westm[inster] hall.
27° Apr.
The businesse of Scotland is much talked on and what the issue will be none know,
all expect.[386] *Oh Lord I beseech thee bringe good out of it get thy selfe glory & a*
name for the Lords sake.
28° Apr.
The Lord is pleased to give me some imployment here I blesse him for it.
29° Apr.

Newes here that the Scottish B[isho]ps are fled through feare & come
hether to London.
27° April 1638
I prayed and went to the hall & could not yet dispatch Wm Warrens
businesse the businesse in Starr=chamber to day I think was betweene
the doctors & Apothecaryes.[387]
28 April.
this day Justice Joanes[388] & Judge hutton argued the case of the
shipmoney, Judge Joanes fluttred in his argum[en]t, meteorlike hunge
betweene heaven & earth & yet in the end concluded ag[ains]t Mr
hampden.
but Justice hutton delivered his opinion freely and

and playnely against the businesse shewinge it to be contrary to the
lawes of the Realme & answerd the argum[en]ts brought on the other
side, wth much applause of the people. Blessed be god for makinge of
him a man of Courage.[389]

---

[386] The Covenant was now rapidly winning support in opposition to the crown's imposition
of the Prayer Book: Gardiner, *History*, VIII, pp. 325–348.

[387] A dispute between the Royal College of Physicians and the Society of Apothecaries,
which lasted for most of the century, over the latter's encroachment on the former's rights:
K. Thomas, *Religion and the Decline of Magic* (Harmondsworth, 1973), p. 14.

[388] Justice William Jones died just in time to avoid impeachment by the Long Parliament:
Jones, *Bench*, p. 139.

[389] Of the minority of five judges who eventually (by June 1638) supported John Hampden,
only Hutton and Sir George Croke did so on general principles as opposed to technicalities.
The aftermath of Hutton's verdict was his being accused of high treason by Thomas
Harrison, who had been presented to the rectory of Crick by William Laud as Master of St
John's College, Oxford. Harrison claimed that Hutton, while riding on the East Midlands
circuit, encouraged Northamptonshire folk to resist this prerogative tax, the legitimacy of
which had been asserted by orthodox divines. Clearly Harrison expected his views to fall
on sympathetic ears, but the verdict went heavily against him: Jones, *Bench*, pp. 125–128;
Fielding, 'Peterborough', p. 133.

29° April. 1638
[*crossed out:* I went to dr. Sto] We p[ro]cured good Mr Pearne to preach at our Church in the wall[390] who dealt faythfuly & was wonderfully assisted both in prayer & preachinge blessed be thy name oh Lord. Lord hold him still as a starre in thy hand for the Lords sake.
graciously affected in dutyes this day I blesse the Lord.
30° Apr.
I prayed and went about my occasions & Lord

1° 2° 3° 4° 5 6 7 8 9 10 11° 12 13 14° [*crossed out:* 15 16 17° 18] Maii 1638. [*rest of page blank*]

[*blank page*]

15° Maii 1638. Tuesday in Whitsun weeke
I prayed and came out of London to day my father & my mother & my deare wife & sweete Children & my brother came with me to Islington where we broke our fast and I came afterward to dunstable, one Mr Bourke[391] a papist came alonge with me; I used what arguments I could to convince him of his error & prayd unto the Lord in his behalfe Lord heare me for thy gloryes sake.
16° Maii
I prayed and we came out somewhat early and came to Wellingborow m[a]rket in due time he went afterward to my Lord Brud[e]nells. I heare ill newes of the sicknesse at Old.[392]
17° Maii
my cousin Wm. Ragdale Wm. Vincent & his brother[393] are gone towards London

to day. The Court at Grafton [Regis] to day.

---

[390] All Hallows', London Wall.
[391] Possibly Lord Thomas Brudenell's kinsman Thomas Brooke of Madeley, Shropshire, who was impeached for treason against Parliament during the Civil War as a delinquent papist. He was the son of Sir Basil Brooke (d. 1646), a leading Catholic close to the king, and his wife, Etheldreda Brudenell: M. Bennett, 'Brooke, Sir Basil (1576–1646)', in *ODNB*.
[392] Old was badly hit by the plague, recording eighteen plague burials for April and May, after which, in the words of the parish register, God turned 'from wrath to mercie': J.F.D. Shrewsbury, *A History of Bubonic Plague in the British Isles* (Cambridge, 1971), p. 398; J.C. Cox, *Parish Registers* (London, 1910), p. 157 (quotation).
[393] William Vincent of Finedon had two brothers, Francis and Augustine. They were the nephews of Augustine Vincent, Rouge Rose Pursuivant of Arms, who had conducted the visitation of Northamptonshire in 1618: Metcalfe, *Visitation of Northamptonshire 1618*, p. 150.

18° Maii
I prayed and went to Abington to Mr Bullivants and thether came
to me Mr Sam. Martin Mr Goodman[394] John Cole John Cox James
ffr[yers] Mrs Crick Nan[395] & Temp[er]ance, who relate to me the
miseryes of North[amp]ton.
I wrote to Mr Maior[396] from Abington by Mr Martin & sent 20s
inclosed & gave him lib[er]ty to dispose of the p[ro]fitts of my court
to the use of the poore & towards my taxe.
19° Maii
I have heard lately that old good wife Arnold is dead at Old.
The sicknesse is somewhat dangerous there. I went to Pitchley to
day to Mr downes & to my uncle Tebots[397] & to Rob. Langleyes[398] at
harowden I was wonderfull sleepy in the afternoone with a stupid
sleepinesse that I was much afrayd

20 Maii 1638. Sab.[bath]
I am now at Wilbye & am in great distresse through feare of beinge
sick for I feel my selfe very aguish & feverish & know not what will
become of me if I should be sick, Lord I pray thee in m[er]cye looke
uppon me p[ar]don my sinnes wch might p[ro]voke thee to wrath
Lord heale me for thy m[er]cyes sake & blesse this thy Sabath unto
me for the Lords sake & blesse my deare wife sweete Children & whole

[394] George Goodman was a key member of Woodford's godly clique. He served as bailiff of
the town from 1636 until 1637 and chamberlain from 1643 until 1645. He was a sidesman at
All Saints' from 1634 until 1635, when he reported the parish's failure to create an east end
altar, and a churchwarden in 1643. Ramsden claimed that he received communion sitting
from Thomas Ball on 3 September 1637: Markham and Cox, *Northampton*, II, pp. 562, 568;
Vestry Minutes, pp. 21–38; PDR, CB64, fo. 75r–v; TNA, SP16/474/80.
[395] Ann Spicer.
[396] William Collis.
[397] Everard Tebbot of Old, whose nuncupative will of 1643 mentioned his wife, Ann
(Woodford's aunt), and Gilbert Tebbott: TNA, PROB/11/193.
[398] A member of the godly Langley family of Harrowden. In 1620 William Langley had
been reported for gadding from his own parish (whose vicar was Thomas Nicholas) to
hear sermons at Robert Bolton's parish of Broughton. Robert Langley appeared in the
ecclesiastical court in 1626 accused of insulting James Forsyth, minister at Old, 'sayinge yt
the Judmt of god was come upon that town because I [. . .] did not preach upon Wensdaies
being fastinge daies lately appointed by the Kinge'. In 1636 Robert appeared again, this
time admitting gadding in the afternoon away from his own parish (where now Thomas
Campion was vicar, a client of George Charnock from the Catholic recusant family of
Wellingborough) to Wilby (where Andrew Perne was the minister), Pytchley (John Barker and
his curate, John Seaton), and Hardwick (John Baynard) 'to hear the minister[s] there deliver
doctrine accordinge to trueth'. The silenced minister mentioned on 20 May is possibly
another member of the family, James Langley, unbeneficed at this stage but instituted as
vicar of Harrowden on 29 May: PDR, CB48, fo. 465r–v; PDR, CB58, unfoliated, under
May 1626; PDR, CBA63, fo. 408r–v (first quotation); PDR, CBA20, fo. 248v; Longden,
Clergy; Longden MS, 30 October 1622 and 29 May and 6 July 1638.

family for the Lords sake & bringe me to them againe wth safty &
peace & comfort.
Mr Pearne preached both times very p[ro]fitably I prayse the Lord.
I dyned at Mr Pentlowes & supped at Mr Pearnes. Mr Langley the
silenced minister was here to day much troubled with a grudging of
my Ague as I suppose.
21° Maii I prayed and went to Rowell[399] fare and

and find my selfe very well all this day I blesse the Lord, I dyned at
John Ponders[400] house with Mr Bullivant Mr Lewes of Waldegrave Mr
Male[401] & Mr Rushworth I went after to see Mr Nicolls at ffaxton who
used me kindly I blesse the Lord & gave me 10s & d[e]l[ive]r[e]d me
50s to send to the poore of North[amp]ton, I went after to Sr John
Ishams, & then to Mr Gourneyes[402] at hanginge houghton where I
intended to have lodged but Mr Rushworth not beinge there, I came
to Wilbye safe & in due time I prayse the Lord
I prayed for practise & ability at the Sess.[ions]
22° Maii 1638
I prayed and went on foot to Wellingborow [*crossed out*: at] to the
Sess.[ions] where they were kept by reason of the sicknesse at
North[amp]ton;[403] and it was there moved by Mr Rainsford[404] for a
weekly allowance to North[amp]ton for their releife & the Country is

---

[399] Rothwell.

[400] The godly Ponder family of Rothwell (Owen, his son John, and John's four children, including William, a minister), together with their friend John James, had been prosecuted for ceremonial nonconformity in the Church courts by Sir John Lambe and Dr Samuel Clarke since at least 1634 (and their friend William Dodson since 1612): Fielding, 'Peterborough', pp. 73, 102.

[401] In 1636 Francis Lewis of Walgrave was reported to the Church courts for omitting to pay the parish clerk's wages. Samuel Male was presented to the vicarage of Litchborough on 9 March 1632 by Sir Samuel Luke of Bedfordshire, who was Sir Valentine Knightley's grandson and later an officer in the Parliamentarian army: S. Kelsey, 'Luke, Sir Samuel (bap. 1603, d. 1670)', *ODNB*; PDR, CBA63, fo. 309r.

[402] John Gurney of Hanging Houghton was a landowner: Isham, *Diary*, p. 160, n. 16.

[403] The county quarter sessions had been adjourned at Northampton on 3 April 1638.

[404] Richard Rainsford of Dallington had been Recorder of Daventry since 1630 and a barrister since 1632. He had married Dr Samuel Clarke's daughter Katherine in 1637. According to Woodford, he was elected Northampton town attorney on 16 January 1638/39 (he lived in St Giles's parish), in which position he served until rising to deputy recorder in 1653 (the recorder was the Earl of Manchester). He was ousted during the Protectorate, but at the Restoration he was knighted and ended his career as Chief Justice of the King's Bench: S. Calkins, 'Rainsford, Sir Richard (1605–1680)', in *ODNB*; NRO 233P/107, unfoliated, under 16 January 1640; Markham and Cox, *Northampton*, II, pp. 103–106.

to pay 100li a weeke over & above the 48li 6s 8d wch is weekly taxed uppon the townes within 5 miles about[405] blessed

blessed be god for this releife, dr Clarke & dr Sibthorpe[406] moved earnestly for it, but Sr Roland St John[407] was somew[ha]t averse. The devillish plot ag[ains]t a p[ro]fessor one Mrs Clarke by one ffolwell of ffosters booth was layd open to day at the Sessions to day,

[405]Following an appeal from the mayor, William Collis, to the recorder, Richard Lane, dated 1 May, complaining about the economic dislocation caused by the disease, Lane had approached the Privy Council, who on 10 May had instructed the justices of the peace to arrange (at their next quarter sessions on 22 May) for Northampton to be provisioned and for a weekly tax to be levied on the county for the town's relief. In the meantime, Lane and Dr Clarke, acting as a justice of the peace, had made temporary provision for relief by ordering a weekly collection of £48 from towns within five miles. The constable of Marston Trussell, to the south of Northampton, recorded raising £4 14s od. Here Rainsford (supported by his father-in-law, Clarke, and Sibthorpe in the teeth of St John's reluctance) is proposing the raising of an additional £100 per week, to be drawn from the county, in addition to that raised by the nearby towns. In June Clarke asserted that the increased county contribution had been achieved (despite resistance) on 22 May, and the market moved to Northampton Heath for safety. Sheriff Sir John Hanbury stated that the combined weekly total of £148 was still being paid on 10 September 1638. Shrewsbury estimates that such relief was generally paid at a rate of 1s per head per week, and that therefore at least 2,960 were in receipt of it out of a total population of less than 5,000. There were problems accounting for the money raised. The town assembly petitioned Parliament in 1640, requesting action to call the justices to account for money in their possession that had been intended for Northampton's relief: Jackson, 'Ship money', pp. 118–121, 150, nn. 17 and 20; Markham and Cox, *Northampton*, II, p. 239; Shrewsbury, *Bubonic Plague*, p. 398. For Woodford's money-raising efforts in the capital, see Diary, pp. 202, 210, 218–220, 230, 252.

[406]A zealous conformist and anti-puritan Church court official, Sibthorpe held an absolutist view of royal power that had come to the fore over his infamous apologia for the forced loan. His first wife was called Douglas Neale. His second wife was Sir John Lambe's sister Susan, and through his brother-in-law he was closely allied with Laud. A royal chaplain, he had been actively involved in the fall of Archbishop George Abbot and Bishop John Williams, and had narrowly escaped impeachment by the parliament of 1629: J. Fielding, 'Sibthorpe, Robert (d. 1662)', in *ODNB*.

[407]Sir Rowland St John, the younger brother of Oliver, first Earl of Bolingbroke, had lived at Woodford since 1621 and had been one of the county's most conscientious deputy lieutenants. However, he enjoyed godly connections – his daughter Judith married Francis Nicolls's son Edward – and Sibthorpe certainly regarded him as one of the puritan conspirators determined to undermine Church and state. He drew up petitions complaining about government policies, but his relationship with the court was not straightforward. He supported the candidacy of his fellow deputy, Thomas Elmes, for knight of the shire for the Short Parliament, and his account of the misconduct of the supporters of the successful candidate (Sir Gilbert Pickering) may have been used in evidence when Elmes appealed, unsuccessfully, against the result. As civil war approached, St John took on the mantle of mediator. He did not sign the county petition of 21 January 1642 in support of the Grand Remonstrance, but was persuaded to present it to Parliament, and was a Parliamentarian in the war itself, albeit a lukewarm one: V.L. Stater, 'The lord lieutenancy on the eve of the Civil Wars: the impressment of George Plowright', *Historical Journal*, 2 (1986), pp. 279–296; Fielding, 'Peterborough', pp. 244–249, 251–260; Temple of Stowe MSS, STT 1876–77, 1880.

ffolwell had p[ro]cured one Pinckerd his man to say he saw another in
the act of incontinencye wth her, which Pinckerd afterward confessed
the truth & cleered her innocencye.[408] I supped wth Mr Raynsford &
Mr Readinge at the Angell where I lodge to night
23° Maii 1638
I prayd & went to the Sessions house & the Lord hath graciously
enabled me to speake in the courses wherein I were reteyned.
I went to Wilby to night & supped with Mr Pearne that sweete man,
& lay at

at Mr Pentlowes, I pray to be defended to morow in my goeinge to
North[amp]ton.
24° Maii 1638
I prayed and went alonge towards North[amp]ton Mr Readinge
overtooke me on the way so we stayed a while at Mr Eakins at Weston
[Favell] and I went alonge toward North[amp]ton, when I came to the
Northgate I met wth a woman that had lived well who complayned
for want of a peck of corne; I went into the towne & wept uppon
it & confessed that sinne was the cause of our mourninge, when I
was about to goe into Mrs Cricks shop Wm[409] desired me to forbeare
for there was one sick betty.[410] yet when Temp[er]ance came from
Church I adventured uppon gods good p[ro]vidence & went into my
house for some things I needed & stayed there a good while, yet I was
troubled at the wormewood & in the leme[411] wch my horse did eate

[408]This was part of a dispute between the godly and their enemies in the parish of Pattishall.
Henry Folwell (a tanner) had previously lived at Northampton, where he had been involved
in a dispute with the mayor and aldermen, but had by now moved to Foster's Booth in
Pattishall parish. Here he had given evidence to the High Commission concerning the
ceremonial nonconformity of the vicar, Miles Burkit, since when, he claimed, Burkit had
persecuted him, including having him here bound over to appear at Northampton assizes.
On 14 May he had written to Archbishop Laud for redress, who had referred the matter to
Sir John Lambe. Mistress Clarke was possibly the wife of William Clarke of Eastcote near
Pattishall, near to whose seat (according to the Church commissioner Richard Powell, the
other, anti-puritan, vicar of Pattishall) 'ye puritans and Nonconformists doe all sitt soe that
their revered gestures cannot be seene' (PDR, Church Survey Book 5, fo. 50r–v). Woodford
and Dr Clarke concurred on her godliness: Clarke reported to Lambe in June 1638 that this
'puritan' had been condemned in the Peterborough Church courts for 'calling the Divine
sermons porradg, and the long puritan sermons Roaste Meate' (TNA, SP16/393/15), and
had successfully appealed against the verdict in the Archbishop's Court of Audience. The
charge of incontinency (a favourite line of attack for the godly's enemies) was part of the same
campaign. Folwell's servant was Thomas Pinckerd: Fielding, 'Peterborough', pp. 102–107,
242 n. 11; TNA, SP16/387/70; Book of Orders, p. 30.
[409]William Spicer, Samuel Crick's stepfather.
[410]Betty was probably Samuel and Mary Crick's servant.
[411]Wormwood was a bitter-tasting plant; leme the husk of a nut.

of, that I suspected came out of the chamber of the sick, I heare she was

was yesterday in my house, I prayed with poore Temp[er]ance, & alone & have besought the Lord for the poore towne, & my poore family Lord be a wall of fire about us for the Lords sake

I went after to Mr Maior[412] to Mr Martin Mr Gifford Mr Bot Mr Bradford Mr Sillesby[413] Mrs Knight[414] &.

I gave away all the silver I had beinge above 10s.

I came away about 3 or 4 a clock or after & came to Long buckby to Mr Bacon where I found kind enterteynemt though I told them that I came from North[amp]ton, and I was indeed much afrayd least I had bene infected & I prayd though distractedly in private, & had too much feare of infeccon.

I gave one 10s as I remember for Perryn.

25° Maii 1638

I prayed, & went to Brockhole[415] to meet with Sam Martin there but he was gone before I came Mr John Bacon [*crossed out*: came] went along wth me to the Porte way[416] towards London. I came & stayed at Mrs ffarm[er]s at Toucester & tooke

hatton alonge with me so we came with saftye to dunstable to night, to Mr Walkers. I was fearefull as I came along to day of beinge Robbed betweene Weedon & Toucester. I was very wett this afternoone.

26° Maii 1638

I came out somew[ha]t late by reason of the Fayre I stayed at St Albans wth Mr downes his man & one Mr Wythers & came safe afterwards to London I blesse the Lord where I found them all well I prayse god.

27° Maii 1638 Sab.[bath]

I prayed and went to dr Stoughtons both times.

---

[412]William Collis.

[413]Matthew Sillesby: see Diary, p. 181, n. 330, on John Sillesby.

[414]The wife of William Knight, mayor of the town in 1626 and 1635: Markham and Cox, *Northampton*, II, p. 252; PDR, Archdeaconry of Northampton Wills, second series, L120.

[415]Brockhall.

[416]The Roman road (or port way) of Watling Street ran through Towcester to Stony Stratford: W. Camden, *Britannia* (London, 1637), p. 506; Pevsner, *Northamptonshire*, p. 435; W.G. Hoskins, *The Making of the English Landscape* (London, 1977), p. 233.

28. Maii
I prayed & went to Westm[inster] hall. my Lord Cheife Baron &
B[aron] denham have delivered their opinions ag[ains]t the Kinge in
the ship money.[417]

29° Maii 1638
I prayed and went to Westm[inster] hall.
30° Maii
This day Sr Richard Wisemans[418] [crossed out: was censured for] busines
beinge an accusacon of my Lord keep[er] for bribery was heard in
Starr=chamber to day.
31° Maii
about this time harrison was tried in the Kings bench for accusinge
Justice hutton of high treason & is fined 10000li to be imprisoned &
make submiss[ion] in Westm[inster] hall to the courts of Justice wth a
pap[er] on his head.[419]
1° Junii
This day (I think) Sr Richard Wiseman censured for accusinge
my Lord keep[er] of bribery & his secretary Mr Tompson & for
asp[er]singe Justice

Jones, he was fined 10000li to the Kinge 5000li to my Lord keep[er]
500li to Mr Tompson 1000li to Justice Jones to be imprisoned to stand
uppon the pillory & loose his eares &.
2° Junii 1638
diverse newes is strong concerninge Scotland, & the marquesse
hambledon[420] is gone or goeinge to them as ambassador from the
Kinge, Lord order every thinge as may be for thy glory for the Lords
sake Amen. This night (I think) Mr Samuel Martin came to London
from North[amp]ton, & his wife. Lord in m[er]cye looke uppon o[u]r
poore towne for the Lords sake Amen.

---

[417] Sir Humphrey Davenport and Sir John Denham: Jones, *Bench*, pp. 126–127.
[418] Sir Richard Wiseman was found guilty of slandering Lord Keeper Thomas Coventry.
Wiseman had accused him of taking bribes, but the Star Chamber found against Wiseman
and he was heavily punished. In 1641 he appealed to the House of Lords but was killed
in the London riots before the case was heard: Jones, *Bench*, p. 106; J.S. Hart, *Justice upon
Petition: the House of Lords and the reformation of justice 1621–1675* (London, 1991), pp. 131–132.
[419] Diary, p. 179, n. 324 on Sir Richard Hutton.
[420] The royal favourite, James, third Marquess and later first Duke of Hamilton (1610–1674),
heir to the premier aristocratic dynasty in Scotland, was royal commissioner to the Glasgow
Assembly of 1638 that abolished episcopacy and the royal supremacy in the Church of
Scotland: J.J. Scally, 'Hamilton, James, first duke of Hamilton (1606–1649)', in *ODNB*.

3° Junii Sab.[bath]

This [*crossed out:* day] morninge I heard the deane of Bristow at Stoughtons[421] who taught very honestly, blessed be thy name oh Lord, and in the afternoone I heard Mr Atkins at Mr Goodwyns,[422] and was graciously affected I blesse the Lord.

4° Junii 1638

I have besought the Lord [*crossed out:* of all things] about my deare wife for a gracious delivery & for a child wth right shape & forme to be a comfort to us & an Instrument of gods glory in due time Lord heare o[u]r poore weake peticons & be still the same god & father unto us as thou hast bene for the Lords sake.

5° Junii

[*crossed out, illegible*] we heare there dyed but 16 of the sicknesse at North[amp]ton this last weeke blessed be thy name oh Lord, so it decreased 10 Lord give us a sanctifyed use of thy stroke and a sudden & happy returne.

6 Junii

Starrchamber day.

This tearme I became bound wth my M[aste]r Mr John Readinge to Sr John hanbury p[ro] 200li to be p[ai]d 14° Nov. next, he desired me to doe him that

that Courtesy and I was suddenly overcome to p[ro]mise him & beinge then at Sr Johns Lodginge the bond was filled up, and I sealled & but in the interim I was much afflicted to thinke what danger I exposed my selfe unto & I remembred the place in p[ro]verbes take a pledge of him that is suerty for another[423] & yet could not then for shame retract Sr John beinge pr[e]sent and fearinge I should then discredit my M[aste]r I after told my wife & we were both much troubled, oh Lord in m[er]cye suffer not my feare to come uppon me deliver me from this danger and give me grace & care to take heed how I expose

---

[421] Edward Chetwind, Dean of Bristol from 1617 until his death in 1639, was associated with the godly minister Richard Bernard, and had obtained his position through the patronage of James Montagu, the Calvinist Bishop of Bath and Wells: K. Fincham, *Prelate as Pastor: the episcopate of James I* (Oxford, 1990), p. 194.

[422] John Goodwin was the vicar and lecturer of St Stephen's, Coleman Street, from 1633 until 1661, and a later Independent. During the 1630s he was accused of failing to conform to Laudian ceremonial but he was abandoning Calvinist predestinarianism and became an Arminian under the Commonwealth; T. Liu, 'Goodwin, John (c.1594–1665)', in *ODNB*; Webster, *Godly Clergy*, p. 327 and *passim*.

[423] Proverbs 20:16: 'Take his garment that is surety for a stranger: and take a pledge of him for a strange woman'. Lord Edward Montagu's father gave him similar advice (taken from Proverbs 11:15): 'He that hateth suertyship is sure': quoted in E.S. Cope, *The Life of a Public Man: Edward, first Baron Montagu of Boughton, 1562–1644* (Philadelphia, 1981), p. 8.

my selfe & family here after for the Lords sake. my M[aste]r afterwards
sealled to me a Counterbond to save me harmlesse but Lord doe thou
in m[er]cy defend me.
7° Junii 1638.
The small pox are much in London, but the sicknesse[424] at a very Low
ebbe blessed be god though they come hether from many p[ar]tes of
the Country that are infected.

8° Junii 1638
The towne very full of people. Mr Robins fayles to pay me money.
9° Junii The Lord doth graciously carry me on through difficultyes:
he is with me in the fire & in the water blessed be his name.
10° Junii Sab.[bath]
I prayed & heard Mr Sedgwick[425] both times, blessed be thy name oh
Lord for so good an instrument in thy church Lord blesse his labors
& endeavors to thy glory & the salvacon of soules for the Lords sake.
11° Junii
I heare that one Bert hath sup[er]seded the outlawry of the Palmers
of Raunston.[426]
12° Junii
I have put in a sup[er]sed[eas][427] to Clayton p[ro] Mr Bott.

13° Junii 1638
Tearme ends to day. I prayed and went to Westm[inster] hall,
14° Junii
I prayed and went to my Chamber.[428]
15° Junii
I am often troubled in respect of outward things but I desire to wayt
uppon the Lord many are in a worse Condicon & yet more contented
Lord p[ar]don my sinne & faylinge helpe me for time to come for the
Lords sake.
16° Junii
The Lord is still gracious to me & my family in p[er]fectinge us in
health blessed be his name.

[424] The plague.
[425] Obadiah Sedgwick was the curate and lecturer at St Mildred's, Bread Street, from 1630
until 1639, the godly protégé of Lord Horace Vere and Robert Rich, Earl of Warwick, and a
future Parliamentarian and member of the Westminster Assembly: B. Donagan, 'Sedgwick,
Obadiah (1599/1600–1658)', in *ODNB*.
[426] Ravenstone near Olney, Buckinghamshire.
[427] A stay of legal proceedings.
[428] His chamber at Clement's Inn.

17° Junii Sab.[bath]
I heard Mr Sedgwick who taught p[ro]fitably

18° Junii 1638
Mr Martin went out of towne to day. This night (as I re[member])
Mr Pyke p[ro]cured his wife to [*crossed out:* seale] dispose of 1000li to
him, which she had lib[er]ty to dispose of, & I refused to be witnesse
knowinge that he had wrought her to it by undue meanes & my father
refused likewise.

19° Junii
This day my father & Mr Bate & my selfe went about to some
North[amp]tonshire men to entreat their liberallity to distressed
North[amp]ton & Sr Paul Pynder[429] gave us 50li blessed be god.

20° Junii
we went agayne in the morninge, and some we found harty [*crossed out:*
others] & charitable & others gave sparingly & some nothinge at all,
in both dayes we gathered about 70li whereof of North[amp]tonshire
men

men about 67li od[d] money; my father & mother wife & I supped
this night at Mr Woolfalls wth Mr Bellamy & ux &

21° Junii 1638
I prayed with my deare wife; and after went to the Carryer
endeavoringe to send downe my money but could not under 10s
so I put the gold in my boots & prayed unto the Lord to p[ro]tect me.
I stayed for hatton at Mr Woodfords in Islington till past 5 a clock &
came safe to St Albans I blesse the Lord & from there from the Red
Lyon I writ back to my deare wife.

22° Junii
I rose early and prayed and came to dunstable to breakfast & to
Grafton [Regis] p[rese]ntly after 12 a clock where I found the Jury &
Court ready.
I went to night to Toucester.

23° Junii 1638
Mr Burkit[430] came downe from Pateshull hether this morninge to me.

---

[429] Sir Paul Pindar was a merchant prince and diplomat with Northamptonshire roots. In
1634 he had donated a full communion service to his birthplace, the town of Wellingborough,
and in 1640 he would give a bell. In 1638 he donated two silver flagons to Peterborough
cathedral: Fielding, 'Peterborough', p. 120; R. Ashton, 'Pindar, Sir Paul (1565/6–1650)', in
ODNB; Pevsner, *Northamptonshire*, p. 452.
[430] Miles Burkit was one of the two vicars of the polarized parish of Pattishall. The poles were
personified by the incumbents. The godly Burkit was the protégé of George Steward, whose

about 12 or 1 I came out & as I went through hardingston I met with
Mr Giffords man John Silby[431] to whom I delivered the 67li 8s & my
letters to be sent to North[amp]ton I came to Wilby in safty I prayse
the Lord. I was at huntsborough hill[432] & saw the miserable afflicted
towne of North[amp]ton belowe me & put up my poore peticons for
it.
24° Junii Sab.[bath]
I prayed and went to heare Mr Pearne who preached p[ro]fitably
morninge & evening. Lord make an instrument of much good to my
soule for the Lords sake.
I was very sleepy to day sinne & faylinge cleaves to all my services.
25° Junii
The fare very small I heare at

Boughton greene[433] by reason of the sicknesse at North[amp]ton.
26° Junii 1638
Mr Newton was at Wilby to day I was somewhat troubled and fearefull
to see him I gave him 22s of the money receaved of my fathers freinds

family owned the manor. However, the remaining Steward brothers supported conformists:
Richard (an Arminian) was Clerk of the Closet to Charles I, and John appointed Burkit's
predecessors – William Paule (the royal chaplain) and Miles's brother, William, a conformist
Church court official. Miles Burkit and his followers were harried constantly by the Church
courts in the 1630s. The iconoclastic attorney William Waters was presented for demolishing
the churchyard cross in 1636, while Miles, after being reported to Sir John Lambe in 1635,
was repeatedly prosecuted by the Church courts (including High Commission in 1637 and
1638), charged with various offences, including support for Burton, Bastwick, and Prynne,
and removing the communion table from its railed enclosure and placing it tablewise in the
chancel to administer the sacraments. The latter episode was quoted by Prynne at Laud's
trial. Burkit's main allies included the godly divines Daniel Cawdrey and James Cranford,
the justice of the peace Sir Richard Samwell, and perhaps Woodford. Ranged against
him were his fellow vicar, Richard Powell, Sir John Lambe, and his clerical conformist
allies, led by Sibthorpe and Clarke, and, ultimately, Laud himself. Burkit was forced to
submit in December 1638, but he was not absolved until after the opening of the Long
Parliament, when he claimed to have suffered for six years, at a cost of £300. One spin-
off of the dispute involved Powell and Samwell (Diary, p. 269, n. 609): Longden, *Clergy*;
Longden MS, 20 March 1634, 17 February 1626, and 19 December 1628; Metcalfe, *Visitation
of Northamptonshire 1618*, p. 138; Longden, *Visitation of Northamptonshire 1681*, pp. 209–210; PDR,
CBA63, fo. 404r–v; W. Prynne, *Canterburies Doome or the First Part of a Compleat History of the
Tryall [...] of William Laud* (London, 1646), pp. 96–97, 488, 494; Fielding, 'Peterborough',
pp. 105–107; HLRO, main papers, 18 January (Burkit) and 21 January (Waters) 1641.
[431] Probably John Sillesby.
[432] Hunsbury Hill stands two miles south-west of Northampton. In 1631 a Mrs Lucas had
been burned at the stake there for poisoning her husband: Pevsner, *Northamptonshire*, p. 355;
Top MS, p. 103.
[433] This contravened the Privy Council's order of early June cancelling the fair at plague-
free Boughton Green (24–26 June) because of the plague at nearby Northampton: Jackson,
'Ship money', p. 120; Isham, *Diary*, pp. 119, 125 and note.

other then North[amp]tonshire men there was in all of that about 2li
7s. I prayed earnestly for him & the Lord heard me.
27° Junii
I prayed and went to Mr Bacons at [Long] Buckby where I found his
daughter sick of the small pox in the house which somewhat troubled
me, but I prayed unto the Lord.
Mr downes came to Mr Bacons to night.
28° Junii
[*crossed out:* The] I prayed as I could, and went to daventry

to the Assizes,[434] one Mr Britten preach't the Assize sermon,[435] Justice
hutton sate in the Crowne Court Baron Trevor for Nisi pr[ius][436] I
returned to [Long] Buckby againe at night wth Mr Watts, & I was
very feverish & ill.
29° Junii 1638
I was somewhat better this morninge (I blesse the Lord) then I was last
night, havinge swet much, Mr Catesby[437] hath recovered 5li damages
ag[ains]t Mr Readinge. I lodge to night wth Mr Rushworth at Mr
Rawlins[438] an apothecar[y] who was sick to night.
30. Junii
I prayed and went alonge wth Mr Rushworth towards Coventry we
were at Mr Reynolds[439] at Braunston, I went after to Baggington & he

[434]The assizes had been moved to Daventry from Northampton owing to the plague.
According to Sibthorpe, the business of the removed assizes was slight: TNA, SP16/393/75.
[435]There are two possible candidates. William Brittaine (Breton) had been rector of Clopton
since 1631 and served in the Church courts at Oundle in 1641. He was the appointee of
Edward Dudley, lord of the manor, and a friend of Edward, Lord Montagu, while his brother
John Breton was master of Emmanuel College, Cambridge. Alternatively, Zaccheus Bredon
had been appointed rector of Croughton in the south of the county in 1631, through the
patronage of Sir Francis Staunton of Bedfordshire: Longden, *Clergy*; Longden MS, 13 and
23 July 1631; TNA, PROB/11/72; PDR, X639-642/8a, fo. 26v.
[436]The final stage of a trial concerning debt in the Court of Common Pleas or the Court
of King's Bench; heard before a jury at the local assizes.
[437]The Catesby family hailed from Ecton and Whiston; the most likely candidates here
are George or Clifton: TNA, SP16/375/82.
[438]Nicholas Rawlins of Daventry had been listed as a physician in 1636: J.H. Raach, *A
Directory of English Country Physicians, 1603-1643* (London, 1962), p. 76.
[439]Edward Reynolds was a moderate Laudian with godly connections. He had been
presented to his living of Braunston by John Reading, acting as the executor of the will of
Isaac Johnson, who was associated with Viscount Saye's Massachusetts Bay Company. A
former incumbent of All Saints', Northampton, but also a royal chaplain, Reynolds preached
conformity to Laudian ceremonial. Indeed, in July 1637 he had been employed to preach
to this effect when Bishop Dee's visitation reached Daventry. He was an Interregnum
vice-chancellor of Cambridge University and Bishop of Norwich after the Restoration:
Longden, *Clergy*; Fielding, 'Peterborough', pp. 20-21, 125, 228-230; Webster, *Godly Clergy*,
pp. 117, 225-226.

to Coventr[y] we had much discourse about the times & the businesse of Scotland. Lord order every thing for the best for the Lords sake

sake Amen.
1° Julii 1638 Sab.[bath]
harry & Wm Bott & I went over this morninge to Coventr[y] & heard one Mr Proctor[440] at Trin[ity] Church a poore preacher.
we heard Mr Gibson[441] in the afternoone at Baggington.
2° Julii
After dinner we went to Coventr[y] & were wth Mrs Ball[442] Mrs Rushworth &
3° Julii
I prayed and came for Wilby, I met wth Mr Prat nere Killesby[443] who came back with me hether, I came after to Mr Bacons & then to Wilby in due time I prayse the Lord. (th) [crossings out]

4° Julii 1638
I prayed and went to Wellingborowe where I met wth diverse of my North[amp]ton neighbors that now live not there. I rec[eive]d a letter from Mr Martin the elder.
5° Julii
[crossings out] I was invited to Mr Pearnes to dinner where dyned Mr Cawdrey & Mr Baynard[444] too. Lord p[ar]don my great abominacons heale my back slidinge sanctify me throughout for the Lords sake Amen.
Mr Pearson came [crossed out: hether] to Mr Pentlowes to day wth his wife one Mr Whitehand & ux Mr Bere &

[440]Robert Proctor was a Cambridge MA who had been vicar of Little St Mary's, Cambridge, from 1620 until 1630, and who served the living of Holy Trinity, Coventry, from 1638 until his death in 1644. I am grateful to Ann Hughes for this reference.
[441]Thomas Gibson obtained his MA from Oxford in 1627 and the following year achieved the living of Baginton, Warwickshire. I thank Richard Cust and Ann Hughes for this reference.
[442]Elizabeth, the widow of Brian Ball, apothecary: Diary, p. 168.
[443]Kilsby.
[444]John Baynard was a member of the godly group centring on the clergyman Robert Bolton and the overseers of his will, Francis Downes and Francis Nicolls. As curate of the Nicolls family's parish of Faxton, Baynard had been presented to the Church courts in 1620 for attracting godly gadders to his sermons, and by 1629 Francis Nicolls had appointed him to the benefice of Hardwick. In the 1630s Baynard became an opponent of religious policy, taking a lead by refusing to read the Book of Sports. During the Interregnum and Restoration periods he continued to enjoy the support of the Downes and Nicolls families, and in 1672 he was licensed as a congregational preacher in the house of Robert Guy: Fielding, 'Peterborough', pp. 26, 51 n. 35, 114 n. 64, 152, 160 n. 15; TNA, PROB/11/111 (Downes); PDR, Archdeaconry of Northampton Wills, third series, A198 (Nicolls).

6° Julii
Mr Pearson sealled Leases to 6 of his tenants this morninge, Mr Wyne
onely is behind. the tenants paid me for my paynes & Mr Pearson
would needs force 10s uppon me besides oh Lord I blesse thee for thy
great goodnesse & p[ro]vidence towards me. I

went afterwards to Ketteringe, where I met wth Mr Peake &
Wm. Cable who gave me instruccons for drawinge a ffeoffm[en]t[445]
betweene them, Lord direct me in it I beseech thee.
7° Julii 1638
I am now to goe to houghton[446] to see the hey that ffr[ancis] Spicer
hath bought for me, & to hardingstone & Wootton Lord I beseech
thee let thy good p[ro]vidence goe along with me let not mine iniquity
deprive me of it for the Lords sake, suffer not evill thoughts to Lodge
within me though my hart is like the raginge boylinge sea thou canst
allay it doe it I beseech thee for the Lords sake.
I went not to houghton as I intended but Mr Runbould & his
wife came hether & after dinner I went alonge wth them towards
Wellingbo.[rough] I was at the Bowlinge greene &
8° Julii Sab.[bath]
I prayed & went to heare Mr Eynesworth[447]

(Mr Pearne beinge absent to day) morninge & evening who preached
very p[ro]fitably, I was dull & heavy with sleepe morninge & eveninge.
I doe often beseech the Lord to be gracious to me & my family oh my
god heare me for the Lords sake.
9° Julii 1638
I was aguish this night & swet much. I prayed & wrote some letters to
London & afterwards went to Easton maudit to Mr Watts & prayed for
grace & favor & wisdome in his eyes & on my iourney consideringe the
distemper of my body I was thinkinge of the day of death & prayed
unto my god about it Lord heare me I afterwards had warre with
corrupcon and evill thoughts.

---

[445]A deed conveying property.
[446]Great and Little Houghton are to the south-east of Northampton.
[447]Samuel Ainsworth, the son of a Northampton tanner, was Perne's curate at Wilby
from about 1636, and the following year was reported to the Church courts for preaching
without a licence. He went on to become the Presbyterian minister of Kelmarsh during
the Interregnum under the Hanbury family and was also connected to the Shuckburghs of
Naseby: PDR, Church Survey Book 5, fo. 134r–v; J. Fielding, 'Perne, Andrew (c.1595–1654)',
in *ODNB*; A.G. Matthews (ed.), *Calamy Revised* (Oxford, 1934), pp. 3–4.

I have bene at Easton where I dyned and now I am at Mr Willoughbyes[448] at Grendon whether I am come to bringe Mrs Allen[449] & here I find that the children

here have lately had the mesles & this the first day of their goeinge abroad so that here I am in danger of infeccon too, Lord pr[e]serve me thou art he in whom I desire to trust in all humility of soule, and I pray thee Lord to Looke uppon me in the condicon that I am now in & helpe from heaven for the Lords sake, corrupcon doth much abound in my soule the old man is alive wthin me & graces are weake, [crossed out, illegible] I and my family are compelled to flee from our habitacon my selfe in one place my wife in another, & my wife is now neare unto the time of travell, if I looke uppon my body I see it subiect to aguishnes & infirmity, & my outward estate in danger of ruine by my debts which I owe, nay the whole Kingdome is in a forlorne condicon gods ordinances in many places mixed wth base ceremony & sup[er]stition, oh Lord I come unto thee beseechinge thee to looke uppon me in m[er]cye in the mom[e]nt thou wilt be seene I have tasted of thy goodnesse formerly & thou art still the same, Let thy grace be sufficient for me to p[ar]don my sinnes & heale my corrupcons hide

hide me by the wings of thy p[ro]vidence for a while even me & mine untill thy indignation be overpast & then bringe us to the place of o[u]r desires & let thy comforts & thy blessinge come along wth us in the meane while sanctifye the absence of me & my wife from one another to each of us and Lord I pray thee be with my deare wife in the houre of her travell & though thou hast layd uppon all sorow in bringing forth yet I beseech thee so moderate it by thy m[er]cy & lend such strength & ability to thy poore handmayd that we may have great occasion to blesse thee for the continuance of thy great m[er]cye and Lord I pray thee for the infant that shall be borne by thy gracious p[ro]vidence oh Lord give it right shape & forme & continue its life unto us & make it an instrument of thy glory & member of thy true Church and a comfort to us the parents, and Lord looke uppon me & my whole family in regard of our bodyes give them health & strength oh Lord thy Judgments are much abroad the pestilence rageth in the Countrye the small pox in the Citty of London oh Lord I pray thee

---

[448]Philip Willoughby owned a manor at Grendon and was the farmer of the parsonage. He was a servant of Spencer Compton of nearby Castle Ashby, the second Earl of Northampton, and of James, the third Earl, and a Royalist during the Civil War: Isham, *Diary*, p. 156, n. 38; PDR, Church Survey Book 5, fo. 85v.

[449]Helen, the wife of Henry Allen of Easton Maudit.

that thy good p[ro]vidence may be a wall of fire about me & my family let us be a family blessed & watered by thee notwithstandinge all o[u]r faylings which I pray thee reforme in us all for

for the Lords sake, and for my outward estate oh Lord thou seest my debts & straights and I confesse I deserve to be in them for my want of dilligence & for my p[ro]fusenesse & other sinnes & faylings but I pray thee thou who showest m[er]cye wthout desert, thou who hast upholden my hart & estate all this while be gracious unto me, it is a more blessed thinge to give then to receave Lord I know & beleive that thou hast all power and all blessings in thine hand oh Lord I pray thee in due time pay my debts & supply me & my family graciously [*crossed out, illegible*] & give us a sanctifyed use of every m[er]cy for the Lord Xt his sake And oh my god looke in m[er]cye uppon the whole Kingdome blesse his Ma[jes]ty and make him strong for thee and in thy cause to p[ro]mote thy glorious gospell & to extirpate all pop[er]y Idolatry sup[er]stition & p[ro]phanenesse and come forth oh Lord amongst thine adversaryes who doe plott against thee & seeke to defile thine ordinances with base humane inventions, if they belong unto thee bringe them in, if not confound them oh Lord confound & curse them and all their machinacons for thy gloryes sake & send forth into all the corners of the land and establish in all congregacons able ministers of the gospell that may build up thy church and put all iniquity to silence that the harts of thy people may greatly reioyce for the Lords sake
I carryed Mrs Allen home to Easton and returned to Wilby at night, & was pr[e]served from a fall in the meadow nere the mill blessed be the Lord.
10° Julii 1638. I prayed and went to speake wth

wth Mrs Pryor at hardingston who had no money for me to day for the fine I have left with her, I met wth harry fflemminge[450] of North[amp]ton who had bene lately shut up. I sent by him 16d to T[homas] Cr[utchley] & 12d to John ffreind, the sicknesse greatly increaseth at North[amp]ton and the miseryes there are many Lord stay thy hand in due time & better us by this affliccon for the Lords sake. I went after to Wootton to goodman Watsons about the Lady

---

[450] Henry Fleming was a public notary who worked for the ecclesiastical courts and lived in St Giles's parish, Northampton. By 1640 he was a freeman of the town: NRO, 241P/42, unfoliated, under the disbursement section for 1634; NRO, 233P/107, unfoliated, 16 January 1640; Finch (Hatton) MSS, F(H) 3501.

Smithes[451] businesse after that I came to houghton ground[452] where my
hey is & spake there wth John Cox of North[amp]ton & & returned
safe home againe blessed be the Lord.

11° Julii 1638
I prayed and went to Wellingborow my horse halted much but I have
shod him & he goeth somewhat better which I acknowledge a great
m[er]cy for I am determined for London to morow if god p[er]mitt.
I dranke with daniel Simonds of North[amp]ton to day at the Angell.
Lord pr[e]serve me in all dangers for the Lords sake Amen.

12° Julii 1638
I prayed and went to Wootton & so to Grafton [Regis] where I
kept Court and then came to ffenny stratford that night where I
was compelled to stay by reason of great thunderinge & lighteninge
& rayne which fell there, I intended els to have gone to dunstable,
yet in this I observe gods great p[ro]vidence for here I met wth Mr
Crumpton who was bound in a bond wth Tom hall to James Warren[453]
which bond is lost, and I was threatned about it so Mr Crumpton first
menconed the businesse & not knowinge of the losse of the bond hath
sealled another to his use & sent it by me blessed be thy name oh
Lord for hearinge my poore prayers form[er]ly made unto thee in this
behalfe.

13° Julii
I prayed and came to dunstable to breakfast I met after wth one Mr
Bannier a Londoner who came alonge wth me to London where I
found my wife & family all very well I blesse the Lord oh blessed be thy
name for pr[e]servinge & comfortinge of us Mr Readings daughter
Elizab was xxned[454] to day.

14° Julii 1638
I prayed and went [crossed out: aboro] abroad, and met wth Mr
Readinge who is offended because the 100li not yet payed, Lord helpe
us & direct every thinge for the best for the Lords sake.
I was at Mr dillinghams.[455]

15° Julii Sab.[bath]
I prayed and went to dr Stoughtons where he preached morninge &
eveninge very p[ro]fitably and boldly, Oh Lord I blesse thee for this

[451] The widow of John Rowland (d. 1636), lord of the manor of Wootton, who went on to
marry Sir Arthur Smithes: *VCH Northamptonshire*, IV (London, 1937), p. 293.
[452] Either Great or Little Houghton near Northampton.
[453] For the Warrens of Old, see Diary, p. 226, n. 482.
[454] Christened.
[455] His house was situated in the parish of Whitefriars: see Diary, p. 141, n. 190.

good instrum[en]t in thy church. Lord throwe downe & destroy all pop[er]y and arminianisme for the Lords sake
Oh that we might enioy thy blessed ordinances in their power & purity!
16° Julii
I prayed and went to my Cousin Ragdales & my Cousin Starkyes, I dyned at my cousin Ragd. I went after to my Masters. Mr John somewhat complayned of beinge ill a gent was buryed this afternoone at the temple of the small pox.

17° Julii 1638
I went along wth my wife & children into More feilds[456] this morninge. my wife not well in the afternoone.
I heard dr Stoughton at the fun[er]all of one Mrs Edmonds.
18° Julii
Mr Bifield Mr Bellamy my father & I have bene advisinge how to rayse some more money for North[amp]ton, alderman Abel[457] hath advised us to peticon the Court of aldermen so we have drawne a peticon, & we were wth my Lord Maior[458] to acquaint him with our intent who doth rather incourage then otherwise.
19° Julii
I prayed and went with my father & to attend the Court of Aldermen, & o[u]r peticon was pr[e]ferred, but fayled in reg[ar]d it was in the name of North[amp]tonshire men & not of the towne. I p[ai]d Mr Kingsman[459] 5li p[ro] Mr Pentlow; old Mr Martin & ux & Mr Sam came to the towne last night, & I now met wth them & supt wth them.

20° Julii 1638
I prayed and had gracious comforts in the duty & went after to St Antholins[460] to heare Mr Wm Martin but he fayled so I heard another who preached indifferent well.

---

[456]Moorfields, London's first civic park, was north of the city, near to the Haunches' parish of All Hallows', London Wall: N.G. Brett-James, *The Growth of Stuart London* (London, 1935), pp. 452–454.
[457]William Abell (1584–1665), vintner and politician, was a native of Oundle in Northamptonshire, where his grandfather, William, had endowed the school. He was a London alderman in the 1630s but lost popularity with the godly when, as Sheriff of London in 1637, he arrested Henry Burton. He was also associated with an unpopular wine monopoly: D. Freist, 'Abell, William (b. c.1584, d. in or after 1655)', in *ODNB*.
[458]Sir Richard Fenn.
[459]Richard Kinsman of Broughton: Metcalfe, *Visitation of Northamptonshire 1618*, p. 103; PDR, Church Survey Book 5, fo. 131; Isham, *Diary*, p. 118, n. 2.
[460]St Antholin's lecture in Budge Row was served by members of a seminary run by the godly divine Charles Offspring (who worked in co-operation with other London ministers such as William Gouge). From 1627 until 1633 the lecture had been run by the Feoffees for Impropriations: Webster, *Godly Clergy*, pp. 26–27, 55.

I heare that young Mr John Readinge is sick of the small pox, & that he raged vehemtly the last night, oh Lord in m[er]cy looke uppon him spare his life & doe him good by this affliccon for the Lords sake.

21° Julii

I prayed and went to alderman Abels & met wth him who would put us uppon it to peticon the Archb[isho]p for a more g[e]ne[ra]ll gathering in London.

I met wth Mr Bolt in the morninge and informed him what my father intended about movinge for the reversion of the clarkship of Weavers hall for me uppon Wednesday next; which thinge I beseech thee oh Lord to effect if it be thy will that it may be for thy glory & the good of me & my poore family Lord I humbly seeke & sue

sue unto thee for thou hast all strength yea thou art the Lord my god, Mr Gregg sent this morning to me for the money that I owe him & Mr Enyon[461] above 10li Lord I pray thee direct & supply me in it for the Lords sake Amen.

22° Julii 1638 Sab.[bath]

I prayed & my wife and I went this morninge to dr Stoughtons church where we heard a scottish man preach uppon that text 4 John[462] god is a sp[iri]t & will be worshipped in sp[iri]t & truth, who dealt faythfully ag[ains]t will worship & sup[er]stition, in the afternoone I heard one at Bow-church[463] who preached very honestly & well uppon that text Ep[h]raim shall say what have I to doe wth Idolls.[464]

my brother heard Mr Simons[465] out of the Canticles who did excellently and amongst other things shewed that there was much m[er]cye in every p[ro]mise & fayth was the midwife to bringe it forth & that it was fayth that added a seale to them to make them effectuall; oh Lord how sweet is thy word blesse it to me & mine for the Lords sake. And

*****

---

[461]James Enyon of Flore, a Royalist who was knighted in 1642: PDR, Church Survey Book 5, fo. 102r; G. Isham (ed.), *The Correspondence of Bishop Brian Duppa and Sir Justinian Isham 1650–1660*, Publications of the Northamptonshire Record Society XVII (Lamport, 1955), p. 210.

[462]Verse 24: 'God is a spirit: and they that worship him must worship him in spirit and in truth.'

[463]The incumbent of St Mary le Bow was Jeremy Leech, who was sequestered during the Civil War, accused of Royalism: R. Newcourt, *Repertorium Ecclesiasticum Parochiale Londinense*, 2 vols (London, 1708–1710), I, p. 440.

[464]Hosea 14:8.

[465]Joseph Simonds was the rector of St Martin's, Ironmonger Lane, and later fled to the Netherlands: Webster, *Godly Clergy*, p. 257; T. Webster and K. Shipps (eds), *The Diary of Samuel Rogers, 1634–1638*, Church of England Record Society XI (Woodbridge, 2004), p. xlvii.

And now Lord I pray blesse me & mine in soules & bodyes estates &
& Lord be gracious to my deare wife in her condicon & in her to me
& my family for the Lords sake.
I have prayd ag[ains]t that hierarchy of B[isho]ps ag[ains]t
sup[er]stition & & for health to me & o[u]r pr[e]servac[ion] from
infeccons diseases & for supply of o[u]r necessityes &. Lord heare my
poore prayers for the Lords sake and blesse us this night for the Lords
sake.

23° Julii 1638
I prayed and had great & gracious assistance in publiq prayer I blesse
the Lord, I went after wth Mr Bate & [*crossed out:* about] to some of
the North[amp]tonshire men who gave us somethinge for the poore
of North[amp]ton.
Mr Robins gave me to night 6li p[ro] my horse & 6s for my sadle and
I have bene downe in Bermondsey to day wth Mr Bannyer wth whom
I came up, and have bought his horse of him for 7li Lord I pray thee
graunt that this horse may be p[ro]fitable and serviceable unto

unto me, and not an occasion of hurt or danger in any respect and
that both he and all other temp[or]all [*crossed out:* m[er]cyes] goods
& m[er]cyes may be blessed unto me for the Lords sake. My lady
Smithes came to towne to day. grac[iously] affected in private prayer
wth my deare wife this night I prayed about the child to be borne &
about her delivery & about the reversion of &

24° Julii 1638
we are now goeinge forth againe [*crossed out:* about] to the
North[amp]tonshire men Lord p[ro]sp[er] us give us grace in their
eyes for the Lords sake.
we have receaved since of diverse of them moneyes for the poore of
North[amp]ton.
I have heard that there dyed 42 the last weeke of the sicknesse at
North[amp]ton.⁴⁶⁶ Mich Smith & his wife goodwife Nelson & all her
children Arthur hutton Mrs ffoster Watts the Loader & Lord stay thy
hand in due time for the Lords sake and pr[e]serve Mrs Cricks house
& the rest of the houses of thy children there for the Lords sake.

25° Julii 1638. St James day.
I prayed and went this morninge to Mr Robins his house but I find
he is gone to Gravesend wch disappoynts me for payinge Mr Gregge,
Lord helpe me & direct me for the Lords sake.

---

⁴⁶⁶The outbreak was reaching its height during the summer: compare this with weekly
totals of twenty-six, sixteen, and twenty-nine for the period 27 May to 17 June: TNA,
SP16/393/15.

I am now waytinge for the Lords p[ro]vidence about the revercon of
the Clarkship of weavers hall my father is now there.

as I was writinge a messenger came for me to dinner there, but the
thinge was not moved, Lord bringe it about in thy due time if it be thy
will for the Lords sake.

Mr Colson chosen M[aste]r for the next yeare.

my new cloathes came home this morning Lord graunt they may not
be a snare to me.

26° Julii

I prayed and went about my occasions, & then to dinner to the weavers
hall at the 3 cranes Taverne nere dow-gate.

I am p[ro]vidinge to goe into the country.

I sent for my horse from Mr Banniers & sent the 7li by Richard
Becket;[467] Lord make my horse serviceable unto me.

27° Julii 1638

I prayed wth my wife & wth my family and came away for the Country.
and came to dunstable that night to Mr Walkers wth one Mr
Sedgwick[468] a minister at or nere Slapton.

28° Julii

I prayed and writt to my deare wife, and afterwards we came away &
p[ar]ted at hockly[469] I came after to Newport [Pagnell] where I dyned
& then came to Wilby in due time I prayse the Lord.

I had many gracious mocons as I came alonge & eiaculacons in fayth.
Lord heare my poore weake and unworthy prayers for the Lords
sake.

29° Julii Sab.[bath]

I am now about to goe to heare Mr Pearne where there is likewise a
sacram[en]t.

[467] A servant of Robert Haunch: Diary, p. 355.

[468] Obadiah Sedgwick's brother, John (an Oxford BD), had married a Northamptonshire
woman – Ann, the daughter of Fulke Buttery of Marston St Lawrence – in 1632. The living
mentioned by Woodford (which was probably a curacy) has not been confirmed – Hugh
Alloway was the rector of Slapton, appointed by Sir Henry Wallop – but perhaps more likely
locations were nearby Stuchbury chapel (where Sedgwick's father-in-law was the patron),
or the Butterys' home parish of Marston St Lawrence, where the incumbent was Francis
Cheynell, a godly minister who was suspended by Sir John Lambe in 1638 for refusing to
bow to the altar. Around this time Sedgwick was also lecturer at St Giles's, Cripplegate,
London: Bridges, History of Northamptonshire, II, pp. 253–54; Webster, Godly Clergy, p. 260; B.
Donagan, 'Sedgwick, Obadiah (1599/1600–1658)', in ODNB; R. Pooley, 'Cheynell, Francis
(bap. 1608, d. 1665)', in ODNB; Longden MS, 27 September 1617, 29 July 1619, 15 May
1627, 13 October 1635; Longden, Visitation of Northamptonshire 1681, pp. 39–40; Webster and
Shipps, Diary of Samuel Rogers, p. 160n.

[469] Hockliffe, Bedfordshire.

oh Lord I beseech thee pr[e]pare me for thy blessed ordinances graunt that I may reape benefit by them

them, give me the fayth spirit & affeccons of a xxian that I may be alive & quickned & may feele a sensible increase of grace & decay of sinne for the Lord xt his sake.

Oh Lord blesse my deare wife & children & whole family, make us all gracious & holy, keepe me and them from infeccon in these contagious times, the small pox doe wonderfully increase yet thou art able to defend & preserve; the sicknesse rageth exceedingly in North[amp]ton but thy p[ro]vidence guideth & disposeth of all things Lord looke uppon our outward estate & Condicon in thy due time pay o[u]r debts & supply us, in the meane while give us to walke holyly in our low condicon & to live by fayth wth much cheerfullnes & freedome from carkinge cares & melancholly & Lord looke uppon my deare wife in her condicon give her a gracious & comfortable delivery uphold her spirits & stay her mind uppon thee her god, make her likewise a nurse if it be thy will, & lord give us comforts in the Child that shall be borne give it right shape & forme & make that & the other instrum[en]ts of thy glory in thy due time for the Lords sake, oh Lord I would bringe

bringe before thee this day all my desires burdens & feares I pray thee looke uppon me wth pitty give me the hand of fayth & the shoulder of fayth for the Lords sake.

some gracious comforts in gods holy ordinances this day I blesse the Lord.

I dyned at Mr Pearnes.

dr Roane[470] an enimy came this afternoone to heare & (I doubt) to entrap Mr Pearne, but he preached faythfully, the Lord make it effectuall uppon us all that heard & uppon that sup[er]stitious doctor, I besought the Lord for his convercon Lord thou art able to doe it.

I was graciously ravisht in private prayer to night I blesse the Lord, and I prayed (according to Mr Sedgwicks[471] direccon) for strong assistance

---

[470] Dr William Roane had been born in Wellingborough, the son of Anthony and Eleanor Roane. His parents were close to Thomas Jones, the conformist vicar of Wellingborough, and his father had been presented to the Church courts in 1607 for heckling the lecturer as he condemned the pride displayed in wearing sumptuous clothes. William was an official in the court of the Laudian Archdeacon of Buckingham, Robert Newell, and an ally of Robert Sibthorpe, with whom he co-operated in 1639 to prosecute Miles Burkit: B. Levack, *The Civil Lawyers of England* (Oxford, 1973), p. 266; K. Fincham and N. Tyacke, *Altars Restored: the changing face of English religious worship, 1547–c. 1700* (Oxford, 2007), p. 209; Longden, *Clergy*; PDR, CB40, fo. 114v; Temple of Stowe MSS, STT 1891.

[471] Probably John, whom Woodford had met on 27 July.

in this gracious assurance. Oh Lord be with me & mine for the Lords sake.

30. Julii 1638

I prayed and afterward writt to my deare & holy wife. oh Lord be with her & my family I am drawinge the bookes for Mr Peake. towards night I have bene very melancholly Lord

Lord I wayt uppon thee for thou art he in whom I desire to trust, I have had litle quiet sleepe these 2 nights past oh my god looke uppon me in m[er]cy give me sweet refreshinge rest helpe me against direfull melancholly give me abilityes & cheerefullnes in my callinge and thy blessinge for the Lords sake and Lord graunt that I may heare good newes from London I commend my selfe & all mine to thy sure p[ro]teccon & gracious blessinge keep us & delight in us to doe us good for the Lords sake.

helpe me in my outward condicon in thy due time in the meane while give me fayth & patience & cheerfullnes till thy eares are prest to heare me for the Lord xt his sake & let me now lye downe in thine armes I humbly beseech thee my gracious father.

31° Julii 1638

I prayed and went along in the morninge wth Mr Sandford[472] to Wellingborowe well &

dranke of the water[473] which wrought very well with us, Lord give us health & sanctifye it to us for the Lords sake Amen.

we dyned at the Angell & had dr Milles[474] wth us I spent about 2s [crossed out: of] uppon my dinner & was much afflicted after to thinke of my p[ro]fusnes & prayed to the Lord for thriftinesse oh Lord bestow it uppon me for the Lords sake.

1° August. 1638

I prayed and went alonge againe to the well which wrought wth us againe.

Mrs Pentlowe & her daughters were here & we dyned at Kemptons &.

I supped at Mr Pearnes [crossed out, illegible].

---

[472]William Sandford (fl. 1618–1646) was a Gray's Inn barrister: Prest, Barristers, p. 337.

[473]The town took its name from its iron-rich or chalybeate springs. It had become a fashionable spa following visits by the Duchess of Buckingham in 1624, the king and queen in 1627, and the queen alone in 1628; Oliver Cromwell also found the waters efficacious against depression: W. Camden, Britannia (London, 1637), p. 510; VCH Northamptonshire, IV, pp. 137–138; J. Morrill, 'Cromwell, Oliver (1599–1658)', in ODNB.

[474]Or Dr Willis: one of that name discovered healing wells at Astrop in the south of the county in 1664: Isham, Diary, p. 134, n. 28.

2° Augusti
I prayed and Mr Sanford & I went along to Grafton [Regis], & came thether safe & in due time; the Court very small by reason

of Toms his absence we returned to Wilby againe at night.
Mr Pentlowe forth at Boughton[475] I prayed in the family.
3° Augusti 1638.
I am now goeinge to Ketteringe wth Mr Sandford Lord I pray thee be with us in our Journey let thy good p[ro]vidence be manifested to us in carryeinge of us out, in o[u]r returne & in all o[u]r wayes this day for the Lords sake Amen
[crossed out: I] we were at Ketteringe & I was somew[ha]t imoderate in the wyne so that when I was returned [crossed out: fro] home & had supped & prayed I felt some illnes, Lord make me exceedinge watchfull for time to come for the Lords sake;
This day I heard that yesterday Mr ffowler was chosen to be Maior at North[amp]ton & henry hill & John Coate Bayleifes.[476] Lord make them instrum[en]ts of thy glory & blesse the government of the towne for the Lords sake Amen.
4° Aug.
some comforts in duty I blesse the Lord, I

I have this day [crossed out: sentt] receaved from my deare & good wife a letter wherein she desires my prayers for her in the Condicon she is in beinge nere her time, & she informes me that litle Sam is not well, oh my god looke uppon me & my family delight in us all to doe us good establish thy covenant wth every one of us in a speciall manner be assistant & gracious to thy handmayd give her strength to bringe forth & comfort in it, give the infant right shape & forme & make it an instrum[en]t of thy glory for the [altered from: thy] Lords sake, & [left margin: symbol of a hand with finger pointing at the next word] looke uppon my poore sick child Lord give it health & continue it unto us still if it be thy will for the glory of thy name & the comfort of us the parents and the rest in like manner for the Lords sake.

---

[475]Great Bowden, Leicestershire: Diary, p. 225. Pentlow was in the process of taking out a lease of the parsonage. He owned it by 1657: TNA, PROB/11/263.
[476]Election day was the first Thursday in August. Richard Fowler (d. 1649) occurs in the parish and town records from 1628 on, as do Henry Hill (who had served as churchwarden) and John Cole. Like Cole, Hill had had a brush with the conformists in the Church courts: in 1614 Dr David Owen had accused Hill's maidservant, Mary Crist, of refusing Easter communion at his hands after he and his allies, Lambe and Sibthorpe, had secured the expulsion from All Saints' of the popular godly vicar, Robert Catelin, and his replacement by Owen: TNA, PROB/11/208 (Fowler); Vestry Minutes, pp. 21–29; Fielding, 'Peterborough', p. 72; PDR, CB44, fo. 42r–v.

my father writes to me that he is in great want of money Lord supply that good & upright & charitable man for the Lords sake Amen.
Mr Pentlowe came home to night from Bowden.

5° Augusti 1638. Sab.[bath]
oh Lord I pray thee blesse this Sabath unto me, let me gaine a greater measure of grace & decay of sinne and blesse my whole family this day likewise for the Lords sake.
my mother & I dyned at Mr Pearnes to day. Mr Pearne preached excellently both morninge & eveninge blessed be the name of the Lord for it; in the afternoone he shewed how we ought to make a good use of sinne to be humbled by it, to goe out of o[u]r selves to be contented in all condicons & & oh Lord I humbly beseech thee graunt that I sinne not neverthelesse if I doe sinne, yet graunt that iniquity may not be my ruine, so order things by thy mighty & overrulinge hand that good may be brought out of evill, oh Lord pr[e]serve me from sinning against thee and make me such a one as thou wouldst have me be for the Lords sake.
6. Aug.
I prayed and wrote letters to London & after that went towards Old, & in the

way I was almost uppon holcot Pesthouses⁴⁷⁷ before I was aware & I thought I smelt somethinge a litle before that, but I have besought the Lord & have desired to rely uppon his gracious p[ro]vidence
I came to Old to my cousin dexters where they used me very kindly, I went after to Scaldwell where my Cousin Rickards⁴⁷⁸ wife was layd uppon the biere at her dore ready to be carried to buryall, lord make me mindfull of my mortallyty & pr[e]pare me for eternity for the Lords sake.
I came after to my uncle woodfords, & lay at my cousin dexters.
I gave my Aunt Ragdale⁴⁷⁹ 12d.
Mr Pentlowe & Mr Sanford went to harborow⁴⁸⁰ or Bowden to night.

---

⁴⁷⁷Holcot had been hit hard by the plague or pest. There were sixty plague burials there during 1638; contrast this with the yearly average of seven: J.F.D. Shrewsbury, *A History of Bubonic Plague in the British Isles* (Cambridge, 1971), p. 398.
⁴⁷⁸John Rickards of Scaldwell (d. 1638) or his son James: PDR, Archdeaconry of Northampton wills, second series, L172.
⁴⁷⁹The wife of one of the sons of John Ragdale of Old. Daniel's wife was called Frances, while the names of Henry's and John's wives are unknown: PDR, Archdeaconry of Northampton Wills, second series, P104.
⁴⁸⁰Market Harborough, Leicestershire.

7° Aug. 1638.
I prayed in secret & brokefast at my cousin dexter & went after to my
Aunt dexters[481] to John Warrens to Mr fforsithes &. I gave my cousin
Emme 2s.[482] Lord blesse it to them & me for the Lords sake.
Mr fforsith spake ag[ains]t puritans, but I have prayd for the rootinge
out all Idolatry sup[er]stition & will worship & the restauracon &
establishm[en]t of

that which is in spirit & in truth[483] oh my god graunt it for the Lord
Xt his sake.
I am much troubled wth the grudginge of my ague.
I came safe home to Wilby I blesse the Lord.
8 Aug. 1638
This day twelvemonth my boy John was borne blessed be thy name oh
Lord for blessinge & increasinge my family, & now Lord graunt that I
may not be afflicted by any evill tidings from London, but that I may
heare that thou hast dealt graciously with us in a further blessinge &
increase & lord make it truly a blessinge, & good Lord uphold our
outward & sinkinge condicon consider o[u]r strengths thou art god
the deliverer, oh Lord if thou wilt thou canst supply me abundantly
& surely thou wilt helpe & uphold when I can once be in danger of
the world without the cares of the world, livinge cheerfully by fayth &
reioycinge in thee the god of my salvacon though there be no oxe in
the stall &. when I can once serve & glorify

glorify him in a lowe condicon, then thus & thus will he doe for me
oh Lord give me contentacon & fayth & dilligence & frugality for the
Lords sake: and patience for thy time is the best time, sanctify thy
m[er]cyes to me that I doe or shall enioy for the Lords sake.

---

[481] Ann (née Turland), the widow of Woodford's maternal uncle Stephen Dexter.
[482] John Warren of Old was possibly married to Woodford's cousin Emme Warren, who
is mentioned here, and was either the daughter of his uncle Henry Woodford or of one of
his mother's Dexter siblings. The other Warrens mentioned in the diary (Thomas, William,
and James) were probably related. In 1631 John had claimed exemption from the status of
knighthood and had been supported by his parish priest, James Forsyth; he was the overseer
of the will of Woodford's father in 1636. Forsyth, rector of Old from 1620 until 1643, was a
fervent anti-puritan whom Bishop Dee had selected to preach at his primary visitation in
1634, and who had in the same year been the promoter of a High Commission case against
Francis Nicolls and John Sawyer for holding illegal conventicles (Diary, p. 195, n. 367). A
close ally of Sir John Lambe and his informer, Humphrey Ramsden, Forsyth had clashed
with the godly Langley family of Harrowden: HMC, *Report on the Manuscripts of the Duke of
Buccleuch and Queensberry*, III (London, 1926), p. 361; PDR, Archdeaconry of Northampton
wills, second series, C168; Longden, *Clergy*; TNA, SP16/414/163; PDR, CB58, unfoliated;
PDR, A42, fo. 566r–v.
[483] John 4:24.

Lord blesse me in goeinge to Wellingborow this day for the Lords sake.

I rec'd to day of h[enry] Parnell in full dischardge of Richard Wards debt to me – 5s.

I met there with Mat Sillesby, I heard to day of the death of Mr Trueman[484] & at North[amp]ton & that there dyed the last weeke about 25. Lord stay thy hand for the Lords sake.

I heare as if the Scottish businesse was determined Lord put an end to it as may be for thy glory

9° Aug.

I prayed, and my mayne worke this day was the p[er]fectinge Mr Peakes deed, whom I have appoynted to meete & sealle it as uppon this day sevennight at Scaldwell if god p[er]mit.

10° Aug. 1638

[*two lines crossed out, illegible*] blessed be thy name oh Lord, I prayed and went towards Ketteringe, where I met wth one Mr Battin[485] s[er]v[an]t to the Earle of holland; one Richard Langley is become my clyent to day blessed be thy name oh Lord.

[*one and a half lines crossed out, illegible*] Oh Lord I deserve to be cast out of thy pr[e]sence to have my porcon wth the damned, yet Lord p[ar]don all my sinnes & transgressions & have m[er]cy uppon my poore soule for the sake & merits of the lord Christ alone;

I heard to day that a voyce is heard often in ffarminge woods nere Brigstock & a grievous groaninge, & its conceaved it comes by reason of [*crossed out:* a] the great murther of the woman & child done at Brigstock or neare it, not discovered.

I came home early.

11° Aug. 1638

I prayed but wth much dullnes & estrangednesse from my deare & good god & father in the morninge, in the afternoone I had some more comfort in the dutye I blesse the Lord Oh Lord hide not thy face from me, thy favor is better then life I confesse thou mightest glorify thy Justice in my destruccon, but Lord deale with me in m[er]cye, & I pray thee good father sanctify me keepe me from all sinnes especially (that [*crossed out, illegible*]) for the Lord xt his sake.

[484]Richard Trueman, the father of the minister of the same name, was the godly owner of the saddler's shop; his will was proved by Thomas Crutchley: PDR, Archdeaconry of Northampton wills, second series, G100.

[485]Holland had appointed Richard Batten in May 1638 to collect fines imposed on delinquents in the Northamptonshire forests: Pettit, *Royal Forests*, p. 91.

I have bene much troubled this day in the consideracon ([*crossed out, illegible*] of the debts I owe & that I dayly runne further in I find that I am lately indebted 14li more to Mr Watts wch I receaved of Mr Robins at the tearme, but for this my father is bound to Mr Watts in this bond of the 100li.) to Mr Bott almost 5li to Mr Goodere 4li of North[amp]ton money paid almost 40s, to Mr Pearne p[ai]d 22s to Mr Gregg & Mr Enyon about 10li [*above:* paid 4li] to Mr Coles

for hey paid 3li so that my hart is allmost [*left margin: trefoil symbol*] oppressed & swallowed up wth the cares of this p[rese]nte world; oh my god what shall I doe I have no helpe nor hope but in thee my estate is like wholly to be ruined unlesse thou beare it up by thyne owne power now for the Lords sake looke uppon my lowe condicon [*crossed out:* the] let the [*crossed out:* lif] lives & estates & comforts of me & my deare wife be pleasinge in thine eyes oh how easy a matter it is for thee to helpe say but the word & we shall be supplyed, thou feedest all things livinge with the openinge (as it were with the turninge) of a hand oh my god bestow this m[er]cye uppon us and sanctifye it for the Lords sake in the meane while uphold o[u]r harts stay them uppon thee, graunt that we may reioyce in thee the god of o[u]r salvacon & be pr[e]served from melancholly [*crossed out:* for] & [*crossed out:* the] from sinne for the Lords sake I heare to day that John Ball the

Carryer is dead at North[amp]ton;
Oh Lord blesse the Sabath to morow to me & my deare wife for the Lords sake.
my wife not yet brought to bed, Sam. recovered & well againe I p[er]ceave by the letter, blessed be god.
12° Aug. 1638 Sab.[bath]
Mr Pearne preached both times to day very p[ro]fitably blessed be god, Lord keep him & establish him, oh that thy gospell might breake forth that the bright shininge of it might enlighten all the world, that Pop[er]y like dagon may fall before it, that men might offer pure sacrifices unto thee in all places, even worship thee with a spirituall worship which thou mightest take delight in Lord heare the poore prayers of thy servants for the Lord Xt his sake.
Mr Watts was here in the afternoone

my mother & I dyned at Mr Pearnes.
13° Aug. 1638
[*two lines crossed out, illegible*] & oh Lord deliver me from the straights & inciursions of sinne, oh Lord that I could live and not sinne against thee truly thy law is holy, and thy favor is better then life it selfe, for the Lord Jesus Xt his sake helpe from heaven,

[*crossed out:* I was feard that Mr Gray[486] was ill & went over to Wellingborow to inquire]
I have bene busy in writinge the deeds betweene Wm. Cable & Mr Peake.
14° August
I heard that Mr Gray the clarke of the peace was ill & I went over to Wellingborowe wth Mr Pentlowe to enquire Lord order ev[e]ry

eve[r]y thinge for the best for the Lords sake.
15° August 1638.
This day should have bene a fare at North[amp]ton[487] but the Lord hath pr[e]vented it wth the sicknesse Lord returne unto us againe in m[er]cye and heale us for the Lords sake.
I went to Wellingborow m[ar]ket, where goodman Odell paid me 20s.
16° August
I prayed and went wth Mr Pearne to Sr xxofer Yelvertons at Easton [Maudit], where we dyned and stayed till about 6 a clock there we met Mr ffinch Mr Eccleston Mr Richard Lane Mr Twisden Mr Rudd &.[488]
Mr Watts & I seemed somewhat to differ uppon the reckoninge of what I and my father had receaved, but we concluded in the end, we are now both of us indebted to

to him in 222li when my father hath rec[eive]d the 10li from Mr Robins or him [*crossed out:* for] whereas I owe him 136li for a 100li whereof he hath my bond then there was besides 22li & 14li rec[eive]d of Mr Robins which 14 is conteyned in my fathers bond of 100li, wch bond I have now left with [*crossed out:* him] Mr Watts & is payable on St James day. Oh Lord thou seest it good that we should lye under the heavy pressure of debts, but Lord susteyne us worke graciously for us thou art the almighty & all-sufficient god, in the eye of man there is

---

[486]Francis Gray of Wellingborough served as the clerk of the peace from 1623 until his death in 1642: J.H. Burgess, 'The social structure of Bedfordshire and Northamptonshire 1524–1764' (unpublished DPhil thesis, University of York, 1978), pp. 178–180.

[487]The Feast of the Assumption of the Blessed Virgin.

[488]The Kentish Twysdens and Finches were relatives of the Yelvertons of Easton Maudit. Sir Christopher Yelverton was married to Ann Twysden, whose parents were Sir William (d. 1629) and Ann Twysden, the latter the daughter of Sir Mayle Finch and sister of Heneage, Roger, Thomas, and John, one of whom is probably referred to here. Thomas Rudd was a justice of the peace and former mayor of his home town of Higham Ferrers. A military engineer and mathematician who had served in the Low Countries, he became a Royalist ally of Edward, Lord Montagu in the Civil War and died in 1656: P.D. Halliday, 'Twisden, Sir Thomas, first baronet (1602–1683)', in *ODNB*; D.L. Smith, 'Twysden, Sir Roger, second baronet (1597–1672)', in *ODNB*; M.-L. Coolahan, 'Twysden, Anne, Lady Twysden (1574–1638)', in *ODNB*; A. Saunders, 'Rudd, Thomas (1583/4–1656)', in *ODNB*.

no likelyhood I should ever pay wthout the sale of my land, but I will wayt uppon thee, thou hast said blessed is the man that trusteth in the Lord & whose hope the Lord is, Lord I pray thee helpe me to pay Mr Gregg if it be thy will for the Lords sake.

17° August 1638
I prayed, and carryed my mother behind me to Old, then I went to Scaldwell to seale

sealle the writings betweene Wm. Cable & Mr Peake, it was late before we had done I came againe to Old, where I met wth Mr Coles & Mr Wright Londoners who came lately from Newcastle.
I sent this day by Sam. More to North[amp]ton to Mr Maiors[489] 11li more which we gathered in London.

18° Aug. 1638.
I lay to night at my Cousin dexters; my mother & I came away about 1 a clock, & came safe to Wilby.
I heare Mr Bacon hath sent for me to come to Burton [Latimer] to him on Munday,[490] & to be with him at daventry on wednesday next Lord p[ro]sp[er] my Journey.
I have heard from my deare wife & family they are all well blessed be thy name oh Lord, oh how unworthy am I of so great a m[er]cy give me to walke more worthy of it for the Lords sake.
my wife not yet brought to bed, oh my god

god looke uppon us in m[er]cye, helpe thy handmaid graciously in thy due time for the Lords sake, and Lord continue all o[u]r healthes unto us for the glory of thy blessed name and pr[e]pare us for thy sabath approachinge and keepe us from all evills especially sinne [*crossed out:* s], keep me from all sinnes especially that sinne for the Lords sake.

19° Aug 1638 Sab[bath]
Mr Baynard preached both times to day here at Wilby, most faythfully & in the afternoone shewed the causes of the pestilence that now rageth in many places vizt Idolatry Corrupcon of gods worship oppression & oh Lord remove both the Cause & the stroke for the Lords sake.

---

[489] Still William Collis.
[490] Thomas Bacon here requested Woodford to provide continuing assistance in his Star Chamber case against George Plowright concerning ship money.

I dyned at Mr Pearnes wth Mr Baynard Mr Pearne (it seemes) pr[eached] at Kettering[491] to day.

20° Aug 1638
I prayed and wrote letters to my deare wife and then went to Burton [Latimer] to Mr Bacon, whom I [crossed out: found] heard was fishinge at his mill, [crossed out: and stayed] so I went downe, but I found him wth Capt Owsley[492] at Mr No hensmans[493] at Isham.
21° August
we dyned at Mr Bacon wth a venison pasty that p[ro]vided by Mrs Kimbould,[494] and Mr Bacon & I and Mr John [crossed out: took] went to Mr downes at Pitchley so he & we went to [Long] Buckby where the scowringe (a very comon disease now) hath bene much, and hath bene lately in Mr Bacons house but I pray unto the Lord to be kept. goodman Dingley a godly man in [Long] Buckby[495] whom I well know is lately dead of the scowringe.
22° August.
we went to daventry to the sheafe to sit uppon the Commission there betweene the

*****

[491] Andrew Perne was here preaching at the invitation of the minister, Thomas Harris. Kettering had previously possessed its own combination lecture, which had taken place on a Friday. In 1630 Bishop William Piers had introduced regulations to exclude from it those ministers regarded as puritan, but the prohibited clergy had returned and preached in opposition to Laudian policies. It seems to have been abolished as part of Laud's metropolitan visitation in May 1635, which was partly organized by Lambe: Longden MS, 6 May 1633; Fielding, 'Peterborough', p. 125.

[492] Either Richard or Robert Ouseley, the sons of Sir John Ouseley, lord of the manor of Courteenhall. Their father had also been a captain in the local militia (1614): VCH Northamptonshire, IV, p. 243; P.R. Brindle, 'Politics and society in Northamptonshire, 1649–1714' (unpublished PhD thesis, University of Leicester, 1983), p. 126; Metcalfe, Visitation of Northamptonshire 1618, p. 190; J. Wake (ed.), A Copy of Papers Relating to Musters, Beacons, and Subsidies etc in the County of Northampton AD 1586–1623, Publications of the Northamptonshire Record Society III (Kettering, 1926), p. cxxii.

[493] Possibly the Morris Henchman of Isham (perhaps the same high constable referred to by Sibthorpe as a puritan for his obstructiveness over ship money collection) who gave evidence in the High Commission case of Alban Eales, who in 1634 had obtained archiepiscopal institution to the rectory of Isham while it was still occupied by Richard Rainsford, and who was forced to resign and pay costs: TNA, SP16/261, fos 121r–v, 127v, 192r–v; TNA, SP16/318/6; Longden, Clergy.

[494] The wife of Thomas Kimbould of Northampton.

[495] Constable John Dingley of Long Buckby had been arrested by the Privy Council (with Richard Robins and others), accused of failing to support Sheriff Sir Robert Banastre's agents, who were distraining the goods of those who had refused to pay ship money around the beginning of 1638: Jackson, 'Ship money', pp. 145, 157 n. 88; PDR, Archdeaconry of Northampton wills, first series, Book AE, fo. 112.

Kings Attourney & Mr Bacon & al. for the examinacon of the late high sheriffe Sr John driden. dr Pocklington & Mr Sea Com[missione]rs p[ro] Att[ourney] K[ing's] were there & Mr downes for Mr Bacon. I met there wth old Mr Martin & diverse North[amp]ton men & came to [Long] Buckby at night.

23° August 1638

Mr Bacon & I and Mr Edmund[496] came from [Long] Buckby in the morninge and came to Mr [crossed out: danes] downes his house whether we were invited to a feast & there we found my Lady harvey Mr Palmer of Stoke &.[497]

we went to Burton [Latimer] afterward.

24° August

I went to Ketteringe after I had bene to see them ffish where I went

with my Cousin Oughton[498] & my Client Mr Some &. I came againe to Burton [Latimer].

25° August 1638

I went wth Mr Bacon againe to fish, who offered to give me 20s, for my Journey & to daventry, but I gave it him againe & desired that & the rest when I shall goe to the tearme.

---

[496] Edmund Bacon, the brother of Thomas and John.

[497] Lady Harvey might be Christian, the widow of the godly Judge Sir Francis Harvey of Cotton End, who had survived his death in 1632, or Mary, the widow of Sir Francis's son, Sir Stephen, who predeceased his father. Sir Francis had made provision in his will for his orphaned grandsons to be educated at university and the inns of court, fervently 'hopeinge they will follow their father's good example to lyve religiously' (TNA, PROB/11/88). The Harveys were a large dynasty of lawyers taking their lead from the judge: his son, Sir Stephen, three of his sons-in-law, and four of his nephews attended the Middle Temple. The family enjoyed godly connections with the Nicolls family of Hardwick and the Sawyers of Kettering, both of whom were closely allied with Francis Downes of Pytchley, who is the host here. The Palmer referred to is Edward (1588–1642), son of Anthony Palmer (d. 1633), squire of Stoke Doyle and kinsman of Sir Richard Knightley. Anthony had previously protected the Elizabethan puritan extremist William Hackett, whose career had ended in execution, although he later patronized many moderate ministers, some of whom served in the Church courts. A Middle Temple barrister since 1616, Edward had married Sir Stephen Harvey's sister Frances. He acted as recorder of the soke of Peterborough from 1629 and Woodford mentions him as such on 11 January 1638/39. He served as escheator for Northamptonshire from 1630 until 1631 and as a justice of the peace. He was also an ally of Bishop John Williams of Lincoln and a member of the Company of Mineral and Battery Works. He supported Sir Gilbert Pickering at the shire contest for the Short Parliament but was a Royalist in the Civil War: TNA, PROB/11/88 (Sir Francis Harvey); TNA, PROB/11/41 (Anthony Palmer); W. Prest, 'Harvey, Sir Francis (c.1568–1632)', in *ODNB*; Pevsner, *Northamptonshire*, p. 353; Metcalfe, *Visitation of Northamptonshire 1618*, pp. 98–99; BRO, St John (Bletso) MSS, DDJ 1369; NRO, Finch (Hatton) MSS, F(H) 133; Venn; Fielding, 'Peterborough', p. 28; Prest, *Barristers*, p. 383; Sheils, *Puritans*, pp. 118, 137, 139.

[498] Richard Oulton?

I came afterward to Wilby, and found that Mr Watts my good freind
had sent me a side of venison which I gave to Mrs Pentlowe, blessed
be the Lord for the love & helpe of freinds
26° Aug. Sab.[bath]
Mr Pearne preached both times, very holily I blesse the Lord.
I dined at Mr Pearnes, where there were 2 gentlewomen, one of them
one of Sr Gerard harveyes[499] daughters a good woman

27° Aug 1638
my mother & diverse freinds invited to Mr Pentlowes here to a venison
pasty after dinner Mr Thomas Pentlowe came who wantinge his
coppyes of his Bill and answer in the Court of Wards inter him & Mrs
Sill[500] we went towards London to get Coppyes out of the office, we
came to Lathbury[501] to Oagles his house to night.
28° Aug.
[crossed out, illegible] afflicted with [crossed out, illegible] & we came
to London about 5. a clock & went to the office, & not findinge
Mr Beesly I wrote to him to Kentish towne to come the next
morninge.
afterward I went to my wife and my family & freinds & found them
in health I blesse the Lord, but my wife not delivered

29° Aug. 1638.
my wife & I were speakinge in the morninge of her stayinge so long
before her delivery, & she was sayinge her mother thought she should
stay till xxmas, and presently after before I arose she began to fall in
travell we prayed together in private so the midwife was sent for &
came & then I went about my occasions to the office for Mr Pentlow.
I came home againe about 2 or 3 a clock & my wife was still in travell,
I stayed there a while with my father & in the hall, & in the hall I
prayed unto the Lord with some gracious affeccon & confidence in
the Lord & then I went away to the temple againe and as I returned
I called at my cousin Ragdales in stayninge lane & there I heard

[499] Sir Gerard, the son of John Harvey and Mary (née St John of Bletso, Bedfordshire, which
was adjacent to the Harveys' parish of Thurleigh), was a soldier who had been knighted
by the Earl of Essex at Cadiz. By 1634 he was living at Cardington near Bedford, his
elder brother, Oliver, having inherited the family manor. Sir Gerard had married Dorothy
Gascoigne, who was also related to the St Johns; their daughters were Ann, Elizabeth, and
Dorothy: F.A. Blaydes, *The Visitations of Bedfordshire 1566, 1582 and 1634*, Harleian Society
Publications, XIX (London, 1884), p. 116.
[500] Philippa Sill was the widow of Wellesbourne Sill (d. 1634), who had owned the rectory
of Westbury in Buckinghamshire. She was acting on behalf of their son, Wellesbourne, a
royal ward: *VCH Buckinghamshire*, IV, p. 267; TNA, WARD 7/89/249.
[501] In Buckinghamshire.

the good newes that my wife was delivered of a daughter, Blessed be thy name oh Lord oh how gracious hast thou bene unto me in hearinge my poore prayer, & in bringinge me up in thy good p[ro]vidence to be here at this time & to give the child right shape & forme &

& life, to give my wife now so much cheerfullnes Lord vouchsafe blessings & m[er]cyes still to me & my family for the Lords sake, I gave thanks in private wth my deare wife for this great m[er]cye to us while my wife was in travell I framed likewise those prayers at the end of the booke.[502]
now Lord sanctify my child for the ordinance of baptisme & sanctify the ordinance to the child, & make the Child thine owne by grace & make that and the other two blessings & comforts to us their parents, and make my wife also a Nurse to it if it be thy will for the Lords sake Amen.
the child lay crosse it seemes in the wombe a great while, blessed be thy name oh Lord for sendinge helpe & ayd.
v[i]d[e] prayer in thend of the book[503]
30° Aug. 1638.
I prayed wth my deare wife and came away from London about two or three a clock and came to St Albans wth Mr Pentlowe to Mr Walkers safe blessed be god. I wrote back to my wife

31. Aug. 1638
we prayed together, and came to Breakfast at dunstable, and afterward we met with Mr harley & one Mr Wooddard a wine Cooper in London, we stayed a litle at Wooburn and afterward at Olney[504] at the Swanne & came to wilby somewhat late.
1° Sept.
I prayed and went to Mr Pentlow at Broughton and after to Mr Tanfeild at Cransley to aske advise about Inter[rogatories] for Mr Pentlowe, & came home safe I put my name R. W. uppon an ash tree which stands by it selfe alone amonge some Bushes neere hardwick or Orlibeere,[505] and I p[ro]mised to acknowledge gods goodnesse here after if the Lord shall bringe me to a better & more plentifull Condicon. I was graciously affected and inflamed with the Love

---

[502] See p. 403, additional entry dated 29 August 1638.
[503] See ibid.
[504] That is, Woburn, Bedfordshire, and Olney, Buckinghamshire.
[505] Orlingbury.

of god as I went alonge in the morninge, and prayed to the Lord
with

with the teares of Love, blessed be thy name oh Lord.
2° Sept. 1638. Sab.[bath]
Mr dyke[506] of Wellingborow preached in the morninge at Wilby & Mr
Pearne in the afternoone, very graciously & well blessed be thy name
oh Lord.
3° Sept.
I prayed, and wrote to my wife, and afterward went to Broughton and
then to Lodington to Mr Tanfeilds then we came away and went to
Mr downes so Mr downes & his man & Mr ffosbrooke & his man, and
Mr Pentlowe & I came alonge to Toucester.

4° Sept. 1638
Mr Smith & one Mr danvers[507] Commissionrs p[ro] Mrs Sill we sate
Closse about the Commiss[ion] all the day.
Mr ffletcher solicitor p[ro] def[endan]t & I were Clerks to take the
deposicons.
Mr downes & Mr ffosbrooke were Com[missione]rs p[ro] Mr Pentlow
5° Sept.
we sate closse at the Commission againe to day and made an end
about one a clock in the morninge.
Mr downes went away in the afternoone to Banbury.
6° Sept.
we came from Toucester about 12 a clock and I came safe to Wilby
I prayse the Lord Mr ffosbrooke Mr Pentlow & & I stayed at Meeres
Ashby by the way

[506] Possibly Jeremiah Dyke, son of Jeremiah Dyke, the godly minister of Epping, Essex,
from 1609 until 1639. He had proceeded MA from St Catherine's College, Cambridge, in
1636, and had been ordained a deacon at Peterborough on 20 May 1638. He may now
have been based at Wellingborough prior to his ordination as a priest at Peterborough on
10 March 1639: Venn; Webster, *Godly Clergy*, pp. 49, 154, 159n, 260; Longden, *Clergy*.

[507] Probably John Smith of Northampton, attorney, who was connected to the godly
minister Thomas Knightley, and who acted as the overseer of the will of Jeremiah Lewis,
minister of All Saints'. Samuel Danvers, a future Parliamentarian, was the son of Sir John
Danvers of Culworth (the regicide and brother of Henry, Earl of Danby), and cousin of
Francis Downes of Pytchley: S. Kelsey, 'Danvers, Sir John (1584/5–1655)', in *ODNB*; J.J.N.
McGurk, 'Danvers, Henry, earl of Danby (1573–1644)', in *ODNB*; NRO Finch (Hatton) MSS,
F(H) 133; Longden, *Clergy*; *Records of the Honourable Society of Lincoln's Inn*, 2 vols (London, 1896),
I (*Admissions, 1420–1799*), p. 221.

7° Sept.
I prayed and went to Ketteringe, where I

I was in Company wth Mr Kimbould[508] Mr Maunsell[509] Mr Lamb of
Cranford Mr Eakins of Barton Segrave Mr Kiplinge;[510] what did I
in that company, my hart did arise in it, & I was sad inwardly, Lord
p[ar]don my faylinge let me never goe into such Company againe
unlesse I have a callinge; And Lord if it be thy will take off the necessity
from my body & the affection from my mind of usinge Tobacco, oh
Lord helpe me against every faylinge crucify every Corruption in me
for the Lords sake.
I came to lodge at Mr downes his house at Pitchley.
8° Sept 1638
I prayed and came safe to Wilby, but first Mr downes reteyned me to
be for him ag[ains]t one Mr Clynt,[511] Lord give me favor still in his
eyes, blessed be thy name oh Lord for all thy goodnesse.

[508]Thomas Kimbold of Northampton was a counsellor at law who worked in the
ecclesiastical courts from 1629 until 1638, and the father-in-law of Sir John Lambe, who
married his daughter, Elizabeth: Longden, *Visitation of Northamptonshire 1681*, pp. 99–100; J.
Fielding, 'Lambe, Sir John (c.1566–1646)', in *ODNB*.
[509]John Maunsell, squire of Thorpe Malsor (1605–1677), supported the Grand
Remonstrance and was a prominent justice of the peace during the Commonwealth.
In 1672 his house was licensed as a congregational meeting place. In the latter half of
1637 he lived in Northampton, where he was involved in an acerbic dispute with his
lodger, Humphrey Ramsden, a supporter of Laudian ceremonial. Ramsden claimed that
Maunsell had been William Prynne's chamber-fellow at Lincoln's Inn, and that Maunsell
hated Laudian ceremonial but did not openly challenge him: 'and I was ever jealous
of him, knowing hee did not inwardly approve of what I did; and I have heard him
wish yt these Ceremonies had never beene thought of, for they are a burden to ye
Consciences of many good men, and that those who are called Puritans are for the
most part religious, conscionable, honest men, and when Prin[ne] suffered condigne
punishment, he said no doubt but he tooke it patiently and joyfully, wheras his Adversaries
might have quakeing hearts': TNA, SP16/414/163 (quotation); Isham, *Diary*, p. 154,
n. 30.
[510]Robert Eakins had been presented to the rectory of Barton Seagrave in 1632 by his
father, Thomas. He had conformist connections – Robert Sibthorpe helped him to buy
the advowson of his living – and was sequestered from the benefice by Parliament in
1644: Longden, *Clergy*; Temple of Stowe MSS, STT 1881; A.G. Matthews (ed.), *Walker
Revised* (Oxford, 1948), p. 278. Michael Kipling was a public notary who had worked
for the Peterborough Church courts since 1633 but around the period 1637–1639 was
registered in the Diocese of York: PDR, CBA63 and PDR, Church Survey Book 5,
passim.
[511]Francis Downes, squire of Pytchley, was engaged in a dispute with John Clynt, a minister
from Wichenford, Worcestershire, over the tithes of Cransley parish. Downes was married
to Alice, the sister of Sir Henry Robinson of Cransley (d. 1637), and through his wife had
controlled part of the manor since 1627 (he also owned property at Broughton, Isham,
and Loddington). Downes was Alice's second husband – she had previously been married

I went to Broughton before I came home but Mr Pentlowe could spare me no money although he owes me about 11 or 12li.
[crossed out: one line, illegible]

[crossed out: one word, illegible] Oh Lord when will it once be that I shall have selfe denyall, that thou wilt kill my corrupcons before my face, Lord passe by mine Iniquityes Lord heale my soule.

I ingraved R.W. uppon an Ash tree in the litle mount[512] in Mr Pentlowes closse here at Wilby. I am now in trouble & straights, but the Lord is able to send inlargement.

good newes from my wife I blesse the Lord Mrs Kimbould came hether to Wilby to night I heare there dyed 20. at North[amp]ton this weeke

9° Sept 1638 Sab.[bath]

Oh Lord make this thy Sab.[bath] a comfortable day unto me, Lord give me the leggs of fayth to runne but out of my selfe unto free grace; if I remayne at home restinge uppon myne owne grace or p[er]formances I am utterly lost & damned forever, oh give me a Christ for his sake give me salvation freely, Oh Lord breath thy spirit into the words of thy servant this day who shall speake to us in thy name, for the Lords sake.

Lord thinke uppon my most deare wife & Children blesse them and cause them to p[ro]sp[er], let not my faylings & sinnes be layd to their chardge, keepe us all from sinne make us a holy family unto thee, p[ro]sp[er] us every way (if thou seest good) for the Lords sake Amen

to John Washbourne of Wichenford – and when the living of Cransley fell vacant in 1639 the right to present to it lay with the crown, which was the guardian of the patrons (Alice's son John Washbourne and Sir Henry's heir and namesake) in their minority. There followed a competition to win the royal patronage (involving a dispute in the Court of High Commission) between Downes, who tried to prefer his candidate, John Baseley, and John Goodman, a conformist client of Sir John Lambe and later of Sir John Isham. Goodman ultimately achieved the living for himself. The Washbourne family resided at Pytchley manor after 1663 and it was from among their papers that the Ishams obtained for their collection a separate manuscript (NRO Isham (Lamport) MSS, I(L) 2570) describing sympathetically the death of the puritan divine John Barker, who was executed at Northampton in 1637 for murder, which had probably belonged to Barker's patron, Francis Downes: *VCH Northamptonshire*, IV, p. 164; NRO Isham (Correspondence), I (C) 3228, and I (L) 708, 731, 735, 736, 740; TNA, PROB/11/176 (Robinson) and PROB/11/183 (Downes); Isham, *Diary*, p. 102, n. 13; Fielding, 'Peterborough', pp. 42, 55 n. 73; Longden MS, 21 August 1639 and 11 June 1641; Longden, *Clergy* (Goodman).

[512] A popular garden feature providing a viewing point: Isham, *Diary*, p. 68, n. 56.

Lord stay thy hand at North[amp]ton if it be thy will

Mr Pearne preached in the morninge & Mr Eynesworth in the afternoone.
Mr Kimbould came hether this morninge
10° Sept. 1638
I prayed and went alonge with Mr Kimbould to goe to Kerby to Sr xxofer hattons.
in Ro[th]well my horse slipt & fell downe on his side & my foote was under him & was much hurt that I feared my legg had either bene broke or out of Joynt.
I was in great payne of it. I dyned at Ro[th]well wth Mr hill of Lodington Mr Baseley &[513] we came to Sr xxofers about 4 a clock I was in great payne of my foote hardly able to goe.
there was an interlude to day at Kerby called the New hunnt, we saw litle of it cominge late. we went back to dr Beales to bed at Cottingham[514] in the great Chamber there is a shamefull Crucifix.

11° Sept. 1638
we went this morninge againe to Kerby my foote a litle better blessed be god.
another interlude acted to day called [crossed out: the] Masculine humors, one hostead[515] was the poet. I dyned in the p[ar]lo[u]r; blessed

[513]The conformist Joseph Hill had been the incumbent of Loddington, owing to crown patronage, since 1618. He served in the Church courts from 1622 until 1631 and was named by Bishop Piers in 1630 as a conforming minister permitted to serve the Kettering lecture: Longden MS, 24 June 1618; Longden, Clergy; TNA, SP16/531/135. The godly minister John Basely was the sole lecturer at the town of Rothwell, although he was not the vicar until 1641; he received bequests from the godly justices of the peace Francis Downes and Francis Nicolls: TNA, PROB/11/111; PDR, Archdeaconry of Northampton Wills, third series, A198.
[514]I have not been able to identify 'The New Hunt'. The Laudian royal chaplain, Dr William Beale, had been vice-chancellor of the University of Cambridge since 1635, but before that had been active in the Peterborough Church courts. He had obtained the rectories of Cottingham in 1625 and Paulerspury in 1637 – the former by royal patronage during Hatton's minority and the latter by the influence of Archbishop Laud himself: N.W.S. Cranfield, 'Beale, William (d. 1651)', in ODNB; Longden MS, 4 February 1625 and 31 October 1637; Fielding, 'Peterborough', p. 43.
[515]Peter Hausted, a native of Oundle, was Dr Edward Martin's curate at Uppingham, Rutland, and was one of a number of conformists who flourished under Hatton's protection. Martin, who had been Laud's domestic chaplain when Laud was Bishop of London, was a conformist partisan as President of Queen's College, Cambridge, where he had protected Hausted, his chaplain, from charges of crypto-popery. Both Martin and Hausted preached at the primary visitation of Bishop Dee in 1634, and struggled to impose Laudianism in their

be thy name oh Lord for givinge me any favor in the eyes of Sr xxofer[516] & we came againe to dr Beales at night & were Mr Canons[517] guests I thinke.

12° Sept I prayed and came from Cott[ingham] to Wellingborowe m[ar]ket in good time & to Wilby at night

13° Sept.

I prayed and went to keepe grafton [Regis] Court which was very small & came home againe to night.

I met with Rob. ffowler & Mr Yorke & wrote to Mr Maior elect.[518]

14° Sept. 1638

I prayed and went to Ketteringe, where I met wth Stephen dexter[519] & Thomas Cr[utchley] sent for me to the towne side,[520] & I went & spake to the Justices in the behalfe of North[amp]to[n]. I met wth Mr Rushworth & we came late to Sr Wm. Willmers[521] house at Siwell.

15° Sept.

James Lewes was at Siwell wth us this morninge, we had discourse which much warmed my hart blessed be the Lord. I went to ffax[t]on afterward, to have shewed Mr Nicolls the letter sent from

---

parish in the teeth of great opposition. Hausted was also connected to the conformist earls of Northampton, Spencer Compton and his son James. Hatton's household functioned as a miniature court, affording patronage to many (mainly conformist) artists and ministers. He accepted the dedication of Hausted's sermons in 1636 and also clearly delighted in his plays (and those of his rival, Thomas Randolph, another Northamptonshire man and a former disciple of Ben Jonson). He pursued various antiquarian projects with William Dugdale and Roger Dodsworth and employed the musician George Jeffreys, who lived locally and who went on to be Charles I's organist at his Civil War headquarters at Oxford. *Masculine Humours* is not listed as part of Hausted's canon. *VCH Northamptonshire*, IV, p. 89; A. Milton, 'Martin, Edward (d. 1662)', in *ODNB*; W.H. Kelliher, 'Randolph, Thomas (bap. 1605, d. 1635)', in *ODNB*; D. Kathman, 'Hausted, Peter (c.1605–1644)', in *ODNB*; J.P. Wainwright, 'Jeffreys, George (c.1610–1685)', in *ODNB*; Fielding, 'Peterborough', pp. 46, 118–120; L.C. Loyd and D.M. Stenton (eds), *Sir Christopher Hatton's Book of Seals*, Publications of the Northamptonshire Record Society XV (1942), pp. xx–xxx.

[516] Sir Christopher Hatton.

[517] Thomas Canon was another Hatton protégé as rector of Church Brampton. A Church court official by 1640, he was ejected from his living as a delinquent. He served as a chaplain in the royal army: Longden, *Clergy*.

[518] Robert Fowler was the son of the mayor elect, Richard Fowler: TNA, PROB/11/208. Yorke might have been a member of the puritan family from Hardingstone: Sheils, *Puritans*, p. 57.

[519] Probably the son of either Gregory Dexter senior or his brother, Alexander.

[520] Kettering lay east of the River Ise. Woodford would have crossed either Hall or North Bridge back to the town side of the river.

[521] Sir William Willmer of Sywell (a future Royalist) steadfastly refused to pay ship money around this time and was involved in disputes with the parishioners of Sywell and Byfield; Jackson, 'Ship money', p. 167; C.W. Foster, *A History of the Willmer Family* (Leeds, 1888), p. 56.

North[amp]ton of the arr[angements][522] in the east div[ision] & Mr Nicolls was not at home.

I was at Mr Mosses[593] as I went. I had many grac[ious] eiaculac[ons] [*crossed out:* &] peticons & meditat[ions] in my Journey I blesse the Lord, I came home safe to Wilby.

I had newes to day that my daughter Sarah was like to dye on munday last blessed be thy name oh Lord shewinge m[er]cye.

16. Sept. 1638. Sab.[bath]

I prayed and went to church where Mr Eyneswo[rth] preached in the morninge; I dyned at Mr Pearnes, Mr Pearne preached in the afternoone, Lord make thine ordinances very fruitfull for the Lords sake Amen.

one Mr harrington & ux is at Mr Pearnes

I had grac[ious] affeccons in private prayer to nig[ht] I blesse the Lord 17° Sept. Mr Pentlowe went towards oxford to day.

I prayed and went to Wootton about my Lady Smethyes busines.

Thomas Cr[utchley] came to me there & told me that there have dyed but 2 at North[amp]ton since Friday Lord cease it for thy m[er]cyes sake.

some grac[ious] comforts in private dutye at night I blesse the Lord.

I came to Wilby. Mr Bere brought home Mrs Susan Pentlow to night. I often seeke the Lord for good to me & my family The Lord will heare me an unworthy sinner for his m[er]cyes sake.

18° Sept. 1638

I prayed and employed my selfe allmost all the day in castinge up accounts & & was somewhat pestered wth melancholly. Lord ease me thy poore servante for the Lords sake. The Sheriffs Bayleifes came to this towne to day to distreyne for shippmoney[524] but the women assembled & some men and affright them, there was much running wth forkes & Cowlestaves & Ah Lord reforme whats amisse both in the church & Comon weale for the Lords sake.

much refreshinge comfort in the good word of god.

---

[522] Possibly arrangements for holding the county quarter sessions at Wellingborough again (as on 22 May 1638), owing to the persistence of the plague at Northampton. The sessions were duly held at Wellingborough on 2 October 1638: Diary, p. 244.

[593] John Mosse had been presented to the rectory of Hannington in 1611 by the conformist Bishop William Barlow of Lincoln: Longden MS, 9 November 1611; Longden, *Clergy*.

[524] This might refer to an incident in which the Constable of Wilby, Francis Freeman, who had been accused of dilatoriness in collecting ship money, fell foul of Sheriff Sir John Hanbury's distraining bailiffs: Jackson, 'Ship money', p. 222.

19° Sept.

I prayed and went to Wellingborowe where the Justice seate was to day held there in the Scholehouse by Mr Lane Attorn[ey] primar[y] deputy p[ro] my Lord of holland.[525]

on Munday last was the Swanimote at Weldon, where were called 4 men & a Reeve out of every towne wthin the new bounds of the forest & diverse of

them sworne; Oh Lord what will these things come to in the end thou alone knowest, Lord order every thinge for the best, and gayne thy selfe glory by bringinge good out of evill for the Lords sake Amen. Mr Maior ffo[wler] gives me ease to stay away at Mich[aelmas] wch I pray

I was very melancholly this day, & had many sad cogitacons but I desired to lift up my soule unto the Lord.

Mr Pentlowe came home to night.

I find much comfort in readinge the good word of god.

20° Sept. 1638

I prayed and went on the way towards London wth [*crossed out:* Mr] Mr Sandford & ux I went wth them beyond hardwater mill[526] & there tooke leave, I prayed the Lord allmighty to blesse them, after I were gone.

I went after to Woollaston to my ill tennant ffuller. I went after to Wellingborow Court & dyned wth the steward there.

I came home from thence; but have bene very melancholly this day.

oh my god helpe me against this heavy infirmity for the Lords sake.

in my melancholly I did desire to wayt uppon the Lord & did remember that heretofore when god hath bene about to [*left margin: trefoil symbol*] bestow uppon me any new m[er]cy he hath excercised me wth some affliccon or other & who knowes but this may have a mercy at the end of it; however oh my god give me a sanctifyed use of it and patience for the Lords sake.

21° Sept. 1638

I prayed and went to Ketteringe wth Oliver Mr Pentlowes man and came home againe wth him safe blessed be thy name oh Lord.

22° Sept.

I prayed and came downe out of my

*****

[525]Richard Lane, attorney general to Prince Charles, was Holland's deputy in the forest court, which is here being held at Wellingborough, instead of Northampton, owing to the plague: Pettit, *Royal Forests*, p. 91.

[526]A watermill on the River Nene situated at Great Doddington, just south of Wilby.

chamber and found Mr Midleton a Sargeant at armes & on[e] Mr Winstanley[527] his freind belowe in the hall they were to goe they s[ai]d to Kettering so I havinge some occasion to Broughton went along wth them to Ketteringe & then Mr Midle[ton] told me he came to appr[e]hend Mr ffr[ancis] Sawyer (of which I knew nothinge before) so he sent for him & arrested him,[528] & tooke bond for him to appeare at Wilby on Tuesday morninge & we came home to Wilby againe safe (blessed be god)

23° Sept 1638 Sab.[bath]

Mr Baynard preached both times here to day Mr Pearne beinge absent, o[u]r strangers[529] did not like the length of the sermons, Lord convert them unto thee draw them after thee for the Lords sake.

24° Sept.

I stayed at home all this day, & was busy

busy some p[ar]te of it in makinge Mr Pent[low's] will. This day Mr Midleton went to take one Walker an high Constable at hardingston,[530] & afterward came to Wilby againe.

25° Sept. 1638

Mr Sawyer came hether to the Sargeant at Armes[531] & they went for dunstable to night.

---

[527] A Mr Winstanley held the position of Keeper of the Privy Lodgings and Galleries at Whitehall in 1660 and was presumably the same individual: R.O. Bucholz, 'Dependent sub-departments house and wardrobe keepers 1660–1837', in *Office Holders in Modern Britain, Volume 11: court officers 1660–1837* (2006), pp. 119–135.

[528] Statements by Sheriff Sir John Hanbury's agents dated 6 and 8 September 1638 claimed that Sawyer, whose brother John was a leading godly magistrate, had delayed paying his ship money. When they attempted to distrain a horse, Sawyer, his wife, and servants had attacked them, Sawyer threatening to 'knock all your brains out'. The council reacted quickly, despatching Sergeant Henry Middleton to arrest Sawyer on 16 September, and ordering Attorney General Sir John Bankes to examine him by 29 September: Jackson, 'Ship money', pp. 159–163; TNA, PC 2/49/422, 440.

[529] That is, Middleton and Winstanley.

[530] William Walker was the Chief Constable of Wymersley Hundred, immediately south of Northampton. His parson, the conformist Charles Stockwell of Hardingstone, had reported Walker to the justice of the peace Robert Sibthorpe for stating that ship money was an 'oppression', that the king was 'under a law as any subject', and that (referring to the recent verdict against John Hampden) 'some judges had determined it to be law, but the best and most honest had not'. Arrested by Middleton at the council's behest, by 30 September Walker was being examined by Attorney General Sir John Bankes. He was eventually released, but was repeatedly harried in the local courts by Sibthorpe, who clearly also regarded him as a puritan: Jackson, 'Ship money', pp. 128–129 (quotations), 130; Longden, *Clergy*.

[531] Henry Middleton.

Lord I beseech thee shew m[er]cye to this Kingdome, amend and reforme what ever is amisse for the Lords sake. Mr Pentlow & I & Mr Eynesworth were ringinge in the afternoone.

26 Sept

I prayed and went to Wellingborowe & went afterwards to Old. Mr Bacon was

was at Wellingborowe to day & Mr Edmund &.

I was afterward wth Mr Bulliv[ant] before I came for Old. [crossed out: one line, illegible]

27° Sept. 1638.

I prayed and afterward kept the Court Baron for my Cousin dexter, Mr fforsith dyned there.

W[illia]m dexter[532] of London came thether at night.

28° Sept.

I came away from Old in the morninge to Ketteringe wth my Cousin dexter. I met there wth Mr Rushworth, who desired me to stay wth him at the red Lyon in Ketteringe to night, one Mr Ramsey supped with us. I prayed wth Mr Rushworth wth some Comfort & enlargem[en]t I prayse the Lord.

29° Sept. 1638 Mich[aelmas] day.

Mr Rushworth hath taken a shop to day at Ketteringe under the Swan, we were there in company wth Mr Miller Mr Pettiver & & their wives, I was troubled to be in such Company Oh Lord pr[e]serve me [crossed out: from] for time to come, we reproved Baxter[533] the host for his swearinge Lord bestowe grace upon him if it be thy will. I came to Wilby to night.

30° Sept Sab.[bath]

I prayed for a blessing uppon the ordinances; Mr Eynesworth preached in the morninge, & Mr Perkins in the afternoone, very well & boldly Lord make thy word fruitfull for the Lords sake Amen.

1° Octob.

I prayed in the morninge wth some

******

---

[532] Gregory Dexter senior was lord of Knightley's manor at Old. William Dexter of London was a relation, possibly the scrivener mentioned on 1 December 1638: *VCH Northamptonshire*, IV, pp. 202–203.

[533] John Baxter was the host of the Swan. He achieved a degree of revenge against the godly by supplying Sir John Lambe with information regarding a clerical conference held at his inn on 25 August 1640 in opposition to the 'Etcetera' oath: TNA, SP16/465/8; Introduction, p. 86, n. 208.

enlargem[en]t I prayse the Lord, and I did beseech the Lord to supply me wth moneyes for London for I was in distresse & could get none either of my tenant or where any was owinge to me; I went afterward to Broughton & there I rec[eive]d a letter that Mr ffosbrooke was not come home of whom I was to receave the Com[missio]n; about wch thinge maynly I went beinge to be payd to carry it up, so I went to Ro[th]well to the visitacon⁵³⁴ & there by gods p[ro]vidence I met wth him & he had brought it wth him & I there received it, & Mr Spencer offered to lend me tenne pounds till my returne & so I went to his house & receaved it & 30s more in p[ar]te p[ro] the fine, blessed be thy name oh Lord for thy gracious & seasonable supplyes.

as I came from Scaldwell I met wth Sr Thomas Cave⁵³⁵ nere holcot goeinge to Wellingborow Sess[ions] who shewed me much Love I blesse the Lord I came to Wilby somew[ha]t Late.

2° Octobr 1638

I prayed and went to Wellingborowe to the Sess[ions]⁵³⁶ & there I was reteyned in some businesses I prayse the Lord & Mr Leet⁵³⁷ & I had much discourse [crossed out: at] concerninge Religion as we lay in bed together. Lord draw us both neerer unto thee for the Lords sake.

3° Octob.

we lay at Mr Prats to night, I prayed in secret in the morninge there & had gracious enlargem[en]t I blesse the Lord, and havinge much doubted before of my inability to speake to the Justices in the causes I had, I besought the Lord & remembered the encouragem[en]t that

---

⁵³⁴The Michaelmas visitation of John Quarles, who had been Archdeacon of Northampton since 1629. Little is known about his churchmanship: his only extant visitation articles (dated 1639) are unexceptional (although they do contain the requirement to bow at the name of Jesus) and are completely silent on the position of the communion table. The conformist Simon Gunton preached at Rothwell on Friday 5 October, while at Northampton on 3 and 4 October Quarles himself preached, along with Lionel Goodricke, the vicar of Little Houghton and client of the godly lord of the manor, William Ward: Longden, *Clergy*; Longden MS, 10 July 1638; PDR, CB70, fo. 24r.

⁵³⁵Sir Thomas Cave, squire of Stanford on Avon, supported conformist ministers such as Anthony Scattergood and William Laud himself, whom he had presented to Stanford in 1607. Cave's sister Eleanor had married the diplomat Sir Thomas Roe: TNA, PROB/11/17; Longden MS, 6 November 1607; H. de Quehen, 'Scattergood, Anthony (bap. 1611, d. 1687)', in *ODNB*; M. Strachan, 'Roe, Sir Thomas (1581–1644)', in *ODNB*.

⁵³⁶The county's quarter sessions had also been held at Wellingborough (instead of Northampton) on 22 May 1638, owing to the plague.

⁵³⁷This might be Gregory Leet of Badby or one of his descendants. Around 1604 Leet was accused in the Church courts of receiving communion either sitting or standing and of refusing to receive kneeling: PDR, CB37, fo. 208r; Longden, *Visitation of Northamptonshire 1681*, p. 87.

was given to Moses, & remembred that I likewise was in my callinge
& I prayed for favor & wisdome & the Lord graciously heard me
for I

I was enabled & had much favor I prayse the Lord. I came after to
Wilby. Mr Eynesworth was at Mr Pentlowes to night to take his leave
to goe from the towne, oh Lord graunt that thy blessings may goe
along wth him & his ministry for the Lords sake.
4° Octob. 1638
I prayed and tooke my leave & came for London I met wth Wm. Spicer
at hardingston by appoyntment & payd him there 25s in p[ar]te of the
50s for Midsom[mer] & Micha[elma]s rent so there is still 25s behind.
Mr Walker was there pr[ese]nt who wth Mr Sawyer is lately come
from the Lords of the Counsell. I called at Wootton of Watson, &
came after to Grafton [Regis] to keep Court, I met there wth one Mr
Peake of Nottingham, we after met wth other company & came safe
to dunstable blessed be god. I prayed wth him. Lord draw him unto
thee for the Lords sake.
5° Octob.
we prayed againe & came forth somewhat early

early wth one Mr Sutton a Londoner borne at Newnham, we had
some good discourse on the way. we eate somethinge at St Albans
at Mr Walkers at the Red lyon, and came safe to London blessed
be god. where I found my family well I prayse the Lord, onely my
wife is troubled wth sore breasts Lord be gracious to us make her
a nurse if it be thy will & give us still matter of prayses for the
Lords sake Amen. p[ar]don o[u]r sinnes for the Lord Xt his sake
Amen.
I heard dr Stoughton p[ar]te of a good sermon.
6° Octobr 1638.
I prayed and after went to my chamber,[538] & am afflicted wth
melancholly oh Lord helpe me & be gracious unto me for the Lords
sake out of the depths I cry unto thee for thou art the Lord my
god.
I was too longe at the horne Taverne wth Mr Greene[539] & Mr Weston,
Lord keepe me that I goe not out to the creature to trust in that for
comfort & cure of melancholly

---

[538] At Clement's Inn.
[539] Theodore Greene of Marston Trussell, a lawyer of Clement's Inn, had been an attorney
since at least 1633, when he acted for Thomas Bacon; he represented Justinian Isham from
1638: NRO 55P/57, p. 63; Isham, *Diary*, pp. 72 n. 26, 73 n. 27.

here is newes that the Queene mother of ffraunce[540] is cominge over Lord pr[e]serve & keep this Kingdome [*crossed out: few words, illegible*]

7° Octobr 1638. Sab.[bath]
I prayed and went wth my wife to heare dr Stoughton in the morninge, and a stranger there in the afternoone, who preached both very faythfully Lord hold thy servants as starrs in thy right hand that no adversary may stop their mouthes for the Lords sake.
8° Octobr.
I prayed and went to see my horse, which I heare is not well, I prayed unto the Lord for his recovery Lord deale graciously wth me thy poore servant for the Lords sake.
Mr Pyke came hether to night wth his family I am much subiect to melancholly Lord helpe me for the Lords sake.
I stayed too longe wth Mr Weston Mr Leastinge & Lord graunt that I may hang uppon thee for comfort & not uppon the creature for the Lords sake.
9° Octob. tearme began to day.
I prayed & went to Westm[inster] hall where I met wth

with Mr Winstanley keep[er] of the Lodgings at Whitehall who shewed me the chambers, I was in the Kings chamber where I saw the 4 gospells the acts of the apostles & the Apocalipse in books all sett forth wth pictures; Lord pr[e]serve & keep thy true religion still amongst us, Lord blesse the Kings Ma[jes]tye & make him a nursinge father to the Kingdomes committed to him for the Lords sake
I have given my wife above 5li. Lord supply us with thy bounty for the Lords sake Amen Mr Winstanley hath p[ro]mised me if I can heare of any place in the Kings gift he will beg it for me, Lord direct me in thy blessed p[ro]vidence as thou seest best for the Lords sake.
10° octob. 1638.
I prayed and went to the hall wth Mr Sanford we dyned at the place called heaven.[541] I heard dr Stoughton in the afternoone my wife hath

---

[540] The Catholic Marie de Medici, widow of Henri IV, and mother of Louis XIII and Queen Henrietta Maria.
[541] Heaven was a tavern located in Old Palace Yard adjacent to Westminster Hall. It is mentioned in Jonson's *Alchemist* (1612), was used by Pepys in 1660, and was referred to by Butler in *Hudibras* (1677): H.B. Wheatley (ed.), *The Diary of Samuel Pepys*, 8 vols in 3 vols (reissued London, 1962), I, pp. 33 and note, 215, 261.

beene wth dr Gourdon[542] for advice who hath pr[e]scribed her a purge
Lord blesse it to her for the Lords sake.
I met wth ffilkins of Wellingborow neer charing crosse.
11° Octob
I prayed with my wife, & since my father tells

me that I must pay the 50li to Mr Readinge that remaynes & I am
troubled because not able to doe it, but in the sorowes of my hart oh
Lord I come unto thee & beseech thee to be gracious Lord rayse both
my father & me from our necessitous condicon supply us from heaven
abundantly by thy good p[ro]vidence, & keep up o[u]r harts to wayte
uppon thee p[ar]don the sinnes of us & our familyes for the Lords
sake.
Lord blesse my wives phisick unto her for the Lords sake this day.
Lord blesse me this day in all my undertakings & shew me thy
p[ro]vidence for the Lord Xt his sake I was this day wth Mr Midleton
& Mr Winstanley & too longe
12° Octob. 1638
I prayed and went to the hall, & after that to dinner in ffish street
wth Mr Midleton Mr Winstanley & & stayed there till night, Lord
what doe I doe in such Company, thou hast called me to holinesse &
moderacon Lord bestow it uppon me for the Lords sake. oh Let not
the cares of the world & melancholly cause me to put forth my hand
unto evill but let me find cherefullnes in attendinge uppon

uppon thee wthout [*crossed out:* the] such squeezinge the Creature for
that which it cannot yeild wthout thee.
Mr Winstanley & I have talked about findinge out some place or
revercons for him to begg of the Kinge & to put in my name, Oh
Lord wthout thee no purpose can be established Thou alone dost
all things graunt successe if it be thy will to thy glory for the Lords
sake.
13° Octobr 1638
I prayed and went to the hall, my hart heavy and dull and I have
bene much troubled that I was wth that Company yesterday, Lord
p[ar]don me thy poore servant & have m[er]cy & heale for the Lords
sake.

[542]Dr Aaron Gourdon (Guerden) was a native of Jersey who had obtained his degree in medicine from Rheims University in 1634 but who was currently practising illegally in London. In 1640 the court of physicians charged him with operating without a licence. In 1649 he was appointed master of the mint: J. Morrill, 'Guerden, Aaron (c.1602–1676?)', in *ODNB*.

14° Octob. Sab.[bath]
I prayed and went to dr Stoughtons Church both fornoone &
afternoone & heard him both tymes. Lord continue him & make
us fruitfull under thy meanes of grace for

for the Lords sake Amen.
15° Octob. 1638.
I prayed wth some comfort & fayth in the trouble of my hart in
the morninge & went after to the hall wth my brother. there I was
informed of one Mr Bendbowe[543] Clerke of the patents that he could
give me light about revercons and afterward by gods p[ro]vidence I
met wth him who tells me to morow morning at his house in Greenes
Lane I shall see the booke
16° Octob.
I prayed and went to Mr Bendbowes & his man shewed me the booke
so I find onely 3 revercons grannted of the 7 auditors[544] places and I
have since told Mr Winstanley of it but I p[er]ceave he makes now
much question about it, yet hath p[ro]mised me to inquire; I had
some comfort in thought that the Lord may perhaps make this day a
ground of comfort (as (this time 4 years it was an occasion of much
sorow & temptacon)

but Lord I desire wholly to submitt to thee, be gracious unto me I
pray thee & let me find thy favor not accordinge to what I have done
(for then I cannot escape p[er]dition) but for thy m[er]cyes sake in the
Lord Xt.
Mr Pentlowe is come to the towne here wth his daughter Susan:
Oh blessed be thy name still for preservinge me notwithstandinge the
temptacon that seized uppon me this day 4 yeares.
17° Octob. 1638
I prayed wth some inlargem[en]t in private in the morninge & then
went to Westm[inster] hall wth about 12d beinge all the money I had
left, so that I am not able to followe my occasions as I should; and my
hart is heavy in the Consideracon of my debts & wants. Oh base hart
be Contented, doth [left margin: trefoil symbol] not god take notice of
thee doth not he see what condicon is left for thee; oh my all-sufficient
father have m[er]cye on me give me cheerfullnes & contentednes in

---

[543]Possibly some relation of John Benbow of Westminster (d. 1625), who had been a
Chancery clerk: J.B. Hattendorf, 'Benbow, John (1653?–1702)', in *ODNB*.
[544]The seven Auditors of the Exchequer were crown-appointed officials responsible for
receiving and auditing crown revenue.

my estate keepe me from direfull melancholly & the cares of this
p[rese]nte world

world that they may never overwhelme me, & give me dilligence &
thriftynesse & ability in my way, and oh my god if thou seest good
supply me of thy fullnesse pay my debts for me & bestow uppon me
wth a more liberall hand & sanctifye it for the Lords sake.
[*left margin: trefoil symbol*] I have bene in this debt & want about 15.
yeares, it may please the Lord in the end to supply me by his good
p[ro]vidence, Abraham wayted 20. yeares for [*crossed out: an*] the
p[er]formance of a promise oh Lord quiet my hart pay Mr Readinge
& helpe both me & my father for the Lords sake Amen.
18° Octob. 1638
I prayed and went to Westm[inster] hall, where I met wth harry
Weltden [*crossed out: &*] who told me of the great debts that he was in,
& I was afflicted in the thoughts of mine, But Lord thou art able to
helpe, I heard that the Maior[545] of North[amp]ton is resolved to keepe
me out of my office this yeare because I have bene absent but Lord I
pray thee

thee give me grace & favor in their eyes there for the Lord Xt his sake
and now that I intend shortly to goe downe [*crossed out: I be*] thether
I beseech thee oh Lord doe thou goe [*crossed out: alonge*] downe with
me as thou didst p[ro]mise to goe downe with Jacob into Egipt keepe
me there from the stroke of thy destroyinge Angell, defend me & my
habitacon & my whole family, give me great favor in the eyes of the
townesmen & let thy p[ro]vidence be wth me there & with my whole
family beside for the Lords sake Amen.
I dranke a pint of sack wth John Snart.[546] I heare that Crutchley is in
towne its lamentable wet weather.
After I came home my wife & mother & were earnest with me to pay
for the wine at Baptiz[in]g about 15s & for money for the midwife
having layd out it or all of the first; but I had not above 12d left, [*crossed
out: I*] beinge compelled to come home wantinge 3s 6d to pay Mr
Killermaster[547] in Mr Pentlowes businesse and then my father told me

[545] Richard Fowler.
[546] John Snart (Smart) was a Northampton hosier who married Thomas Pentlow's daughter
Susan. He served as churchwarden of All Saints' from 1639 until 1640, when Humphrey
Ramsden claimed that he received communion sitting: Vestry Minutes, pp. 21, 34–36; TNA,
SP16/474/80.
[547] The barrister Thomas Kittermaster of Warwickshire had been admitted to Lincoln's
Inn in 1634: *Records of the Honourable Society of Lincoln's Inn*, 2 vols (London, 1896), I (*Admissions,
1420–1799*), p. 225.

I must pay the 50li to Mr Readinge that he had payd me & disbursed
for me [*crossed out:* 4] neere 400li allready & shewed me his

his booke of accounts where he reckons for every box of Marmalad[e]
given to any of the Lawyers & & about 14li or 15li for interest money
for money which he borrowed it seemes to pay Mr Readinge, wch
is nothinge to me at all, but there is rather interest due to me from
the time that I was marryed till now for much of the porcon, & he
reckoned for the wyne & sugar plums at Sams Baptizinge[548] & all which
much troubled me & I was very melancholy I feared least it should
unfit me for my callinge yet I desired then in the midst of sorrow to
[*crossed out:* stay] looke up unto the Lord; Lord heare my weake desires.
before night I went to Mr Warrens[549] & heard one Mr Leech[550] preach
very well at Bowe.
my wives milke gone wth greife Lord helpe us.
19° Octob. 1638. the weather extreme rayny.
some comfortable sleepe this night I prayse the Lord & some
refreshinge in prayer in secret & I have much blamed my selfe in
my too much [*left margin: trefoil symbol*] deiectednes and carefullnes
about my debts & the things of this world, & in my forgetfullnes of
heaven & eternall happinesse my everlastinge inheritance, Lord I pray
thee that my care for heaven & my comfort in spirituall things may
swallow up my too much carkinge care about and false

false esteeme & pleasure in the Creature as Moses serpent devoured
the rest Lord I pray thee uphold my hart give me the comforts of the
holy ghost let them dwell in my soule & fill my sayles, and I beseech
thee oh Lord supply me in thy due time in things temp[or]all of thine
abundant bounty for I thy poore servant am now in straights and god
forbid that I should forget such a m[er]cy and Lord sanctifye it unto
me when it comes, & give me fayth & patience to wayte uppon thee
and I beseech thee oh my father give me grace & favor in the eyes of
the Mayor bayleifes & inh[ab]itants of North[amp]ton when I come
downe & make me an instrument of good in that Corporacon & Lord
blesse my deare wife & children & whole family pr[e]serve us in life
& sanctifye o[u]r harts more & more & sanctify comforts unto us for
the Lords sake, and blesse me now in my goeinge out & cominge in,

---

[548]Samuel had been born at his grandparents' house (the Two Wrestlers) in All Hallows'
parish, London Wall, on 15 April 1636: N.H. Keeble, 'Woodford, Samuel (1636–1700)', in
ODNB.
[549]Presumably lodgings belonging to William Warren of Old, with whom Woodford had
travelled to London on business on 25 April 1638.
[550]Jeremy Leech, the incumbent of St Mary le Bow.

helpe me to borrow some money for my necessityes & keep me from
melancholly for the Lords sake
Lord stay me uppon thy sure word for the Lords sake.
20° Octob. 1638.
I have borrowed 40s of Mr Pentlowe to be p[ai]d

to his wife in the Country, blessed be thy name oh Lord for supplyinge
me in this necess[ity].
I have payd Mr hillesly for the wyne at the Baptizing
I was to search in Allhallowes Lombard str[eet] p[ro] mort Joh[ann]is
Watkin⁵⁵¹ 1608 – p[ro] Mr Bacon.
21° Octob. 1638 Sab[bath]
I went to day to the Kings Chappell at Whitehall where I heard 2
severall men preach in the morning one before the Kinge & thother
before the houshold. dr Beale preached before the Kinge, & preached
ag[ains]t supr[a]lapsarians & p[ro] Confession to, & absolucon by
the Church, Oh Lord establish true doctrine & a pure worship in his
Church & blesse his sacred Ma[jes]ty & give him to discerne betweene
things that differ and make him a sp[ec]iall instrument of thy glory
for the Lords sake Amen.
I dyned at Mr Midletons house a Sergeant at Armes wth Mr
Winstanley &.
I came after to Lincolnes Inne & heard Mr Cowell, that good man.
22° Octobr.
I went not to the hall to day its said the

queene mother of ffrannce comes into London on Thursday next, my
deare child Sarah is very ill, but I have prayd unto the Lord & I trust
the Lord will be gracious.
we have got a nurse to day that lives about Edmunton, for o[u]r child
blessed be god.
23° Octob. 1638
my deare child is still very sick, but the Lord is able to recover her, I
now pr[e]pare for my Journey into the Country to morow, & prayed
for my Comfortable arrival at North[amp]ton & for favor in the eyes
of the Maior & Bayleifes there & for preservacon from the devouringe
pestilence

---

⁵⁵¹ Possibly some relation of the Watkin brothers of Watford, wool dealers connected to
the Ishams: M.E. Finch, *The Wealth of Five Northamptonshire Families 1540–1640*, Publications
of the Northamptonshire Record Society XIX (Oxford, 1966), p. 31, n. 4.

24° Octob.
I prayed and tooke my leave of my wife & and came by gods m[er]cye
to dunstable with one Mr Porter[552] of Birmingham, & there we met
wth good Mr Bostock[553] the Counseller & wth one Mr Pinson[554]
a godly Attourney of Birmingham, Mr Bostock was sick of the
stone

25° Octob. 1638
Mr Bostock prayed excellently with us this morninge so I came to
Grafton [Regis] Court & dyned there, & came home after with Mr
Scryven,[555] where I found Mrs Cricks family all in health blessed be
god.
I supt at Mr Martins
26° Octobr.
I prayd & went to Mr Martins where I stayed a g[rea]t p[ar]t of this
rayny day. I dyned wth him & supped at Mrs Cricks I think.
27° Octobr
I had diverse occasions of writs & to day I blesse the Lord. I have
wrote diverse letters to London.
I have found Mr Maior & the bayleifes very lovinge I blesse the
Lord.

*****

[552] Robert Porter was a member of the minor gentry living at Edgbaston, Birmingham,
and later a supplier of swords to the Parliamentarian army: TNA, SP28/201/47. I thank
Richard Cust and Ann Hughes for this reference.

[553] According to William Prynne, Archbishop Richard Neile had connived to have Bostock's
house searched for seditious books by pursuivants during his absence in London in 1637.
Prynne has Bishop John Bridgeman of Chester informing Neile of 'one Bostock a Yong
Lawyer, but an old Puritane': W. Prynne, *A New Discovery of the Prelates Tyranny* (London,
1641), p. 225. John Bostock of Tattenhall near Chester, counsellor at law, served during the
Civil War as clerk to the council of war based at Nantwich. His godly credentials took a
hammering in 1643, when his employers found him guilty of adultery and sentenced him
to perform a penance in the market square: J. Hall (ed.), *Memorials of the Civil War in Cheshire
[. . .] Providence Improved by Edward Burghall*, Lancashire and Cheshire Record Society XIX
(1889), pp. 61–62.

[554] William Pinson of Birmingham, a puritan nonconformist, was charged before the Court
of High Commission. Proceedings continued until November 1640, when he was discharged:
TNA, SP16/388, fo. 167; *CSPD*, 1640, pp. 379, 384, 389, 428; *CSPD*, 1640–1641, pp. 383,
388, 392.

[555] John Scryven, shoemaker, appears as a member of the Northampton trained band in
1612 and was active in the vestry of All Saints' parish from 1621 until 1640, repeatedly acting
as churchwarden and sidesman: J. Wake (ed.), *A Copy of Papers Relating to Musters, Beacons, and
Subsidies etc in the County of Northampton AD 1586–1623*, Publications of the Northamptonshire
Record Society III (Kettering, 1926), p. 156; Vestry Minutes, pp. 15–35; Book of Orders,
p. 57.

28° octobr. 1638. Sab.[bath]
Mr Ball preached both times out of 3. Jonah[556] I have had gracious
comforts & enlargem[en]t in prayer last night & to day I blesse the
lord. I dyned at Mr Sam. Martins to day & supped at his fathers.
young Mr Martin is ill.
29° Octob.
I prayed and went to the Court, where the gayne was but small but
the Lord will increase it in his due time. I dyned wth Mr Bayleife hill.
Oh Lord I blesse thee that thou hast brought me home againe to my
owne habitacon Lord blesse me & pr[e]serve me here for the Lords
sake.
30. Octob.
I prayed and went out wth Mr Martin Mr Knight & Mr Woollaston[557]
3 of the aldermen to Coventry to renew the bond for Mr Wheatleys
money[558] there, we came safe to the Kings head in Coventry I wrote
to Mr Goodere

31° Octobr 1638
I prayed and went to the Lecture where one Mr dyamond,[559] a country
minister preached very honestly & well, blessed be thy name oh Lord.
we were wth Mr Legg the Maior of Coventry[560] & the Aldermen in
the Counsell house[561] there. Mr Goodere came to us.

[556] In which is described how God decided not to punish the people of Nineveh when they
renounced their evil ways.
[557] For William Knight, see Diary, p. 206, n. 414; he later made a charitable benefaction
to the town: Markham and Cox, *Northampton*, II, p. 361. Richard Woollaston had been a
wealthy wood merchant in Northampton since at least 1617 and had become mayor of the
town by 1622. As churchwarden of All Saints' around 1616–1617 he had denied inviting
Leicestershire ministers to preach in the parish without a licence, saying that the minister of
All Saints', Jeremiah Lewis, had invited them: Pettit, *Royal Forests*, pp. 63, 70 n. 52; Markham
and Cox, *Northampton*, II, p. 552; PDR, CB45, fos 52r–52v.
[558] Thomas Wheatley, alderman of Coventry and ironmonger, had, by his will of 1566,
bequeathed money to the corporation of Northampton to be loaned to 'artificers' of the town
at 4 per cent interest. The charity, which was to be overseen by the mayor and corporation
of Coventry, was still in operation in 1648: TNA, PROB/11/49; Book of Orders, pp. 100,
103; Markham and Cox, *Northampton*, II, p. 360.
[559] Tristram Dymond, a Cambridge MA in 1612, was the vicar of Foleshill near Coventry
from 1612 until his ejection in 1662: Venn.
[560] Godfrey Legg had been Sheriff of Coventry in 1627 and had supported the non-
corporation candidate in the 1628 parliamentary election. He had been admitted to
Coventry Council in 1635 and served as mayor from 1637 until 1638: Coventry City Record
Office, Coventry Council Minute Book A14(a), fo. 332r; B. Poole, *Coventry, its History and
Antiquities* (London, 1870), p. 372. I am grateful to Richard Cust and Ann Hughes for these
references.
[561] St Mary's Hall, a medieval structure.

1° Nov.

This day the New maior of Coventry one Mr fforest[562] was sworne:
the minister that preached there had litle in him, Oh Lord restore &
establish thy Gospell in that Citty for the Lords sake.

I dyned in the counsell house there, & one Mr Naylor[563] an arminian &
I had much dispute about pr[e]destinacon the Lord much moved my
hart to defend his truth but I found few there that favoured it, I was
too earnest & hasty in my argum[en]t, Lord p[ar]don my frayltyes &
infirmityes in the Bloud of the Lord Xt.

2° Nov. 1638

we came from Coventry this morninge & came home safe at night
I blesse the Lord but we find the sicknesse broke out in 2 or 3 fresh
houses & one widow Evans dead of it, Lord stay thy hand in thy due
time & give us a sanctifyed use of it for the Lords sake.

I heard from my deare wife to day, & that shee & my family are in
health & that litle Sarah is recovered againe blessed be thy name oh
Lord. Oh how gracious the Lord is.

I heare the queene mother came into London on wednesday last in
g[reat] pompe. I supped wth old Mr Martin.

3° Nov.

we had indifferent good market here to day blessed be god and I had
some new imploym[en]t in my practise, yet I was very melancholly this
day through the Thorny cares of this p[rese]nte world, & consideracon
of my debts oh Lord helpe thy poore s[er]vant in regard of sinnes &
debts to p[ar]don those & pay these, oh when will it

once be, but thy grace is sufficient for me to forgive & crucify sinne
in me, & to supply me wth temp[or]alls, Lord give me to [*crossed
out:* belei] beleive, for thou canst doe all things, I have observed thy
gracious p[ro]vidence to thine in thy holy word, thou art still the same
Lord I beleive helpe my unbeleife stay up my hart against base &
carkinge cares make me paynfull like the Ant make me thrifty delight
in me & my family to doe us good every way for the Lords sake.

---

[562] Thomas Forest became alderman of Bayley Lane ward in 1641 and took up the mayoralty
again in 1646, when another man was ejected by Parliament: Coventry City Record Office,
Coventry Council Minute Book, A14(b), fo. 19r; TNA, SP28/248, 24 August 1646; C.H.
Firth and R.S. Rait, *Acts and Ordinances of the Interregnum, 1642-1660*, 3 vols (London, 1911), I,
p. 1244. I am grateful to Richard Cust and Ann Hughes for this reference.

[563] Possibly connected to James Naylor, who was a receiver of Parliament's monthly
assessment from 1647 until 1648 and Sheriff of Coventry in 1650: Coventry City Record
Office, Coventry Council Leet Book A3(b), p. 194; TNA, E179/240/278. Again, I thank
Richard Cust and Ann Hughes.

Mr Crompton p[ai]d me the 9li to day for James warren an extent
was served on Mr Judkins[564] goods here to day.
4° Nov. 1638 Sab.[bath] sacram[en]t.
Mr Ball preached p[ro]fitably in the morning & Mr Newton in the
afternoone I desired at the sacram[en]t to stirr up my poore soule to
beleive & to renew my Cov[enan]t, oh Lord give me fayth & keep me
& mine from sinne & pay o[u]r debts for the Lords sake I dyned at
Mrs Cricks & supped at Mr Martins.

5° Nov. 1638. powder treason day.
Mr Ball preached very p[ro]fitably blessed be thy name oh Lord, it
was a sermon to stirre up gods people to wayte on god for deliverance
& to live by fayth Lord pr[e]vayle wth us by it.
I dyned beinge invited to Mr Maiors,[565] wth Mr Newton & ux Mr
Bayleifes[566] & ux & blessed be thy name oh Lord for the favor thou
givest me in their eyes.
I supped at Mrs Cricks. And now Lord take me into thy p[ro]teccon
this night keepe me from sinne, blesse my deare wife my children
my whole family build us up yea surely thou wilt doe it, in soules
in Comforts in o[u]r outward condicon, but the way must be
thine owne oh that I had fayth oh that I could wayte uppon the
Lord.
6° Nov.
I was graciously affected & enlarged in prayer in

in the morninge & against that sinne which I had much strife & conflict
with this morninge & some dayes before & and then I went to the
Court, afterward I dyned wth [crossed out: Crutchley] Mr Trueman[567]
the new sadler & at Crutchleyes my hart smote me for beinge in
Company there wth Mr Burgins &. Lord give me I pray thee wholly
to forsake & reiect such company for the Lords sake [crossed out: half
line, illegible] Oh my god when will it once be that thou wilt purge
me from all my filthines for Jesus Xt his sake subdue the power of
corrupcon wthin me; Mr Sam. Martin was with me to night & blames
himselfe for keepinge company sometime wth those that feare not
god in drinkinge wine & takinge tobacco wth them now & then,
and I as iustly I may did likewise condemne my selfe for the same;
and we have resolved in gods feare & wth his helpe to reforme in

[564] Thomas Judkin: Diary, p. 147, n. 209.
[565] Richard Fowler's.
[566] Henry Hill and John Cole.
[567] Presumably the son of the saddler Richard Trueman: Diary, p. 227, n. 484.

that p[ar]ticuler, Lord assist us for Xt his sake for thou art god all sufficient.

I am afrayd I have lost some bonds of the Court, but I have prayed unto the Lord to be delivered from such a feare & danger I supped at Mrs Cricks

one dyed of the sicknesse at North[amp]ton.

7° Nov. 1638

beinge full of melancholly & sensible [*crossed out: of*] in some measure of the naughtinesse of my hart & nature I cast my selfe downe before the Lord, & the Lord hath surely heard me & will yet doe good unto me.

I went to Wellingborow, [*insert: trefoil symbol*] and as I went I was greatly affected to teares, in seeinge a Kennell of hounds in hot pursuite after a hare,[568] I wondered at & adored & gods wisdome in puttinge such an instinct into the creature & gave thanks to him that had given to me reason, when I saw the poore doggs runne wth such Confidence & yet [*crossed out: saw*] they saw nothing I condemned my selfe, that am so much for sence & have so litle fayth that I cannot relye uppon the p[ro]mises, yea uppon gods most precious excellent & sure p[ro]mises, which traine would lead me to what I desire both in regard of soule & body & and when I heard their hideous & violent cry after the poore timerous hare, I thought that after the Commission of sinne thus doe conscience & the wrath

wrath & Judgem[en]ts of god follow the poore sinner oh Lord give me ever to revere & adore thy wisdome & thy power, to beleive thy promises to repent of & avoyd sinne for the Lord Xt his sake. I met wth Mr Watts at Wellingborow who though he wants 100li yet I prayse god he doth not aske me for what I owe him Lord give me still favor in his eyes, I sent goodw[i]f[e] Chapman 16s p[ro] interest money by my mother I came to Mr Pentlowes to Lodge. I have bene very melancholly this day But I have desired to encourage my selfe in the Lord Oh Lord stay my hart on thee forever give me sweet sleepe this night & safe p[ro]teccon under the shadow of thy blessed Wings for the Lords sake Amen. & blesse my deare wife sweet Children & whole family.

8° Nov. I prayed & went to Broughton to keepe Court there, where I found them ready Lord I pray thee graunt that there may come

---

[568] Hare coursing was a popular sport among the gentry, who kept greyhounds for the purpose. Woodford's client John Bernard quarrelled with Alexander Eakins over the issue: Diary, p. 127; Isham, *Diary*, pp. 30–31.

no trouble by keepinge of the Court so longe after Mich[aelmas]. Mr Bentham dyned

dyned wth us, it was late before we had done at night in the morninge [*crossed out:* as] at prayer I had some gracious enlargem[en]t, & as I came along I encouradged my soule to wayte uppon god for power ag[ains]t Corrupcon, & for supply of temp[or]all things, the Lord will heare my poore desires & will shew m[er]cy unto me in his due time, The Lord o[u]r god is gracious he is a rock yea the rock of ages, oh that thy spirit & thy word might ever dwell plenteously in my soule, that thy Love might ever inflame my hart that I might be an instrument of thy glory in the world that I might serve thee in this my generacon I prayed to the Lord to be rescued from the feare about the Losse of any bonds at North[amp]ton.

9° Nov. 1638
I prayed and went to Ketteringe wth Mr Pentlowe of Broughton; I met there wth Mr Rushworth, I refused to goe to the swan to Mr Lewes & & blessed be thy name oh Lord oh

oh Lord teach me to avoyd the occasions of evill forever for the Lords sake Amen. I heare to day that Rob. Yorke an Attourney at harborowe[569] (sometime my schole-fellowe at Brixworth) is lately dead of the small pox, yet I am still in the land of the livinge blessd be thy name oh lord, Lord give me to improve thy continued m[er]cyes for the Lords sake, & Lord increase my practise & give me abilityes for it & give me ever the peace of a good conscience; I came to Old at night, & had some good meditacon on the way. at Old my mother & I sealled a bond of 10li 16s dated 17° Octob last to be payd 18° Octob 1639 [*crossed out, illegible*] to ffrancis Chapman widow [*crossed out:* in Old] at her house in Old, the debt is onely mine, Lord helpe me to pay all my debts in thy due time if it be thy will & fit me for such a m[er]cye.

I came to my Cousin dexters house. I heard to day that my Aunt Margret Wale is dead long since. I heard to day that George hodges[570] that lived once here at Old hath committed Adultery wth a mayd at Wellingborow, oh Lord shame is the end of sinne, & this is a fruit of his drunkennesse, fence my heart for ever ag[ains]t such abominacons

[569]Market Harborough, Leicestershire.
[570]One Hodges was the usher of Wellingborough school from 1637 until 1649: D.K. Shearing, 'A study of the educational developments in the Diocese of Peterborough, 1561–1700' (unpublished MPhil thesis, University of Nottingham, 1982), biographical appendix.

for the Lords sake Blessed be thy name oh Lord for keepeinge of me all my life time as thou hast done

10° Novembr. 1638
I prayed and came afterward to hanginge houghton to Mr Rushworths house there, & from thence I came along wth him & came to North[amp]ton safe I blesse the Lord, in goeinge to houghton from Old I sought the Lord [*left margin: trefoil symbol*] for [*crossed out:* grace] m[er]cye & grace & supply in my necessity & for blessinge & gods good p[ro]vidence, And sure the m[er]cy of the great & gracious god shall shine uppon my soule in the face of Jesus Christ to p[ar]don my sinnes, The power of the Almighty god through the spirit of the Lord Jesus Christ shall Crucify & kill my strong Corrupcons for his grace is sufficient for me both to forgive & to mortify the Bounty of the all-sufficient god, possessor of heaven & earth shall pay my debts, feed & cloath me & my family, The proteccon of the all-seeinge god shall ever more mightily defend me & mine under the shadowe of his blessed wings shall be my refuge; his good blessinge & gracious p[ro]vidence shall direct us & lead us forth & order every thing for the best, Oh Lord helpe me to live by fayth and let me have comfort & cheerfullnes from that.
I heare to day that Mr Bechins[571] an Attourney the Steward of daventry is dead; yet the Lord hath graciously spared me and given me a longer time to work out my salvacon oh Lord give me to improve my span of time.
The sicknesse increases here Lord stay it.

11° Nov. 1638 Sab.[bath]
Mr Newton preached p[ro]fitably both times to day I dyned wth Mr Maior[572] to day; blessed be thy name oh Lord for his favor Lord continue it if it be thy will.
I was witnesse to Wm Spicers girle Elizab. to day, which was borne on Thursday night last.
I supped at Mrs Cricks, & prayed & was graciously enlarged both there & at home in private Oh Lord I blesse thee for it, Oh shew me thy glory I pray to find the order for Mr Some which I have for the pr[e]sent lost

---

[571]Joseph Bechins paid Daventry corporation's ship money contribution in 1636, and was presented to the Church courts throughout 1636 and 1637 for maintaining too high a pew within the chancel of the church and because his wife had allegedly brawled in church: Jackson, 'Ship money', pp. 50, 63 n. 80; PDR, CBA63, fo. 395r–v; Church Survey Book 5, fo. 63r.
[572]Richard Fowler.

I p[ai]d Mr Watts 15s wch was sent him.

12° Nov.

I prayed and went to the Court which doth somewhat increase blessed be god.

I dyned wth Mr Cole the Bayleife to day. and supped not at all, I was wth Mr ffisher at night who informed me how god delivered him from the violence of the prison[er]s when they had cast him into the dungeon⁵⁷³ &.

Easton brought me a load of Coles to day and my hey came from houghton grounds⁵⁷⁴ 6. load. I p[ai]d about 13s 6d p[ro] the carriage

13° Nov. 1638

I prayed & am oft graciously affected in the duty I blesse the Lord.

hatton came to me againe to day from Toucester we afterward ingrossed the Lease & counteapt⁵⁷⁵ about dodington Mills from Mr Pentlowe to William Broad. I prayed to the Lord wth some enlargem[en]t I blesse the Lord, & to be defended both I & my family from the devouringe pestilence.

14° Nov.

I prayed and went to Wilby where I dyned & then to Wellingborowe, & was brought home safe againe I blesse the Lord, the Lord [crossed out: put] moved my hart often in the way & gave me some meditacons I blessed his name, I heard by Mr Pentlowe that dr Oldsworth⁵⁷⁶ preached excellently & boldly on 5 Nov blessed be thy name oh Lord

---

⁵⁷³There were frequent jailbreaks from the three jails in the town: Fisher may have been referring to the escape of Matthew Longstrap mentioned by Woodford on 11 November 1637: Markham and Cox, *Northampton*, pp. 175–178.

⁵⁷⁴Either Great or Little Houghton to the south-east of Northampton.

⁵⁷⁵Counterpart.

⁵⁷⁶Dr Richard Holdsworth, Master of Emmanuel College, Cambridge, and Archdeacon of Huntingdon, probably preached this sermon at his London parish of St Peter the Poor (Pentlow had been in London around 20 October and did not return with Woodford on 24 October: Diary, pp. 251–252). He was one of the most famous preachers of his generation but, as a moderate Calvinist, was under pressure from both sides of an increasingly polarized political and ecclesiastical scene: P. Collinson, 'Holdsworth, Richard (1590–1649)', in *ODNB*.

that thou raysest any to stand up for thee & thy truth. Mr Twigden[577] the Alderman dyed to day.

15° Nov. 1638
I prayed & went to Grafton [Regis] Court where I gayned about 5s I blesse the Lord, I was somewhat late ere I came home & met with a divine who came alonge with me to North[amp]ton I went afterward to the hind beinge sent for about an arrest made on a woman, I got about 3s 4d blessed be thy name oh Lord
Mr Twigden buryed to day.
16° Nov.
I thought to have gone to Ketteringe to day but by reason of the rayne I stayed at home
17° Nov.
St hughs fare kept here to day 3 have dyed of the sicknesse this last weeke
Mr Goodere came hether to night
18° Nov. Sab.[bath]
Mr Newton preached both times p[ro]fitably

19° Nov. 1638
I kept the court in the morninge and came along to dunstable very safe blessed be god though somwhat late, and there I lodged at the white hart wth Mr Trueman & Mr Goodere, we discoursed of the badnesse of the times Lord amend them for the Lords sake.
20° Nov.
we prayed and came to London safe, where I found my deare wife & children in good health I prayse the Lord.
21° Nov.
I prayed and went to the hall, about my occacons. And dyned wth Mr Bacon & Mr Poulton[578] in Bredstreet at the mermayd, Lord I blesse thee for Mr Bacons Love & practise.

---

577 John Twigden had been mayor of the town from 1632 until 1633 when he was involved in investigating rumours, details of which were forwarded by Sir Robert Banastre to the Privy Council, that the Catholic recusant Lady Digby of Gayhurst, Buckinghamshire, was raising troops to hinder Charles I's visit to Scotland. This would be either Mary, the widow of Sir Everard Digby, who had been executed for his part in the Gunpowder Plot, or Venetia (née Stanley), the wife of Mary's son Sir Kenelm: Markham and Cox, *Northampton*, II, p. 552; M. Nicholls, 'Digby, Sir Everard (c.1578–1606)', in *ODNB*; TNA, SP16/237/45 and SP16/239/61, I–IV.
578 The Poultons (Pultons) of Desborough were Thomas Bacon's maternal relations. The individual here mentioned is probably George: PDR, CBA16, fo. 250r–v; PDR, CBA20, fo. 250r–v; PDR, CB50, fo. 143r–v; PDR, CBA63, fo. 18r–v; PDR, CB64, fo. 37r–v.

22° Nov.
I prayed and went about my occasions.

23° Nov. 1638
I prayed and went to the hall I thinke, & about my occasions.
24° Nov.
there is much talke about the Scottish busines Lord direct every thinge
for the best for the Lords sake & thou who causest every thinge to worke
togeth[er] for the to thine owne, bringe good out of this to thy church
for the Lords sake.
25° Nov. Sab.[bath]
I heard Mr davyes a goodman, in Colemanstreet at Mr Goodwyns
church in the morninge & Mr Goodwyn there in the afternoone, Lord
keepe open the mouthes of thy faythfull ministers, & restore those that
are silenced for the Lords sake
26. Nov.
I prayed and went about my occasions I have concluded to have the
chamber in Clements Inne, Oh Lord graunt that I may

may have comfort & practise in it if it be thy will. And Lord looke
uppon me in my indebted & necessitous condicon for the Lords sake.
Mr Wyckes[579] dyed suddenly this day. Lord fit me for death.
27° Nov. 1638.
I prayed and went about my occasions Lord I blesse thee that I have
any thinge to doe its thy m[er]cy to give me practise & enable me for
it in any measure. I receaved a letter from hatton who certifyes me
that two dyed of the sicknesse the last weeke. Lord stay thy hand in
due time for the Lords sake
my father is much deiected about the death of Mr Wicks
28° Nov.
Its said that warre is concluded against Scotland and that the Earles
of Arundell & of Essex[580] shall be the gen[er]alls of horse & foote Lord
pr[e]vent the evill that hangs over this Kingdome if it be thy will.
*****

---

[579]John Wikes, squire of Haselbech, whose pew was condemned as too high in the church
survey of 1637: PDR, Church Survey Book 5, fo. 138r–v; Isham *Diary*, p. 60, n. 10.

[580]Thomas Howard, Earl of Arundel, was identified with the Catholic interest at court. A
hardliner against the Scots, he was appointed to command the English forces in the north.
Robert Devereux, third Earl of Essex, held meetings with the Covenanters in London, and
in 1640 signed the petition of twelve peers calling for the summoning of Parliament and a
treaty with the Scots: R.M. Smuts, 'Howard, Thomas, fourteenth earl of Arundel, fourth
earl of Surrey, and first earl of Norfolk (1585–1646)', in *ODNB*; J. Morrill, 'Devereux, Robert,
third earl of Essex (1591–1646)', in *ODNB*.

29° Nov. 1638
I and my wife are much subiect to care & trouble about our outward condicon, & by reason of the bond which I have entred into wth Mr Readinge my master as suerty to Sr John hanbury, Lord p[ar]don my faylinge in it, & pr[e]ven[t] my feare for the Lords sake
30. Nov. St Andrew
I prayed and went to Mr Robins about Mr Watts his occasion, & to Mr dillingham where I dyned, & afterward I spake wth Mr Pardoe, Mr Weekes was buryed to day, who was borne, made free marryed & buryed uppon this day.
1° dec.
my master hath bene earnest with me for the 50li arrere from me or my father, I told him of

of the bond not satisfyed to Sr John hanbury. I was greatly troubled & deeply melancholly in the thoughts of that & the debts I owe, I after met with my father who poore man is likewise much troubled in the thoughts of his owne debts; Ah Lord when shall it once be that thou wilt deliver us out of this sad & heavy condicon, I endeavored to have borowed 50li of Mr dexter[581] the scrivener but could not.
I came home in the afternoone, & my deare wife & I prayed in this great trouble & [left margin: trefoil symbol] commended our heavy condicon to the Lord and we entred covenant wth him & p[ro]mised that if the Lord please to pay o[u]r debts & give us ease this way that he shall forever be o[u]r god & we will be his people & will prayse & exalt his name. Lord heare us & helpe us for the Lords sake.
2° dec.1638. Sab.[bath]
I prayed and went to dr Stoughtons church where he preached excellently concerninge

temptation, I [crossed out: letter, illegible] and my wife receaved the sacram[en]t there I desired to bringe my sinnes my infidelity my burdens before the Lord, Lord ease me in thy due time for the Lords sake.
Mr Sedgwicks brother[582] preached there in the afternoone very p[ro]fitably, The Lord did graciously enable me in prayer in the family my wife & I have this day sought the Lord together

---

[581] Possibly the William Dexter of London mentioned on 27 September 1638.
[582] That is, Obadiah Sedgwick's brother, John, a Northamptonshire minister.

3° dec.1638.
I went downe to Mr Robins & as I went beinge very melancholly I called uppon my Uncle dexter[583] & gave him his morninge draught [*crossed out:* for] he had p[ro]mised me a payre of gloves which he then gave me, I went to the other end of the towne afterward about my occasions, but my hart hath bene marvellous sad, & the cares of this present world doe much op> oppresse me considering my debts & danger, Oh Lord heare my poore prayers if it be thy will, & give me to live above the creature by thy fayth for the Lords sake my wife rode behind my father to day to see litle Sarah who is very well blessed be god.

4° dec. 1638
I prayed and came to St Albans alone about Sunsett, where I lay. I was extremely melancholly as I came along my debts & feares did wonderfully seize uppon me yet I repelled my troubles & would not give way to them & the word of god is often sanctifyed unto me & much refreshinge, yea like the honey that Jonathan tasted wth the end of his rod. Oh Lord cure my melancholly & enable me to live by fayth for the Lords sake.
grac[iously] enlarged in peticon in my sorow.
5° dec.
I slept well this night I blesse the Lord and prayed wth much fayth in my sorow and came along wth Mr Wedland, & after wth Mr Chamberlayne & Mr Cooke,[584] and to North[amp]ton safe I prayse the Lord, I supped at Mr Martins wth Mr Sam. Martin & Mr Rushworth, I am very melancholly. I pray earnestly unto the Lord, & sure the Lord doth heare me.

6° dec 1638.
I was very heavy & direfully sad in the morninge before day I rose about 6 a clock & prayed and went to Grafton [Regis] Court, I was very melancholly & greatly oppressed with cares as I rode alonge but I endeavoured to hang uppon the Lord, and the [*crossed out:* sp] holy & gracious spirit of the Lord is pleased continually to bringe to memory & dart in [*crossed out, illegible*] places of scripture sentences out of gods word to warne me & to comfort & susteyne me when I was doubtinge that to morow morninge before day would be very sad & direfull I remembred take no thought for to morow & sufficient to the day

---

[583] First name unknown, the brother of Woodford's mother, Jane. He possibly resided in the parish of St Bartholomew by the Exchange: T.C. Dale (ed.), *The Inhabitants of London in 1638* (London, 1931), p. 36.
[584] Francis Cook, the Kingsthorpe attorney, died in 1638. Perhaps this is one of his sons, Francis or Tempest.

is the evill thereof,[585] I had then trouble enough why should I make this day more evill & troublesome by caringe for the morowe and I rem.[embered] the 50th of Isayah[586] let him stay himselfe uppon his god oh thou art the surest stay [crossed out: becas] because the strongest most durable, thou art the rock of ages, everlasting strength, and art not thou exceeding gracious as Abraham said shall not the Judge of all the world doe Right, so I thy poore

poore servant say shall not the father of all the world shew m[er]cye?, Lord I have sinned against thee exceedingly but p[ar]don thy servant helpe me in my distresses either pay my [left margin: trefoil symbol] debts if it be thy will, or worke my hart & make it suitable to my condicon, oh that I could live by fayth in this condicon as I trust I shall in some measure through the strength of god, & I am thinkinge if I can live by fayth in this disadvantage of direfull melancholly surely I should have a most comfortable life if this were removed as one that can dannce in Wooden shoes would surely be more nimble in pumpes, I kept the Court at Grafton [Regis] we had a Jury. I came home wth Tho Pidgeon[587] who was almost drunke Lord convert that p[er]secuter to thee if it be thy will.

7° dec.1638.

I was not altogether so melancholly before [above next word: trefoil symbol] day this morning as I feared I should but

diverse scriptures came into my mind & did me much comfort, I afterward prayed in private to many teares & besought the Lord

---

[585] Matthew 6:34.

[586] Verse 10.

[587] Thomas Pidgeon was a joiner by trade but also a Church court apparitor. In October 1637 Sibthorpe had visited the chapel of Upton, of which his colleague Dr Clarke was the parson, and had ordered that the communion table (standing in mid-chancel) be cut short, railed, and placed altarwise at the east end. According to the churchwardens, Clarke procured Pidgeon to do the work. They were obstructive, so Clarke excommunicated them. They appealed to the Court of Audience, then the Court of Arches, of which Sir John Lambe was the dean, for an inhibition overthrowing the verdict of the lower court, but claimed that Lambe informed them that Archbishop Laud had ordered that no inhibitions were to be issued to the counties of Northamptonshire, Bedfordshire, or Buckinghamshire without his express permission. The wardens were forced to pay Pidgeon for his work. Eventually, their petition to the Long Parliament resulted in a verdict by the House of Lords that Clarke pay for a new communion table in the traditional position. Pidgeon is encountered again in September 1640, being interrogated by Sibthorpe about derelictions in his duty in failing to arrest William Walker, a constable resisting ship money, and failing to distribute prayers supporting the king's military effort against the Scots: PDR, Church Survey Book 5, fo. 68r–v; HLRO, main papers, Garfield and Woolfe vs. Clarke, 22 December 1640; TNA, SP16/468/76.

earnestly who hath heard me & will surely doe me good will ease
me of these thorny cares though which way I know not but the Lord
doth all things & can doe this, I am much troubled that these thorny
cares should seize uppon me, who am a xxian who have a better hope
then after the creature, after all these things doe the gentiles seeke[588]
which have no god wch know no heaven or true happinesse, nay
their contempt of these things many of them I meane, may shame me
Lord p[ar]don this horrid sinne of mine lay it not to my chardge give
me sweetly to repose my selfe in thee And stretch thy mighty arme
from heaven & helpe me thy poore servant, Lord thou hast said to
the upright shall arise light in darknesse, thou hast sayd for he shall
deliver the needy when he cryeth & Lord heare my poore prayer for
the Lords sake.
I tooke the Antimoniall cup[589] to day but it hath not wrought wth me.

I went after to Mr Martins, and there I receaved some comfort & ease
of my mellancholly for the pr[e]sent I blesse the Lord.
8° dec 1638 Lad[y] day fare to day. [*trefoil symbol*]
I am very mellancholly, but Lord thou art still my helpe & hast bene
ever Mr Stancy[590] told me of one who through affliccon & melancholly
because of his former Lewdnesse was become a foole, wch thinge did
much smite me but I will yet hope in the Lord who is my strength &
my sheild, oh my god shall any that trust in thee be ashamed? I have
had some comfort in readinge thy word I blesse thy name, at such
time as I am afrayd I will trust [*margin:* 6 ps.[alm]] in thee, Thy vowes
are uppon me oh god and if thou please [*crossed out, illegible*] to helpe
me out of these debts & yet to susteyne me & my family by thy helpe I
will never forget such a m[er]cy, but shall serve thee more comfortably
& cheerefully when thou hast enlarged my steps, heaven & earth are
thine Lord supply me of thy bounty or stay my hart for the Lords sake.
afterward there came to me Goodman Gardner[591] of North[amp]ton
whose businesse I forgot which he had imployed me in & I gave him
his 5s againe he gave me 6d back I thank him.

[588] Matthew 6:32.
[589] The cup was impregnated with the element antimony, an emetic and a popular remedy
for melancholy.
[590] A William Staceye occurs in Northampton in 1591, who was presumably the same as
the William Stansey, tanner, who obtained a loan from Elkington's charity in 1608 on the
recommendation of the godly minister Robert Catelin: Markham and Cox, *Northampton*,
II, p. 308; J. Wake (ed.), *A Copy of Papers Relating to Musters, Beacons, and Subsidies etc in the
County of Northampton AD 1586–1623*, Publications of the Northamptonshire Record Society
III (Kettering, 1926), p. 36.
[591] James Gardiner occurs in 1614: Wake, *Musters, Beacons, and Subsidies*, p. 156.

after that my cousin Wm Woodford[592] came & I told him that I wanted money to pay to Rich

Rise the 32s which I had receaved of his mother to pay him, after that I went to Mr Watts my creditor & was much afflicted & whom I feare & then I came home & was very sad, but the Lord hath brought to my hand the 107 ps.[alm] 40.[593] yet setteth he the poore on high from affliccon & maketh him familyes like a flock & the 1. Sam. 2.8 & pa[ra]llell 113. ps.[alm] 11.[594] he rayseth up the poore out of the dust & lifteth the needy out of the dunghill, oh what emphasis there is in lifting out! for truly I am in the deepe mire & clay & it must be no lesse then liftinge to helpe me out, yet will I trust in thee oh Lord possessor of heaven & earth thy m[er]cy is infinite & thy arme is exceedinge strong help may come though I know not from where, thy vowes are uppon me yet shall I prayse thy name oh god the god of my salvation, Lord blesse me my deare wife children & family [*crossed out, illegible*] & helpe my poore father out of his straights for the Lords sake.
my debts this day are

to Mr Watts_____122li or_____100_____			126 [[595]] of 4li[596]
Wm. Turland_____	X	_____	020—0—0
X to goodwife Chapman_____	X	_____	010—0—0
to Mr Spencer_____	X	_____	010—0—0[597]
to Mr Bott about_____	X	_____	005—0—0
to Mr fflood[598] m[er]cer about_____	X	_____	006—3—0
to Mr Greg about_____		_____	006—0—0
to Mr Enyon_____	X	_____	000-18—0
X to my aunt Ragdale _____	X	_____	004-X-0-0
to Sue [Tue] about _____	X	_____	010—0—0

177 18   0

---

[592] The son of his uncle Henry Woodford of Old.

[593] Misquotation: Psalm 107:41.

[594] Misquotation: Psalm 113:7.

[595] A symbol is used here, consisting of the letter 'e' with a tail running clockwise around it, that is, in the opposite direction to that in the commercial '@', and meaning 'excepting'.

[596] Inserted above the line: 'this 4li is to be accounted in halfes so but 122li'.

[597] Illegible crossings-out above.

[598] Ralph Flood appeared at musters in 1613: Wake, *Musters, Beacons, and Subsidies*, p. 155.

paid 20s

to Mr Goodere_____X_____	004—0—0
to Mr dillingham about_____	004—0—0
to Mr Andr[ew] Broughton Attourney)	
at Mr Greenes_____)____X_____	002—10—0
to Ned Coop[er]⁵⁹⁹ about_____X_____	001—17—0
to hopkins of holcot about_____X_____	001—1—0
to my mother about 5 or_____X_____	004—0—0
to R[ichard] Rise for my Aunt Woodford_X_____	001 * 12—0

[*crossed out:* to my father 14li]

$$19 - 1 - 6$$
$$\underline{177\quad 18\quad 0}$$
$$196\quad 19\quad 6$$

to Edward Brish about_____X_____	2li—10—0
to Mrs Crick about_____	1*—5—0
to Mr Some 6li to be reckoned for Oe⁶⁰⁰ if there be no more	
to my father_____	14—0—0

Oh my god these my debts doe stare me in the face, and satan
continually iniects them seeinge my weaknesse & want of fayth, but
Lord at such time as I am afrayd I will trust in thee I doe even depend
uppon thee in this lowe condicon Lord I beleeve helpe my unbeleife
make me exceedinge dilligent & thrifty [*crossed out, illegible*] but wilt
thou shew a miracle to the dead⁶⁰¹ shall the dead prayse thee am I not
in the

the dust doe I not stick in the dunghill? send forth thine ayd & helpe
me oh god the deliverer Thine is the Kingdome power & glory, my
mouth shall be open to thy prayses others will I encourage to trust in
thee. Lord helpe & susteyne me for Jesus Xt his sake. Lord pr[e]pare
me for the Sabath for the Lords sake.
I wrote to my deare wife & sent the 2 letters inclosed wherein my
father expressed his willingnes to pay the 25li over & above the
400. I encouraged my deare wife to wayt uppon the Lord, and
communicated to her the p[ro]mises which the Lord had brought
to my hand, and that in Mat[thew]⁶⁰² if two agree on earth & to aske

⁵⁹⁹Edward Cooper served as a sidesman in 1636, in 1639 as town bailiff, from 1642 to 1643
as a churchwarden, and as a chamberlain from 1644 until 1646: Vestry Minutes, pp. 21, 32,
38; Markham and Cox, *Northampton*, II, pp. 562, 568.
⁶⁰⁰That is, 'Omne': 'all, everything'.
⁶⁰¹Psalm 88:10.
⁶⁰²Matthew 18:19.

& It shall be done so we [*crossed out:* to] two will agree wth gods helpe to seeke grace & favor.

I went after [*crossed out:* letter] to old Mr Martins where I met wth Sam. Martin, wth whom I had discourse about worldly cares & dependance for temp[or]all things, this conference was blessed unto me he put me in mind that one thinge onely is necessary and that we are to seeke the Kingdome of heaven & the right & & if we walk in gods way & he sees good all these shall be added,[603] he spoke of a place in Job 22.[604] acquaint thy selfe now wth the Lord & be at peace & and in 107. ps[alm][605] fooles are afflicted for their folly & yet they cry & god doth deliver them &.

9° dec. 1638 Sab.[bath] sacram[en]t.

I have some cheerefullnesse this morninge I blesse the Lord, Lord stay my soule uppon thee, & though I have brought affliccon uppon me through mine owne sinne & folly yet I cry unto thee & thou wilt surely have m[er]cy uppon me oh Lord teach me the way unto thee, blesse this thy sabath & thine ordinances to me for the Lords sake

I prayse the Lord my cheerfullnes continues in a gracious measure oh Lord keepe out of my hart those base thorny cares forever, and though I am in debt & that some of them should now be payd & are expected yet I pray thee give me fayth to rely uppon thee in this Condicon and I pray thee keepe me from the fiery temptacons & inieccons of Satan & send me helpe give me ever the sheild of fayth to repell them & helpe me as thou hast done for the Lords sake at such time as I cry unto thee my enimyes shall be turned back, and my creditors shall be my freinds Thou art my god forever uppon thee will I hang & repose my selfe for evermore, blesse me & comfort me

me this night & pr[e]pare me for to morowe & send me blessinge & comfort in the day, manifest thy p[ro]vidence to me in it for the Lords sake.

I have bene at old Mr Martins to reade my notes. Lord blesse them to us. And Lord blesse my deare wife & family & whatever belongs unto me for the Lords sake.

Ile [*crossed out:* cont] count it all Joy[606] when I fall into diverse temptacons I trust & beleive the fruit of them shall be comfortable I

---

[603]Matthew 6:33.
[604]Job 22:21.
[605]Psalm 107:17–19.
[606]James 1:2–3: 'My brethren, count it all joy when ye fall into divers temptations; Knowing this, that the trying of your faith worketh patience'.

meane not the temptacon & enticements of sinne but the fiery darts
of Satan.

10° dec 1638.

I prayed and went to the Court where we had somethinge to doe I
blesse the Lord, Mr Maior[607] invited me to dinner & there I dyned.
I was after at old Mr Martins.

11° dec.

I prayed and went about my occasions, wth some

some Cheerfullnes I blesse the Lord.
I dyned at Mr Samuel Martins, wth old Mr Martin.

12° dec [crossed out: I] 1638

I prayed and went towards Wellingborow I dyned at Mr Pentlowes of
Wilby
the Lord hath in some gracious measure upholden my hart this day.
I came home with James Woolston,[608] & I went after supper to old Mr
Martins where I heard of the death of one Powell of Patteshull[609] a

---

[607]Richard Fowler.

[608]Woolston was rate assessor of All Saints' in 1635 and sidesman in 1636: Vestry Minutes,
p. 32.

[609]Richard Powell had been one of the vicars of Pattishall since 1609. A conformist Church
court official, he had been embroiled in an acerbic dispute with a godly faction in his parish
led by his fellow vicar, Miles Burkit, since at least 1637 (Diary, p. 210, n. 430). Around the
beginning of 1638, Burkit and his supporters retaliated by submitting to the Court of High
Commission a long list of charges against Powell, the most significant being that he had
'preached dangerous and seditious doctrine [. . .] to pswade yor pishoners to stand out and
not pay the ship money' and had 'inveigh[ed] agt Tirants and tyrannical princes that layd
unwell uniust and tyrannical taxes upon their subiects saying that when God gives such a
King he gives him in his wrath [. . .] you intended [. . .] our gratious soveraigne Lord King
Charles and [. . .] the shippmoney' (TNA, SP16/433/46). The godly faction were protected
by Sir Richard Samwell (one of the justices of the peace deputed to assess the case), who had
previously protected Burkit against his accusers in High Commission. Powell was supported
by the conformists Sibthorpe and Clarke, the two remaining justices of the peace detailed
to try the case. They advocated Powell's orthodoxy: he had encouraged loyalty to a just
king and tax, and had volunteered his own payment. His opponents were dismissed as
disobedient schismatical puritans, who had not paid ship money and who opposed the rites
and ceremonies of the Church of England. The conformists, supported by Lambe and
Laud himself, were victorious: in April 1638 the Council exonerated Powell and ordered his
opponents to pay both his costs and their ship money. Furthermore, Sibthorpe and Clarke
(via Lambe and Laud) persuaded Lord Keeper Thomas Coventry to remove Samwell from
the Commission of the Peace: High Commission now also prosecuted him. The Council's
verdict was not overturned until the advent of the Long Parliament, which condemned
Powell's views on ship money as unorthodox and popish, and removed Sibthorpe and
Clarke from the Commission and replaced them with Samwell and John Crewe: Longden
MS, 24 March 1609; PDR, Church Survey Book 5, fo. 50r–v; Jackson, 'Ship money', pp. 125–
127; HLRO, main papers, 21 January 1641 (Petition of William Waters); J.S. Hart, *Justice
upon Petition: the House of Lords and the reformation of justice 1621–1675* (London, 1991), pp. 87–89,
103n.

p[er]secutinge preist, who dyed on the suddaine in the house of office;
it seemes he had his horse forth to have gone to Toucester to have
pr[e]sented about 40. for not beinge Canonicall the Sab[bath] day
before when he went [crossed out: illegible word] up to the Communion
table about 3 times; & he spake to one of the wicked wretches that
were with him to hold his horse he would but goe & untrusse a poynt
& come pr[e]sently; & was there found

found dead immediatly, Thus doth the Lord glorifye himselfe in the
destruccon of his obstinate enemyes oh that thine adversaryes would
lay this to hart that they might convert & turne unto thee that thou
mightest heale them oh Lord make thy people to observe & consider
thy wayes.
Mr Watts sent one it seemes in my absence to day for the bag of money
which he left here on satterday
13° dec. 1638
I prayed, and tooke the sealled bag of money which Mr Watts left here
on Satterday last & rode over to Easton [Maudit] but he was not at
home so I gave it to Mrs Watts his wife who keeps it for him
I told her how I was frighted on Sab.[bath] day night by reason of it,
Lord give me grace & favor in the eyes of Mr Watts still & make him
still a stay & comfort to me in my outward condicon.
Mr Caudrey preached here in my absence.
14° dec.
I have prayed this morninge & sure the Lord will heare

heare in his due time, when I have learnd to live by fayth & wayt
patiently uppon the Lord, my wife doth confirme me in the same too
by her lovinge comfortable & most gracious letter blessed be thy name
oh Lord for bestowinge on me so good a wife oh Lord when thou hast
tried us & given us fayth & humilyty bringe us out of the fire as gold,
inlarge our steps & tents, & give us to pay o[u]r vowes unto thee & to
singe of thy prayses all the day longe
I beinge melancholly & in trouble wrote CXW. 38. in the house of
office for Cares of the world[610] 1638. Resolvinge if the Lord doth helpe
me to be put in mind when I shall sometimes come thether to prayse
his name.
Oh my god save me for the waters come up to my soule;
[crossed out: I] I sit in the dust, in m[er]cye rayse me up, my feet stick
fast in the dunghill let thy goodnesse oh god lift me out,

---

[610]Mark 4:19.

thy servant is in debt & want let thy Bountye supply him abundantly

The fiery iniections & darts of Satan come thick uppon me, the Archer
hath shot sure at me with envenomed arrowes, but Ile take the sheild
of fayth & in the name of god Ile quench them & repell them
At such time as I am afrayd I will trust in thee my hart moveth
towards thee, oh that thou wouldst dwell in the soule of thy servant,
why shouldst thou be like a traveller that stayeth but for a night,
my hart is sad & cares & troubles are ready to seise uppon me, give
me of the wine of thy consolacon then shall I forget my poverty,
let me never goe to Beelzebub the god of Ekron,[611] to the Creature for
helpe seeinge theres a god in Israel that hath made heaven & earth
Oh put a psalme of prayses into the mouth of thy servants of my
family, and shew us that never any trusted in thee & were ashamed
looke uppon the face of thyne annoynted & in him heare the voyce of
thy servant which putteth his trust in thee
Thou wilt heare from heaven & helpe blessed be thy name.

letters are come to the towne for [*crossed out:* musteringe] a list of the
names of men betweene 16. & 60. & in other places they muster, now
my hart is ready to be deiected to thinke that now men will call for
their moneyes, & I shall neither be able to pay nor will my land be
worth any thinge if warrs should come
oh my god in thee the fatherlesse findeth m[er]cye support my hart
keepe my mind in frame for the Lords sake. And doe good to my
deare wife & children & family Lord refresh us with thy m[er]cye &
love let us not afflict o[u]r selves wth vayne feares but teach us to live
by fayth for the Lords sake Amen.
15° dec.1638.
I prayed & went about my occasions, I have bene very melancholly
this day but it hath bene more in my head then in sadnesse. Lord send
forth thine ayd & helpe me for the Lords sake.
hatton offended me to night in beinge absent & at an alehouse wth
dick[612] at Mr Readings & Mr Bartons[613] man, & I corrected him
Lord I

I beseech thee blesse it unto him & doe him good by it for the Lords
sake.

---

[611] 2 Kings 1:3, 6.
[612] Richard Odell.
[613] Possibly Henry Barton, who, with John Fisher, had been reported to the Church courts
in 1604 for omitting to report the nonconformity of Robert Catelin, the incumbent at All
Saints': PDR, CB37, fo. 163r.

16° dec.1638. Sab.[bath]

Mr Ball preached very p[ro]fitably both times to day & I did behold the goeinge of my god in the sanctuary even in this publiq ordinances & I was greatly affected to teares in heareinge the eveninge sermon I did receave the Lord by fayth in some gracious measure, I doe sometimes even stirre up my selfe to be Joyfull seeinge my many exigencyes, according to the Commannd of the Apostle count it all Joy[614] &. Satan [*crossed out:* doth] hath much followed me this day with fiery darts, & often iniects my debts likewise But the Lord will helpe, the Allsufficient & gracio[us] god will in his due time save & deliver.

I went to old Mr Martins after supper & read my notes.

17° dec.

I prayed & went to the Court. I dyned

after at Mr Maiors[615] &.

18° dec. 1638

I prayed and went about my occasions the Lord is pleased graciously to uphold my hart & still to susteyne me in difficultyes blessed be his name.

19° dec.

I prayed and went to Wellingborow & returned safe againe at night I blesse the Lord.

20° dec.

I prayed and went to the Lecture, where Mr Newton preached very p[ro]fitably a sermon ag[ains]t Adultery. I dyned at Mr daniel Readings wth Mr downes his man towards night I came to old Mr Martins where I expressed too much foolish choler because I was then invited to dyne wth the Maior & Ald[er]men uppon St Thomas day. Oh Lord what a world of

of pride & wickednesse there is in this soule of mine I beseech thee p[ar]don my sinne & heale my soule for the Lords sake.

I was invited to come to the dinner to morow

21° dec.1638. St Thom. day.

I prayed & went to heare Mr Ball, it was uppon occasion of the Legacy of Alderman ffreeman,[616] This day one house [*crossed out:*

---

[614] Diary, p. 268, and n. 606.

[615] Richard Fowler.

[616] As part of his charitable bequest, Sir Ralph Freeman had made provision for an annual sermon at All Saints' parish on St Thomas's day: TNA, PROB/11/165.

looked] arrested at the suite of Sr Rob. Bannestre,[617] who would shew no m[er]cye to the debtor as he told him, more then he would to a dogg, so the Bayleifes were leading him to the Gaole out uppon the Southbridge he leapt over & was drowned.

I dyned with the Aldermen to day at Mr ffarrens oh Lord I pray thee give me more & more favor still in their eyes if it be thy will.

22° dec

no newes yet of the man that was drowned, oh Lord keepe the harts of all thine in p[er]fect peace & let their minds be stayed on thee for the Lords sake

23° dec. 1638 Sab.[bath]

Mr Newton preached p[ro]fitably in the morninge & Mr Ball in the afternoone, blessed be thy name oh Lord for any comfort thou art pleased to afford me by thy blessed ordinances.

24° dec.

I went to the Court in the morninge, & after to Wellingborowe & returned home safe againe I blesse the Lord.

25° dec. xxmas day

Mr Ball preached p[ro]fitably out of 1 Tim[othy] 3. 16.[618] blessed be thy name oh Lord that we enioy wholsome doctrine, oh how sweet is thy [crossed out, illegible] word, Lord let thy light breake forth more for the Lords sake Amen.

26. dec.

I went to Wilby towards night, where I found Mr Pentlowe of Broughton who

stayed for me,

27° dec 1638.

I prayed & went to [Earl's] Barton to get some money of Mr Baynes my Clyent[619] if I could, but he did not furnish me so I borowed a gunne of him that I might have a pawne for my money. I dyned at Mr Pentlowes wth my mother aun[t] & divers others.

---

[617]A vigorous ship money sheriff and enthusiastic Laudian beautifier of his parish of Passenham: K. Fincham and N. Tyacke, *Altars Restored: the changing face of English religious worship, 1547–c. 1700* (Oxford, 2007), pp. 259–261; Fielding, 'Peterborough', pp. 120–121.

[618]On the mystery of godliness.

[619]Nicholas Baynes of Earl's Barton was the son of Nicholas Baynes, vicar of Ecton from 1592 until 1611, who, with the anti-puritan Church court official Richard Butler, had supported the conformist candidates for convocation in 1593 against the godly candidates supported by Thomas Stone, a former *classis* member. Like his father he attended Clare Hall, Cambridge, and became a clergyman: E.A. Irons, 'A calendar of a court book', *Northamptonshire Notes and Queries*, new series, 3 (1911), pp. 170–171; Longden, *Visitation of Northamptonshire 1681*, p. 147; PDR, Church Survey Book 5, fo. 134r–v.

28° dec.
I rose early & prayd & Oliver & I went towards Kingston wthin 5 miles of Cambridge to seale the Condic[ional] Lease to Mr Pentlow. Mr Pearson went alonge wth me to Cambr[idge] to night my brother[620] & henry Spencer supt wth me, I hired one goodman Totnam to goe along wth me in the morninge.
Mr Pearson gave me 1li.
I heard of the m[ise]rable end of Mr Ryley who lat[e]ly hang'd himselfe.

29° dec 1638
I prayed wth my brother, & was cominge out of Cambr[idge] wth my guide & his Brother about 4 a clock or more, they went along wth me to Barkway. I stayd there wth them a litle & bayted[621] my horse at Ware, & came in indifferent good time to London I blesse god & safe, my wife was at Mrs Wilsons fun[er]all
I find them all well blessed be the Lord.
30. dec. Sab. [bath]
we went to heare Mr Maiho both times who dealt faythfully, blessed be god.
31°. dec.
I dyned at Sr John Wolstenholmes with Mr Welden,[622]
1° [crossed out: ffebr] Januar New yeares day.
I heard good Mr Simons preach excell[en]tly at Ironmonger lane to day. I dyned at home

2° Januar. 1638/39.
Mr Smart[623] was at my fathers this morninge & brought a barrel of oysters, which we eat & afterwards dyned here, I went after into the other end of the towne, was wth Mr dillingh[am] who shewed me the Journall of the p[ro]ceedings of the Scottish assembly.[624] Its feared there will be warrs, oh Lord bringe glory to thy selfe & enlargem[en]t, to thy gospel that the harts of thy children may reioyce.

---

[620] His brother-in-law, Samuel Haunch, was studying at St Catherine's College, and Henry, the son of William Spencer, the godly incumbent of Scaldwell, was attending Emmanuel College before intrusion into the living of Wadenhoe in 1644: Venn; Longden, Clergy.
[621] Fed and watered.
[622] That is, Henry Weltden.
[623] John Smart (Snart): Diary, p. 249, n. 546.
[624] In November 1638 the Scottish Assembly had abolished episcopacy and established a Presbyterian form of church government, provoking a military response from the English, the First Bishops' War: Gardiner, History, VIII, pp. 349-392; A. Hughes, The Causes of the English Civil War (London, 1991), pp. 36-37.

3° Januar
I came out of London betweene 11. & 12. and came to dunstable
that night, I met wth one Mr Smith & Mr White [*crossed out, illegible*]
thother of Lancash[ire] this of dublin I prayd & lodged wth Mr White
he seemed to be much affected, oh Lord blesse my poore words to
him for the Lords sake.

4° Januar 1638/39
I prayed againe wth Mr White,
I was compelled to borow 5s of Rob[er]te the Chamb[er]laine at the
white hart where I lay. Lord supply me in thy due time for I am runne
in debt this tearme 4li which I rec[eive]d to bringe downe to my aunt
Ragdale 32s I should have payd Ric Rise, & 50s I borowed of Mr
Andrew Braughton, & this 5s.
I came home in due time safe I blesse the Lord.
I had no vittayles in the house to eat to night nor money.
I p[ai]d the 5s againe to Mr Walker for Rob. on Friday 25° Januar
5° Januar
The Lord hath graciously supplyed me blessed be his name.

6° Januar Sab.[bath] sacr.[ament]
Mr Ball preached in the morninge, Mr Newton in the afternoone,
gracious Comforts in the dutyes of the Sabath I blesse the Lord,
Lord blesse thy word sacram[en]t & ordinances whereof I & my
servant have this day bene p[ar]takers.
7° Januar
Mr Pentlowe of Broughton was here in the morninge I went after to
the Court, & after that to Mr Pentlowes of Wilby to lodge there all
night.
8° Januar 1638/39
I prayed and went in the frost to Ketteringe in the morninge to
the Sessions there, & the Lord graciously upheld my hart from
melancholly, the lord in m[er]cy did suspend it, I dyned at Goodwife
Bullocks & supped wth o[u]r Aldermen at the Lyon, & lodged
wth Bennoni Coldwell at goodwife Bullocks [*crossed out:* wth] with
whom I had much good discourse & comforts in it & in prayer wth
him

9° Januar 1638/39
I dispatched my occasions at the Sessions, having much favor from
the Justices I blesse the Lord, the Lord gave me ability to speake freely,
blessed be thy name oh Lord for all thy goodnesse. I came after to
Wellingborowe & then home safe I blesse the Lord.

10° Januar.
I prayed and went in the morninge towards Peterborough, beinge sent by the Maior & Aldermen to move at the Sess[ions] there for an arrere of the tax grannted by the Soken to North[amp]ton when visited,[625] Crutchley went along with me, we came thether safe, though somewhat late blessed be our good god for his gracious p[ro]vidence we lodged at one Troughtons house at the Woolsack & milstone.
I prayed wth Crutchley. Lord doe us both good.
11° Januar.
I prayd againe & went to speake with Mr Palmer the recorder, & after to the Sess[ions] house where the Lord enabled me graciously to speake & I

found much favor, I moved in the morninge & afterw afterward I went to see the Minster, & was over them when they were at their service, and I sent up my poore prayers to the Lord, to establish a holy & spiritual worship, & to remove the inventions of men.
12° Januar 1638/39
I prayd & we tooke horse about 4. a clock & came safe to North[amp]ton about 3 in the afternoone & my service to the towne was well taken I blesse the Lord.
13° Januar 1638/39 Sab.[bath]
[crossed out, illegible] A stranger sent by Mr Ball preached both times very well, And the Lord hath graciously appeared to me this day, oh come tast & see how good the Lord is[626] I supped to night at Mr ffishers wth him his sonne & Wm Bott.

14° Januar 1638/39
Court to day, after Court I gave account to diverse of the Aldermen of my Journey & successe & they seemed to take it very well blessd be the Lord. I dyned at Mr ffishers afterward I rode to [Long] Buckby to Mr Bacons, but in the way I met wth a great storme, rayne hayle snow & great thunderings & lightening but the Lord graciously pr[e]served me.
we had newes afterward of great hurt done uppon Churches by this thunder towards London, thou art god alone & there is none besides thee.

---

[625] The soke or liberty of Peterborough possessed its own justices of the peace and sessions. It is not known for what visit to the county town Peterborough is here paying a levy.
[626] Psalm 34:8.

15° Januarii
I went from [Long] Buckby to day after dinner & came home safe,
wth one Scarborough the watchmaker[627]
16° Januar
I prayed in the morninge wth great fayth & comforts & went towards
Wellingborowe in the frost but goeinge betweene North[amp]ton &
Abington over

the lands ends, my horse foot fell into a chinker[628] or footinge & fell
downe & threw me downe & the horse was not able to rise a pretty
space, so that I feared his legg had bene broke as the horses was that
Will. Loe[629] was drivinge to Olney lately, but it was not so I prayse the
lord, yet much bruised or streyned so that he halted, yet I rode him to
Wellingborowe & there dressed him, he was after very lame so that I
was compelled to borowe one of ffr[ancis] ffreeman of Wilby to bringe
me home I behold gods goodnesse in pr[e]servinge in the fall that my
horse & I were not both straynd.
Mr Rainfford[630] chosen towne Counsell to day.
17° Januar 1638/39
I prayed, & went & heard Mr Newton at the Lecture, & wrote out
p[ar]te of Mr Pentlowes breviats for the hearinge.
18° Januar.
Mr Pentlowe of Broughton come to me wth whom I dyned at the
Rose & crowne[631]

19° Januar 1638/39
diverse Clyents with me to day I blesse the Lord, the Lord doth
graciously supply me susteyninge me in difficultyes blessed be his
name.
20° Januar. Sab.[bath]
Mr Ball preached both times to day. The Lord is gracious to me in
comfortinge me in his word & ordinances blessed be thy name oh
Lord.

---

[627]William Scarborough, watchmaker, gained his freedom in 1636, and served as a night
watchman in 1656, and bailiff in 1659: Freemen of Northampton, unpaginated, dated 1636;
Markham and Cox, Northampton, II, pp. 457–458, 562.
[628]A narrow, deep, cleft.
[629]The son and heir of the Northampton ironmonger John Loe.
[630]Richard Rainsford.
[631]This was located in Market Square and had been established after 1585: Markham and
Cox, Northampton, II, pp. 306–307.

21° Januar.
some gracious supply from the Court to day. I dyned wth Mr Maior.[632]
Mr Bacon came to the towne wth Mr dowsinge[633] who was goeinge to
Cambridge.
22° Januar.
I was busy about the Breviats
goodman Wright went for the horse Mr

Pentlowe was to lend me, & brought him.
I sent a breast of veale to Mr Samuel [*crossed out:* 23° Januar 1638
I praye] Martins to night to suppe with them beinge my weddinge
night this day 4 yeare the Lord ioyned me & my deare wife together
in that holy ordinance of mariage Blessed be thy name oh Lord for
p[ro]vidinge for me so good & fit a yoakfellowe, since o[u]r cominge
together o[u]r sinnes have bene many but Lord p[ar]don & wash
them away in the bloud of Jesus Xt & be gracious unto us, let us
live more holily the ffifth yeare then before let us & o[u]r family
increase dayly in grace, Thou hast shewed us great & sore troubles
since our cominge together, but hast in m[er]cye susteyned give us
more comforts, (sanctifyed) this 5th yeare then before if it be thy will,
thou hast given us offspringe blessed be thy name, Lord make them
thine I beseech thee, make us wise & holy parents & them gracious &
dutifull children our debts are many graunt that many of them may
fall off this yeare if it be thy will, & pr[e]vent the warre wth Scotland
I pray if thou seest good

however let thy truth & gospell be established in power & purity
amongst us, oh Lord heare oh Lord have m[er]cy, graunt these things
& what else thou knowest necessary for the Lords sake.
23° Januar 1638/39.
I prayed and went to Wellingborowe, where I spake with diverse.
I supped at old Mr Martins to night, I was at Mr Maiors[634] & Mr Collis
his house
24° Januar.
I prayed, and came to Grafton [Regis] Court & afterward to hockly[635]
wth one goodman Rechuds a Carryer of Loughborowe, an honest
religious man I hope. I prayed wth him wth comfort I blesse the Lord
we lodged at the swanne there

---

[632] Richard Fowler.
[633] Thomas Dowsing, vicar of Long Buckby, lived at the University of Cambridge: PDR,
CB67, unfoliated.
[634] Richard Fowler's.
[635] Hockliffe, Bedfordshire.

25° Januar
I prayed, & we came forward towards London, I came to towne about
4. a clock

where I found all well, I blesse the Lord, unlesse litle Sam. who had
his foot somewhat burnt wth a warminge panne, blessed be the Lord
for correctinge of us gently & in m[er]cye Lord sanctify thy whole
p[ro]vidence to me & mine for the Lords sake.
26° Januar 1638/39
I prayed and went towards Westm.[inster], but Mr Pentlowe came not
to me till about 1. a clock, we reteyned for counsell Mr Lane Mr hatton
& Mr Reynolds[636] in his cause against Mrs Sill in Cur[ia] Wardor[um]
27° Januar Sab.[bath]
I prayed and went to dr Stoughtons both times he preached very
excellently uppon, for thine is the Kingdome &. Lord hold him as a
starre in thy right hand for the Lords sake.

28° Januar 1638/39
I prayed with some comfort, & remembred Mr Pentlowes businesse
to be heard to day in Cur[ia] Ward[orum] the cause was some what
broken that the counsell did much doubt of it, & we were in some feare
they would have given the defendant costs but the Lord so ordered it
that there was allowed my clyent [crossed out: 460] 400li or there abouts
he paying about 120li p[ro] rent & about 11li p[ro] barley blessed be
thy name oh Lord.
29° Januar.
Mr Pentlowe & I goeinge to Westm[inster] went into white hall &
there in the Long walke I met wth my M[aste]r Mr Readinge, who
threatens that he will have above 100li of us still, though he would
have bene content with 50li not long since or threatens that he will put
in a bill against us in the Court of requests; I am too much troubled,
for then I thinke, that will discover to

the world that I give money for the place & then another may step
in & get it from me, but Lord Ile trust in thee, mine eyes are towards
thee, change things if it be thy will turne my feares into Joy & deliver
me in thy due time from my debts & melancholly, find out a way
of thine owne, for worldly helpe fayleth, the summer brooke of the
creature is dryed up, & in the broken Cisterne there is no water,
drop downe (then) yee heavens from [crossed out: on high] above &

[636]There was a Buckinghamshire barrister called Thomas Lane. Robert Hatton was a
Middle Temple barrister and bencher based in Surrey. Robert Reynolds was the third most
senior counsellor in the Court of Wards: Prest, Barristers, pp. 64, 367, 375.

let the skyes poore downe righteousnesse (45 Isai[ah] 8.) let the word
of [*crossed out:* of] the god of truth be p[er]formed unto thy servant
wherein thou hast caused me to trust, thy testimonyes have bene my
song in the house of my pilgrimage, I have desired to wayt patiently
for thee, shew me the soveraignty of thy power & fill me with fayth &
peace, blesse me & my deare wife & family for the Lords sake blesse
me in my callinge strengthen me in it

30° Januar 1638/39
still much noyse of Warre, & that the Kinge hath sent letters to
the noble men to contribute towards warre with or defence against
the

Scotts.[637] Lord bringe a good effect out of this trouble for the Lords
sake.

31° Januar 1638/39.
I rise & goe & move in the strength of the Lord, or desire to doe so,
though I have p[ar]ticuler troubles in regard of wants & & the publiq
is much amisse, Oh God allmighty & allsufficient thou canst remedy
all this when thou pleasest.

1° ffeb.
Oh my god looke uppon us in regard of the publiqe, the foundacons
are shaken & what shall the righteous doe, set up pure doctrine &
holy worship amongst us, maynteyne thine owne Cause & children,
let iniquity stop her mouth & be confounded, spread thy gospell into
all the world for the Lords sake.

2° ffeb. 1638/39.
I p[ai]d Ric Rise the 32s for my Aunt Woodford Lord helpe me to
pay the rest of my debts in thy due time, confirme & strengthen me by
fayth that worldly sorow may not cause death, Lord I pray thee that I
and my family may live in thy sight & uppon thy blessed p[ro]vidence.
Mr Smart dyned at my fathers.

3° ffeb. Sab.[bath]
I heard dr Stoughton in the morninge & receaved the sacram[en]t
wth comfort I prayse the Lord, Oh Lord I blesse thee for givinge of us
a holy rest & holy ordinances to comfort us in the worst condicons.

4° ffeb.
comforts in duty I blesse the Lord.

the Lord is pleased still to uphold my hart though I meet with many
difficultyes, blessed be thy name oh Lord, And I encourage my selfe

---

[637] The king's summons to the nobility: Gardiner, *History*, VIII, p. 384.

in the Lord & oppose his blessed p[ro]mises to my carnall feares &
cares.
5° ffeb. 1638/39.
still noyse of warre ag[ains]t Scotland, and a p[ro]clamacon came
lately forth for all gentlemen of the North p[ar]ts to repayre to their
houses in the Country by the 1 of M[ar]ch[638] 2 books come lately forth
one called a p[ro]clamac[ion][639] wherein was shewed the rebellion of
the Scots & the lawfullnes & necessity of Bishops wth 5 argum[en]ts for
them: another booke called the declinator,[640] wch was a p[ro]testacon
of the Scottish B[isho]ps against the Assembly. Oh Lord pitty & helpe
thy poore church set up pure doctrine & holy worship amongst us for
the Lords sake.
6. ffeb.
I prayed & havinge writt in diverse letters I went to Westm[inster]
hall, Mrs Pilkingtons[641]

businesse in the Court of Wards put off againe, I considered how god
had delivered me out of her husbands hand, & how his were now
inplunged in law, but I desired to lift up my hart unto the Lord to
deliver her
7° ffeb. 1638/39
I prayed and went about mine occasions, though I am in diverse wants
of moneyes yet the Lord graciously supplyes me blessed be thy name
oh Lord for thy goodnes

---

[638] For the proclamation, dated 29 January 1639, see J.L. Larkin (ed.), *Stuart Royal
Proclamations II: royal proclamations of King Charles I, 1625–1646* (London, 1982), pp. 648–650.
[639] Possibly either the proclamation of 29 November 1638 dissolving the Assembly or that
of 19 December 1638 denouncing its continued sitting and its proceedings: D. Stevenson,
The Scottish Revolution 1637–1644: the triumph of the Covenanters (Newton Abbot, 1973), p. 126;
P.H. Brown (ed.), *Register of the Privy Council of Scotland*, 8 vols (Edinburgh, 1899–1908), VII,
pp. 91–102.
[640] Part of the ill-organized opposition to the Covenant, the *Declinator* (which complained
about abuses in the elections to the Assembly and about the Assembly's membership) was
read at the 27 November 1638 session but was ineffective: Stevenson, *Scottish Revolution*,
pp. 119, 121.
[641] Ann, the widow of Woodford's rival, Thomas Pilkington. She was the daughter of the
godly alderman Edward Mercer, who had written to Robert Cecil in 1605 to protect the
puritan minister Robert Catelin. Mercer had been presented to the Church court accused of
sending his children (perhaps including Ann) to be taught by the free school's master, Simon
Wastell, who had been excommunicated for nonconformity. In 1607 he was involved in a
Star Chamber suit initiated by John Lambe against the writers and circulators of scurrilous
verses attacking the personnel of the Church courts: Sheils, *Puritans*, p. 83; PDR, CB37,
fo. 193r; TNA, STAC8/205/19 and STAC8/205/20; Metcalfe, *Visitation of Northamptonshire
1618*, p. 129.

8° ffeb.

I prayed & went towards the temple & returned early & afterwards went along wth my wife my father mother Mr Woolfall Mrs Woolfall Mrs Bellamy Mr Smart & Mrs Susan[642] to Edmunton to see litle Sarah my child, we had a coach we found the Child very well blessed be the Lord Lord blesse all my children, surely Lord thou wilt graciously p[ro]vide for them. I humbly cast my selfe & my whole family uppon thee for Xt his sake delight in us to doe us good

9° ffeb. 1638/39

I prayed & went about mine occasions, my father went in the afternoone to speake wth Mr Readinge who served a subpena uppon him so that I have bene much troubled & very sad & melancholly but I desired to looke unto the Lord & to quiet my discontented & wranglinge spirit; Lord why should I be thus cast downe Thou hast made heaven & earth thine are the fullnes thereof, man suffereth for his sinne Let me put my mouth in the dust doe graciously for me sanctifyeinge this affliccon unto me & deliveringe me in thy due time, my lady Smethes payd me her bill, & Mr Warren payd me to night blessed be thy name oh Lord

10. ffeb. Sab.[bath]

I prayed and we went to heare dr Stoughton who preached excellently concerninge prayer in the forenoone & a stranger there in the afternoone, I had gracious rest this day from mine unquiet thoughts & many comforts I blesse the Lord

11° ffeb. 1638/39.

I have had much deliverance from my melancholly this day I blesse the Lord.

Lord keepe defend uphold & supply me still for the Lords sake, my wife much troubled wth melancholly by reason of this affliccon, oh Lord shew us how to live by fayth for the Lords sake Amen.

12° ffeb

This morninge Mr Readinge hath served me wth a subpena, & yet the Lord pleased graciously to uphold my hart, Lord I have need of affliccon sanctyfye it to us for the Lords sake God is mine helper why should I feare what man can doe unto me,

Thou art my hidinge place, let my defence be the safe mountions of rocks

Stay up my soule by fayth & let not mine eyes fayle in lookinge for thee

[642] Susan Pentlow, whom John Smart would marry on 26 September 1639.

Let [crossed out: my c] our consciences be kept pure & ungashd yea not
scrupled in the least measure in this businesse
Turne thou the hart of him that is against me

speake thou unto him that he may not hurt me Instruct us what we
ought to doe & let us harken unto thee
teach us to order o[u]r affayres with discrecon that they may not have
the upper hand through o[u]r indilligence
put an end to this difference if it be thy will by thy gracious p[ro]vidence
without the determinacon of law,
Are we not both thine, pr[e]serve thy gospell from imputacon, we are
both of us vessells wherein there is no pleasure & thou mayest Justly
[crossed out, illegible] breake us one against another,
but oh let us live in thy sight, & let thy m[er]cye pr[e]vent o[u]r ruine,
keepe me still in the place if it be thy will & let no strong hand
pr[e]vayle against me. Lord heare my prayer & let my cry come unto
thee, uphold o[u]r harts by thy selfe give a gracious yssue & supply
me & my family for the Lords sake.
The Lord hath graciously upholden my hart this day
13° ffebr 1638/39
I prayed and went about my occasions, and Mr

Readinge & I have [crossed out, illegible] entred into bonds to referre the
difference betweene us to dr Stoughton & dr Gouge[643] oh Lord I pray
thee direct them to give a righteous sentence, even accordinge to thine
owne will, for alas oh Lord we are weake & exceedinge shallow, & too
too p[ar]tiall in iudginge things that concerne our selves I pray thee
direct them from heaven, & give harts to Mr Reading my father & I to
be fully satisfied, & compose the businesse graciously, truly Lord we
are vessels very unusefull therefore thou mightest breake us in peeces
one against another but spare us for the Lords sake lay not uppon us
o[u]r iniquityes but delight to shew m[er]cye unto us for the Lords
sake.
14° ffebr. 1638/39.
I prayed and went to the B[isho]p of Winton to be made Almoner
p[ro] Com[itatu] North[amp]ton[644] which was granted me & I entred

[643]William Gouge, minister of St Ann's, Blackfriars, was perhaps the most celebrated
preacher in London. He was living quietly under the protection of London businessmen
and Robert Rich, Earl of Warwick, but from 1639 until 1648 he published various tracts
dealing with godly ethics which were to be highly influential. He and Stoughton made
an adjudication shortly before 26 April 1639 (Diary, p. 302): B. Usher, 'Gouge, William
(1575–1653)', in ODNB; Webster, Godly Clergy, pp. 56–57.
[644]The Bishop of Winchester was lord high almoner to Charles I and is here appointing
Woodford county almoner for Northamptonshire. Bishop Walter Curll had achieved this

into bond of 200li to give account at Easter & Mich[aelmas] tearme
allways what should [*crossed out:* g] come to my hand, Lord blesse me
& defend me in the place for the Lords sake:
Afterward my wife & I came forth for North[amp]ton though very
melancholy, & my wife wept & seemed to be discontented

discontented, I was sad yet desired to lift up my hart to the Lord of
heaven & earth, Mr Goodere came alonge with us neare to [South]
Mim[m]s, & then returned back to London but at Co[l]n[e]y Mr
ffarren & Mr Ayre⁶⁴⁵ overtooke us, & went no faster then we & drew us
along to Redburne⁶⁴⁶ to the Swan there blessed be thy name oh Lord
for thy p[ro]vidence in this
15° ffebr 1638/39
I prayed & we came along through gods m[er]cy with much comfort
& not much wearyed though the horse trotted all, and we came home
in due time to North[amp]ton Blessed be the Lord.
[*crossed out:* I] we came on Andrew Gills horse.
Mr Martin & diverse came to see us.
16° ffebr.
blessed be god that the sicknesse is thus ceased here in North[amp]ton,
& That the Lord hath brought us home againe to the place of our
habitacon,
Temp[er]ance & the Child came home safe in the Wagon to night
blessed be god
Oh Lord I prayse thy name for all thy m[er]cyes though we meet wth
many straights, yet thou art unto

unto us thy children as a place of broad rivers & streames of water,
Isa.[iah][33:21] Oh my god I pray thee have m[er]cy uppon me & my
poore family, thy word is my delight & the very Joy & reioycinge of
my hart & my rock & confidence wherin thou hast caused my soule
to trust, I pray thee shew me thy glory, I pray thee make me sick of
Love to the Lord Xt & enflame my soule, p[ar]don my sinnes & heale
my corrupcons give me all grace especially fayth and all spirituall
endowments especially holinesse, and Lord looke thou uppon me in

royal appointment in 1637 through the patronage of Archbishop Laud, and was an anti-
Calvinist supporter of Laudian ritualism: M. Dorman, 'Curll, Walter (1575–1647)', in *ODNB*;
K. Fincham and P. Lake, 'The ecclesiastical policies of James I and Charles I', in K. Fincham
(ed.), *The Early Stuart Church, 1603–1642* (Stanford, 1993), p. 38.
⁶⁴⁵Probably Edward Eare (Diary, p. 298, as Ned Eyre). Constable Eare of Burton Latimer
had become embroiled in the Burton ship money dispute when Sibthorpe had accused
Thomas Bacon, Eare's landlord, of threatening to evict him unless he ignored his duty to
collect the levy: Jackson, 'Ship money', pp. 34–36.
⁶⁴⁶South Mimms, Colney, and Redbourn, Hertfordshire.

regard of my outward Condicon thou seest my debts, & how here one
creditor expects money & there another which I cannot pay yet shall
I sink under the burden & suspend my fayth and be discouraged? no
when I looke to thy word, & to the workmanship of thy hands the
sunne moone & starres which thou hast made, I will say what ayleth
thee oh my soule, why art thou so disquieted within me? trust still in
god for [*crossed out, illegible*] the Lord Jehovah is the work of ages; oh my
god though I am in great debts to 200li yet thou my father possessest
heaven & earth I have no way to extricate my selfe; But I beseech thee
oh Lord to helpe, thou wilt surely helpe & it shall goe well with me,
for thy power is boundlesse, nay tis easy to thee speak but the word &
the egiptians shall lend & give liberally

liberally to the Israelites, all the creatures wayte uppon thee to obey
thee and thou delightest in doeinge good to thine, oh manifest thy
p[ro]vidence that my wife & I may reioyce in thy favor & be as they
that dreame when thou shall free us from our incumbrances, & let thy
m[er]cy confirme o[u]r fayth & beare thy love engraven uppon it &
be sanctifyed oh Lord heare & have m[er]cye for the Lords sake
my mother came to us to day.
17° ffebr. 1638/39 Sab.[bath]
Mr Ball preached both times, & I had gracious enlargem[en]t &
comforts in this Sabath blessed be thy name oh Lord.
18° ffebr.
Court to day, where the Court but small but Lord do thou blesse my
gaynes unto me.
19° ffebr.
great noyse here of the warres ag[ains]t Scotland oh Lord

Lord doe thou order every thinge for the best for the Lords sake thou
holdest the [*crossed out:* reg] reignes of the world in thine owne hand.
20° ffebr 1638/39
we prayed and I and my wife went to Wilby, & I after to Wellingborowe,
after that I was sent for to [*crossed out:* with] goodman Tompson &
goodman Basse[647] to take instruccons of them for their wills, Lord be

---

[647] That is, William Tompson and George Basse, both of Wilby. Basse was presented to
the Church court in 1619 accused of receiving communion either sitting or standing (but
not kneeling, as required by the court) at Broughton during the incumbency of Robert
Bolton. He went on to serve as churchwarden at Wilby in 1635 and was reported in
1637 (as was Tompson) for maintaining a pew which was too high. The will made for
Tompson by Woodford was later superseded: PDR, Church Survey Book 5, fo. 134r–v;
PDR, X639–642/8, unfoliated, under Wilby; PDR, CB48, fo. 273r–v; PDR, Archdeaconry
of Northampton wills, third series, C128.

blessed for these good men, [*crossed out:* if] as thou hastest many away
so fournish thy church with more for the Lords sake
21° ffebr
we lay at Mr Pentlowes to night, after dinner we came home safe
blessed be god, And lord we prayse thee for the comfort of freinds we
doe enioy
I went alonge with Mr downes to duston
22° ffebr
I prayed unto the Lord & then tooke the Antimonial Cup which
wrought well wth me (blessed be god) Mr

Mr Attourney[648] came home to day, Lord give me favor in his eyes &
rayse me more freinds if it be thy will
23° ffebr. 1638/39
I prayed and went about my occasions & the Lord hath graciously
enabled me for them
24° ffeb. Sab.[bath]
Mr Ball preached both times very p[ro]fitably in his former manner
to set forth a body of religion oh Lord blesse his labors to us, & enable
him graciously more & more for thy service.
25° ffebr.
I prayed and went to the Court, where Mr d[aniel] Readinge did
[*crossed out:* much] abuse me in some words Lord p[ar]don him, &
p[ar]don my faylings rash anger pride & all other corrupcons &
transgressions

26° ffeb. 1638/39
Justice hutton dyed at London [*crossed out:* they] its said this day in the
morninge, thus I have lost another mortall friend; but oh my Lord
thou art the immortall god, rayse me up more if it be thy will, & doe
thou be to me all in all
I was wth Mr Attourney[649] to day who shewed me favor blessed be god
27° ffeb.
To day Justice Bartlet[650] came in wth the Sherriffe blessed be the Lord
that we have meetings againe in this place:[651]

---

[648]Richard Lane.
[649]Richard Lane.
[650]Sir Robert Berkeley.
[651]This refers to the resumption of the assizes at Northampton at the end of the outbreak
of plague: the sheriff involved was Philip Holman, an official charged with the unenviable
task of collecting the arrears of ship money in Northamptonshire, as well as a new writ for
1638. A London scrivener made good, Holman was lord of the manor of Warkworth, and a
patron of godly ministers. Warkworth itself was exempt from ecclesiastical jurisdiction and

I was much troubled when Mr Attourney[652] shewed me the defects in dentons plea ad[versus] A[lexander] Eakins.

28° ffeb.

one Mr Challenor[653] preached the Assize sermon to day excellent well & honestly.

I had too much carnall feare to day about my causes that were for tryall;

see at the other end of the booke.[654]

the first cause which was inter Denton [*symbol meaning plaintiff*] & Eakins & Andrewes def[endan]ts went for us to night, blessed be the Lord

[*crossed out:* 29° ffeb] 1° Martii 1638/39

This morninge the other cause went for denton too; oh Lord it is not in vayne to rest quietly & cast all uppon thy p[ro]vidence, I pray thee inable me greatly for my callinge, & give me imploym[en]t & industry & much comfort in it, & sanctify every m[er]cy to me & mine for the Lords sake Amen.

Two prisoners are condemned one for murther thother p[ro] horsstealinge. Lord make them wholsome examples to others, & Lord give them repentance & fayth.

---

possessed no incumbent, although Holman maintained his own chaplain. He promoted the careers of two very different godly ministers at Marston St Lawrence, whose advowson was owned by the Blencowe family: in 1633 he had appointed Charles Chauncy, the vocal opponent of Laudian altar policy, who preached at Warkworth before emigrating to New England in 1638; and in 1637 Chauncy's replacement, the more moderate minister Francis Cheynell, nephew of Sir Gervase Clifton, whose appointment was advocated, to his own astonishment, by Archbishop Laud and the High Commission. Holman also enjoyed godly connections with John Crewe, Richard Knightley, Lord Saye, Thomas Ball, and Edward Reynolds: Jackson, 'Ship money', pp. 176–181, 195; Fielding, 'Peterborough', pp. 20, 96; Bridges, *History of Northamptonshire*, II, pp. 182, 217; Longden MS, 28 August 1633 and 28 October 1637; Longden, *Clergy*; TNA, SP16/311/33; Webster, *Godly Clergy*, pp. 221–224; F.J. Bremer, 'Chauncy, Charles (bap. 1592, d. 1672)', in *ODNB*; R. Pooley, 'Cheynell, Francis (bap. 1608, d. 1665)', in *ODNB*; Nottingham University Library, Clifton MSS, CL C600.

[652] Richard Lane.

[653] Either Thomas Chalenor, the son of Jonas Chalenor, who had been deprived from the living of Byfield in 1605 for nonconformity, or Jonas himself, who had lived in Shropshire since his deprivation. Thomas seems an unlikely candidate: he had been the vicar of Geddington (and the client of the Catholic Sir Thomas Tresham) until 1637, and was possibly still the schoolmaster there. He had preached at Archdeacon John Quarles's visitation in 1630, but Bishop Piers's officials thought him too indifferent to contribute to the Kettering lecture in 1630 and by 1632 he was being presented for negligence in serving his cure: Longden, *Clergy*; Sheils, *Puritans*, pp. 75, 81, 82; Longden MS, 23 September 1626 and 14 June 1637; Fielding, 'Peterborough', p. 64; PDR, CBA51, fo. 19r; PDR, CB40A, fo. 80r; TNA, SP16/531/135.

[654] See p. 402, additional entry dated 28 February 1638/39.

2° Martii

This day the Judge went out of towne towards Warrick, Lord graunt that he may proceed iustly in all his accons in the Circuite that he may Judge for thee, for the fatherlesse & the widow & the oppressed.

Lord pr[e]pare us for the Sabath & the sacram[en]t to morowe for the Lords sake

3° Martii 1638/39 Sab.[bath]

Mr Ball preached in the morninge & Mr [*crossed out:* Newto] James Lewes in the afternoone, I was somewhat dull in dutyes this day but I desired to lift up my hart unto the Lord, & to bringe my burdens before him.

4° Martii

I prayed against rash anger for a blessinge & went after to the Court where the Lord sent me some supply, though the Courts are worse by farre then they have bene, Lord be gracious to me and my family

I went in the afternoone wth Mr Rushworth & instead of comfortinge my selfe wth gods creatures I through want of moderacon was sick, oh Lord forgive this sinne & all the rest in the blood of Jesus Xt make me watchfull for time to come, & bringe good out of this evill, crucifye in me the body of death for the Lords sake.

5° Martii

The two poore men that were condemned at the

the Assizes for murther & horsstealinge were this day executed, the murtherer was very penitent blessed be the Lord

6° Martii 1638/39

I prayed and went to Wellingborowe, & I rode uppon my horse this first day since he was sinew-streyned in the frost & he goes now indifferent well blessed be god. Oh Lord I pray thee blesse what I doe possesse, & let thy gracious countenance shine uppon me [*crossed out:* f] & my family from the begininge of the yeare to the end thereof for the Lords sake.

This day at Wellingborowe I first heard of & saw the p[ro]clamacon & declaracon[655] come forth against the Scotts shewinge that they strike at the Roote of monarchicall governm[en]t &.

---

[655]Charles I had issued a declaration on 27 February 1639 describing the actions of the Scots as seditious, challenging monarchical government under the pretence of religion: J.L. Larkin (ed.), *Stuart Royal Proclamations II: royal proclamations of King Charles I, 1625–1646* (London, 1982), pp. 662–667.

Oh good Lord looke uppon us what will these things come to? Thou
alone knowest, for thou hast the orderinge and disposinge of all things,
oh Let thy gospell breake forth like the glorious sunne from under a
Cloud, that the eyes of the adversayes

adversaryes may be inlightened, or they may be so ashamed that
they may hide them selves in obscurity, let thy truth be so manifested
& effectually declared that all iniquity may stop her mouth, why
should dumb dogs that cannot barke remayne snarlinge at thy faythfull
servants, why should Idle drones eat the fat & drinke the sweete
& serve thy people, why should p[ro]phanenesse be established or
countenanced by a law, why should the haters of truth be increased &
flourish, why should the pr[e]cepts of men be taught for doctrines, why
should we cut off a dogs neck before thee & offer thee swines blood
instead of the sacrifice wthout blemish, why should carnall ordinances
& an earthly sanctuary still remayne & the worship in spirit & in
truth[656] be yet refused why should the whore of Rome the mother of
fornicacon & all the abominacons that are in the earth remayne under
these heavens & breath in thy ayre, why should not Babilon fall & be
cast rather into the botome of the sea like a milstone???[657] Oh send
forth thy light & thy truth & save us, The opposers of god & true
religion have said we will devoure at once; they are in our hands, now
shall we pr[e]vayle against those that they esteeme the offscowring
of

of the world, & stayne with opprob[r]y[um] callinge them puritans
sectaryes &. But Lord though thou seemest to hide thy face, & to give
thy people into their hand yet we will trust in thee, though they kill
us all the day long yet will we never forsake thee, though the plowers
shall plow uppon o[u]r backs & make long furrowes, though thou
shalt cast us into the place of dragons, yet will we boast of thee all the
day long, for though thou seemest to stand farre distant from us, & to
be like a stranger & a wayferinge man unto us which lodgest but for a
night & threatenest not to returne yet will we reioyce in thee & wayt
patiently for thee, for we know thou doest regard us, & though thou
dost not give us any playne demonstracon from heaven that thou wilt
succour & helpe, yet thou hast given us thy word to be neare unto us
even in o[u]r mouthes, & we have the mind of Xt. Oh give us fayth
to make all o[u]r owne. And Lord blesse me & my family build us up
& pull us not downe plant us & pluck us not up, keep us in health, &

[656] John 4:24.
[657] The fate awaiting those who condemned God's 'little ones', in Matthew 18:6, Mark
9:42, and Luke 17:2.

give us supply in our straights & wants but above all give us the grace
of thee o[u]r god in o[u]r harts for the Lords sake, And now oh my
god

god that my deare wife is with child againe I prayse thee for it, & I
blesse thee for the yssue thou hast allready given me & for givinge
them right shape & forme & the use of reason & understandinge, now
Lord I pray thee send me another sonne if it be thy will (yet Lord I
humbly submitt unto thee doe as may be most for thy glory) but I
beseech thee give it right shape & forme & make it a speciall blessinge
& keepe my wife till the time of her delivery & give her then a gracious
houre, & give her likewise the blessinge of the breasts & give us still
cause to prayse & blesse thee for the Lords sake.
7° Martii 1638/39
I prayed and went along wth the Coron[e]rs[658] to inquire of the death
of one Joane Shrewsbury, after that I went to Grafton [Regis] Court,
where I too much abounded in passion against a miller which the
Lord sent thether but to trye me, oh Lord subdue my strong passions
& lusts in me for the Lords sake I came home safe I blesse the [*crossed
out:* Lord] Lord.

8° Martii 1638/39
I prayed & went about my occasions, Oh Lord blesse & guide me in
all my undertakings, that they may be for the glory of thy name & the
good of me thy poore servant [*crossed out:* for the] & my family for the
Lords sake.
9° Martii.
we heare newes & Rumors still of Warrs wth Scotland, Lord I pray
thee looke uppon us & save us, establish thy gospell & set it up in
power & purity for the Lords sake.
10. Martii 1638/39 Sab.[bath]
Mr Ball preached both times very well Lord increase his gifts & p[ar]ts
& make him an instrum[en]t of thy glory.
11° Martii
Court to day, the gayne is very

small, by reason as we suppose of the rumors of warrs now with
Scotland, Lord pr[e]vent this evill that we feare, & blow over the
cloud that we feare will breake uppon us for the Lords sake

---

[658] Probably four of the following: Richard Woollaston, William Knight, Abraham Ventris,
Roger Sargent, Thomas Martin, and John Gifford: Book of Orders, pp. 51, 60.

12° Martii 1638/39
horses & wagons for the warrs come dayly through the towne which
are goeinge towards yorke for there I thinke must be the Rendezvous
of the army.
There is a declaracon[659] or proclamacon lately [*crossed out, illegible*] come
forth wch doth in effect declare the Scotts to be rebells & traytors &
its commannded to be read in churches &.
13° Martii.
I prayed and went to Wellingborowe, & the Lord brought me home
safe I am too often troubled in the thoughts of my debts Lord pay
them in thy due time for the Lords sake.
14° Martii
Mr Newton preached at the Lecture to day

Lord keepe it up still I humbly pray thee & graunt that religion may
flourish still in this place for the Lords sake.
15° Martii 1638/39
I have letters from London to day I think and I p[er]ceave their feares
there, & they refuse[660] to send 3000 souldiers to the Kinge or to give
him 50000li they feare the french there about the suburbs wch are
thought to be in number 50 or 60 thousand familyes & not wthout
armes; oh Lord deliver us from the violence of that nacon for the
Lords sake.
16° Martii
o[u]r markets here are very dead, people want moneys & those that
have it are loath to p[ar]t wth it, Lord supply me thy poore servant,
worke uppon the harts of my creditors that they may spare me for the
Lords sake.

17° Martii 1638/39 Sab.[bath]
Mr Ball preached both times to day, very p[ro]fitably blessed be
god.

---

[659] See Diary, p. 288, n. 655.
[660] In April 1639 the City of London refused to lend the king money to fund the campaign
against the Scots: K. Sharpe, *The Personal Rule of Charles I* (London, 1992), p. 822.

18° Martii
Court to day but the p[ro]fitts there very small. Mrs Isham Mr
Justinian Isham his wife[661] dyed not many dayes since a good woman
as it is said.
19° Martii
I prayed and went over to Long Buckby to have spoken wth Mr Bacon
but when I came I found him from home, & as I returned I met wth
Mr Watts goeinge towards Coventry
20° Martii
I prayed & went towards Wellingborowe I was in such want of money
that I was fayne to leave the hostler unpayd at the Angell Oh Lord
supply me in thy due time for the Lords

Lords sake, susteyne me in the meane time I humbly pray thee.
21° Martii 1638/39
Mr Cranford preached here at the Lecture to day, an excellent sermon
to incourage to stand for the truth in times of greatest darknesse &
danger, this was a word in season Lord uphold him & stand by him in
his troubles & dangers for the Lords sake.
22° Martii
The times in the apprehencon of all seeme to be very doubtfull; &
many feares we have of dangerous plotts by french & papists, Lord
pr[e]serve us & send us peace & truth for the Lords sake.
23° Martii
This day about 60 or 70 horses &

men belonginge it seemes to the Earle of Essex came [*crossed out:*
through] to the towne & were goeinge towards yorke.
24° Martii 1638/39 Sab.[bath]
Mr Ball preached p[ro]fitably both times to day in the morninge the
Kings p[ro]clamacon against the Scots was read by Mr Johnston.

---

[661] Justinian Isham of Lamport (1611–1675) had married Jane Garrard (the daughter of Sir
John Garrard of Lamer, Hertfordshire) in 1634. The couple had been based at Shangton,
Leicestershire, but had travelled to Sir John Isham's at Lamport for the birth of their son.
Jane had died on 3 March after childbirth and had been buried on 5 March. Justinian
employed Thomas Stanton to build a monument to her in the chancel at Lamport, and in
1642 praised her ('a Religious and Discreet woman') to their daughters, recommending that
they read the same books as she had, which included works by the puritans Daniel Featley
and Richard Sibbes. Justinian himself was a prominent patron of conformist ministers
before and during the Commonwealth period: R. Priestley, 'Isham, Sir Justinian, second
baronet (1611–1675)', in *ODNB*; Fielding, 'Peterborough', pp. 46–47; G. Isham (ed.), *The
Correspondence of Bishop Brian Duppa and Sir Justinian Isham 1650–1660*, Publications of the
Northamptonshire Record Society XVII (Lamport, 1955); Pevsner, *Northamptonshire*, p. 285;
NRO, Isham (Correspondence), I(C) 3415 (quotation).

25° Martii 1639
A great fare[662] here to day & though I had litle or no money in
the morninge yet my tenant brought me rent & god supplyed me
graciously
26° Martii
I prayed & went to Court to day where Mr Giffords cause v[e]rs[u]s
Skynner went ag[ains]t Mr Gifford I went towards night to Long
Buckby to Mr Bacon.
this eveninge it seemes the Earle of Arundell g[e]n[er]allissimo of the
Army [*crossed out:* lodged in] came hether to

North[amp]ton, & the Maior[663] & Aldermen fayled to pr[e]sent their
service to him.
27° Martii 1639 A[nn]° Re[gis] Car.[oli] [*crossed out:* 15°] 15°[664]
I lodged at Mr Bacons this last night, stayed dinner & then came
home, & I find here that Mr Maior is gone from the towne to attend
the Earle of Arundel beinge served wth a warrant to that purpose,
Mr Collis Mr Gifford Mr ffarren & John Lewes went along wth
him.
Mr Sargent Midleton was here at the towne to night.
28° Martii
I prayed and went to Grafton [Regis] Court where the Leet was kept
likewise, it was a pretty good court to me to day blessed be god. I
came home with one Mr Symcock of harborowe[665] from whom I had
a p[ro]phecy. I supped at Mr Rushworths
I p[ai]d 5s more in p[ar]t p[ro] my neast of Boxes so I have p[ai]d 10s
ab.[out] 3s behind
old Mr Sillesby dyed this eveninge.
Mr Maior[666] came home againe to night.

29° Martii 1639
I have p[ai]d 9s to day towards the 50li assessm[en]t in the parish
towards the church.[667]

[662]Lady Day.
[663]Richard Fowler.
[664]Woodford is here recording the beginning of Charles I's fifteenth regnal year: C.R.
Cheney (ed.), *Handbook of Dates for Students of English History*, Royal Historical Society Guides
and Handbooks IV (London, 1978), p. 26.
[665]Market Harborough, Leicestershire.
[666]Richard Fowler.
[667]A meeting of the vestry ordered this assessment on 20 March 1639: Vestry Minutes,
p. 34.

I am about Mr Bacons occasions, abbreviatinge the deposicons in Starr-chamber,[668] oh Lord I pray thee direct me in it,
We supped at Mr Sam. Martins to night.
Mr Sillesby [*crossed out:* dye] was buryed to day.[669]
30° Martii
I have sent the 8li to London to my father wch I rec[eive]d of Mr Spencer to that end, I sent Mr harvey[670] 20s towards a sp[ec]ial dedimus[671] p[ro] yorke &.
great pr[e]paracons for Warre against the Scotts Good Lord bringe good out of it for thy poore despised church for the Lords sake.
I have p[ai]d Ned[672] 24s for mault.
31° Martii Sab.[bath]
I have bene dull this day. Mr Ball preached both times to day very well.
Lord keepe open the mouthes of thy ministers still & make them faythfull.

1° April 1639
I prayed and went to the Court, wich is at a lower ebb then it use to be, but Lord blesse unto my gaynes, graunt that I may never covet or take more then I can Justifye unto thee & thy vicegerent in me

---

[668] The Star Chamber case of *Plowright vs. Bacon* over ship money. The court official gave notice on 30 March 1639 that the hearing would take place on 10 May: Temple of Stowe MSS, STT 1876, 12 April 1639.
[669] Duplicate entry: see Diary, p. 298.
[670] Probably the Harvey whom Woodford on 6 November 1639 describes as his chamber-fellow at Clement's Inn, part of the legal dynasty of Hardingstone and Weston Favell. Stephen Harvey was the younger son of Stephen Harvey of Weston, the brother of the godly judge, Sir Francis Harvey. Stephen senior had left Weston to become a wealthy London merchant and member of the Society of Grocers, and had married Sir Ralph Freeman's sister Elizabeth, although he retained close contacts with his roots – his lawyer was his kinsman William Adams, the Hardingstone barrister, and in his will of June 1636 he provided the money to construct a monument in Hardingstone church dedicated to his parents, William (d. 1606) and Ann. His religious affiliations were ambiguous: the preamble to his will was godly and he forbade any sordid funeral ostentation, but made bequests to various ministers including the conformist Samuel Baker, chaplain to Bishop William Juxon. His son Stephen, Woodford's proposed room-mate, was admitted to the Middle Temple on 26 November 1641 and called to the bar on 21 November 1651: H.A.C. Sturgess (ed.), *Register of Admissions to the Honourable Society of the Middle Temple from the Fifteenth Century to the Year 1944*, 3 vols (London, 1949), I, p. 140; TNA, PROB/11/171; Metcalfe, *Visitation of Northamptonshire 1618*, pp. 98–99; J.J. Howard and J.L. Chester (eds), *The Visitations of London AD 1633, 1634, and 1635*, 2 vols (London, 1880), I, p. 358; N. Tyacke, *Anti-Calvinists: the rise of English Arminianism c. 1590–1640* (Oxford, 1987), p. 218n; A. Hunt, 'Baker, Samuel (d. 1658)', in *ODNB*.
[671] A writ empowering one who is not a judge to perform an act as if he were a judge.
[672] Edward Oakley.

my conscience, p[ar]don my Ignorances, & discover things unto more
cleerely for the Lords sake.

2° April

This day the deputy lieutenants have bene busy in pressinge souldiers
at the Castle for the Northerne expedicon, Oh Lord what will these
things come to, Order all things by thy over-rulinge p[ro]vidence that
glory to thee & good to thy church may result out of them for the
Lords sake

goodwife Crutch[ley] dyned wth us to day, I had comfort &
enlargem[en]t in good discourse wth her Mr Bullivant & I had
much discourse about the Scottish businesse & when we consider
p[ro]ceedings, & how iustly the Lord may bring uppon

uppon us the Judgem[en]t of the sword, we see o[u]rselves environed
wth feares & dangers, I was afterward somewhat troubled in regard
of these feares, & my debts & because Mr Watts calls for the 20li of his
money, And I sought the Lord who revealed himself graciously unto
me in prayer, the Lord will surely keepe & defend supply & comfort
me & mine, I have prayed for p[ar]don of sinne power ag[ains]t it,
helpe in my debts defence from dangers that the Lord would build
& plant me & my family blesse me my wife ch[ildre]n & those that
belong to me Lord heare all my peticons for the Lords sake.

John Ball[673] dyed this morning I think.

3° Apr. 1639

my wife was called to Mrs danbyes[674] Labor this morninge betweene
3 & 4 Lord stand by the poore woman give her a gracious deliverye &
comfort for the Lords sake.

I am this day 33 yeares old I think & my wife 22 blessed be thy name
Lord thou hast continued so longe under the meanes of grace, Lord
continue

continue [crossed out: I] us still together if it be thy will to thy glory
& the good & comfort of ourselves & others, Lord thou hast tried us
many yeares whether we will be fruitfull or not, thou mightest now
pluck us up, but oh spare us still for thy m[er]cyes sake, & thou who
art the author of every good gift powre downe grace abundantly into
o[u]r soules & make us more fruitfull this yeare then ever & blesse us
& o[u]r family make us Instruments of thy glory & vessells of m[er]cye
d[e]l[ive]r me thy poore s[er]v[an]t this yeare if it be thy will from my
straights in the world & sanctify the m[er]cye unto me, & now that

[673]Diary, p. 296, n. 676, on Lawrence Ball.
[674]John Danby was married twice: to Sarah and Alice. This was probably the former:
TNA, PROB/11/232.

I am goeinge abroad doe thou ever graciously guide & blesse me &
grannt me a comfortable Journey & returne for the Lords sake.
Mrs danby brought to bed of a sonne
I am goeinge to Wellingborow if the Lord please.
The Lord carryed me alonge graciously & brought me home safe.

4° April 1639
I prayed, & afterward went to the Lecture [*crossed out, illegible*] where
one Mr . . of Rushden a Germa[n][675] preached very honestly & well,
The souldiers went away this day towards yorke which were pressed
here.
Lord looke uppon the miserable & distracted Condicon of the land
reforme what is amisse & setle peace & thy gospell in this & the
neighbor nacon for the Lords sake.
5° April
I was this day at the buriall of John Ball a scholler sonne to Lawrence
Ball,[676] I was a litle melancholly to see Burgins & some other take place
before me on purpose yet I laboured to keepe downe my base proud
spirit Lord I that am so ready to take uppon me in my necessitous
condicon wha[t] should I doe if I had my desired supply. Lord I desire
wholly to submitt unto thee crucifye every corrupcon & blesse me for

for the Lords sake, Mr Rogers preached excellently at the fun[er]all,
Lord I blesse thee for it.
I rec[eive]d a letter at night from my father earnestly callinge uppon
me for money. Oh Lord looke graciously uppon me thy poore servant
for the Lords sake for I know not what to doe but my helpe standeth
in the name of the all sufficient Lord who hath made heaven & earth
susteyne & graciously uphold my father & me in our Condicon.
Mr Martin & ux Mr Rushworth & ux supped wth us here to night.

---

[675]Friedrich Schlör of the Rhineland had been inducted to the living of Rushden on
16 September 1637 and on 26 September licensed to preach anywhere in the Diocese of
Peterborough. During the Civil War he was intruded into the rectory of Old after the violent
death of Peter Hausted, the previous incumbent, at the siege of Banbury: Longden MS,
16 September 1637; Longden, *Clergy*; PDR, Miscellaneous Book XVIA, fo. 9r; Fielding,
'Peterborough', pp. 46, 118–120; D. Kathman, 'Hausted, Peter (c.1605–1644)', in *ODNB*.
[676]John Ball attended Queen's College, Oxford, gaining a BA in 1635 and an MA in 1638.
Both father and son were members of the godly grouping in the town: John witnessed the
will of the saddler Richard Trueman, and Lawrence that of the ironmonger John Loe.
Lawrence's father, Lawrence senior, who had been mayor in 1592, had been among the
corporation members who had written to the Secretary of State Robert Cecil in 1605 to
protect Robert Catelin, their minister, from deprivation. Lawrence the younger occurs in
the parish records from 1628, and served as a churchwarden in 1636 and as mayor in 1641
(Diary, p. 394): Foster; Sheils, *Puritans*, p. 83; Vestry Minutes, pp. 21–32, 35; Markham and
Cox, *Northampton*, II, p. 552.

6° April 1639
many men & horses & wagons goe through the towne dayly to yorke,
Lord get glory to thy selfe & bringe good to thy poore church out of
the pr[e]sent businesse for the Lords sake.
the Lord hath sent a gracious & seasonable

seasonable rayne uppon the land after 2 month or 10 weekes drought
or there [*crossed out:* abbo] abouts blessed be thy name oh Lord.
7° April 1639 Sab.[bath]
Mr Ball preached both times to day Lord strengthen his voyce more
if it be thy will I & my wife & hatton rec[eive]d the sacram[en]t to
day blessed be thy name oh Lord for thy holy ordinances: Lord make
them effectual uppon us for the Lords sake.
8° April
Court to day where the gaine but small blessed be the name of the
Lord for any supply.
we supped at Mr Rushworths wth Mr Martin & ux the Assembly have
not agreed to give money to convey souldeirs[677]

9° Apr. 1639
I prayed & went about my occ[asi]ons & have bene very dilligent this
day & doe find much comfort in it I blesse the Lord; the Lord hath
graciously moved my hart in private prayer this eveninge to meltinge
affeccons through fayth of gods m[er]cye the Lord will surely blesse
& sanctify me & mine.
10. April 1639.
I prayed and went to Wellingborow, and the Lord brought me home
safe, blessed be thy name oh Lord for thy good p[ro]vidence to me &
my family
11° April
much newes [*crossed out:* letter] & talke of the Scottish businesse oh
Lord that it may goe well with thy church & people ruine antixt[678] in
thy due time & all his

his cursed adherents, blesse the Kings Ma[jes]ty I humbly pray thee,
Lord convert his soule unto thee & make him a blessed instrument

---

[677]The deputy lieutenants of the county had written to the corporation of Northampton to
request this coat and conduct money, but the town's assembly rejected the request by a large
majority. The mayor, Richard Fowler, by his sole authority, next ordered the constables to
collect it, but most defaulted over a levy which lacked the assembly's approval. By 21 July
the assembly had paid the levy out of corporation funds: Markham and Cox, *Northampton*,
II, p. 436; *Book of Orders*, pp. 53, 57–59.
[678]Antichrist.

of thy glory in these churches let his eyes scatter all Idolatry pop[er]y sup[er]stition & p[ro]phanenesse let the good be accepted of him for the Lords sake.

Mr Sillesby[679] buryed about this day I think.

12° April 1639

I prayed and went about my occasions, we supped at Mr Samuel Martins to night blessed be thy name oh Lord for the comfort of freinds [crossed out: make] let not our metings be an occasion of excesse, but make us moderate & make them occasions of much good & comfort to us in these sad times.

13 April

[crossed out, illegible]

my wife hath bene sad havinge heard about a week since of Sams illnesse, but we desire to wayt uppon the Lord & seeke his face for o[u]r poore child whom the lord bestowed uppon us at first, uppon o[u]r poore requests.

14° April. 1639. Easter day.

Mr Newton preached both times o[u]r table is still brought downe blessed be the Lord, Lord keepe us still from sinnfull innovacons[680]

15° April

I prayed with & for my famyly, & went afterward with Ned Eyre[681] to Burton Latimer wth Mr Bacons bookes & a breviat which I had drawne, Mr John Bacon met me there

16° Apr.

we went in the morninge from Burton [Latimer] to Mr Palmers[682] to Carleton to advise with & to shew him the breviat, who liked it well we came back that night to desborowe[683] to Mr Pultons a papists house where I conceive I supped wth a demure priest which was there as I

[679]Duplicate entry: see Diary, p. 294.

[680]Ramsden had written to Lambe on 20 March 1639 declaring that Northampton men still regularly received communion sitting and advising him to send informers to the parish at Easter. Note Woodford's description of the position of the communion table, which had apparently been unrailed in the middle of the chancel since at least 16 June 1638 (Introduction, p. 62): TNA, SP16/414/163.

[681]Constable Edward Eare of Burton Latimer, who was involved in the Plowright vs. Bacon ship money dispute.

[682]Geoffrey Palmer of East Carlton was a high-flying lawyer who had already represented the county gentry against the king's revival of the forest laws and is clearly sympathetic to Woodford's and Bacon's ship money dispute here: Diary, p. 114, n. 85.

[683]Desborough.

was informed, we had much discourse of gen[er]all papists in divinity & my hart was affected I blesse the Lord.

17° April 1639
Mr Bacon againe served, (the warrant or coppy came to him this morninge to desb[orough]) againe to appeare before the Lords of the Councell.[684]
I came afterwards to Wellingborowe ffare where I met wth hatton & Richard ffarmer.
Mr Snart was at Mr Pentlowes as I came by
18 April
I prayed & went wth Richard ffarmer to Grafton [Regis] Court, where I met with a french Captayne who was goeinge downe to newcastle & told me much of the Scottish affayres.
19. April
I prayed and went to keepe Mr Pentlowes Court at Wilby, & the Lord graciously enabled me for it I could not come away from Wilby to night it beinge late my wife supped at Mr Rushworthes.
20. Apr.
I came home from Wilby this morninge

the Earle of Leic[ester][685] came to the towne this eveninge, many poastings to & fro betweene yorke & London, Lord bringe not o[u]r feares uppon us if it be thy will, but susteyne us & teach us how to carry o[u]r selves in theise darke times, & keepe us from sudden feares keepe o[u]r harts in a holy & good temp[er], and turne againe the streames [crossed out: waters] in the North, and make us like people that dreame by thy great deliverance & helpe us to awake to thy prayse & singe of thy m[er]cyes & tell them to [crossed out: the] o[u]r children. much practise to day I blesse the Lord.

[684]Bacon had been summoned to appear before the Court of Star Chamber on 10 May concerning his ship money dispute with Plowright. This second summons, to appear on 17 May, concerned a second Star Chamber case. The subject of this was Plowright's impressment (on 4 April) as a soldier for the Scottish wars by Deputy Lieutenant Sir Rowland St John after Plowright, as Constable of Burton Latimer, had failed to produce any recruits. Sibthorpe had intervened by writing to his court contacts, Sir John Lambe and Richard Kilvert. Shortly afterwards, Plowright was released and appeared before the council to accuse Bacon of conniving with St John over his impressment. Accordingly, after 17 April Bacon was imprisoned in London. St John was also arrested. On 30 April Bacon gave bond to appear before the Council on 17 May and was released: V.L. Stater, 'The lord lieutenancy on the eve of the Civil Wars: the impressment of George Plowright', *Historical Journal*, 2 (1986), pp. 285, 287, 289; Introduction, pp. 79-81.
[685]Robert Sidney, second Earl of Leicester, had been recalled in February 1639 from his ambassadorship to France. He returned to France in August: I. Atherton, 'Sidney, Robert, second earl of Leicester (1595-1677)', in *ODNB*.

21° April 1639 Sab.[bath]
Mr Newton preached in the morninge, thearle of Leic[ester] was at
Church, but went away p[os]t prand[ium]. Mr Bullivant preached in
the afternoone.
22° April.
Court to day, where the Lord graciously sent me some supply, & kept
me from passion though John hall[686] p[ro]voked me blessed be thy
name oh Lord for all thy m[er]cyes.
my mother & Bridget Wheelok[687] came to night

23° April. Georges ffare, & the quarter sess[ions] here to day. I moved
for the Constable of hartwell & was heard I blesse the Lord. Lord
I blesse thee for the dayly bread thou bestowest uppon me, for the
practise thou sendest me for the abilityes & successe thou bestowest
uppon me Lord I pray thee increase my practise my abilityes successe
& dayly bread continually if it be thy will, & let me ever admire &
prayse thee in it & be more humble & graunt that I may ever keep
a good conscience voyd of offence both to thee & men let not what I
have be a feare unto me; Lord pay my debts for me in due time, & in
the meanewhile susteyne me graciously: setle us here if it be thy will
as a nayle in a sure place, or p[ro]vide a hidinge place for us for the
Lords sake.
my wife & I had some difference to night, Lord p[ar]don it in us &
make us more watchfull forever.
24° April
I prayed & went about my occasions, & was closse at worke all day &
had much comfort in it I blesse the Lord.

---

[686] John Hall, a sergeant: TNA, SP16/474/80.
[687] Bridget seems to have been a friend of Woodford's mother, Jane; James Wheelock is
mentioned in the will of Woodford's father: PDR, Archdeaconry of Northampton wills,
second series, C168.

25° April
I prayed & went to the lecture, Mr Castle[688] preached

preached there very well. I was wth Mr Ball in p[os]t merid[iem].
Newes from yorke to day that the godly & gracious Lord Sea & Lord
Brooke[689] are committed at yorke for refusinge an oath oh Lord bringe
good out of all this trouble for the Lords sake

[688] William Castle (Castell) had, in 1627, obtained through crown patronage the benefice
of Courteenhall. In 1630 he had been involved in a controversy over the possession of the
living of Paulerspury. The eventual victor was William Beale, who accused Castle and Peter
Fawtrart of Guernsey of acting in a puritan conspiracy against him. The case resurfaced at
Archbishop Laud's trial, when Laud was accused of exploiting crown patronage to favour
men of his own faction. Castle was suspended at Bishop Piers's primary visitation in July
1631 for failing to hold May Day prayers, and he may have tried his hand at being a Virginia
planter around this time. At the metropolitical visitation of the diocese in May 1635 he
was described as a puritan who bragged of sitting with his hat on during service. At Dee's
1637 visitation he was charged with always editing the Prayer Book service, never wearing a
surplice, using an alternative catechism to that in the Prayer Book (asking 'strong questions
[like] what was the first sinne? what was the forbidden fruit? what the Divell ys?': TNA,
SP16/366/17), and fighting with his parishioners who were playing on the bowling leys. His
opposition to the altar policy was dramatic. He initially prevented the churchwardens from
railing the communion table, but after an admonition from Dr Clarke he promised on 25
June 1636 to allow it. His strategy was similar to that employed at All Saints': he permitted
the creation of a rail at the bottom of the chancel steps, enclosing a long table which was not
placed against the eastern wall of the chancel. The Church court official complained about
the rails and ordered the apparitor to measure the table, whereupon Castle pushed him
away, claiming he could as easily live in New England. Castle asserted that his parishioners
did not approach the rails at the communion (the charge stated they came within the rails),
that they should not, and that he would never encourage them to do so, and that it was as
appropriate to bow at the other parts of the Trinity as at Jesus' name. In 1639 Sibthorpe
claimed that Castle was the most averse clergyman in the diocese to the clerical contribution
towards the cost of the Bishops' Wars: NRO, Spencer (Althorp) MSS, A19; Longden MS,
13 April 1627; Fielding, 'Peterborough', p. 43; PDR, CB1, fo. 414r–v; PDR, CBA63, fo.
392r–v; TNA, SP16/308/52; TNA, SP16/36/17; PDR, Church Survey Book 5, fo. 8gr–v;
Temple of Stowe MSS, STT 1891; Webster, *Godly Clergy*, p. 220; P. Gordon, 'William Castell
of Courteenhall: a seventeenth century pioneer of missionary work', *Northamptonshire Past
and Present*, 8 (5), (1993–1994), pp. 354–362.

[689] Robert Greville, second Lord Brooke, lived at Warwick Castle, and William Fiennes,
Viscount Saye and Sele, at Broughton Castle, Oxfordshire. They were connected through
marriage and conviction with a network of puritan opponents of royal policy from the 1620s
onwards, ranging from such aristocratic figures as Francis Russell, Earl of Bedford, and
Robert Rich, Earl of Warwick, to gentry figures such as John Pym, Oliver St John, Richard
Knightley, and many godly ministers with whom they also collaborated on New England
colonial ventures in the 1630s. Both inveterate opponents of Charles I and supporters of the
Covenanters, with whom they were probably already in touch, they are here being briefly
imprisoned at York for refusing to fight for the king against the Scots, and for refusing
to swear an oath of loyalty to the king on the grounds that it had not been approved by
parliament: A. Hughes, 'Thomas Dugard and his circle in the 1630s: a "Parliamentary-
Puritan" connexion?', *Historical Journal*, 29 (1986), pp. 771–793; A. Hughes, 'Greville, Robert,
second Baron Brooke of Beauchamps Court (1607–1643)', in *ODNB*; D.L. Smith, 'Fiennes,
William, first Viscount Saye and Sele (1582–1662)', in *ODNB*; Gardiner, *History*, IX, pp. 11–12.

my mother went home to day

26. April 1639

I prayed and have bene about my occasions wth some dilligence, I have prayed for my deare wife who is gone to drink wth Mrs danby, wth Mrs Maioresse[690] &.

I have heard this day by my fathers letter that dr Gouge & dr Stoughton have ended the businesse betweene me & Mr Readinge, Lord be praysed for it, good Lord p[ro]vide money for us to pay him for the Lords sake I humbly pray thee.

27° April.

I prayed & went about my occasions, & practise wch I prayse the Lord is much increased I hope Lord give me more abilityes for it dayly & graunt that I may see & acknowledge thee

thee in all thy m[er]cy towards me & mine for the Lords sake.

28° April Sab. [bath]

Mr Newton preached this day both times Mr Ball not beinge yet recovered of his ague.

29° April

I prayed and went to the Court where we had diverse tryalls & we could not end it till about 6 or 7 at night there was Mr Clarke Mr Rainsfford & Mr Paynter Counsellors[691] & Mr Readinge & Mr danby[692] Attourneyes.

its sayd that Perkins the host & vintener at the swan was dead diverse times the last night, he havinge caught a surfeyt wth drinkinge I sate up very late to night to ingrosse a feoffm[en]t [*crossed out:* for] inter Stephen harrington & John Warren of Old, to the use of Richard Yule &.

*****

[690]That is, Richard Fowler's wife, Martha, the executrix of his will in 1649: TNA, PROB/11/208.

[691]John Clarke, Lincoln's Inn bencher, Parliamentarian, and later judge, was lord of the manor of Guilsborough and Dr Samuel Clarke's cousin. Henry Painter was the son of the ecclesiastical lawyer William Painter. He had become wealthy – in 1632 the vestry had assigned seats to him and his close friend William Rushton, the future steward. He was also the trusted confidant of Sir Robert Banastre: Prest, *Barristers*, pp. 334, 351; Bridges, *History of Northamptonshire*, II, p. 567; Longden, *Visitation of Northamptonshire 1681*, pp. 51–55; Metcalfe, *Visitation of Northamptonshire 1618*, p. 70; Vestry Minutes, pp. 28, 32; TNA, PROB/11/285 and PROB/11/179; Fielding, 'Peterborough', pp. 120–121; Jackson, 'Ship money', pp. 66–100.

[692]Daniel Reading and John Danby.

30. April 1639
I prayed and went to Walgrave to Mr Bawds[693] to keepe Court & after
Court I went to Old.
[*crossed out:* 31 April] 1° Maii I lay at Old to night.
I [*crossed out:* pr] went in the morninge & deliverd possession of Stephen
harringtons land to John Warren, Blessed be thy name oh Lord that I
still keepe my fathers inheritance oh my god if it be thy will give it me
still for if any Creditors should call I should be forced to doe the like,
but Lord helpe me to pay my debts wthout the sale of it if it be thy will
that the name of my deare father that bred me thus may not suffer yet
Lord I humbly cast my selfe downe at thy foot & desire to wayt uppon
thy good p[ro]vidence helpe me to doe so patiently & cheerfully for
the Lords sake
I went after to Wellingborow where I heard that Wm Perkins of
North[amp]ton is dead

dead Lord make him an example to me & all others that heare of
it that we may learne moderacon in the use of thy m[er]cyes for the
Lords sake.
I came home safe (though late) I blesse the Lord.
2° Maii 1639
I prayed & went to the lecture where Mr Atterbury preached, Mr
Watts my creditor dyned here
I went to the fun[er]all of Perkins in the afternoone where Mr
Newton preached he was accompanied wth the souldiers having bene
a souldier.
3° Maii
I was wth the B[isho]p of Winchester[694] this morning who is
Lord Eleemosyner,[695] I went afternoon to fflemings where I was
commissioner wth Mr Britten[696] for taking the answere & exam[ini]ng
Wootton men.

4° Maii 1639
I went againe to examine the def[endan]ts ad[ver]s[us] Lady Smithes,

---

[693] Either Ferdinando Baude, or his son William, lords of the manor of Walgrave and
Catholic recusants linked to the Brudenells of Deene: *VCH Northamptonshire*, IV (London,
1937), pp. 218–219; PDR, CB42, fo. 406r–v; M.E. Finch, *The Wealth of Five Northamptonshire
Families 1540–1640*, Publications of the Northamptonshire Record Society XIX (Oxford,
1966), pp. 85n, 91, 95n; Metcalfe, *Visitation of Northamptonshire 1618*, pp. 67–68.
[694] Walter Curll.
[695] Lord High Almoner to Charles I: Woodford was probably rendering his Easter account
to his superior, Curll, as promised at his installation on 14 February 1638/39: Diary, p. 283.
[696] This is a continuation of Lady Smithes's case. Britten might be John Britten of
Wellingborough: PDR, Church Survey Book 5, fo. 133r–v.

Oh lord pay my debts for me in thy due time, litle Johns eyes are much amisse wth Rhewme, but I have prayed unto the Lord for him & for Sam who hath a dangerous cough & for my litle girle who is or hath bene very ill.

5° Maii Sab. [bath]
I desire to draw nere unto god in dutyes & but I am subiect to much dullnesse infidelity & Lord in m[er]cy Looke uppon me & my poore family for the Lords sake
Mr Perkins preached here to day both times very p[ro]fitably, he [crossed out: is] hath supped here & is to lodge wth us to night.

6° Maii
I prayed & went to the Court, and afterwards towards London, goeinge downe the hill beyond grafton [Regis] my horse fell downe with me & he lay uppon my legg in a Rut but the Lord graciously delivered me without hurt

hurt, To thee oh Lord be prayse & glory, thou keepest from dangers & helpest in them blessed be thy good p[ro]vidence oh Lord.
I have often prayed to be delivered from the bond wherein I stand for security for Mr Readinge to Sr John hanbury for 200li, & to be helped in the paym[en]t of the 6oli to Mr Readinge & straights that have much pinched me. I came safe to dunstable where I met wth Mr Bullivant & Mr Burkit at Mr Walkers & wth Mr Steward[697] of Pateshull

7° Maii 1639
I came safe to London I blesse the Lord Mr Steward & Mr Burcot & I came out & broke fast at St Albans, where I first heard of the death of good dr Stoughton who dyed yesterday,[698] & where my Creditor Mr Watts overtooke me & Wm. Spence[r] oh Lord I pray thee that what I feare may not over take me in thy due time deliver me from my bonds & ingagem[en]ts of debt & set me at lib[er]ty if it be thy will in the meane while I kisse the rod & accept the burden sanctifye it to me for the Lords sake; I came to my new chamber in Clem[en]ts Inne and

and I have prayed unto the Lord to blesse me in it & I trust the Lord hath heard me in [crossed out: it] what I have prayed, I am to lodge at my fathers

---

[697]Presumably Miles Burkit's patron, George Steward. Steward and his wife, Ann, were (like Burkit) the subjects of suits in the Court of High Commission. Steward claimed that these were the result of the malice of Sir John Lambe's conformist ally Henry Alleyn: TNA, SP16/434/fos 16r, 125v, 143v, 191v; TNA SP16/434A/fos 11r, 30v, 50v.

[698]According to P.S. Seaver, 'Stoughton, John (bap. 1593, d. 1639)', in ODNB, Stoughton died on 4 May 1639.

8° Maii 1639
I prayed & went to my Chamber, my deare Child Sam is very ill with
an extreame Cough and sniffinge, and I am doubtfull least it should
be a Consumpcon But Lord my god I beseech thee heare & have
m[er]cy heale him if it be thy will he is a sonne of o[u]r poore prayers
let him be so still I humbly beseech thee thou bringest downe to death
& raysest up againe, let not the sinnes of us his parents p[ro]voke thee
to correct us thus if it be thy will Lord p[ar]don o[u]r sinnes & faylings
and sanctifye us throughly for time to come we desire [*crossed out:* him]
humbly to give him unto thee and to submit unto thy disposinge hand
helpe us by fayth & patience to wayt uppon thee Lord I pray thee
blesse me & my family for the Lords sake.
9° Maii
I goe on wth Mr Bacons businesse who is much oppressed by the
malice & violence of wicked men that p[er]secute him Lord I pray
thee sanctifye it unto him, & breake this snare if

it be thy will, thou sittest above & orderest all things Lord looke downe
& ridd him from these vexacous suites if it be thy will
10° Maii 1639
I prayed in the morninge with some meltinge affeccons & fayth the
Lord I trust will spare my child & uphold me in difficultyes & will goe
on to blesse me,
I am desired to goe to the Counsell table wth Mr Bacon, and I am
apt to thinke that dr Sibthorpe will therefore set himselfe against me
& ruine me but Lord I will trust in thee I am in my callinge thou
canst deliver me from the mouth of the Lyon & from the fingers of the
wicked & the violen[t] man oh Lord doe thou safguard me I humbly
pray thee. This businesse is since put off till Sr Rol[an]d St John comes
to towne.[699]
11° Maii I prayd & went about my occasions, I am p[ro]vidinge
br[ev]iates for Mr Bacons cause, my deare child Sarah came to my
fathers to night & is recovered & in p[er]fect health blessed be god
*****

[699] This refers to the Star Chamber hearing of the *Plowright vs. Bacon* ship money dispute,
but it is clear that the Council postponed the case until St John arrived, although he was
not involved in the ship money, only the impressment, case. Indeed, Sibthorpe's letter to
Lambe (dated 16 May) makes it clear that Lambe, to Sibthorpe's chagrin, had abandoned
the ship money case, and it disappears from the records: Temple of Stowe MSS, STT 1885.

12° Maii 1639 Sab.[bath]
I went to dr holdsworths in the morninge, & in the afternoone I heard Sh[e]reife harrisons Chaplaine at dr Stoughtons church,[700] who preached very well.

13° Maii
I pray often to the Lord for my deare wife children & family & to be delivered from my great straights by reason of my debts, Oh my good father heare me if it be thy will of thy grace & bounty for the Lords sake; I payd the Nurse 40s & gave her 2s 6d Sarah went away to day, oh Lord let thy blessinge rest uppon her for the Lords sake.

14° Maii
No newes yet from the North but of

of Warre, oh Lord by thee all warrs are husht and gone, bringe good, even a setled peace to thy poore church out of this Commotio[n] Lord helpe with thy might for the Lords sake.

15° Maii 1639
Oh Lord keepe me in my straights, give me favor in the eyes of my creditors, & lift me up out of the mire & clay in thy due time for the Lords sake, & heale my deare children Sam of his Cough John of his weake & sore eyes & blesse us all sanctifye us for thy selfe

16. Maii
I heare that the Archb[isho]p hath renounced the havinge a hand in bringinge men up to the rayles to receave the sacrament oh Lord thou art able to bringe shame & conf

confusion of face uppon all fauvo[u]r[er]s & p[ro]moters of sup[er]stition & Idolatry Oh Lord set up thine ordinances in their power & [crossed out: illegible letter] purity that we thy poore children may be built up by them growinge in grace & holinesse abundantly; oh that thou [crossed out: who] wouldest please to heare & comannd deliverance for thy poore church

17° Maii 1639
Mr Bacons cause at the Counsell table was heard to day & Plowright the p[er]secuter is to be imprisoned in the gate house & to make submission to Sr Roland St John at thassizes & to pay some chardges to Mr Bacon.

---

[700] The identity of Sheriff Sir Gilbert Harrison's chaplain is elusive. Both Stoughton and Edward Chetwind (the Dean of Bristol, who died the next day, 13 May 1639) had been his clients: Seaver, 'Stoughton, John'; J.M. Rigg, 'Chetwynd, Edward (1576/7–1639)', rev. V. Larminie, in ODNB; A.B. Beaven, The Aldermen of the City of London, 2 vols (London, 1908–1913), II, pp. 63–65.

18° Maii
Mr Collis dyed as yesterday or this day as I heard I think.

19° Maii 1639 Sab.[bath]
my father & I went over to hackney[701] this day & heard Mr Goodwyn of
Colemanstreet both times who preached p[ro]fitably, I went & came
wth Mr Everet nere B[isho]ps gate & another honest man we had
good discourse on the way concerninge the Church of god [crossed out:
two letters, illegible] the Lord will surely looke uppon his poore church in
the end, when his church is fit for deliverance & when ungodly men
have filled up the measure of their sinnes
20° Maii
greatly afflicted wth ([crossed out, illegible]) oh my god let thy grace I
pray thee be sufficient for me, heale the fountayne of sinne that is
ready to buble up continually dry it up I pray thee, let me live to thee
forever for the Lords sake.

21° Maii 1639
I am oft troubled to thinke that I shall be much put to it for want of
moneyes [crossed out: to fa] about my callinge & occasions this tearme
but the Lord hath helped me in many straights formerly & will still
be gracious for his names sake, oh thou the great & allsuffic[ien]t god
possessor of heaven & earth uphold & supply me graciously for the
Lords sake
[crossed out: eclipse]
22° Maii 1639
This day there was an eclipse of the sunne about 4 & 5 a clock in the
afternoone oh Lord suffer not thy glorious gospell so to be eclipsed but
[crossed out: let] that it may breake forth againe in beauty & excellency
for the Lords sake.
23° Maii Ascencon day[702]
I went this day to a stationers to buy p[ar]chm[en]t, to make writts,
where I used to

to buy but the M[aste]r desired me to forbeare for he durst not sell
me any I told him he need not so scruple it for it was not sabath day,
he said no were it Sab.[bath] day he might doe it wthout danger but
if to day he should be called in question oh Lord I pray thee establish
& countenance thy Sabaths amongst us, & [crossed out: give] so order

---

[701] A suburb where the godly divine Calybute Downing was the incumbent: B. Donagan,
'Downing, Calybute (1606–1644)', in ODNB.
[702] According to Ramsden, James Cranford delivered the Thursday lecture at Northampton
on this day: TNA, SP16/474/80.

that we may have lib[er]ty to worke the 6. days Lord reforme what ever is amisse amongst us for the Lords sake.

24° Maii 1639
I pray to the Lord to be pr[e]pared to pay Mr Readinge & be d[e]l[ive]r[e]d from Sr John hanburyes bond.

25° Maii
This day my father & I borowed of Mr Perke 60li & p[ai]d it for Mr Readinge at Sr John hanburyes in the afternoone & there I rec[eive]d

receaved the bond wherein I was bound wth him to Sr John hanbury & pulled my seale from it, oh my god blessed be thy name that these two great businesses & feares are determined in one day blessed be thy name for hearinge [*crossed out:* my] o[u]r poore prayers deliver me still from my wants & feares if it be thy will

26° Maii 1639 Sab.[bath]
I heard Mr Cranford both times at Bowe Church in Cheape side,[703] who preached faythfully, Lord blesse thine ordinances to me for the lords sake

27° Maii
Tearme ended this day and so shall the tearme of my life when I have bene in action in the world so long as the Lord appoynts oh

oh Lord fit me for eternitye oh lord assure me of thy Love & favor & give me to walk as he that doth enioy thee make me even as holy I pray thee if my mortallity will beare it as an angell of light, oh helpe me to be above the creature, above smooth pleasures & the thorny cares of this pr[e]sent life for the Lords sake.

28° Maii 1639
I have now at two severall times this tearme rec[eive]d of Mr Bacon 5li—4s but one peice wanted 18d.
I p[ai]d Mr Tourney 20s Mr Gregg 10s. Lord be blessed for supplyeinge graciously. I left Mr Tapper 10s in p[ar]te of this tearme all the rest p[ai]d before.

29° I prayed and came forth early dyned at dunstable & came home to North[amp]ton & found my family well blessed be god & Johns eyes very well recovered againe

blessed be god. I came home about 8. a clock very weary.

30° Maii 1639
I prayed & went to Grafton [Regis] Court where I gayned litle or nothinge.

---

[703] Cranford was preaching at St Mary le Bow, whose vicar was Jeremy Leech: R. Newcourt, *Repertorium Ecclesiasticum Parochiale Londinense*, 2 vols (London, 1708–1710), I, p. 440.

31° Maii
[*crossed out:* Mr Martin Mr Rushworth & ux & Mr [*illegible*] supped here with us to night], the newes uncertayne from Scotland, Lord create a holy & good peace betweene the two nacons if it be thy will, for the comfort of thy church
1° Junii
[*crossed out:* Mr] I prayed and went about my occasions,

2° Junii 1639 Sab[bath] Sac:[rament]
I prayed & went to heare the word & to rec[eive] the sacram[en]t. Lord p[ar]don our unfittinge of o[u]r selves, o[u]r passion o[u]r Idlenes o[u]r deadnesse & dullnesse oh the [*crossed out:* h] 7. abominacons[704] that are in my soule oh the denne of dragons that harbor in me oh the multitude of locusts that swarme in my hart! helpe from heaven oh my god thou most holy & omnipotent god p[ar]don & heale remove from thy pr[e]sence & from my affeccons my sinnes for the Lords sake.
This day I prayed unto the Lord for my poore child John who is in great misery & danger wth his eyes, & I recorded the prayer in the end of the booke[705]
3° Junii
I am greatly subiect to deadnes & coldnesse in dutye oh Lord quicken me
4° Junii
I have prayed for my deare wife & family for my poore child; we are apt to fall out wth o[u]r servants who are apt to be negligent & to displease us & to answere againe but lord p[ar]don the rebellions ag[ains]t thee wch thou mightest call us to account for and give me grace to lay to hart & to be humbled for all my stubornesse & Idlenesse in my Masters service, thou art a iust god yet spare me for thy m[er]cyes sake.
5° Junii
I prayed and went to Wellingborowe ffare with Mr Smart & I came home at night safe againe blessed be god.
6° Junii
Mr Martin Mr Rushworth & ux supped wth us to night & Mr Rogers Mr Ball preached to day
*****

[704] Proverbs 6:16–19.
[705] See p. 401, additional diary entry dated 2 June 1639.

7° Junii 1639
I prayed to be enabled for keepinge the Sess[ions][706] Gaole d[e]l[ive]ry
& leet this day & the Lord did graciously carry me through the worke
blessed be thy name oh Lord.
8° Junii
I prayed & went about my occasions the Lord still sends me
imploym[en]t graciously
9° Junii Sab.[bath]
I was this day at St Sepulchres church wth Mr Maior & the Bayleifes[707]
to heare one Thorne[708] a new vicar there, but it appeares by his sermon
what he is, Lord weed up the darnell & the Cockle[709] that the wheate
may grow & be very fruitfull.
10° Junii
I am pr[e]paringe Mr Watts & their answere ad[ver]s[us]

ad[ver]s[us] Temple[710] & I pray to be directed, the Lord onely gives
abilityes
11° Junii 1639
Sessions here to day, but I have bene busy at home in p[er]fectinge
the answere, my uncle Wale[711] my mother & dyned here, my tenant
brought me 23 hundred Coles in a Load.
12° Junii
I was busy still about the same answere; The Lord hath now graciously
cured my childs eyes so that there is no [*crossed out:* paine] web or

---

[706]The town's sessions not the county's.

[707]Richard Fowler, Henry Hill, and John Cole.

[708]Previously a protégé of Bishop John Williams, Giles Thorne had been ejected from
Oxford in 1631 by William Laud himself after preaching against altars. He seems to have
changed sides and by 1639 was Sir John Lambe's appointee as vicar of St Sepulchre's
parish, Northampton, but retained the living only until 1640. He was later ejected from
a Bedfordshire living as a maintainer of the Book of Sports but was restored after 1660,
awarded a doctorate, and declared in his will that he had lived 'and will dye in the truly
ancient Catholick and Apostolick [. . .] Church of England'. Henry Storke, one of Thorne's
students at Oxford, wrote to Lambe in 1640 acknowledging his generosity to Thorne and
asking for the living of St Giles: Longden, *Clergy*; Longden MS, 7 June 1639; C. Hill, *A
Turbulent, Seditious, and Factious People: John Bunyan and his church 1628-1688* (Oxford, 1988),
p. 26; R.M. Serjeantson, *A History of the Church of St Giles, Northampton* (Northampton, 1911),
p. 54; K. Fincham and N. Tyacke, *Altars Restored: the changing face of English religious worship,
1547-c. 1700* (Oxford, 2007), pp. 185, 186 n. 43.

[709]Harmful weeds growing in corn fields.

[710]The godly John Temple of Frankton, Warwickshire, a strenuous opponent of court
policy, connected by kinship to Viscount Saye and Sele and by political affiliation to both
Saye and Lord Brooke; also a future Parliamentarian captain: A. Hughes, *Politics, Society, and
Civil War: Warwickshire, 1620-1660* (Cambridge, 1987), pp. 54, 97, 103, 109, 113, 153.

[711]Uncle Wale was a widower: Woodford heard of the death of his wife, Woodford's aunt
Margaret, on 9 November 1638.

pearle[712] in them & but litle sorenesse, blessed be thy name oh Lord
Lord continue it to thy glory & make me truly thankfull
13° Junii
I prayed & went alonge wth Mr Watts to

to [*crossed out:* Cran] Brockhole & daventry to have met wth a
Comm[i]ssion[e]r or two to have put in the answere but they fayled
to meet so I went to Long Buckby where [*crossed out:* they] Mr Bacon
used me kindly. I sent to xxofer[713] Meadcroft executor of Amye henman
p[ro] obad[iah] Wallop.
14° Junii 1639
xxofer Meadcroft came over this morninge & p[ai]d me the 3li for
obad[iah] Wallop[714] wch doth stead me in my pr[e]sent necessity I
came home safe to my deare wife we supped at Mr Sam. Martins.
15° Junii
my neighbors of Old brought me home this day 4 loads of Wood
from Mausley wood & I dyned them, blessed be god for the good
p[ro]vision of fewell I have
Sr John hanburyes corpse came through the towne to day; oh Lord I
blesse thee that I was delivered out of the bond before he dyed.

16° Junii Sab.[bath] 1639.
Mr Newton preached in the morninge & Mr Ball in the afternoone.
17° Junii
I prayed and went to the Court, where I had some supply I blesse
the Lord afterward assined the Leete booke & dyned wth Mr Maior[715]
Mr ffisher Mr Knight Mr Woollaston Mr Readinge Mr danby & at
Crutchleyes.
18° Junii
I prayed and went to Sr John Ishams to take the fine from Stephen
harr[ington] & his wife to John Warren, & came safe home I blesse
the Lord.
19° Junii
I prayed with my deere wife, with my family & in secret & came out
of North[amp]ton this morninge for London about 5. a clock in

in the morninge & before I came at Stratford I overtooke Mr Butler
& Mr Ashton goeinge tow[a]rd London & afterwards Sr Arthur

---

[712]Thin, white, opaque growth over the eye like a cataract.
[713]Christopher.
[714]Woodford had passed this money to Wallop by 30 November 1639: *Diary*, p. 334.
[715]Richard Fowler.

haslerigge,[716] so I had company inough to London I prayse the Lord
& came thether about 8. a clock at night very weary & sore by reason
of my trotting horse

nere St Albans I met with Mr Whalley & Mr Spice[r] who informed
me of the welcome newes of peace with Scotland[717] at which I was
much affected even to teares to see gods great m[er]cy blessed be thy
name oh Lord.

20. Junii 1639
I prayed and went forth wth Mr Watts and I am somewhat ill & sore &
distemp[er]ed in body & which much troubles me I feare I shall want
money for my occasions this tearme but oh my god how easily canst
thou supply me both the Judges are thine the cattell uppon a thousand
mountaynes[718] surely I will trust in that god who hath allwayes helped
me hetherto lay not my former p[ro]fusenes & indiligence in my
callinge to my chardge but p[ar]don & doe good to me thy poore
s[er]v[an]t & my family for the Lords sake.

21° Junii 1639
The good newes of peace with Scotland & much Love from the Kinge
to them is still confirmed, oh Lord my god I blesse & prayse thy name
for it, oh Lord give thy church & people dayly more & more grace
in the eyes of his Ma[jes]ty let his eares be open to their peticons &
his hand ever ready to helpe them, but make him to frowne uppon
the wicked and such as have evill will at Sion & would hinder the
building of thy temple amongst us, oh that thy light might breake
forth & that the bright shinninge thereof might [*crossed out:* might]
shame & confound all opposers, powre out uppon thy servants the
spirit of fervent prayer & unwearied supplicacon, that thou [*crossed out:*
might] mayest delight to heare & answere us in

in m[er]cye graunt these for the Lord Xt his sake

---

[716]Sir Arthur Haselrig was based in Leicestershire but was also lord of the manor of
Alderton, Northamptonshire. Through his Greville marriage he was associated with the
puritan Saye–Pym–Knightley group's opposition to the royal policies of the 1630s and with
their colonial ventures. He was one of the Five Members, a Parliamentarian officer, and
ultimately a regicide. His chaplain at this time was Samuel Fisher, the son of Woodford's
friend John Fisher: C. Durston, 'Hesilrige, Sir Arthur, second baronet (1601–1661)', in *ODNB*;
S. Villani, 'Fisher, Samuel (bap. 1604, d. 1665)', in *ODNB*; Bridges, *History of Northamptonshire*,
II, pp. 281–282.
[717]This refers to the Truce of Berwick (18 June 1639) concluding the First Bishops' War.
The king agreed to a meeting of the Scottish Assembly and Parliament, and both armies
agreed to disband: B. Coward, *The Stuart Age: England 1603–1714* (London, 2003), pp. 180,
520.
[718]Psalm 50:10.

this morninge (as I rem[ember]) I had great discourse with Nich Tew[719] & 2 or 3. others [*crossed out:* whereof] beinge all unlesse one of them sep[ar]atists or greatly inclininge, my hart doth much hate or distrust the antichristian power that is amongst us and vayne ceremonyes & some weake rudim[en]ts yet why I should sep[ar]ate because of some imp[er]feccons I am not yet wholly convinced oh Lord enlighten me thy poore servant for the Lords sake, And lord I pray thee purge thy floore blowe away the chaffe that is amongst o[u]r doctrine & in o[u]r discipline let pop[er]y & Arminianisme hide them selfe reforme what ever is amisse, looke uppon the imprisonm[en]ts of thy servants formerly & at this day & uppon all their sufferings & uppon all their prayers & vouchsafe to heare in m[er]cy for the Lords sake. I

I had hot dispute wth Anthony in St dunstans Churchyard ag[ains]t Arminianisme, I had great comforts in duty at night to teares & I have prayed for my deare child Sam.
22° Junii 1639
I prayed & went about my occasions
Lord let it goe well with thy church & people confound the plots of wicked & sup[er]stitious men & set up thine ordinances in lustre & purity.
This day the kings counsell wa[i]ved day till Tuesday to answere about the ha[beas] cor[pus] p[ro] the London[e]rs[720]
23° Junii Sab.[bath]
Mr Calamy preached admirably in the morninge uppon the 51°. ps[alm].17 the sacrific[es][721] the Lord was pleased to affect me in some gracious measure.

[719]Nicholas Tew was a London radical who was arrested in 1644 for publishing works by John Lilburne and William Walwyn. He was a General Baptist and later a Leveller: A. Sharp, 'Lilburne, John (1615?-1657)', in *ODNB*; B.J. Gibbons, 'Overton, Richard (*fl.* 1640-1663)', in *ODNB*.

[720]See also Diary, p. 314. This is probably the case of the London merchant Richard Chambers, and others, who had in 1629 led opposition to the payment of tonnage and poundage. In 1636 he had commenced an action in King's Bench against Sir Edward Bromfield who, as Mayor of London, had jailed him for his refusal to pay ship money. The judges had not permitted the issue of its legality to be raised. Nevertheless, the case seems to have continued, as Woodford's comments demonstrate. Gardiner describes the ongoing case a year later in June 1640, when Sir Robert Heath was acting for Bromfield: Jones, *Bench*, pp. 76–77, 88, 123; Gardiner, *History*, IX, p. 161; *CSPD*, 1640, pp. 307–309, 335.

[721]'The sacrifices of God are a broken spirit: a broken and a contrite heart, O God, thou wilt not despise.' Edmund Calamy was elected to succeed John Stoughton as perpetual curate of St Mary Aldermanbury in May 1639 on the latter's death. A client of Robert Rich, Earl of Warwick, and a famous puritan divine who had left the diocese of Norwich after pressure from its Arminian bishop, Matthew Wren, Calamy was admitted to St Mary's on 26 October 1639, although it is clear that he was already preaching there on a probationary basis (see also Diary, p. 315): S. Achinstein, 'Calamy, Edmund (1600-1666)', in *ODNB*.

a stranger preached in the afternoone
24° Junii 1639 Midsom day.
I prayed & followed my occasions, & the Lord is pleased to make my Chamberfellowe[722] a great helpe to me in my affayres blessed be thy name oh Lord
25° Junii
This day I exchanged the fr[ench] history plut[arch's] lives & the imp[er]iall history for L[or]d Cookes entryes[723] wth Anthony.
This day the Londoners beinge Prisoners for not paying ship-money were brought to the K[ing's] Bench barre wth expectacon of w[ha]t the Kings Counsell would say ag[ains]t their baylinge, so havinge nothing to say they were bayled.
Oh Lord turne the streame of things for the Lords sake, oh Let thy lawe & o[u]r good lawes fflourish amongst us.
26. Junii
men & horses come dayly out of the

Scotland, Lord thou hast turned againe the Rivers in the North hast dryed up the [*crossed out, illegible*] waters of many people, Lord confirme & sanctifye this peace unto us let it be of moment, a meanes to advance thy gospell & to disappoynt Antixt[724] & his cursed adherents for the Lords sake
27° Junii 1639
The Lord hath in some measure graciously recovered my Child Sam of his lamenesse. Lord sanctifye it unto us, & sanctifye us all to thy selfe for the Lords sake.
28° Junii
I have had bills this tearme come from Mr fflood & Mr Ricroft Lord I pray thee helpe me to pay all my debts in thy due time, both the Judges are thine Thou dost still uphold me blessed be thy name &

& thou commanndest my creditors to have patience Lord uphold me still & supply me graciously for the Lords sake.

---

[722] Stephen Harvey.
[723] Woodford gained a useful professional handbook: *A Booke of Entries: Containing Perfect and Approved Presidents of Courts, Declarations, Informations, Pleints, Inditements, Barres [. . .]* (London, 1614), which included a preface by Sir Edward Coke. For this he exchanged Plutarch's *Parallel Lives* and two other works whose identities are less clear. Possible candidates are: STC 11273, P. de Comines, *An Epitome of All the Lives of the Kings of France* (London, 1639) and STC 23525.7, N. C., *The German History Continued. The seventh part [of the Swedish Intelligencer]* (London, 1634) or an earlier number in this series.
[724] Antichrist.

29° Junii 1639
St Peters day. Lord I pray thee bringe things about so in thy due time that it may be lawfull [*crossed out, illegible*] by mans law also to worke uppon the Six dayes, & not to p[ro]phane the Seaventh
30° Junii 1639 Sab.[bath]
Mr Calamy preached excellently in the morninge at Aldermanbury Church & a stranger in the afternoone Lord setle & confirme[725] Mr Calamy there if it be thy will & make him a speciall instrument of thy glory for the Lords sake

1° Julii 1639
I prayed & went about my occasions in which the Lord is pleased to give me successe & to blesse me.
2° Julii
I am imployed about a businesse of Sr xxofer[726] yelvertons this tearme by Mr Watts his meanes Lord give me still more & more favor in their eyes if thou seest good
3° Julii
The tearme ends this day. I pray to be carryed home safely.
4° Julii
I have payd 14li for goodman houghton to Mr dent & Mr Baud which Mr Watts sent me.
I came out of the towne in the afternoone &

& met on the way wth Mr Massingbergh[727] & his brother, & with a very wild gent & we came to Mr Walkers at St Albans but before I met wth them I went to see my sweet Child Sarah at Nurse [*crossed out: in the forest*] neare Edmunton in Enfeild Chase & left her very well I blesse the Lord blessed be thy name oh Lord that thou art pleased to watch over me & my family Lord continue o[u]r healths to thy glory for the Lords sake.
5° Julii 1639
I had much discourse wth the gent & often intreated him to leave his swearinge, Lord convert him unto thee if it be thy will for the Lords sake.
I came home safe I prayse the Lord & found my wife & family well the Lord be blessed for it.

[725]Calamy was preaching on a temporary basis, pending final approval by the parish: *Diary*, p. 313. He was formally admitted in October: Achinstein, 'Calamy, Edmund'.
[726]Christopher.
[727]Richard Massingberd served as bailiff of Northampton in 1654, chamberlain from 1660 until 1661, and mayor in 1667; his brother has not been identified: Markham and Cox, *Northampton*, II, pp. 562, 568, 553.

6° Julii
diverse to speake wth me this day, oh Lord

I blesse thee that thou hast placed me in an honest callinge hast
given me some abilityes for it, & imploym[en]t in it, lord increase my
abilityes & practise dayly if it be thy will to thy glory for the Lords sake
7° Julii 1639 Sab.[bath] sacr.[ament]
Mr Ball preached in the morninge Mr Newton in the afternoone, I
did desire to draw neare to the Lord this day in the word sacram[en]t
& prayer, Lord p[ar]don my faylings & accept my weake desires for
the Lords sake.
8° Julii
I prayed & went to the Court, some gracious supply there I blesse the
Lord Lord let me pay my debts in thy due time I pray thee for the
Lords sake

9° Julii 1639
I prayed and went to Oxford wth Mr Watts about Sr xxofer[728]
Yelvertons businesse wth Mr hide & the Keats[729] & Christ Church.[730]
we came thether about 2 a clock the act ended this day.
we called at Kirtlington
10° Julii
This place here is p[ro]digiously p[ro]fane I p[er]ceave for
drunkennesse swearinge & other debauched Courses, stage playes
& Lord reforme these seminaryes if it be thy will for the Lords sake.
11° Julii
we could not dispatch o[u]r businesse as we hoped, I heard a latin
sermon in St Maryes.[731] I was in the library[732] &
*****

---

[728]Christopher.

[729]Hide is possibly Edward Hide, a rich Warwickshire attorney. John and Jerome Keyte
were brothers. John was a Gray's Inn barrister, an Oxford graduate who lived in the town:
C.W. Brooks, *Pettyfoggers and Vipers of the Commonwealth: the 'lower branch' of the legal profession in
early modern England* (Cambridge, 1986), p. 258; Prest, *Barristers*, p. 336.

[730]On 28 October 1639 the Dean and Chapter of Christ Church, Oxford, the owners
of the rectory of Sir Christopher Yelverton's parish of Easton Maudit, appealed to Lord
Keeper Thomas Coventry to subpoena Yelverton in Chancery for ruining the rectory:
British Library, Add. MSS 14,030, fo. 181v; Bridges, *History of Northamptonshire*, IV, p. 17.

[731]St Mary's is the university church. It is not known who preached this latin sermon, but
Oriel College owned the advowson and one Henry Eccleston (a fellow) served as vicar from
some time during 1639 until 1646. I am grateful to Anna Petre of the University Archives
for this reference: G.C. Richards and C.L. Shadwell, *The Provost and Fellows of Oriel College,
Oxford* (Oxford, 1922); N. Tyacke, *Anti-Calvinists: the rise of English Arminianism c. 1590–1640*
(Oxford, 1987), p. 33.

[732]The Bodleian Library.

12° Julii 1639
we sealled [*crossed out, illegible*] the writings to day, & in the afternoone
betweene 3 & 4 a clock Mr Blomely & Sam & I came forth and I
came to North[amp]ton this night presently after 9 Mr Blomeley lost
me about Toucester & his way too, blessed be thy name oh Lord for
bringinge me safe home, I met wth Langley & Mr Ball of Whitmore[733]
at oxford townesend.

13° Julii
my horse growne very lame with my Journey.
my child John in my absence had a sparke fell into the Corner of his
left eye, & the eye so swelled that it was much doubted whether it were
not out but the lord pr[e]served it & hath in a great measure healed it
blessed be thy name oh Lord.

14° Julii Sab[bath]
Mr Ball preached both times & I was

graciously affected especially in the morninge sermon, & in prayer
after I came from church blessed be thy name oh Lord for the Messiah
thou hast sent to redeeme thy church, & for the holy spirit thou
hast likewise sent to comfort thy people blessed yea thrice blessed
be thy name that thou hast made me thy poore creature in any sort
acquain[ted] wth these things.

15° Julii 1639
I had a good p[ro]fitable Court to day blessed be god

16° Julii
I prayed & went about my occasions

17° Julii
The Judges vizt Lord Chefe Baron davenport & Judge Berkley

18° Julii 1639
I prayed & went abroad & at dinner I went wth Mr Bagshawe & ux
& Rich Ward[734] to acknowledge a fine to my Clyent John Lad before
Justice Berkley.
Mr Pentlowe lodges here to night.

---

[733] John Ball was the minister of Whitmore in the parish of Stoke-on-Trent, Staffordshire.
He enjoyed Northamptonshire connections to John Dod and his patron, Richard Knightley
of Fawsley, and was a key player in the ecclesiological debates of the 1630s. He was perhaps in
Oxford to attend the University's Act: J. Sutton, 'Ball, John (1585–1640)', in *ODNB*; Webster,
Godly Clergy, passim.
[734] Ward was bailiff of the town by 1681: Longden, *Visitation of Northamptonshire 1681*, p. 153.

19° Julii

at dinner againe, one Steffe & ux acknowledged a fine to my Clyent Wm hills of Walgrave[735] blessed be thy name oh Lord for the practise thou art pleased to send me, thou hearest prayers blessed be thy name.

20° Julii

The Judges went out of towne to day. 2 condem'd blessed be thy name oh Lord who hast moved the Justices of peace to [crossed out: shew] ioyne together & unanimously to shew their dislike of the B[isho]ps base articles that are come out for the visitac[ion][736] here on Tuesday next Lord throw downe pop[er]y & all sup[er]stition in thy due time for the Lords sake.

21° Julii 1639 Sab.[bath]

Mr. [entry blank]

22° Julii

The Lord continues to supply me graciously at the Court still I blesse his name.

23° Julii The Bps visitacon here to day & a frothy sermon[737] Lord amend things amisse & visit these visitors & reforme all

---

[735]Hills had been elected churchwarden of his parish in 1635: PDR, X639–642/8, unfoliated, under Rothwell deanery. Steffe might be Richard Steph of Wollaston, who occurred at musters there from 1605 until 1612: J. Wake (ed.), *The Montagu Musters Book 1602–1623*, Publications of the Northamptonshire Record Society VII (Northampton, 1935), pp. 12, 122.

[736]The articles mentioned here are those of the new bishop, John Towers, and they are being circulated in advance of his primary visitation of Peterborough diocese. The justices' petition to the bishop survives in the papers of Deputy Lieutenant Sir Rowland St John, who was probably instrumental in its composition. (Two earlier protests, originating at the assizes of 1629 and 1633 and probably drafted by St John, had complained to Lord Lieutenant William Cecil, the Earl of Exeter, of previous bishops' taxing the parishes to provide hoods for their ministers.) The 1639 document requests the bishop to moderate some of his 'very strict and unusual' articles and not to 'presse new things to be practised in the worship and service of God wch are not enjoyned by the Rubrick and Canons of the church of England'. Towers's articles were ultra-Laudian and anti-puritan. The priest was to administer the communion from within the rails of an east end railed altar only to communicants who received at the rails kneeling. Towers insisted on strict ceremonial conformity, the necessity of auricular confession, and the Church's power of absolution. However, Woodford's depiction of the protest of the justices of the peace as unanimous was disingenuous; the issue split the bench. The two justices delegated to present the grievances to Towers were Sibthorpe and Clarke: St John claimed that there were 'arguments that were contraverted betwixt Dr Clark and Sir Miles Fleetwood concerning some of the particular Articles, wch was drawn on by Dr Clark': BRO, St John (Bletso) MSS, DDJ 1361 (quotations), 1323, 1331; K. Fincham and N. Tyacke, *Altars Restored: the changing face of English religious worship, 1547–c. 1700* (Oxford, 2007), pp. 240–241, 250–253; J. Fielding, 'Towers, John (d. 1649)', in *ODNB*; Fielding, 'Peterborough', pp. 93–134.

[737]Towers's primary visitation at Northampton lasted for two days. The consecration ceremony had taken place at Lambeth on 13 January, when the rabidly Laudian Peter Heylin had attacked 'popular prelates' such as John Williams and Joseph Hall who threatened the

I prayed and went along wth hatton to Coventry to take a fine before the Judge to Mr Pentlowe from Mrs Child Mr Prat & ux. I came safe thether, but Mr Prat & his wife disagreed. I spake wth the Maior of Coventry about the businesse I was imployed in from Mr Maior here but could not pr[e]vayle by reason of mistake in the bond sent & want of a letter of Attourney to receive the 40li[738]

24° Julii

I lay at the Starre to night, This morninge poore

poore Mrs Prat was fayne to abate [*crossed out:* the]10li her husband had p[ro]mised her, & then they acknowledged the fine before Justice Berkley. afterward we came home safe & in due time I blesse the Lord I heare there was a most wicked raylinge sermon here to day the second day of the visitacon, oh Lord I beseech thee appeare for the manifestacon of truth & for the good of thy children, make no Long tarryeinge, oh let thy seasonable m[er]cye pr[e]vent us, for the Lords sake

25° Julii 1639 St James fare[739]

I prayed & after dinner went downe to the fare with my wife & we went to Mr Parker wth Mr Whalley & reteyned him in the busines inter White & Mr Cawdrey & Mr Whalley.

26 Julii

I prayed & went about my occasions.

27° Julii

good newes out of Germany blessed be god of victorious conquests by the p[ro]testants.[740]

*****

Church by failing to exert proper control over the godly. It is not known who delivered the two Northampton sermons, which were, judging from Woodford's reaction, equally aggressive in their Laudianism: K. Fincham and P. Lake, 'Popularity, prelacy, and puritanism in the 1630s: Joseph Hall explains himself', *English Historical Review*, 111 (1996), pp. 876n, 877.

[738] The Mayor of Coventry was Thomas Forest (Diary, p. 253), the Mayor of Northampton was Richard Fowler, and the matter under discussion was probably Wheatley's charity: *ibid.*, p. 254.

[739] An important annual fair held on land near the west gate of the town formerly owned by St James's Abbey: Markham and Cox, *Northampton*, II, pp. 187–188.

[740] Presumably the success enjoyed by the partnership of the Elector Palatine and Bernhard of Weimar, who crossed the Rhine at the head of an army but who died on 28 June: Gardiner, *History*, IX, p. 57.

28° Julii 1639 Sab.[bath]
[*crossed out:* Mr] Oh Lord I blesse thee for the continuance of thine ordinances Lord make them fruitfull unto us for the Lords sake.
29° Julii
Court here to day & the Lord doth graciously carry me through my imployment.
30° Julii
I am in trouble often by reason of my debts but the Lord is possessor of heaven & earth the allmighty god is my father who maynteynes all the world oh Lord I will trust in thee.
31° Julii
Oh Lord graunt that it may goe well wth thy Church here & in Scotland & all places; that thou mayst get thy selfe a name;
I stayed this day from Wellingborow to

to p[er]fect & seale the writings betweene Mr White Mr Cawdrey & Mr Whalley but Mr Sillesby who was to ioyne in them came not home.
1° Aug. 1639
This day I sealled [*crossed out, illegible*] the writings & delivered possession, blessed be thy name oh Lord for the practise I find & for my abilityes for it.
2° Aug.
Blessed be thy name oh Lord for my seasonable supplyes & for my recovery from my melancholly.
3° Aug.
the Lord is pleased still to uphold me in

difficultyes & to blesse me in my way blessed be thy name oh Lord
4° Aug. 1639 Sab.[bath]
sacram[en]t to day. I prayed to the Lord for a blessinge uppon it, Lord heare my weake prayers.
5° Aug.
Court to day, the last before the vaccacon,
6° Aug.
The Lord is grac[iously] pleased to send me imploym[en]t in my callinge blessed be thy name oh Lord
7° Aug.
my debts come oft in my minde but Lord

Lord rebuke the Cares of the world & send me supply for the Lords sake

8° Aug. 1639
This day Mr danby is elected Maior & one Mr Bryan & Edward
Cowper Bayleifes,[741] oh Lord blesse the governement of this towne
make us instruments of thy glory for the Lords sake.
9° Aug.
much discourse about the eleccon yesterday.
[crossed out: Mr]
10° Aug.
invited this day to dyne wth Mr Bacon on Munday,

11° Aug. 1639 Sab.[bath]
The Lord is grac[ious] to us in continuing his ordinances in their
power in a grac[ious] manner, oh Lord establish them to us & o[u]r
posterity for ever.
12° Aug.
I prayed & went to [Long] Buckby & there dined wth Mr Bacon, &
others who were there, & came home safe againe I blesse the Lord.
[crossed out: I went to seale writings at]
13° Aug.[742]
I often pray for my deare wife who is nere her time, & feares that Mrs
Parsons [crossed out: will] the midwife will be fetched away before we
shall use her.
my wife was very ill to day.

14° Aug. 1639
I prayed & went to Wellingborow though litle the better in resp[ec]t
of practise but the Lord is allsufficient
15° Aug.
Mrs Parsons is here, but my wife is pretty well & doub[t]full she shall
stay till the midwife be gone, but Lord we desire to wayte uppon thee
forever.
16° Aug.
This day my deare wife brought to bed of another girle betweene 8
& 9 at night, the Lord graciously ordered all Conveniences, Blessed
be thy name oh Lord for upholdinge my deare wife & my selfe & for
shewinge m[er]cy unto us, oh Lord
*****

[741]John Danby and Edward Cooper. John Bryan, esquire, was allotted John Reading's
seat in the church of All Saints' in 1637 and was made free of the borough in 1639: Vestry
Minutes, p. 33; Book of Orders, p. 53.
[742]See p. 400, additional entry dated 13 August 1639.

make the Child an instrument of thy glory & a vessell of m[er]cye & a
comfort to us the parents & feed us & cloath us all for the Lords sake
[*crossed out:* see the prayer in the latter end of the booke.][743]
17° Aug. 1639
Mrs Parsons was sent for away this morninge & is gone, blessed be
thy name oh Lord for orderinge all things so graciously in thy good
p[ro]vidence
18° Aug. Sab.[bath]
Blessed be thy name oh Lord for the sweetnesse that is in thy word
& for thy blessinge uppon me & mine for addinge to my family &
feedinge of us Lord doe us good still spiritually & corporally for the
Lords sake.

19° Aug. 1639
I had occasion about Mr Watts his businesse to day & ingrossing
p[ar]te of the deed p[ro] Mrs Bussy[744] from Mr Spencer;
20° Aug.
I prayed & went to Wilby to execute the deed from Mr Spencer to
Mrs Bussy & delivered poss[essio]n to Mr Pearne Attourney p[ro]
Mrs Bussy I have p[ro]cured Mr Perne to preach at the baptizing of
my Child.
21° Aug.
I prayed & went to Wellingborow & p[ro]cured Mrs Susan Pentlowe
& Mrs Anne Coles[745] to be witnesses to my

Child on Tuesday next.
22° Aug. 1639
in the afternoone I went toward Lutterworth about the Commission
concerninge Mr Watts, who came to me at Thorneby & we went
to Lutt[er]w[or]th togeth[er] where wee found Mr Cranford & Mr
Pentlow o[u]r Commissioners, & sate up late.

[743]See p. 401, additional entry dated 16 August 1639.
[744]Elizabeth Harvey, the daughter of Sir Gerard Harvey of Bedfordshire, had married
Cecil Bussy, the son and heir of Andrew Bussy of Cheshunt, Hertfordshire. Bussy had been
buried at Harvey's parish of Cardington, Bedfordshire, in 1632. This Mrs Bussy perhaps
belonged to the same family: *VCH Bedfordshire*, III (London, 1912), p. 237; F.A. Blaydes,
The Visitations of Bedfordshire 1566, 1582, and 1634, Harleian Society Publications, XIX (1884),
p. 116.
[745]The daughters of Thomas Pentlow of Wilby and George Coles of Northampton
respectively: TNA, PROB/11/263 and PROB/11/185.

23° Aug.

Mr Temples commission[e]rs vizt Mr Sprig & Mr More[746] came in the morninge. we were at goodwife youngs house.

24° Aug.

the Commission is adiourned by their Com[missioners]

Comm[issione]rs to Banbury on Tuesday Sevenight red Lyon.

I came home safe I blesse the Lord

25° Aug 1639 Sab.[bath]

Mr Ball preached both times very p[ro]fitably uppon the Cov[enan]t of workes & Cov[enan]t of grace.

26° Aug.

I sent to one Mr Eakins of Chester[747] to be witnesse to morow but he was not at home.

27° Aug.

I sent to him againe this morninge who came willingly, and Mr Perne preached very p[ro]fitably blessed be thy name

name oh Lord, and we agreed to have the child named Susannah havinge first prayed for a blessinge upon the ordinance, Mr Newton Baptized her

28° Aug. 1639

I prayed and went to wellingborow & was reteyned to appeare p[ro] Mr Pent[low] ad[ver]s[us] Mr Lane.

Mr Bates of London here to night & Mr hollis.

29° Aug.

I was wth Mr Bates this morning. I supped at Mr Rushworths to night at a venison pasty.

30° Aug.

this day Mr Coldwell & I comp[ro]mised a

a businesse betweene Mr Peach & Mr [crossed out: Clarke], hart, I dyned at Mr Whalleys at a venison pasty.

---

[746]Simon Moore was appointed to the curacy of Frankton, Warwickshire, by the Temple family, and was chaplain to John Temple of Frankton. He also occurs as the lecturer at Atherstone in 1629 and was probably still acting as such on 24 November 1639, when Woodford refers to him in connection with the town. His later career was as a Congregationalist in Worcestershire. I am grateful to Ann Hughes for this reference. See also A. Hughes, *Politics, Society, and Civil War: Warwickshire, 1620–1660* (Cambridge, 1987), p. 70; Lichfield Record Office, B/A/4/18 and B/V/1/62.

[747]Either George Eakins of Chester, who died in 1658, leaving his estate to his wife, Alice, and mentioning John and Thomas Eakins; or Thomas Eakins, described in 1631 as of Chester: TNA, PROB/11/280; HMC, *Report on the Manuscripts of the Duke of Buccleuch and Queensberry*, III (London, 1926), p. 363.

This day my poore child is gone to nurse to goodwife Iblethy, Oh Lord thou who denyest this blessinge of the breasts to us blessed be thy name thou p[ro]videst the breasts of others for us Lord I pray thee blesse the Child and graunt that she may p[ro]sper & come on as beinge blessed by thee for the Lords sake.

31° Aug. 1639

Mr Smart came hether to day I was too immoderate in squeezinge comfort out of the Creature of wine & tabacco this day with him & others, & my [crossed out, illegible] Corrupt passion broke forth to Edward chadwick who was my adversary about the businesse of Mr Pilk[ington], oh Lord it greiveth me

me to the hart that I have no more moderate[ion] oh that I were as holy as an angell of light oh that I could doe thy will in earth as the angells doe it in heaven Lord fill me with thy grace & spirit that I may obey thee p[er]fectly for the Lords sake

1° [crossed out: Aug.] Sept. 1639 Sab.[bath] & sacram[en]t.

Oh Lord my god how have I sinned & dep[ar]ted from thee since the last sabath since the last sacram[en]t I feed or may feed uppon these precious dayntyes but yet I th[r]ive not but am a very starvelinge in grace & godlines & stand as it were at a stay if not goe backward, oh what a heavy bias of Corrupcon doth lead me aside what a body of death doe I beare about with me continually, Oh that thou wouldst mortify Corrupcon in me oh that thine ordinances might this day be made effectuall to that very end

end though the spirit of Xt comes not as a mighty & rushinge wind yet let it this day breath & blow in his ordinances uppon my soule oh Lord how unacquainted & ignorant I am of thy power in these ordinances of thine owne appoyntinge, and Lord seeinge there is a burden of debt & want lyes uppon me & makes me often (through want of fayth) to runne to the Creature & squeeze that for pr[e]sent Comfort oh Lord I pray thee if thou seest good commannd a greater measure of wealth to serve me for the payment of my debts & the mayntenance of my family in the meane while give me to live by fayth & to be thrifty, & diligent in my callinge, and seeinge thou hast graciously added to my family, which is matter of Joy & Comfort, I pray thee oh my god continue me & my family in health & safty

safty that we may still reioyce in thee & may dayly prayse thy name forever Lord heare & helpe & have m[er]cy & doe good to me & mine for the Lords sake

some comforts in gods blessed ordinances I prayse his name.

2° Sept. 1639
I prayed & went to the Court where there were many entryes & I blesse the Lord for all his goodnesse.
After dinner I went alone to Banbury & came hether in good time I blesse the Lord safe, I went about the Commission inter Temple [*symbol meaning plaintiff*] & Watts & al def[endan]ts, I found at the red lyon there Mr Pentlow & Mr Robins &.

3° Sept 1639
we heard an indifferent sermon by a stranger at the Lecture at Banbury we have much endeavored an agreem[en]t in this businesse but cannot yet compasse it
one of Mr Sprigs sonnes who came lately from Scotland dyned wth us & shewed us some godly & good determinations of the assembly[748] there blessed be thy name oh Lord.
4° Sept.
Mr Pentlowe & I came out somewhat late from Banbury & I came home safe I blesse the Lord & found my famyly in health &.
5° Sept.
Mr Pearne & diverse good ministers

dyned in the towne to day at Oagles his
Mr Smart & Mrs Susan Pentlowe were contracted this morninge.
6° Sept 1639
Oh Lord that thy Church & cause may p[ro]sper & that thow wouldst build up me & my poore family for the Lords sake
7° Sept.
I am too apt to be troubled wth the Thorny cares of this p[rese]nte World but oh my god helpe me for the Lords sake
8° Sept Sab.[bath]
Mr Ball preached p[ro]fitably both times

9° Sept 1639
no Court to day by reason of the absence of the Bayleifes[749]

---

[748] Following the Peace of Berwick (concluding the First Bishops' War), the Scottish Parliament had met on 31 August 1639 and had ratified the previous acts of the General Assembly (which had abolished episcopacy and installed a Presbyterian system of church government), and had then continued with an ecclesiastical and constitutional revolution: R. Cust, *Charles I: a political life* (Harlow, 2005), p. 250; A. Hughes, *The Causes of the English Civil War* (London, 1991), pp. 36–37; B. Coward, *The Stuart Age: England 1603–1714* (London, 2003), pp. 180–181.
[749] Henry Hill and John Cole.

10 Sept.
my wife churched to day in the house by Mr Newton, who with his
wife, Mr Rushworth & ux Mrs Crick & dyned here we had a venison
pasty blessed be the Lord for all supplyes & Comforts.
trayninge here to day.
11° Sept.
I prayed & went to wellingborowe to day.
12° Sept
I prayed and went to keepe the Co[u]rt I

I sent hatton to Grafton [Regis] but no Co[u]rt there.
13° Sept 1639
I prayd & went to Sr John Ishams havinge bene sent for on the Saterday
before, who hath reteyned me to keepe his Court Lord enable me for
it give me still grace & favor in his eyes & in the eyes of others & Let
me ever acknowledg thy p[ro]vidence in all my imploym[en]t Sr John
gave me a peece of Venison
14° Sept.
Troubled wth cares by reason of continual expence of money but Lord
I beseech thee supply me graciously for the Lord Xt his sake.

15° Sept 1639 Sab.[bath]
Mr Newton preached both times excellently blessed be god.
16° Sept.
Court to day where I was too much p[ro]voked to day by John hall
Lord p[ar]don & heale
17° Sept
The Justice seate[750] here to day oh Lord that Justice & right may
pr[e]vayle & that all oppression may cease for the Lords sake
I bought a gowne of Mrs Pilk[ington] p[ro] 45s.
18° Sept
I sent hatton to Wellingborowe I have diverse times gracious affeccon
in [crossed out: I bought a gowne of]

in seeking the Lord I blesse his name I have bought me cloathes Lord
send me well to pay for them & weare them.
19° Sept. 1639
I have bene greatly enflamed this day with the Love my gracious &
lovinge god & father in readinge meditac[ion] & prayer, these ioyes
have swallowed up base cares blessed be thy name oh Lord And Lord

---

[750]This was the primary forest court. In May 1638 the Earl of Holland was still collecting
(through Richard Batten) composition fines imposed in 1637. The collection (by a Mr
Keeling) continued as late as 1641: Pettit, *Royal Forests*, pp. 88–91.

heale the eyes of my poore child John Cleere his sight, & above all
give him a spirituall eye in thy due time to see his owne misery & thy
m[er]cye for the Lords sake.
20° Sept.
good newes still out of Scotland blessed be god that the worke of
reformacon is like to goe on there & that a peace shall be concluded

21° Sept 1639
St Mathewes day to day, oh Lord that we might once leave this
dedication of dayes to Saints & dedicate all o[u]r dayes to thee o[u]r
god & to thy service
22 Sept. Sab.[bath]
Lord I blesse thee for thy Sabaths which the world love not, Lord let
me more delight in them then ever I have done for the Lords sake.
23 Sept.
Court to day where the Lord doth weekly supply me of his owne
goodnes blessed be his name I went late to Burton [Latimer] wth
hatton
24 Sept
I prayed and kept court to day for Mr Bacon, Mr harvey kept for the
Lord Vaux[751]

25° Sept 1639
I prayed and went afterward to Wellingbo[rough] & thence to Old
& Lamport to Sr John Ishams where I had kind enterteynem[en]t
blessed be thy name oh Lord for his favor & the favor & Love of other
freinds & Clyents oh Lord thou dost all.
26 Sept
I kept Sr John Ishams Court to day[752] where the Lord did graciously
enable me,
This day Mr Smart was marryed at Wilby to Mrs Susan Pentlowe oh
Lord I beseech thee blesse them & doe them good for the lords sake
27° Sept
we prayed and went early to Wilby & from there after dinner I brought
my

*****

---

[751] Edward Vaux, fourth Baron Vaux of Harrowden (1588–1661), was a leading Catholic
recusant magnate: H.R. Woudhuysen, 'Vaux, Thomas, second Baron Vaux (1509–1556)', in
ODNB; Metcalfe, *Visitation of Northamptonshire 1618*, p. 203; G. Anstruther, *Vaux of Harrowden*
(Newport, 1953), *passim*.
[752] This is confirmed by the Lamport manorial records: NRO, Isham (Lamport) MSS, I(L)
121 m 5.

my wife home, oh Lord I blesse thee for the Comfort of freinds & all thy m[er]cyes.

28° Sept 1639

My poore John's eyes are very ill but I pray unto the Lord to helpe him oh Lord how dull I am in duty helpe me ag[ains]t it for the Lords sake, I sent Mr M[aio]r elect[753] a roundlet of claret of 6 gal[lons].

29° Sept. Sab.[bath]

blessed be thy name oh Lord for thine ordinances wch by thy goodnesse we doe enioy.

30 Sept.

This day Mr danby was sworne Maior Mr Bryan & Mr Coop[er][754] Bayleifes Mr Recorder[755] was not here, the Lord graciously enabled me to give the oathes, dick Odell came to me this

day[756] oh Lord if we remayne together I pray thee make him a blessing to o[u]r famyly & give us all to doe o[u]r dutyes in o[u]r severall relacons for the Lords sake

1° Oct.

the Sess[ions] here to day for the Country I pray for imploym[en]t & abilityes there

2° Oct.

the Lord hath sent me diverse clyents & given me successe & abilityes in my undertakings blessed be thy name oh Lord.

I dyned at Mr Maiors.

3° Oct

I supped to night wth Mr More at the Swan, where I drunke too much wyne with him for it made me a litle ill

afterward, oh Lord make me to take heed for time to come forever, I bought my cane of Mr Smith to night for halfe a crowne, oh Lord blesse that good man Mr Moore[757] & continue him still to be a faythfull preacher of thy gospell

4° Oct 1639

Mr Sprig Mr Moore Mr Pent[low] & Mr Cranford sate this day uppon the businesse inter Temple [*symbol meaning plaintiff*] & Watts & al def[endan]ts. [*crossed out:* but we can ma]

---

[753]John Danby.
[754]John Bryan and Edward Cooper.
[755]Richard Lane.
[756]Richard Odell, probably the son of Goodman Odell, is here commencing his service with Woodford: Diary, p. 166.
[757]Simon Moore.

5° Oct.
we sate still uppon the Commission but can make no end of the
businesse oh Lord send peace betweene them if it be thy will.
my brother[758] came hether to day from Cambr[idge]

6° Oct. Sab.[bath]
I prayed to the Lord to blesse his word & the sacram[en]t to me this
day Lord graunt that I may manifest the strength of thine ordinances
throughout my life for the Lords sake.
7° Oct
Court to day, where the Lord still supplyes me graciously blessed be
his name
8° Oct
my boyes eyes still amisse but the Lord I trust in his due time will looke
uppon him in m[er]cy
9° Oct.
the great Navy of the Spaniard lyes still uppon the Coast & the duch
attend uppon it.[759]

10° Oct. 1639
Lecture to day blessed be thy name oh Lord for upholdinge o[u]r
Lecture & thine ordinances here amongst us.
11° Oct blessed be thy name oh Lord for thy p[ro]vidence in sendinge
me this practise & these writinges for Sr John Isham & I acknowledge
all to come from thy gracious hand, sanctify every m[er]cy to me for
the Lords sake
12° Oct m[ar]ket day, whereby I have great imploym[en]t continually
I blesse the Lord
13° Oct Sab.[bath]
god is pleased to send many comforts & incouragem[en]ts often by
his blessed ordinances oh Lord I prayse thee for thy goodnesse

14° Oct 1639
Court to day, blessed be the Lord for sendinge me supply in my wants.
15° Oct.
worldly cares doe oft thrust in uppon me but the Lord is my stay how
should I beare a debt of 200li did not the Lord succor me

---

[758] Samuel Haunch, Woodford's brother-in-law, and a Cambridge student.
[759] A proposed treaty with France against the Habsburgs was a casualty of the Scottish War,
and Charles I had drifted towards an alliance with the latter. After the Treaty of Berwick,
Olivares had obtained from Charles naval protection for a Spanish fleet of reinforcements
for Flanders, but after being attacked by the Dutch under Admiral Tromp this had been
forced to retreat to Dover. On 11 October Tromp routed it: Gardiner, *History*, IX, pp. 56–84.

16° Oct

I prayed and went to Wellingborow, blessed be thy name my good father for the favor thou givest me in the eyes of men, & the practise I have, & abilityes in any measure for it, oh my god goe on I pray thee to blesse thy s[er]vant & his family for the Lords sake

17° Oct.

I prayed & went about my occasions blessed be thy name for my callinge oh Lord

18 oct. St Luke

I prayed & went to Wellingborowe fare

& returned safe I blesse the Lord.

19° Oct 1639

many businesses & much distraccon this day but the Lord is pleased graciously to carry me through them

20° Oct Sab.[bath]

Blessed be the Lord for continueinge his Sabaths & ordinances. Lord make thy people fruitfull under them

21° Oct

Court to day blessed be the Lord for carryinge me through the businesse of the day.

22° Oct.

I prayd & went about my occasions, oh Lord that I may p[er]forme earthly businesse wth heavenly affeccons

23° Oct 1639

I prayed & went to Wellingborowe, & the Lord is pleased to rayse me up much above my melanch[oly] oftentimes blessed be thy name oh Lord

24° Oct

I prayed & went to the Lecture.

25° Oct

I prayed & went about my occasions,

26. Oct.

much businesse I blesse the Lord but the Lord stands by me in it blessed be thy name oh Lord

27° oct Sab.[bath]

oh Lord graunt that we may once enioy thine ordinances in their power & purity, that the gospe[l] may have free passage that many soules may be gayned unto thee dayly for the Lords sake

28° Oct 1639

no co[u]rt to day beinge Symon & Jude

29° Oct.
I prayed & went to the Court, where I had still supply I blesse the Lord
30. Oct.
I prayed & went to Wellingborow [*crossed out:* again] & thus I desire to move in the sphere that god hath placed me in, & desire to wayt uppon him for a blessinge
31° Oct.
I prayed & went to the lecture
1° Nov. All s[ain]ts
I prayed & went to Sr John Ishams to seale some writings, but when I came there hatton had mistaken & written very false so that they could not serve at which I

I was troubled, but I desired to cast my selfe uppon the Lord, I sate up till 4 a clock writinge one of the same againe, & Wm Bott was mistaken in the other
2° Nov. 1639
I prayed & went about my occasions & writ over another p[ar]te of the Indent[ure] & sent them to Sr John Isham at night, blessed be thy name oh Lord for enablinge me,
3° Nov. Sab[bath] & sacram[en]t
I prayed & went to p[ar]take of gods ordinances Lord blesse these & every ordinance to me for the Lords sake.
4° Nov.
I prayed & went to the Court, & doe meet wth fayre carriage from Mr Maior[760] I blesse the Lord

5° Nov. 1639
I prayed & came forward to London with dick & we met wth Mr Ward[761] of houghton & his man about Road Lane, & came safe to dunstable I blesse the Lord.
6° Nov.
I prayed & we came forward, and came safe to London nere night, where I found my fathers family very well I prayse the Lord but my

[760]John Danby.

[761]William Ward (1605–1674) was lord of the manor of Little Houghton and the patron of the godly ministers Thomas Martin, Richard Trueman, and Lionel Goodrick. A Parliamentarian, he was a particularly diligent justice of the peace during the Civil War and Commonwealth and served as sheriff of the county from 1646 to 1647: Longden, *Visitation of Northamptonshire 1681*, p. 226; P.R. Brindle, 'Politics and society in Northamptonshire, 1649–1714' (unpublished PhD thesis, University of Leicester, 1983), pp. 135, 138, 143; Longden MS, 27 May 1657 and 10 July 1638.

Cousin Spencer is very weake still but there is great hope the Lord will recover him.

I ly at Clements Inne with my good Chamb[er]fell[ow] Mr harvey.

7° Novembr.

I prayed and went about my occasions my Chamberfellowe hath found out a society of honest younge men in o[u]r house blessed be god for it, Lord increase thy graces in us all to thy glory for the Lords sake

I p[ai]d 34s p[ro] Mr Some which he gave me.

8° Nov.

The Lord hath given me a competent & comfortable imployment this tearme I blesse the

the Lord, and the Lord will graciously assist me to goe through it

9° Nov. 1639

It is much doubted that there will be warre with Scotland,[762] but Lord I pray thee divert it if it be thy will for the good of thy poore Church & Children o[u]r honest society met to night at Mr Ratcliffs Chamber, where we had some dispute which way we should goe as most p[ro]fitable in o[u]r meetings, Lord sanctifye o[u]r meetings make us of one hart & mind

10° Nov.

I heard Mr Calamy in the morninge, & a godly man there in the afternoone, wth much comfort I blesse the Lord; I dyned at my fathers, & we met againe at night at Clements Inne

[11 November omitted]

12° Nov.

I prayed & went about my occasions.

13° Nov. 1639

I receaved bad newes of Johns eyes, but the Lord is a pr[e]sent helpe in time of trouble

14° Nov.

my debts doe dayly [above: trefoil symbol] pinch me, but my god is the possessor of all the world he that doth uphold me under the burden can ease me of it when he pleases, when all meanes hide them selves oh Lord I will trust in thee, though an host of cares come against me through my god I shall doe valiantly & not be surprised strengthen my fayth oh my god in thy great & true p[ro]mises for the Lords sake.

---

[762] When the Scottish Parliament had again proposed the abolition of episcopacy, Charles I had attempted to prorogue it on 31 October 1639, but it had continued to sit, and thereafter war (the Second Bishops' War) seemed inevitable: Gardiner, *History*, IX, pp. 49–55; K. Sharpe, *The Personal Rule of Charles I* (London, 1992), pp. 834–837.

15° Nov.
The Lord is very gracious to me in assistinge me in my way blessed
be thy name oh Lord
16. Nov.
I was troubled to thinke of the great affliccon by reason of Johns eyes,
and I put downe a prayer in the l[atte]r end of the booke⁷⁶³
o[u]r company met at Clem[ent's] Inne

17° Nov. 1639 Sab.[bath]
I prayed and went to a Church wthout Aldegate hopinge to have heard
a goodman but I saw I was disappoynted⁷⁶⁴ & came to Aldermanbury.
we met againe in Clem[ent's] Inne to seeke the Lord
18° Nov.
I prayed & went about my occasions.
19° Nov.⁷⁶⁵
I heare that Sam. is very ill at my fathers the Lord is able to recover
him.
This day I have good newes from North[amp]ton about John I blesse
the Lord.
20° Nov.
Sam still [*symbol of a hand with finger pointing down at the next word*] remaynes
very ill, Lord we are not able to beare many m[er]cyes together unlesse
thou give greater strength thou doest in goodnesse exercise us Lord
make us gayners by every passage of thy p[ro]vidence towards us.

21° Nov. 1639
I prayed & went about my occasions, & desired to wayt uppon the
Lord for Sam &.
22° Nov.
There is some hope the intent of Warre against Scotland⁷⁶⁶ will not
goe on as we heare.

---

⁷⁶³See p. 399, additional entries dated 16 and 17 November 1639.
⁷⁶⁴'The incumbent of St Botolph's, Aldgate, was the strongly Royalist writer Thomas
Swadlin (1600–1670), who was possibly the source of Woodford's disappointment: G.
Burgess, 'Swadlin, Thomas (1599/1600–1670)', in *ODNB*.
⁷⁶⁵See two additional entries at the end of the diary (pp. 398–400) both dated 19 November
1639.
⁷⁶⁶This possibly refers to the Scots' despatch of commissioners (Lords Dunfermline and
Loudoun) to present their demands to the king in London, but the hope of peace was
short-lived, as they were promptly dismissed back to Scotland and the English government
began to prepare for war: Gardiner, *History*, IX, pp. 73–75.

23° Nov.
I went with my Chamb[er]fellow[767] dyned at Mr hollands an honest mans at the red lyon at the upper end of Newgate market & went to Guildhall in the afternoone, to heare Mr Newmans Cause tried.
we met at Clem[ent's] Inne
24. Nov. Sab.[bath]
I heard honest Mr Moore of Atherston[e] at the Church ag[ains]t Londonstone & at St Magnes[768] wth some refreshinge I blesse the Lord.
we met at Clem[ent's] Inne.
25° Nov[769]
I prayd & went about my occasions

26. Nov. 1639
I goe in hand wth the Bill v[e]r[u]s[770] Mr Temple ad[versu]s Watts.
27° Nov.
I am pinched for want of money but the Lord is gracious.
28° Nov.
Tearme ends, I want money for my occasions, to fetch out my fines & But the Lord will p[ro]vide.
29° Nov.
Mr More prayed excellently at my fathers wth my Cousin Spencer, whereat I was greatly affected I blesse the Lord to teares Lord fill me wth thy spirit & fit me for thy service.
Mr More Mr Goodere & I came out of towne & came safe to dunstable I blesse the Lord
my father lent me 5s & Mr Goodere lent me about 6s

30° Nov 1639
we prayed, and Mr Goodere & I came safe to North[amp]ton in due time I blesse the Lord, where I find my family well I prayse god, & John much recovered of his eyes.
This tearme I have p[ai]d Mr ffloods money above 6li & Obadiah Wallop his 3li Mr Pike was with me in vayne Lord enable me to pay him next tearme

---

[767] Stephen Harvey.
[768] This was Simon Moore. The minister of St Swithin's, Londonstone, was the later Royalist Richard Owen, and that of St Magnus was the puritan Cornelius Burges: A.G. Matthews (ed.), *Calamy Revised* (Oxford, 1934), pp. 352, 354; R. Newcourt, *Repertorium Ecclesiasticum Parochiale Londinense*, 2 vols (London, 1708–1710), I, pp. 399, 543; T. Liu, 'Burges, Cornelius (d. 1665)', in *ODNB*.
[769] See p. 398, additional entry dated 25 November 1639.
[770] The grand jury must have found the plaintiff's (Temple's) bill of indictment a 'true bill': that is, they considered there was enough evidence to justify a hearing.

1° dec. Sab.[bath]

Mr [*entry blank*]

2° dec.

Court here to day where the Lord is pleased to supply me graciously

3° dec. my mother went home

I went to Sr John Ishams & dyned there and afterward went to deliver possession to my Aunt Ragdale

I lay at my cousin dexters.

4° dec.

I prayed and went to wellingborow and came home safe at night I blesse the

the Lord

5° dec.

I prayed and went to the Lecture where the Lord graciously refreshed me

6° Dec.

I prayed and laboured in my callinge blessed be thy name oh Lord for health & abilityes

7° dec.

I prayed & had many occasions this day I blesse the Lord

8° dec Sab.[bath]

I prayed & heard Mr Ball both times with some p[ro]fit I trust.

I heare newes to day of a Parliam[en]t intended[771]

9° dec.

the ffare[772] here to day we have bought a

a hog cost 38s blessed be thy name oh Lord for givinge food & rayment, Lord I deserve not the least Crum of bread I eat make me to prize every m[er]cy & to be truly thankfull, thou givest us thy good creatures to dye & serve us oh give us to live to thy service for the Lords sake

10° dec. 1639

I prayed and followed my occasions.

11° dec.

[*left margin: trefoil symbol*] I prayed and went to Wellingborow this shortest day. Ah lord my time in this world is like [*crossed out:* this] a short winter day, cloudy & pinchinge & soone ended give me in this

---

[771]Woodford is here in receipt of breaking news. The Council had only agreed to call a parliament on 5 December 1639: Gardiner, *History*, IX, pp. 75–76.

[772]This was the annual fair at the feast of the Conception of the Virgin Mary (8 December). It lasted for three days, starting on the day before the feast, but if this fell on a Sunday, as here, then all buying and selling was postponed until the Monday, in line with a sabbatarian order of the town assembly of 1605: Markham and Cox, *Northampton*, II, pp. 187–189.

my day to worke out my salvacon wth feare how doth that glorious lampe of thine the sunne runne dayly about the earth goe forward & turne back againe to [*crossed out:* lil] light us to serve thee in o[u]r callinge; how dost thou draw the curtayne of the night uppon us that we may retire

retire & consider of thy goodnesse, oh my god give me to improve every inch of time thou affordest, why should I loose the pr[i]son[er] time that cannot be called back, oh Lord p[ro]sper & blesse me & my family every way for the Lords sake.

12° dec 1639
I prayed and went to the Lecture where I rec[eive]d comfort I blesse the Lord in the unfoldinge of the true & exceedinge g[rea]t p[ro]mises of god.

13° dec.
I prayed, and sate at my occasions. The newes of the Parliam[en]t still is confirmed Lord bring it to passe if it be thy will, & give grace & wisdome to the Country & Corporacons to make choyce of gracious & able men & thou blesse the worke in their hands pr[e]vent the plots of thine adversaryes for the Lords sake

14° dec 1639
much imploym[en]t in my callinge I blesse the Lord. Lord increase my practise if it be thy will & enable me for it more, & give me to be truly thankfull, oh pay my debts for me that I may be able to looke Mr Watts & other Creditors in the face, & that my hart may be melted into thankfullnes to thee my god.

15° dec Sab.[bath]
Mr Ball preached both times very p[ro]fitably on the agravac[ion] of Adams sinne. Lord blesse it to me & my family, oh what a great & pr[e]sumptious sinne it was, Lord give me to be humbled for it for my hand was in it, oh heale the wound that it hath made in my nature for the Lords sake.

16° dec.
Court to day, where the Entryes very few but the Lord made it up in some other

other things I blesse the Lord. I was wth Mr Marston[773] at Mr ffarrens & wth Mr Readinge & Mr Goodere after, Lord give me more to avoyd the socyety that is not p[ro]fitable as Mr Readinge,[774] Lord blesse &

---

[773]John Marston occurs in 1628: Vestry Minutes, p. 21.
[774]That is, Daniel Reading.

doe good to Mr Goodere whom thou hast endued with the grace of
thy sp[iri]t.
17° dec. 1639
I prayed and went about my occasions
18° dec
I prayed and went to Wellingborow I had very g[rea]t comforts in
duty in the morninge I blesse the Lord.
19° dec.
I prayed and went to the lecture, where I rec[eive]d much refreshinge
I blesse the Lord I went downe to Mr Ball at night
20° dec.
The Aldermen & Mr Rec[order][775] dyned to day at Mr ffarrens, Lord
thou art able to give

give me more favor in their eyes, I pray thee bestow it uppon me if
thou seest good.
There was a fire tonight at Kingsthorpe
21° dec 1639
some new imploym[en]t this day I blesse the Lord
I have wrought another g[rea]t trip[ar]tite Indent[ure] beinge up
about 3 a clock; blessed be the Lord for bestowinge health uppon me
& for makinge of me diligent in some measure in my callinge, that so
he may make good the p[ro]mise unto me.
I heare to day that Mr Jones of London (Mrs Pentlowes father) is dead,
another warning to me Lord pr[e]pare me for death
22° dec Sab.[bath]
Mr Cawdrey preached both times, I have found too much
straightenednes in duty this day Lord enlarge me more & more

23° dec 1639
I have desired to seeke the lord earnestly in private this morninge,
but my hart hath still bene heavy & dull but Lord accept me in and
through thy beloved, The Lord will surely blesse me & increase his
graces in me, will pay my debts for me, & build upp me & my family.
Lord manifest thy p[ro]vidence towards me this day graciously supply
of thyne owne bounty at the Court & otherwise in this my necessity &
Lord give me favor in the eyes of the Maior & recorder & keepe me
from rash anger & Idle speeches dwell thou in my hart for the Lords
sake.

[775] Richard Lane.

I want neere 50s to pay the interest of Mr Watts his 6 score pound
for which I am bound wth him, to Mrs Pilk.[ington] & more & Lord
p[ro]vide.
24° dec.
I prayed & went about my occacons Mr Greg was

was with me to day &.
25 dec 1639 xxmas day.
I prayed & we went to heare Mr Ball my hart much streightned & I
am too subiect to melancholly & Thorny cares the Lord will helpe me
26° dec.
John James of Olney was with me to day & p[ai]d me 40s of that
he owes me blessed be thy name oh Lord for any supply, I was very
melancholly to night yet my wife encouraged me in the Lord blessed
be thy name oh Lord for any comfort
27° dec.
I prayed & went about my occacons young Mr Martin supped wth
me here to

to night & his wife.
28 dec. 1639
I had much comfort in [*crossed out:* private] secret prayer [*above next
word: double trefoil symbol*] this morninge I blesse the Lord.
Lord I beseech thee appeare to me more & more, Lord how sweet
thy pr[e]sence is, & how refreshinge thy Comforts! well! have I hope
of heaven & shall I be deiected? the creature indeed could not truly
comfort me were I voyd of god & grace, but spirituall comforts can
susteyne a man in the absence of the Creature, oh my god be gracious
unto me, truly Lord thou art exceedinge gracious, but my sinnes
hinder the Current of thy favors, thy goodnesse would flowe uppon
me in abundance as the waters when the windowes from on high are
opened & the botles of heaven unstopped or the fountaynes of the
great deepe unsealled, did not my sinnes so dam them up that I can
be but bedeowed & sprinkled with

with a few drops, the fatherly bowells of thyne infinite Compassion
doe yerne towards me thy unworthy servant, but I so behave my selfe
that they are much restrayned, & thou art oft constrayned to lay hold
of thy correctinge rod, but oh my gracious god put my hart into a holy
frame, & make me fit for the receavinge of m[er]cyes that so all the
good that thou hast p[ro]mised may be made good uppon me that I
may boast in the Lord all the day longe, and may set forth thy lovinge
kindnesse faythfullnesse & truth, that I may teach transgressors thy

way & sinners may be converted unto thee,[776] that I may encourage those that are in want to wayt uppon thee and may be liberall to the hungry & distressed soule, ah my god supply me

me wth moneyes to pay my debts & maynteyne me & my family, I have trusted & will trust in the allsufficient god possessor of heaven & earth who hath taken the care & Chardge of me & mine Lord I beleive helpe my unbeleife, & make me more holy every day then other, & Lord blesse my dear wife powre grace uppon her soule abundantly make us meet helpers one unto another, make us to know in a greater measure the good & the excellency of this ordinance of matrimony & blesse & p[ro]sp[er] the sweet childen thou hast given us oh make them thine by grace, Lord blesse o[u]r servants give them to doe their dutyes to us & we to them take away the rebelliousnes & risinge of spirit that are amongst us, Lord Convert them unto thee make sinne their greatest sorowe that Christ may be their greatest Joy, & uppon him the altar I offer up this poore supplicacon Lord blesse thee that thou hast recovered Mr

Mr Whalleyes sick child which was nere unto death[777] I blesse thee for sendinge me moneyes to pay the interest of 48s of the 120li wch Mr Watts hath of Mrs Pilkington I blesse thee for movinge my hart to come away so soone out of the Company of Mr daniel Readinge & some others at Mr ffarrens, Lord I blesse thee for thy p[ro]vidence of this day & for all thy goodnesse to me & mine at all times,
Lord order things I pray thee for the best in the businesse betweene Mr Temple & Mr Watts &. Lord enable me more for my callinge & give me more practise & give me ever the peace of an honest Conscience for the Lords sake.
Lord pr[e]pare us for thy Sabath to morow for the Lords sake Amen.

here I neglected to put downe many dayes through many occasions, uppon Tuesday 21° Januarii[778] I went towards London about Mr Watts his businesse, I went to dunstable the first night & uppon Wednesday I came safe to London, & sought god earnestly about the occ[asi]on,

[776] Based on Psalm 51:8, 13.
[777] This was Peter Whalley's son Daniel, who became both deaf and mute until cured at the Restoration by Dr John Wallis, who paraded the results before the king and the Royal Society: G. Ford, 'Where's Whalley? The search for Sir Samuel uncovers a Whalley–Cartwright alliance in Northamptonshire', *Northamptonshire Past and Present*, 62 (2009), pp. 36–37.
[778] See additional entries at the end of the diary: dated 22 January, 23 January (two entries), and 25 January 1639/40 (pp. 396–398). These entries cover Woodford's stay in London from 22 to 27 January 1639/40, when he made no entry in the main diary.

& on Friday we had a heareinge[779] before the M[aste]r of the Roles & Baron henden,[780] & the businesse went very well for us I blesse the Lord, v[id]e the latter end of the booke.

I came from London on Munday 27° Januar to Barnet that night, & the next day home I blesse the Lord[781]

on thursday 6° ffebruar[782] I went towards London againe & came thether safe on friday & stayed there till friday 21. ffebr & came to ffenny stratford[783] that night & came home safe on Satterday I blesse the Lord.

Blessed be my gracious god for his good hand of p[ro]vidence towards me all this while Lord sanctifye thy m[er]cyes to me for the Lords sake.

23° ffeb. 1639/40. Sab.[bath]

Mr Pinchester[784] preached both times very p[ro]fit

p[ro]fitably I blesse the Lord.

24° ffeb 1639/40

Court here to day where the Lord supplyed me graciously

25° ffeb[785]

I prayed & went about my occ[asi]ons.

26. ffeb.

This day the Judges, my Lord Cheife Baron[786] & Justice Berkley came in to the towne wth Sr xxofer[787] yelverton sheriff

27° ffeb.

Mr Palmer[788] preached the Assize sermon very p[ro]fitably

---

[779] In Chancery: see additional entries detailed in previous note. The judges referred the matter to the Warwick Assizes, where it was tried: Diary, p. 341.

[780] Sir Charles Caesar (1590–1642) had been Master of the Rolls since 1639. Archbishop George Abbot had appointed him the judge of the Court of Audience for life, and there is some evidence that he helped to stymie Laudianism through his control of this archiepiscopal appellate jurisdiction, as Sibthorpe suspected. Sir Edward Henden was a judge on the Oxford circuit, and a Civil War Royalist: L.M. Hill, 'Caesar, Sir Charles (1590–1642)', in *ODNB*; Fielding, 'Peterborough', p. 106; A. Fletcher, *The Outbreak of the English Civil War* (London, 1981), pp. 301, 359.

[781] See p. 397, additional entry dated 1 February 1639/40.

[782] See p. 395, additional diary entry dated 15 February 1639/40.

[783] Buckinghamshire.

[784] Perhaps Edward Pinchester, who had graduated BA from Magdalen Hall, Oxford, in 1614: Foster.

[785] See p. 395, additional entry dated 25 February 1639/40.

[786] Sir Humphrey Davenport.

[787] Christopher.

[788] John Palmer, unbeneficed at this time, was presented to the living of Ecton by his father-in-law, Clifton Catesby, in 1641. The grandson of the godly divine John Dod, he was closely connected to the godly Yelverton family of Easton Maudit and their kinsman Lord Grey of Ruthin: Sir Christopher mentioned him as a cousin in his will of 1654. He conformed at

28. ffeb.
The Assizes ended to night there beinge not

not much to doe, John Ponder & some others have endited a curate[789]
for not deliveringe them the sacram[en]t unlesse they would come up
to the rayles
29° ffeb. 1639/40
I went alonge to Warwick wth Mr Pentlow & henry Coop[er], we
came thether in the Close of the eveninge; I went about the tryall at
Law inter Mr Temple & Watts &.
1° Martii Sab.[bath]
Mr Venners preached in the morninge at Wa[rwick] & Mr Bryan[790]
in the afternoone, very honestly & p[ro]fitably, & I was refresh[e]d to
see the good Lord Brooke
2° Martii
an unworthy man preached this day before the Judge, Lord set up
shining lights

3° Martii 1639/40
This morninge the cause inter Temple & Watts & was heard, & its
gone against my Clyents dam[ages] to 890li ah my god I pray thee
bringe good out of this both for them & me thou art able to doe it give
me yet favor in the eyes of Mr Watts if it be thy will & furnish me that
I may pay him & all others to whom I stand indebted mine eyes are
towards thee.

---

the Restoration and served as Archdeacon of Northampton from 1665 until 1679: Longden,
Clergy; TNA, PROB/11/217; Longden MS, 18 November 1641.

[789]This appeal to secular law was a favourite means of redress for the godly against the
policies of their Laudian opponents: the townsmen of Northampton used it against the
ceremonialist Humphrey Ramsden; the godly cleric Miles Burkit against the Church court
informer Henry Folwell; and the parishioners of Towcester against their Laudian vicar,
John Lockwood. The curate in question in this instance might be James Flint of Rothwell,
a Cambridge graduate who had been licensed to preach during Laud's metropolitical
visitation in 1635 as schoolmaster of Rothwell, had been ordained a priest the same year,
and had subscribed in 1636 when he also proceeded MA. He was killed by Captain Francis
Sawyer at Wellingborough in 1642: Fielding, 'Peterborough', pp. 235–241; Longden, *Clergy*;
PDR, Miscellaneous Book 7A; PDR, X620/66, fo. 88v; PDR, X639–642/8, unfoliated,
under Rothwell.

[790]Richard Venour, vicar of St Mary's, Warwick, and John Bryan, vicar of nearby Barford,
were key members of the circle of godly ministers which revolved around Robert Greville,
second Lord Brooke, whose seat was Warwick Castle. Both (and especially Bryan) were close
friends of Thomas Dugard, the godly schoolmaster of Warwick, who had Northamptonshire
godly contacts with Richard Knightley, Thomas Hill, and Charles Chauncy. Both went on
to be moderate Presbyterians in the 1640s and 1650s, but, while Venour conformed at the
Restoration, Bryan was ejected: A. Hughes, 'Thomas Dugard and his circle in the 1630s: a
"Parliamentary–Puritan" connexion?', *Historical Journal*, 29 (1986), pp. 771–793.

4° Martii

we came from Warr[ick] to day, & by gods p[ro]vidence about 2 or 3 mile on thisside we met wth one Mr Taylor of Birmingham a godly man & his freind, I rec[eive]d much good & comfort in discourse & conference wth Mr Taylor, Lord goe along with him & blesse him for the Lords sake. I came home safe I blesse the Lord.

5° Martii

Mr Wm Martin preached well at the Lect

lecture here to day. Mr Glede[791] hath bene wth me to intreat my voyce for Sr xxofer[792] hatton to be K[nigh]t of the shire, but I delivered my selfe so to him that he p[er]ceaves how I stand affected, Lord I pray thee direct me & defend me from evill that may come uppon me for doeinge that wch is right[793]

---

[791] Possibly the Richard Glede mentioned in the will of John Hampden's uncle, Sir Edmund of Abington, in 1627. Clearly there was debate over who should be the court candidate for knight of the shire. The final choice was Thomas Elmes of Warmington. He enjoyed godly connections (unlike the conformist Sir Christopher Hatton) and may therefore have been regarded as a more promising candidate. Hatton's consolation prize was the borough seat of Higham Ferrers (part of Queen Henrietta Maria's jointure), where he was steward. He won, after a contest as closely fought between court and country as at the shire level. A sympathizer with Laudian reforms, he looked for support to Sir John Lambe, Francis Gray (clerk of the peace), John Digby (the Laudian vicar), and Thomas Rudd (a justice of the peace). Forearmed with legal decisions from Chief Justice Sir Robert Heath and Geoffrey Palmer, Hatton triumphed by polling the ordinary townsfolk instead of the capital burgesses as was traditional. His opponent was Edward Harby of Adstone, friend of the Knightleys and Drydens and related to the aldermanic family that dominated the corporation, which refused to accept the principle of the widening of the franchise and was forced to concede. Hatton was re-elected by the borough for the Long Parliament, at which time he was also elected at Castle Rising, Norfolk, but rejected the seat in favour of continuing at Higham, allowing his uncle, Sir Robert Hatton, to claim the Norfolk seat: Fielding, 'Peterborough', p. 247; TNA, PROB/11/53; A.N. Groome, 'Higham Ferrers elections in 1640: a Midland market town on the eve of Civil War', *Northamptonshire Past and Present*, 2:5 (1958), pp. 243–251; Longden MS, 5 December 1635; PDR, CB65, fo. 50v; M.F. Keeler, *The Long Parliament* (Philadelphia, 1954), pp. 208–209.

[792] Christopher.

[793] Two weeks before the election Woodford was clearly no floating voter. It is apparent that both sides had been canvassing in the environs of Northampton well in advance of the poll; indeed, St John claimed Sir Gilbert Pickering's agents had been campaigning at quarter sessions, markets, and other public occasions since the calling of the parliament in December 1639. Pickering's supporters tried to discredit Elmes by claiming that he was supported by papists and by associating him with unpopular royal policy. Thomas Pentlow was later charged that on 18 March he dissuaded Richard Knighton of Irthlingborough (who had been an opponent of ship money) from voting for Elmes by claiming that, as a deputy lieutenant, Elmes was questionable in Parliament for his part in raising coat and conduct money for the wars in Scotland. Pickering's followers among the Northampton godly (Thomas Ball, John Gifford, and Thomas Martin) were also charged with applying similar pressure to the mayor, John Danby, claiming Elmes's lieutenancy rendered him

from the 5[th] to the 19[th] I neglected my Journall by reason of divers occasions but had many passages of gods good p[ro]vide[nce] towards me not to be forgotten. M[aste]r at Graft[on] my horse fell into the mud as I went & where I was in company 12° Martii wth ffoliat & Arundell[794] preists & diverse other lea[r]n[e]d drunkards the Lord kept me that I ranne not to the same excesse, blessed be thy name oh Lord for all thy goodnesse yet I had cause to be humbled for want of that moderacon that should have bene in m[e] Lord p[ar]don the sinne of thy servant & mak[e] me a gayner by all my faylings, I came home early on Friday morninge had come there over night but that I stayd for company that fayled

16° Martii 1639/40
I prayed & after Court went to Mr Bacons
17° Martii
I stayd at Mr Bacons takinge Instr[uction] p[ro] leases blessed be thy name oh Lord for imploym[en]t & abilityes for it
18° Martii

ineligible. Ball allegedly sent a letter to John Ward, godly minister of Spratton, eliciting support for Pickering, and Ward read this publicly after evening prayer. Elmes's supporters were similarly far from idle. Spencer Compton, Earl of Northampton, was canvassing for him in the Hundred of Spelhoe, in which Northampton lay. Elmes also enjoyed active support in the township of Kingsthorpe. Dr Clarke campaigned in Spelhoe, in which his benefice of St Peter, Northampton, was situated, and in Guilsborough Hundred, where lay his benefice of Winwick. Richard Mottershed of Kingsthorpe acted as Compton's agent, writing on 14 March to the beleaguered John Ward of Spratton, a future Parliamentarian, to request his voice for Elmes. The Mottersheds were a recusant family, and Richard had been presented for six months' recusancy as recently as 1632. Clarke himself had presented him in 1628, and for not bringing his children to be catechized: PDR, CBA2, dated 10 September and 2 October 1628. Finally, on the eve of the election St John sent his agent, Christopher Clarke, to canvass for Elmes in the village of Hardingstone. Clarke possibly resided at Potterspury, where in 1608 his father had appointed Paul Boughton to the vicarage: Bodleian Library, Bankes MSS, 42/55, 44/13, 65/62, and 18/5; BRO, St John (Bletso) MSS, DDJ 1369; PDR, CB55, fo. 83r–v; Longden, *Clergy*; Metcalfe, *Visitation of Northamptonshire 1618*, p. 82; Longden MS, 25 February 1608.

[794] Edward Foliot and Emmanuel Arundel were ministers from the parishes of Alderton and Stoke Bruerne, which were adjacent to Grafton Regis, where the manorial court was held. They were the clients of Sir Francis Crane and the crown (in Sir Christopher Hatton's minority) respectively and both were conformists (Arundel was a Church court official) removed by Parliament in the 1640s. One of the charges made against Arundel in 1646 was indeed drunkenness, but he was also accused of imposing Laudian ceremonial, and of issuing a document in the form of a royal proclamation condemning Parliament as a collection of Brownists and rebels: Longden, *Clergy*; Longden MS, 25 August 1634 and 16 December 1625; A.G. Matthews (ed.), *Walker Revised* (Oxford, 1948), pp. 276, 278.

I came from Burton [Latimer] to Wellingborow & p[rese]ntly
after I had bene there Sr Gilb[er]t Pickeringe[795] came through the
towne [*crossed out:* & I was] goeing wth some Company towards
North[amp]ton to stand to be a K[nigh]t of the shire ag[ains]t Mr
Elmes,[796] I was much affected to see him & prayed in my hart for him
& came along wth him to North[amp]ton

[795]Pickering (1611–1668), the lord of the manor of Titchmarsh, lived at Titchmarsh Grove.
He was the godly candidate for the shire election and enjoyed a staunchly puritan pedigree.
The son of Sir John Pickering, he was the grandson of Sir Gilbert Pickering, a zealous
witchfinder who had been exposed to the puritanism of the Brownes, his wife's family, the
most radical of whom was the separatist Robert Browne. The tone was set for the rest
of Gilbert's life at his christening in 1611, which was performed by Sampson Sheffield, a
Rutland puritan who was curate for the Knightleys' friends, the Drydens, and who had
been suspended from an Oxfordshire living for nonconformity. In the words of the Church
court presentment that ensued, Sheffield had christened baby Gilbert 'without the surplice,
and did not use the Crosse in baptisme nor the Questions and answeres as by the book of
common prayer is apointed'; his denial was typically equivocal: 'he did signe with the water
and that he doth not remember that he did use the [questions and answers] appointed in
the booke' (PDR, CB43, fo. 18v). Pickering's father was connected to many other godly
divines (such as Robert Bolton and Jeremiah Whitaker) and sent his son to study under John
Preston (and later Thomas Ball) at Cambridge. He promoted others in conjunction with
Lord Saye and Sele and Sir Henry Yelverton. When he died in 1628 his will, with its ultra-
godly preamble, mentioned Christopher Sherland and Sir Miles Fleetwood as friends, and
placed the wardship of his son in the hands of Sir Erasmus Dryden, Francis Nicolls, Robert
Horsman, and Edward Bagshaw. In 1638, Sir Gilbert married Elizabeth, daughter of Sir
Sidney Montagu, Charles I's Master of Requests. He was a member of the tribunal which
tried Charles I in 1649, but withdrew from the court and did not sign the death warrant.
He went on to be a Cromwellian courtier: Sheils, *Puritans*, p. 40; M. Gibson, 'Devilish sin
and desperate death: Northamptonshire witches in print and manuscript', *Northamptonshire
Past and Present*, 51 (1998), pp. 15–21; P.C. Almond, *The Witches of Warboys: an extraordinary story
of sorcery, sadism, and satanic possession* (London, 2008), pp. 31–33, 41, 47–49, 61–63; Metcalfe,
Visitation of Northamptonshire 1618, p. 127; Longden, *Visitation of Northamptonshire 1681*, p. 171;
Fielding, 'Peterborough', pp. 17–18; TNA, PROB/11/19; T. Venning, 'Pickering, Sir Gilbert,
first baronet, appointed Lord Pickering under the protectorate (1611–1668)', in *ODNB*; P.R.
Brindle, 'Politics and society in Northamptonshire, 1649–1714' (unpublished PhD thesis,
University of Leicester, 1983), p. 110.

[796]Deputy Lieutenant Thomas Elmes of Warmington, although the court candidate, was
not without Protestant conviction. In 1633 it had been reported to the Church courts that
the Warmington lecture was supplied by Elmes's domestic chaplain, Mr Leach. After his
ordination at nearby Peterborough in 1639, the Essex minister Ralph Josselin was invited by
Elmes to deliver his first sermon at Warmington. The family enjoyed other godly contacts:
Thomas's son Anthony had married Grace Knightley, the sister of Richard of Fawsley; his
daughter Frances was the wife of Sir Arthur Haselrig. Indeed, Elmes's survival in county
government until 1650 (though demonstrating little loyalty to Parliament) may have been the
result of these godly contacts: Fielding, 'Peterborough', p. 161, n. 24; *VCH Northamptonshire*,
III (London, 1930), pp. 114–121, 229–230; TNA, SP14/44/7; TNA, PROB/11/186; Brindle,
'Politics and society', pp. 118–119; C. Durston, 'Hesilrige, Sir Arthur, second baronet (1601–
1661)', in *ODNB*.

19° Martii
I prayed & went to the Castle where

after the writt was read the Earle of North[amp]ton⁷⁹⁷ Earle of
Westm[or]land⁷⁹⁸ Earle of Peterburgh wth others⁷⁹⁹ mounted their
horses & [*crossed out:* so] Rode betweene the companys callinge men to
come to Mr Elmes his company but the company⁸⁰⁰ of Mr Crewe⁸⁰¹ &

⁷⁹⁷Spencer Compton, the courtier and future Royalist, was Lord Lieutenant of
Warwickshire, and the political opponent of Robert Greville, Lord Brooke. He had raised
soldiers to fight the Scots and obtained one of the Warwickshire county seats for his son
James, later the third earl: M. Bennett, 'Compton, Spencer, second earl of Northampton
(1601–1643)', in *ODNB*.
⁷⁹⁸Mildmay Fane of Apethorpe, second Earl of Westmorland, was a deputy lieutenant
who had become associated with court policy, for example serving as a commissioner
for knighthood fines in 1631. He had accompanied the king's army to Scotland in 1639
and became a devoted Royalist, attempting against all the odds in 1642 to execute the
commission of array with Lord Montagu and Sir Christopher Hatton: S. Wright, 'Fane,
Mildmay, second earl of Westmorland (1602–1666)', in *ODNB*.
⁷⁹⁹John Mordaunt (1599–1643), first Earl of Peterborough, lived at Drayton House. He
had previously served as Deputy Lieutenant of Northamptonshire and was raised to the
lord lieutenancy in 1640. The Mordaunts were a recusant family and, owing to John's
father's involvement in the Gunpowder Plot, James I had placed him under the wardship
of Archbishop George Abbot to ensure that he received a Protestant education. He had
been a courtier in the 1620s, a close ally of the Duke of Buckingham, and had been raised
to an earldom in 1628, but in the 1630s he was an opponent of ship money and refused
to contribute towards the Bishops' Wars. He served in the Parliamentarian army, although
Parliament was suspicious of his religious background, until his death in 1643: V. Stater,
'Mordaunt, Henry, second earl of Peterborough (bap. 1623, d. 1697)', in *ODNB* (John's son).
Sir William Fitzwilliam of Milton, a later Royalist, also supported Elmes, who, despite St
John's denial, provided entertainment for his supporters on election day.
⁸⁰⁰As for Pickering's followers, St John's account agrees in tone with the charges later
brought against the Northampton puritans regarding their behaviour: 'Multitudes' of men
who 'make profession of the most syncear practice of the Gospell' cried 'Weel have no
Deputy Lieutenants! Take heed of Deputy Lieutenants no Deputy Lieutenants!' (BRO, St
John (Bletso) MSS, DDJ 1369), or 'A Pickering a Pickering. No deputy lieutenants, no Elmes'
(Bodleian Library, Bankes MSS, 44/13), to disrupt the proceedings. Gifford, Whalley, John
Spicer, Martin, Friend, Pentlow of Wilby, and Collins were so charged. Francis Nicolls
also admitted supporting Pickering. St John claimed that the barrister Edward Palmer did
likewise. Palmer was the son of Anthony Palmer of Stoke Doyle, who was connected to
Lord Lieutenant William Cecil, Earl of Exeter, and was a patron of conformist Church
court ministers: Bodleian Library, Bankes MSS, 65/62; Fielding, 'Peterborough', p. 28;
TNA, PROB/11/41.
⁸⁰¹John Crewe of Steane Park was the son of Sir Thomas Crewe (d. 1634), Speaker of
the House of Commons, who had pursued a career in opposition to government policy.
In 1628 Sir Thomas had delivered the impeachment charge against the Arminian Roger
Mainwaring, and had been a feoffee for impropriations from 1632. He had been a member
of a powerful puritan network of opposition to government policy which had included Lord
Saye and Sele, Richard Knightley, and Christopher Sherland. He had also supported a
bewildering array of godly divines. John Crewe continued his support for puritan ministers
such as John Barker, Charles Chauncy, and many moderates, but Thomas Ball and Lord

Sr Gilbert who stood nere together was the greatest, [*crossed out:* yet]
so the Lords would goe to pollinge & this night there were abou[t] 7
score more sworne on Mr Elmes his side then on Sr Gilberts[802]
Mr Elmes yealded the first place to Mr Crewe wthout pollinge
20° Martii
pollinge still, I was sworne for Sr Gilb[er]te,[803]
21° Martii
pollinge still,[804] & I was sent this morninge to Mr Bagshawes about an
occasion. I came home againe about one a clock and about 2 or 3 a
clock Sr Gilb[er]t was declared Knight of the shire to the Joy of the
harts of gods people.

22° Martii 1639/40 Sab.[bath]
some comfort this day in gods ordinances.

Saye considered him insufficiently godly, even though Sibthorpe regarded him (and, indeed,
St John) as key members of a puritan conspiracy to overthrow Church and state. If the more
fervent godly preferred Pickering, then it seems that Crewe owed his popularity at the
election to his stance on ship money. There is no definite evidence on whether he paid, but
Reginald Burden, Lambe's conformist ally as rector of Aynho, informed him in 1637 that
Crewe's attitude was disrupting the collection of the tax in the whole area. Crewe went on
to become a moderate Parliamentarian: M. Jansson, 'Crewe, Sir Thomas (1566–1634)', in
ODNB; Fielding, 'Peterborough', pp. 19–21, 127–128; Jackson, 'Ship money', p. 217; Brindle,
'Politics and society', pp. 108–110.

[802] St John averred that Elmes's lead was 186 (Elmes having polled 350 and Pickering 164),
as opposed to the 140 quoted here by Woodford: BRO, St John (Bletso) MSS, DDJ 1369.

[803] St John claimed that, on this second day, Pickering's brother John and Sheriff Sir
Christopher Yelverton employed delaying tactics designed to disrupt Elmes's count. He also
claimed that by the end of the day Elmes still led Pickering 510 : 430 (*ibid.*).

[804] St John asserted that it was only now that Pickering's tally started to exceed Elmes's.
He complained that Pickering's cousin, Robert Horsman, loudly insisted that the oath of
allegiance should be tendered on the spot to one of Elmes's recusant supporters, and that
Sheriff Yelverton barely reprimanded him for the stunt. Elmes's older brother, William,
lord of the manor of Lilford and a justice of the peace, had complained to Yelverton about
the conduct of the election, stating that he would seek redress. From 8 April onwards
the Privy Council summoned before it those whose names were supplied by the Earls
of Peterborough and Northampton: these included the Northampton men (Ball, Gifford,
Martin, Spicer, Friend, Whalley, Thomas West, Matthew Watts) and others from nearby
parishes (Pentlow, Edward Pickering of Bugbrooke, Henry Collins, constable of Broughton,
John Ward, John Eakins of Ringstead, and Edward Arnold of Heyford). On 3 May the king
in council ordered the Attorney General, Sir John Bankes, to investigate the charges made
against them. On 6 May the Council ordered Bankes to consult with Lord Chief Justice Sir
Robert Heath as to whether further action should be taken. Around 10 May, Ball, Pentlow,
and the rest stated that they were in the custody of the Council's messengers and petitioned
the Council for a swift resolution. Finally, on 6 December, the king in council discharged
them, conceding that they did not mean any disrespect to the office of deputy lieutenant *per
se*: BRO, St John (Bletso) MSS, DDJ 1369; TNA, PC 2/52/427, PC 2/52/456, PC 2/52/461,
and PC 2/52/469; TNA, SP16/452/16, SP16/452/56, SP16/452/110, and SP16/473/24;
VCH Northamptonshire, III, pp. 114–121, 228–230.

23° Martii
Court to day
24° Martii noyse of Warrs wth Scotland I kept Court at Blissworth[805]
the burgesses chosen for North[amp]ton Mr Tate Mr Knightley[806]
25° Martii 1640
ffare[807] here at North[amp]ton
26. Martii
I prayed & went to Stoke [Bruerne][808] where I kept Court & came safe
home that night I blesse the Lord.
27. Martii I prayed & went to the sessions here kept this day for
the towne & the Lord carryed me graciously through the worke &
supplyed me graciously

28° Martii I prayed & attended my occ[asi]ons
29° Martii 1640 Sab.[bath]
some refreshinge by gods ordinances Lord helpe me against the thorny
cares of the world for the Lords sake.
Mr Ball preached both times. I & my deare wife rec[eive]d the
sacram[en]t.
30° Martii
I prayed & went to the Court.

[805] Sir Francis Crane had leased this manor to Sir Robert Cooke for thirty-one years in
1635: *VCH Northamptonshire*, IV (London, 1937), p. 225.
[806] Zouch Tate of Delapré Abbey, Northampton, and Richard Knightley of Fawsley both
came from godly families. Knightley was not the Richard (d. 1639) who had been connected
to Saye and Sele, Pym, and Dod (and who was the grandson of the Elizabethan Sir Richard)
but hailed from the Staffordshire branch of the family (he was the Elizabethan Sir Richard's
nephew). He was married to the daughter of the Solicitor General, Sir Edward Littleton,
who had prosecuted John Hampden for the crown. Knightley's son, another Richard, who
was knighted at Charles II's coronation, married John Hampden's daughter Elizabeth. Tate
and Knightley had both signed Crewe's and Pickering's election indenture and were both
later Parliamentarians. On 18 April 1640 Knightley presented a petition of grievances from
the borough whose tenor was the same as the county petition presented the previous day
by Pickering. Tate's and Knightley's own indenture, dated 26 March, was signed by Mayor
John Danby, whom Ball *et al.* were accused of coercing to poll for Pickering at the shire
contest (Diary, p. 342, n. 793). Henry Lee claimed that Tate was elected unanimously, but
without his knowledge, then informed of the *fait accompli*: Fielding, 'Peterborough', pp. 21,
44, and n. 77; D.W. Hollis, III, 'Tate, Zouch (1606–1650)', in *ODNB*; Longden, *Visitation of
Northamptonshire 1681*, pp. 103–104, 106, 108, 239–240; TNA, C219, 41, 1, part 2, 158; E.S.
Cope and W. Coates (eds), *Proceedings of the Short Parliament 1640*, Camden fourth series XIX
(London, 1977), pp. 158, 235; J.D. Maltby (ed.), *The Short Parliament (1640): diary of Sir Thomas
Aston*, Camden fourth series XXXV (London, 1988), p. 12; Top MS, p. 93.
[807] Lady Day.
[808] Stoke Bruerne (adjacent to Grafton Regis) was a manor formerly owned by Sir Francis
Crane, and in it was situated his mansion of Stoke Park. His will stipulated that his widow,
Marie, be permitted to live there for the rest of her life; she died in 1642: W. Hefford, 'Crane,
Sir Francis (c.1579–1636)', *ODNB*.

31° Martii
I prayed & went & kept Alderton Co[u]r[t][809] & came home safe that
night I prayse the Lord.
1° April
I prayed & went this heavy Snowy frosty morninge to Grafton [Regis]
to keepe the Leete there, it hath snowed all this day, I lodge at Grafton
[Regis] this night Rich ffarmer marryed to day.
2° April 1640
I kept the 3. weeks Court this morninge & after that I rode to Potts
Perry[810] to keepe Court there, & then came to Mr Butlers to Alderton
to bed It hath snowed almost all this day.
3° April
This day I am 34 I thinke Lord [*left margin: trefoil symbol*] blesse thee for
sparinge my life so long & givinge me so large a time of rep[en]tan[ce]
sanctify thy patience towards me pr[e]seve me still to thy glory & the
good of my family my wife this day 23. Lord cont[inue] us both
together long to thy glory & o[u]r mutuall comfort for the Lords sake.
Sam. this day (as beinge good Friday) is [*left margin: trefoil symbol*] 4.
yeares old Lord pr[e]serve & blesse make him a vessell of m[er]cy &
an instrum[en]t of glory to thee & comfort to us. I went from Alderton
to Greenesnorton[811] to keep Court & there I met wth Mr

Wilkinson[812] & another or two in whom Jesus Xt was formed wch was
a great Comfort to me, I came home to night safe I blesse the Lord;
& was brought safe over the wall[813] I blesse the Lord.
4° April 1640
I prayed and went about my occasions & the Lord graciously carryed
me through them.

---

[809] Sir Arthur Haselrig was tenant of this Crane manor: Bridges, *History of Northamptonshire*,
II, p. 281.
[810] Potterspury had belonged to Sir Francis Crane as part of the honour of Grafton: *ibid.*,
II, p. 316; Pettit, *Royal Forests*, pp. 192–193.
[811] Green's Norton had been another Crane manor: Bridges, *History of Northamptonshire*, II,
p. 241.
[812] George Wilkinson of Green's Norton and his wife had resisted receiving communion
at the altar rails around December 1636. Wilkinson had been the servant of Judge Sir
Thomas Chamberlain (d. 1625), Lord Keeper Ellesmere's manorial steward, who had been
connected to other godly lawyers in the area, including Sir Thomas Crewe and Sir Henry
Yelverton: PDR, CBA2, fo. 422r–v; D. Ibbetson, 'Chamberlain, Sir Thomas (d. 1625)', in
ODNB; TNA, PROB/11/151; Prest, *Barristers*, p. 349.
[813] The town gates were closed at night and Woodford would have been allowed in by the
town watch: Markham and Cox, *Northampton*, II, p. 454.

5° April Easter day
Mr Ball preached in the morninge Mr holmes[814] in the afternoone, both very p[ro]fitably.
6° April
This day I sent my deare wife & litle John towards London wth hatton & dick[815] & Wm Spicer we besought the Lord for his good p[ro]vidence in o[u]r severall iourneys, I went towards Lamp[ort] before my wife set forth, I was there about the Commission betweene Tho Knighton & his mother[816] Mr Cawdrey good Mr Cawdrey was there too

[crossed out: 6] 7 April 1640
about 4 a clock we ended o[u]r commission & I came along wth Mr Kimbould & ffleminge to North[amp]ton in the great raine & could not receave any newes of my deare wife & was in feare of the men that were to come back in resp[ec]t of the waters but did desire to wayte uppon the Lord. I supped at Mr Rushworthes.
8° April I prayed & went to Wellingborow ffare, great hurt done this night in Cotton end & South quarter to the value of 1000li or as some say 2000li wth the violent & sudden overflowinge of the waters in the night & g[rea]t lamentacon made, Lord sanctifye this thine hand, oh how [crossed out: fr] vayne are temp[or]all things. I went to Broughton this night.
9° April
I kept Mr Pentlowes Court of Broughton this day, I had much good discourse wth Mr Bentham about the church & p[a]rliam[en]t.

[crossed out: 9] 10 April 1640
I came along wth dick to holcot & there I stayd & wrote to Rob. Wyne & dick went back wth the letter to Ketteringe.
a g[e]n[er]all fast was held this day [crossed out: fo] amongst xxians privately in England Scot.[land] Germany ut dic[itur] p[ro] successe of the p[ar]liam[en]t.

---

[814]William Holmes, a graduate of Emmanuel College, Cambridge, was married to Mary. Ordained a priest in 1640, his first position was as curate of All Saints', to replace Charles Newton. He counted Peter Whalley and John Spicer among his friends. He was intruded into the living of Guilsborough during the Civil War and conformed at the Restoration: Longden, Clergy; Isham, Diary, p. 138, n. 19.
[815]Richard Odell.
[816]Knighton (d. 1672) was an attorney residing at Brixworth. His father, William Knighton (d. 1610), had owned a manor in the adjacent parish of Little Creaton through his wife, Elizabeth, daughter of Edward Twigden. The subject of the dispute between mother (who had remarried to Gifford Bullock) and son is not known: Isham, Diary, p. 168, n. 12; VCH Northamptonshire, IV, pp. 102–103.

11° April
I prayed & had great & extraordinary comforts to many teares I blesse
the Lord, the Lord shewed m[er]cy to me stayed me wth fflagons &
comforted me wth apples[817] & I prayed unto him in an accepted time
for my selfe & wife & children & [*crossed out:* I] for my deare bretheren
abroad in the world, this was a blessed day I was lifted up above the
prosp[er]ity & adversity of the world, oh my god that I could soare up
above on the wings of fayth & dwell allwayes above the midle region,
12° April Sab.[bath]
some comforts in gods ordinances this day I blesse the Lord, Mr Ball
preached in the morninge & Mr holmes in the afternoone.

13° April 1640
This day the p[ar]liam[en]t begins, Lord make it a meanes of good
to thy Church & this Comon wealth,[818] take notice of thy adversaryes
& those that plott against thy truth & gospell breake their plotts &
confound their devices seeing they imagine mischeife against thee let
them not bringe to effect what they [*inked out, unintelligible*] intend set
up holy doctrine & pure worship amongst us for the Lords sake
Court to day & the Lord graciously carryed me through the businesses
of the day.
14° April
Quarter Sess[ions] here to day Sr Rob. hatton[819] gave the Charge

[817]Song of Songs 2:5.
[818] A charge by the freeholders of the county to their newly elected MPs, John Crewe and Sir
Gilbert Pickering, presented to the House of Commons by Pickering on 17 April, chimes well
with Woodford's concerns and, as here, lists religious concerns ahead of secular: 'of late we
have been unusually and unsupportably charged, troubled and grieved in our consciences,
persons and estates by innovations in religion, exactions in spiritual courts, molestations
of our most Godly and learned ministers, ship money, horse money, conduct money, and
enlarging the forest beyond the ancient bounds and the like: for not yielding to which things
or some of them, divers of us have been molested, distrained and imprisoned'. They urged
the calling of annual parliaments to prevent these problems: TNA, SP16/450/25, printed
in Cope and Coates, *Proceedings*, pp. 157, 234, 275.
[819]Hatton (1589–1661) was the uncle of Sir Christopher Hatton of Kirby and a
Northamptonshire justice of the peace living at Long Buckby. By 1640 he was living at
Benefield, but also owned land in Kent and Cambridgeshire. In 1637 the Hundreds of
Rothwell and Guilsborough had elected Lord Thomas Brudenell and Hatton to referee a
ship money rating dispute that they were conducting with Sheriff Sir Robert Banastre, and
in 1642 he was named in the Northamptonshire Commission of Array. Like his nephew, he
was a fervent Royalist and was only able to achieve a seat in the Long Parliament outside
the county (at Castle Rising, Norfolk), through the influence of the Howard family, and that
only when the first choice, his nephew Sir Christopher, turned it down: Metcalfe, *Visitation of
Northamptonshire 1618*, p. 226; NRO, Isham (Lamport) MSS, I(L) 2529; Finch (Hatton) MSS,
F(H) 133; Jackson, 'Ship money', pp. 79–86; M.F. Keeler, *The Long Parliament* (Philadelphia,
1954), pp. 57, 208–209.

I attended Mr Pearsons businesse v[e]rs[u]s Rob Wyne p[ro] the Inquir[y] de dampn[820] Mr Readinge was against me.

in the eveninge about 9 of the Clock there was a strange streame of light came out of the Northwest closse by the moone as then it was & came quite over which I saw &

called diverse to see it, ah Lord thou shewest signes & wonders in heaven above & in the earth beneath & yet we remayne hardned still oh worke mightily in thy church & for it for the Lords sake

Good Lord I pray thee looke uppon my poore child John & Cure his eyes, & pay my debts for me in thy due time & susteyne me graciously in the meane time [crossed out: s] & sanctifye them to me for the Lords sake.

15° April 1640
I was this day for one Bowyer of Toucester in another inquiry of damages, & the Lord inabled me graciously, I blesse the Lord for it

16° April
Mr Ball [inserted: 2 the[ssa]l[onian]s] preached very well at the Lecture blessed be god

17° April 1640
I prayed & went to Slapton[821] & kept the Court there & the Lord graciously enabled me for it & brought us home safe at night

I have still good newes from London I blesse the Lord about Johns amendm[en]t Lord p[er]fect it I humbly beseech thee

18° April
I prayed & went about my occasions, & the Lord is please to give me good imploym[en]t I blesse the Lord, I sate up late about the bus[ines]s concerning Mrs ffarmer & Mr Watts.

19° April Sab.[bath]
some Comforts & grac[ious] abilityes in duty this day I blesse the Lord

20° April 1640
Court to day where the Lord enabled me graciously.

& then till the 1° of maii many passages of gods good p[ro]vidence towards me which through businesse I have not expressed.

---

[820] Abbreviation meaning 'damages'.
[821] Sir Henry Wallop was the lord of the manor: Bridges, *History of Northamptonshire*, II, p. 253.

1° Maii
I prayed & went to Ould to seale the writings inter Alex Ibs[822] & Wallis
& beinge his wives Joynture. after that I went to Sr John Ishams and
there I supped but I p[er]ceave his carriage was altered towards me
in respect that I was for Sr Guilb[er]t Pickering at the eleccon,[823] but
Lord my god I desire to wayte uppon thee & to trust thee with my selfe
family estate & what ever concernes me; I beseech thee direct & order
every thinge so as may be for the glory of thy great & holy name & the
good [crossed out: of] & sp[irit]uall Comfort of me thy poore servant
for the Lords sake.

2° Maii
many occ[asi]ons, at North[amp]ton, & the Lord sent me another
Client [crossed out: vrss] vizt Mr Morley to draw writings inter him &
Mr harbert[824]

3° Maii 1640 Sab.[bath]
Mr Perkins preached well here both times & we heard good newes of
the p[ar]liam[en]t.

4° Maii
I prayed & went early to the Court by reason of the visitacon here to
day,[825] & after Court I went towards London, & came safe to dunstable
I & dick & his father, though I was somewhat affrighted on the way
wth two in o[u]r company. I lay at Mr Walker

5° Maii
as I came towards London I heard it at highgate that some s[ai]d
the Parliam[en]t was [crossed out: to be] broke off & when I came to
London I found it so indeed, & the harts of good people were much
deiected but Lord thou art o[u]r refuge in the time of trouble a sure
defence, oh save us thy people & rescue us & bringe thine enimyes to
p[er]petuall shame, Let thy gospell flourish for the Lords sake
*****

---

[822] Presumably the son of Alexander Ibbs, the rector of Old, who had died in 1606: Longden, *Visitation of Northamptonshire 1681*, p. 259.

[823] Isham sympathized with the Royalists in the Civil War but was harassed by both sides and attempted to remain neutral, unlike his more dedicated Royalist offspring Justinian and Elizabeth: NRO, Isham Correspondence, I(C) 3424, 3427, 3273; G. Isham (ed.), *The Correspondence of Bishop Brian Duppa and Sir Justinian Isham 1650–1660*, Publications of the Northamptonshire Record Society XVII (Lamport, 1955), pp. xxxviii–xli; R. Priestley, 'Isham, Sir Justinian, second baronet (1611–1675)', in *ODNB*; K. Aughterson, 'Isham, Elizabeth (bap. 1608, d. 1654)', in *ODNB*.

[824] Possibly Valentine Morley, the rector of Harlestone since 1603 and a Church court official. Alderman John Harbert had been mayor in 1629, when he was among the godly clique which brought Thomas Ball to the town: Markham and Cox, *Northampton*, p. 552; Longden MS, 18 January 1603 and 11 November 1629.

[825] Archdeacon John Quarles's Easter visitation: PDR, X622/6.

6° Maii 1640 O

The Studyes of the good Lord Sea, Lord Brooke[826] & have bene searched, Lord graunt that all the malice of thine adversaryes may turne unto thy prayse, blesse me & my family for the Lords sake

7° Maii

I prayed & went about mine occasions the times are very doubtfull & mens harts full of feares, Lord settle us & thy glorio[us] gospell in due time for the Lords sake

8° Maii

[crossed out: I was at the hall & dyned] I was wth Mr Pentlowe at night who d[e]l[ive]r[e]d me 3 peec[es] from Mr Pearson

9° Maii

I prayed & went to Mr Pearson & to my uncle dexters, & I heard that that morninge

a libell was found which was a sumons to all Apprentices & to meete the next holiday (as I then heard) in St Georges feilds to pull downe the Archb[isho]ps house at Lambeth

10° Maii 1640 Sab.[bath]

I heard Mr Calamy in the morninge & one Mr Wilson[827] [crossed out: illegible letter] in the afternoone there, I was very dull this day oh my god lay it not to my charge but quicken me & make me more to delight in thee my god & to find more tast & sweetnesse in thine ordinances for the Lords sake.

This [crossed out: night] eveninge a drum was beat up in Southwarke & Charge given to the trayne bond[828] there to [crossed out: p] guard the Archb[isho]ps house.

[826] Charles I blamed Lords Saye and Sele and Brooke (and the Earl of Warwick, Pym, and Hampden, whose houses were also searched) for the failure of the parliament. All were suspected of dealing with the Scottish Covenanters, but no incriminating material was found. In addition, John Crewe, who had chaired the Committee on Religion, was arrested and confined in the Tower and ordered to relinquish the petitions forwarded to that committee by ministers silenced in the 1630s. After making a submission, he was ordered to be released on 10 June: Gardiner, *History*, IX, pp. 129–130; J.D. Maltby (ed.), *The Short Parliament (1640): diary of Sir Thomas Aston*, Camden fourth series XXXV (London, 1988), pp. 148–149; TNA, PC 2/52/479, PC 2/52/537, and PC/2/52/544.

[827] Thomas Wilson (1601–1653) was a godly divine presented by Maidstone puritans to the living of Otham, Kent, where he was suspended from 1635 until 1639 for refusing to read the Book of Sports and was repeatedly called before the High Commission: J. Eales, 'Wilson, Thomas (c.1601–1653)', in *ODNB*.

[828] That is, the trained band, London's citizen militia.

11° Maii
about 12 or one [*crossed out:* or 2] of Clock in the night diverse hundreds were gathered together to assault the Archb[isho]ps house, & the archb[isho]p was compelled to take a grey cloake as was s[ai]d & to [*crossed out:* esp] escape over

over Thames,[829] oh Lord god bringe good out of all these troubles & feares for the Lords sake
12° Maii 1640
we here of diverse other libells, and the state of things in the Kingdome is very [*crossed out: illegible word*] doubtfull & uncertaine.
13 Mr Maior[830] of North[amp]ton & Mr Knight are come up the Maior beinge sent for for not collectinge conduct money[831] &.
Mr Maior I heare would not keepe a Court in my absence, Lord looke uppon me in m[er]cy & give me favor in the eyes of the corpora[tion] if it be thy will for the Lords sake
14° Maii[832]
This day the traine bond in these p[ar]ts towards Clem[en]ts Inne were commannded to gather p[rese]ntly & meet at Arundell house[833] & to attend; oh Lord thou who commanndest the waves to be still commannd these stormes to cease, thou art able to doe it oh Lord put forth thy power for the Lords sake.

*****

[829] Laud was widely blamed for the dissolution of the Short Parliament, and the 1,200 apprentices refused to move from Lambeth Palace until 2.30 a.m., much to the distress of local justices of the peace. When they discovered that he had fled to Whitehall, they threatened to return. The house of Laud's deputy, Sir John Lambe, was similarly attacked. Meanwhile, on 8 May the Northampton Assembly had enacted that the mayor, bailiffs, and burgesses should carry arms during the period of emergency and that the nightly town watch should be overseen by one bailiff and one council member: Gardiner, *History*, IX, pp. 132–133; K. Sharpe, *The Personal Rule of Charles I* (London, 1992), pp. 906–907; Book of Orders, p. 57.
[830] John Danby.
[831] John Danby was the mayor and William Knight an alderman. In April 1640, the deputy lieutenants had for a second time demanded coat and conduct money from the town to support the war against the Scots (the first such demand was in 1639). On 27 April the town assembly instructed Danby to reject this but not to detail the names of those who opposed it. Danby is here being summoned to London to account for this non-payment. He appealed twice to the assembly, on 2 and 13 July, to grant the money but was both times refused: Markham and Cox, *Northampton*, II, pp. 436–437.
[832] See p. 400, additional entry dated 14 May 1640.
[833] The house on the Strand belonging to Thomas Howard, Earl of Arundel: R.M. Smuts, 'Howard, Thomas, fourteenth earl of Arundel, fourth earl of Surrey, and first earl of Norfolk (1585–1646)', in *ODNB*.

15° Maii 1640

This last night we were much affrighted by reason that about 12. a clock in the night one knocked vehemently at [*crossed out:* the] my fathers dore & p[ro]claymed that all the trayned men must suddenly repayre to their Captaine uppon payne of death as it was s[ai]d; whereuppon my father sent Richard Becket wth his armes, & in the morninge we heard they were the Apprentice[s] & others that had pulled downe the white Lyon & delivered the prison[e]rs there, & their fellowes that were committed a litle before;[834] oh Lord thou art able to silence all these troubles, doe it for the glory of thy blessed name & the comfort of thy people for the Lords sake.

16° Maii

the Apprentices as they are called have let the prisoners this night out of the white lyon, & one of them was found dead there oh Lord bringe good out of all theise evills & peace & quietnesse out of these distemp[er]s for the Lords sake

17 Maii Sab[bath]

comforts in gods ordinances I prayse the Lord

*****

---

[834] The apprentices who had attacked Laud's palace on 11 May 1640 had threatened to return when they found that the 'fox' had fled. On 15 May, 3,000 returned to Lambeth, attacked the White Lion prison, and sprang their colleagues who had been arrested on 11 May, and all the other inmates too, causing the mayor to take emergency crowd control measures: Sharpe, *Personal Rule*, p. 907.

17° Maii 1640

tearme ended this day. ffrancis ffreeman[835] in some hope of getting out of the fleete &.

I came safe home & was there before Whitsontyde[836] & left my wife at London & went & came hether againe 16° Junii 1640 & there stayed till 1° Julii & then came out of the towne wth Mr Walden & ux Mr Smart & ux Mr downham & ux[837] & lay at dunstab[le] at the crowne & through the next day wth my wife & [crossed out: I who]

8. Julii thassizes here, & I observed not th[is] my Journall through occ[asi]ons till 2° Aug. & therefore have not recorded many

---

[835]Constable Freeman's offence related to ship money, and developed into a minor constitutional cause célèbre. He had run foul of Sheriff Sir John Hanbury's distraining bailiffs in September 1638 and had been sent for by the Privy Council. In December 1639 he was again arrested by Davenport, a Council messenger, for refusing to collect the tax. Freeman refused to accompany Davenport unless he produced a warrant, upon which Davenport drew his sword but was detained by Freeman's neighbours until the constable had effected his escape. These neighbours constituted the godly clique dominating the village: Thomas Pentlow was lord of the manor; John Hackney and Constable William Lord had in 1636 been reported to the Church courts for failing, as churchwardens, to present for gadding to their parish the radical puritan Robert Welford of Earl's Barton, who was the friend of William Tompson, another of Freeman's rescuers; Valentine Cave was closely connected with the Pentlows, the Hackneys, and the Ragdales, Woodford's godly relations, who were represented in the person of Robert Ragdale. Around 10 January 1640 Freeman and the others had been brought before the Council. Freeman and Pentlow had been committed to the Fleet prison, and had appeared before the Council around 28 January. Pentlow had been released on 14 February on paying fees, but Freeman had been kept in custody. Woodford is here hopeful for his release, which was realized on 23 May. Woodford had been in London during the time of their troubles and almost certainly provided support of some kind (see Diary, pp. 339–340). In jail, Freeman had applied to the judges of King's Bench for habeas corpus but had been denied bail (except by Justice Croke), despite there being no reason given for his arrest. Simultaneously, Pentlow et al. had been prosecuted in the same court for rescuing Freeman, and this case was still pending in November 1640. Following Freeman's petition to the House of Lords dated 1 December 1640, the House declared that, since the Privy Council warrant for his arrest had not shown due cause, it was contrary to the Petition of Right, as was the judges' denial of bail. Attorney General Bankes was ordered to abandon proceedings in King's Bench. Freeman was possibly the Captain Francis Freeman who was charged with holding Ranter beliefs by his Parliamentarian colonel, John Okey, in 1650, and was obliged to defend his position in print: J.S. Hart, *Justice upon Petition: the House of Lords and the reformation of justice 1621–1675* (London, 1991), pp. 87–88; Jones, *Bench*, pp. 141, 189–190; TNA, PC 2/51/230, PC/2/51/264, and PC/2/51/307; TNA, SP16/441/86; TNA, PROB/11/223; PDR, Archdeaconry of Northampton wills, third series, C128; PDR, CBA63, fos 417r–v, 425r–v; K. Thomas, *Religion and the Decline of Magic* (Harmondsworth, 1973), p. 161; C. Hill, *A Turbulent, Seditious, and Factious People: John Bunyan and his church 1628–1688* (Oxford, 1988), pp. 92–93; A. Hessayon, 'Calvert, Giles (bap. 1612, d. 1663)', in *ODNB*; C. Durston, 'Okey, John (bap. 1606, d. 1662)', in *ODNB*.

[836]24–26 May 1640.

[837]Robert Durham: Markham and Cox, *Northampton*, II, p. 462.

remarkab[le] passages of gods p[ro]vidence towards me in the time,[838] but Lord I blesse thee for all thy goodnesse to me, I have bene often deiected but thou hast raysed me up againe I have bene since in many wants but thou hast graciously supplyed me blessed be thy nam[e] oh Lord

O

The high sher[iff][839] distreynes somewhat violently

violently for ship money, & great noyse hath bene of Brasse or copper money to come out, but Lord pr[e]vent & amend these wayes if it be thy will in thy due time
many souldiers are gone & dayly goe into the north but are vehemently bent ag[ains]t papists & will scarce be ruled by their captaynes. Oh Lord looke uppon us in this nacon reforme what is amisse send forth thy light & thy truth, scatter Idolatry sup[er]stition & p[ro]phanesse for the Lords sake
I have [*above: double trefoil symbol*] now diverse burdens uppon me but a shoulder of fayth would beare them away & not be sensible of any pinchinge, my debts oft looke me in the face & my hart is ready to be daunted & say it will allwayes be thus I shall never be able to pay but goe backwards rather then forwards, thus infidelity takes hold on me & bringeth worldly sorow whereby I sinne against

the bounty & the power of my god, who possesseth all things, but Lord Ile trust in thee helpe me to hang uppon thee forever did david thinke of a Kingdome when he was keepinge sheepe, did Joseph dreame of such a p[ro]vidence that the King should dreame & he expound it & so attayne to that high place, how came Mordecai[840] or daniel the 3 ch[ildre]n[841] & to their pr[e]ferm[en]t but by thee, oh Lord Ile pray unto thee & wayt for thee, oh Lord that I ought nothinge to any man but love! Oh Lord sanctify my pr[e]sent Condicon unto me make me a gayner by it sp[irit]ually & uphold me under the burden; and Lord looke uppon my deare wife in her pr[e]sent condicon now great wth

---

[838]Though Woodford did not resume chronological diary-keeping until 2 August, he had clearly left a large space after this 8 July entry, which he later filled with a long discursive section and with entries that included information from 6 August (the mayoral election, which he went on to repeat in the chronological section) and the heading 'postin August 11° 1640'.

[839]Sir Christopher Yelverton.

[840]A Jewish hero and nemesis of Haman: see Diary, p. 184, n. 334.

[841]Shadrach, Meshach, and Abednego, three companions of Daniel: Daniel 1:7; 3:12–30.

Child, Lord give her a gracious delivery give her strength to bringe forth pr[e]serve her life give the child right shape & forme continue the life of it & of the rest, make them instruments of thy glory & vessels of m[er]cy give us great comf

comforts in them [*crossed out:* make them instruments of thy glory & vessels of m[er]cy] give us still matter of prayses & thankfullnes; and Lord blesse thy holy church throughout the world my deare bretheren in the comon Savior uphold them in all their troubles satisfy them in all their doubts supply them in all their wants make us all more zealous for thee & for thy truth, p[ro]sp[er] all their honest & godly designes, establish a holy & sure peace in these Kingdomes cast out as unsavoury salt the accursed B[isho]ps that hinder the spreadinge of thy truth & gospell they hate the light because their deeds are evill,[842] they set up those whom thy soule hateth but lord let thy thunder breake through the Cloud uppon them, & let thy lighteninge consume their hierarchy [*crossed out:* not] put it into the hart of his royall maiesty to love the good & hate the evill to discerne betweene those that differ that those that feare the Lord may be precious in his eyes oh Lord give him davids hart & Solomons wisdome that he may improve the talent betrusted to him to the good of this so great a people over which thou hast set him let him scatter sinne & iniquity

iniquity with his very looke, convert his queene unto thee & blesse his royall posterity that they may be famous in Jacob[843] & doe worthily in this our Ephratah,[844] oh when will it once be that thou wilt bowe the heavens & come downe & dwell amongst us, & make us a Kingdome of preists a holy nation oh let holy doctrine & pure worship be set up, & let Justice flow downe like a streame, that the throne may be established let us not linger any longer after the fleshpots of Egipt, & thinke it was well with us when we sacrificed to the Queene of heaven & burnt incense to her, but make it playne to o[u]r soules that it shall be o[u]r happinesse to have communion with thee & to rest under the shadowe of the allmighty, And Lord looke uppon this poore towne here, & now that thou hast so ordered it that a good man is chosen to succeede in the place of Maioralty & good bayleifes,[845] in despite of all

---

[842] John 3:19.
[843] i.e. Israel.
[844] Bethlehem.
[845] The mayoral election did not take place until 6 August, by which time Woodford had resumed chronological coverage: Diary p. 360.

adverse power, to the ioy of thy people & the vexacon of the enimyes
of religion & strictnes Lord be with thy servants whom thou

thou hast chosen, comfort them & carry them through the imployment
that they may discharge it faythfully to the good of this corporacon
[crossed out: th] & the comfort of thy people; And Lord blesse my good
chamberfellow[846] direct him in this great businesse of a [crossed out:
letter] wife if thou seest them both fit for one another bringe it about
remove obstacles, create instruments vouchsafe an accomplishment
of it in m[er]cy to thy glory & their mutuall comfort Lord heare &
helpe & have m[er]cy for the Lords sake Amen.
postin[847] August 11° 1640. [rest of page blank]

[crossed out: 19° June 1640[848]
some comforts in duty this day I blesse the Lord oh Lord p[ar]don all
my sinnes & heale my nature for the Lords sake] [rest of page blank]

[one blank page]

2° Aug. 1640 Sab.[bath] & sacr[ament]
oh Lord sanctifye my hart to thy service this day let thine ordinances
come with power & pr[e]vayle uppon me, let me this day by fayth
eate the flesh & drinke the bloud of the Lord xt & Lord looke uppon
all my burdens & give me fayth to beleive for sustentacon under them
& deliverance from them if it be thy will espec[ially] helpe me against
sinne oh my god for the Lords sake
the Lord was graciously pr[e]sent wth me I prayse his name for it.
3° Aug.
I prayed & went to the Court where we had many tryalls & all carryed
very well I blesse the Lord. We came to dinner & went againe & stayed
allmost till 6. a clock in thafternoone.
4° August
I prayed & went to Toucester as I had done

done 2 or 3 dayes before & yet I find litle encouragem[en]t in goeinge
thether oh my god I pray thee direct me & guide & blesse me from
heaven oh that I could live by fayth uppon thee

---

[846] Stephen Harvey.
[847] Woodford's own Latin term ('postinde') meaning 'afterwards'.
[848] Woodford was in London at this time: Diary, p. 356.

5° Aug. 1640
I prayed & went to Wellingborowe & met there wth Mr Pentlowe of
Broughton & some others but with no money of what is due to me,
oh my god helpe me thy poore servant & his family for the Lords sake
I prayed for gods good p[ro]vidence in the eleccon of the Maior & &
p[ro] Math hudsons wife that is ill.
I heare this day that Mr downes dyed on Sab[bath] day last.
6° Aug.
This day we begane to reade 1 Gen[esis] & Math[ew] Lord sanctify
& blesse thy holy word to us in o[u]r family & build us up by it for the
Lords sake
Mr Ball preached the Lect[ure] sermon & afterward Mr ffisher Mr
Tompkins[849] & henry Sprig chosen notwithstanding all the opposicon

opposicon of Mr danby now Maior Mr Knight & al the Lord himselfe
hath done it by his owne power & arme oh Lord carry them through
the worke thou requirest of them & make them instrum[en]ts of thy
glory for the Lords sake Lord heale my poore child that is now wth
goodman Sheppard for the Lords sake.
7° Aug. 1640
the adversaryes are much fretted, but the worke of god shall goe on &
prosper I stayed at home this day & wrote Lord p[ro]sp[er] me in my
callinge for the Lords sake
[crossed out: This last night Mrs downham miscarried & the child]
8° Aug.
my wife hath bene very ill this day, but Lord stand by her continually
for the Lords sake this day Mr Watts was here but the Lord inabled
me to converse with him wthout too much deieccon Lord rescue me
in thy due time poore Mrs Robins of London & Mr Burrowes[850] were
here to day Lord uphold them in their condicon & save them from it
for

for the Lords sake. This last night Mrs downham miscarryed & the
child dead Lord sanctifye it to them.

[849] John Fisher and Martin Tompkins.
[850] Thomas Burrowes: Markham and Cox, Northampton, II, p. 461.

9°Aug 1640 Sab.[bath]
Mr Coxall[851] Mr ffishers sonne in lawe preached both times this day
very p[ro]fitably blessed be the Lord, & my hart in some good frame
I blesse the Lord.
10 Aug.
I prayed and went to Toucester fare where I have yet but small
incouragem[en]t, Lord direct me in the thing for the Lords sake I
met there wth Mr Palmer[852] of Stoke Mr Tompkins &
11° Aug.
I am heavy wth my wants & debts, but my god is the Creator, & can
bringe forth what I am not aware of Lord Ile trust in thee helpe me
for ever to doe so wth comfort for the Lords sake.
12° Aug.
great expectacon of this great busines

of Scotland, the Lord hath some great worke to doe we trust in the
behalfe of his church to root out Idolatry & sup[er]stition & to purge
& purifye the sonnes of Levi.[853] Lord stand up in thine owne cause fight
for those that stand for thee & though the enemyes be great & mighty
& full of carnall wisdome & policy yet who hath an arme like thee,
thou hast bid us not to despise the day of Small things, thou canst to
the shame of thine enimyes bringe destruccon [crossed out: illegible letter]
uppon them whence they did least expect it good lord be gracious for
the Lords sake.
I sent hatton to Wellingborow.
13° Aug. I stayd at home & followed mine occ[asi]ons, Lord p[ro]sp[er]
me thy poore servant in all mine undertakings to the glory of thy name
& the good & comfort of my family cause the oyle in the Cruse & the
meale in the barrell[854] to hold out by thy blessinge & pay my debts for
the Lords sake
14° Aug.
I went to h[anging] houghton to day wth Mr Rushworth & dyned wth
Mr Gourneyes & was after wth Sr John

*****

[851] Possibly Esdras Coxall of Peterhouse, Cambridge, who had proceeded MA in 1618 and
had been ordained a priest at Peterborough the following year. Alternatively he might be
Richard Coxall, another Peterhouse MA (1629), who was beneficed in Lincolnshire from
1630 until 1641: Venn.

[852] Edward Palmer, barrister and lord of the manor of Stoke Doyle: Diary, p. 345, n. 800.

[853] Malachi 3:3: 'And he shall sit as a refiner and purifier of silver: and he shall purify the
sons of Levi, and purge them as gold and silver'.

[854] 1 Kings 17:16. A cruse was an earthenware container for liquids.

John Isham at the Bowlinge greene, who beleives not that the Scots will come, I came home at night wth some yorkeshire men who report that they are already come.

15 Aug. 1640

[*crossed out:* S] Lady Day[855] ffare here to day. I was in great want of moneyes yet the Lord graciously supplyed me wthout borowinge, Lord why should I be so deiected in my wants hath it not bene my case to be in straights many hundered times & thou hast delivered me & shall I not beleive for time, oh Lord how hard it is to beleive Lord I beleive helpe mine unbeleife for the Lords sake.

16° Aug. Sab.[bath]

one Mr Chambers[856] preached here both times very p[ro]fitably, Lord I blesse thee for this sweete refreshinge Sabath

17° Aug. 1640

this day I have shewed my book to some Lord deliver me from danger & blesse & prosper thy people

now about 7 a clock at night my wife is fallen very ill & the women are with her & we suppose it is her travell & the midwife goodwife Edwards is now come blessed be god but Lord we desire not to trust in the meanes but to hope in thy wonted m[er]cy for a gracious event Lord I beseech thee looke uppon my dear wife strengthen her to bringe forth by thine own power & give us still matter of prayses for the Lords sake.

postin[857] about 8 a clock at night oh my god shew m[er]cy for the Lords sake & blesse o[u]r children, make them instruments of thy glory & vessells of m[er]cy for the Lords sake.

18° Aug.

my deare wife was brought to bed betweene 2 & 3 of the Clock this morninge of a sonne blessed be thy name oh Lord, thou didst send strength where it did lack blessed be thy name for it, Lord make this poore child a blessinge an

an instrument fit for thee to worke by & a vessell of m[er]cy & grace thou art he that doest every great & mighty worke oh that I could wayt uppon thee forever for me & mine helpe me to doe so for the Lords sake.

---

[855] The Feast of the Assumption of the Virgin Mary.

[856] Possibly either Thomas Chambers, a godly preacher from Suffolk, or Humphrey Chambers, a godly Somerset divine imprisoned by Bishop Piers for his defence of the sabbath: Webster, *Godly Clergy*, p. 47; A.G. Matthews (ed.), *Calamy Revised* (Oxford, 1934), pp. 107–108.

[857] Woodford's own Latin term ('postinde') meaning 'afterwards'.

19° Aug. 1640
I prayed & went to wellingborowe where I met wth Mr Robinson.[858]
20° Aug.
I stayed at home about my callinge Lord blesse me in it give me to use dilligence & a good Conscience in it & then doe thou be pleased to add a blessinge for the Lords sake & Lord make me thrifty
21° Aug.
I prayed & went to Stony stratford[859] about a Commission inter Knight [*symbol meaning plaintiff*] & Knight[860] def[endan]t wth Mr Parker we came home late.

22° Aug. 1640
I have taken paynes this day in my callinge [*crossed out:* I heare my] Mr Readinge came to towne here yesterday with Nath[aniel].
23° Aug. Sab.[bath]
Mr holmes preached in the morninge & Mr Ball in thafternoone; and now the litle infant is very ill, oh Lord I have not bene thankfull for the m[er]cy nor walked worthy of it sure thou hast sent it & therefore thou mightest onely shew it unto me & take it away againe but oh my god thou hast heard me in the rest Looke downe from heaven I pray thee Lord heale it if it be thy will thou bringst downe to the gates of death & raysest up againe Lord be gracious & take off o[u]r harts from the creature for the Lords sake Amen. my wife & I prayed afterward for the poore child.
the child began to suck prety well at night blessed be god after I was in bed,

24° Aug. 1640
the Child I heare suckt very well in the night but since that is very ill & we & others much feare that it will dye,
But Lord my god I come unto thee oh that it might be in an acceptable time the yssues of life & death are in thy hand, pardon o[u]r unwillingnesse to submit unto thee why should so much of o[u]r affeccons breake out uppon the Creature like a mighty streame or torrent, & we be so dry & barren towards thee, Lord forgive this sinne of o[u]rs in runninge too much to broken Cisternes & so litle to thee

[858] Thomas Robinson of Wellingborough had been presented to the Church court in 1635 for omitting to pay a levy: PDR, CBA63, fo. 84v.

[859] Buckinghamshire.

[860] One of the disputants might have been John Knight, a client of Sir John Lambe as vicar of St Giles's, Northampton, who moved to the living of Stony Stratford, Buckinghamshire, in 1640: Longden, *Clergy*; Longden MS, 2 September 1640; TNA, SP16/485/101, SP16/485/102, SP16/485/105, and SP16/485/106.

the fountayne of livinge waters[861] let the remission of this & all other
o[u]r sinnes be p[ro]nounced from heaven uppon us, And oh my god
now that my Child is in this weak condicon, my litle younge poore
helplesse child I desire to cast him uppon thee even from the womb
bestowe him againe uppon me that I may stirre up my selfe more
then I have bene to be thankfull, oh Lord I know that of Abraham old
Abraham & he as good as dead then didst rayse & multiply a seed like

like the starres of the heaven for multitude, & if Isaac had bene
sacrificed thou couldst have given him againe from the dead, oh
that I had the fayth of Abraham oh that I could by fayth hang uppon
thee I beseech thee if it be thy will bestowe this m[er]cy as a pledge of
thy love and as a speciall engagement to further duty, oh thou hearer
of prayers accept my poore peticons neverthelesse not mine but thy
will be done, bringe it wthin the arke of thy Covenant make it a vessell
of m[er]cy [crossed out: for] oh give an eare & speake a word for the
Lords sake Amen.
This eveninge [crossed out: after about] about 9 a clock I went for Mr
Ball to desire him to come & baptize my poore child who was ill, & so
had bene from Saterday so he came & Baptized it in the Chamber.
25° Aug. 1640
This morninge the poore child is very much changed and like to dye
in a very short space I

I have sought the Lord in this behalfe, & have confessed & desired
to lament my sinnes before him, when I receaved it at the first I
rec[eive]d it after a carnall manner, & spent the day unp[ro]fitably
& not in prayses to my god Lord pardon this & all my sinnes, and I
have humbly vowed before the Lord (if he please to rayse this dead
child up againe to health & to give it me againe as it were from the
dead) through his strength & grace to walke more holily & precisely
& circumspectly & not to forget so great a m[er]cye & Lord if thou
please to doe so make it I pray thee a m[er]cy unto me & give it me
in Love oh that my sonne Thomas might live before thee, yet not my
will but thine be done oh thou hearer of prayers sanctifye this to me
& my family whether it be m[er]cy or correcon & let even afflicon be
in great m[er]cye, heare from heaven for the Lords sake Amen.
The poore child [crossed out: illegible word] cryes very much & seemes

to be nere unto death, oh my father I pray thee have m[er]cy on the
soule of it, that it may be rec[eive]d into everlastinge glory, and seeinge

[861]Jeremiah 2:13, Israel's rejection of God.

thou art life it selfe though the blood seemes to be setled & death nere
approachinge, if it be thy will restore it againe unto us in m[er]cy &
let us never forget such a favor if thou seest good graunt this for the
Lords sake Amen; how shall we sing of thy prayses & speake of thy
goodnesse
26° Aug. 1640
the poore child continued ill. I prayed & went to Wellingborow.
27° Aug.
This morninge about 7 a clock after my deare wife & I had commended
o[u]r poore child Tom into the armes of the lord by prayer it died,
the first exp[er]ience of affliccon in this kind wch we have had, Lord
sanctify it to us we were much afflicted & I

I went to looke for comfort in gods word & the first place was ps[alm]
42. why art thou cast downe & I shall yet prayse him & oh Lord
helpe us to be bettered by this exercise blessed be thy name that thou
remaynest still o[u]r god, thou art better then all the comforts of the
creatures, oh make us gayners hereby for the Lords sake.
It was buryed this afternoone. dust I am & to dust I shall returne[862]
28° Aug 1640
I prayed & went to Scaldwell to seale John Mabots[863] writings, & did
oft lift up my hart to the Lord in my iourney
29° Aug.
I prayed & went about my occ[asi]ons Mr Watts my creditor not here
to day whereby my hart the more stayed. I owe him now 100li or 102li
& no more I p[ai]d Mrs Pilk[ington] the rest for him.

30° Aug. 1640 Sab.[bath]
one Mr Rathbone[864] preached here to day both times singulerly blessed
be the Lord for it, oh make all thy p[ro]phets zealous.
31° Aug.
I prayed & went to Mr Rathbone, no Court to day.

---

[862] Genesis 3:19.

[863] In the 1637 church survey, John Mabot's seat in Scaldwell church was described as being
too high: PDR, Church Survey Book 5, fos 14r, 136r–v.

[864] William Rathbone (Rathband), who may have enjoyed Northamptonshire roots, was
a godly minister and supporter of Presbyterianism connected to Simeon Ashe, Edmund
Calamy, and the Northamptonshire divines Thomas Hill and Daniel Cawdrey: Foster;
Webster, *Godly Clergy*, pp. 302, 306, 327, 330.

1° Sept.
I prayed & went to Toucester newes that the Scots tooke new castle
on Satterday night last, Lord direct every thing for the best for the
Lords sake
2° Sept.
I prayed & went to wellingborowe & was wth Mr Pentlowe.
the newes confirmed that the Scots have taken Newcastle

3° Sept 1640
I prayed & went to the Court
4° Sept.[865]
I met this day with Mr ffisher Mr Goodman Wm Turland & & we kept
some howers in seeking the Lord, Lord p[ar]don my dullnes heare
o[u]r poore prayers doe good to thy church blesse us & o[u]r familyes,
pay the debts of me thy poore servant in due time Ile ever wayt uppon
thee till thou send deliverance stay up my hart in the meane while for
the Lords sake
I have mistaken in a busnesse inter Collis & Garret[866] whereof Mr
Raynsford & doe take advantage, oh Lord I pray thee extricate me
out of this evill & let me see thy good p[ro]vidence towards me for
the Lords sake pr[e]pare me for thy Sab[bath] & sacram[en]t, heale
poore John keepe us all under thy wings for the Lords sake
*****

---

[865]At a meeting of the town assembly, the deputy lieutenants' demand that the
Northampton trained band be placed under their control was rejected: Book of Orders,
p. 59.
[866]This is the widow of William Collis, the former mayor. Richard Garret occurred in 1628
and may be the same who won the contest for the mastership of the house of correction
against Woodford's preferred godly candidate, John Cole: Vestry Minutes, p. 21; Diary,
p. 372; Markham and Cox, *Northampton*, II, pp. 177–178.

5° Sept. 1640
my cousin Greg dexter Jun[ior][867] here to day, litle Johns face we hope
doth amend.
6° Sept. Sab.[bath] sacr.[ament]
we prayed & I went to the publiq ordinances where I laboured to have
my hart affected but I had litle comunion oh my god. oh my god hide
not thy face from me but helpe me to live by fayth uppon thee for the
Lords sake
7° Septemb.
Court to day where the Lord was pleased to Cary me through wth
difficulty conc[er]ninge Mrs Collis her busines & oh Lord helpe me

[867]In 1632, Gregory Dexter junior (c.1610–c.1700) had been apprenticed to Elizabeth Allde, the owner of a London printing house closely allied with that operated by the Purslow family. Both were situated at Newgate Market in the parish of Christ Church. In 1637, while still an apprentice, he had been charged by the High Commission with illegally printing Prynne's Instructions to Church Wardens. The pamphlet contained an initial letter 'C', which appeared to be the pope's head or an army, depending on which way it was turned. The result of the court case is unknown, but he does not appear as a printer again until 1641. He had befriended Richard Oulton, who took over the management of the works from his mother (Allde), and who may also have been connected to Old: in 1638 he took as apprentices William Isham and Robert Jenison (perhaps he is the Cousin Oughton referred to by Woodford on 24 August 1638). In 1639 Dexter gained his freedom of the Stationers' Company. He married Abigail Fuller before October 1642. From 1641 Dexter and Oulton established a partnership dedicated to printing radical material. That year the fruits of their collaboration included John Milton's anti-episcopal tract Of Prelatical Episcopacy, Pym's speeches, Thomas Stirry's A Rot amongst the Bishops, and from New England works by John Cotton, and Henry Burton's anonymous work, The Protestation Protested. The latter led to Dexter's imprisonment in the Gate House and interrogation by the House of Commons. The following year they printed works by the Northamptonshire man Praisegod Barebone, and Northamptonshire's petition in support of the Grand Remonstrance. In the autumn Dexter may have served briefly with the Parliamentarian army. He was certainly absent, as it was Abigail alone who was interrogated by the House of Lords and committed to the King's Bench for publishing the anonymous King James His Judgement of a King and of a Tyrant. Extracted out of his speech at Whitehall to the Lords and Commons in Parliament 1609. In 1643 he printed works by John Goodwin and Andrew Perne, as well as one by the New England radical Roger Williams: A Key into the Language of America. Williams and Dexter became friends. Dexter's radicalism had left him in bad odour with the prevailing Presbyterian establishment at Westminster, but it was his publication of Williams's radical bombshell, The Bloudy Tenent (1644), that Parliament ordered burned by the hangman, which precipitated his flight to Providence, Rhode Island, with Williams, its founder, in 1644. Dexter's remaining life was taken up as an administrator, politician, and pastor. He served as town clerk of Providence, rose to president of the colony in 1653, and in 1655 was ordained a minister of the first Baptist church in America: I. Gadd, 'Allde, Edward (1555×63–1627)', in ODNB; B.F. Swan, Gregory Dexter of London and New England 1610–1700 (Rochester, NY, 1949); idem, 'A note on Gregory Dexter', Rhode Island History, 20 (1961), pp. 125–126; Stationers' Company, London, Apprentices' Register Book 1605–1666, fo. 123; Freemen's Register Book 1605–1708, fo. 49; Journal of the House of Commons, volume 2: 1640–1643 (London, 1802), pp. 268–270; Journal of the House of Lords, volume 5: 1642–1643 (London, 1767), pp. 386–388.

to doe my duty allwayes & not to be troubled at the event of things but allwayes submitt willingly

8° Sept.

the ffare[868] here to day the newes concerninge the p[ro]ceedings of the Scots very uncertayne &

& what the event will be the Lord alone knoweth oh Lord deliver thy poore church suffer not adversary & popish power to pr[e]vayle against thy truth thou sittest at the stearne & hast the guidance of all things doe good to thy Church and cause for the Lords sake Amen I supped at Mr Giffords this night wth my M[aste]r

9° Sept 1640

I prayed and went to Wellingborowe. Mr Gifford Mr Whalley & went along wth me to Wilby, they goeinge towards storbridge[869] we have continuall discourse of the publiq Lord create peace & deliverance if it be thy will

I met wth a copy of a peticon to the Kinge from Lord essex War[wick][870] & divers others

10° Sept

I prayed & followed my occ[asi]ons after I had shewed the Lords peticon.

11° Sept.

I prayed & followed my callinge I supped

at Mr Rushworths at a venison pasty &.

12° Sept 1640

we heare this day from London of theincrease of the sicknesse & that a child the next dore to o[u]rs there dyed suddenly which hath troubled us & my wife & I Jarred she beinge desirous to have them downe & I to have them to the Nurses 9 miles off there, Lord I pray thee direct every thinge for the best I beseech thee pr[e]serve us all in life & health if it be thy will to thy glory & give us matter of prayse & thankfullnesse, for the Lords sake

---

[868] The feast of the Nativity of the Blessed Virgin.

[869] The fair held on Stourbridge Common, on the outskirts of Cambridge, was the most important in the region. Northampton corporation paid an annual tribute to Cambridge corporation (until 1733) for the goods that they transported back to Northampton, which was the subject of some dispute between the two bodies. Aldermen Gifford and Whalley are making this payment: Markham and Cox, *Northampton*, II, p. 535.

[870] The petition advertised dangers threatening the Church and state, and called for a parliament to punish those royal servants responsible and for an Anglo-Scottish peace treaty. Drafted by Pym and St John, it was signed by twelve peers including Warwick, Brooke, Saye and Sele, and Bolingbroke: Gardiner, *History*, IX, p. 199.

13° Sept. Sab.[bath]
this day my wife churched, & Mr holmes Mrs Crick & & goodman
Iblethy ffayery ffrend[871] Johnson dyned here,
I am much subiect to the thorny cares of this p[rese]nte life but I have
prayed unto the Lord to quiet my hart under the affliccon & I

I have [above: trefoil symbol] discoursed wth my soule in the pr[e]sence
of god about the folly that its guilty of in sinfull Carkinge, [crossed out:
oh] I have remembred thexample of Job & how patient he was in the
losse of these outward things, & what know I but the Lord may suffer
me to be in this condicon of debt to try me onely oh my god stay my
hart & if thou seest good supply me, but not myne by thy will be done
oh my god, powre out [crossed out: of] uppon me the sp[iri]t of fayth
& prayer for the Lords sake. Oh my god Ile trust in thee, thou will
lengthen out the oyle & the meale & when thou pleasest thou canst
give me so much oyle that I must get more vessells till I have inough
to pay all my debts happy it is to be in thy pr[e]sence & to enioy thee!
14° Sept.
I prayed & went to the Court & was invited to Mr Maiors[872] to dinner
to venison.

15° Sept 1640
I prayed & went not to Toucester in respect that some Knights &
gent[ry] of the Country met here at North[amp]ton to frame a
peticon[873] to the Kinge about greivances where I was p[rese]nte &
beinge desired put to my hand, & Sr Guilb[er]t Pyke[ring] & Mr
Knightley were chosen to goe downe to yorke to pr[e]sent the same.
16 Sept
I prayed & went about my occ[asi]ons to We[llingborough] &

---

[871]John Friend was the sexton of All Saints' parish from 1625 and was related to the
man of that name described by John Lambe in 1605 as spreading rumours of a papist
uprising in the town. In 1637 Ramsden claimed that the sexton stayed within the rails of the
communion table and aided the minister in administering the communion. In 1641 Friend
served as a sidesman. John Friend junior, a barber, was presented to the Church courts in
1637 for socially denigrating Ramsden's informant, the curate Christopher Young. Friend
later served as bailiff (1647), chamberlain (1655–1657), and mayor (1665 and 1668), while
his brother Jeremiah was sexton by 1665: TNA, SP14/12/96; TNA, SP16/474/80; Vestry
Minutes, p. 36; Markham and Cox, Northampton, II, pp. 417, 456–459, 551–552, 562; PDR,
Church Survey Book 5, fos 69r–71v.
[872]John Danby.
[873]This has not been identified, but several other petitions were current calling for
the redress of grievances and the summoning of parliament, and these were also the
Covenanters' demands: Gardiner, History, IX, pp. 198–206; K. Sharpe, The Personal Rule
of Charles I (London, 1992), p. 915.

17° Sept
I prayd & went alonge wth Mr Kimbould to harborowe[874] about a commission p[ro] my Clyent Burnet, we came to Mrs Boults where my Lord Litleton & the Kings Attourney[875] were to lodge the same night goeinge downe into the North. I lifted my hart up unto the Lord

18° Sept. 1640.
I lodged at harborowe & towards night in a g[rea]t wind we came away & came home safe blessed be god.

19 Sept
I prayed ag[ains]t thorny cares & went about my occ[asi]ons

20° Sept Sab.[bath]
Mr Lewes preached here in the morninge very well & in the afternoone I & my wife went over to Abingdon[876] I beinge witnesse to Mr Bullivants Child Nathaniel

21° Sept
I prayd & after my wife & I went downe to Mr Balls house to ioyne wth many of gods people in seekinge the Lord in the behalfe of his church & o[u]r selves, the Lord be blessed for [crossed out, illegible] a sweet gale of his sp[iri]t uppon his servants in duty

22° Sept 1640
I prayed & went about my occ[asi]ons

23 Sept
I prayed & went to Wellingborowe & from thence to Burton [Latimer] wth Leases & to keepe Court.

24° Sept
I prayed & went to kepe the Court & did dispatch in a short while

25° Sept
we sealled some Leases to Mr Bacons tenants I met there wth Mr Jarton wth whom I had much discourse of the pub[lic] & likewise about melancholly wth wch he hath bene much afflicted & we stirred up one another to live by fayth in the p[ro]mises of god.

26. Sept.
I pray'd & came for North[amp]ton
*****

[874]Market Harborough, Leicestershire.
[875]Edward, Baron Littleton, and Sir John Bankes.
[876]Abington, Northamptonshire.

27° Sept. 1640. Sab.[bath][877]
Mr ffisher[878] & Mr holmes preached this day Mr [*crossed out:* ho] ffisher
did very well blessed be god but oh my father make my hart better let
me be a gayner by the enioym[en]t of thyne ordinances for the Lords
sake Amen.

28° Sept
Court this day where the Lord did graciously carry me through though
in difficultyes about mistakes.

29° Sept
Mr Recorder not here this day the Lord graciously enabled me for my
part[879] blessed be thy name oh Lord Lord make this man a blessing to
this towne & a m[er]cy to me in p[ar]tic[ular] if it be thy will for the
Lords sake

30° Sept. 1640
I remayned [*crossed out:* &] at home this day, Lord doe good to me &
my family

1° Oct
I prayed & went to a Commission at Toucester inter Waters & Bland[880]
where I met wth Mr Cranford Mr Kimbould & Mr Saunders[881]

2° Oct.
I prayed & went to keep Blissworth Court & came to Toucester againe
at night

3° Oct.
This morninge we ended the Com[missio]n & hatton & I came for
North[amp]ton.

4° Oct Sab.[bath]
Lord make thine ordinances that I enioy fruitfull unto me for the
Lords sake

*****

---

[877] Sibthorpe interrogated his apparitor, Thomas Pidgeon, on 28 September, demanding
to know if he had delivered to Thomas Ball the official prayer 'for his Majesty's safety
and success against his rebellious subjects' (TNA, SP16/468/76). Pidgeon claimed to have
handed it to the churchwarden, Peter Whalley, but it had not been read on the following
Sunday (20 September), whereupon Sibthorpe ordered him to pass it to the curate, William
Holmes, on Sunday 27 September before morning prayer, but Holmes refused to accept it,
while Whalley told him he had no authority to do so, so it was still not read.

[878] John Fisher, the mayor, or his son, Samuel: Diary, p. 95, n. 1.

[879] The swearing in of the new mayor, John Fisher, to whom Woodford as steward would
tender the oath, the recorder, Richard Lane, being absent.

[880] Either William or Thomas Waters, godly attorneys living in Pattishall (Diary, p. 156,
n. 242). Bland's identity is unconfirmed, but there was a family of that name living at
Eastcote in Pattishall parish. This was possibly the John Bland described in the diary as
John Crewe's man: *ibid.*, p. 383.

[881] William Saunders of Potterspury: Isham, *Diary*, p. 69, n. 4; PDR, CB55, fo. 82.

5° Oct. 1640
Court here to day, blessed be thy name oh Lord for supply
6° Oct.
Sess[ions] here to day John Cole moved for the house of Correccon
but Garret[882] carried it, Lord be wth the other thy servant & doe him
good
7° Oct
I prayed & went to keepe Court at Stoke [Bruerne], & returned safe
at night I blesse the Lord.
8° Oct.
I prayed & went & kept Court at Grafton [Regis], where I met wth a
minister & had some comfort in discourse with him

9° Oct
I prayed & went & kept Court at Morend[883]
10° Oct.
I had much imploym[en]t & busines at home I blesse the lord
11° Oct.
Lord I blesse thee for thy Sabaths & ordinances make me fruitfull for
the Lords sake
12° [crossed out: Oct] 13. 14 15 16. 17. 18. much [en]cumb[e]re[d] wth
the cares of this pr[e]sent world, oh my god the burden is heavy but
if I could keepe closse to thee & indeed depend uppon thee my peace
should be as a River Lord helpe me & doe me good, and we pray
often [crossed out: illegible word] for the publike & for a blessinge on the
Parliam[en]t to begin [word destroyed] Nov next[884]

19° Oct. 1640
Court to day. I went after to wellingb[orough] ffare & came to lodge
at wilby
20. Oct.
I kept Court at Wilby but wth too much wranglinge & difference,
Lord give the glorious grace of meeknes & humility to thy people &
love & unanimity that we may be knit together in the bond of true &
xxian Love for the Lords sake.

---

[882]John Fisher had been the master of the house of correction since 1619 and had now
apparently retired upon being elected mayor. The fact that there was competition for the
post suggests that it was profitable. The successful candidate was Richard Garret; Cole was
one of Woodford's godly friends: Markham and Cox, *Northampton*, II, pp. 177–178.
[883]Moor End was a hamlet of Potterspury in Whittlewood forest: Pettit, *Royal Forests*, pp. 14,
76.
[884]Charles I had sent out writs on 24 September to summon a parliament to meet on 3
November 1640, the Long Parliament: Gardiner, *History*, IX, p. 208.

21° Oct

I prayed & went to Broughton to keepe Court where I met wth Sam. Boulton[885] to whom I shewed the reply.[886] Lord looke on that younge man and make him a blessed sonne of so good a father.

22° Oct.

I prayed & was goeinge at about 2 a clock & came to North[amp]ton about 5 in the morn

morninge & after went to Slapton to keep Court & from there came to Mr Butlers at night to Alder[ton].

23° oct. 1640.

I prayed & went to keepe Court (a p[ur]chased Cou[rt] at Pott[ers] Pury, & after that came safe home I blesse the Lord.

24° Oct.

many occasions this day, Lord enable me for my calling & doe good to thy servant & his family for the Lords sake Amen.

25. Oct Sab.[bath]

Lord p[er]petuate thy Sabaths & ordinances to me & my posterity forever & let them be a signe betweene thee & us to these Kingdoms 26 Oct. Court 27. 28. 29. 30. 31. still sub[jec]t to worldly newes Lord helpe me

1 Nov. 1640. Sab.[bath]

oh my god that thy Sabaths may be a delight to the whole nacon, that they may be more sanctifyed

2° Nov.

Court to day the Lord graciously enables me for my calling blessed be his name lord succeed me in it for the Lords sake.

3° Nov.

This day Mr Whalley Mr Goodman Mr Rushworth & I met together to read pray & conferre, which meetinge we purpose to be constant in if god p[er]mitt, we rem.[embered] the church of god & the p[ar]liam[en]t begininge this day[887]

---

[885]Samuel Bolton was the son of the famous puritan divine Robert Bolton, who had bequeathed his library to him: PDR, Archdeaconry of Northampton wills, second series, J90; *VCH Northamptonshire*, V (Woodbridge, 2005), p. 158; S. Wright, 'Bolton, Robert (1572–1631)', in *ODNB*.

[886]The reply may have been a piece of either English or Scottish propaganda relating to the Bishops' Wars or may simply refer to paperwork in a law suit.

[887]The Long Parliament began on this day. Pickering continued to sit for the shire but his uncle, Sir John Dryden, replaced Crewe for the first slot: Crewe now sat for Brackley. The Northampton borough election on 20 October 1640 caused controversy. Woodford himself was absent at Wilby. Tate and Knightley had been chosen for the Short Parliament, and the corporation (comprising the godly mayor, John Fisher, and the bailiffs, Henry Sprig and

4° Nov.
I prayed & went to Wellingborowe then

then to Burton [Latimer] to seale some writings, whether I came safe
I blesse the Lord.
5° Nov. 1640
I made hast in the morning & came to Wilby & heard Mr Pearne, &
after dinner came safe home I blesse the Lord.
6° Nov & 7; many exp[er]iences of gods favor yet I am greatly troubled
wth worldly thorny cares Lord pull them out for the Lords sake.
8° Nov. Sab.[bath]
Lord sanctify unto me all thine ordinances that I have bene at any
[crossed out: illegible letter] time made a partaker of for the Lords sake
9° Nov.
I prayed & kept Court & after came for Lond

London, wth old Mr Martin; & we lay at Brickhill at the Lyon
10° [crossed out: Oct] 1640
we prayed & came & got safe to London I blesse the Lord.
11° [crossed out: Oct]
blessed be god p[ar]liam[en]t sits still, & are unanimous.
12. 13. 14. [crossed out: Oct] Nov.
Lord I blesse thee that those 3 precious men Mr Burton Mr Prynne
& dr Bastwicke are yet in life and sent for back
15 oct.
I prayed & went to Mr Calamyes blesse be thy name oh Lord for
continuing thy servants bold & [crossed out: enowing] & courage in thy
words

16 Nov. 1640
the Parliament goes on very well blessed be god Lord give them
heavenly wisdome & p[ro]sper them for the Lords sake

Martin Tompkins, the aldermen, and the Common Council) re-elected them for the Long,
but when the freemen attempted to substitute the future Royalist John Bernard for the godly
Knightley, Fisher locked the Guildhall doors against them, confirmed the election of Tate
and Knightley, and jailed a freeman for supporting the Tate–Bernard ticket. A petition of
ninety-one freemen was submitted to the House of Commons requesting referral of the case
to the Committees for Privileges and Elections. The petitioners asserted the right of the
freemen to choose their representatives. This was a reversal of the usual civic state of affairs,
where the freemen were generally more radical than the ruling oligarchy, and illustrates
the domination of the Northampton corporation by the godly clique. However, the MPs
continued to sit: Fielding, 'Peterborough', p. 249; Longden, *Visitation of Northamptonshire 1681*,
p. 66; NRO Finch (Hatton) MSS, F(H) 3501; D. Hirst, *The Representative of the People? Voters
and voting in England under the early Stuarts* (London, 1975), pp. 88–89.

17° Nov

This day was held a publiq fast here in London[888] & some adiacent parishes by [crossed out: comann] his Ma[jes]t[y']s p[ro]clamacon for removinge Judgem[en]ts & a blessinge upon the Parliament, god did wonderfully enlarge the harts of his ministers & people, I was at Aldermanbury Church about 14 houres together where 3 ministers prayed & preached one after another, Mr Calamy & 2 strangers, Mr Marshall doctor Burges[889] preached before the house of Comons at Westm[inster] in [St] Margarets, & delivered glorious things with extraordinary zeale & fervor, this hath bene a heavenly day Lord heare the prayers of thy people worke a holy reformacon & make this nacon a pray [word destroyed] the whole earth for the Lords sake

18° Nov. 1640

I prayed and went about my occasions. I oft pray to the Lord to be upholden under the burden of debts & to be eased of thorny Cares by lively fayth Lord looke on thy poore servant for the Lords sake.

19° Nov 20. [crossed out: 21°]

still god goes on very graciously with the Parliament, though some feare the braking of it up for its said his Ma[jes]ty is greatly solicited to it & great sumes of money (as its s[ai]d) many hundred thousand pownds are offered to that end; But Lord confirme the hart of his Ma[jes]ty, and make strong his resolucon to continue it for the good of thy church & people & this nacon for the Lords sake.

---

[888] The proclamation dated 11 November ordered a fast in London on 17 November and countrywide on 8 December: Diary, p. 380; J.L. Larkin (ed.), *Stuart Royal Proclamations II: royal proclamations of King Charles I, 1625-1646* (London, 1982), pp. 734-736; Gardiner, *History*, IX, p. 237.

[889] Stephen Marshall (vicar of Finchingfield, Essex) and Cornelius Burgess (St Magnus, London) delivered the first two sermons ordered by Parliament for its fast days. The sermons argued that Arminians were attempting to reverse the Reformation and reinstate popery, and encouraged the chosen people to join themselves to God by an everlasting covenant. These two and others in the clerical circle sponsored by Francis Russell, Earl of Bedford, had been meeting at Calamy's house from the beginning of the parliament and it was from among them that 'Smectymnuus' was formed, which produced tracts from 1641 calling for a limited form of episcopal government: A. Fletcher, *The Outbreak of the English Civil War* (London, 1981), pp. 93-94; T. Webster, 'Marshall, Stephen (1594/5?-1655)', in *ODNB*; T. Liu, 'Burges, Cornelius (d. 1665)', in *ODNB*; Webster, *Godly Clergy*, pp. 318-319; Gardiner, *History*, IX, p. 237.

21° Nov.

still doubts of the Parliam[en]ts breakinge up but Lord pr[e]vent it if it be thy will this day a popish preist stab[be]d Justice heyward in Westm[inster] hall wth a rusty dagger[890]

dagger, & is taken, and I trust the Lord will bringe good out of it to his Church.

22° Nov. 1640

I heard Mr Pearne both times, once at Allhal[lows] in the wall & once at Mr Jacksons Church[891] Lord make his doctrine p[ro]fitable to me for the Lords sake

23° Nov.

the Parliam[en]t still continues blessed be god Lord smite thine implacable enimies,[892] & reioyce the harts of thy people

24° Nov.

haynous things are against the Lieutenant of Ireland,[893] & he is now committed to the tower.

---

[890]Peter Heywood, a Westminster justice of the peace, had been crossing Westminster Hall holding a list of Catholic recusants marked out for removal from the area when he was stabbed by a man. Pym advocated the implementation of the penal laws against Catholics: Gardiner, *History*, IX, pp. 239–240; TNA, SP16/459/55.

[891]Perne preached at All Hallows', London Wall, and at St Michael's, Wood Street, where Arthur Jackson was the incumbent. Jackson was a godly opponent of Laudianism in the 1630s. He had been one of the London ministers meeting on 6 August to reject the 'Etcetera' oath, which had so much influenced the Northamptonshire clergy (Perne among them) to follow suit. He was an active Presbyterian from 1644: T. Liu, 'Jackson, Arthur (*c.*1593–1666)', in *ODNB*.

[892]The Northamptonshire MP, Sir John Dryden, shared Woodford's hopes for the new parliament and also his assessment of the dangers threatening it: 'heere want not skillful agents for this greate worke' and though 'Tobia and Sanballa [Tobiah and Sanballet were enemies of the Jewish hero Nehemiah] hinder what they may yet the walls go up fast [...] the ruines are such both in Church and Common welth that soom yeares will hardly repair all breaches': NRO, Dryden (Canons Ashby) MSS, D(CA) 906, Sir John Dryden to his uncle, 26 November 1640.

[893]Thomas Wentworth, Earl of Strafford, had been Lord Deputy of Ireland since 1632 and Lord Lieutenant since 1640, and was regarded by the leaders of the Long Parliament as one of the two main perpetrators of the evils of the Personal Rule, the other being Archbishop Laud. However, the method of his condemnation (by bill of attainder introduced by Sir Arthur Haselrig after a failure to prove the charge of treason) opened up divisions in the Parliamentary opposition: B. Coward, *The Stuart Age: England 1603–1714* (London, 2003), pp. 171–172, 190–195; R.G. Asch, 'Wentworth, Thomas, first earl of Strafford (1593–1641)', in *ODNB*; Fletcher, *Outbreak*, p. 10.

25° Nov. 26. 27°

My Chamberf[ellow][894] is gone downe to Missenden to [*word destroyed*]
Randall[895] & is in hope that god will bringe about [*word destroyed*]
match betweene him & Mrs Randall, Lord [*word destroyed*] thy selfe in
the thinge for the good of them [*word destroyed*] for the Lords sake.

28° Nov. 1640 tearme ends to day.

Oh blessed be the Lord for this day for this day; those holy [*crossed out:
Mar*] livinge Martirs Mr Burton & Mr Prynne came to towne, & the
Lords p[ro]vidence brought me out of the Temple to see them, my
hart reioyceth in the Lord for this day its even like the returne of the
Captivity from Babilon.

there went to meet them about 1500. or 2000. horsemen, & about 100.
Coaches and the [*crossed out: pro*] streets were all thronged wth people,
and there was very great reioycinge; Lord keepe them & be with
them and bringe confusion of face uppon their Cursed & malicious
adversaryes let them fall before them even as haman before Mordecai
for the Lords sake and bringe safe home the 3d. banished man[896] safe
for the Lords sake.

This day Mr ffarren & Mr Rushworthes cause was heard against
doctor Clarke & doctor Sibthorpe before the grand Committee.[897]

*****

[894]Stephen Harvey. The Missendens are near Amersham, Buckinghamshire.

[895]Possibly some relation of John Randall (1570–1622), a London minister born at Great
Missenden. He acted as tutor to the Northamptonshire puritan divine Robert Bolton at
Lincoln College, Oxford, and a posthumously published sermon of 1631 was dedicated to
Richard Knightley. He left behind eight sisters. A Richard Randall was mentioned in the
will of Stephen Harvey's father in 1636: S. Wright, 'Randall, John (1570–1622)', in *ODNB*;
TNA, PROB/11/171.

[896]Dr John Bastwick returned on 4 December: Gardiner, *History*, IX, p. 242.

[897]Farren and Rushworth were appealing to the Long Parliament's Grand Committee on
Religion against their excommunication by Samuel Clarke for refusing to create a railed
altar at All Saints' and against his collaboration with Lambe to initiate a High Commission
case against them (which was still pending), forcing them to comply with the altar policy,
albeit only between March and June 1638: see *Diary*, pp. 166 n. 278, 298 n. 680.

29° Nov Sab.[bath]

I prayed and went to Mr Calamyes church where good Mr Ash[898] preached, & gave thanks for the safe returne of Mr Burton, who was there pr[e]sen[t] wth good Mr Prynne also. Lord my soule doth bless thee for their returne.

I heard Mr Marshall in the afternoone at Milkstre[et][899] his subiect was harts hipocrisy Lord make me upright for Jesus Xt his sake

30° Nov.

the newes much about towne that the mouthes of the Scots will be stopped by granntinge all things & the feare is the p[ar]liam[en]t will not last after their returne, but Lord worke for the best helpe us not to trust in parliam[en]t or Scots or any thinge save thee the livinge god for the Lords sake

I saw good Mr henderson at Mr dillinghams & there was wth him Mr Archibald Johnston[900]

1° dec 1640

I am busy in pr[e]paringe the declar[ation] v[e]r[u]s[901] Wilby men[902] ad[versu]s Mr Pentlowe & I have much indeavored an agreement but in vayne & meet with many wrongfull aspersions from those that are good Lord pardon my faylings in any kind, & doe thou blesse those

---

[898] Simeon Ashe was chaplain to Lord Brooke, but less radical than his patron. He spent most of the next twenty years in London but did not hold a living until 1655, although he acted as assistant from 1651 until 1655, as here, to his friend and ally, Calamy, at Aldermanbury. He preached and lectured throughout the city and was connected to many of the lay and clerical opponents of the Personal Rule. During the 1640s he was a Parliamentarian army chaplain, then a staunch supporter of Presbyterianism. He was a close friend of the Rutland minister Jeremiah Whitaker, who was Jonathan to Ashe's David, and preached Whitaker's funeral sermon in 1654. They both organized the posthumous publication of the works of Christopher Love, who had been executed in 1651 for plotting a Presbyterian-Royalist uprising in the city: A. Hughes, 'Ashe, Simeon (d. 1662)', in *ODNB*.

[899] Dr Spright occurs as incumbent of St Mary Magdalene's, Milk Street, in 1636, and a Mr Jones in 1642: R. Newcourt, *Repertorium Ecclesiasticum Parochiale Londinense*, 2 vols (London, 1708–1710), I, p. 471.

[900] Dillingham was back in London having returned from exile in France. Alexander Henderson and Archibald Johnston, Lord Wariston, were two of the leading Covenanter commissioners despatched to London to continue negotiations with Charles I following the Second Bishops' War. Johnston was the more radical of the two, repeatedly pressing for Charles's offending counsellors to be sent to Scotland for trial as incendiaries: J. Coffey, 'Henderson, Alexander (c.1583–1646)', in *ODNB*; *idem*, 'Johnston, Sir Archibald, Lord Wariston (bap. 1611, d. 1663)', in *ODNB*; Diary, p. 274; K. Sharpe, *The Personal Rule of Charles I* (London, 1992), pp. 818–819; Fletcher, *Outbreak*, p. 179.

[901] 'True declaration': that is, the statement of the plaintiffs, the Wilby residents.

[902] Pentlow was engaged in a dispute with his tenants over their leases, one of whom was Woodford's cousin Robert Ragdale. Woodford records that the two sides were reconciled, apparently without recourse to the courts, between 21 February and 26 April 1641 (Diary, p. 387); *VCH Northamptonshire*, IV (London, 1937), p. 147.

that speake ill of me & doe them good & make me a gayner by it & in
thy due time bringe forth my righteousnes & uprightnes her[e]in as
the Light, Lord create agreement & Love betweene Mr Pentlowe &
me & them remove pride & pr[e]iudice let us be base & low in o[u]r
owne eyes for the Lords sake.

2° dec.
my horse came to towne this day &
great hopes of good from god by meanes of this parliam[en]t Lord
give them holy wisdome & zeale & successe for the Lords sake.

3° dec. I prayed and came forth wth Mr

Rushworth, & Mr Watts overtooke us so we came safe to Redburne[903]
blessed be god.
dick was wth me

4° dec. 1640
we came safe & in good time to North[amp]ton blessed be god though
I very sore & weary

5° dec. [*crossed out:* Sab]
I prayed & went about my occasions wch but few to day

6° dec. Sab.[bath] sacr.[ament]
I prayed & heard Mr Ball [*crossed out:* &] in the forenoone & Mr holmes
in thafternoone.
I had too much dullnes in hearinge prayinge & receavinge but Lord
p[ar]don & heale for the lords sake. I heare of imputacons uppon me
still by Wilby men, Lord p[ar]don them & comfort me

[7]° dec. Court to day where the Lord sent me supply blessed be the
Lord.
[Mr] danby & I went downe with Mr

Rushworth to the Registers office havinge a war[ran]t from the
parliam[en]t to search there concerninge dr Clarke & dr Sybthorpe
&[904] Lord remove these idle & unprofitable servants of thine & send
out those that are faythfull for the Lords sake.

---

[903]Redbourn, Hertfordshire.

[904]This is the case of *Farren and Rushworth vs. Clarke and Sibthorpe* at the Long Parliament's
Grand Committee for Religion: Diary, p. 377. The registrar for the Diocese of Peterborough
was Thomas Thirlby: PDR, CB67, *passim*. The churchwardens' case (and the conformists'
High Commission suit against them) was, however, still pending on 6 February 1641 (HLRO,
main papers), when they petitioned the House of Lords for redress: the Lords' final verdict
is unknown.

8° dec 1640

This day a publiq fast was kept by p[ro]clamac[ion][905] for remov.[ing] Judg[e]m[en]ts & a blessinge on the parliament, Mr holmes preached in the morninge, & Mr Ball stood about 4 houres & dim[i] in the afternoone & prayed & preached very well blessed be god, Lord remove B[isho]ps & Idolatry & sup[er]stition & pesteringe Ceremonyes & thy plagues out of the Land, & send forth thy light & thy truth for the Lords sake

9° dec.

the fare[906] held here to day

10. dec 1640

I prayed & went to the Lecture where Mr Newton preached very p[ro]fitably blessed be god

11° dec.

I prayed & went wth Mr Goodman to account wth Crutchley. I hear blessed newes from London of the sweet goeinge on of the Parliam[en]t Lord be blessed for it

12° dec.

subiect to melancholly through want of having sent to diverse that ought me money they fayled & I borowed 8s of Mr Rushworth Lord looke on my lowe estate for the Lords sake

the Smith sent for money & I wanted & the weight players & Mathew Watts & I wanted; Lord helpe me

13° dec. Sab.[bath]

Mr Ball & Mr holmes preached, the Lord [g]raciously enlarged me in my family

14° dec. 1640

I prayed & went to the Court, where the Lord graciously enabled me & supplyed me of his owne bounty.

15° dec.

I sent hatton to Toucester, & my wife & I went downe to Mr Balls to dinner where dyned Mr Gifford & my debts pinch me Lord enlarge me for the Lords sake

16° dec.

I prayed & went to Wellingborowe & after that to Burton Lat[imer]

17° I came from Burton [Latimer] to Wilby & so to North[amp]ton.

*****

[905] A royal proclamation of 11 November had ordered a fast in London on 17 November and throughout the kingdom on 8 December: Diary, p. 375, n. 888.

[906] The annual fair on the feast of the Conception of the Blessed Virgin fell on 8 December: it was delayed because of the public fast on that day.

18° dec 1640
I prayed & followed my callinge
19° dec.
in g[rea]t want of moneyes, but my god is able to helpe, I did lately give my deare wife the litle oyle & the meale. Oh my god lengthen it out for the Lord Xt his sake.
20° dec Sab.[bath] Mr Lewes preached both times the Lord is often pleased to breake in graciously uppon me in duty, though truly my hart is mervaylous full of infidelity in respect of the things of this life, when I rem[embered] that Mrs Pilk[ington's] money calls for about 4li use & another about 14s oh my god that the [*left margin: trefoil symbol*] extorconer the usurer may not catch all that I have, oh that the oppressed might goe free, that the sighing of the needy might come before thee yet not mine but thy will be done.

21° dec S[t] Tho.[mas's] Day.
Mr Ball preached[907] to day & I dyned wth Mr ffisher Maior & the Aldermen & at ffarrens being invited, Lord I blesse thee for the Love I meet wth all it is by thy merciful p[ro]vidence
22° dec.
hatton caryed this day to Mr Lynes[908] the declarac[ion] of Mr Allawayes[909] Charity to Slapton.
hatton brought 6s 8d p[ro] the writing 3ce[910] done & abr[i]d[ged]
23° dec
I prayed & went to Wellingborowe, & am still informed that Wilby men doe cast imputacons uppon me, but the Lord of heaven knoweth that I am innocent, Lord bring forth my righteousnes herein as the light for the Lords sake & in the meane wh[ile] let me beare it as the Lord Xt [*crossed out: would doe if they*] did the reproches that fell on [him]

24° dec. 1640
I prayed & went about my occ[asi]ons, a small market here to day

[907]This sermon had been instituted by the legacy of Sir Ralph Freeman: Diary, p. 272, n. 616.
[908]In the 1637 church survey of Slapton parish, one Mr Line was presented for building a seat which was too high: PDR, Church Survey Book 5, fo. 33r–v.
[909]Hugh Alloway (d. 1650) had been presented to the living of Slapton in 1627 by Sir Henry Wallop of Hampshire and Northamptonshire, who also presented ministers such as the godly Richard Trueman to the living of Dallington. The details of Alloway's Slapton charity are not known, although by his will of 1650 he made provision for the poor of Much Marcle, Herefordshire: Longden, *Clergy*; Longden MS, 15 May 1627 and 21 September 1625.
[910]Thrice.

25. dec. xxmas day.

Mr Whalley Mr Goodman Mr Rushworth & I met this morninge at Mr Rushworths, & read & prayed Lord blesse o[u]r meetings for the Lords sake.

26 dec Mrs Crick Wm Spicer & Iblthy & dyned

no market here to day the parliament was adiourned from Tuesday or wednesday last till Tuesday next, Lord p[ro]sp[er] them for the Lords sake the Lord hath done great things allready the Lieu-tenant of Ireland is in the Tower the Archb[isho]p Cant[erbury] under the black rod, the Lord Keeper[911] rune away b[isho]p Wren bound to appeare & 6. Judges,[912] oh my god arise thou & the arke of thy strength for the [Lord's] sake

[word destroyed] buryed. John James here about his peticon[913]

27° dec 1640 Sab.[bath]

Mr [crossed out: Lewes] Perkins preached both times very well

28° dec. This day another eleccon of K[nigh]ts in Warrwickshire[914]

29° dec.

I prayed and went to Toucester wth about 2d in my purse, & could get no moneyes in there, but the Lord sent one who ought me money that payd about 8d for my reckoninge, Lord helpe me to want & to abound, & all with cheerfullnes & moderac[ion]

30° dec.

I prayed & went to Wellingborowe & had private and lovinge discourse with my cousin,[915] & afterward I learned that my cousin had much

[911] Lord Keeper John Finch had been threatened with impeachment on 21 December and had fled into exile: Jones, *Bench*, p. 143.

[912] Chief Justice Sir John Bramston, Chief Baron of the Exchequer Sir Humphrey Davenport, Justices Sir Robert Berkeley and Sir Francis Crawley, and Barons of the Exchequer Sir Thomas Trevor and Sir Richard Weston: *ibid.*, pp. 137–148.

[913] John James's later petition to the House of Lords (vs. Lambe and Clarke) was dated 9 February 1641. The issue raised by his case (and that of the churchwardens of Upton vs. Samuel Clarke) was referred by the Long Parliament's Committee for Religion to the House of Lords, who stated that henceforth an ecclesiastical judge in an inferior court would be disallowed from holding office in the superior court to which appeals were directed: J.S. Hart, *Justice upon Petition: the House of Lords and the reformation of justice 1621–1675* (London, 1991), pp. 72–73, 75, 77–78, 106–109.

[914] The original return had been voided. Owing to the influence of his father, Spencer Compton, Earl of Northampton, James Compton was re-elected for one of the county seats: M.F. Keeler, *The Long Parliament* (Philadelphia, 1954), p. 139.

[915] Robert Ragdale, who was a tenant of Pentlow at Wilby.

abused me & s[ai]d to Mr Pentlowe that I was the occ[asi]on of the
suite & that hell swarmed wth Lawyers[916] oh

oh my God I humbly appeale to thee, & I confesse I never so
p[er]formed any worke before thee in all my life but thyne eyes could
discerne many blemishes in it, but Lord to those men I am righteous,
thou knowest oh my god that I drew the writings (as I p[er]ceaved
they had agreed) accordinge to the best skill thou hadst bestowed
uppon me without partiallity & without leaninge unlesse to the party,
thou knowest how I laboured for many monethes together wth a
most earnest & harty desire usinge meanes & words to put off these
suites, yet Lord thou seest how uncharitably they use me, oh my god
I acknowledge I have deserved ten thousand times more from thee
(though not from them) therefore I desire wth all patience to cast this
burden uppon thee, make my cursed hart submit Lord they are but
the instruments thou usest to doe me good by, helpe me to

to love them to pray for them to 'seeke their good And love I pray thee
blesse them & doe them good, and give me grace & favor in their eyes
yet againe if it be thy will, and if [crossed out: illegible letter] thou pleasest
& that it may be for thy glory cleere mine innocency thine owne way
for the Lords sake.
Arthur Nicholls agreed wth Mr Pentlowe, & p[ai]d me money towards
the Charges.
I lodg at wilby to night
31° dec. 1640
I prayed & came for North[amp]ton this morninge wth Mr Crewes
man John Bland who Lodged there.
1° Januar. Mr George Coles buryed to day.[917]
O[u]r company met againe at Mr Rushworths & I p[er]formed duty
but my hart was very dull & the Lord for my sinnes in too much
carking care as I may supose wtheld

himselfe much from shininge, Lord accept of my paynfull &
straightned prayers. my wife & I & Mr Martin & ux dined at Mr

[916]This slur on the legal profession was a seventeenth-century commonplace: Prest,
Barristers, pp. 283–284.
[917]He was buried in the church of St Sepulchre, Northampton, in the parish where he had
lived. A brass plaque was erected detailing Coles's twelve children and his two deceased
wives, Sarah and Eleanor; he was survived by a third, Catherine: TNA, PROB/11/185;
Markham and Cox, *Northampton*, II, p. 364; Bridges, *History of Northamptonshire*, I, p. 448.

Rushworthes & my wife & I & cousin Greg Dexter[918] supped there too, my cousin lodgeth wth us to night
I was grac[iously] enlarged in pub.[lic] pr[ayer] in fam.[ily]
2° Januar. <u>1640/41</u>
my cousin went away this morninge before dinner, Lord be with him who hath adventur[ed] himselfe much in thy cause.[919]
3° Januar Sab.[bath] sacr.[ament]
I have much deadnes & streightendnes in duty this day Lord pardon & enlarge for the Lords sake, Mr Ball pr[eached] in the morninge Mr holmes in the afternoone Mrs Wilson dyed in the morninge Mrs Garret[920] in the afternoone.
4° Januarii
Mrs Garret buryed to day Mr Ball preached

5° Januarii 1640/41
Mrs Wilson buryed to day & Mr Bullivant preached.
6° Januarii
John Rolles[921] buryed to day & James Lewes preached Lord thou art pleased to preach to us by thy word & by example, oh teach to profit, to consider our mortality & pr[e]pare for death for the Lords sake
7° Januar
oh my god looke uppon me in my pr[e]sent necessityes & helpe & supply in thy due time for the Lords sake.
8° Januar
I & my wife dyned to day at Mr Parkers with Mr fflint Mr Ball & still good newes from the p[ar]liam[en]t blessed be god, lord p[rotec]t them for the Lords sake

9° Januar 1640/41 [crossed out: &]
I had litle or no moneyes at all in the morning but the Lord first sent me 16d to buy a dimi[922] then more to supply me that the oyle & meale held out till night blessed be thy name oh Lord.
10° Jan Sab.[bath]
Mr holmes preached in the morninge Mr Ball in the afternoone, the Lord did grac[iously] [crossed out: el] enlarge me in family dutys in the afternoone I blesse the Lord.

---

[918] Gregory Dexter junior.
[919] Gregory Dexter junior. For the cause to which Woodford is alluding see Diary, p. 367, n. 867.
[920] Mrs Wilson has not been identified. Mrs Garret might be the wife of Richard Garret, newly appointed master of the house of correction: Diary, p. 372.
[921] One John Roles appears in the vestry records in 1628: Vestry Minutes, p. 21.
[922] A half-measure.

11° Jan
Court to day where the Lord graciously supplyed me
from 11 Jan to the 1. ffeb. 1640/41, through occasions I have not kept
this booke, & so not recorded many gracious p[ro]vidences of god
manifested to me, some times I have inioyed the Lord in [*crossed out:*
dut] prayer & meditacon &

& bene sometimes dull espec[ially] by reason of want of fayth to
depend uppon the great & allsufficient god in respect of my debts &
necessityes, but lord increase my fayth empty me of my selfe & helpe
me to wayte for the Lords sake.
I drew a peticon for North[amp]tonshire ag[ains]t episcopacy[923]
1° ffebr 1640/41
Court to day where the Lord sent me some supply I blesse the Lord
2° ffebr
I prayed & came to dunstable this night safe wth Mr Goodere blessed
be god.
3° ffebr
I came safe to London I prayse god where I find the p[ar]liam[en]t
continue & my freinds well blessed be god
4° ffeb [*crossed out:* &]
I am subiect to melancholly & distrust of

the Lord for outward things, but Lord helpe me; I supped this night
wth blessed Mr Burton who suffered for the name of Jesus Xt;
5° ffeb 1640/41
Lord my debts are [*above: trefoil symbol*] many & urgent & my straights
even pr[e]sent straights are multiplyed but Lord Ile wayt uppon thee
Lord stay my hart & refresh me from thy selfe, & in thy due time supply
me, didst not thou give Cirus the hiden treasures of darknes,[924] hast
not thou 10 thousand p[ro]videnc[es] to helpe thou liftest the beggar
from the dunghill[925] Lord doe me good & my wife mother & family
good for the Lords sake I had a recovery at Bar p[ro] Mr Campio[n][926]

---

[923] The only reference yet found to a Northamptonshire petition against episcopacy. Since
Woodford drew it up at some time within the period of 11–31 January 1641, it must have
been among the twelve county petitions (from the south, east, and East Midlands) which
arose in response to the London Root and Branch petition of 11 December 1640: Fletcher,
Outbreak, pp. 91–92.

[924] Isaiah 45:3. Cyrus II was an Old Testament ruler of Babylonia who was lenient to the
Israelites.

[925] 1 Samuel 2:8.

[926] Richard Campion, signatory of the indenture confirming the knight of the shire result
for the Short Parliament. Alternatively, Thomas Campion or his son John, who occur in

6° ffeb.

much good newes from the p[ar]liam[en]t this week I blesse god about 300000li[927] given to their br[ethere]n the Scots that there shall be no pub.[lic] goeinge [?after] &. Lord goe on to build thy temple [amo]ng us for the Lords sake

7° ffeb. 1640/41 Sab.[bath] & sacram[en]t
I heard Mr Calamy this morninge & Mr Whitaker[928] this afternoone & rec[eive]d the sacram[en]t in the morninge my hart was affected I blesse the Lord & the Lord enlarged me in duty
8° ffeb. 9. 10. 11. 12. 13. I was very busy about my occasions & the Lord in some gracious measure rescued me from Thorny Cares that I followed my callinge wth more diligence my brother admitted this weeke of Grays Inne[929] Lord p[ro]sper him & doe him good for the Lords sake. Mr Knight answ[er] on Satt[er]day
14° ffeb. Sab.[bath]
I prayed and went to Aldermanbury in the morninge where sweet Mr Spirestoe[930] preached the glorious gospell out of 7 Hebrews[931] therefore he is able to save unto the uttermost & my hart was greatly affected in hearinge & prayer I blesse the Lord, in the afternoone I heard a Scotish minister at the Scotish house before the Commissioners,[932] a singuler able good man

1640: TNA, C219, 41, 1, part II, 159; Freemen of Northampton, unpaginated, under John Campion, dated 1640.

[927] As part of the Treaty of Ripon, which concluded the Second Bishops' War in October 1640, Charles I was obliged to pay the Scottish army £850 per day while it remained on English soil: B. Coward, *The Stuart Age: England 1603–1714* (London, 2003), p. 182; Gardiner, *History*, IX, p. 214.

[928] Jeremiah Whitaker was the rector of Stretton, Rutland. A client of the Cecils, earls of Exeter, and of Sir John Pickering, he was a leader of opposition to the religious policies of the 1630s. He refused to read the Book of Sports, to convert afternoon sermons into catechizing sessions, or to contribute towards the clerical levy to support the Bishops' Wars. He was a leading figure in the clerical conference held at Kettering on 25 August 1640 to co-ordinate resistance to the 'Etcetera' oath and support for Covenanter propaganda. He later served in the Westminster Assembly and developed into a committed London Presbyterian, collaborating with Simeon Ashe and Matthew Newcomen: J. Fielding, 'Whitaker, Jeremiah (1599–1654)', in *ODNB*.

[929] Samuel Haunch is recorded by Venn as being admitted on 20 February.

[930] William Spurstowe had been appointed to the living of Great Hampden, Buckinghamshire, by John Hampden, and he was later chaplain to Hampden's regiment during the Civil War. He was a Presbyterian, and part of 'Smectymnuus': Webster, *Godly Clergy*, pp. 260, 318; S. Achinstein, 'Spurstowe, William (d. 1666)', in *ODNB*.

[931] Hebrews 7:25.

[932] The Scots sent treaty commissioners to negotiate with the English in talks which had been postponed at Ripon and now resumed at Westminster, leading to a treaty in August. Various Scottish ministers (Robert Baillie, George Gillespie, and Robert Blair) were preaching to great acclaim in London pulpits: Coffey, 'Henderson, Alexander'; D. Stevenson, 'Baillie, Robert (1602–1662)', in *ODNB*; *idem*, 'Blair, Robert (1593–1666)', in

15° ffeb. [*crossed out:* 16] I prayed and went about my occasions, Lord doe good to me & my family for the Lords sake.

16° ffeb. 1640/41
This day the Kings Ma[jes]ty was pleased graciously to assent to a trienniall parliam[en]t, which hath occasioned much reioycinge in the City & very many bonefires, Lord helpe us to returne new prayses for every fresh m[er]cy by Jesus christ.
17° ffeb.
This day the Lieu-tenant of Ireland was caryed from the Tower to the upper house of Parliament to put in his answere,[933] I saw him upon the water as he was goeinge, he hath gotten time for a weeke longer, in the afternoone I attended the Committee for ship money about Mr Bacons busines.
18° ffeb.
I prayed & went about my occasions & about 3 a clock in the afternoone came out wth dick onely & we met wth good company & came to Redburne[934]

19° ffeb. 1640/41
we came safe home by gods m[er]cy about 5 a clock in the afternoone where I found my family in health & my mother [*crossed out:* wife] rid of her ague
20. ffeb.
I prayed and attended my occasions, Good Lord blesse me in all my wayes for the Lords sake.
26° April 1641 being munday in sept[imana] pe[nali]s[935]
by reason of many occasions I have neglected this Journall, & so many [*crossed out: illegible letter*] p[ro]vidences that I have since met with are not here recorded as the agreem[en]t of Wilby businesse betweene Mr Pentlowe & his tenants my Childrens (vizt [*symbol of a hand with finger pointing at the next word*] Sam & Sarah) beinge sick of the small pox at London & their recovery, my supportment under my many debts, & for the enioym[en]t of the pr[e]sence & countenance of my gracious God & Lovinge father sundry times since in prayer & in meditacon uppon the highway & otherwise, for deliveringe me in my f[all]
*****

ODNB; K.D. Holfelder, 'Gillespie, George (1613–1648)', in *ODNB*; Gardiner, *History*, IX, pp. 214, 238.
[933] Strafford is here preparing for his trial before the Lords for treason; the trial started in March: Coward, *Stuart Age*, pp. 189–194, 520.
[934] Redbourn, Hertfordshire.
[935] Holy Week.

wth my horse, when my leg was under him that the Lord [*crossed out:* h] doth still continue my health & parts, & enables me in some measure for my callinge, & so restraynes my melancholly & feares & worldly cares that they doe not devoure me & many other blessings & m[er]cyes wch I have in this space receaved from the hand of my God, & the dore of hope that the Lord hath opened for his poore Church in generall & my selfe in particuler I desire to exalt the name of the Lord & to prayse him for his goodnes, and Lord I beseech thee [*left margin: trefoil symbol*] for a continuance of thy favors; Good Lord forgive my sinnes & heale my soule purge my conscience from dead workes, Lord make me as holy as an angell of light that I may doe thy will on earth as it is done in heaven, let the deaw of grace be distilled into my soule continually & the light from on high be darted into my hart dayly that my strength & tallne

tallnes may be as the Cedars & my smell as Lebanon, that the North & South wind of that spirit of thine which bloweth where it listeth may breath uppon my garden[936] that my savor may be as a feild which the Lord hath blessed, oh Let the heavens drop downe from above & the skyes powre downe righteousnes,[937] blesse thine ordinances I have bene yesterday made p[ar]taker of, & Lord helpe me in my straights thou knowest my debts Lord I desire to owe nothinge to any man but Love, and God forbid I should ever put forth my hand to receave the least peny of unlawfull gayne to extricate my selfe out of this misery Ile trust in thee forevermore, are not the Catle thine uppon a thousand mountaynes[938] & the treasures of darknes[939] Lord pay my debts for me I beseech thee that I may serve thee wth

wth more enlargement, yet not mine but thy will be done oh most gracious & wise god, Lord helpe me to sell my land if it be thy will, or helpe me or [*crossed out:* su] susteyne me which way thou pleasest, if thou withholdest the sufficiency of furniture I pray thee bestowe uppon me that of supply, And for my family oh my God I pray thee save all o[u]r soules & let us grow up before thee as Calves of the stall, let my house be a Church & let mount Gerizim[940] be amongst us, let the good will of him that dwelt in the bush inhabite with us, let the everlastinge armes embrace us Continually let us be unto thee as [*crossed out:* thy] a litle vineyard of red wyne water us night & day, in

[936] 2 Kings 19:23; Song of Songs 4:11, 16.
[937] Isaiah 45:8.
[938] Psalm 50:10.
[939] Isaiah 45:3.
[940] An alternative location of worship to Jerusalem: John 4:20.

the name of my god I blesse my poore family; And looke uppon thy
[*crossed out: illegible word*]

distressed Church, thine anncyent people the Jewes seeme to be
forgotten by thee returne oh shulamite returne,[941] where are thy
bowells? for the Lords sake ingrafte them in againe, o[u]r elder sister
hath no breasts[942] what shall we doe for o[u]r sister, oh we desire to
speake for her who is obstinate & refuseth to come in, Lord inlighten
her, oh that all Isr[ael] might be saved accordinge to thy p[ro]mi[se]
the unmarried hath more children then she that hath an husband,
Lord we blesse thee for the great fruitfullnes of the gentiles, the Lord
increase us a thousand fold, but Lord let not the wife be allwayes
barren, & bring in the remaynder of the gentiles in America[943] &
otherwhere, and [*crossed out: send a*] let the spirit of reformacon passe
through this I[s]land & Ireland & the adiacent Kingdomes pull downe
that cursed Antichrist of Rome that B[abilon]

Babilon the great[944] may fall in these o[u]r dayes if it be thy will, that
the voyce of the Bride groome & the Bride may be heard no more in
her [*crossed out: e*] that the light of a Candle may be seene no more in
her[945] and Lord thou seest how the wicked B[isho]p[s] limbs of him
here in this Kingdome have even darkned the sunne in the heavens
thereof & brought up a fog over the whole nacon Lord cutt them off
roote & branch[946] in one day forever extirpate their hei[r]archy, & set
the Lord Christ uppon his throne amongst us, Lord thou seest how
they & some of their adherents have sought to enslave us & bringe us

---

[941] Song of Songs 6:13.

[942] Song of Songs 8:8.

[943] William Castle was advocating just such a missionary effort. In *A Petition of W C Exhibited to the High Court of Parliament* (London, 1641) he encouraged the conversion of native Americans as part of the international godly response to the international popish plot led by Spain and the papacy. Supporters of his lobby included national figures (Scottish and English) but the core was a group of twenty-five (mainly puritan) ministers from Peterborough diocese. Castle went on to expand his thesis in *The Jesuits Undermining of Parliament and Protestants with their Foolish Phancy of a Toleration* (London, 1642), in which he gave full-blown support to the international popish plot interpretation of current domestic and foreign affairs espoused by the Protestation Oath and Grand Remonstrance. He encouraged Parliament to arm against papists at home and to pursue an aggressively Protestant policy against Spain and the papacy abroad. A 1640s tract published by Whitaker, Calamy, and Marshall (*The Clear Sunshine*) reported on the progress of the missionary project: Fielding, 'Peterborough', pp. 255, 261 n. 9; P. Gordon, 'William Castell of Courteenhall: a seventeenth century pioneer of missionary work', *Northamptonshire Past and Present*, 8:5 (1993-1994), pp. 354-362.

[944] Revelation 17:5.

[945] Revelation 18:23.

[946] Sir Edward Dering presented the Root and Branch Bill to Parliament on 27 May 1641: Fletcher, *Outbreak*, p. 100.

into bondage both in respect of soule & body but Lord breake the yoke
of the oppressor as in the day of Midian strengthen the Parliam[en]t
to that end Lord guide them & doe good to us for the Lords sake.

8° Junii 1641
Lord looke uppon me in my lowe [*above: trefoil symbol*] Condicon, my
debts are very many & my sinnes are more, Lord send helpe & graunt
that I may yet live comfortably [*crossed out:* &] in the feare of the Lord
wth my family for the Lords sake. Lord supply me wth moneyes for
my Journey into the country & while I am here
14° Julii at London
the Lord graciously supplyed me wth moneyes when I was in the
Country so that I have payd 7li to Su[947] in full & & 3li for my p[rese]nte
money Lord cary me out of towne wth Comfort & bringe me through
my many businesses wth gracious successe Lord pardon my sinnes
increase grace in me blesse me & my deare wife now that she [*crossed
out: illegible letter*] is nere her time[948] give strength to bring forth uphold
her graciously & make the child a vessell of m[er]cy & a comfort to
us the parents & blesse o[u]r whole family feed us cloath us & pay
o[u]r debts for the Lords sake and oh my God still p[ro]sp[er] the
Parliam[en]t for the L[ords] sake

21° Julii 1641
my mother haunch & I & Richard came out of London & came safe
to Redburne[949] that night Mrs Eliz hatch[950] buryed this day it seemes
22° Julii
we prayed & came towards North[amp]ton & came through Newport
[Pagnell] in regard of the sicknes raginge at Stony Stratford, & came
home & found my wife & family well blessed be god, & my wife not
yet brought to bed
Mr dod the yonger[951] preached [*crossed out:* yester] the Lecture to day
my mother & John & Susan at Old.
23° Julii
my sister Rushworth is very ill & troubled in Conscience: Lord looke
uppon her in m[er]cye for the Lords sake

[947]Susan Tue.
[948]Their son Nathaniel was not born until 7 September 1641.
[949]Redbourn, Hertfordshire.
[950]Possibly a relation of Thomas Ball's third wife, Jane Hatch, a widow: J. Fielding, 'Ball,
Thomas (1590–1659)', in *ODNB*.
[951]Two of John 'Decalogue' Dod's sons – John and Timothy – became ministers. Timothy
was a minister at Daventry and is the more likely candidate: J. Fielding, 'Dod, John (1550–
1645)', in *ODNB*; K. Gibson, 'Dod, Timothy (d. 1665)', in *ODNB*.

24° Julii
The Lord graciously supplyed me wth money blesse the Lord ah thou
art a god of trust & makest good all thy p[ro]mises oh that [I] c[o]uld
wayt uppon thee & trust in thee p[er]fectly

25° Julii Sab[bath] 1641
Mr holmes preached in the morninge Mr Ball in the afternoone, &
spake as desirous of a reconciliacon of the differences that are now in
the towne, Lord reconcile them & bringe good out of these evills
This night beinge about to beginne repeticon Mr S Martin came for
me to goe p[rese]ntly to Mrs Rushworth who was in mighty horror
roringe sometimes most hideously & cryeinge out she was damn'd
she was damn'd, she should be in hell to all eternity, & that she had
neglected so great salvacon, woe & alas that Jesus Christ had cast her
off forever & the like fearefull expressions, as that she was allready in
hell & but after 2 or 3 houres the Lord stayed her in some measure
in the midest of her horrors she acknowledged she loved god & his
children, & that she had iniured god but he had done her no iniury at
all, oh my God create peace for thy servant, oh let her make thee the
eternall god her refuge & let be undern[eath] the everlastinge armes
though she [*word destroyed*] d[arknes]

darknes & sees no light yet let her [*crossed out:* stay] trust in the Lord
& stay her selfe uppon her god, oh Lord hide not thy face too longe
be not wrath very sore why wilt thou follow a leafe driven by the
wind of thy tempest after thou hast throughly humbled her give her
revivinge & strengthen her weake body to beare the worke, & let this
thinge be a speciall lesson to me & other of thy servants to learn
to serve thee wth feare & come before thee wth tremblinge yet with
full assurance of fayth & make us more watchfull against sinne wch
breaks the comunion betweene thee & us Lord heare & helpe &
shew m[er]cy for the Lords sake my cousin Emme warren & Cousin
Turland⁹⁵² supped here to night
26° Julii 1641
the fare⁹⁵³ to day.
27° Julii
Court to day & many causes entred, the Lord graciously supplyed me
this Court that it was worth
*****

---

⁹⁵²Probably Thomas Turland of Old, whose wife, Ann, may have been the sister of
Woodford's cousin William Woodford – certainly one of that name witnessed her husband's
will in 1659: TNA, PROB/11/294.
⁹⁵³The annual St James's Fair.

worth about 3li to me, Lord be blessed for my seasonable supplyes at London & here.

I paid Su. 7li at London the residue of the 12li wch I ought her & have in the bond blessed be god.

28° Julii 1641

I prayed & went to Wellingborowe where Mr Waggner[954] preached at the Lecture there Lord uphold that & other lectures graunt that thy gospell may have free passage throughout these Kingdomes that Satan may like lighteninge fall downe from heaven for the Lords sake oh my god whereas there have bene differences betweene Wilby men & me, & that I have receaved much wrong from them (as I conceave havinge done the busines about their Leases wth all iustice & integrity of spirit accordinge to the best of the knowledge & skill bestowed uppon me & havinge done what I could to keepe off the suite,) Lord bringe forth my sincerity (if it be thy will) as the light to the glory of thy na[me]

this I humbly referre unto thee, & Lord give me a hart to beare iniuryes with all patience & cheerfullnes & make me a gayner in my soule by this p[ro]vidence of thine & Lord give me yet grace & favor in the eyes of those men if it be thy will thou canst in thy good p[ro]vidence find out a way to unite us Lord I wayt uppon thee give me fayth & patience for the Lords sake

29° Julii 1641

Mr Ball preached at the Lecture to day

oh Lord what great things hast thou done for this Kingdome how hast thou made the cursed B[isho]ps & their Clergy which were as the head to be now as the tayle & thy faythfull & godly ministers & people to triumph Lord goe on wth this great worke to the savinge of many thousand soules to the pullinge downe of will-worship & to the exaltinge of that in spirit & truth[955] for the Lords sake.

Mrs Parsons is here wth my wife & hath bene here in the towne about a fortnight, & is to goe to Mrs Lewes at Brixworth, & the houre is not yet come wch makes us apt to be troubled, But oh Lord thou wilt doe ev[e]ry

ev[er]y thinge for the best, Lord order every conveniency give her a gracious delivery In thy due time the sentence on her is to bringe forth in payne & on me to get my bread in the sweat of my browes, Lord

---

[954]Not identified. There are glimpses of the operation of the Wellingborough lecture between 1607 and 1642; it seems to have been administered by the ruling body of the town, the feoffees: Fielding, 'Peterborough', p. 166, n. 24.

[955]John 4:24.

stand by her thy servant & support her graciously Lord many have
lately dyed in Childbed, [*crossed out:* whe] wee shall the better see &
acknowledge thy great m[er]cy to us in pr[e]servinge thy handmayd
oh Lord build up & continue o[u]r family still, thou hast gathered
us doe not scatter us for the Lords sake & Lord give the child right
shape & form & continue it & the rest in life & let the blessings of
the everlastinge & all-sufficient god be uppon them in spiritualls &
temporalls especially spiritualls oh my god, & [*crossed out:* though] give
grace to me thy poore servant to wayt uppon thee to beleive in thee
p[er]fectly for heaven & earth increase grace in my soule give me to
labor & be dilligent in my callinge, & blesse me from heaven pay my
debts in thy due time keepe my father & his family from the pestilence
which rageth in London for the Lords sake.

30 Julii 1641
good Mrs Rushworth is very ill the Lord will be gracious
31° Julii
the Lord is pleased to carry me through my wants & imployments that
I still subsist blessed be the allmighty & most gracious God.
1° Aug. Sab.[bath]
I heard Mr Ball in the morninge, & Mr Symmer[956] in the afternoone
Lord pardon my dullnes & prophaninge thy Sabath & ordinances
continually.
2° Aug.
last Court before the vaccacon this day, blessed be the Lord for
supplyeinge me this day graciously
3° Aug.
we had a fast this day in publiq blessed be god, though not
commannded publiquely, Mr Rathbone Mr Baynard & Mr Ball
excercized, Lord Let prayers ascend to thee, & blessed be thy name
for this gracious season & lib[er]tye Lord sanctfye it to us

4° Aug. 1641
I went this day to wellingborow, & did heare that this day there is a
fast at Bedford, Lord doe good to this Kingdome & nacon
I came home safe I blesse god.

---

[956] Archibald Symmer from Aberdeen occurred as curate at Great Oakley from 1629 until
1642 owing to the patronage of Sir Thomas Brooke. He was also connected to Sir John
Hanbury: Fielding, 'Peterborough', p. 26; PDR, CB68, fo. 106r-v.

5° Aug.
Mr Ball preached at the eleccon of the Maior & there are chosen Mr
Lawrence Ball Maior Jonathan Whishton[957] & John holmes Bayleifes
oh my god overrule them & direct them in such a manner that they
may be a speciall blessinge to this towne for the Lords sake.
This day my deare sister Mrs Rushworth dyed
6° Aug.
oh Lord fit me for my dissolucon for the Lords sake.
7° Aug.
Mr Rogers preached excellently at the fun[er]all of Mrs Rushworth[958]
This day Tho. Warren of Old here on whom I trust the Lord hath
shewed much m[er]cy & converted him a sinner from his evill way
Hosanna in the highest to o[u]r god, Lord confirme him in thy truth
for the Lords sake

8° Aug. 1641 Sab.[bath]
Mr Symmer preached at Allhallowes in the morning Mr Ball in the
afternoone
9° Aug. my deare wife still troubled in regard she hath missed her
account, Lord thy time is the best give her a gracious delivery in due
time & blesse her & the child & my whole family for the Lords sake.
10. Aug. I was this day at the ffare in Toucester
11° Aug. I was not at Wellingborow [*crossed out:* I think I eat a plum or
two & was somew[ha]t ill at night] Judge Reeve[959] came in to day.
12° Aug.
The Assizes began to day Mr Waters[960] of dodington preached here.
13° 14° Aug. The cause went ill for Mr Trueman[961]

---

[957]Whishton had served as a sidesman in 1636. He was elected mayor on 6 August 1657
after a bitterly disputed poll in which John Smart, the bailiffs, and the council supported
Whishton against candidates nominated by the sitting mayor (Joseph Sargent) and aldermen:
Markham and Cox, *Northampton*, II, pp. 33–34, 553.

[958]Joan Rushworth's burial is confirmed by the parish records: NRO 223P/1, dated 7
August 1641.

[959]Edmund Reeve had been knighted and appointed justice of the Court of Common Pleas
in 1639. He supported Parliament during the Civil War: D.A. Orr, 'Reeve, Sir Edmund
(*c.*1589–1647)', in *ODNB*; Jones, *Bench*, p. 143.

[960]Anthony Waters had been vicar of Great Doddington (by crown presentation) since 1619.
He served as a commissioner for the church surveys of 1631 and 1637 and was regarded by
Sibthorpe as an ally in 1639. The moderately godly Royalist Thomas Jenison of Irchester,
who was later to side with Lord Montagu against the more fervent George Catesby and
Francis Sawyer concerning the iconoclastic attack on Isham cross, bequeathed his divinity
books to Waters in 1646: Longden MS, 24 February 1619; Temple of Stowe MSS, STT
1876; Fielding, 'Peterborough', pp. 25–26, 260; TNA, PROB/11/229.

[961]Richard Trueman was the incumbent of Dallington, which was identified in the
anonymous *A Certificate from Northamptonshire. Touching pluralities. Defect of maintenance. Of not
preaching. Of poor ministers* (London, 1641) as a very poor vicarage.

15° Aug. Sab.[bath] I heard Mr holmes & Mr Ball

16. Aug. the ffare[962] kept here to day oh how men buy & sell & get gayne, oh give me to make godlines great gayne for the Lords sake

ffinis huius.

Additional diary entries

25° ffeb. 1639/40[963]

now that I am in distresse by reason of many debts & straights drop downe ye heavens from above & let the skyes powre downe plenty, let him that is in the mire be lifted out, let the beggar be raysed from the dunghill,[964] let not him that trusteth in god be ashamed, let the time of gods gracious visitacon hasten, ah my god I like peter am afrayd that I shall even sinke in these waters, yet how can I seeinge thou holdest me by the hand, oh Lord I will stay for thee thy time is the best time, helpe me to wayt patiently for thee pull out these faythlesse thorny worldly cares, let thy sweet spirit refresh & comfort me enable me for my callinge & blesse me in it, Lord order my iourney for Warrick if it be thy will & succeed o[u]r cause graciously if thou seest good

[blank page]

15° ffeb. 1639/40[965] beinge in g[rea]t distresse & too deepe melancholly wth the thoughts of my debts & feare of runinge further,

oh my god & father gracious & allsufficient I pray thee pardon the rebellion & pride of my spirit that I cannot submit unto thee in that condicon which I am in Lord helpe me that I may for time to come, & helpe me to wayte uppon thee for releife & supply, but Lord wilt thou shew a miracle to the dead, wilt thou yet bringe me out of this great gulfe of debts & wants which I have much brought uppon my selfe through my want of diligence & thrift? truly Lord both the Judges are thine & the cattell uppon a thousand mountaynes,[966] thenioym[en]t of these things comes neither from the east or west but from my deare father who setteth up one & pulleth downe another, Lord say but

---

[962]The annual fair held on the feast of the Assumption of the Blessed Virgin.

[963]See p. 340, main diary entry dated 25 February 1639/40.

[964]1 Samuel 2:8.

[965]See p. 340, main diary entry for 6 February 1639/40: Woodford was in London at this time.

[966]Psalm 50:10.

the word & every creature shall delight to supply me, Lord thou hast ten thousand p[ro]vidences for my good which I ne're thought of, if thou pleasest, oh Lord let the good of my selfe deare wife & family be precious with thee, uphold my spirit in my pr[e]sent state & sanctifye unto me what is uppon

uppon me, & when thou shalt enlarge my steps let me breake forth in prayses & be ravished with thy tender m[er]cy let temporalls come by vertue of the covenant & prove pledges of thy love & g[rea]t engagem[en]ts to holy & ready service, oh that thine eare might [*crossed out: illegible letter*] incline to this poore prayer of thy servant, heare oh Lord & helpe for the Lords sake Amen.

25° Januar 1639/40[967]
Lord why am I so slack to prayse thee, apt I am to cry & howle unto thee in time of trouble; but when helpe & comforts come how longe I am before I reflect thy goodnesse uppon thee againe by thanksgivings, doe the outgoeings of the morninge & the evening prayse thee? doe the sunne & moone & starrs in their places shine forth thy glory & the rest of the creatures reioyce in prayses before thee? and shall I thy poore Creature, to whom thou hast caused also thy spirit to breath uppon me & hast embraced me in the everlastinge armes of thy love, & kissed me with the kisses of thy mouth[968] and hast recorded sweet & precious & excellent p[ro]mises which belong to thy poore servant his poore wife & family, shall I be slow & backward to give unto the Lord the prayses due unto his name? Oh [*crossed out: I*] accept of the poore prayses

which I here offer upp unto thee, let it be accepted as a sacrifice of a sweet savor in the nostrills of thee my good god in Jesus Xt my deare & blessed Savior, thou hast multiplyed thy m[er]cyes uppon me & hast dealt bountifully with me, what were I that thou shouldest move me oftentimes by the spirit in my infancy, that thou shouldest shew me my sins & after seale my savio[u]r to me? that thou should[est] Carry me through my youth & keep me clenil[y] from many great & scandalous sines which my Corrupt nature would have thrust me into, that thou shouldest deliver me from so many horrours [*crossed out: h*] so many fiery darts & heavy temptacons of Satan, that thou shouldst susteyne me under so many debts & troubles, that thou shouldst besto[w]

[967]This additional entry, together with one for 22 January and two for 23 January 1639/40 (pp. 397–398) cover a visit to London to which the diarist barely alludes in his main diary entry for 21 January 1639/40 (p. 339).
[968]Song of Songs 1:2.

uppon me so good a wife, & sweet children that thou shouldst give
me imploym[en]t, & abilityes in any kind, that thou shouldst heare
my prayers that I lately put up unto thee [*crossed out: illegible word*]
about o[u]r late hearinge in Channcery that thou shouldst so order
things, ah my god while I have breath will I prayse the[e] while I have
a beinge will I never forsake thee, oh keepe me closse unto thee &
accept of me & my poore prayses for the Lords sake
[*word destroyed*] cold affect[ions] p[er] occ[asi]on Mr Wats busine[ss]

23° Januarii 1639/40[969] I have had litle sleepe here to night in respect
of thoughts of Mr Watts his busines & my debts, yet I receaved much
comfort in remembringe that the Lord can bringe light out of darknes
oh my god thou canst create comfort for those that wayte uppon thee,
mine eyes are lifted up towards, and my hand is stretched out to lay
hold on thy precious p[ro]mises, oh my god blesse me, create the
fruit of the lips peace unto me,[970] who knowes but thou oh god mayest
enlarge my steps, & take from my shoulder this burden of debts I desire
patiently to wayt for my god, And oh my Lord I humbly supplicate
thy blessed Ma[jes]ty in this p[rese]nte acc[ti]on about which I am
now come oh Lord thou seest how we are streighted & how they boast
vindicate me thy poore servant, manifest thy gracious p[ro]vidence,
give me matter of prayses herein for the Lords sake

23° Januar 1639/40[971]
This day the new Lord keep[er] ffinch tooke his place, oh Lord put
good men into places.
I am now much troubled wth the thought of my debts & about Mr
Watts his cause but put me hereafter in mind oh looke that I may
speake a song of prayse unto the Lord in the day when he shall enlarge
my steps, & looke uppon me oh my god in the pr[e]sent businesse of
the hearinge to morowe, that I may behold thy p[ro]vidence in it &
learne to wayte uppon thee forever for time to come; oh my good god
pitty me & my poore family for the Lords sake.
1° ffeb 1639/40[972]
diverse of Pisford are served wth subp[oen]as, & one or two of them
would come to me & the rest consult wth ffleminge, but Lord if it be
thy will direct them to me in thy good p[ro]vidence & enable me for

[969]See p. 339, main diary entry for 21 January 1639/40.
[970]Isaiah 57:19.
[971]See p. 339, main diary entry for 21 January 1639/40.
[972]Woodford was back in Northampton at this date: see p. 340, main diary entry dated 27
January 1639/40.

the imployment & blesse me in it, Lord my eyes are towards thee doe me good for the Lords sake Amen.

22° Jan 1639/40[973]

I am now at dunstable almost ready to take horse for London & my hart is sad through my melancholly temp[er] & cares of the world &. Ah my god to thee I fly be gracious to me for the Lords sake Lord supply me all my wants p[ro]vide for me & my family thou hast kept me & my deare wife this 5. yeares oh manifest thy bounty & thy goodnesse to us still & I pray thee looke uppon me in respect of the pr[e]sent businesse for Mr Watts & in Canc[974] thou seest the strength & the runinge of those that solicite the cause against me & thou seest their boastinge but oh my god thou hast helped me, thou knowest how much it doth concerne me, the whole disposinge of the matter will be from thee, Lord manifest thy good p[ro]vidence to me even for the Lords sake Amen.

25° Nov. 1639[975]

oh my god I prayse thee for the health & outward good which thou bestowest uppon me & my poore family, but espec[ially] I prayse thee for workinge grace uppon us in any measure goe on towards I pray thee with all thy grace & goodnesse & sanctifye all m[er]cyes & meanes thou usest to doe us good, blesse the cristian society in this house[976] whereof by thy grace I am a member let us goe on fruitfully to thy glory & bestowe thy blessings uppon us and now Lord pr[e]pare me for my Journey order my occasions & all my affayres I humbly pray let me behold thy p[ro]vidence in my endeavors & carry me & mine safe to o[u]r Journeyes end at North[amp]ton, and oh my god enable me for my p[ar]ticuler callinge more & when thou hast filled my hart to beare & receave so great a m[er]cy as to be out of debt worke wonderfully for me & take this heavy burden off my shoulders, Lord let me be a blessinge to my family at home & let us enioy much comfort in one another for the Lords sake.

19° Nov 1639[977] my deare child Sam. is very ill I heare & swooned 4 times yesterday.

---

[973] See p. 339, main diary entry for 21 January 1639/40.

[974] The Court of Chancery.

[975] See p. 334, main diary entry for 25 November 1639.

[976] This refers to the godly meetings at Clement's Inn: see, for example, main diary, pp. 332-334.

[977] See main diary entry for 19 November 1639 (p. 333) and p. 400, further additional entry for that date.

Oh most blessed Lord I pray thee continue his soule in life, strengthen
his fayntinge spirits I humbly pray thee, we receaved from thee at first
by peticon & he hath bene continued unto us by thy m[er]cye & often
raysed up from weaknes, oh be the same god still unto us lengthen
his days to many yeares & fill his soule wth thy grace [*crossed out:* &]
that thou mayst have much glory from him & we much comfort in
him, oh strip us not of the m[er]cyes thou hast bestowed uppon us for
o[u]r abuse of them, but shew m[er]cy freely, oh my god heare me for
him & heare me for the rest of my family, recover Johns eyes keepe
Sarah and Susannah in health, & oh my god as we desire the evill
of sorow to be removed from o[u]r family so I pray thee purge from
us the evill of sinne Lord shew us the way wherein we should walke
& overcome & inflame o[u]r harts to walke therein circumspectly &
watchfully shininge in o[u]r conversacon to others, oh Lord heare &
give an answere of peace for the Lords sake
postin⁹⁷⁸ apud Clem.[ent's] Inne.
Blessed be thy name oh Lord for raysinge up my poore child againe
oh Lord sanctifye this m[er]cye to us for the Lords sake.

16° Nov 1639⁹⁷⁹ my deare child John is very ill wth his eyes so that we
feare continuall blindnesse
But oh my god & father my continuall refuge in all affliccons I pray
thee in m[er]cye Looke upon us is it not easy with thee to heale?
yea say but the word & the scales or specks shall fall from his eyes art
not thou willinge to helpe! yea thou delightest in the p[ro]sp[er]ity of
thy children, oh bow downe thine ears & heare stretch forth thy hand
& helpe thou hast hetherto blessed the family of thy servant & we
subsist by thy speciall yea even miraculous p[ro]vidence deliver us we
pray thee from such a feare & evill as is now uppon us in o[u]r child,
lay not the sinnes of us his parents uppon us thus if it be thy will but
p[ar]don o[u]r misdoeings, oh that thou wouldst rend the heavens &
come downe that all mountaynes of sinne & pride may flow downe at
thy pr[e]sence that there may be a way made for the Lord of hosts,
& that he may dwell & rule in o[u]r family, oh Lord I pray thee fit
me here & my wife in the country & o[u]r whole family to seeke thee
earnestly & p[ro]fit much to morow by the dutyes of thy Sabath &
graunt me comfortable newes from home if it be thy will for the Lords
sake
oh give an answere from heaven for the Lords sake.
postin⁹⁸⁰ die sept[im]o d[e]c[im]o in my chamber at Clem[en]ts Inne

---

⁹⁷⁸ Woodford's own Latin term ('postinde') meaning 'afterwards'.
⁹⁷⁹ See p. 333, main diary entry for 16 November 1639.
⁹⁸⁰ 'Afterwards'.

19° Nov.[1639][981] I have good newes of the Amendm[en]t of Johns [eyes] blessed be thy name oh Lord, oh goe on to p[er]fect them [*several words destroyed*] Lords sake Amen.

14° Maii 1640[982]

Ah my god thou seest how my hart is downe & how it faynts through the badnesse of the times & feare of want & fear of man, & how I runne unto the creature for comfort & how I sit very loose from thee & see thee not many times in a long while, ah my good god be gracious to me infuse thy grace & comforts more into my soule lett me feare thee more & the creature lesse, pay my debts for me be a hidinge place to me & my family carry us uppon eagles wings[983] & teach us oh Jehovah to depend uppon thee and put things here in frame stirre up thy selfe & come & save us, turne the harts of thine enimyes & establish & comfort the soules of thy children for the Lord Jesus Xt his sake.

13° Aug. 1639[984]

betweene 2 & 3 a clock in the morninge my wife was very ill, and I rose & sent for the midwife Mrs Parsons to Mr Wests[985] & called some freinds, and my w[ife] hath since bene somewhat better & doth yet continue ill, Oh Lord my good god who art the god that hearest the peticons of thy children when they cry unto thee, & who art a readye helpe at hand in the time of trouble & sorowe, Oh Lord o[u]r helpe is in thee who hast made heaven & earth we desire to have o[u]r eyes up onely to thee as o[u]r confidence remember not against us former iniquityes but deale graciously wth thy servants as thou wert wont, let the sence of thy favor come wth the sence of payne, & let thy hand mayd feele her Joy surmount her greif very much let her fayth remayne fixt uppon thee [*crossed out: illegible letter*] immovably & give us also this exp[er]ience of thy power & goodnesse & give us to make more use of it then heretofore to receave it wth more fruitfullnesse & more obedience Lord thou art strength it selfe & canst communicate it where it is wantinge make us glad parents I humble pray thee of a fourth child & make that an Instrument of glory & a vessel of
*****

---

[981] See main diary entry for 19 November 1639 (p. 333) and p. 398, further additional entry for that date.

[982] See p. 354, main diary entry dated 14 May 1640.

[983] Isaiah 40:31.

[984] See p. 321, main diary entry for 13 August 1639.

[985] Possibly one of the brothers John and Thomas West, who lived at Cotton End to the south of Northampton: Longden, *Visitation of Northamptonshire 1681*, pp. 239–240.

of mercye & a comfort to us give us fayth to stay o[u]r selves uppon
thee & shew thy selfe glorious and gracious on o[u]r behalfe for the
Lord Xt his sake who is the foundacon & meritorious cause & meanes
of all o[u]r mercyes, its now halfe an houre past 7. Lord send the good
houre in thy due time & stay o[u]r harts & strengthen them in thee &
fit us for such a m[er]cye & heare the poore prayers that have bene
put up unto thee in this behalfe.
my wife hath bene very well since[986] but now is ill againe uppon friday
16° Aug. [*crossed out:* &] about 5. a clock; oh my Lord we thy poore
servants desire still to wayte uppon thee, thou alone art o[u]r helpe &
o[u]r sheild, hold under thy hand & graunt my deare wife a gracious
& speedy delivery uphold her spirits & give her seasonable ease I
humbly pray thee give the infant right shape & forme & make it an
instrument of thy glory & a comfort to us the parents for the Lord Xt
his sake amen. Lord let us not trust in the midwife or in freinds but in
thee the livinge god forever for those that know thy name will surely
trust in thee,
Blessed be the Lord that he hath bestowed a gracious delivery on my
deare wife of another daughter, she was borne betweene 8. & 9. at
night.

2° Junii 1639. Whitsunday[987]
my poore child John is in great distresse by reason of his eyes which
are much swelled wth rheume so that he cannot looke up & he cryes
vehemently & we are in much trouble & heavinesse for him, but Lord
I desire to looke up unto thee for helpe I pray thee pitty the distresses
of thy poore servants vouchsafe ease & cure to the poore child say but
the word & he shall be whole, say but unto him let there be light &
he shall see againe thou gavest him unto us at the first Lord continue
him in m[er]cy if it be thy will & make him an instrument of thy glory
& a comfort to us his parents, oh Lord build up & doe good to me
& my family, & put an end to the troubles of these times & bringe
great good out of them to thy poore church & children, & pr[e]vent
Bloodshed, Lord helpe me thy poore servant in my many straights of
debts & troubles supply me & uphold me for the Lords sake
This day 3. yeares my father was buryed Lord fit me for death Let it
not come unawares or unwelcome to me for the Lords sake.
*****

[986] See p. 321, main diary entry for 16 August 1639.
[987] See p. 309, main diary entry for 2 June 1639.

28° ffeb. 1638/39.[988] At the Assizes [*crossed out:* of] at North[amp]ton Justice Bartlet[989] onely came Justice hutton my good freind dyed on Tuesday morninge last at London, Oh Lord thou hast deprived me of another freind, but I pray thee doe not thou forsake me & then I shall not want them any more then I doe the starrs when I have the sunne, thou canst give me more in stead of him if thou pleasest oh Lord I desire to wayt uppon thee evermore, blesse me & my family for the Lords sake.

yesterday I was much troubled at a sp[ec]iall plea [*crossed out:* inter] p[ro] denton ad[versus] Eakins Mr Attourney[990] findinge fault with it, for layinge so many abbuttalls & & for puttinge in Selions,[991] & not hades[992] onely & denton layd a fault uppon me though indeed his confidence & the counsell to which we shewed it before were rather faulty, Lord lay not to my charge my faythlesse melancholly.

now we have another acc[ti]on ag[ains]t Eakins p[ro] comon & for ought I see o[u]r witnesses are not hasty to come in.

Oh my Lord thou who art Justice it selfe; I beseech thee so to order in thy p[ro]vidence that defects or mistakes on other side may not sway in these but that right & truth may be manifested & sett

forth order every circumstance for that end graciously I humbly beseech thee, and keep my hart this day & the whole Assizes in a holy & heavenly temp[er], & give me grace & wisdome in the eyes of men in the measure thou seest fittest oh Lord heare & have m[er]cye for the Lords sake.

afterwards towards night [*crossed out:* the] the cause wherein denton was pl[ain]t[iff] was tried & they brought in witnesses on the def[endan]ts p[ar]t who swore punctually, & much possessed the Judge yet afterwards our witnesses beinge of more credit & number were sworne, & though it was offered to wthdraw a Juror if Eakins would forbeare his cause [*crossed out:* but] yet he refused & the verdict was given p[ro] [*symbol meaning plaintiff*] the next morninge theother was tried wherin Eakins was pl[ain]t[iff], which cause we much doubted & the counsell seemed to despayre of in regard of defects in the pleadinge, & of o[u]r witnesses & though their witnesses swore dangerously & as my clyent sayth very falsly, yet I lifted up my hart to the Lord for the orderinge of it Justly, & the verdict passed likewise for us, oh Lord thou heardest my poore prayers blessed be thy name & hast vindicated thy

---

[988] See p. 287, main diary entry dated 28 February 1638/39.
[989] Sir Robert Berkeley.
[990] Richard Lane, attorney to Charles, Prince of Wales.
[991] Strips of arable land in an open field.
[992] Probably 'hide', the amount of land thought to suffice for the support of a family.

servant, oh p[ar]don my too much distractednesse & want of fayth to wayt uppon thee, and accept of my poore prayses & confirme me by this in matters of greater moment. Thine is Kingdome power & glory & the soveraignty of them receave graciously me thy poore creature & my weake [of]f[e]rings for the Lords sake Amen.

29 Aug. 1638 v[id]e the same day in the booke.[993]
Oh Lord looke uppon my poore wife, who is now in travell, & whom thou hast called to this worke Lord put under thine hand give her strength & patience & a cheerfull spirit & speciall comunion wth thee our good god grannt her a gracious & speedy delivery, And Lord blesse the child wth right shape & forme and make it thine by grace & adopcon, And graunt to us the parents & them the Children still to continue & live together to thy glory & the mutuall comfort one of another, make my deare wife a Nurse too if it be thy will. Lord thou mightest say unto me as [*crossed out:* david] Solomon to Shimei thou knowest the sinnes whereunto thy hart is privy, & thou mightest bringe them uppon my head,[994] but for the Lords sake lay them not to my chardge but p[ar]don them and delight to doe good to me & my family; and supply me wth moneyes for my occasions for the Lords sake Amen.
my deare wife began to travell about 7 in the morninge and is still in great payne now at or after 4 in the afternoone, [*word destroyed*] Lord what shall I say thou holdest [*word destroyed*]

[*fourteen blank pages*]

[993] See p. 234, main diary entry dated 29 August 1638.
[994] I Kings 2:44.

INDEX

Places are in Northamptonshire unless otherwise stated (with the exception of well-known towns).

Lightning Source UK Ltd.
Milton Keynes UK
UKOW04n1612120915

258444UK00003B/42/P